MW00398161

AMERICAN ORIGINS

David B. Trimble

Preface

This volume of genealogy is a result of thirty-five years of research on the author's ancestry. However, so much additional data and so many collateral lines were obtained in the course of that research, that the scope of the work has been expanded into four volumes:

American Beginnings (Barnwell, Dunlap, Johnson, King, Lewis, Shaw, Shearman, Taylor, and Trimble families).
Southwest Virginia Families (Buchanan, Crockett, Gillespie, Graham, James, Kincannon, Lamie, McDonald, Montgomery, Robinson, and Thomson families).
American Origins (Bare, Collier, David, Davidson, Easley, Freiley, Gash, Gist, Hickman, Hinds, Jarratt, McPherson, Marriott, Nevill, Pennington, Robertson, Stroud, Stubblefield, Trail, West, and Wolfe families).
Hiestand Family of Page County, Virginia (Hiestand and Boehm families).

The material on the author's ancestry was generally obtained by original research, which is detailed in the bibliography; the collateral lines were usually obtained from interested descendants, who are identified in the bibliography.

This genealogical volume is intended to be a reference work, and it is hoped that others will be able to find useful information in it. The author also hopes that additional information will be obtained following the publication of this material, so that it, too, can be published in the future.

1974   Dr. David B. Trimble
                                  607 River Road
                                  San Antonio, Texas   78212

American Origins

BARE of Hawkins County, Tennessee

George Peter Bar moved from Germany to America in the Rowand from Rotterdam, landing at Philadelphia, Pennsylvania, on September 29, 1753, with his family after being becalmed at sea for several weeks and suffering many hardships.[1]

On November 5, 1770, Bar bought 100 acres near the head of Swan Ponds in Frederick (now Berkeley) County, (West) Virginia, from Jacob Morgan for £100; on March 19, 1782, he acquired from Jane Morgan an additional eight acres he was already using. On April 2, 1787, he and his wife, Catherine, sold his 108 acres to George Tabler for £320.[2]

Peter Bare, as the name was Anglicized, then moved from Swan Ponds but his later residence has not been located. The names of his children are not definitely known, but probably include the following:[3]

a. Catherine Bare, born c1753; died c1835 in Scott County, Virginia; married c1778 in Berkeley County, (West) Virginia, to John Wolfe (see p. 267).
b. Peter Bare, born c1756; died 1829 in Hawkins County, Tennessee; he moved from Berkeley County, (West) Virginia, to Washington (now Scott) County, Virginia, about 1791, and lived about three months with the Wolfe family; he then moved about 20 miles away and in August, 1801, he moved to Hawkins County, Tennessee. On November 27, 1804, he bought land on Poor Valley Creek; on August 2, 1816, he bought 90 acres in the same area; he sold two tracts to George Williams on January 4, 1823, and April 28, 1824. He and his wife Edy had the following children:[4]
   (1) Peter Bare, born c1781; lived in Hawkins County, Tennessee, in 1850.
   (2) Henry Bare.
   (3) Michael Bare.
   (4) George Bare.
   (5) Matthias Bare.
   (6) Nancy Bare.
   (7) Barbara Bare.
   (8) Deborah Bare.
   (9) Susan Bare.
   (10) Jacob Bare lived in Clinton County, Ohio, in 1833.
   (11) James Bare.

***

REFERENCES

[1]Ralph Beaver Strassburger and William John Hinke, Pennsylvania German Pioneers (Norristown, Pennsylvania: Pennsylvania German Society, 1934), I, 570; the same family tradition with minor variations has persisted among descendants of at least three children of Catherine Bare Wolfe.
[2]Frederick County, Virginia, Deed. Bk. 14, p. 12; Berkeley County, (West) Virginia, Deed Bk. 5, p. 702, Bk. 8, pp. 38, 40.

[3]Deposition of Peter Bare, Chancery Court Papers, 1821, Wythe County, Virginia, states that Peter Bare and Catherine Wolfe were brother and sister; Berkeley County, (West) Virginia, tax lists, 1783, name only Peter Bare, Sr., and Peter Bare, Jr.

[4]Ibid.; Hawkins County, Tennessee, Deed Bk. 6, p. 341, Bk. 8, p. 75, Bk. 11, pp. 414, 415, Will Bk. 1, p. 40.

* * *

COLLIER of Surry County, Virginia

Edward Collier of Charles City County, Virginia, bought 300 acres on Chippokes Creek called Cabin Point in 1659; in 1668, he sold the land to Richard Rogers, at the same time granting a power of attorney to his "cousin," John Collier.[1]

John Collier resided in Surry County, Virginia, in 1668 and died there early in 1676; an inventory of his estate was filed on May 27, 1676. His wife Mary made a pre-marital contract on September 24, 1677, with John Rawlings, by which Rawlings gave up all claims to Mary's estate. John Rawlings made his will in August, 1702, and his estate was probated on May 25, 1703. The children of John and Mary Collier were as follows:[2]

1. a. Thomas Collier, born c1665.
   b. John Collier, born c1668; raised by Thomas Sowerby and served in the Surry County militia in 1687. An inventory of his estate was filed in 1693 and William Goodman was appointed guardian of his orphans.[3]
   c. Mary Collier, born c1672.
   d. Joseph Collier, born c1674; died 1727 in Surry County, Virginia; married Jane Halso, daughter of William Halso; children:[4]
      (1) John Collier died 1732 in Surry County, Virginia; married Sarah Briggs, daughter of Samuel Briggs; children:
         (a) Mary Collier married Moses Johnson; lived in Sussex County, Virginia.
         (b) William Collier.
         (c) Thomas Collier.
         (d) Grace Collier.
         (e) Benjamin Collier.
         (f) Charles Collier.
         (g) Henry Collier.
      (2) Joseph Collier.
      (3) William Collier.
      (4) Thomas Collier.
      (5) Mary Collier.
      (6) Jean Collier.
      (7) Elizabeth Collier.
      (8) Sarah Collier.

The children of John and Mary Rawlings were as follows:[5]

   a. Elizabeth Rawlings, born c1680; married c1700 in Surry County, Virginia, to _____ Partin.
   b. John Rawlings, born c1684.
   c. Gregory Rawlings, born c1688.

***

1. Thomas Collier, who was born c1665 in Surry County, Virginia, resided with his step-father, John Rawlings, and Thomas Sowerby, probably his grandfather, after the death of his father. In 1687 he was a horseman in the Surry County Militia; in 1704 he owned 550 acres of land there, and in 1714 and 1721 he was sheriff of the

3

county. He made his will on February 15, 1727/8, stating that he lived on Mill Swamp and owned land in both Surry and Isle of Wight Counties; his estate was probated on March 20, 1727/8. His children were as follows:[6]

a. John Collier, born c1692; died 1716 in Surry County, Virginia; married c1712 to Jane Thomas; children:
   (1) Thomas Collier.
   (2) John Collier.
b. Sarah Collier, born c1695; married c1715 in Surry County, Virginia, to William Marriott (see p. 125).

(see p. 125).

**

REFERENCES

[1]Surry County, Virginia, Deed Bk. 1, pp. 143, 321; at that time, cousin probably meant nephew.
[2]Ibid., Bk. 2, pp. 151, 172, 211, Bk. 5, p. 279; Mary Collier Rawlings was probably the daughter of Thomas and Ann Sowerby, who raised some of her children by Collier and left them property.
[3]Surry County, Virginia, Order Book 1671-90, p. 413, Deed Bk. 5, p. 49.
[4]Ibid., Deed Bk. 7, p. 115; Deeds and Wills 1730-38, Bk. 1, p. 246.
[5]Ibid., Bk. 5, p. 279.
[6]Ibid., Court Orders 1683, Militia list 1687; Virginia Quitrents of 1704; Surry County, Virginia, Deeds 1715-30, p. 795.

**

DAVID of Manakintown, Virginia

Pierre David, born about 1690, belonged to a family that had moved from Bolbec, Normandy, to London; he was a member of the group of French Huguenots that settled Manakintown, Virginia, although he probably did not arrive there until about 1712. He married Anne _____ about 1713 and on March 3, 1715, he received a grant from the colony of Virginia for 88 acres on the south side of the James River. He was a vestryman of King William Parish in Henrico (now Powhatan) County, Virginia, from 1721 until his death. He made his will on May 28, 1729, leaving his property to his wife Anne and his four children; the estate was probated on August 18, 1730.[1]

Pierre and Anne David were godparents of John Chastain on September 26, 1721; Anne David was godmother of Judith Chastain on May 10, 1727, of Jacob Amonet on June 15, 1732, and of Lucy and Magdalene Robinson on March 15, 1741.[2]

On February 14, 1744/45, Anne David and her son Peter sold her husband's 88 acre farm to Benjamin Harris for £100. She made her will on October 18, 1750, leaving her property to her three surviving children, and the estate was probated in November, 1750; the sale of her personal property brought £124.17.10.[3] The children of Pierre and Anne David were as follows:

1. a. Peter David, born c1715.
   b. Isaac David, born c1717; dsp c1741 in Goochland (now Powhatan) County, Virginia.
   c. Marianne David, born c1720; died in Sullivan County, Tennessee; married (1) c1745 in Goochland (now Powhatan) County, Virginia, to William Burton (2) c1751 in Cumberland (now Powhatan) County, Virginia, to Stephen Easley (see p. 26); children:
      (by first marriage):
      (1) Lewis Burton, born c1747; died young.
      (2) Ann Burton, born March 15, 1749.
      (by second marriage): (see p. 26).
   d. Anne David, born May 10, 1722; married c1744 Daniel Easley (see p. 29).

**

1.   Peter David was born about 1715 in Henrico (now Powhatan) County, Virginia, and married there about 1737 to Elizabeth Morriset, born March 1, 1721, daughter of Pierre and Elizabeth Morriset. On April 20, 1742, he sold 229 acres which had belonged to his brother Isaac to Stephen Mallet; on November 2, 1745, he became warden of King William Parish; on January 9, 1752, he sold the 125 acres where he lived on the lower side of Manakin Creek to David LeSoeur for £40; on March 22, 1755, he sold land to Jesse Weaver. He moved to Henry County, Virginia, where he made his will on December 21, 1781; the estate was probated on November 25, 1785. Peter and Elizabeth David had the following children:[4]

a. Anne David, born January 15, 1738/39.
b. Elizabeth David, born c1740.

```
     c.  Mary David, born c1743.
2.   d.  Peter David, born July 1, 1748.
     e.  Judith David, born c1750.
     f.  Jean David, born c1753.
3.   g.  Isaac David, born c1756.
     h.  Magdalene David, born c1758.
     i.  Phoebe David, born c1760.
     j.  Abraham David, born July 8, 1763; died 1854 in Franklin County,
         Virginia; married December 15, 1803, Rachel Edmond; children:
         (1)  Isaac David married December 18, 1827, to Malinda Powell.
         (2)  Susan David.
         (3)  Phoebe David.
         (4)  Sarah David.
         (5)  Elizabeth David.
         (6)  John P. David married August 24, 1851, to Happy A. Hines.
```

***

```
2.        Peter David was born July 1, 1748, in Goochland (now Powhatan)
     County, Virginia, and died about 1798 in Madison County, Georgia;
     married (1) c1771 Elizabeth White (2) November 8, 1793, in Franklin
     County, Virginia, to Elizabeth Hale; his children were as follows:5

     (by first marriage):
     a.  William David, born 1772; died 1822 in Elbert County, Georgia;
         married Lucy White.
     b.  Lucy David, born c1774; married February 4, 1794, John Allen,
         died 1827 in Putnam County, Georgia.
4.   c.  Judith David, born 1784.
     (by second marriage):
     d.  Morriset David married May 2, 1819, in Elbert County, Georgia,
         to Elizabeth David.
     e.  Samuel David married May 26, 1826, in Elbert County, Georgia,
         to Harriet Threlkeld.
     f.  Isaac David married July 3, 1823, in Elbert County, Georgia,
         to Martha Sartin.
```

***

```
4.        Judith David was born in 1784 and died October 15, 1828, in
     Putnam County, Georgia; married in 1807 Micajah White, born 1788;
     died 1826.  Their children were as follows:6

     a.  Elizabeth Brown White, born June 26, 1808; died November 2,
         1851, in Selma, Alabama; married February 4, 1823, in Putnam
         County, Georgia, to Leland Allen, born February 2, 1799; died
         1890; children:
         (1)  Fernandia Allen.
         (2)  Saphronia Allen.
         (3)  Judith Allen.
         (4)  Micajah H. Allen.
         (5)  Louise Marion Allen.
         (6)  Elizabeth Brown Allen.
         (7)  James M. Allen.
         (8)  George W. Allen.
         (9)  Mary Allen.
```

6

       (10) John Judson Brown Allen.
       (11) Leland Allen.
       (12) Columbus D. Allen.
       (13) Oliver Henry Allen, born September 2, 1846; died March
             30, 1926, in Austin, Texas; married December 3, 1872,
             in Limestone County, Texas, to Martha Anne Granade, born
             September 6, 1856; died May 16, 1903, in Temple, Texas;
             children:
             (a) Lycurgus Leland Allen.
             (b) Ada Allen married March 3, 1897, Hillery Lee Peoples,
                  born September 14, 1874; died January 15, 1939, in
                  Dallas, Texas; children:
                  /1/ Foster Peoples married (1) Dr. Roger W. Gray;
                       (2) Robert L. Harper.
                  /2/ Hillery Lee Peoples, dsp.
                  /3/ Allen Harlan Peoples, born September 15, 1906;
                       married May 24, 1942, Gertrude Hand.
                  /4/ Ann Peoples married Eugene Lawson.
                  /5/ Ruth Peoples married Alex Meletio.
             (c) Claud Allen.
             (d) Granade Allen.
       (14) Virginia Anne Allen.
       (15) Francis Americus Allen.
       (16) Julia Allen.
   b. Jesse White.
   c. Sophronia White.
   d. James White.
   e. John White.

                              ***

3.   Isaac David was born about 1756 in Cumberland (now Powhatan)
   County, Virginia, and died about 184? in Madison County, Georgia;
   married (1) Lucy White (2) October 10, 1798, to Susannah Vaughn;
   his children were as follows:

   (by first marriage):
   a. Patience David married Benjamin M. Davis.
   b. Charity David married _____ Brooks.
   c. Isaiah David.
   d. Celia David married _____ Baldwin.
   e. Henry David.
   f. Elizabeth David married August 20, 1807, Alexander Vaughn;
       lived in Elbert County, Georgia.
   g. Mildred David married February 4, 1808, George Wiley.
   h. Caroline David married _____ Glore.
   i. Locky H. David married Bird Moon.
   j. Jacob White David, born 1795; died August 30, 1871; married
       January 2, 1817, in Elbert County, Georgia, to Margaret All-
       man; lived in Harris County, Georgia; children:
       (1) Henry Clay David married Gussie Biggers.
       (2) Susan David, born September 30, 1820; died October 15,
            1906; married November 12, 1847, George Slayton.
       (3) James A. David married October 13, 1848, Mary E. Fuller.
       (4) John Isaac David, born October 12, 1824; died September
            8, 1880; married (1) Clarissa Slayton (2) Eliza Josephine
            Blackmon (3) Mrs. Nancy (Meadows) Jones.

                               7

(5)   Jacob White David, born May 5, 1825; died January 5, 1873, in Huntsville, Alabama; married Parthenia Brantley.

(6)   Lavonia David, born 1827; married January 15, 1858, James Henry Brawner.

(7)   Jane Amelia David, born February 22, 1828; died September 20, 1905; married November 2, 1849, Thomas Scroggins.

(8)   William Jerome David, born February 12, 1830; died September 12, 1889; married November 2, 185?, Elizabeth Victoria Taylor.

(9)   Sarah A. David.

(10)   Margaret Louise David, born January 28, 1835.

(11)   (Dr.) Francis Columbus David, born March 10, 1837; died July 26, 1911, in Huntsville, Alabama; married (1) October 27, 1857, Sarah Ann Jones, born October 22, 1840; died January 7, 1866; (2) Rebecca Taylor Ogletree.

(12)   Clementine David married 1857 William Lednum.

(13)   Elizabeth David married Green McCreary.

(14)   Josephine Augusta David, born July 11, 1845; died March 8, 1894; married Henry Clay Blackmon.

***

REFERENCES

[1] Kenn Stryker-Rodda (ed.), _Genealogical Research_ (Washington, D. C.: The American Society of Genealogists, 1971) II, 259; Roll of "French Protestant Refugees at King William Parish," Henrico County, Virginia, c1714; list of tithables, King William Parish, 1712-1738; list of vestrymen, King William Parish, published in Robert A. Brock, _Huguenot Emigration to Virginia_ (Baltimore: Genealogical Publishing Company, 1962); Virginia Land Grants, State Archives, Richmond, Virginia; Goochland County, Virginia, Will Bk. 1, p. 214.

[2] List of baptisms in King William Parish, published in Brock, pp. 75, 86-89, 97-98, 100, 102.

[3] Goochland County, Virginia, Deed Bk. 4, pp. 104, 549; Cumberland County, Virginia, Will Bk. 1, p. 28.

[4] List of baptisms in King William Parish; Goochland County, Virginia, Deed Bk. 4, p. 104; Cumberland County, Virginia, Deed Bk. 2, pp. 1, 226; Henry County, Virginia, Will Bk. 1, p. 119; records of Mrs. Kelly McAdams.

[5-6] Records of Mrs. Hillery L. Peoples.

[7] Records of Mrs. Kelly McAdams.

***

DAVIDSON of Brown County, Ohio

Joshua Davidson was born in April, 1753, in Scotland, and
is first mentioned in contemporary records when he enlisted in
the Revolutionary service on the Monongahela River in Pennsylvania on August 13, 1776.[1] He served in Captain James Montgomery's and Captain Van Swearingen's companies, Colonel Aeneas
Mackey's and Colonel Daniel Brodhead's 8th Pennsylvania Regiment;
he served as a sergeant until April 19, 1779, when he received
a commission as ensign; he resigned his commission on March 20,
1780. He crossed the Trenton with his regiment, fought at the
battles of Boundbrook, Brandywine on September 11, 1777, Paoli
on September 20, 1777, and spent the winter of 1777/78 at Valley Forge. In March, 1778, he accompanied his regiment back to
Pittsburgh, where he guarded the frontier against Indians. On
one occasion during this Indian campaign when he was assigned
to guard prisoners, he and General Anthony Wayne got into an
argument; he raised a musket to shoot Wayne, who was approaching
him with a drawn sword, when, fortunately, bystanders intervened.
Part of his military service was in the artillery, which left
him partially deafened.[2]

After leaving the Revolutionary service, Davidson served
as a private and sergeant in the Washington County, Pennsylvania,
militia, in 1781 and 1782, completing seven years of military
service. About 1783 in Washington (now Allegheny) County, he
married Eleanor Beam, who was born about 1763 in Germany; in
1784 he lived in Peters Township and in 1785, in Dickinson Township in Washington (now Allegheny) County, Pennsylvania. In
1787, he signed a petition to form Allegheny County from Washington and Westmoreland Counties, and he lived there in Mifflin
Township in 1791.[3]

About 1794, Joshua Davidson moved to Bracken County, Kentucky,
where in May, 1798, he was sued by the trustees of Newtown and
by Nathaniel Patterson for not performing assumption; on June
30, 1798, he sold Nathaniel Patterson his personal property. He
was sued for debt by John Brown on October 4, 1802.[4]

In 1806, Davidson moved to Clermont (now Brown) County, Ohio,
and built a cabin on John Brown's survey #1795, just south of
New Hope, and set up business as a millwright in what is now Scott
Township. He was appointed overseer of the poor in the township
in 1811; he also served as an election judge on April 6, 1812,
and April 5, 1813, and as chairman of the election judges on
April 4, 1814. He applied for a pension for his revolutionary
service on August 8, 1818; it was granted on September 21, 1833.[5]

Joshua Davidson bought 191 acres on White Oak Creek, part
of survey #1795, on February 6, 1833, from Joseph and Sally Davidson for $100.00; he sold it to his son-in-law, Moore Ralston,
on October 29, 1835, for $855.00. After the death of his wife
about that time, he retired to live with his son-in-law, John
Bingaman; he was well-known for the stories of the Revolution which
he like to tell, although he was deaf and blind in his old age.
He left no property at his death on August 18, 1844, in Brown

9

County, Ohio.[6] His children were as follows:[7]

1. a. William Davidson, born March 19, 1784.
2. b. John Davidson, born December 31, 1785.
   c. Jonathan Davidson, born c1787; dsp between 1821 and 1844 in Brown County, Ohio.
3. d. Elizabeth Davidson, born c1789.
   e. Ruth Davidson, born c1791; died before 1844.
   f. Eleanor Davidson, born April 21, 1793; died June 8, 1869, in Brown County, Ohio; married April 20, 1817, in Clermont (now Brown) County, Ohio, to John Bingaman.
   g. Joseph Davidson, born c1793; died after 1844; married (1) c1823 to Nancy _____ (2) December 25, 1827, in Brown County, Ohio, to Sarah Howland.
4. h. Mary Davidson, born February 2, 1796.
   i. Rachel Davidson, born c1797; died between 1821 and 1844.
5. j. Nancy Davidson, born c1799.

***

1.   William Davidson was born March 19, 1784, in Washington (now Allegheny) County, Pennsylvania, and died March 9, 1839, in Brown County, Ohio; married July 15, 1813, in Clermont (now Brown) County, Ohio, to Susan Knaus, born June 23, 1793, and died February 13, 1859, daughter of Henry and Catherine Knaus. Their children were as follows:[7]

   a. Henry Davidson, born May 5, 1814; died January 5, 1892, in Brown County, Ohio; married November 6, 1839, to Elizabeth Holden; born 1813; died 1879; children:
      (1) Martha Davidson, born August 1, 1840; dsp May 3, 1862.
      (2) Mary Davidson, born October 9, 1844; dsp January 13, 1917.
      (3) Frances Davidson, born July 14, 1847; died November 13, 1932, in Champaign, Illinois; married John W. Brookbank, born February 3, 1842, in Higginsport, Ohio; died September 12, 1920, in Danville, Illinois; children:
      (a) Alva Brookbank, dsp.
      (b) Mary Brookbank.
      (c) George E. Brookbank, born July 9, 1875; died July 20, 1946, in Champaign, Illinois; married November 21, 1904, to Jane Thorwell Prichett, born April 16, 1869; died April 23, 1942; child:
         /1/ Lois Frances Brookbank, born July 21, 1906; married November 24, 1927, to Robert Rankin McKay, born September 11, 1905; children:
         /a/ Patricia Lou McKay, born December 25, 1928; married May 29, 1947, to Andrew Shelton Huson; children:
            1. Shelley Huson.
            2. Pamela Huson.
            3. Stacey Huson.
            4. Scott Huson.
         /b/ Robert Rankin McKay, born March 1, 1933.
         /c/ Karen Sue McKay, born September 11, 1940.
      (d) Bessie Brookbank.

(e) Henry Brookbank, dsp.
   (f) William Brookbank.
  (4) Ella Davidson, born c1850; died young.
  (5) Julia Davidson, born 1854; married 1877 to Franklin
    Pierce Hite.
 b. Joshua Davidson, born October 20, 1815; died January 13, 1848;
   married March 25, 1841, to Nancy Printy.
 c. Walter Davidson, born September 19, 1817; dsp May 5, 1842.
 d. Mary Davidson, born October 25, 1819; died July 21, 1843;
   married November 7, 1839, to Peter H. Green.
 e. Thomas Davidson, born March 19, 1822; died October 17, 1864;
   married July 10, 1845, to Eliza D. Talbot.
 f. Elizabeth Davidson, born April 18, 1824; died 1906; married
   March 26, 1862, to William B. Mookler.
 g. Catherine W. Davidson, born May 12, 1826; died February 27,
   1871; married August 10, 1858, to Matthias Drake.
6. h. Ann Carr Davidson, born September 18, 1828.
 i. Sarah F. Davidson, born June 10, 1830; died January 2, 1913;
   married February 20, 1856, to Elias C. Abbott.
 j. John Davidson, born April 13, 1834; dsp February 23, 1842.

***

6.   Ann Carr Davidson was born September 18, 1828, in Brown
County, Ohio, and died July 1, 1901; married June 25, 1852, to
Chester Green Bartholomew, born November 25, 1830; died May 17,
1896; their children were as follows:[8]

 a. Inez Vilena Bartholomew, born March 9, 1853; died August 4,
   1927; married 1884 to Thomas C. Eliason; children:
  (1) Wood Eata Eliason, born November 16, 1884; died July 6,
    1957; married October 10, 1907, to Pearl M. Davis; chil-
    dren:
    (a) Doris Pearl Eliason, born December 20, 1913; mar-
     ried June 24, 1939, to Edwin Leonidas Godfrey;
     child:
     /1/ Thomas William Godfrey, born October 15, 1953.
    (b) Inezetta Eliason, born March 26, 1916; married
     November 24, 1940, to R. Carl Stiver; dsp.
    (c) Woodice Esther Eliason, born April 8, 1922; married
     December 31, 195?, to Orville Hoos; child:
     /1/ Robert Hoos, born December 7, 195?.
  (2) Gaar Ghent Eliason, born March 9, 1888; married October
    31, 1917, to Sarah Charlene Burgess; children:
    (a) Gaar Ghent Eliason, born August 14, 1918; married
     (1) June 11, 1938, to Bertha Doddridge (2) Febru-
     ary 11, 1949, to Mrs. Gladys Beatrice (Owens) Webb;
     children (by first marriage):
     /1/ Ronald Eliason, born June 6, 1940; dsp July
      18, 1940.
     /2/ Carolyn Rene Eliason, born May 21, 1942; mar-
      ried May 21, 1961, to Jack Lee Frame.
    (b) Donald Dean Eliason, born February 22, 1922; mar-
     ried January 16, 1943, to Dolores Turner; children:
     /1/ Donna Joene Eliason, born April 22, 1944.
     /2/ Thomas Dean Eliason, born August 31, 1947.
     /3/ Kathryn Jean Eliason, born August 31, 1947.

11

<u>/4/</u> Rebecca Sue Eliason, born August 15, 1949.
<u>/5/</u> Douglas Duane Eliason, born March 31, 1959.
<u>/6/</u> Beth Anne Eliason, born October 28, 1960.
(3) Nina Gladys Eliason, born April 12, 1890; dsp March 16, 1908.

b. Homer G. Bartholomew, born 1854; dsp 1910; married Letitia McMahan.
c. Virgil G. Bartholomew, born 1856; died 1924; married Mary Fowler; children:
    (1) Chester G. Bartholomew.
    (2) Othneil Aid Bartholomew.
    (3) Marian Bartholomew married Bernard DeWeese.
d. Thomas B.-Bartholomew, born 1858; dsp 1942; married Jessie Partridge.
e. William E. Bartholomew, born 1860; died 1925; married Mary Taylor; children:
    (1) Inez Bartholomew.
    (2) Winnie Bartholomew.
    (3) Lula Bartholomew.
    (4) Thomas Bartholomew.
    (5) Lesley Bartholomew.
    (6) Mildred Bartholomew.
f. Samuel M. Bartholomew, born 1862; died 1943; married Lou ____.
g. Edwin Harris Bartholomew, born 1864; dsp 1869.
h. Lorin Chester Bartholomew, born 1865; dsp 1943.
i. Lucy Mary Bartholomew, born 1867; dsp 195?.
j. Susan Isolene Bartholomew, born 1870; dsp 1870.

***

2.   John Davidson was born December 31, 1785, in Dickinson Township, Washington (now Allegheny) County, Pennsylvania, and lived there until about 1794, when the family moved to near Augusta in Bracken County, Kentucky. About 1806, he moved to Scott Township, Brown County, Ohio, but he returned to Bracken County, where <u>on June 17, 1810, he married Mary West</u> (see p. 260). About 1813, he settled near Georgetown, in Pleasant Township, Brown County, Ohio. He was elected overseer of the poor of the township on April 1, 1816. [9]

        On June 15, 1822, John Davidson bought 127 acres on White Oak Creek, part of survey #2789, for $253.50, and an adjacent 58 acres on September 24, 1829, for $232.00, both from William Clark and Joseph Wells. On July 7, 1827, he acquired 81 acres, part of survey #2523, in exchange for 90 acres on White Oak Creek with William White's heirs, and on March 11, 1833, he bought 40 acres from James McKinney for $509.17. On August 10, 1827, he sold 15 acres to Michael Weaver for $140.00 and 20 acres to Andrew Donaldson for $150.00, and on September 24, 1835, he and his wife Mary sold 147 acres on White Oak Creek to Samuel Horn for $4,750.00. [10]

        John Davidson and his family moved to Vermilion County, Illinois, in 1835, and acquired 40 acres, the southeastern quarter of the northwestern quarter of Section 25, Township 19 north, Range 13 west, by U. S. patent; he sold it to John Gilgas on February 23, 1839, for $75.00. [11]

12

In July, 1836, he moved to Van Buren County, Iowa, and settled near Farmington, where he built a mill on Indian Creek.
Davidson worked, not only as a farmer, but also as a miller, millwright, and surveyor at various times. Between 1839 and 1841, he
purchased 845 acres in Van Buren County from the U. S. government
for $1,056.00. In October, 1839, Davidson surveyed the road from
Farmington to the Missouri state line for $2.00. He took an active
interest in politics and local affairs as a Democrat in his early
years and then as a Whig until 1852; he represented Van Buren
County in the making of the first Iowa constitution. He was also
a devoted member of the Methodist Church.[12]

Davidson sold 24 acres of his Van Buren County land to Lloyd
Rollins and 116 acres to John Burris on December 6, 1840, and
acreage to Hiram Brown on August 4, 1845, all part of Section 11,
Township 67, Range 8. On September 29, 1846, he sold 40 acres to
his son, George W. Davidson, and on November 8, 1847, he sold
lot 3, block 2, in the town of Harrisburg to his granddaughter,
Celestine Jane Davidson, for $118.00. In February, 1849, he sold
160 acres, the southeastern quarter of Section 33, Township 68,
Range 8, to John Folker, and moved from Van Buren County.[13]

In 1860, John Davidson was living in Cooke County, Texas, where
Mary West Davidson died in 1867. He then moved to Fannin County,
Texas, where on July 20, 1868, he bought 125 acres on Sloan's
Creek, four miles south of Bonham, from G. W. Grant for $250.00;
he sold it to William E. McDade for $500.00 on September 14, 1869,
after moving earlier in the year to Marion County, Texas, to live
with his son, Ben Davidson, in whose home he died on January 15,
1873.[14]

The children of John and Mary West Davidson were as follows:[15]

7. a. John Wesley Davidson, born September 6, 1812.
   b. Eliza Davidson, born c1813; died c1843 in Van Buren County,
      Iowa; married February 23, 1835, in Brown County, Ohio, to
      Gibson Hesler; children:
      (1) Elizabeth Hesler, born c1835.
      (2) Francis Hesler, born c1837.
      (3) Sarah Hesler, born c1839.
      (4) Amanda Hesler, born c1841.
   c. Nancy Davidson, born c1815; died before 1890 in Van Buren
      County, Iowa; married January 11, 1836, in Vermilion County,
      Illinois, to Samuel Hesler.
8. d. Benjamin Franklin Davidson, born November 28, 1816.
9. e. George Washington Davidson, born December 18, 1818.
   f. Christopher Columbus Davidson, born c1821; died between 1860
      and 1865.
   g. Oliver Ellsworth Davidson, born c1823; died between 1860 and
      1870 in New Orleans, Louisiana; married (1) _____ c1852
      (2) June 14, 1860, in Fannin County, Texas, to Sarah E. Hill;
      children (by first marriage):
      (1) William Davidson, born c1853.
      (2) Martha Davidson, born c1857.
   h. Thomas P. Davidson, born c1826; died before 1890.
   i. Mary Ann Davidson, born c1828; died December 18, 1886, in Van
      Buren County, Iowa; married March 7, 1849, in Clark County,

Missouri, to James Schoolcraft.
j. Mathilda J. Davidson, born September 30, 1830; died June 25, 1850, in Van Buren County, Iowa; married April 4, 1849, in Van Buren County, Iowa, to Daniel McCoy.
10. k. Susan Davidson, born c1833.

***

7.   John Wesley Davidson was born September 6, 1812, in Clermont (now Brown) County, Ohio, and died May 6, 1893, in Van Buren County, Iowa; married April 2, 1834, in Brown County, Ohio, to Esther Ervin. Their children were as follows:[18]

a. Celestine Jane Davidson, born c1835; married James F. Bailey; child:
  (1) Ella Bailey, born 185?; died 1898; married Henry T. Shepherd; children:
    (a) Harry Armstrong Shepherd, born c1878; married Eva Mae Gaston; children:
      /1/ Byrle B. Shepherd.
      /2/ Stanley Theodore Shepherd married Thelma Gentry; lived in Ft. Madison, Iowa; children:
        /a/ Robert Shepherd.
        /b/ Sally Shepherd.
      /3/ Lloyd Shepherd.
      /4/ Donald Edward Shepherd.
b. Corrina Davidson, born c1837; died young.
c. Corwin Marion Davidson, born November 7, 1840; died July 23, 1908; married December 23, 1869, to Alice Burthena Irwin; children:
  (1) John Davidson, dsp.
  (2) Ella Davidson married _____ Johnson; lived in Hannibal, Missouri.
  (3) Esther Davidson married _____ Glover; lived in Kahoka, Missouri.
  (4) Earl Davidson.
d. E. M. Davidson, died young.
e. John A. Davidson, born c1844; married October 28, 1872, to Mary Fulton; children:
  (1) Harry Nay Davidson married Irene McClelland; children:
    (a) Bessie Nina Davidson married M. F. Browne; lived in San Antonio, Texas.
    (b) Daisy Lamar Davidson married _____ Stansky; lived in Chicago, Illinois.
  (2) Nellie Davidson married February 4, 1905, to Robert Orion Fidlar; children:
    (a) Ruth Davidson Fidlar, born May 11, 1909; dsp December 10, 1913.
    (b) Robert Leon Fidlar, born November 15, 1910; lived in Miami, Florida.
    (c) Delbert Charles Fidlar, born May 25, 1914; lived in Kalamazoo, Michigan.
  (3) Nina Celestine Davidson, born January 17, 1885; married September 22, 1927, to J. L. Glockle; dsp.

***

8.   Benjamin Franklin Davidson was born November 28, 1816, in Clermont (now Brown) County, Ohio, where he lived until 1835 and attended school with the future President U. S. Grant. In 1835 he moved with his family to near Catlin in Vermilion County, Illinois, where he married Susan Wolfe (see p. 269) on December 18, 1840. He moved about 1843 to Van Buren County, Iowa, and to Clark County, Missouri, about 1848. In 1849 he moved to Crawford (now Sebastian) County, Arkansas, and continued to work as a farmer, millwright, surveyor, and Methodist preacher.[17]

About 1855, Davidson moved to Fannin County, Texas, and on March 12, 1857, he bought 320 acres on Timber Creek about seven miles north of Bonham from Josiah Clark for $517.00. He sold 40 acres of the land on February 20, 1860, to Lafayette Winburn for $80.00, and 160 acres of it on February 5, 1861, to Solomon N. Phillips for $440.00. On July 13, 1861, he bought an additional 120 acres on Bois d'Arc Creek from B. F. Keene for $600.00.[18]

On July 19, 1861, at Bonham, Ben Davidson enlisted in the Bonham Dragoons, Independent Militia Volunteers, 14th Brigade of the Texas Militia, and on March 16, 1864, he enlisted for six months at Camp Lubbock in Company F, 1st Infantry Regiment, 3rd Brigade of Texas State Troops. After the death of his brother Oliver E. Davidson in the Civil War, he raised his daughter Martha. In 1868, he and his wife sold their part of the estate of her father, Henry Wolfe, in Vermilion County, Illinois.[19]

Ben Davidson sold the farm on Bois d'Arc Creek, four and a half miles northeast of Bonham, to B. E. Brown for $800.00 on June 11, 1869, and moved to Marion County, Texas, where on September 14, 1869, he bought 195 acres on the Daingerfield road about 10 miles from Jefferson from William E. McDade for $1,839.00, and an additional 100 acres about 10 miles west of Jefferson on September 25, 1869, from A. J. B. Garrett for $150.00.[20]

In 1873, Davidson was a Marion County school trustee, and in 1878, he was a trustee of the Kellyville Circuit, Jefferson District, of the North Texas Conference of the Methodist Church. He sold 25 acres of his farm to James Cole on January 15, 1877, and on October 29, 1881, he sold one acre to J. P. Beamer for $5.00. On March 9, 1882, he traded his remaining 170 acres in Marion County to J. W. Wright for 159 acres about a mile and a half west of Sipe Springs in Comanche County, Texas, and moved there.[21]

Davidson was interested in the political protest movement which resulted in the formation of the Populist Party, and on November 2, 1886, he was elected Comanche County surveyor on the Human Party ticket, but he died August 16, 1887, before completing his term of office.[22] He was a Mason and a Methodist, never financially successful; he was tall, of heavy build, with blue eyes and brown hair.[23]

The children of Ben and Susan Wolfe Davidson were as follows:[24]

a.   Ann W. Davidson, born October 6, 1841; died April 9, 1903, in Anson, Texas; married June 26, 1862, in Fannin County, Texas, to John B. Darnell; children:

15

   (1) Mattison Davidson Darnell, born September 15, 1863; dsp
     November 16, 1919.
   (2) Delura Darnell married William Bolding.
   (3) Reese Darnell, born September 15, 1868; married Della
     Chancellor; child:
     (a) John B. Darnell married Lee _____ ; dsp; lived in
       Ft. Worth, Texas.
   (4) Jerusha Darnell, dsp 1929.
   (5) William Darnell married Emma _____ ; children:
     (a) Ann Darnell married Lloyd Smith; dsp; lived in Ft.
       Worth, Texas.
     (b) Burrell Darnell; lived in California.
 b. Nancy Davidson, born July 12, 1844; dsp September 6, 1865.
 c. Martha Davidson, born September 3, 1847; dsp October 8, 1847.
 d. Henry Wolfe Davidson, born December 4, 1848; dsp January 8,
   1928, in Denton, Texas.
11. e. William Franklin Davidson, born October 15, 1851.
 f. Arnetty Bell Davidson, born September 1, 1854; dsp October
   12, 1868.
12. g. Joshua Ellen Davidson, born February 7, 1857.
 h. Susan Davidson, born January 6, 1860; died March 12, 1895,
   in Savoy, Texas; married December 15, 1881, to John Taylor
   Alderson; children:
   (1) John Malcolm Alderson, born 1890; dsp February 26, 1968,
     in Alpine, Texas; married June 14, 1921, to Eleanora
     Seidenstricker (one adopted son).
   (2) Susan Elizabeth Alderson, born January 19, 1893; married
     Samuel Ewing Davis; child:
     (a) Jean Davis, born June 14, 1918; married (1) _____
       (2) _____ (3) Raymond S. Green; lived
     in Galveston, Texas; children (by third marriage):
     /1/ Raymond S. Green, born 1951.
     /2/ Sammie Sue Green, born 1953.
 i. Benjamin Soule Davidson, born December 7, 1862; died August
   9, 1939, in Lubbock, Texas; married May 16, 1899, in Anson,
   Texas, to Effie Nevill (see p. 141); child:
   (1) Mary Zella Davidson, born July 1, 1901, in Anson, Texas;
     married November 23, 1921, in Denton, Texas, to Homer
     Buchanan Trimble (see David B. Trimble, *American Begin-*
     nings).

***

11.   William Franklin Davidson was born October 15, 1851, in Sebastian County, Arkansas; died December 15, 1916, in Mullin, Texas;
married (1) February 27, 1888, in Comanche County, Texas, to Emma
Louisa McKeehan (2) September 4, 1899, in Democrat, Texas, to
Jane Gray. His children were as follows:[25]

(by first marriage):
a. James Ira Davidson, born January 10, 1889; married Frances
  Leach; lived in Waxahatchie, Texas; child:
  (1) James Ira Davidson, born 1920; dsp.
b. Benjamin Franklin Davidson, born November 30, 1890; married
  Cecil Bellamy; lived in Austin, Texas; children:
  (1) Benjamin Franklin Davidson, born November 24, 1918; mar-
    ried Allene Evans; dsp.

16

  (2) James Dickerson Davidson, born September 28, 1920.
  (3) Lewis Edgar Davidson, born September 11, 1923.
  (4) William Theodore Davidson, born November 9, 1925.
  (5) Molly Joyce Davidson, born December 14, 1927.
  (6) Eugene Verle Davidson, born November 25, 1930.
  (7) Marion Bernice Davidson, born November 23, 1934.
  (8) Grace Edna Davidson, born June 28, 1936.
  (9) Cecil Ira Davidson, born September 15, 1937.
 c. Mary S. Davidson, born November 15, 1894; married John M.
  Gray; lived in Brownwood, Texas; children:
  (1) Ronald Gray, dsp.
  (2) Donald Gray.
  (3) Katie Gray married Perry H. Cox; lived in Brownwood,
    Texas; child:
    (a) David Cox.
 d. Willie Lou Davidson, born February 9, 1898; dsp July 10, 1898.
 (by second marriage):
 e. Rosa Maggie Davidson, born March 23, 1902; dsp August 5, 1902.
 f. William Caswell Davidson, born c1905; married Martha _____;
  lived in Goldthwaite, Texas.
 g. George Jones Davidson, born c1908; married Irene _____; lived
  in Brownwood, Texas.

***

12. Joshua Ellen Davidson was born February 7, 1857, in Fannin
County, Texas, and died February 17, 1920, in Weatherford, Texas;
married December 25, 1878, to Benjamin Franklin Bailey, born February 9, 1852; died April 1, 1926. Their children were as follows:[26]

 a. Claude Eugene Bailey, born September 26, 1880; died 1968; married (1) Lallie Ira Davis (2) Billie Boozer; children:
  (by first marriage):
  (1) Max Blendon Bailey, born August 17, 1905; dsp March 9,
    1907.
  (2) Richard Eugene Bailey, born October, 1908; dsp; lived in
    Stillwater, Oklahoma.
  (3) Ida Louise Bailey, born and died November, 1913.
  (4) Mary Ellen Bailey, born November, 1913; married William
    Hunnicutt; lived in Pomona, California; children:
    (a) Penelope Hunnicutt, born December 29, 1941.
    (b) Barbara Hunnicutt.
  (5) Jack Blendon Bailey, born August, 1925; married Margaret
    _____; dsp; lived in Tulsa, Oklahoma.
  (by second marriage):
  (6) Minnie Will Bailey, born 1942; lived in Lincoln, Alabama.
 b. Myrtle Bailey, born August 18, 1889; married Sim R. Brown;
  children:
  (1) Ellen Elaine Brown, born October, 1917; married (1) Roy
    _____ (2) Harold Grantham; dsp.
  (2) Ladene Elizabeth Brown, born September 26, 1918; married
    (1) Jack White (2) Guy Davis; lived in Temple, Texas;
    child (by first marriage):
    (a) Gretta White, born August 21, 1942.
 c. Benjamin Franklin Bailey, born September 21, 1892; dsp June
  5, 1966; married June 23, 1925, to Zelda Lurene Winchell; dsp.

***

17

9.   George Washington Davidson was born December 18, 1818, in Brown County, Ohio, and died May 6, 1910, in Van Buren County, Iowa; married (1) December 20, 1840, in Clark County, Missouri, to Hannah Amanda Tompkins (2) April 9, 1889, in Van Buren County, Iowa, to Nancy A. Pervines. His children (all by first marriage) were as follows:[27]

    a. Sarles Taylor Davidson, born 1841; died in Kansas; married Nancy Paddleford; children:
       (1) Lila Davidson, born c1867.
       (2) Georgeann Davidson, born c1869; died young.
       (3) George W. Davidson, born c1869; lived in Kansas.
       (4) C. May Davidson, born c1874.
    b. Johanna Davidson married John Ray; lived in LaBelle, Missouri; children:
       (1) Emma Ray married John Sutton.
       (2) Annis Ray married _____ Minke; lived in LaBelle, Missouri.
       (3) John Ray.
13. c. James Davidson, born December 20, 1845.
    d. Mary Davidson, born c1848; married William Scott; lived in Greeley, Colorado; children:
       (1) George Scott.
       (2) Elizabeth Scott.
       (3) Myrtle Scott.
       (4) Roy Scott.
       (5) Leta Scott, dsp; lived in Greeley, Colorado.
    e. Mariah Davidson, born May 8, 1852; died March 22, 1897; married June 13, 1874, to Samuel Sylvester Giles; children:
       (1) Oran Giles, born April 25, 1876; married Hulda _____.
       (2) Maggie D. Giles, born July 15, 1878; dsp October 8, 1883.
       (3) Earl B. Giles, born September 25, 1882; married Ada _____; lived in Quincy, Illinois.
       (4) Charlotte Giles, born May 17, 1885; married August 1, 1902, to Charles Welch; children:
          (a) Viola Welch.
          (b) Perry Welch.
       (5) Eva Lena Giles, born August 10, 1887; died February 7, 1957; married September 1, 1904, to Fred Welch; child:
          (a) Velma Lee Welch.
       (6) Presley Giles, born August 26, 1891.
    f. Sarah Davidson, born c1856; married James Tompkins; lived in Riverside, California.
    g. Ella Davidson, born c1859; married (1) Pierce Bradford (2) Albert Woods (3) J. H. Bennett; children (all by first marriage):
       (1) Stella Bradford, dsp.
       (2) Bruce Bradford, dsp.

***

13.   James Davidson was born December 20, 1845, at Bonaparte, Iowa, and died June 27, 1937, in Ft. Worth, Texas; married March 18, 1875, to Josephine Giles. Their children were as follows:[28]

    a. Elizabeth Davidson, born January 10, 1877; married August 18, 1898, to John Haney Anderson; children:

18

(1) Oletha Anderson, born July 30, 1899; married June 25, 1922, to Walter Howard Hinton; lived in Altus, Oklahoma; children:
  (a) Betty Jo Hinton, born October 25, 1925; dsp.
  (b) Robert Howard Hinton, born April 17, 1931; married Donna Lee Milburn; lived in Altus, Oklahoma; children:
    /1/ Holly Lee Hinton, born December 27, 1969.
    /2/ Howard Milburn Hinton, born December 28, 1972.
(2) Theresa Marie Anderson, born July 5, 1901; married March 21, 1923, to Rubin Leslie Krueger; child:
  (a) Margaret Elizabeth Krueger, born December 24, 1927; married August 27, 1949, to Raoul Barton Beasley; child:
    /1/ Leslie Denise Beasley, born 1957.
(3) William Bryan Anderson, born September 18, 1907; married (1) Arvilla _____ (2) Gwendolyn Watts (3) Grace Shappard (4) May 17, 1947, to Mrs. Dora (Neeley) Skaggs; dsp.

b. Hurder Davidson, born July 3, 1879; dsp July 4, 1880.
c. Glen Davidson, born December 1, 1881; died December 23, 1967; married (1) December 24, 1902, to Daisy Dickson (2) Mary _____; children (by first marriage):
  (1) Howard Leslie Davidson, born December 30, 1903; dsp October 15, 1970; married Elsa Mix; lived in Oklahoma City, Oklahoma.
  (2) Gertrude Glendine Davidson, born August 12, 1916; dsp.
d. Emmett Davidson, born September 25, 1886; dsp March 7, 1958; married (1) 1908, Valley De Rosier (2) Hattie Carr.
e. Thurman Allen Davidson, born November 7, 1888; married Mae Mellick; lived in Oklahoma City, Oklahoma; children:
  (1) Rose Mary Davidson, born July 11, 1918; married (2) March, 1946, to Victor B. Sellers; dsp; lived in Tampa, Florida.
  (2) Betty Jean Davidson, born January 31, 1921; married 1943 to Robert E. Van Zant; lived in Glendale, California; children:
    (a) Robert E. Van Zant, born November 1, 1946.
    (b) Allison B. Van Zant, born February 16, 1953.
    (c) Deborah Suzanne Van Zant, born July 16, 1954.
    (d) Valerie Van Zant, born 1963.
f. Lulu Belle Davidson, born June 21, 1890; dsp February 7, 1910.
g. Iza Mae Davidson, born 1894; dsp December 23, 1968; married September 18, 1918, to Ray J. Noblitt.

***

10.   Susan Davidson was born about 1833 in Brown County, Ohio, and died November 8, 1886, in Montague County, Texas; married c1852 to Jacob Gardenhire. Their children were as follows:[29]

a. Elmira Gardenhire, born c1853; married John W. Evans; lived in Homer, Texas.
b. Sarah J. Gardenhire, born c1855; dsp; lived in Dixie, Oklahoma.
c. Mary B. Gardenhire, born c1856; married A. B. Hill; lived in Spanish Fort, Texas.
d. Thomas Milton Gardenhire, born c1858; lived in Dixie, Oklahoma.

19

e. John D. Gardenhire, born c1860; married November 26, 1882, to Julia Bingham; children:
    (1) Jesse James Gardenhire; lived in Duncan, Oklahoma.
    (2) Thomas Gardenhire; lived in Fontana, California.
    (3) Hannah Gardenhire; lived in Portland, Oregon.
    (4) Essie Gardenhire.
f. Lillie Gardenhire, born c1863; married August 3, 1881, to R. R. Turner; lived in Dixie, Oklahoma.
g. Emma L. Gardenhire, born c1865; married Daniel E. Raglin; lived in Dixie, Oklahoma.
h. Tennessee A. Gardenhire, born c1868; died March 6, 1894; married Martin Jerry Welch; children:
    (1) Marion Lee Welch, born June 14, 1890; lived in Lefors, Texas.
    (2) Columbus Washington Welch, born March 8, 1892; lived in Wichita Falls, Texas.
i. Eva Gardenhire, born c1870; married M. B. Pruitt; lived in Leon, Oklahoma.
j. S. Jarvis Gardenhire, born c1872; married January 18, 1892, to Lucy Johnson; lived in Spanish Fort, Texas.
k. Arminta Gardenhire, born c1874; married 1891 to F. N. Dennis; lived in Spanish Fort, Texas.

                              ***

3.   Elizabeth Davidson was born about 1789 in Allegheny County, Pennsylvania, and died after 1860 in Bracken Coutny, Kentucky; married about 1811 in Clermont (now Brown) County, Ohio, to Thomas Myers; their children were as follows:[30]

a. Caroline Myers, born c1813; married _____ Baker; children:
    (1) Mary E. Baker, born c1831; married _____ Mettam.
    (2) Amanda Baker, born c1833; married _____ O'Neal.
b. Amanda Myers, born c1815; married _____ Perrine; children:
    (1) Julia Perrine, born c1842.
    (2) Elizabeth Perrine, born c1844; married James Wilson.
    (3) Louisa Perrine, born c1846.
    (4) Garrett Perrine, born c1849; died young.
c. Susan Myers, born c1818; died October, 1876, in Bracken County, Kentucky; married October 7, 1834, to William Champe Marshall, born 1807; died 1873, son of Martin Pickett Marshall and Mildred Taliaferro; member of Kentucky legislature, Commonwealth attorney, Mayor of Augusta, Kentucky; children:
    (1) Mary T. Marshall, born August 19, 1836; married November 23, 1860, William C. Middleton, who died in 1871; lived in Cincinnati, Ohio.
    (2) Elizabeth Marshall, born July 28, 1839; married September 5, 1867, John Ewing.
    (3) Martin P. Marshall, born February 3, 1843; lived in Kansas.
    (4) William T. Marshall, born March 30, 1844; lived in Cincinnati, Ohio.
    (5) George C. Marshall, born November 17, 1845; married Maria Bradford, daughter of Dr. Johnson Bradford and Maria Stuart; dsp; lived in Uniontown, Pennsylvania.
    (6) Matilda B. Marshall, born January 12, 1847; married June 4, 1868, Samuel Blaine; lived in Washington, Pennsylvania.
    (7) Robert P. Marshall, born April 7, 1848; married 1882 Mrs.

_____ Laughlin; lived in Mahoning, Pennsylvania.
- (8) Margaret P. Marshall, born March 5, 1851; married December 29, 1876, Dr. Thomas Bradford, son of Dr. Johnson Bradford and Maria Stuart.
- (9) Charles L. Marshall, born December 14, 1852.
d. Alfred N. Myers, born c1825; married (1) Louisa _____ (2) Sarah _____; child (by first marriage):
  (1) Louisa Carter Myers, born c1849.
e. Lucy Myers, born c1827; dsp 186?.

* * *

4. Mary Davidson was born February 2, 1796, in Bracken County, Kentucky, and died January 28, 1858, in Brown County, Ohio; married June 18, 1820, in Brown County, Ohio, to Lot Stratton, born March 24, 1798; died January 28, 1866, son of William Stratton and Katherine Keethler; their children were as follows:[31]

a. Louisa Stratton, born c1821; died 1860; married A. G. McCall.
b. Napoleon Bonaparte Stratton, born August 6, 1823; died October 6, 1866; married September 23, 1846, to Barbara Ann McKinzie, born March 29, 1830; children:
  - (1) Mary Louise Stratton, born June 30, 1847; died August 19, 1954.
  - (2) Clara Stratton, born May 24, 1849.
  - (3) Anastatia Stratton, born July 19, 1850.
  - (4) Amanda Evelyn Stratton, born December 26, 1851.
  - (5) Roderick Random Stratton, born June 13, 1854; died January 8, 1937; married July 20, 1878, Tabitha Jane Pitzer; children:
    - (a) William Albert Stratton, born October 25, 1878; died February 15, 1931.
    - (b) Robert Stratton, born November 18, 1883; lived in Stillwater, Oklahoma.
  - (6) Lot Stratton, born May 22, 1860; died August, 1954.
  - (7) Rachel Lucinda Stratton, born June 23, 1863; married _____ Patton.
c. Francis Marion Stratton, born October 1, 1825.
d. Nancy Jane Stratton, born c1827; married (1) James Ringold Robertson (2) Newton Louderback; children:
  (by first marriage):
  - (1) James Ringold Robertson, born July 11, 1854; married Emily E. Wardlow; children:
    - (a) Clarence C. Robertson; lived in Georgetown, Ohio.
    - (b) Robert B. Robertson, died 1936.
    - (c) William C. Robertson.
    - (d) Bertha May Robertson.
  (by second marriage):
  - (2) Francis Marion Louderback.
e. (son), born c1829.
f. Albina Stratton, born c1831.
g. Susan Stratton, born March 13, 1833; dsp February 18, 1854.
h. Martin Van Buren Stratton, born January 13, 1835; dsp March 17, 1859.
i. Thomas B. Stratton, born February 25, 1837; dsp January 25, 1859.
j. Lucinda Stratton, born c1839; dsp.

* * *

5. Nancy Davidson was born about 1799 in Bracken County, Kentucky, and died after 1850; married July 28, 1822, in Brown County, Ohio, to Moore Ralstin. Their children were as follows:[32]

21

a. (daughter), born c1823.
b. (son), born c1825.
c. Amanda Ralstin, born c1827.
d. Marcus Ralstin, born c1828.
e. Elizabeth Ralstin, born c1829.
f. (daughter), born c1831.
g. Jane Ralstin, born c1833.
h. William Ralstin, born c1834.
i. Matilda Ralstin, born c1836.
j. Ellen M. Ralstin, born c1844.

***

REFERENCES

[1]Revolutionary Pension #S16099, National Archives, Washington, D. C.; History of Brown County, Ohio (Chicago, W. H. Beers & Co., 1883), pp. 462, 625; Portrait and Biographical Album of Jefferson and Van Buren Counties for 1890 (Lake Publishing Company, 1890), p. 405; family tradition states that he had a brother who served with the British in the American Revolution and that the two brothers quarreled bitterly because of it and never met again.

[2]Pennsylvania Archives (Philadelphia, 1853; Harrisburg, 1874-1935), 5th Series, III, 317.

[3]Pension, #S16099; Pennsylvania Archives, 5th Series, IV, 396, 6th Series, II, 221; Portrait and Biographical Album... , p. 405; Washington County, Pennsylvania, tax lists.

[4]Bracken County, Kentucky, Record Book, 1797-1805, pp. 33-34, 325, Deeds C, 54.

[5]History of Brown County, Ohio, p. 624; Pension #S16099; Record Book, Clark Township, Clermont (now Brown) County, Ohio, owned (1960) by Robert Stratton.

[6]Brown County, Ohio, Deeds K, 197, M, 282, Estate Settlement File 7465; History of Brown County, Ohio, p. 625; Last pension payment record, Records Division, National Archives, Washington, D.C.

[7]Records of Lois Brookbank McKay and Inezetta E. Stiver.

[8]Records of Inezetta E. Stiver.

[9]Bible record belonging (1967) to David B. Trimble; Bracken County, Kentucky, tax lists, 1811, 1812; Record Book, Clark Township.

[10]Brown County, Ohio, Deeds C, 90, G, 520, F, 84, H, 41, K, 309, 310, F, 112, I, 14, M, 230, 231, 232.

[11]Vermilion County, Illinois, Entry Book, Deeds E, 520.

[12]U. S. Land Office Records, Washington, D.C., patents #2856, 5389, 5495, 8410, 5371; Van Buren County, Iowa, Road Book, p. 320; Portrait and Biographical Album... , p. 405.

[13]Van Buren County, Iowa, Deeds C, 18, 20, 0, 67, G, 198, H, 218, I, 507.

[14]Cooke County, Texas, census of 1860; Fannin County, Texas, Deeds P, 546, R, 87; Bible record owned (1967) by David B. Trimble.

[15]Portrait and Biographical Album... , p. 405.

[16]Records of Stanley T. Shepherd.

[17]Bible record belonging (1967) to David B. Trimble; Brown County, Ohio, school census book; statement of Benjamin S. Davidson; Portrait and Biographical Album... , p. 405; Crawford County, Arkansas, census of 1850.

[18]Fannin County, Texas, Deeds J, 213, M, 435, N, 334, 116.

[19]Pension record, Texas State Archives, Austin, Texas; Marion County, Texas, census of 1870; statement of Benjamin S. Davidson; Vermilion County, Illinois, Deeds.

22

[20]Marion County, Texas, Deeds E, 472, 48.

[21]Ibid., I, 499, L, 410, P, 193; Comanche County, Texas, Deed Bk. 2, p. 483.

[22]Comanche County, Texas, Record of Official Bonds, p. 159; Bible record belonging (1967) to David B. Trimble.

[23]Statement of Benjamin S. Davidson.

[24]Bible Record belonging (1967) to David B. Trimble; records of John Malcolm Alderson.

[25]Records of Benjamin F. Davidson.

[26]Records of Myrtle B. Brown.

[27-28]Records of Oletha A. Hinton.

[29]Kaufman County, Texas, Deeds C, 108, H, 614, I, 287, 557, 558, 559, L, 137, O, 243; Montague County, Texas, Estate Files #251, 280, 289, District Court Cause #1225, Deeds T, 333, U, 225; Cooke County, Texas, Deed Bk. 7, p. 485, Bk. 9, p. 326, Bk. 29, p. 6, Bk. 31, p. 361, Bk. 33, p. 556.

[30]Bracken County, Kentucky, census of 1850, 1860.

[31]Brown County, Ohio, census of 1850.

***

EASLEY of Virginia

William Parker lived in Henrico County, Virginia, as early as 1664, when he bought 100 acres from Robert Bullington; he had probably moved from England shortly before. At about the same time he married Katherine _____ ; he died by 1677 and was buried on his farm. His widow then married John Milner, who was born about 1639 and died in 1684, leaving property to his wife's children. The children of William and Katherine Parker were as follows:[1]

1. a. Ann Parker, born c1665.
   b. Mary Parker, born c1669; married 1689 in Henrico County, Virginia, to William Burton.
   c. William Parker, born c1671; lived in Henrico County, Virginia, in 1726.

***

1. Ann Parker was born about 1665 and received property from the estates of her father and step-father; about 1683 she married Robert Easley, who had moved, probably from England, to Henrico County before December 15, 1680.[2]

Robert Easley was involved in several law suits between 1684 and 1711 with Mrs. Katherine Milner, his mother-in-law, William Randolph, William Sutton, John Johnson's estate, Giles Webb, and Abraham Womack. On June 1, 1692, he was fined for swearing, while William Byrd stated in 1709 that "I had some complaints against Robin Easley, which seemed to be the effect of quarreling," and "Will Bass gave me a sad account of Robin Easley, who is a lazy fellow." On October 6, 1711, Easley received the local militia prize for wrestling.[3]

Easley received a grant from the colony of Virginia on October 20, 1704, for 315 acres on the east side of Reedy Creek in Henrico County; with Thomas Jefferson, Thomas Turpin, and John Archer, he received a 1500 acre grant in Henrico County. He made his will on December 17, 1711, giving his three older children 500 acres on Fine Creek and his three younger children 400 acres between Fine and Manakin Upper Creek; he died shortly afterwards and his estate was probated in March, 1712, by his widow.[4]

After the death of her husband, Ann Easley was sued in 1712 and 1713 by Robert Blaws, William Byrd, Abraham Womack, Joseph Pleasants, John Woodson, and John Bolling, which consumed much of the proceeds of the estate. She made her will on April 12, 1720, dividing her property among her six children, and the estate was probated on June 6, 1720.[5]

The children of Robert and Ann Easley were as follows:

2. a. John Easley, born c1685.
3. b. Warham Easley, born c1688.
   c. Margaret Easley, born c1692; married (1) Thomas Dupray (2) James Watson.[6]
4. d. William Easley, born c1695.
   e. Elizabeth Easley, born c1698.[7]
   f. Robert Easley, born c1704; dsp 1736 in Amelia County, Virginia.[8]

***

24

2.   John Easley was born about 1685 in Henrico County, Virginia; about 1710 he married Mary Benskin.

****

Jeremiah Benskin moved to Henrico County, Virginia, probably from England, before 1690; on December 1, 1696, he sold Henry Ascough 308 acres in Henrico County for five shillings. He made his will in April, 1690, leaving his property to his wife Elizabeth and daughter Mary; the estate was probated on June 3, 1703. His widow married Robert Williams on October 12, 1703, and his daughter was raised by John Bolling. Benskin received posthumously a grant from the colony of Virginia of 324 acres on the south side of the James River at the mouth of Lower Westham Creek for transporting seven persons into the colony.

****

John Easley lived on the 324 acre grant which had been granted to Jeremiah Benskin, his father-in-law; in August, 1711, he petitioned for acquisition of his wife's estate, then in the hands of John Bolling. He was involved in law suits with Philip Purcell, Edward Watkins, William Byrd, William Finney, John Bolling, and John Martin between 1709 and 1724. On October 6, 1735, he bought 400 acres on Powhick Creek in Dale Parish, Henrico County, from Henry Cary for £24; in 1736 he paid quit rents on both tracts. In November, 1739, he and his son John acknowledged a deed to his brother Warham. He died shortly before April, 1742, and his will was probated by his brother Warham as his executor in May, 1742.[10]

The children of John and Mary Easley, probably among others, were as follows:

5. a. John Easley, born c1712.
    b. William Easley, born c1715; died before 1753 leaving a child:
        (1) Benskin Easley, born c1740; married Elizabeth _____; served in 5th Virginia Regiment, Continental Line, in American Revolution; lived in Dinwiddie County, Virginia; died c1778.
6. c. Stephen Easley, born c1718.
    d. Robert Easley, born c1724; dsp 1751 in Chesterfield (now Powhatan) County, Virginia.[11]
7. e. Warham Easley, born c1726.

***

5.   John Easley was born about 1712 in Henrico (now Powhatan) County, Virginia, and married about 1733 Joyce Allen, daughter of William and Mary Allen of Albemarle County, Virginia. On October 2, 1739, he acquired the 400 acre plantation settled by his uncle, Warham Easley, probably in exchange for his father's 324 acre plantation; the land was located on the south side of the James River between Deep Creek and Watson's Branch in Goochland County. He made his will in 1746, leaving his property to his wife and children, and the estate was probated in August, 1746. His widow married Joel Chandler, who with William Allen, was appointed guardian of his children;[12] The children of John and Joyce Easley were as follows:[13]

    a. Judith Easley, born c1734; married John Wright; lived in Goochland County, Virginia.
    b. Samuel Easley, born c1736.
    c. John Easley, born c1738; died c1785 in Greenville County, South Carolina; married Ann Gowen.
    d. William Easley, born c1740; died 1796 in Halifax County, Virginia;

25

married Jane Scruggs, daughter of Drury Scruggs and Mary Carter.

    e.   Robert Easley, born c1742; died 1806 in Anderson County, South Carolina; married (1) Elizabeth Coleman (2) Mary Allen (3)Catherine Benson.

    f.   Millington Easley, born c1744; died c1803 in Greenville County, South Carolina; married Elizabeth _____ .

***

6.   Stephen Easley was born about 1718 near Manakin Town, Virginia, and married Mrs. Marianne (David) Burton (see p. 5) c1751. He was appointed administrator of the estate of his brother Robert in January, 1752, and on March 2, 1753, he sold Warham Easley for Ł24 his interest in 150 acres in Chesterfield County on the north branches of Powhick Creek and the James River which he had inherited from his father, John Easley, and his brother, Robert Easley.[14]

About 1762, Stephen Easley moved to Antrim Parish in Halifax County, Virginia, and on February 19, 1763, he bought 1,000 acres on Sandy Creek in Halifax County from Daniel Easley for Ł100; he also bought 150 acres on the south side of Banister River from Daniel Easley for Ł50 on April 22, 1763. He bought 75 acres on the south side of Banister River from Joshua Powell on June 21, 1770, and 175 acres from George Brown for Ł150 on November 12, 1777.[15]

On March 26, 1770, Stephen Easley and his wife Marianne gave her daughter Ann Burton 200 acres in King William Parish in Cumberland (now Powhatan) County on Buck Branch; on May 20, 1773, he gave his daughter Sarah Stubblefield 200 acres in Antrim Parish, Halifax County, and on the same date he sold another 200 acres to William Childress for Ł30. On May 20, 1780, he sold Robert Chappell 325 acres on the south side of Banister River for Ł2,000; on March 15, 1781, he sold 400 acres to George Ridley for Ł9,000; on May 12, 1781, he sold 200 acres on Broomstraw Branch to John Chappell for Ł8,125.[16]

Stephen Easley then moved to Sullivan County, Tennessee, where in October, 1782, and October, 1783, he received grants totaling 1,733 acres on Horse Creek, a branch of the Holston River. On May 18, 1798, he sold a 300-acre grant to Elijah Butler for Ł100, and on January 25, 1811, he sold 220 acres to Caleb Smith and William Pierce for $600.00.[17]

There is no record of the death of Stephen and Marianne Easley; they had the following children:[18]

    a.   Sarah Easley, born December 1, 1752; died in Hawkins County, Tennessee; married July 15, 1772, in Halifax County, Virginia, to Robert Loxley Stubblefield (see p. 212).

    b.   Robert Easley, born November 25, 1754; married (1) March 10, 1778, in Halifax County, Virginia, to Winifred Dixon (2) 1807 in Sullivan County, Tennessee, to Mrs. Mary Pope (see p. 267).

8. c.   Thomas Easley, born November 23, 1756.

    d.   Daniel Easley, born December 4, 1759.

    e.   Stephen Easley, born May 16, 1763.

9. f.   Peter Easley, born October 15, 1765.

***

8.   Thomas Easley was born November 23, 1756, and died November 21, 1842, in Hickman County, Tennessee; married 1782 to Ecleo Wade; moved to Geor-

26

gia, then South Carolina, and in 1811 to Hickman County, Tennessee, where he settled on Duck River near Centerville. The children of Thomas and Ecleo Easley were as follows:[19]

a. Elizabeth Easley, born October 11, 1783; married Ripley Copeland.
b. John Easley, born November 9, 1784.
c. Mary Easley, born January 23, 1786; dsp 1789.
d. Thomas Wade Easley, born December 25, 1786; married Katherine Blankenship.
e. Anna Easley, born July 16, 1788; married Adam Wilson.
f. Stephen Easley, born October 26, 1789; dsp 1815.
g. Edward Easley, born March 28, 1791; married Frances King.
h. Warham Easley, born December 14, 1792; married Grace Baxter.
i. William Moody Easley, born September 22, 1794; married (1) Sarah Harvill (2) Mary Norris.
j. Mary Ann Easley, born February 4, 1796; married John W. Nunnlee.
k. Robert Easley, born January 1, 1797; married August 20, 1819, Elizabeth P. Lewis.
l. Ecleo Easley, born July 15, 1799; married William N. Nunnlee.
m. Sarah Easley, born October 27, 1801; dsp c1822.
n. James Daniel Easley, born May 7, 1804; married January 24, 1826, Elizabeth Warren.
o. Nancy Easley, born August 23, 1805; married Joseph A. Nunnlee.
p. Phoebe David Easley, born March 13, 1809; dsp c1823.

＊

9.   Peter Easley was born October 15, 1765; died about 1819 in Posey County, Indiana; married December 1, 1785, in Sullivan County, Tennessee, to Elizabeth Vincent, who was born March 21, 1766, and died about 1840 in Hickman County, Tennessee. Their children were as follows:[20]

a. Frances Easley, born August 21, 1786; married Michael Light.
b. John Easley, born August 6, 1788; married Mary Hamilton.
c. Vincent Easley, born October 2, 1790; died May 16, 1864; married September 12, 1821, Nancy Wilkerson Hamilton.
d. Robert Easley, born May 24, 1793.
e. Moses Easley, born October 24, 1795.
f. Winifred Easley, born July 7, 1798; married _____ Powers.

＊

7.   Warham Easley was born about 1726 in Henrico (now Powhatan) County, Virginia; in April, 1742, he chose his uncle Warham Easley as his guardian. On March 2, 1753, he bought his brother Stephen's interest in their father's 324 acre plantation; on August 6, 1762, he sold the land to Charles Clark. In 1766 Easley bought 200 acres on the branches of Ward's Fork in Charlotte County, Virginia, from George Anderson for £90; he bought 12 adjoining acres from John Simms for £8 in 1772. Easley sold the 212 acres to Richard Moore in 1779 and moved to Surry (now Stokes) County, North Carolina; about 1785, he moved to Henry County, Virginia, to a plantation on the North Carolina line. He made his will on August 12, 1790, and died shortly afterwards.[21]

Warham Easley married about 1752 Ann Woodson, daughter of John Woodson and Mary Miller; she was born about 1736 and made her will on August 24, 1801; the estate was probated in October, 1801. The children of Warham and Ann Easley were as follows:[22]

27

a. John Easley, born c1754; lived in Stokes County, North Carolina, in 1790.
b. Miller Easley, born c1756; died August 19, 1834, in Grainger County, Tennessee; married August 2, 1782, Mary Lyon.
c. Susanna Easley, born c1760; married Joseph Francis.
d. Joseph Easley, born April 11, 1764; died February 14, 1849, in Shelby County, Kentucky; married February 24, 1785, in Stokes County, North Carolina, Mary Catherine Deatherage.
e. William Easley, born c1766; married February 2, 1792, in Surry County, North Carolina, to Sarah Smith; lived in Jackson County, Missouri.
f. Warham Easley.
g. Judith Easley, born c1774; died 1823 in Dallas County, Alabama; married December 7, 1790, in Stokes County, North Carolina, James Strother Gaines.

***

3.   Warham Easley was born about 1688 in Henrico County, Virginia, and about 1721 married Sarah (Raibone) Barnes, daughter of Richard Raibone and widow of John Barnes.[23]

        Easley bought land from Samuel Burton in 1720, John Barnes in 1722, and William Barnes in 1724. He sold 363 acres in St. James Parish, Henrico County, to John Farrar for £30 in 1726. He received grants from the colony of Virginia for 2,000 acres on October 13, 1727, and 400 acres on September 17, 1731. He bought 150 acres on the south side of James River on August 4, 1729, from Thomas Cardwell for £100 and 100 acres on the north side of James River on November 3, 1729, from Henry Bailey for £25. On August 15, 1729, he sold Alexander Kilpatrick 400 acres on the south side of James River; on August 19, 1729, he sold Thomas Cardwell 400 acres in the same area; and on October 15, 1734, he sold James Barnes 400 acres nearby. On January 14, 1736, he sold land to John Phelps, and the same day sold Thomas Dupray 100 acres on Watson's Branch.[24]

        Easley sold his nephew, John Easley, Jr., 400 acres on the south side of James River on October 2, 1739, undoubtedly in exchange for John Easley's 324 acre plantation called Westham. On June 2, 1746, he gave his son Roderick that 324 acres and another 500 acres on Deep Creek and the same day gave his son Robert the 250 acres bought from Thomas Cardwell and Henry Bailey.[25]

        Warham Easley made his will on September 24, 1747, leaving his property to his two sons; the estate was probated in November, 1747, the personal property being valued at £338. The children of Warham and Sarah Easley were as follows:[26]

a. Robert Easley, born c1722; died 1750 in Chesterfield County, Virginia; married December 23, 1744, Hannah Bates, daughter of John Bates and Susannah Fleming; child:[27]
    (1) Susannah Easley, born c1746.
b. Roderick Easley, born c1724; died 1768 in Halifax County, North Carolina; married Elizabeth Weldon, daughter of Samuel Weldon and Elizabeth Allen; moved to Halifax County, North Carolina, where he bought 240 acres from Robert Green in 1764 and 534 acres from Joseph Blake in 1765; children:[28]
    (1) James Easley died 1799 in Halifax County, North Carolina; married (1) Elizabeth Norwood; (2) Frances _____.
    (2) Daniel Weldon Easley died c1831 in Greene County, Alabama; married (1) Elizabeth Finch.

    (3) Samuel Easley married Rhoda _____; lived in Greene County,
        Alabama.
    (4) Roderick Easley married 1772 Elizabeth Ellis.
    (5) Benjamin Easley lived in Wilkes County, Georgia, in 1792.

                                ***

4.   William Easley was born about 1695 in Henrico County, Virginia;
married Mary _____; he sold 57 acres on the north side of James River
to Joseph Mayo on March 7, 1726; he bought 275 acres on Fine Creek and
the south side of James River from Thomas Jefferson and sold it to
Joseph Mayo on May 16, 1737. On March 20, 1738, he sold the 275 acres
given to him by his father's will to William Walker. He evidently left
Cumberland County, Virginia, in 1753 to escape prosecution for debt.
No further mention of him has been found. He had the following child:[29]

    a. Warham Easley married Elizabeth _____; lived in Halifax County, Vir-
        ginia, in 1792.[30]

While there is no proof, William and Mary Easley may have also had the
following children:

    b. Thomas Easley, died c1759 in Lunenburg County, Virginia.[31]
    c. Pyrant Easley married Elizabeth _____; lived in Pittsylvania County,
        Virginia.[32]
    d. Daniel Easley, born c1720; died 1786 in Halifax County, Virginia;
        married (1) Anne David (see p.   5); (2) Elizabeth Echols. On
        September 23, 1751, he bought 400 acres on Pole Cat Branch of Lower
        Manakin Creek from Matthew Branch, Jr., for ₤35; on May 13, 1761,
        he sold the land to William Stone and moved to Halifax County, where
        on April 16, 1761, he bought 591 acres on Banister River from William
        Russell; on May 20, 1762, he bought 154½ acres on Banister River from
        Brady Owen. He sold Stephen Easley 150 acres on April 22, 1763, and
        1,000 acres on February 19, 1763; on February 20, 1772, he sold
        Richard Carter 400 acres for ₤60, and on May 21, 1778, he sold his
        son John the land John lived on for ₤5. On October 17, 1782, he
        bought 100 acres from John Clardy and on September 16, 1784, he
        bought 204 acres from James Bailey. Daniel Easley made his will on
        January 12, 1786, and the estate was probated on January 19, 1786.
        His children were as follows (all by his first marriage except per-
        haps Daniel):[33]
        (1) Marianne Easley, born October 3, 1746; married March 15, 1781,
            Daniel Parker.
        (2) Martha Easley, born July 20, 1750; dsp.
        (3) Phoebe Easley married _____ Adams.
        (4) John Easley, born c1757; died July 15, 1782; married c1778
            Sarah Mann, daughter of Robert and Phoebe Mann; children:
            (a) Elizabeth Easley, born c1779; married January 25, 1796,
                William Stone.
            (b) Robert Easley, born March 23, 1781; died September 10, 1859;
                married October 31, 1799, Nancy Stone, born November 6,
                1783; died September 6, 1853, daughter of John Stone and
                Dollie Hoskins.
        (5) Isaac Easley, born c1761; died 1810; married c1782 Judith Eas-
            ley; children:
            (a) Isaac Easley, dsp c1824 in Wilson County, Tennessee.
            (b) John Scruggs Easley, born October 13, 1793; died 1868;
                married November 6, 1821, Agnes Clark White.
            (c) William A. Easley.
            (d) Mary Easley married Thomas Donohoe.

                                29

    (e) Nancy Easley married Richard A. Cook.
    (f) Judith Easley married Fountain Scates.
    (g) Martha Easley, born October 11, 1801; died June 14, 1899,
        in Campbell County, Virginia; married September 29, 1824,
        to Joel Hubbard.
    (h) Daniel Easley.
    (i) Phoebe Easley.
    (j) Elizabeth Easley.
(6) Ann Easley.
(7) Daniel Easley, born June 25, 1765; died March 21, 1820, in Harrison County, Ohio; married November 24, 1791, Edith Anderson, born September 26, 1772; died March 6, 1820; children:
    (a) Sarah Easley, born February 13, 1793; died August 25, 1866; married January 2, 1812, Jonathan Bogue.
    (b) Mary Ann Easley, born October 17, 1794; died November 1, 1870; married April 24, 1813, Job Bogue.
    (c) Ruth Easley, born August 20, 1796; died April 3, 1875; married December 18, 1814, Henry Person David.
    (d) John Easley, born September 9, 1798; died January 25, 1873; married November 30, 1820, Nancy Kinsey.
    (e) Daniel Easley, born June 2, 1800; dsp January 5, 1825.
    (f) Rachel Easley, born June 14, 1802; dsp April 7, 1820.
    (g) Richard Easley, born September 22, 1804; married June 11, 1827, Elizabeth Valentine.
    (h) Isaac Easley, born August 2, 1806; died 1861; married April 8, 1830, Mary Norris.
    (i) Stephen Easley, born August 8, 1808; died April 22, 1847; married April 24, 1839, Subina Cadwallader.
    (j) Phoebe Easley, born June 29, 1811; died August 22, 1899; married April 19, 1831, Daniel Knock.
    (k) Thomas Easley, born April 7, 1814; died December 4, 1849; married March 2, 1837, Lydia Ann Buck.

***

REFERENCES

[1] Henrico County, Virginia, Wills & Deeds Bk. 1, p. 46, 1677-92, pp. 97, 249, 251, 286; Orphan's Court Book, 1677-1739, pp. 6, 14-15.

[2] Ibid., Orphan's Court Book, 1677-1739, pp. 6, 14-15; Wills & Deeds 1677-92, p. 286; Court Records Bk. 1, p. 175.

[3] Ibid., Court Records Bk. 2, pp. 170, 313, 346, 354, 1707-09, p. 39, 1710-14, pp. 82, 96, 103, 106, 112, 116, Bk. 5, p. 322; Louis B. Wright and Marion Tinling (eds.), The Secret Diary of William Byrd of Westover, 1709-1712 (Richmond, Virginia, The Dietz Press, 1941). pp. 34, 89, 417.

[4] Land Patent Bk. 9, p. 624, Bk. 10, p. 378, State Archives, Richmond, Virginia; Henrico County, Virginia, Wills & Deeds, 1710-14, part 1, pp. 116, 129, Order Book, 1710-14, pp. 112, 116, 123.

[5] Henrico County, Virginia, Order Book, 1710-14, pp. 138-140, 148-149, 159, 162, 170, 173, 186, 188, 192, 196, 204; Miscellaneous Records Bk. 2, p. 483.

[6] Ibid., Wills & Deeds, 1710-14, part 1, p. 116; Orphan's Court Book, 1677-1739, p. 54.

[7] Although there is no proof, she probably married (1) Philip Martin and (2) Alexander Kilpatrick; Henrico County, Virginia, Wills & Deeds, 1714-18, p. 165, Orphan's Court Book, 1677-1739.

[8] Amelia County, Virginia, Will Bk. 1, p. 2.

[9] Henrico County, Virginia, Wills & Deeds, 1688-97, p. 704, 1697-1704, pp. 325, 351, Orphan's Court Book, 1677-1739, pp. 93-95, 98; Land Patent Book 9, p. 623.

[10]Henrico County, Virginia, Orphan's Court Book, 1677-1739, p. 106, Order Book, 1707-09, p. 166, 1710-14, p. 224, 1719-24, pp.69, 123, 186, 194, 329, Deeds & Wills Bk. 2, p. 506, Order Book, 1737-46, pp. 41, 181; tithe lists, 1736.

[11]Chesterfield County, Virginia, Deed Bk. 1, p. 518, Order Book 1, p. 166.

[12]Albemarle County, Virginia, Wills A, 33; Goochland County, Virginia, Deed Bk. 3, p. 271, Will Bk. 5, p. 159, Order Book 6, pp. 218, 492.

[13]For descendants, see Virginia Easley DeMarce, A Tentative Outline of U. S. Easley Lines Primarily to the Year 1800 (n.p., 1970).

[14]Bible record of Stephen Easley's family, published in LeRoy Reeves, Ancestral Sketches (Lynchburg, Virginia: J. P. Bell Company, 1951); Chesterfield County, Virginia, Order Book 1, p. 166, Deed Bk. 1, p. 518.

[15]Halifax County, Virginia, Deed Bk. 4, pp. 291, 286, Bk. 8, p. 11, Bk. 10, p. 346.

[16]Cumberland County, Virginia, Deed Bk. 4, p. 372; Halifax County, Virginia, Deed Bk. 9, pp. 43, 63, Bk. 12, pp. 2, 99, 94.

[17]Sullivan County, Tennessee, Deed Bk. 1, pp. 143, 146, 144, 168, Bk. 3, p. 194, Bk. 6, p. 127.

[18]Bible record of Stephen Easley's family ... ; Halifax County, Virginia, Marriages; Sullivan County, Tennessee, Deed Bk. 5, p. 23.

[19]James D. Easley, A Genealogy and Family History of the Easley and McCullough Families (Ft. Worth, Texas, n. d.).

[20]LeRoy Reeves, Ancestral Sketches, pp.100ff.

[21]Henrico County, Virginia, Order Book, 1737-46, p. 178; Chesterfield County, Virginia, Deed Bk. 1, p. 518, Bk. 4, p. 458; Charlotte County, Virginia, Deeds; Henry County, Virginia, Will Bk. 1, p. 191.

[22]Patrick County, Virginia, Will Bk. 1, p. 37; for descendants, see Virginia Easley DeMarce, A Tentative Outline of Easley Lines ...

[23]Henrico County, Virginia, Miscellaneous Records, 1718-26, pp. 493-494, Court Minutes, 1719-24, p. 155, Wills & Deeds, 1732.

[24]Ibid., Court Minutes, 1719-24, pp. 76, 178, 354, Deeds & Wills 1725-37, pp. 46, 240, 252, 178, 172; Land Patent Book 13, p. 218, Bk. 14, p. 369; Goochland County, Virginia, Deed Bk. 2, pp.28, 155.

[25]Goochland County, Virginia, Deed Bk. 3, p. 271; Henrico County, Virginia, Deeds & Wills, 1744-48, pp. 152-153.

[26]Henrico County, Virginia, Deeds & Wills, 1744-48, pp. 316, 327.

[27]Goochland County, Virginia, Marriages; Chesterfield County, Virginia, Order Book 1, pp. 79, 135, 528.

[28]Henrico County, Virginia, Deeds & Wills, 1748-50, p. 7; Halifax County, North Carolina, Deed Bk. 9, pp. 60, 271, Will Bk. 1, p. 221; for descendants, see Virginia Easley DeMarce, A Tentative Outline of Easley Lines ...

[29]Henrico County, Virginia, Deeds & Wills, 1725-37, p. 9; Goochland County, Virginia, Deeds; Cumberland County, Virginia, Order Book, 1752-58, p. 97, Deed Bk. 5, p. 91.

[30]Halifax County, Virginia, Marriages, Deed Bk. 9, p. 10, Bk. 10, p. 58, Bk. 15, p. 559.

[31]Lunenburg County, Virginia, Order Book, 1759-61, pp. 24, 42, Will Bk. 2, p. 253.

[32]Pittsylvania County, Virginia, Deed Bk. 5, p. 479, Bk. 8, p. 359, Bk. 10, p. 115, Bk. 11, pp. 174, 298.

[33]Cumberland County, Virginia, Deed Bk. 1, p. 411, Bk. 3, p. 165; Halifax County, Virginia, Deed Bk. 3, pp. 102, 302, Bk. 4, pp. 286, 291, Bk 8, p. 357, Bk. 11, p. 17, Bk. 12, p. 252, Bk. 13, p. 81, Will Bk. 2, p. 174; for descendants, see Virginia Easley DeMarce, A Tentative Outline of Easley Lines ...

***

FREILEY of Monroe County, Kentucky

Nicholas Freiley, who was probably born about 1735, either in Germany or of German ancestry, bought 185 acres on the west branch of Conococheague Creek near Fort Loudon in Peters Township, Cumberland (now Franklin) County, Pennsylvania, from the heirs of Mesech James for £200 on August 27, 1771. The land, which was probably divided, with Freiley retaining 150 acres, was located at the mouth of Bear Valley. Freiley died before 1781, when his widow, Christina, was taxed on the land, two horses, and three cattle. She was granted administration of the estate on October 23, 1783, and was still living in Franklin County, Pennsylvania, in 1790.[1] Their children, among others, were as follows:[2]

1.
  a. Christian Freiley, born February 14, 1759.
  b. Barbara Freiley married _____ Harding.
  c. Mary Freiley married Andrew Campbell.

While there is no proof, Nicholas and Christina Freiley probably also had the following children:[3]

  d. Nicholas Freiley died c1787; married Hannah _____.
  e. Joanna Freiley married Richard Harris; child:
     (1) Rebecca Harris married Cornelius Gough.

***

1.   Christian Freiley was born February 14, 1759, and lived on Conococheague Creek in Cumberland (now Franklin) County, Pennsylvania, as early as 1771. He served as a private in the 7th Company, 4th Battalion, of the Cumberland County militia in 1780 and 1781. He was a blacksmith and in 1782 paid taxes on his father's land and on two horses and two cattle. On November 11, 1783, he sold his interest in his father's land to Colonel James Chambers for £80; it later became part of the Nor'East Iron Furnace.[4]

Freiley moved to Augusta County, Virginia, where on September 27, 1787, he married Elizabeth Harding, who was born March 15, 1766, and who had moved to Augusta County from Franklin County, Pennsylvania, also.[5] The family moved to Washington County, Tennessee, where on August 23, 1797, he bought 65 acres on Cedar Creek from Nathan Shipley for £40; he sold the land back to Shipley on August 27, 1801, for $133.33. He paid taxes in Washington County from 1793 to 1799.[6]

Freiley moved to Barren (now Monroe) County, Kentucky, about 1800, and on June 13, 1801, he joined the Mill Creek Baptist Church near Tompkinsville. He bought 100 acres on the East Fork of Barren River from Thomas Means in 1807 and the same year sold four acres of it to Thomas Howser. He made his will in November, 1810, naming his wife and children as beneficiaries, and he died December 14, 1810; the estate was probated in February, 1811.[7]

Elizabeth Freiley, who also joined the Mill Creek Church in 1803, lived with her son-in-law, Daniel Pennington, after the death of her husband, and died December 20, 1854, in Monroe County, Kentucky.[8] The children of Christian and Elizabeth Freiley were as follows:[9]

  a. Esther Freiley, born May 5, 1788, in Augusta County, Virginia; died

April 30, 1854, in Monroe County, Kentucky; married August 20, 1805, in Barren (now Monroe) County, Kentucky, to Daniel Pennington (see p. 162).

b. Nicholas Freiley, born September 4, 1789.
c. Edward Freiley, born September 14, 1791; married August 20, 1810, in Barren (now Monroe) County, Kentucky, to Mary Hagan.
d. Mary Freiley, born February 14, 1794; died December 23, 1882, in Monroe County, Kentucky; married March 4, 1815, in Barren (now Monroe) County, Kentucky, to Thomas Means.
e. John Freiley, born November 12, 1796.
f. Adam Freiley, born April 18, 1799.
g. Jonathan Freiley, born November 26, 1801.
h. Samuel Freiley, born January 1, 1805.
i. Thomas Freiley, born March 9, 1808; evidently died before his father made his will.

***

REFERENCES

[1]This is probably the same Nicholas Freiley who lived in East Nantmill Township, Chester County, Pennsylvania, from 1765 to 1769; Franklin County, Pennsylvania, Deed Bk. 3, p. 169; Pennsylvania Archives, 3rd Series (Philadelphia, 1853, Harrisburg, 1874-1939), XX, 476; Cumberland County, Pennsylvania, estate file B, p. 41; Franklin County, Pennsylvania, census of 1790.

[2]Cumberland County, Pennsylvania, Deeds 1-G, 132, 133; Franklin County, Pennsylvania, Deed Bk. 1, p. 110.

[3]Franklin County, Pennsylvania, Wills A, 124; Frederick Adams Virkus (ed.), The Abridged Compendium of American Genealogy (Chicago: A. N. Marquis & Company, 1925) V, 91.

[4]Bible record belonging (1960) to Mrs. Nina Hicks Alspaugh; Pennsylvania Archives, 3rd Series, XX, 633, XXIII, 704, 748; Cumberland County, Pennsylvania, Deeds 1-G, 132.

[5]Bible record belonging to Mrs. Nina Hicks Alspaugh; Augusta County, Virginia, Marriages; Elizabeth Harding was probably a daughter of Edward (died c1781) and Esther Harding and sister of Samuel, Edward, Anna, and Rebecca Harding; see Pennsylvania Archives, 3rd Series, XXIII, 704; Augusta County, Virginia, Marriages.

[6]Washington County, Tennessee, Deed Bk. 6, p. 240, Bk. 11, p. 220, tax lists 1793-1799.

[7]Mill Creek Church Minutes, p. 23; Barren County, Kentucky, Deeds A, 320, 327, Will Bk. 1, p. 154; Bible record belonging to Mrs. Nina Hicks Alspaugh.

[8]Mill Creek Church Minutes, p. 43; Monroe County, Kentucky, census of 1850; Bible record belonging to Mrs. Nina Hicks Alspaugh.

[9]Bible record belonging to Mrs. Nina Hicks Alspaugh; Barren County, Kentucky, Marriages.

***

GASH of Harford County, Maryland

Thomas Gash was probably born in England about 1665; he was a planter in Baltimore (now Harford) County, Maryland, as early as 1701. He made his will on April 4, 1704, leaving all his property to his son Thomas, and the estate was probated on April 15, 1704. His child was as follows:[1]

1. a. Thomas Gash, born c1692.

***

1.   Thomas Gash was probably born about 1692 in England; when his father died, he was left in the custody of Lawrence Draper and was educated by him; he inherited his father's entire estate when he was 21 and became a planter in Spesutia Upper Hundred, Baltimore (now Harford) County, Maryland. He married Johannah Gilbert, who was probably a daughter of Thomas Gilbert, on December 22, 1715. In 1722 he bought 60 acres, part of "Beedle's Reserve," from Francis Holland; in 1732 he patented "The Scotchman's Generosity" of 50 acres, and in 1737 he bought 50 acres of "St. Martin's Ludgate" from Thomas White, all of which he sold to Benjamin Osborn in 1737. In 1740 he bought "Gash's Purchase" of 100 acres from Robert West; he sold it and part of "New Westwood" to Edward Wakeman in 1750 and Bernard O'Neal in 1753.[2]

Gash made his will on April 1, 1758, leaving his property to his wife; at her death it was to be divided between his son Thomas and his daughter Blanche; the estate was probated on June 7, 1759. His children were as follows:[3]

a. Johannah Gash, born November 8, 1716; married January 22, 1732, to Robert West (see p. 259).
b. Sarah Gash, born July 16, 1719; married July 13, 1736, to Thomas Burchfield, born August 8, 1712, son of Thomas Burchfield and Mary Wilson; children:
    (1) Aquilla Burchfield, born August 9, 1738.
    (2) Thomas Burchfield, born January 13, 1739/40; dsp April 5, 1740.
    (3) Hannah Burchfield, born June 3, 1741.
    (4) Mary Burchfield, born July 14, 1743.
    (5) Sarah Burchfield, born October 16, 1746.
    (6) Elizabeth Burchfield, born May 17, 1749.
c. Mary Gash, born June 8, 1721; dsp November, 1724.
d. Blanche Gash, born c1723; dsp January 29, 1724/5.
e. Mary Gash, born December 10, 1725.
f. Michael Gash, born May 19, 1728; married Elizabeth _____; lived in Bedford County, Virginia, in 1776.
g. Thomas Gash, born October 30, 1730; married Elizabeth _____; lived in Harford County, Maryland, in 1783; children (among others):
    (1) Martha Gash, born c1764.
    (2) Hannah Gash, born c1766.
    (3) Elizabeth Gash, born c1773.
    (4) Mary Gash, born c1775.
h. Blanche Gash, born May 8, 1733.

***

REFERENCES

[1]Baltimore County, Maryland, tax lists, 1701 et seq., Will Bk. 3, p. 252.
[2]Ibid.; St. George's Parish Register, Harford County, Maryland, in Maryland Historical Society Library, Baltimore, Maryland; Baltimore County, Maryland, Deeds IS#G, 84, IS#K, 490, HWS#1A, 43, TR#D, 245, BB#1, 158; Maryland Land Patents AM#1, 245.
[3]Baltimore County, Maryland, Will Bk. 30, p. 688; St. George's Parish Register.

***

GIST of Monroe County, Kentucky

Christopher Gist and his wife, Edith Cromwell, were in Baltimore County, Maryland, on February 12, 1679, when he proved his importation right to 150 acres which he then assigned to Daniel Carroll. On March 7, 1682, Gist and his brother-in-law, Richard Cromwell, bought 245 acres called South Canton on the south side of the Patapsco River at Fishing Point and Curtis Creek from Robert Clarkson; they sold 84 acres of it to William Cromwell on June 14, 1682. Gist received a patent for 100 acres called Lowe's Neck on the south side of the Patapsco in 1683, and on August 7, 1688, Rebecca Lightfoot conveyed 320 acres called Rebecca's Delight to him.[1]

Christopher Gist made his will on February 17, 1690/1, and it was probated on March 10, 1690/1, giving his estate to his wife and child, his mother, and his brother-in-law, Richard Cromwell.[2]

Edith Gist married Joseph Williams in 1691; he died in 1692 and she married John Beecher the same year. She made her will on May 23, 1694, leaving her property to her son; her estate was probated on June 19, 1694.[3]

***

Richard Gist, the only child of Christopher and Edith (Cromwell) Gist, was born about 1683 in Baltimore County, Maryland. In March, 1692/3, his mother gave him a slave, and on February 21, 1693, Thomas Hammond gave him 225 acres called Gist's Rest, formerly Rebecca's Delight, and including the 100 acres previously given to his father. Gist lived with his uncle Richard Cromwell, who willed him property in 1717, until his marriage to Zipporah Murray, a Quaker, on December 7, 1704.[4]

On September 10, 1705, Gist sold Gist's Rest to Richard Cromwell, and on July 6, 1711, Josephus Murray gave his sister Zipporah Gist 100 acres called Brother's Good Will; Gist moved to the new plantation and bought an adjoining 100 acres from Murray on October 31, 1724. Gist acquired several other tracts in Baltimore County - 200 acres called Turkey Cock Hall, 725 acres called Adventure, 300 acres called Green Spring Traverse, 190 acres called Addition to Green Spring Traverse, 400 acres called Gist's Search, 249 acres called Gist's Lime Pits, 200 acres called Addition, 100 acres called Pleasant Green, 83 acres called Milford, 50 acres called Gist's Meadows, and 24 acres called Gist's Inspection.[5]

Richard Gist operated a plantation on his large land holdings; he helped build a rolling road to carry tobacco to market, and by 1721 had become a merchant, trading his tobacco and other crops through Philip Smith, a London merchant, and others. He owned a small sailing vessel, and after Baltimore was laid out, he moved his offices and warehouse there.[6]

On January 2, 1728, Gist was appointed by the vestry of St. Paul's Church in Baltimore County to purchase a site for a new building, and in 1729 he was appointed to help select a site for a new town, which became Baltimore; he bought lot #48 on Calvert Street in January, 1729, and built a house on it, acquiring lot #47 later.[7]

In 1726, Gist became deputy surveyor of the Western Shore of Maryland; on March 2, 1727/8, he became one of the justices and commissioners of Baltimore County, and after February 1, 1735, he was presiding justice. After 1739 he represented Baltimore County in the Maryland Assembly. In March, 1736, he became captain in the county militia and took an active part in the Maryland boundary dispute with Pennsylvania.[8]

Richard Gist gave his son Christopher 300 acres on September 5, 1728; he gave 284 acres to his son Nathaniel on March 28, 1731, and 216 acres to his son Thomas on March 8, 1738. He died without a will in August, 1741, and his widow and son Christopher inherited his property.[9]

Zipporah Gist was living on August 18, 1759, when she sold John Mercer lots 47 and 48 in Baltimore and two tracts of land which had belonged to her husband. On April 25, 1760, she sold her dower rights in the remainder of her husband's estate.[10]

****

Thomas Morgan died in 1698 in Baltimore County, Maryland, leaving three daughters - Jemima (who married (1) James Murray and (2) Thomas Cromwell), Sarah (who married _____ McLane), and Martha (who married Nicholas FitzSimmons).[11]

Jemima Morgan married (1) James Murray, who died in 1704 in Baltimore County, Maryland, leaving perhaps among others, the following children:

a. Josephus Murray died 1772 in Baltimore County, Maryland.
b. Nicholas Murray.
c. Morgan Murray.
d. Jabez Murray.
e. Zipporah Murray married December 7, 1704, in Baltimore County, Maryland, to Richard Gist.

****

Richard Gist and Zipporah Murray had, probably among others, the following children:[12]

a. Christopher Gist, born c1705; died July 25, 1759, in Virginia; married c1728 to Sarah Howard.
b. Nathaniel Gist, born c1707; married c1731 to Mary Howard; lived in Sevier County, Tennessee.
c. Edith Gist, born c1709; married Abraham Vaughn.
d. William Gist, born c1711; died November 19, 1794, in Baltimore County, Maryland; married October 22, 1737, to Violetta Howard.
e. Thomas Gist, born July 13, 1712; died May 24, 1787, in Baltimore County, Maryland; married July 2, 1735, to Susanna Cockey.
f. Jemima Gist, born c1714; died c1747 in Baltimore County, Maryland; married William Seabrook.

In addition, Richard Gist and Zipporah Murray probably had the following children, although there is no proof:[13]

g. Ruth Gist married William Lewis.
h. John Gist, born c1722; died 1778 in Loudon County, Virginia; married Mary _____.
1. i. Benjamin Gist, born c1725.

***

37

1.   Benjamin Gist was born about 1725 and lived in Lunenburg County, Virginia, in 1750, when he married Mary Jarratt (see p. 68). On November 6, 1752, his wife's parents, Thomas and Rebecca Jarratt, gave him 100 acres on the south side of Stony Creek in Cumberland Parish; he and his wife Mary sold the land back to Jarratt for £35 on March 2, 1756.[14]

Gist then moved to Sandy Creek in Orange County, North Carolina, where he petitioned to build a grist mill on February 17, 1761; he was appointed a road overseer in 1763, and in May, 1765, his term as constable expired.[15]

Benjamin Gist and his family then moved to the Fair Forest area of Union County, South Carolina, with a Baptist congregation, and on November 3, 1767, he had 500 acres surveyed on Fair Forest Creek, for which he received a grant on July 8, 1768; he later sold the land to William Wofford.[16]

Gist moved to Washington (now Greene) County, Tennessee, before February 23, 1778, when he took office as justice of the peace; on April 23, 1778, he was appointed one of the commissioners to locate a site for the county seat. He was appointed a county tax collector on August 27, 1778, and the same year was active as a militia captain guarding the frontier against Indians; in 1780 he served at the Battle of Boyd's Creek against the Indians.[17]

On October 23, 1782, Gist received a 400-acre grant on Lick Creek in Greene County which he sold to Thomas Russell on November 4, 1788. On September 20, 1787, he received a 400-acre grant on Gist's Branch on the north side of Nolichucky River; he sold 200 acres of it to John Carter on May 5, 1789, and the remaining 200 acres to William Young on May 25, 1791. On January 12, 1793, he received a 395-acre grant on the south side of the Little Chucky River, which he sold to Charles Lowery on February 12, 1795.[18]

Benjamin Gist was active in the Baptist Church in Tennessee; in November, 1783, he was on the Sinking Creek Church rolls and in October, 1789, he represented the Beaver Dam Church at a meeting of the Holston Association at Buffalo Ridge Meeting House in Washington County. He also represented the Association at Big Creek Meeting House in Hawkins County in June, 1791, and Coon's Meeting House in Jefferson County in August, 1797.[19]

In 1784, Gist was appointed to take tax inventories for Green County, Tennessee, and he became a justice of the peace in May, 1785. On December 14, 1784, he was elected a delegate to the second convention called to organize the State of Franklin, and in 1787 he signed a "petition of the inhabitants of the Western Country" for the creation of a new state.[20]

Benjamin Gist moved to Knox County, Tennessee, in 1793, and on August 19, 1793, he sold John Wilson part of the plantation in Greene County where he had formerly lived; he sold Thomas Russell the remainder of the land, 410 acres, on May 13, 1798. On February 4, 1794, Gist was a justice of the peace in Knox County and one of the tax collectors; on March 8, 1799, he was a justice of the Court of Pleas and Quarter Sessions.[21]

In the fall of 1799, Gist moved to Line Creek of Big Barren River in Smith (now Macon) County, Tennessee, where on April 28, 1801, he bought 250 acres from William Sanders; in 1802 he paid taxes on this land in Jackson County, and on December 6, 1804, he sold Alexander Lowery 55

acres from the eastern portion of his plantation. He continued to be
active in Baptist Church work; on January 11, 1800, he was appointed to
visit all members of the Mill Creek Church near Tompkinsville, Kentucky,
and on May 9, 1800, he became an elder in the Mill Creek Church, which
he represented at a conference on Beaver Creek the same year.[22]

Benjamin Gist, then residing in Jackson (now Clay) County, Tennessee, on June 3, 1808, sold John Carter 159 acres on Lick Creek in Greene
County, part of a 400-acre grant. Gist probably died soon afterwards, but
the destruction of the Jackson County records makes further information
difficult to obtain. Although there is no proof other than association
of names in several locations, the following were probably, among others,
his children:[23]

a. Joseph Gist, born August 27, 1751; died August 31, 1844, in Monroe
   County, Kentucky; married (1) January 25, 1773, in Union County,
   South Carolina, to Hannah Breed (2) January 7, 1816, in Barren (now
   Monroe) County, Kentucky, to Mrs. Elizabeth (Belew) Springer.
b. Mary Gist, born May 5, 1755; died December 2, 1822, in Connersville,
   Indiana; married 1776 in Greene County, Tennessee, to James Stevenson.
c. John Gist, born c1757; died c1819 in Barren (now Monroe) County,
   Kentucky; married c1789 in Hawkins (now Knox) County, Tennessee, to
   Hannah (probably Geron).
d. Thomas Gist, born October 10, 1764; died c1837 in White County, Tennessee.
e. Amy Gist, born c1769; married May 25, 1790, in Greene County, Tennessee, to Alexander Lowery.
f. Ann Gist, born c1771; married June 22, 1790, in Greene County, Tennessee, to James McClain.
2. g. Benjamin Gist, born September 15, 1773.

***

2.   Benjamin Gist was born September 15, 1773, in Berkeley-Craven (now
Union) County, South Carolina; about 1777 the family moved to Greene
County, Tennessee, and about 1793 to Beaver Creek in Knox County, Tennessee. In 1793, he married Rhoda Hinds (see p. 66) and worked as a
surveyor with Watson Reed in several East Tennessee counties.[24] About
1800 he moved to Jackson (now Clay) County, Tennessee, and on January
20, 1804, he received a 50-acre land grant in Barren County, Kentucky,
where he was a member of the Mill Creek Baptist Church. He was taxed on
land in White County, Tennessee, from 1810 to 1813, and probably lived
there during part of that time. His wife Rhoda died between 1817 and
1820 and he later married Rebecca _____.[25]

During the War of 1812, Ben Gist served in the Jackson County militia, being commissioned captain of the 48th Regiment on January 31, 1814.
It is difficult to locate information concerning him because of the destruction of the Jackson County records, but on June 16, 1818, he received
a 100-acre grant on Trace Creek in Jackson County.[26]

On June 28, 1823, he and Thomas Miller, deacons of the Mill Creek
Christian Church (the congregation had seceded from the Baptists), received a deed to 38 acres of land from Samuel Wilson as long as the site
was used as a place of worship, and on August 18, 1834, he and Alexander
Rush, Sr., as trustees for the public, received a deed from Peter White
of three and a half acres on Line Creek "for the purpose of a public
meeting house to be free for all sects or denominations of Christians."[27]

39

On December 3, 1824, Ben Gist recorded a claim to a stray hog in Jackson County. In 1837 he signed a petition to form a new county from Jackson. On October 24, 1842, he bought 50 acres consisting of an island in Obed's River at the mouth of Iron's Creek in Overton County, Tennessee, from George W. Sevier for $150.00. On March 9, 1843, he was made executor of the will of his older brother, Joseph Gist.[28] Ben Gist died before 1850, leaving the following children, all by his first marriage:[29]

a. Sarah Gist, born July 29, 1794; died January 30, 1857, in Boone County, Missouri; married October 2, 1811, in White County, Tennessee, to Philip Barger.
b. Mary Gist, born October 4, 1795; married William Fraim and probably had no children; lived in Monroe County, Kentucky, in 1840.
c. Watson Gist, born August 15, 1797; died August 17, 1863, in Moniteau County, Missouri; married c1817 in Jackson (now Clay) County, Tennessee, to Sarah Ann Hayes.
d. Bayless Gist, born December 9, 1799; died 1840 in Monroe County, Kentucky; married May 8, 1822, in Monroe County, Kentucky, to Nancy Ray.
3. e. Hiram Gist, born October 3, 1801.
f. Levi Gist, born July 13, 1803; died April 7, 1851, in Jackson (now Clay) County, Tennessee; married c1827 in Monroe County, Kentucky, to Ruth McPherson (see p. 94).
g. Elizabeth Gist, born August 10, 1805; died May 22, 1861, in Monroe County, Kentucky; married c1825 in Jackson (now Clay) County, Tennessee, to John Hayes.
h. Rhoda Gist, born October 17, 1807; died in California; had a child by John Chism; married John Thompson.
i. Lucinda Gist, born October 28, 1814; died in Missouri; married (1) c1835 to James L. Cloyd (2) Charles W. Copass.

***

3.   Hiram Gist was born October 3, 1801, in Jackson (now Clay) County, Tennessee, where he lived on Line Creek. About 1823 he married Margery McPherson (see p. 94) and about 1831 he moved to Monroe County, Kentucky. Between 1840 and 1850 he moved back to Jackson (now Clay) County. In 1836 he paid taxes on 384 acres in Tennessee, and in 1838 he received a grant of 120 acres on Barren River in Monroe County. He was a farmer and also operated a store with his brother Levi. The destruction of the Jackson and Monroe County records makes it difficult to locate information concerning him. He died about 1853 in Jackson County.[30]

On May 5, 1871, Margery McPherson Gist sold her farm on Line Creek to J. W. Clement and then lived with her son Jehu. In 1881 the family sold their furniture in Clementsville, went by wagon to Nashville in October, and then traveled by train to Tulare, California, where Margery Gist died on May 6, 1882. The children of Hiram and Margery Gist were as follows:[31]

a. Rhoda Gist, born February 25, 1824; dsp January 8, 1899, in Monroe County, Kentucky; married October 29, 1860, Michael Chism.
b. Eleanor Gist, born c1826; dsp c1855.
c. Adeline Gist, born December 1, 1827; dsp October 3, 1914, in Mitchell County, Texas.
d. Abigail Gist, born January 18, 1830; dsp June 7, 1922, in Mitchell County, Texas.
4. e. Lucinda Gist, born April 28, 1832.
f. Mary Gist, born June 13, 1834; died May 14, 1919, in Anson, Texas;

married September 2, 1855, in Jackson (now Clay) County, Tennessee, to Daniel Boone Hestand (see David B. Trimble, Hiestand Family of Page County, Virginia).

  g. Levi Hinds Gist, born April 27, 1836; died January 7, 1905, in Tulare County, California. He served as a sergeant in the 37th Kentucky Regiment in the Civil War; moved to Tulare County, California, in 1881 and bought land there on September 16, 1882, from A. G. Tryon; he was also a carpenter. He married January 10, 1872, in Coffee County, Tennessee, to Lucy Jayne Nevill (see p. 140); children:

    (1) Ida Gist, born c1873; died c1896; married March 30, 1889, J. J. Duncan; children:

        (a) Goldie Duncan, died young.

        (b) Lucy Duncan, died young.

    (2) Beulah Gist, born c1875; married Herbert Riley; child:

        (a) Earl Riley, died young.

    (3) Porter Gist, born April 23, 1878; dsp July 25, 1958, in Oakland, California; married Frieda Schaefer.

  h. Hiram Gist, born February 14, 1838; dsp April 18, 1898, in Tulare County, California.

5. i. Jehu McPherson Gist, born June 28, 1840.

***

4.   Lucinda Gist was born April 28, 1832, in Monroe County, Kentucky, and died July 20, 1895, in Clay County, Tennessee; married August 8, 1859, to Robert Hamilton Silvey, born October 31, 1831, in Roane County, Tennessee; died April 8, 1897, in Clay County, Tennessee. They had the following children:[32]

6. a. Mary Ellen Silvey, born February 10, 1861.

7. b. Kittie Emma Silvey, born December 12, 1862.

  c. Hiram Jeffers Silvey, born November 30, 1864; died December 11, 1942; married October 29, 1891, to Sarah Jane Hayes, born October 6, 1863; died September 6, 1907; children:

    (1) Paul Silvey, born August 9, 1892; married June 14, 1922, Gladys McCord; children:

        (a) Hiram Hayes Silvey, born August 5, 1929.

        (b) Imogene Silvey, born May 23, 1931.

    (2) Trigg Silvey, born October 21, 1894; dsp May 3, 1937.

    (3) Nannie Lou Silvey, born January 23, 1897; married January 18, 1931, Samuel J. Birdwell; lived in Gallatin, Tennessee; child:

        (a) Sam Joe Birdwell, born February 20, 1938; dsp May 21, 1938.

    (4) Ermine Silvey, born May 9, 1899; dsp January 13, 1936; married September 5, 1920, to Benton R. Harlin.

    (5) Kirkpatrick Silvey, born September 20, 1901; married May 16, 1934, to Jeanette Langford; dsp.

    (6) Ruth Silvey, born December 27, 1903; dsp January 15, 1904.

    (7) Lockie Silvey, born June 8, 1906; married November 6, 1926, to William Cecil Dickerson; child:

        (a) Richard Cecil Dickerson, born October 9, 1934.

8. d. Alter Elizabeth Silvey, born December 3, 1865.

  e. Robert Jehu Silvey, born 1868.

  f. William Levi Silvey, born 1870; dsp 1923 in Gamaliel, Kentucky.

  g. Benjamin Bedford Silvey, born November 8, 1872; died May 5, 1945, in Gamaliel, Kentucky; married December 29, 1897, to Julia Isabelle Payne, born October 15, 1877; died December 22, 1940; children:

    (1) Electa Silvey, born September 3, 1898; dsp; lived in Los Angeles, California.

    (2) Clel Thurman Silvey, born May 27, 1900; married December 19,

41

1939, to Bernice Kitten; child:
    (a) Bedford John Silvey, born July 16, 1940.
  (3) Glade Silvey, born October 11, 1907; married Clifton Thurman, born 1914; died 1944; dsp.
9. h. Preston Howard Silvey, born August 31, 1874.

***

6.   Mary Ellen Silvey was born February 10, 1861, and died July 15, 1942, in Monroe County, Kentucky; married George Washington Marshall, who was born October 10, 1861, and died February 16, 1948, in Monroe County, Kentucky, the son of James Andrew Marshall and _____ Sims. Their children were as follows:[33]

a. Robert Haskell Marshall, born December 25, 1881; died October 5, 1943, in Louisville, Kentucky; married August 30, 1912, to Flossie Tinsley. Children:
  (1) Robert Woodrow Marshall, born July 8, 1913; married 1937 to Margaret T. Woods; lived in Louisville, Kentucky. Children:
    (a) Robert Woods Marshall, born August 8, 1938.
    (b) Philip Haskell Marshall, born October 1, 1939.
    (c) Sue Ellen Marshall, born March 20, 1947.
  (2) Mildred Marshall, born September 28, 1921; married 1941 to Darrel Wade Swope; lived in Louisville, Kentucky; child:
    (a) Darrel Wade Swope, born July 6, 1947.
  (3) Ruth Marshall, born April 28, 1925; married October 1, 1944, to Edward F. Kaiser; lived in Louisville, Kentucky; children:
    (a) Joan Marshall Kaiser, born November 17, 1945.
    (b) Diane Roberts Kaiser, born November 28, 1946.
    (c) Kenyon Edward Kaiser, born November 26, 1953.
b. James Claud Marshall, born January 14, 1884; married (1) October, 1912, Texie May Harlin (2) November 19, 1938, Emily Ray; lived in Gamaliel, Kentucky; children (all by first marriage):
  (1) James Erf Marshall, born July 1, 1913, married August 1, 1940, Catherine Martin; children:
    (a) Mary Ellen Marshall, born October 6, 1941.
    (b) James Carroll Marshall, born June 29, 1943.
  (2) Mary Catherine Marshall, born September 13, 1915; died September 17, 1952; married February 1, 1939, Arthur Proffitt; child:
    (a) James Arthur Proffitt, born September 17, 1952.
  (3) Robbie May Marshall, born September 9, 1921; married 1941 Elmer Martin.
  (4) Dorothy Marshall, born October 28, 1923; married October 24, 1945, Warren H. Gardner; child:
    (a) David Hughes Gardner.
  (5) George Mervin Marshall, born July 8, 1929.
c. Pearl Marshall married Robert Short; dsp; lived in Bowling Green, Kentucky.
d. Only Homer Marshall, born October 2, 1890; married February 8, 1917, to Virginia Moulder, born April 22, 1899; lived in Celina, Tennessee; children:
  (1) Iris Marshall, born April 18, 1918; married October 25, 1935, Carl Hulon Dowell; lived in Florida; children:
    (a) Polly Ellen Dowell, born August 15, 1936.
    (b) Hugh Moulder Dowell, born December 11, 1940.
  (2) Donnie Marshall, born February 10, 1920; married February 1, 1941, Billy Edwin Williams; lived in Detroit, Michigan; child:
    (a) Edwin Marshall Williams, born April 18, 1943.
  (3) Lockie Mae Marshall, born October 28, 1921; married November 5,

42

1941, Aury Clifton; lived in California; child:
(a) Shirley Faye Clifton, born June 22, 1945.
(4) Doye Kate Marshall, born December 30, 1923; married August 14, 1945, Wilburn Covington Simmons.
(5) Ina Pearl Marshall, born September 13, 1930; married October 30, 1946, James Cleve Scott; lived in Indianapolis, Indiana; children:
(a) James Cleve Scott, born August 24, 1948.
(b) Philip Duane Scott, born February 21, 1953.

***

7.   Kittie Emma Silvey was born December 12, 1862, and died August 28, 1949, in Gamaliel, Kentucky; married July 3, 1881, to James Andrew Marshall, born August 22, 1863, and died December 26, 1951, son of James Andrew Marshall and _____ Sims. Their children were as follows:[34]

a. Hugh Gist Marshall, born April 28, 1882; married June 20, 1911, to Catherine Maud Trout; lived in Ft. Worth, Texas; dsp.
b. Howard Preston Marshall, born February 2, 1884; dsp January 21, 1953; married (1) September 12, 1910, Rena Malson (2) Hallie Pulley.
c. Otia Edna Marshall, born January 21, 1887; married March 3, 1906, to Cyrus Russell; lived in Ft. Worth, Texas; children:
(1) Lillian Juanita Russell, born January 20, 1907; married (1) Ernest Ragsdale (2) Charles Beals.
(2) Lois Oleta Russell, born May 10, 1908; married Ross Trigg.
(3) Robbie Russell married William Parsons; dsp.
(4) Gypsy Hazel Russell.
(5) Marshall Kemp Russell, died young.
(6) Edna Geneva Russell married Oscar Hix.
d. Witt Marshall, born October 19, 1888; married (1) June 4, 1911, Nannie Crabtree (2) May 30, 1929, Roxie Clark; dsp.
e. Luther Clinton Marshall, born September 26, 1890; married December 18, 1912, to Beatrice Barton; lived in Ft. Worth, Texas; child:
(1) Bettie Maurine Marshall married Chris Cuffman; dsp.
f. Iva Lucinda Marshall, born April 4, 1892; married October 3, 1920, to John T. Lewis; lived in Dallas, Texas; child:
(1) Iva Louise Lewis, born October, 1921; married Charles Bates.
g. (Dr.) Fred Edward Marshall, born December 17, 1894; married July 6, 1924, to Clone Vance; lived in Glasgow, Kentucky; child:
(1) Fred Edward Marshall, born April 14, 1925.
h. Bliss Glearman Marshall, born October 27, 1899; married April, 1933, to Edith Cox; lived in Shawnee, Oklahoma; child:
(1) Georgia Bliss Marshall.
i. Daisy Belle Marshall, born December 8, 1901; married January 30, 1923, to Arnett Mills Duncan; lived in Gamaliel, Kentucky; children:
(1) Hugh Mills Duncan, born January 4, 1925; married October 15, 1949, to Corinne Proffitt.
(2) Roger Lewis Duncan, born May 20, 1926; married November 11, 1943, to Mildred Garman; child:
(a) Wanda Lewis Duncan, born August 31, 1944.
(3) William Marshall Duncan, born December 12, 1929; married April 8, 1952, to Juanita Smith; child:
(a) Pamela Ruth Duncan, born March 10, 1953.
(4) Dixie Dean Duncan, born May 27, 1946.

***

8.   Alter Elizabeth Silvey was born December 3, 1865, and died August 15, 1922, in Portland, Tennessee; married Wiley Smith Woodcock, who was

born August 24, 1858, and died September 29, 1917. Their children were
as follows:35

a. Gipsy Woodcock, born November 21, 1884; died August 28, 1910; mar-
    ried November, 1904, to William Huston Sadler; children:
    (1) Ralph Silvey Sadler, born September 29, 1905; dsp.
    (2) Smith Raymond Sadler, born March 8, 1907; married May 10, 1933,
         to Georgia Lawson; children:
         (a) William Raymond Sadler, born March 10, 1934.
         (b) Betty Alta Sadler, born November 7, 1936.
         (c) Margaret Gipsy Sadler, born August 1, 1944.
         (d) Lynda Sadler, born January 13, 1946.
b. Alta Woodcock, born September 19, 1893; married November 19, 1907,
    to Noah Edgar Rhodes; lived in Mt. Pleasant, Tennessee; children:
    (1) Byno Ryvers Rhodes, born January 25, 1920; married March 18,
         1946, to Mildred Daniels; lived in Harrogate, Tennessee; chil-
         dren:
         (a) Myra Gail Rhodes, born October 20, 1948.
         (b) Byno R. Rhodes, born September 7, 1950.
         (c) Karen Leigh Rhodes, born October 27, 1952.
         (d) William T. Rhodes, born September 25, 1954.
    (2) Noah Edgar Rhodes, born March 17, 1923; married December 28,
         1944, to Ruth Ella Elrod; lived in Brookhaven, Mississippi;
         children:
         (a) Pattye Ruth Rhodes, born December 28, 1949.
         (b) Michael Rance Rhodes, born November 3, 1953.

                              ***

9.   Preston Howard Silvey was born August 31, 1874; married January 17,
    1897, to Zouella Maxey; lived in Comanche, Oklahoma. Their children were
    as follows:36

a. Grace Silvey, born October 11, 1897; married December, 1914, to
    Walter Davis; children:
    (1) Walter David Davis, born December 24, 1915; married July 30,
         1945, to Maxine Speck, born November 21, 1920; lived in Pampa,
         Texas; children:
         (a) Shirley Anne Davis, born April 20, 1946.
         (b) Jimmy Ray Davis, born and died September 4, 1950.
         (c) Mary Grace Davis, born October 16, 1952.
    (2) Lois Beatrice Davis, born October 8, 1917; married February 12,
         1944, to Dwight Carl Plemons, born November 8, 1916; lived in
         Ft. Worth, Texas; children:
         (a) Gerald Dwight Plemons, born December 28, 1944.
         (b) Donald Carl Plemons, born July 30, 1946.
    (3) Eva Blanche Davis, born July 13, 1919; married November 25, 1938,
         to Durwood Boggs, born December 6, 1918; lived in Haskell, Texas;
         children:
         (a) Kenneth Richard Boggs, born November 28, 1939.
         (b) David Robert Boggs, born November 13, 1941.
         (c) Carol Jean Boggs, born May 24, 1950.
    (4) Jack Draper Davis, born June 26, 1922; dsp April 19, 1945, on
         Okinawa.
    (5) George William Davis, born August 17, 1924; married June 8,
         1946, to Inefa Smith; children:
         (a) Jack Randall Davis, born November 26, 1947.
         (b) James Michael Davis, born September 20, 1949.
         (c) Anita Kay Davis, born June 18, 1953.

                               44

b. Bertha Bessie Silvey, born July 7, 1899; married February, 1925, to Homer Worth Bennett; child:
   (1) Patsy Ruth Bennett, born March 23, 1926; married December, 1945, to Cordell Brown; child:
      (a) Cordell Brown, born September 10, 1946.
c. Ray Howard Silvey, born June 28, 1901; dsp.
d. Walter Cliff Silvey, born February 16, 1903; married May, 1938, to Bessie Nunley; children:
   (1) David Cliff Silvey, born July 20, 1943.
   (2) Cynthia Ann Silvey, born October 24, 1945.
e. Fred Pennington Silvey, born January 5, 1905; died August, 1947; married January, 1933, to Fern Coulston; child:
   (1) Joy Fern Silvey, born October 26, 1933; married July, 1949, to Otis Burrow; child:
      (a) William Bobby Burrow, born October 18, 1951.

***

5.   Jehu McPherson Gist was born June 28, 1840, and died January 19, 1918, in Colorado City, Texas; married June 15, 1871, to Dice A. Shields, who was born May 27, 1851, and died May 3, 1885. He moved to Tulare County, California, in 1881 and after his wife's death to Colorado City, Texas; the children of Jehu and Dice Gist were as follows:[37]

10. a. Anthus Claud Gist, born March 24, 1872.
    b. Olivia Gist, born November 12, 1873; married Thomas Field; dsp; lived in Teague, Texas.
    c. Sanford Clyde Gist, born September 20, 1876; died July 21, 1949, in Colorado City, Texas; married December 28, 1898, to Mary Jane Heath; children:
       (1) Merry Mae Gist, born February 15, 1900; married December 28, 1921, Henry Grady Castle; lived in Abilene, Texas; children:
          (a) Henry Grady Castle, born October 4, 1923; married Joyce Linn.
          (b) Delano Davis Castle, born April 13, 1933.
       (2) Lura Gist, born February 27, 1903; married George Ralph Sinclair, born November 27, 1899; lived in Odessa, Texas; children:
          (a) George Ralph Sinclair, born March 14, 1926; married Murrell Dean Robuck; child:
             /1/ Patricia Ann Sinclair.
          (b) Lura Doris Sinclair, born July 6, 1927; married Edward E. Crabtree; child:
             /1/ David L. Crabtree.
          (c) Margaret Joan Sinclair, born December 19, 1929; married Charles R. Ward; children:
             /1/ George Ward.
             /2/ Alan C. Ward.
             /3/ Lianna Ward.
          (d) Richard Gist Sinclair, born August 11, 1937.
          (e) William Sanford Sinclair, born April 11, 1943.
       (3) Dollie Fay Gist, born September 25, 1912; married Dee McArthur; lived in Spur, Texas; children:
          (a) Douglas Gist McArthur, born June 8, 1932.
          (b) Merry Dee McArthur, born July 4, 1942.
    d. Huron Franklin Gist, born January 17, 1879; married Frances Blackshear; children:
       (1) Coleman C. Gist; lived in Rio Vista, Texas.
       (2) Dollie Gist, married _____ Covington.
       (3) Ned Gist.

45

e. Lura Gist, born April 17, 1881; dsp 1884.

11. f. Nollie Huff Gist, born July 10, 1884.

***

10.   Anthus Claud Gist was born March 24, 1872, and died December 27, 1936, in Colorado City, Texas; married September 20, 1893, to Elizabeth Smith; their children were as follows:[38]

a. Julia Della Gist, born September 1, 1894; married (1) February 9, 1913, to Newman Free, dsp February 18, 1920; (2) August 15, 1923, to James Pulaski Hestand (see Trimble, Hiestand Family of Page County, Virginia).

b. Herman Clyde Gist, born February 27, 1896; married March 24, 1918, to Milton Foster; lived in Odessa, Texas; children:
(1) Della Ruth Gist, born October 6, 1919; married December 28, 1945, to J. T. Beckham; children:
   (a) Herman Roy Beckham, born February 15, 1949.
   (b) Jackie Lynn Beckham, born March 17, 1951.
(2) J. M. Gist, born January 12, 1924; married February 9, 1946, to Lucile Rhoton; child:
   (a) Frances Elaine Gist, born September 20, 1946.
(3) Effie Mae Gist, born October 25, 1926; married November, 1946, to Loren Shelfer; children:
   (a) Douglas Michael Shelfer, born October 11, 1948.
   (b) James Darrell Shelfer, born June 17, 1954.

c. James T. Gist, born July 27, 1901; married May 30, 1928, to Eleanor Barker; dsp; lived in Midland, Texas.

d. Fred Morgan Gist, born August 27, 1904; married June 19, 1935, to Velma Inez Graham; lived in Midland, Texas; children:
(1) Fred Graham Gist, born April 20, 1936.
(2) James Edward Gist, born May 28, 1938.

e. Huron Franklin Gist, born June 4, 1907; married November 13, 1927, to Ethel Marie Luce; lived in Colorado City, Texas; children:
(1) Frances Louise Gist born August 11, 1929; married April 11, 1948, to W. Robert Motley; child:
   (a) Huron Jay Motley, born August 26, 1950.
(2) Dorothy Jean Gist, born November 18, 1933; married April 26, 1951, to Jack Bourland; children:
   (a) Robert Bourland, born January 31, 1952.
   (b) Steven Bourland, born April 11, 1955.
(3) Doris Marie Gist, born September 10, 1935; married March 2, 1955, to Billy John Voss.

***

11.   Nollie Huff Gist was born July 10, 1884, and died May 3, 1943, in California; married August 20, 1902, to Ethel Jane Turner, born February 3, 1888; died February 22, 1947; their children were as follows:[39]

a. Olivia Fay Gist, born August 8, 1903; died November 27, 1937; married (1) 1921, Aubrey Connel (2) 1935, Leroy Ham; children:
(by first marriage):
(1) Violet Fae Connel, born March 22, 1923; married (1) November, 1937, Charles Reed (2) 1947, C. R. Peebles; children:
(by first marriage):
   (a) Patsy Jo Reed, born January 12, 1939.
   (b) Twila Reed, born 1943.
   (c) Charles Wayne Reed, born 1945.

(by second marriage):
    (d) (son) born January 9, 1948.
    (e) (son) born October 28, 1953.
  (2) Nollie Norman Connel, born January 12, 1925.
  (3) Van Turner Connel, born June 1, 1928.
  (4) Odie Coquese Connel, born April 18, 1931.
(by second marriage):
  (5) Doria May Ham, born January 26, 1936.
  (6) Dolores Fae Ham, born January 27, 1936.

b. Mamie Alice Gist, born May 11, 1907; married April 12, 1925, Norman
    A. Peugh; lived in Ukiah, California; children:
    (1) Jettie Alice Peugh, born March 3, 1926; married Ernest Eugene
        Pendergrass; children:
        (a) Nancy Madelon Pendergrass, born April 30, 1945.
        (b) Donna June Pendergrass, born January, 1947.
    (2) Norman H. Peugh, born June 27, 1934.
    (3) Edward Allen Peugh, born January 7, 1938.
    (4) Barbara Ann Peugh, born June 29, 1940.
c. Guy Jennings Gist, born May 6, 1910; dsp December 2, 1924.
d. Jack Marcus Gist, born February 4, 1917; dsp December 2, 1924.
e. Newman Huff Gist, born October 20, 1919; married September 14, 1947,
    Verna ____; lived in San Diego, California; children:
    (1) Guy Gist, born February 10, 1953.
    (2) Debbie Gist, born February 10, 1953.
f. Byron Lloyd Gist, born January 30, 1922; married December 31, 1940,
    Marnie Clark; child:
    (1) Gary Gist, born September 6, 1945.
g. Verelda Katherine Gist, born February 10, 1924; married December,
    1940, Ray Stoltz; lived in National City, California; children:
    (1) Rita Stoltz, born April 26, 1942.
    (2) Ronnie Stoltz, born 1946.
    (3) Bobbie Stoltz, born November, 1948.
h. Goldie Ethel Gist, born August 19, 1925; married September 26, 1942,
    Vernon Clark; lived in National City, California; children:
    (1) Pamela Ann Clark, born December 15, 1943.
    (2) Richard Clark, born January 28, 1948.
    (3) Kathy Jane Clark, born December 1, 1951.
i. Betty May Gist, born January 10, 1928; married June 1, 1945, Ray
    Lilly; child:
    (1) Wade Conley Lilly, born November 3, 1946.

***

REFERENCES

[1]Land Patents W. C. 2, 66, I. C. & I. L. C., 18; Land Office, Annapolis, Maryland; Baltimore County, Maryland, Deeds I. R., A. M. 179-183, 193-195, R. M., H. S., 279-281.

[2]Baltimore County, Maryland, Deeds R. M., H. S., 331.

[3]Ibid., Wills Bk. 6, p. 20, Deeds R. M., H. S., 417, 510.

[4]Ibid., Court Proceedings F2, 360, Deeds R. M., H. S., 417, Will Bk. 14, p. 396; Friends' Records, Baltimore, Maryland, 116-30.

[5]Baltimore County, Maryland, Deeds I. R., P. P., 192-194; T. R., A., 140-141; I. S., H, 69; T. R., R. A., 443; T. R., A., 177; Land Patents P. L. 2, 166, Bk. 7, p. 157.

[6]Ibid., Court Proceedings I. S., G, 211, Deeds I. S. H, 427, I. S., I. K., 470.

[7]St. Paul's Parish Vestry records, Maryland Historical Society, Baltimore, Maryland; W. H. Browne and C. C. Hall (ed.), Archives of Maryland (Baltimore: Maryland Historical Society, 1883-19??), XXXVI, 464; Baltimore County, Maryland, Deeds.

[8]Archives of Maryland XL, 508, 574, XLII, 93, 117, 192, 234; Baltimore County, Maryland, Court Proceedings H. W. S., I. A., 357; Pennsylvania Archives (Philadelphia, 1853; Harrisburg, 1874-1935), 1st Series, I, 526.

[9]Baltimore County, Maryland, Deeds I. S., 1, 196, I. S., L., 201, H. W. S., I. A., 189, Account Bk. 20, p. 455.

[10]Ibid., Deeds B., H., 149, 159-160.

[11]This account has been compiled from the wills of Thomas Morgan and James Murray in Baltimore County, Maryland.

[12]These relationships are proven by deeds of Richard Gist and Christopher Gist, and the will of Richard Cromwell, all in Baltimore County, Maryland; see David B. Trimble, unpublished dissertation, University of Texas, 1951.

[13]These relationships are possible because of associations of residence, and because there seems to have been no other Gist family to which these persons might have belonged.

[14]Lunenburg County, Virginia, tax lists of 1750, 1751, 1752, Deed Bk. 3, p. 89, Bk. 4, p. 267.

[15]Orange County, North Carolina, Minutes, Court of Pleas and Quarter Sessions, Bk. 2, p. 47, Bk. 3, pp. 29, 221, 244.

[16]George W. Paschall, History of North Carolina Baptists (Raleigh: The General Board, North Carolina Baptist State Convention, 1930), p. 394; Pre-Revolutionary Land Plats and Land Grants, State Archives, Columbia, South Carolina; Union County, South Carolina, Deeds A, 340, B, 3.

[17]Washington County, Tennessee, Minutes, Court of Pleas and Quarter Sessions Bk. 1, p. 22; William L. Saunders (ed.), The Colonial Records of North Carolina (Raleigh: P. M. Hale, State Printer, 1886-90), XII, 517; Pension of James Stevenson, S4009, National Archives, Washington, D. C.; Samuel Cole Williams, Tennessee During the Revolutionary War (Nashville: The Tennessee Historical Commission, 1944), p. 185.

[18]Greene County, Tennessee, Deed Bk. 1B, pp. 16, 21, Bk. 4, pp. 5, 7, Bk. 2, pp. 230, 326, Bk. B3, p. 292.

[19]Sinking Creek Baptist Church records, 1783-1785, p. 2, Holston Association Minutes, 1786-1850, Historical Commission of Southern Baptist Convention, Nashville, Tennessee.

[20]Greene County, Tennessee, Minutes, Court of Pleas and Quarter Sessions, 1783-1796, pp. 17, 35, 40; Samuel Cole Williams, History of the Lost State of Franklin (Johnson City, Tenn.: The Watauga Press, 1924), p. 39; original petition in State Archives, Raleigh, North Carolina.

[21]Greene County, Tennessee, Deed Bk. 2, p. 437, Bk. 6, p. 286; Knox County, Tennessee, Court Minutes Bk. 1, pp. 208, 293, 317, 319, 395; Hamilton District Superior Court of Law and Equity, Case #963.

[22]Smith County, Tennessee, Deeds A, 75; Jackson County, Tennessee, tax list, 1802; Smith County, Tennessee, Deeds, B, 290; Mill Creek Baptist Church Minutes, pp. 13, 16, 17, 20, Tompkinsville, Kentucky.

[23]Green County, Tennessee, Deed, Bk. 8, p. 220; for descendants of the presumed children of Benjamin Gist, see Jean Muir Dorsey, Christopher Gist of Maryland (Chicago: John S. Swift Company, Inc., 1958); Joseph and Benjamin Gist, Jr., were brothers, according to the will of Joseph Gist, and Mary Gist Stevenson was a daughter of Benjamin Gist according to her husband's pension record; the others mentioned accompanied Benjamin Gist on his various moves.

[24]Bible record belonging (1960) to Mrs. Noma C. Hodson; Wayne County, Kentucky, Wills A, 18; Bledsoe County, Tennessee, Deeds A, 10, 41.

[25]Knox County, Tennessee, Court Minutes; Jackson County, Tennessee, tax list, 1802; Willard Rouse Jillson, The Kentucky Land Grants (Louisville: The Standard Printing Company, 1925), p. 321; White County, Tennessee, tax lists, 1810-1813.

[26]Mrs. John Trotwood Moore, "Records of Commissions of Officers in the Tennessee Militia, 1814," in Tennessee Historical Quarterly, IX, 179; Tennessee Land Grants, State Archives, Nashville, Tennessee.

[27]Monroe County, Kentucky, Deeds E, 6 (re-recorded); Clay County, Tennessee, Deeds G, 450 (re-recorded).

[28]Jackson County, Tennessee, Ranger's Book, 1817-60, p. 80; Original petition, State Archives, Nashville, Tennessee; Overton County, Tennessee, Deeds J, 225; Monroe County, Kentucky, Wills B-1, 2 (re-recorded).

[29]Jackson County, Tennessee, census of 1850; Bible record belonging (1960) to Mrs. Noma C. Hodson; for descendants of these children, see Dorsey, Christopher Gist.

[30]Bible record belonging (1960) to Mrs. Noma C. Hodson; statement of Ferdinand P. Hestand; Jackson County, Tennessee, census of 1830 and 1850; Monroe County, Kentucky, census of 1840; Jackson County, Tennessee, tax list, 1836; Jillson, The Kentucky Land Grants, p. 1286.

[31]Clay County, Tennessee, Deeds A, 198-199; statement of Mary Abigail Hestand Bennett; Bible record belonging (1950) to Olivia Gist Field; records belonging to Porter Gist.

[32]Records belonging to Preston Howard Silvey and Nannie Silvey Birdwell.

[33]Records belonging to James Claud Marshall.

[34]Records belonging to Daisy Belle Marshall Duncan.

[35]Records belonging to Alta Woodcock Rhodes.

[36]Records belonging to Preston Howard Silvey.

[37]Records belonging to Olivia Gist Field and Mrs. Henry G. Castle.

[38]Records belonging to Della Gist Hestand.

[39]Records belonging to Violet Connel Peebles.

***

HICKMAN of Sullivan County, Tennessee

John Peter Hickman was born May 4, 1740, probably in Germany, and married Magdalene about 1763. He lived in Frederick (now Berkeley) County, (West) Virginia, as early as 1722, and was taxed on 96 acres of land there from 1782 to 1785, although there is no record of a purchase or sale of the land. On September 27, 1782, he received 100 acres on Steel Creek in Washington County from the State of Virginia.[1] Peter Hickman's first wife died after 1783, and about 1787 he married again, although the name of the second wife is unknown. On May 4, 1794, he married a third time in Washington County, Virginia, to Mrs. Susanna (Book) Oakwood.[2]

On March 4, 1794, Peter Hickman bought 600 acres on the waters of Steel Creek and two 300-acre tracts on the road from the head of Holston to Long Island in Sullivan County, Tennessee, from Mary Parker, executrix of Anthony Bledsoe, for £200. On August 23, 1796, he and Archibald Brumley bought 160 acres on Beaver Creek in Sullivan County for £80 from Ephraim Smith; on November 10, 1796, he received 60 acres for 30 shillings from the state of North Carolina. On May 19, 1800, he bought 158 acres from William Snodgrass for $30.00. He lived west of Bristol near the present border between Sullivan County, Tennessee, and Washington County, Virginia, although during his early residence there the line fluctuated. It is also possible that some references to Peter Hickman are to his son.[3] Peter Hickman's third wife died in 1808 and he soon married Margaret Parity, who was born October 28, 1732, and who survived him.[4]

On March 13, 1813, Peter Hickman, Sr., and his wife made an agreement with his son Michael, whereby Peter was to remain on his 750 acre farm and receive food and clothing for the remainder of his life, after which the land would be Michael's. At the same time, he gave Michael 224 acres on Steel Creek in Sullivan County, and on March 30, 1813, he gave Michael his 100 acres on Steel Creek in Washington County. On February 3, 1818, he sold his son Adam 250 acres for $625.00.[5]

Peter Hickman could not read or write and perhaps could not speak English, but by hard work he accumulated considerable property. He was a vigorous man and was able to ride a horse the day before his death on March 31, 1825, in Washington County, Virginia.[6] Peter Hickman was the father of the following children:[7]

(by first marriage):
a. Adam Hickman, born August 14, 1764; lived in Sullivan County, Tennessee, in 1834.
1. b. Peter Hickman, born October 17, 1766.
2. c. Michael Hickman, born October 24, 1768.
d. Mary Ann Hickman, born April 13, 1771; married David Walden, born c1758; died October 28, 1849; lived in Blount County, Alabama, in 1833.
e. John Hickman, born February 18, 1774; married Elizabeth King; lived in Alabama in 1834.
3. f. Jacob Hickman, born February 2, 1777.
g. Magdalene Hickman, born May 3, 1780; married William Bullock; lived in Sullivan County, Tennessee.
h. Daniel Hickman, born April 2, 1783.
(by second marriage):

4. i. Hannah Hickman, born c1788.
    j. Anna Hickman, born c1790; died May 24, 1846, in Vermilion County, Illinois; married c1806 in Sullivan County, Tennessee, to Henry Wolfe (see p. 269).

***

1.   Peter Hickman was born October 17, 1766, and married about 1800 in Sullivan County, Tennessee, to Mary Oakwood, daughter of Henry Oakwood and Susanna Book. About 1810 he married Susan Troxell, daughter of Daniel Troxell of Sullivan County. Peter Hickman bought 206 acres adjoining his brother Adam from his brother Michael for $2,000.00 on February 20, 1822. His father-in-law, Daniel Troxell, gave him 160 acres on Back Creek on October 6, 1824. He died about 1825 in Sullivan County, Tennessee, leaving the following children:[8]

(by first marriage):
a. Jacob Hickman, born c1802; lived in Bracken County, Kentucky, in 1831.
b. Michael Hickman, born c1804; lived in Bracken County, Kentucky, in 1831.
c. Catherine Hickman married Frederick Leonard; lived in Washington County, Virginia, in 1831.
(by second marriage):
d. Rosanna Hickman, lived in Sullivan County, Tennessee, in 1831.
e. Elizabeth Hickman, lived in Sullivan County, Tennessee, in 1832.

***

2.   Michael Hickman was born October 24, 1768, and married in Washington County, Virginia, to Catherine Mumpower, daughter of Peter Mumpower. He served in the War of 1812 as captain of the 105th Regiment, Washington County, militia. On April 24, 1798, he bought 240 acres in Washington County, and on June 28, 1799, he sold 221 acres on Back Creek to Frederick Whiteman. He bought an additional 150 acres on Steel Creek from Jacob Susong on March 20, 1811, and sold it to Anthony Sowerbeer in April, 1813.[9] On March 13, 1813, his father, Peter Hickman, gave him 224 acres on Steel Creek and the 750 acre plantation where Peter lived for taking care of him for the remainder of his life. On February 20, 1822, he sold his brother, Peter Hickman, Jr., 206 acres in Sullivan County for $2,000.00.[10] Michael Hickman died June 10, 1825, in Washington County, Virginia, leaving the following children:[11]

a. Peter Hickman, born December 5, 1797; died August, 1840, in Port Gibson, Mississippi; he was a slave trader doing business from Washington County, Virginia. He bought the estates of his father, grandfather, and uncle Peter Hickman. He married Susannah _____, born April 25, 1798; children:
    (1) Joseph Harrison Hickman, born May 17, 1821.
    (2) Elizabeth Margaret Hickman, born March 20, 1823.
    (3) Michael Hickman, born February 9, 1826.
    (4) Margaret J. Hickman, born December 8, 1827.
    (5) Peter P. Hickman, born February 28, 1830.
    (6) Susannah Hickman, born November 8, 1832.
b. Katherine Hickman married Roland Harkins.
c. John Hickman married Sarah Pitts; lived in Crab Orchard Spring, Lincoln County, Kentucky.
d. Ann Hickman married John Saunders.
e. (daughter) married John Swatts.

51

    f. Michael Hickman married Mary Blackburn; lived in Vermilion County,
        Illinois.

***

3.   Jacob Hickman was born February 2, 1777, in Frederick (now Berkeley) County, (West) Virginia, and married about 1800 in Sullivan County,
Tennessee, to Sarah Oakwood, born June 30, 1786, and died June 23, 1858,
daughter of Henry Oakwood and Susannah Book. He moved to Brown County,
Ohio, and about 1830 to Vermilion County, Illinois, where he owned a
large amount of land and raised Hereford cattle descended from stock
bought from Henry Clay in Kentucky. He died April 25, 1841, leaving
the following children:[12]

5. a. John Peter Hickman, born February 5, 1802.
6. b. Susannah H. Hickman, born November 21, 1803.
7. c. Hiram Hickman, born October 21, 1805.
8. d. Morgan Hickman, born c1807.
    e. Nancy Hickman, born June 1, 1809; died December 4, 1886; married
       (1) Beriah M. Dougherty (2) James McCorkle; children (all by first
       marriage):
       (1) Sarah Dougherty married William Hart.
       (2) Malinda Ann Dougherty married _____ Littler.
       (3) Margaret Dougherty married Ewell Jeffers.
    f. Sarah Hickman, born October 20, 1811; died May 23, 1905 in George-
       town, Illinois; married William Hesler, born April 22, 1815; died
       December 9, 1891; children:
       (1) George Harmon Hesler, born September 3, 1842; died 1907 near
           Terre Haute, Indiana.
       (2) Andrew J. Hesler, born January 28, 1844; lived in Kansas.
       (3) Jane Hesler, born 1844; dsp 1916.
       (4) Mary A. Hesler, born September 27, 1846; dsp December 25, 1864.
       (5) Samuel Hesler, born February 28, 1849; dsp February 28, 1857.
       (6) Sarah A. Hesler, born December 17, 1851; died 1929; married
           March 16, 1887, to M. F. Sandifer; children:
           (a) Jean B. Sandifer, born February 24, 1888; married James
               Ross Mason.
           (b) Ethel I. Sandifer, born January 3, 1891; married (1) Feb-
               ruary 11, 1912, to William Allrands (2) _____ Andreas;
               child (by first marriage):
               /1/ Richard J. Allrands, born January 19, 1913.
       (7) William Hickman Hesler; lived in Kansas.
9. g. Andrew Jackson Hickman, born April 25, 1813.
10. h. Mary Ann Hickman, born March 2, 1815.
    i. Jacob B. Hickman, born March 15, 1817; dsp November 30, 1834.
    j. Allen Hickman, born c1819; died December 20, 1854, in Mariesville,
       California; married Laura Ann Hunter; lived in Carroll County, Il-
       linois.
11. k. Hannah Hickman, born 1821.
    l. Samuel H. Hickman, born March 9, 1823; dsp March 6, 1856.
12. m. Richard Collins Hickman, born July 22, 1825.
    n. Loren Margaret Hickman, born January 13, 1828; dsp August 25, 1838.
    o. George R. Hickman, born March 15, 1830; dsp September 20, 1846.

***

5.   John Peter Hickman was born February 5, 1802, and died April 16,
1862; married Elizabeth Singleton, born September 19, 1811; died January
26, 1875. They lived in Vermilion County, Illinois, and had the following

52

children:[13]

a. David K. Hickman, born April 22, 1830; dsp October 9, 1843.
b. Sarah O. Hickman, born December 14, 1831; dsp September 22, 1852.
c. Jacob Hickman, born May 10, 1833; dsp February 10, 1842.
d. Katherine Hickman, born c1835; married _____ Sutton; children:
   (1) James Sutton; lived in Danville, Illinois.
   (2) Elizabeth Sutton.
   (3) William Sutton; lived in Grape Creek, Illinois.
   (4) Charles Sutton.
   (5) Ann Sutton.
   (6) John Sutton.
e. Susan Hickman, born July 10, 1837; died May 25, 1912; married (1) March 8, 1859, to David R. Egy (2) July 6, 1875, **Philip W. Blagg**; **lived in Vermilion County, Illinois; children (all by first marriage):**
   (1) Homer Hickman Egy, born c1860; died May 8, 1895; married Flora Lee (see p. 55); children:
     (a) Leo Egy.
     (b) Frank Egy.
     (c) Elizabeth Egy.
   (2) Mary Elizabeth Egy, born 1863; died 1920; married James W. Elliott; children:
     (a) Grace Elliott.
     (b) Burleigh Elliott.
f. Lura Jane Hickman, born 1840; married Jurgen Peterson; children:
   (1) Frank Peterson.
   (2) Margaret Peterson; dsp.
   (3) Katherine Peterson, born February 24, 1867; died January 29, 1940; married Peter Barry.
   (4) Susan Peterson married _____ Turner.
   (5) Lou Peterson married Joseph Kilpatrick.
   (6) Robert Peterson.
   (7) Raymond Peterson.
   (8) Ralph Peterson; lived in Globe, Arizona.
g. Sidney M. Hickman, born April 3, 1842; dsp October 13, 1842.
h. Laura Ann Hickman, born 1843; died 1905; married Michael C. Reynolds, born September 28, 1825; died April 2, 1878; lived in Vermilion County, Illinois; children:
   (1) Louise Reynolds married _____ Stansbury.
   (2) Katherine Reynolds married _____ Craig.
   (3) Laura Reynolds.
i. Serane Hickman, born May 22, 1846; dsp September 14, 1846.
j. Serilda Hickman, born May 22, 1846; dsp September 27, 1846.
k. Margaret A. Hickman, born September 26, 1847; dsp June 27, 1863.
l. Hannah Louisa Hickman, born 1849; died February 17, 1923; married June 20, 1878, to David Bloomer, born December 24, 1845; died January 9, 1924; children:
   (1) William D. Bloomer, born March 20, 1882.
   (2) Ransom Bloomer, born March 29, 1884; died February 15, 1932.
   (3) Ruby N. Bloomer married Seymour Winans.
   (4) Daisy Isabel Bloomer.
   (5) Beatrice Bloomer married Frank Preston Pritchard; children:
     (a) Lyle Pritchard.
     (b) David Pritchard.
     (c) Fledra Pritchard.
   (6) Jean Bloomer married Ernest Beers.

***

6.   Susannah H. Hickman was born November 21, 1803, and died June 17,

1890; married c1828 William Taylor, born July 8, 1804; died January 10, 1881; lived in Georgetown, Illinois. Their children were as follows:[14]

a. Sarah Taylor, born June 8, 1832; died February 3, 1905; married December 25, 1860, to James H. Gadd, born 1828; died November 19, 1890; children:
    (1) Myra Gadd, born September 15, 1861; married August 5, 1889, to Fred Barrows; lived in Detroit, Michigan; children:
        (a) Walter Barrows, born May 13, 1891.
        (b) Allen Barrows, born October 24, 1892.
    (2) Mae Gadd, born April 7, 1863; died 1937, in Veedersburg, Indiana; married April 4, 1884, to Millard F. Bales, born 1851, died 1920; children:
        (a) Catherine Bales, born February 13, 1885.
        (b) Dorothy Bales, born November 5, 1888.
        (c) Edythe Willard Bales, born August 19, 1890.
    (3) Catha Gadd, born November 16, 1867; married J. Rice Cannady; lived in Los Angeles, California; children:
        (a) Henry Cannady, born February 19, 1900.
        (b) James Cannady, born March 13, 1901.
        (c) Robert Cannady, born December 27, 1902.
        (d) Joseph R. Cannady, born September 12, 1906.
    (4) Frank Gadd, born December 21, 1869.
    (5) Laura Gadd, born August 13, 1872; died April, 1952, in Englewood, California; married September 23, 1899, to Charles A. Smith; child:
        (a) Harry L. Smith, born June 4, 1900.
    (6) Susanna Gadd, born March 23, 1875; married January 14, 1894, to W. Hinds; lived in Terre Haute, Indiana; children:
        (a) Charles L. Hinds, born October 2, 1894.
        (b) Catherine Hinds, born November 19, 1896.
        (c) Florence Hinds.
    (7) Fred W. Gadd, born September 16, 1883.
b. Mary Taylor, born August 13, 1834; married Dr. Dwight Morris; lived in Mattoon, Illinois; children:
    (1) Charles Morris.
    (2) Edward Morris.
c. Catherine Taylor, dsp September 16, 1844.

***

7.   Hiram Hickman was born October 21, 1805, and died October 8, 1882, in Vermilion County, Illinois; married 1828 in Brown County, Ohio, to Martha Ann Allen, born April 11, 1814; died October 4, 1885. Their children were as follows:[15]

a. Martha Jane Hickman, born April, 1833; dsp November, 1862.
b. Mary Ellen Hickman, born c1835; married George Ray; lived in Danville, Illinois.
c. Sarah Hickman, born c1837; married Clark Brant.
d. Hardy Hickman, born c1841; married Iva Snyder.
e. Cornelia A. Hickman, born January 15, 1843; died December 7, 1875; married William E. Wolfe (see p. 271).
f. Lorinda Hickman, born c1845; married George Howell; lived in Iowa.
g. Isabel Hickman, born c1847.
h. Hiram Hickman, born January 4, 1849; died May 24, 1933, in Danville, Illinois; married Martha Griner; children:
    (1) Lou Hickman married Thomas Lloyd.
    (2) Fanny May Hickman married K. Shipps.

         (3) Asa Hickman.
         (4) Alva Hickman.
         (5) Gene Hickman.
         (6) Thelma Hickman.
         (7) Ronald Hickman.
         (8) Dale Hickman.
    i.   Ada Hickman married J. H. O'Connor; lived in Moneta, California.
    j.   Frank A. Hickman, born August 28, 1853; died March 25, 1879.

                                   ***

8.   Morgan Hickman was born about 1807; married Lucy Hunter; lived in
    Knox County, Missouri; their children were as follows:[16]

    a.   Eliza Hickman, born c1835; married Joseph Douglas.
    b.   Sarah Ann Hickman, born c1837; married Mark Ross; children:
         (1) Eva Ross married Charles Baldwin.
         (2) Charles Ross.
         (3) Lucy Ross married Whack Sadler.
    c.   Mary Jane Hickman, born c1840; married Marshall McCall; children:
         (1) Morgan McCall, dsp.
         (2) Nattie McCall, dsp.
         (3) Connie McCall.
         (4) Charles McCall.
    d.   Margaret Hickman, born c1843; married Charles Baldwin; children:
         (1) Frank Baldwin married Anna Greenley.
         (2) Willie Baldwin married Dr. _____ Hayden.
         (3) Charles Baldwin.
    e.   Martha Hickman, born c1850; married Boone Norris; children:
         (1) Morgan Norris married Fleta Applegate.
         (2) Lee Norris married Jenny Lou Robinson.

                                   ***

9.   Andrew Jackson Hickman was born April 25, 1813; died November 21,
    1843; married Hannah Davis Hunter; their children were as follows:[17]

    a.   Isabel D. Hickman, born July 5, 1836; dsp September 11, 1837.
    b.   Samuel Henry Hickman, born December 31, 1837; lived in Missouri.
    c.   William Morgan Hickman, born September 14, 1840; dsp November 20,
         1870.
    d.   Margaret Ann Hickman, born January 22, 1843; died 1914; married Aaron
         Lee, born February 4, 1838; died June 14, 1880; children:
         (1) Flora Lee married Homer Hickman Egy (see p.   53).
         (2) Willard Lee married Nora Hunter; children:
              (a) Edna Lee married Elmer Reinhold.
              (b) Ethel Lee married Leroy Ceibert.
         (3) Nettie Lee, died young.
         (4) Cora Isabel Lee married December 20, 1888, John Rutan; lived in
              Homer, Illinois; children:
              (a) Fred Rutan.
              (b) Allen Rutan.
              (c) Carl Rutan.
              (d) Kenneth Rutan.
              (e) Jennie Rutan.
              (f) May Rutan.
              (g) Mabel Rutan.
              (h) Joseph Rutan.
              (i) Howard Rutan.

                                   55

(5) Iva J. Lee, dsp.
(6) Roy A. Lee married Retta Strong.
(7) Amy F. Lee married John Baird Salladay.
(8) Grace Lee married Perry L. McPheeters; lived in Wheaton, Illinois.

***

10.   Mary Ann Hickman was born March 2, 1815, and died January 19, 1900, in Freeport, Illinois; married November 22, 1834, to John Brown, born June 30, 1811; died July 4, 1891; their children were as follows:[18]

a. Clark J. Brown, born October 3, 1835; died November 5, 1917; lived in Dakota, Illinois.
b. Sarah Jane Brown, born August 10, 1837; died February 15, 1926; lived in Dakota, Illinois.
c. Mary Ann Brown, born October 13, 1839; died July 10, 1919; lived in Dakota, Illinois.
d. John Hickman Brown; lived in Keithburg, Illinois.
e. Caroline E. Brown, born August 21, 1845; died January 18, 1850.
f. Florence Brown married _____ Mack; lived in Spencer, Iowa.
g. Martha Brown married F. B. Walker; lived in Dakota, Illinois.
h. Natalie Brown married H. A. Milliken; lived in Chicago, Illinois.
i. Vincent D. Brown, born October 31, 1851; died September 28, 1915; lived in Spencer, Iowa.
j. Allen Hickman Brown, born December 18, 1853; died October 31, 1916; lived in Dakota, Illinois.
k. James C. Brown; lived in Spencer, Illinois.

***

11.   Hannah Hickman was born in 1821 and died in 1864; married Samuel D. Hunter, born 1821, died 1902; lived in Knox County, Missouri. Their children were as follows:[19]

a. Henry Hickman Hunter, born 1843; married Lavinda James; children:
   (1) Edward Everette Hunter married Dorothy Richardson.
   (2) Carrie Hunter, died young.
   (3) Maude Hunter married George Edmunds; children:
       (a) Margaret Edmunds married Carl Waye.
       (b) Hunter Edmunds.
   (4) Walter Hunter, died young.
   (5) Fanny Hunter married Charles Shumate; children:
       (a) Virginia Shumate married Ed Hunt.
       (b) Hortense Shumate.
       (c) Charlene Shumate.
       (d) Carl Shumate.
   (6) Ona Hunter married Raleigh McKinney; children:
       (a) Ruth McKinney.
       (b) James McKinney.
   (7) Carl Hunter married Pauline _____; children:
       (a) Josephine Hunter.
       (b) Charles Hunter.
   (8) Charles Hunter married Elizabeth _____.
b. Richard Collins Hunter, born 1843; dsp 1844.
c. Sarah Isabelle Hunter, born 1846; dsp 1911.
d. Mary Jane Hunter, born 1848; dsp 1856.
e. George Washington Hunter, born 1850; died 1889; married Lura Hendricks; children:
   (1) Narz W. Hunter married Libbie Naylor.

56

     (2) Frank Hunter married Mary Henry.
     (3) Gertie Hunter married Carl Boyd.
g. James Franklin Hunter, born 1854; died 1934; married Viola Hunsaker;
    children:
    (1) Homer Hunter.
    (2) Essa Hunter married _____ Shory; child:
       (a) Richard Shory.
    (3) Wayde Hunter.
    (4) Lucy Hunter married Joseph Delaney; child:
       (a) Margaret Ann Delaney.
    (5) Richard Hunter.
    (6) Allie Hunter married Ray Chadwick; children:
       (a) Donald Chadwick.
       (b) Bernice Chadwick.
       (c) Lois Chadwick.
       (d) Marjorie Chadwick.
    (7) Ollie Hunter married Mace Wicker.
h. Martha Ann Hunter, born 1857; married Abraham Imbler; child:
    (1) Claude Imbler.

***

12.   Richard Collins Hickman was born July 22, 1825, and died June 3,
1890, in Vermilion County, Illinois; married (1) 1847 Mary Buoy, born
September 15, 1823; died January 23, 1848; (2) 1860 Achsa Pruden, born
November 10, 1840; died October 13, 1927. His children were as follows:[20]

(by first marriage):
a. James R. Hickman, born January 13, 1848; died August 27, 1885; mar-
    ried Catherine Jane Connor, born August 18, 1851; died April 28,
    1923; lived in Vermilion County, Illinois; children:
    (1) Edward Hickman, born 1869; died 1912.
    (2) Nettie Hickman married Owen Stalker; lived in Shell Lake, Wis-
       consin; children:
       (a) Ara Stalker married _____ Lilkey.
       (b) Fay Stalker.
    (3) Hila May Hickman, born February 25, 1874; died February 20, 1900;
       married I. H. Graham.
    (4) Gertrude Hickman married Frank Potts; dsp.
    (5) Achsa Hickman married John Hampton; children:
       (a) Mona Hampton.
       (b) Bessie Hampton.
       (c) Charles Hampton.
(by second marriage):
b. Lucian D. Hickman, born November 13, 1862; dsp January 25, 1863.
c. Charles Pruden Hickman, born March 25, 1864; died August 8, 1938;
    married Margaret Sandusky; child:
    (1) Frederick Allen Hickman, born September 24, 1894; married Wenona
       Williams; children:
       (a) William Charles Hickman.
       (b) Frederick Allen Hickman, died young.
d. Allen Ray Hickman, born January 21, 1866; dsp September 22, 1936;
    married Hetwich Kohler.
e. Oscar Collins Hickman, born February 17, 1868; died February 19, 1939;
    married Edna White; lived in Danville, Illinois; children:
    (1) Frank Hickman married Julia Dodge; child:
       (a) Frances Rose Hickman.
    (2) Howard H. Hickman married Mary Cozatt; child:
       (a) Louise Ann Hickman.
    (3) Alice Hickman, born August 5, 1896; married Frank J. O'Keefe;

57

children:
    (a) Constance O'Keefe.
    (b) Irene O'Keefe, born April 30, 1929; married C. F. Plumer.
  (4) Marian Hickman; dsp November 28, 1897.
  (5) Allen Ray Hickman, born October 9, 1900; married Lottie Lash; children:
    (a) Betty Joyce Hickman.
    (b) Peggy Alice Hickman.
  (6) Robert Hickman, born August 22, 1909; married Lois Chew; children:
    (a) David Hickman.
    (b) Ann Hickman.

13. f. George Wilfred Hickman, born June 14, 1871.

* * *

13.   George Wilfred Hickman was born June 14, 1871, and married January 1, 1896, to Sadie Philora Hopper, born June 26, 1874; died June 29, 1904; lived in Vermilion County, Illinois. Their children were as follows:[21]

  a. Wilfred Hickman, born November 10, 1896; married Cena Lois Gilkison; lived in Fairmount, Illinois; children:
    (1) Janet Elizabeth Hickman, born July 13, 1926; married John Figueras; children:
      (a) Anita Figueras.
      (b) Richard Figueras.
      (c) Julia Figueras.
      (d) John Wilfred Figueras, born September 26, 1957.
    (2) Wilma June Hickman, born July 17, 1933.
    (3) Carol Adeline Hickman, born September 30, 1934.
  b. James Owen Hickman, born November 20, 1897; dsp September 3, 1909.
  c. Vernon Hickman, born October 16, 1900; married Mae Cheuvront; children:
    (1) Helen Anita Hickman, born April 7, 1927; married Harold Dowers.
    (2) George Edward Hickman, born January, 1929.
    (3) Peter Hickman, born December 29, 1931; dsp April 6, 1935.
    (4) Philip Sanford Hickman, born November 21, 1936.
    (5) Glenn Hickman.
    (6) Paul Hickman.
    (7) Kenneth Hickman.
  d. Wayne Hickman, born September 25, 1902; married June 12, 1932, to Miriam Lucille Gilkison; lived in Joliet, Illinois; children:
    (1) Delores Ann Hickman, born May 24, 1933.
    (2) Charles Wayne Hickman, born July 1, 1942.

* * *

4.   Hannah Hickman was born about 1788 in Virginia and died after 1870 in Smyrna Township, Jefferson County, Indiana; she married James Hartsock about 1805 in Sullivan County, Tennessee. They moved to Bracken County, Kentucky, and in 1814 to Jefferson County, Indiana, where Hartsock deserted the family in December, 1824, although he may have returned later. Although there is no proof, their children were, probably, among others, as follows:[22]

  a. John Hartsock, born c1806; died before 1880; married March 4, 1845, to Margaret Wyne; children, perhaps among others:
    (1) Ellen Hartsock, born c1846.
    (2) Ann Hartsock, born c1848.

58

     (3) George Hartsock, born c1853.
     (4) Hannah J. Hartsock, born c1856.
     (5) Elisha B. Hartsock, born c1858; married c1879 Elizabeth T.
           _____; divorced 1884.
b. George Hartsock, born c1808; dsp 1884 in Jefferson County, Indiana.
c. Anna Hartsock, born June 5, 1817; died February 9, 1904, in Jefferson County, Indiana; married c1839 Absolem Bolen, born December 26, 1814, and died July 17, 1890; children:
     (1) Hannah Bolen, born c1840.
     (2) John Bolen, born c1842; lived in Illinois.
     (3) Mary J. Bolen, born c1845; dsp 1940 in Jefferson County, Indiana.
     (4) Martha Bolen, born c1847; died young.
     (5) Hanson Bolen, born c1849; died young.
     (6) Annetta Bolen, born 1852; dsp 1930 in Jefferson County, Indiana.
     (7) Sarah A. Bolen, born c1854; died young.
     (8) Robert Willard Bolen, born 1856; dsp 1924 in Jefferson County, Indiana.
     (9) William Absolem Bolen, born 1857; dsp 1938 in Jefferson County, Indiana.
    (10) Calvin Bolen, born 1860; dsp 1940 in Jefferson County, Indiana.
d. Rachel Hartsock, born May 8, 1821; died March 21, 1884, in Pueblo, Colorado; married October 24, 1843, to Samuel Thomas, born February 2, 1821, and died July 16, 1899.
e. James Hartsock, born August 23, 1822; died June 22, 1901, in Jefferson County, Indiana; married Susan _____, born December 18, 1835, and died October 22, 1917; children:
     (1) Joseph Hartsock, born c1864; dsp.
     (2) Ida Hartsock, born c1868; married _____ Draper; lived in Indianapolis, Indiana.
     (3) Laura Belle Hartsock, born c1870; married Asberry Fisher; dsp.
f. William Henry Harrison Hartsock, born January 13, 1830; dsp June 16, 1895, in Jefferson County, Indiana; married November 9, 1856, to Eliza Lowe, born January 2, 1836.

***

REFERENCES

[1]Original record belonging (1960) to Wayne Hickman; deposition of Adam Hickman, Wythe County, Virginia, Chancery Court records, 1821; Frederick County, Virginia, Deed Bk. 14, p. 12; Berkeley County, (West) Virginia, tax lists (he is not listed in 1791 and 1792); Washington County, Virginia, Entry Bk. 1, p. 45.
[2]Original record belonging (1960) to Wayne Hickman; Washington County, Virginia, Marriages.
[3]Sullivan County, Tennessee, Deed Bk. 2, pp. 682/685, Bk. 3, p. 73, Bk. 4, pp. 623, 629.
[4]Original record belonging (1960) to Wayne Hickman.
[5]Sullivan County, Tennessee, Deed Bk. 7, pp. 122, 196, 195, 258; Washington County, Virginia, Deed Bk. 7, p. 188.
[6]Letter from Anna Wolfe to Jacob Hickman, June 19, 1825, original owned by Wayne Hickman.
[7]Original record belonging (1960) to Wayne Hickman; Sullivan County, Tennessee, Deed Bk. 11, pp. 120, 358.
[8]Original record belonging (1960) to Wayne Hickman; Sullivan County, Tennessee, Deed Bk. 9, p. 270, Bk. 10, p. 100, Bk. 11, pp. 119, 120, 185; Washington County, Virginia, Deed Bk. 3, p. 28, Bk. 5, p. 428.

[9]Original record belonging (1960) to Wayne Hickman; Washington County, Virginia, Will Bk. 5, p. 173, Deed Bk. 2, pp. 76, 542, Bk. 5, pp. 186, 220, 221, Bk. 7, p. 188.

[10]Sullivan County, Tennessee, Deed Bk. 7, pp. 122, 195, 196, Bk. 9, p. 270.

[11]Original records belonging (1960) to Wayne Hickman; Sullivan County, Tennessee, Deed Bk. 10, pp. 213, 293, 294, 396, 398, Bk. 11, pp. 119, 120, 185, 194, 358, 259, 373, 532.

[12]Original records belonging (1960) to Wayne Hickman; Washington County, Virginia, Deed Bk. 5, p. 428.

[13-21]Original records belonging (1960) to Wayne Hickman.

[22]Jefferson County, Indiana, census of 1850, 1860, 1870, 1880; letter from Hannah Hartsock to Jacob Hickman, February 2, 1825, original owned by Wayne Hickman; Madison Courier, Madison, Indiana, December 6, 1873; Jefferson County, Indiana, Marriages, Wills B, 754, D, 318, Cemetery records; records of W. L. Bolen.

**

HINDS of

Knox County, Tennessee, and Wayne County, Kentucky

Joseph Hinds was born about 1705 and married Ruth _____ about 1730; they lived in New Hanover Township, Hunterdon (now Mendham Township, Morris) County, New Jersey, as early as December 6, 1732, when he was surety for the administration of Robert Crosman's estate. On December 11, 1732, he and Samuel Crosman were sureties for the administration of the estate of Stephen Leonard. On April 18, 1749, he was an appraiser of the estate of Joseph Crosman, and on October 30, 1749, he appraised the estate of Timothy Peneton in Mendham Township. On June 19, 1750, he was an executor of the estate of Stephen Thompson in Morris County, and on December 11, 1751, he declined to serve as executor of Jacob Bescherer of Roxbury. In 1753 he apprenticed his son John to Robert Carlile of Roxbury.[1]

Joseph Hinds moved to North Carolina by 1761, and on March 5, 1763, he bought 250 acres on the southeast fork of Polecat Creek in Rowan (now Randolph) County, North Carolina, from Zachariah Cox for £42. After the death of his first wife, he married a widow, Susanna _____, but had no children by her. In 1770 he sold 30 acres to his son Simeon for £5, and left the remainder to his sons Simeon, Levi, and John in his will made on April 14, 1772; he gave cash to his son Joseph; the estate was probated in August, 1772. The children of Joseph and Ruth Hinds were as follows:[2]

          a. Charity Hinds, born November 16, 1731.
          b. Hannah Hinds, born June 2, 1734.[3]
     1.   c. Joseph Hinds, born June 17, 1737.
     2.   d. Simeon Hinds, born March 15, 1740.
     3.   e. Levi Hinds, born August 25, 1742.
     4.   f. John Hinds, born June 9, 1745.
          g. Mary Hinds, born February 6, 1748.

                            ***

1.   Joseph Hinds was born June 17, 1737, in Hunterdon (now Morris) County, New Jersey; served in the American Revolution and received several land grants for his services, including one for 5,000 acres in Maury County, Tennessee; he was a delegate to the North Carolina Constitutional convention. He moved to Randolph County, North Carolina, Knox County, Tennessee, and Wayne County, Kentucky, where he died in 1815, leaving a wife Hannah and the following children:[4]

     a. Joseph Hinds, born c1760; died 1815 in Wayne County, Kentucky; married Margaret _____; children:
         (1) Benjamin Hinds lived in Wayne County, Kentucky, in 1820.
         (2) George Hinds married November 28, 1811, to Mary Hinkle; lived in Wayne County, Kentucky, in 1820.
         (3) Charity Hinds married May 25, 1808, to William Bond.
         (4) Margaret Hinds married John McHenry.
         (5) Jane Hinds married November 11, 1805, to Joel Bond, born January 18, 1784, son of John Bond and Jane Beeson.
         (6) Hannah Hinds married William Reese.
         (7) Joseph Hinds married Amy _____; lived in Madison County, Kentucky, in 1815.

      (8) Stephen Hinds married Sarah _____; lived in Madison County, Kentucky in 1815.
- b. Samuel Hinds, born c1762; died c1830 in Wayne County, Kentucky; married Sarah _____; children:
  - (1) Joel Hinds married Pennina _____; lived in Fentress County, Tennessee, in 1830.
  - (2) Hannah Hinds.
  - (3) Charity Hinds married Samuel Reese; lived in Pulaski County, Kentucky, in 1830.
  - (4) Lucretia Hinds married Daniel Hurt; lived in Pulaski County, Kentucky, in 1830.
  - (5) Jenny Hinds.
  - (6) Levi Hinds married Martha Ann _____; lived in Wayne County, Kentucky, in 1830.
- c. Hannah Hinds.
- 5. d. Levi Hinds, born c1767.
- 6. e. Simeon Hinds, born August 11, 1769.
- f. Charity Hinds.
- g. Mary Hinds.
- h. Phoebe Hinds.
- i. Ruth Hinds.
- j. Sarah Hinds married Ebenezer Byram, son of Ebenezer Byram and Lydia Geren; lived in Jackson County, Alabama.
- k. Abigail Hinds married Joseph Bond, born February 29, 1780; died February, 1853, son of John Bond and Jane Beeson.

***

5.   Levi Hinds was born about 1767 in Rowan (now Randolph) County, North Carolina, and died September 11, 1842, in Madison County, Alabama; married in 1787 to Huldah Byram, died July 25, 1868, daughter of Ebenezer Byram and Lydia Geren; their children were as follows:[5]

- a. Benjamin Hinds, born c1788; married October 17, 1809, to Mary Childress.
- b. Hannah Hinds, born c1790; married Abraham Caldwell.
- c. Byram Hinds, born March 5, 1792; died April 23, 1875; married October 2, 1813, to Elizabeth Childress, born June 5, 1798; died January 14, 1870, daughter of John Childress.
- d. Lydia Hinds, born January 1, 1794; died November 23, 1880; married September 28, 1817, to Henry Rigney.
- e. Chloe Hinds, born c1795; married December 14, 1814, to Solomon Frey.
- f. Mahala Hinds.
- g. Thyrza Hinds, born 1799; married Isaac Morris.
- h. Calvin Hinds, born c1801; married November 6, 1822, to Sophia Culp.
- i. Joseph Hinds, born c1803.
- j. Levi Hinds, born 1805; died 1884; married August 14, 1828, to Eliza M. Connally.
- k. Milly Hinds, born c1807; married Daniel Weaver.

***

6.   Simeon Hinds was born August 11, 1769, in Rowan (now Randolph) County, North Carolina, and died December 13, 1840, in Overton County, Tennessee; married Elizabeth Stone. Their children were as follows:[6]

- a. Nancy Hinds, born July 5, 1797; married _____ Weaver.
- b. Mary Hinds, born December 7, 1798; married Sterling Harris.
- c. Josiah Hinds, born January 30, 1801; lived in Overton County, Tennessee.

62

d. Susan Hinds, born August 15, 1802; married David Masters.
e. Claiborn Hinds, born August 8, 1804; married _____ Goodpasture; lived in Overton County, Tennessee.
f. Elizabeth Hinds, born February 6, 1807; married _____ Laughlin.
g. John Hinds, born October 1, 1809; died July 26, 1862, in Prairie Grove, Arkansas; married May 22, 1841, to Rhoda Webb.
h. Sarah Hinds, born August 31, 1811; died July 12, 1881, in Overton County, Tennessee; married T. Sherral Anderson.
i. James Clinton Hinds, born September 11, 1813; lived in Overton County, Tennessee.
j. Caroline Hinds, born April 25, 1816.
k. Simeon Hinds, born March 29, 1818; married (1) Margaret Gardner (2) Mary Masters; lived in Cookeville, Tennessee.

***

2.   Simeon Hinds was born March 15, 1740, in Morris County, New Jersey, and died October 3, 1778, in Guilford (now Randolph) County, North Carolina; married Sarah _____; their child (among others) was as follows:[7]

a. Nancy Hinds, born c1775; married July 25, 1807, James Jones.

Although there is no proof, the following was undoubtedly one his children:

b. Joseph Hinds, born c1770; died c1820 in Fayette County, Illinois; married c1793 Elizabeth Pugh. He bought 62 acres on Polecat Creek in Randolph County, North Carolina, from Job Lewis for £50 on December 28, 1796, and sold it to Richard Richardson for £100 on March 11, 1802. He then moved to Christian County, Kentucky, and later to Fayette County, Illinois; children:
   (1) John Hinds married (1) Henrietta Woods (2) Sarah _____.
   (2) Sarah Hinds, born c1796; married August 20, 1819, Joseph Hall, son of John Hall; lived in Fayette County, Illinois.
   (3) Eleanor Hinds, born January 19, 1798; died March 4, 1858, in Fayette County, Illinois; married December 14, 1813, John Hall, son of John Hall.
   (4) Ann Hinds, born August 16, 1800; died April 11, 1863, in Ramsey, Illinois, married John Knight, born January 10, 1794; died April 28, 1859.
   (5) Charity Hinds, born c1802; married January 28, 1822, Zela F. Watwood.
   (6) Elizabeth Hinds, born c1804; married George W. McCurdy.
7. (7) Joseph Hinds, born December 28, 1806.
   (8) Mary Hinds, born c1808; married June 1, 1826, Col. Charles Prentiss, died November 22, 1837, in Vandalia, Illinois.
8. (9) Simeon Hinds, born December 12, 1811.

***

7.   Joseph Hinds was born December 28, 1806, and died July 20, 1852, in Fayette County, Illinois; married December 3, 1835, to Nancy C. Knight, born March 11, 1820; died May 10, 1892; their children were as follows:[8]

a. Mary E. Hinds, born c1837; married Elias L. Wicklin.
b. John C. Hinds, born July 15, 1838; dsp May 20, 1856.
c. Francis Marion Hinds, born c1840; married October 13, 1861, Ellie C. Smith.
d. Geneva M. Hinds, born c1848.

63

e. Charles Eugene Hinds, born February 2, 1851; married April 8, 1874, in Black River Falls, Wisconsin, to Belle Barber, who was born March 17, 1854, the daughter of James Barber and Eliza Dugan. Charles and Belle Hinds lived in Racine, Wisconsin, in 1899; children:
(1) James Barber Hinds, born August 18, 1875.
(2) Charles Morton Hinds, born July 12, 1877; dsp April 8, 1878.
(3) Francis Somerfield Hinds, born November 28, 1885.

***

8. Simeon Hinds was born December 12, 1811, in Hopkinsville, Kentucky, and died June 15, 1857, in Fayette County, Illinois; married October 6, 1836, to Jane Alvira Poland, who was born May 16, 1819, in Blount County, Tennessee, and died January 1, 1880. Their children were as follows:[9]

a. Jerome Jasper Hinds, born May 12, 1838; married Clara Belle Bliss; lived in Washington, D. C.
b. John Baxter Hinds, born December 13, 1839; married Josephine Wright; lived in Decatur, Alabama.
9. c. Joseph Monroe Hinds, born January 6, 1842.
d. Adolphus Leonidas Hinds, born February 28, 1846; dsp June 19, 1864, at Vicksburg, Mississippi.
e. Emily Elizabeth Hinds, born April 16, 1848; dsp; married April 11, 1872, in Fayette County, Illinois, to Dr. Louis Phillippe Griffin; lived in Washington, D. C.
f. Albert Morris Hinds, born September 16, 1850; dsp December 1, 1869, in Memphis, Tennessee.
g. Ada Adora Hinds, born February 6, 1853; died February 1, 1884, in Birmingham, England; married William Faucett Ramskill.
h. Ferris Simeon Hinds, born October 31, 1855; married Eliza Spain.

***

9. Joseph Monroe Hinds was born January 6, 1842, and died about 1905 in Manila, Philippine Islands. He served from Illinois in the Civil War, and moved to Decatur, Alabama, afterwards; in 1872 he was appointed U. S. Consul General at Rio de Janeiro, Brazil. In 1873 in Rio de Janeiro, he married Lucia Anita Trillia of Buenos Aires; he returned to Decatur, Alabama, in 1878, and was appointed U. S. Marshal for the Northern District of Alabama in 1882. About 1896 he failed in business and moved to Buenos Aires, later securing a position with the U. S. government in the Philippinne Islands. Joseph and Lucia Hinds had the following children:[10]

a. Grace Elvina Hinds, born 1879; married (1) 1902 Alfred Duggan of Buenos Aires, who died in 1915 (2) 1917 George Nathaniel Curzon, 1st Marquess Curzon of Kedleston, born January 11, 1859, in Kedleston, Derbyshire, England, died March 20, 1925, in London, England; he was Viceroy of India and Foreign Secretary under Lloyd George. The children of Grace Hinds (by her first marriage) were as follows:[11]

(1) Alfred Duggan, born 1903; dsp; lived in Sussex, England.
(2) Hubert Duggan, born 1904; dsp 1943; member of Parliament for Acton, 1931-43.
(3) Marcella Duggan, born 1907; married 1926 Edward Rice of Kent, England; children:
(a) Henry Rice.
(b) Patrick Rice.
(c) Caroline Rice married 1952 Robert Clive, 3rd Earl of Plymouth.

b. Albert Hinds, born 1884; married Mabel Cowes; children:
    (1) Leslie Hinds, born 1910; dsp.
    (2) Josephine Hinds, born c1913; married Gordon Cameron of Buenos
        Aires.
    (3) John Hinds, born c1915; dsp 1939.
c. Anita Hinds, born 1884; married 1913 to Col. A. Dudley; dsp.
d. Trillia Hinds, born 1888; dsp 1919.

***

3.   Levi Hinds was born August 25, 1742, in Morris County, New Jersey,
and moved to Polecat Creek in Rowan (now Randolph) County, North Carolina, by 1761. He married about 1765 to Sarah _____. On February 12,
1775, he and his brother Simeon and their wives sold their interest in
their father's 220 acre farm on the Southeast Fork of Polecat Creek to
their brother, Joseph Hinds. On November 10, 1778, Levi Hinds entered
200 acres on Polecat Creek which were granted to him on October 23, 1782;
in 1779 he was taxed on 16 acres of improved land, 480 acres of other
land, nine cattle, three horses, and £75 cash, for a total value of
£1,065.[12]

        Levi Hinds served in the American Revolution; at the close of the
war he moved to Burke County, North Carolina, and on February 19, 1783,
sold his 200-acre grant in Randolph County to Hiram Geron for £60.[13]

        By about 1788, Hinds lived in Hawkins (now Knox) County, Tennessee,
where he received a grant of 200 acres on the waters of Beaverdam Creek.
In October, 1794, he sued Hiram Geron; he was relieved from taxes in
1798, served as executor of the estate of John Brady on November 6, 1799,
and served on juries many times.[14] Many references to Levi Hinds may re-
fer to his son or nephews, so that it is difficult to differentiate.

        On July 29, 1793, Levi Hinds acquired another 200-acre grant on
Beaverdam Creek in Hinds Valley, which he sold to Jesse Stubbs for £150
on October 31, 1796, and on September 17, 1796, he bought 183½ acres on
the West Fork of Flat Creek from John Beaird for $167.50, and sold it
to Boston Graves for $333.33 on February 4, 1799. He made his home on a
350-acre tract on the South Fork of Beaverdam Creek which he bought from
Thomas Jeffries on December 9, 1801; he sold the 100-acre part on which
he lived to his brother, John Hinds, on February 29, 1804, but continued
to make his home there. He sold another 50 acres of it to John Clibourn
for $250.00 on October 2, 1816.[15]

        Levi Hinds moved to Wayne County, Kentucky, in 1817, and on August
28, 1817, made his will dividing his property among his children; the
estate was probated in January, 1818. On February 18, 1818, his sons
Levi and Joseph sold his remaining 200 acres in Knox County, Tennessee,
to Samuel Tindle for $800.00.[16]

        The children of Levi and Sarah Hinds were as follows:[17]

a. Joseph Hinds died in 1820 in Wayne County, Kentucky; married Elizabeth
   Sharpe.
b. Hannah Hinds married _____ Graham.
c. Levi Hinds.
d. John Hinds married Esther _____.
e. Ruth Hinds married _____ Pierce.
f. Sarah Hinds.

65

g. Rhoda Hinds, born July 19, 1773; died c1819 in Jackson (now Clay) County, Tennessee; married c1793 in Knox County, Tennessee, to Benjamin Gist (see p. 39).

***

4.   John Hinds was born June 9, 1745, in Morris County, New Jersey; he was a justice of the peace in Guilford County, North Carolina, in 1779 and adjutant of the southern part of Randolph County the same year. He served as a captain in the American Revolution and received several land grants in Tennessee for his services, including one of 4,400 acres in Overton County, Tennessee. After the war he moved to Knox County, Tennessee, where he made his will on August 25, 1811, leaving his property to his children as follows:[18]

a. Sylvanus Hinds, born c1778; married Abigail ____; lived in Roane County, Tennessee, in 1810; children:
    (1) John Hinds married Sarah A. Hickey.
    (2) James R. Hinds married October 5, 1825, to Rachel Abel.
    (3) Levi J. Hinds.
    (4) Joseph Hinds.
    (5) Sarah Ann Hinds married ____ Perkins.
    (6) Mary Hinds married March 21, 1829, to Lewis Perkins.
b. Hannah Hinds, born c1780; married February 20, 1800, to Richard Newport.
c. Susannah Hinds, born c1782; married January 8, 1801, to Cavanaugh Newport.
d. John Hinds, born c1784; died 1860 in Roane County, Tennessee.
e. Levi Hinds, born c1786; married Nancy ____; lived in Overton County, Tennessee, in 1810.
f. Simeon Hinds, born c1788; married 1812 to Elizabeth Lockard.
g. Asa Hinds, born c1790.
10. h. Joseph Hinds, born c1792.
i. Abigail Hinds, born c1794.

***

10.   Joseph Hinds was born about 1792 and died 1844 in Roane County, Tennessee; married June 9, 1812, to Susannah Hankins, daughter of Absolem and Ruth Hankins; their children were as follows:[19]

a. Henry Hinds married Margaret Harner.
b. Asa Hinds married October 8, 1836, Ruth Parks.
c. Levi Jackson Hinds, born January 15, 1817; died December 15, 1886; married (1) February 4, 1843, Minerva Owings, born January 18, 1822; died February 27, 1851, daughter of Samuel Sumter Owings and Sarah Randolph; (2) October 1, 1852, Martha Bullard; children:
    (by first marriage):
    (1) Albert Hinds married Susan Harner.
    (2) Ruth Caroline Hinds married (1) Joseph Bacon (2) James Carter Hinds.
    (3) Sarah Ann Hinds married (1) Absalom Rector (2) David R. Billingsley.
    (by second marriage):
    (4) Asa Franklin Hinds married Jane Brown.
    (5) Amanda Hinds married William Long.
d. Eliza Hinds married Simeon C. Geren, born February 20, 1818; died January 27, 1889; lived in Bradley County, Tennessee; children:
    (1) Susan Catherine Geren, born c1842; married ____ Hawk.

(2) William L. Geren, born c1844; married January 10, 1867, Ruth M. Collins.
e. Sarah Ann Hinds married September 4, 1841, Carter Hickey.
f. George Washington Hinds married Elizabeth Robbs.
g. Susan Hinds married John Fooshee.
h. Joseph Hinds, dsp.
i. Anna Hinds died 1848; married 1838 James Christopher Abel, born 1818, son of David Abel and _____ Harner; children:
  (1) Louise Abel.
  (2) Susan Abel.
  (3) George Abel.
  (4) Robert Abel died c1863.
  (5) William Abel.

***

REFERENCES

[1]A. Van Doren Honeyman (ed.), Archives of the State of New Jersey (Somerville, New Jersey: The Unionist-Gazette Association, Printers, 1918-1924), vol. 30, pp. 126, 298, 375, 479, vol. 31, p. 28; apprenticeship agreement belonging (1938) to Harry Burn.
[2]Rowan County, North Carolina, tax list 1761, Deed Bk. 5, p. 355; Guilford County, North Carolina, Deed Bk. 1, p. 92, Wills A, 150; Bible record belonging (1938) to Harry Burn.
[3]This is probably the Hannah Hinds of Mendham Township who married January 2, 1753, in Morris County, New Jersey, Ephraim Leonard; Presbyterian Register, Morristown, New Jersey.
[4]Wayne County, Kentucky, Wills A, 19, Deeds B, 270, E, 239, Marriages.
[5]Records of Mrs. Helen Hinds Stacy.
[6]Records of Mrs. Kate Hinds Steele.
[7]Bible record belonging (1938) to Harry Burn; Simeon Hinds Estate Papers, State Archives, Raleigh, North Carolina; Randolph County, North Carolina, Marriages. The guardian of Nancy Hinds was Zebedee Wood, perhaps her step-father; records of Mrs. Louise R. Turner.
[8-9]Records of Mrs. Louise R. Turner.
[10-11]Records of Alfred Duggan.
[12]Guilford County, North Carolina, Deed Bk. 1, p. 317; North Carolina Land Entries #123, entry 518, grant 122, bk. 49, p. 209, State Land Office, Raleigh, North Carolina.
[13]Index to Revolutionary Army Accounts, V-7-3, VIII-83-4, XI-28-4, State Archives; Randolph County, North Carolina, Deed Bk. 1, p. 42.
[14]North Carolina Land Grant #2735; Knox County, Tennessee, Court Minutes #0, #2, #3, Wills.
[15]Knox County, Tennessee, Deeds A1, 185, B2-1, 39, E2-1, 128, 158, G1, 313, L1, 50, P1, 410.
[16]Wayne County, Kentucky, Wills A, 18; Knox County, Tennessee, Deeds S1, 213.
[17]Wayne County, Kentucky, Wills A, 18.
[18-19]Records of Mrs. B. J. Lamb, Jr.

***

JARRATT of Lunenburg County, Virginia

Thomas Jarratt was in Brunswick (now Lunenburg) County, Virginia, as early as April 3, 1735, when he witnessed a deed. On September 22, 1739, he received a patent for 64 acres on the south side of Stony Creek adjoining James Mize, and on October 1, 1747, he received a patent for an additional 153 acres on the west side of Stony Creek adjoining his own land and that of Francis Wray and James Mize.[1]

On November 6, 1752, Thomas and his wife Rebecca Jarratt gave their son-in-law, Benjamin Gist, 100 acres of their plantation on Stony Creek, and on March 2, 1756, Benjamin and Mary Gist sold the land back to Jarratt for ₤35. Thomas Jarratt then gave the 100 acres to his son Thomas and several of his sons-in-law before 1782, when he was taxed on 117 acres. He was still living in 1788 but died before November 17, 1792, when several of his heirs sold the land to Luke Taylor.[2]

The children of Thomas and Rebecca Jarratt, perhaps among others, were as follows:[3]

a. Mary Jarratt, born c1732; married c1750 in Lunenburg County, Virginia, to Benjamin Gist (see p. 38).
b. Thomas Jarratt, born c1735; bought 100 acres on Stony Creek in Lunenburg County, Virginia, from Solomon Wright on May 14, 1767, and 50 acres nearby from Thomas and Hannah Wright on September 8, 1768. He married (1) Martha Allen, daughter of William Allen of Mecklenburg County, Virginia; (2) Susannah _____. On December 14, 1797, he and Susannah sold their 200 acre farm on Stony Creek to William Bailey for ₤100. He is undoubtedly the Thomas Jarratt who died in 1806 in Abbeville County, South Carolina, and while there is no proof, he probably had, among others, the following children:[4]
    (1) Adda Jarratt died in 1834 in Franklin County, Virginia; children:[5]
        (a) Rebecca Jarratt.
        (b) Lucy Jarratt married October 2, 1809, Peter Campbell.
        (c) Allen Jarratt married October 17, 1805, Mary Spangler.
        (d) Young Jarratt married October 24, 1816, Nancy Hill.
        (e) Wyatt Jarratt.
        (f) Adda Jarratt married November 7, 1815, Winifred Bobbitt.
        (g) Gregory Jarratt.
        (h) William Jarratt.
    (2) Peter Jarratt lived in Lincoln County, Georgia, in 1818.
    (3) David Jarratt married December 18, 1786, Judith Mize.
    (4) Nancy Jarratt married April 2, 1792, John Calliham; lived in Abbeville County, South Carolina.
c. (daughter) married Joseph Wright.
d. (daughter) married John Wright.
e. Eleanor Jarratt married Drury Allen; lived in Anson County, North Carolina.
f. (daughter) married John Wray.
g. Nancy Jarratt married _____ Wright.

***

REFERENCES

[1]Brunswick County, Virginia, Deeds; Land Patent Bk. 18, p. 384,

Bk. 28, p. 221, Virginia State Archives, Richmond, Virginia.

[2]Lunenburg County, Virginia, Deed Bk. 3, p. 89, Bk. 4, p. 267, Bk. 15, p. 503, Bk. 16, p. 346, tax lists of 1782, 1788.

[3]Ibid., Deed Bk. 16, p. 346.

[4]Ibid., Deed Bk. 11, pp. 15, 195; Mecklenburg County, Virginia, Will Bk. 3, p. 15; Lunenburg County, Virginia, Marriages; Deed Bk. 18, pp. 5a, 15; Abbeville County, South Carolina, Estate Settlements.

[5]Franklin County, Virginia, Will Bk. 4, p. 193.

***

McPHERSON of Monroe County, Kentucky

Daniel McPherson, according to family tradition, was born about 1682 near Inverness, Scotland, and was kidnapped while tending sheep on his father's farm when he was about 14 years of age. He was brought to the New Castle, Delaware, area and sold as an indentured servant. After his term of indenture was ended, he worked as a laborer until he earned enough money to buy a farm.[1]

On October 10, 1706, Daniel McPherson of Birmingham bought 300 acres in Kennett Township, Chester County, Pennsylvania, from John Guest for £60, and thereafter made his home in Kennett Square. About 1712 he married Ruth Shires, who had recently moved to America from Great Britain. After Ruth McPherson died about 1747, Daniel sold his land to James House and moved to Salisbury Township, Lancaster County, Pennsylvania. He made his will on February 24, 1755, dividing his property among his children; the estate was probated on August 5, 1755.[2] Daniel and Ruth McPherson had the following children:[3]

a. Ann McPherson, born c1714; died September 22, 1795, in Orange County, North Carolina; married December 15, 1733, in Wilmington, Delaware, to Nathaniel Carter; children:
    (1) John Carter, born September 19, 1734; died September 19, 1815, in Orange County, North Carolina; married Ann Whipple.
    (2) Elizabeth Carter, born August 16, 1736; died February 16, 1832, in Clinton County, Ohio; married William Harvey.
    (3) Hannah Carter, born July 4, 1738; dsp December 3, 1742.
    (4) Mary Carter, born August 8, 1740; died July 11, 1824, in Randolph County, North Carolina; married December 2, 1761, Stephen Harlan.
    (5) Ruth Carter, born January 30, 1742; married Nathan Farlow.
    (6) Nathaniel Carter, born March 23, 1746; died May 15, 1820; married (1) c1768 Sarah _____ (2) March 5, 1791, Mrs. Jane Edwards (3) Jane Collins; lived in Orange County, North Carolina.
    (7) Edith Carter, born August 27, 1749; died May 15, 1830; married Enoch Harlan.
    (8) William Carter, born February 23, 1752; died 1810 in Chatham County, North Carolina; married Mary Elliott.
    (9) Hannah Carter, born December 12, 1754; died May 2, 184?, in Hamilton County, Ohio; married 1796 Henry Justis.
1. b. John McPherson, born November 6, 1718.
2. c. Daniel McPherson, born c1722.
3. d. William McPherson, born c1726.
4. e. Stephen McPherson, born c1728.
    f. Othniel McPherson, born c1732; dsp c1745.

***

1. John McPherson was born November 6, 1718, in Chester County, Pennsylvania, and owned a farm which lay partly in New Castle County, Delaware. He sold land to Nathaniel Ring and in 1765 moved to Orange (now Chatham) County, North Carolina, where he farmed. His three oldest sons were involved in the Regulator Rebellion, although they took an oath to the Crown afterwards. The family was neutral in the American Revolution, and both Whigs and Tories pillaged their farm repeatedly; they lost cattle, horses, crops, and other property. John McPherson became blind several years before his death on March 16, 1798, and was cared for by

70

his daughter Abigail.[5]

About 1740, John McPherson married Mary Green, who was born April 2, 1722, the daughter of John Green and his wife Abigail.[6] Mary McPherson was probably not a member of the Society of Friends, but many times stated that she "listened to the good Quaker in her breast." She was extremely industrious and was noted as a midwife, often riding 15 miles to a case, and her services were much in demand. She was known for her kindness and charity, and her devotion to the family's oath of allegiance or her pacifism kept them neutral in the American Revolution. She was more than six feet tall and of remarkable strength; it was claimed that she could lift a keg of cider or two and a half bushels of wheat.[7]

After the death of her husband, Mary McPherson continued to keep house with her daughter Abigail; she sometimes visited her son Joseph in Stokes County, North Carolina. She remained vigorous to an advanced age, dying of cancer on her face on October 27, 1813, in Chatham County, North Carolina.[8]

The children of John and Mary McPherson were as follows:[9]

a. Ruth McPherson, born January 22, 1742; died in 1802 in Chatham County, North Carolina; married August 20, 1760, to Aaron Evans, born May 1, 1739, and died January 11, 1786, son of Owen Evans and Mary Harlan; children:[10]
    (1) Mary Evans, born May 5, 1761; /married Daniel McPherson?/
    (2) Owen Evans, born August 16, 1763.
    (3) Sarah Evans, born October 8, 1765; married James Emerson; lived in Madison County, Tennessee.
    (4) John Evans, born December 22, 1767.
    (5) Thomas Evans, born January 17, 1770.
    (6) Abigail Evans, born January 17, 1773; married _____ Pyle.
    (7) Ruth Evans, born August 21, 1775; married Isaac Brooks, son of Job Brooks and Catherine Dimmaux; lived in Tennessee.
    (8) Aaron Evans, born October 21, 1777.
    (9) Rebecca Evans, born July 24, 1780.
b. Daniel McPherson, born February 28, 1744; dsp about 1750.
5. c. John McPherson, born April 19, 1746.
6. d. Joseph McPherson, born August 27, 1748.
e. Abigail McPherson, born December 27, 1750; dsp September, 1834, in Alabama.
f. Stephen McPherson, born May 7, 1753; died December 28, 1780, in Surry (now Forsyth) County, North Carolina; married and had a son and a daughter.
7. g. Jehu McPherson, born February 24, 1756.
h. Sarah McPherson, born January 29, 1759; married David Walker.
i. Mary McPherson, born January 12, 1763; married Macajob McGee; lived in Alabama.

***

5. John McPherson was born April 19, 1746, in Chester County, Pennsylvania; he moved to Orange (now Chatham) County, North Carolina, in 1765, where he participated in the Regulator Rebellion. He married Sarah Harlan, daughter of Aaron Harlan and Sarah Hollingsworth, about 1775 and moved to Union County, South Carolina, where on January 6, 1775, he was granted 150 acres on Lower Fish Dam Creek; on January 23, 1775, he bought

an additional 100 acres on Lower Fish Dam Creek from Elizabeth Rinchard for 10 shillings. He sold both tracts to Nathan Glen on December 22, 1787, for £160. On February 17, 1786, he bought 350 acres on the south side of Fair Forest Creek on Mitchell's Creek in Union County from John and Martha Wood. He died in 1789, and on January 1, 1790, his widow Sarah and his brother Jehu asked for letters of administration on his estate. Sarah McPherson later moved to Barren (now Monroe) County, Kentucky, with her sons, and died there. Their children were as follows:[11]

a. Aaron McPherson, born November 25, 1776; moved to Barren (now Monroe) County, Kentucky, about 1800, and about 1827 to Moniteau County, Missouri, where he died February 14, 1853; married March 24, 1811, to Lucinda Bray, born July 15, 1790; died September 17, 1828; children:[12]
   (1) Nancy McPherson, born November 20, 1811.
   (2) Sarah McPherson, born May 9, 1813; dsp October 19, 1828.
   (3) Phoebe McPherson, born April 7, 1815.
   (4) Joseph Bray McPherson, born June 21, 1817; died June 15, 1901, in Lane County, Oregon; married March 9, 1841, Julia Ann _____, died January 12, 1879; children:
     (a) Aaron McPherson, born c1842; dsp.
     (b) Lewis F. McPherson, born c1844.
     (c) Hester Ann McPherson, born c1850; married August 24, 1865, James M. Gearhart.
   (5) Lucinda McPherson, born June 24, 1819; married January 15, 1854, Montgomery C. Barger; child:
     (a) E. B. Barger lived in Eugene, Oregon.
   (6) John Green McPherson, born August 18, 1821; died September 26, 1848, in Moniteau County, Missouri; child:
     (a) John Green McPherson, born November 8, 1848.
   (7) William McPherson, born December 30, 1823; dsp May 2, 1901, in Eugene, Oregon.
   (8) Aaron Harlan McPherson, born November 19, 1826; dsp June 10, 1830.
b. Stephen McPherson, born c1781; died 1831 in Union County, South Carolina; married Elizabeth _____; children (probably among others):[13]
   (1) John McPherson.
   (2) (daughter) married Amos Lee.
8. c. Joshua McPherson, born June 17, 1783.
d. Joseph McPherson, born c1785; moved to Barren (now Monroe) County, Kentucky, about 1800, and then to Moniteau County, Missouri, where he lived in 1850; married (1) October 27, 1813, to Mary Grasty; (2) Malinda _____.
e. John McPherson, born c1788; lived in Barren (now Monroe) County, Kentucky, 1810-16.

***

8.   Joshua McPherson was born June 17, 1783, in Union County, South Carolina, and died August 29, 1872, in Lane County, Oregon; his children (among others) were as follows:[14]

9. a. Elizabeth McPherson, born July 17, 1817.
10. b. James C. McPherson, born February 25, 1820.
   c. Harlan McPherson, born c1822.
   d. Rhoda McPherson married John Bowen.

In addition, although there is no proof, Joshua McPherson probably had the following children:

e. John McPherson, born c1809; married Sarah _____, born c1810; children: (among others):
    (1) Caroline McPherson, born c1839.
    (2) Hardin McPherson, born c1841.
    (3) Sarah McPherson, born c1843.
    (4) John McPherson, born c1845.
    (5) Rachel McPherson, born c1849.
f. Rebecca McPherson, born c1811; dsp.
g. Amy McPherson, born c1815; dsp.
h. Ann McPherson, born c1820.
i. Rachel McPherson, born c1826.

        ***

9.   Elizabeth McPherson was born July 17, 1817, in Barren (now Monroe) County, Kentucky, and moved to Moniteau County, Missouri, in infancy; moved to Oregon in October, 1853, and died November 7, 1882, in Lane County, Oregon. Married March 15, 1834, to Robert Morris, who died in 1848; their children were as follows:[15]

a. Eleanor Morris, born c1838; died 1895 in Salem, Oregon; married (1) Bluford Miller, born 1830; died June 14, 1857; (2) Alexander D. Scott, died July, 1876; children:
    (by first marriage):
    (1) Bluford Miller, died young.
    (by second marriage):
    (2) Charles Scott lived in Montana.
    (3) William Scott lived in Marion County, Oregon.
    (4) Lewis H. Scott lived in Wasco County, Oregon.
    (5) John H. Scott, born September 10, 1865; County Judge at Salem, Oregon; married December 18, 1901, Maude Alice Martin, daughter of James Martin.
    (6) Mary E. Scott.
    (7) Clara G. Scott.
    (8) Elmer H. Scott.
    (9) Alexander D. Scott.
   (10) Alwilda Scott, dsp.
11. b. Ann Morris, born August 8, 1840.
c. Thomas B. Morris, born December 13, 1842; died April 23, 1872.
d. Rachel Morris, born c1845.
e. Howard G. Morris, born October 25, 1847; died January 28, 1876.

        ***

11.   Ann Morris was born August 8, 1840, and died June 17, 1924, in Woodburn, Oregon; married August 19, 1856, Benjamin Franklin McKee, born March 9, 1837; died June 8, 1927, son of James McKee and Elizabeth McWilliams; their children were as follows:[16]

a. Elizabeth McKee, born August 31, 1857; died November 2, 1889; married D. F. Strom.
b. Martha McKee, born 1859; married John Chalmers; lived in Portland, Oregon.
c. Nettie McKee, born January 5, 1861; died July 20, 1945, in The Dalles, Oregon; married January 14, 1879, Lewis Melvin Woodside, born 1858; died 1926, son of Francis A. and Nancy Woodside; children:
    (1) L. D. Woodside, born March 12, 1882; lived in Maupin, Oregon.
    (2) Fred Woodside, born July 29, 1884.

73

  (3) Walter Woodside, born March 29, 1886; lived in Portland, Oregon.
  (4) Mattie Woodside, born July 16, 1887; married November 10, 1903,
     Peter J. Olsen, born 1876; died 1954; lived in Klamath Falls,
     Oregon; children:
     (a) Alice Olsen, born August 1, 1904; married April 26, 1929,
       Otto Vitus, born 1904; dsp December 10, 1948; lived in Kla-
       math Falls, Oregon.
     (b) Ivan Olsen, born January 12, 1908; lived in Madras, Oregon.
     (c) Raymond Olsen, born June 7, 1912; lived in Roseburg, Oregon.
     (d) Gertrude Olsen, born January 22, 1916; married Gordon
       Shirley; lived in Hanford, California.
  (5) Lewis Woodside, born March 1, 1894; lived in Maupin, Oregon.
  (6) Lela Woodside, born January 29, 1895; married Walter Driver;
     lived in The Dalles, Oregon.
  (7) Ralph Woodside, born July 26, 1905; lived in Maupin, Oregon.
 d. Olive McKee, born 1862; died December 22, 1882; married Thomas Palmer; lived in Belle Passe, Oregon.
 e. Clara McKee, born 1864; married George Bradley; lived in Portland,
   Oregon.
 f. Rodney McKee, born 1867; died 1941; lived in Belle Passe, Oregon.
 g. Eva McKee, born 1876; married _____ Malloy; lived in Portland, Oregon.
 h. Benjamin McKee, born 1877; dsp 1879.

***

10.   James C. McPherson was born February 25, 1820, and died March 28,
1885, in Lane County, Oregon; married (1) September 28, 1843, Mary Ann
Stout, died December 15, 1844; (2) October 3, 1847, Mary Ellen Scott, born
September 23, 1830, daughter of Robert Scott; his children were as follows:[17]

(by first marriage):
 a. Benjamin McPherson, born July 12, 1844; married August 9, 1866, Mary
   L. Simmons; children:
  (1) Harlan McPherson, born c1867.
  (2) Malvina McPherson, born c1869.
(by second marriage):
 b. Preston J. McPherson, born August 6, 1848; died April 26, 1909, in
   Eugene, Oregon; married October 12, 1872, Catherine Landis.
 c. Girren McPherson, born August 18, 1850; dsp November 4, 1850.
 d. Pierson M. McPherson, born September 24, 1851; married July 4, 1871,
   M. A. Spencer; lived in Lane County, Oregon; children:
  (1) Seth McPherson, born c1872.
  (2) Walter McPherson, born c1874.
  (3) Chandos McPherson, born 1876; dsp 189?.
  (4) Vennie McPherson.
  (5) Dorena McPherson.
  (6) Lula McPherson.
  (7) Adell McPherson.
  (8) Wade McPherson.
 e. Robert H. McPherson, born March 10, 1854; dsp January 22, 1863.
 f. Joshua R. McPherson, born January 5, 1856; married October 8, 1876,
   Mary Edwards; lived in Lane County, Oregon; children:
  (1) Lena McPherson, born April 29, 1882; married Lee Davis; lived
     in Lane County, Oregon; children:
     (a) Etta Davis.
     (b) Charles Davis.

                    (c) Sarah Davis.
                    (d) Emma Davis.
                    (e) Francis Davis.
                    (f) Margie Davis.
                    (g) Richard Davis.
              (2) Edna McPherson, born November 25, 1885; married Carl Carpenter;
                   lived in Lane County, Oregon; children:
                    (a) Mildred Carpenter.
                    (b) Margaret Carpenter.
         g.   Martha E. McPherson, born October 7, 1857; dsp December 24, 1862.
         h.   Joseph H. McPherson, born June 12, 1859; dsp January 30, 1863.
         i.   Andrew K. McPherson, born March 6, 1861.
         j.   Mary Arrena McPherson, born March 17, 1863; dsp December 30, 1886.
         k.   James M. McPherson, born November 2, 1864.
         l.   Rodney E. McPherson, born September 4, 1866; dsp March 3, 1888.
         m.   Ennis L. McPherson, born September 29, 1873.

                                        ***

6.   Joseph McPherson was born August 27, 1748, and moved to Orange
         (now Chatham) County, North Carolina, in 1765. He was a spectator in
         the Regulator Rebellion, but took no part in the fighting; he later took
         an oath of allegiance to the Crown. Many years later he wrote two ac-
         counts of the Rebellion, one of which was published in part. He was a
         carpenter and millwright, and for a time worked in an iron furnace. He
         married Abigail Piggott on July 25, 1776; she was born January 18, 1757,
         the fourth child of William Piggott and Sarah Pike.[18]

              In 1780, Joseph McPherson moved to Surry (now Forsyth) County, North
         Carolina, where he lived between Salem and Muddy Creek Meeting of the
         Society of Friends, which he probably joined about the time of his mar-
         riage. He paid for his farm by working as a carpenter in the neighbor-
         hood; the farm consisted of 192 acres with two orchards, and he was pri-
         marily interested in raising cattle.[19]

              Joseph McPherson was strongly interested in education and promoted
         the establishment of schools in his neighborhood; he wanted his children
         to receive the best education possible. His life as a farmer was unevent-
         ful. Abigail, his wife, died June 28, 1827, and Joseph lived with his
         daughters Abigail and Lydia after he lost his farm on a security debt.
         He suffered a fall before his death which rendered him helpless, and he
         died January 14, 1835, in Forsyth County, North Carolina.[20]

              The children of Joseph and Abigail McPherson were as follows:[21]

         a.   Mary McPherson, born June 23, 1777; married c1806 to Joshua Lindley,
              born March 21, 1778; died August 16, 1850, son of Thomas Lindley and
              Sarah Evans.
         b.   Hannah McPherson, born June 12, 1779; married October 23, 1811, to
              Thomas Hussey; lived in Morgan County, Indiana.
         c.   Sarah McPherson, born February 21, 1781; married November 28, 1822,
              to Solomon Dixon, son of Simon Dixon and Elizabeth Allen.
         d.   Ruth McPherson, born August 20, 1782; dsp; lived in Indiana.
         e.   Jane McPherson, born August 20, 1782; dsp.
         f.   Stephen McPherson, born November 25, 1784.
11.   g.   John McPherson, born November 7, 1786.
         h.   William McPherson, born October 23, 1788.
12.   i.   George D. McPherson, born November 30, 1790.
         j.   Ann McPherson, born October 28, 1792; dsp; lived in Indiana.

k. Abigail McPherson, born May 16, 1795; dsp; lived in Miami County, Ohio.
l. Lydia McPherson, born June 14, 1797; dsp; lived in Miami County, Ohio.
m. Joseph McPherson, born January 18, 1799.
n. Jehu McPherson, born April 19, 1801; died February 27, 1847; married May 2, 1833, to Isabel Parsons; children:
   (1) Martha Ann McPherson, born July 30, 1834; dsp 1912; married September 25, 1853, to Harvey Pearson.
   (2) William Yautes McPherson, born February 25, 1836; dsp April 16, 1839.
   (3) Lucinda Jane McPherson, born May 21, 1838; dsp April 8, 1839.
   (4) Lydia Emeline McPherson, born April 18, 1840; married February 10, 1870, to Joseph Washburn; child:
      (a) Mattie Washburn married Thomas Campbell; lived in Summit, New Jersey.
   (5) James Wesley McPherson, born June 15, 1841; dsp December 6, 1862.
   (6) Sarah Delphina McPherson, born November 4, 1843; dsp November 12, 1847.
   (7) John Calvin McPherson, born November 12, 1846; dsp.

***

11.   John McPherson was born November 7, 1786, in Surry (now Forsyth) County, North Carolina, and moved to Martinsville, Indiana, about 1831. He later moved to Richland, Iowa, and finally to Plymouth, Kansas, where he died November 11, 1871. He married June 16, 1811, to Ruth Kirkpatrick, who was born March 9, 1792, and died November 22, 1864, in Richland, Iowa. Their children were as follows:[22]

a. Hugh Reeves McPherson, born June 10, 1818; died June 19, 1863, in Richland, Iowa; married March 7, 1851, Martha Triggs.
b. Martha Green McPherson, born March 30, 1820; died May 22, 1861, in Plymouth, Kansas; married October 12, 1850, John Triggs.
c. Abigail Ruth McPherson, born August 14, 1822; died July 20, 1871, in Plymouth, Kansas; married July 22, 1861, John Triggs, died December 25, 1877.
d. Joseph Shires McPherson, born December 8, 1824; died December 31, 1898, in Trenton, Nebraska; married July 10, 1847, Nancy Ann Deere.
e. John Jehu McPherson, born June 6, 1827.
f. Lydia Naomi McPherson, born May 26, 1830; dsp March 14, 1898.

***

12.   George D. McPherson was born November 30, 1790, in Stokes (now Forsyth) County, North Carolina, and died about 1875 in Wayne County, Indiana. He married August 12, 1814, Charity Hicks Locke, daughter of John Locke and Lucretia Hicks; their children were as follows:[23]

13. a. Joseph W. McPherson, born May 30, 1815.
     b. Lucretia H. McPherson, born May 30, 1815; married January 20, 1831, Phenton Riley; lived in Paw Paw, Illinois.
     c. Abigail McPherson, born c1817; married April 2, 1835, Samuel Lenington.
14. d. John Locke McPherson, born October 30, 1818.
     e. Elizabeth J. McPherson married Rufus K. Mills; lived in Randolph County, Indiana.
     f. (daughter).

***

13.   Joseph W. McPherson was born May 30, 1815, in Warren County, Ohio; died July 4, 1907, in Guthrie County, Iowa; married December 24, 1835, in Wayne County, Indiana, to Sarah Lenington, daughter of Abraham Lenington and Elizabeth Bowles. Their children were as follows:[24]

15. a. George Bestwick McPherson, born c1836.
     b. Abraham Lenington McPherson, born February 18, 1839; died January 3, 1913, in Elgin, Oklahoma; member of Iowa legislature; married Elizabeth S. Hain in Des Moines, Iowa; children:
       (1) Della McPherson, dsp.
       (2) Frankie McPherson, dsp.
       (3) Bertha McPherson married L. L. Stine; lived in Woodward, Oklahoma.
       (4) Evertt McPherson lived in Elgin, Oklahoma.
       (5) Grace McPherson married C. W. Stickle; lived in Woodward, Oklahoma.
       (6) Roscoe E. McPherson lived in Deadwood, South Dakota.
       (7) David H. McPherson lived in Higgins, Texas.
     c. John B. McPherson, born c1841; died 1901 in Kansas City, Missouri.
     d. Augustus W. McPherson, born c1843; lived in Los Angeles, California.
16. e. Mary Jane McPherson, born August 16, 1845.
17. f. James Monroe McPherson, born c1848.
     g. Rufus K. McPherson lived in Portland, Oregon.
     h. Emma C. McPherson married Edward L. Pugh; lived in Des Moines, Iowa.
18. i. Eunice Exaline McPherson, born May 9, 1856.
     j. Myrtle E. McPherson, married John Fowler; lived in California.

***

15.   George Bestwick McPherson was born about 1836 in Wayne County, Indiana. He married Mary Ellen Harbour and lived near Rapid City, South Dakota; their children were as follows:[25]

     a. Charles P. McPherson married Clara M. Flathers; children:
       (1) Ethel S. McPherson married Valentine Wollen (see p. 79).
       (2) Edward S. McPherson married Rozella Young.
       (3) George B. McPherson married Florence Tennis; lived in Sturgis, South Dakota.
       (4) Ruby E. McPherson married Ole Otterberg; children:
         (a) Richard C. Otterberg married Zula E. Benton; children:
           /1/ Richard E. Otterberg.
           /2/ Mary Ellen Otterberg.
         (b) Leonard G. Otterberg.
         (c) Neva Louise Otterberg married Max E. Patterson; children:
           /1/ Neena A. Patterson.
           /2/ Tina L. Patterson.
           /3/ Kathline Patterson.
           /4/ Max E. Patterson.
     b. Viola M. McPherson married Charles Runkel; children:
       (1) Fred Runkel.
       (2) Nina Runkel.
       (3) Francis Runkel.
     c. Ranswell B. McPherson, born January 13, 1877; died April 20, 1944; married April 19, 1911, Edith I. Long, born March 8, 1872; died November 1, 1943; child:
       (1) Margaret Independence McPherson, born July 4, 1913.
19. d. Eugene McPherson.
     e. Glenn McPherson lived in Rapid City, South Dakota.

***

19.   Eugene McPherson married Ida M. Thierse; they lived in Sturgis,
South Dakota, and had the following children:[26]

   a. Edna McPherson, born April 13, 1908; married June 29, 1929, Vernon
       L. Watkins; lived in Alexandria, Virginia; child:
       (1) Linda Mae Watkins, born January 11, 1939.
   b. Earl Eugene McPherson, born December 14, 1909; married November 11,
       1942, Celeste Karrells; lived in Sturgis, South Dakota; children:
       (1) Kathleen McPherson, born December 11, 1947.
       (2) Mary McPherson, born March 16, 1950.
       (2) Wayne McPherson, born May 9, 1951.
       (4) Lawrence McPherson, born May 21, 1957.
   c. Arnold E. McPherson, born July 21, 1911; married January 18, 1941,
       Maxine Phillips; lived in Sturgis, South Dakota; children:
       (1) Eugene McPherson, born February 8, 1945.
       (2) David McPherson, born June 6, 1948.
       (3) Marcia McPherson, born April 16, 1958.
   d. Mary L. McPherson married Charles Keffeler; children:
       (1) Darleen Keffeler.
       (2) Duane Keffeler.
       (3) Kay Keffeler.
       (4) Roger Keffeler.
   e. Joseph B. McPherson married Elma Hedman; lived in Sturgis, South
       Dakota; child:
       (1) Fred McPherson.
   f. Glenn T. McPherson married Rosalind Kammerer; children:
       (1) Jay McPherson.
       (2) Terry McPherson.
   g. Donald R. McPherson, born August 29, 1927; married June 9, 1950,
       Mable Keffeler; lived in Sturgis, South Dakota; children:
       (1) Harvey McPherson, born May 21, 1952.
       (2) Judith McPherson, born November 25, 1955.
       (3) Cheryl McPherson, born May 18, 1961.
       (4) Ross McPherson, born December 15, 1962.
   h. Dale W. McPherson, born October 2, 1929; married April 20, 1958,
       Dorothy Bostic; lived in Rapid City, South Dakota; children:
       (1) Kevin McPherson, born March 26, 1959.
       (2) Todd McPherson, born September 30, 1962.

                              ***

16.   Mary Jane McPherson was born August 16, 1845, in Guthrie County,
Iowa, and died February 28, 1925, in Cass County, Nebraska; married September 21, 1865, to William Childers Wollen, born September 11, 1844, in
Spencer County, Iowa; died February 25, 1930, in Cass County, Nebraska,
son of Mathias Wollen. Their children were as follows:[27]

   a. Arch Melvern Wollen, born 1867; died October 26, 1950, in Omaha, Neb-
       raska; married Jessie A. Stock; children:
       (1) Walter Wollen, dsp.
       (2) Floyd Wollen.
       (3) Violette Wollen married _____ Collister; child:
       (a) DeVonne Collister married _____ Foote; lived in Denver,
            Colorado.
   b. Ernest A. Wollen, born October 26, 1868; dsp February 14, 1873.
20. c. August Herbert Wollen, born August 15, 1871.
21. d. Effie Dale Wollen, born August 30, 1873.
   e. March Centennial Wollen, born March 17, 1876; died March 22, 1953;

                              78

married Carrie Reed; child:
(1) Philip Wollen.
f. Roscoe Delmont Wollen, born April 21, 1877; died January 30, 1969, in Omaha, Nebraska; married January 1, 1907, Barbara Loew, born 1882; died 1915; children:
(1) George Lawson Wollen married 1946 Corinne Pangborn; lived in Everett, Washington.
(2) Ruth Evelyn Wollen married 1938 George C. Rose; lived in Omaha, Nebraska.
g. Roy Wollen, born January 24, 1880; died June 21, 1957, in Lake City, Iowa; married March 11, 1905, Thressa Quinn; children:
(1) Kenneth Wollen married 1928 Violet Brock; children:
(a) Sharon Wollen married James Shultz; lived in Wells, Minnesota.
(b) Nancy Wollen married James Conley; lived in Tucson, Arizona.
(c) Leslie Ann Wollen married K. T. Mathews; lived in Mankato, Minnesota.
(2) Alice Wollen married Theodore X. Cox; lived in Great Falls, Montana; children:
(a) (Dr.) Theodore X. Cox; lived in Armour, South Dakota.
(b) Carmelita Cox married James Bullock; lived in Missoula, Montana.
(c) Patricia Cox married Dr. Rudy Strnot; lived in Lincoln, Nebraska.
(3) Mary Jane Wollen married Lawrence J. Ritter; lived in Sac City, Iowa; children:
(a) Lawrence J. Ritter; lived in Vermillion, South Dakota.
(b) Kathleen Ritter married William Cramer; lived in Decorah, Iowa.
(4) Beryl Moynette Wollen, born 1923; died 1951; married 1941 Ralph Fisher; children:
(a) Ronna Fisher married D. E. Peel; lived in Perry, Iowa.
(b) Raylyn Fisher married Edward Abell; lived in Alamogordo, New Mexico.
(c) Lindy Fisher married Steven Baker; lived in Iowa City, Iowa.
h. Heloise Olivia Wollen, born February 21, 1882; married Wilburn Countryman; lived in Phoenix, Arizona.
i. Valentine Wollen, born 1884; died October 6, 1955; married Ethel S. McPherson (see p. 77); children:
(1) Mabel Ellen Wollen.
(2) Edna Ethel Wollen married Lyle Ward; lived in Brookings, South Dakota.
(3) (son).
22. j. Florise Vivian Wollen, born September 17, 1888.
k. Flossie Evelyn Wollen, born September 17, 1888; died September 11, 1962; married Robert Baker; children:
(1) Robert Wollen Baker.
(2) Warren E. Baker; lived in Indianapolis, Indiana.
(3) Vivian Baker married _____ Hanson; lived in Weeping Water, Nebraska.

***

20.   August Herbert Wollen was born August 15, 1871, in Cass County, Nebraska, and died January 4, 1953, in Garnett, Kansas; married January 1, 1895, Jennie Alberta McKenzie, born April 12, 1875; died October 5, 1964. Their children were as follows:[28]

23. a. George William Wollen, born July 5, 1896.

b. Alberta Florine Wollen, born 1898; married Aart A. Velthoen; lived in Garnett, Kansas; dsp.
c. Lloyd P. Wollen, born December 31, 1899; married Ethel Florence Stafford; lived in Bakersfield, California; children:
   (1) Esther Mae Wollen married Calvin Barnes; lived in Saugus, California; children:
     (a) Alison Lynn Barnes.
     (b) Leslie Sue Barnes.
   (2) Nancy Joy Wollen married Kenneth Tinker; lived in El Segundo, California; children:
     (a) Janice E. Tinker married Rod Allan; child:
       /1/ Faith Ann Allan.
     (b) Glen Lloyd Tinker.
   (3) Linton Lee Wollen married Kathleen Dee; lived in Merced, California; children:
     (a) Denise Lee Wollen.
     (b) Debra Sue Wollen.
d. Ethel Glen Wollen, born November 3, 1902; married Donald Hawley, born March 1, 1903; lived in Bellflower, California; child:
   (1) Herbert Clark Hawley married Kathy _____; lived in Placentia, California; children:
     (a) Karen Jean Hawley.
     (b) Brad Alan Hawley.
24. e. Orville Ray Wollen, born 1906.
f. Ina Marie Wollen, born March 11, 1909; married William E. Smith; lived in Milpitas, California; child:
   (1) William Joseph Smith married Irene _____; lived in Santa Rosa, California.
g. Mary Genevieve Wollen, born August 20, 1912; married Franklin Lee; lived in La Junta, California; child:
   (1) Laura Alberta Lee married (1) _____ Bartholomew (2) D. R. Taylor; lived in Milpitas, California; children:
    (by first marriage):
     (a) Randy Lee Bartholomew.
     (b) Robert Kevin Bartholomew.
     (c) Russell Ray Bartholomew.
    (by second marriage):
     (d) Danelle Renee Taylor.

***

23.   George William Wollen was born July 5, 1896, and died in 1950 in Garnett, Kansas. He married Iva S. Todd and had the following children:[29]

a. George William Wollen married 1938 Ruth Demler; lived in Topeka, Kansas; children:
   (1) Lorigene Marie Wollen married Robert Crow; children:
     (a) Laura Crow.
     (b) Renee Crow.
     (c) J. W. Crow.
   (2) Glen Edwin Wollen married Benita _____; child:
     (a) Elizabeth Ruth Wollen.
   (3) Carol Jean Wollen married Joseph Ehalt; children:
     (a) Jean Marie Ehalt.
     (b) Patricia Jane Ehalt.
     (c) Jacqueline Ann Ehalt.
     (d) Janette Kay Ehalt.
     (e) Pamela Jo Ehalt.

(f) Penny June Ehalt.
b. (Dr.) Olin Glen Wollen married Maxine Sarver; lived in Ottawa, Kansas; children:
   (1) James William Wollen.
   (2) Terry Sarver Wollen married Judy Lewis; children:
       (a) Andrew Wollen.
       (b) Kristy Wollen.
   (3) Jane Ann Wollen married Joseph Works; lived in Humboldt, Kansas; children:
       (a) Beth Works.
       (b) Anthony Works.
   (4) Sarah Beth Wollen, born 1951; married Victor Mitchell; lived in Ottawa, Kansas; child:
       (a) Robert Mitchell, born 1972.
   (5) Rebecca Sue Wollen, born 1959.
c. Juanita Marie Wollen married Robert Webber; lived in Milpitas, California; children:
   (1) Geraldine Ann Webber married Marshall Smith; children:
       (a) Mark Smith.
       (b) Stephanie Smith.
   (2) Patricia Jean Webber married Frank Martinez; children:
       (a) Kathy Martinez.
       (b) Jerome Martinez.
   (3) Susan Gay Webber married Mark Fuller; child:
       (a) Andrew Fuller.
   (4) Roxena Webber married Thomas Alderete; children:
       (a) Alison Renee Alderete.
       (b) Christopher Alderete.
d. Alberta Jean Wollen married Lester Schulte; lived in Omaha, Nebraska; children:
   (1) Ronald Schulte.
   (2) John Wayne Schulte.
   (3) David Michael Schulte.
   (4) Mary Kay Schulte.
e. (Dr.) Marvin Eugene Wollen married Sally Brown; lived in Olathe, Kansas; children:
   (1) Catherine Fern Wollen.
   (2) Teresa Kay Wollen.
   (3) Cynthia Sue Wollen.
   (4) Liliana Rae Wollen.

***

24.   Orville Ray Wollen was born in 1906 and married Opal Hawley. They lived in Santa Barbara, California, and had the following children:[30]

a. Ray Jeanette Wollen married _____ Bartlett; lived in San Jose, California; children:
   (1) Lynne Ellen Bartlett.
   (2) Julie Ray Bartlett.
b. Alice Lavon Wollen married John Henry Harper; lived in Santa Maria, California; children:
   (1) John Henry Harper.
   (2) Victoria Ann Harper.
   (3) Paul Harper.
   (4) Susan Harper.
   (5) Kathy Harper.
c. Barbara Jean Wollen married _____ Sturtevant; lived in Santa Barbara, California; children:

        (1) Donald Sturtevant.
        (2) Daniel Sturtevant.
        (3) Darla Sturtevant.
     d. Rex Leroy Wollen married Kay _____; children:
        (1) Naomi Opal Wollen.
        (2) Anita Ann Wollen.

                              ***

21.   Effie Dale Wollen was born August 30, 1873, and died October 17,
     1951, in Lincoln, Nebraska. She married 1895 William Melvin Mapel and
     had the following children:[31]

     a. Audrey Mapel married W. O. Ward; lived in Lincoln, Nebraska; child:
        (1) Merle E. Ward, born 1920; married 1947 Mildred R. Boettger, born
             1922; children:
             (a) Mary Beth Ward, born 1952.
             (b) Barbara Rose Ward, born 1953.
             (c) William E. Ward, born 1956.
             (d) John R. Ward, born 1958.
     b. Goldie Mapel married (1) M. P. Ward, died 1954; (2) Samuel Baker;
         lived in Weeping Water, Nebraska; children (all by first marriage):
        (1) Thelma Ward, born 1918.
        (2) Jack Ward, born 1923.
        (3) Gene Ward, born 1926.
        (4) Ted Ward, born 1940.
     c. Howard Mapel married Clara Meyer; children:
        (1) Roberta Ione Mapel married Ralph Wilcox; lived in Chadron, Neb-
             raska; children:
             (a) Judy Jean Wilcox, born 1946; married 1969 John Novak; child:
                  /1/ John Alan Novak, born 1970.
             (b) Betty Jo Wilcox, born 1952.
             (c) William Roy Wilcox, born 1953.
        (2) Vada Ruth Mapel married James Regan; lived in Chadron, Nebraska;
             children:
             (a) Penny Ann Regan married Pat Rollins; child:
                  /1/ Donald Eugene Rollins.
             (b) Sandra Regan married (1) 1967 Daniel Tobin (2) Donald
                  Broderick; children (by first marriage):
                  /1/ Tracy Lynn Tobin.
                  /2/ Susan Ann Tobin.
             (c) Rhonda Sue Regan.
             (d) James Robert Regan.
        (3) Dorothy Jean Mapel married Daniel Boyer; child:
             (a) Shar Lee Boyer married 1966 Michael Caban; child:
                  /1/ Michael Don Caban.
     d. Stanley Mapel married Wuanita Chandler; child:
        (1) Raymond Mapel; lived in Jacksonville, Florida.
     e. Harlan Mapel married Adeline Baller; lived in Lincoln, Nebraska;
         children:
        (1) Donald Mapel married Sandi Ray.
        (2) Dwaine Mapel married Donna Hendrickson; children:
             (a) David Harlan Mapel.
             (b) Deann Marie Mapel.
        (3) Suzanne Mapel married John Thompson; children:
             (a) Christopher John Thompson.
             (b) Kelly Lyn Thompson.

                              ***

22.   Florise Vivian Wollen was born September 17, 1888, and married John
Noell; they had the following children:[32]

a.   Flossie Evelyn Noell, born 1915; died 1971; married 1933 Arthur R.
     Bothwell; children:
     (1)   Robert Arthur Bothwell married 1953 Annalee Summers.
     (2)   Keith Thomas Bothwell married 1955 Anna Perkins; children:
           (a)   Keith Randall Bothwell.
           (b)   Connie Sue Bothwell.
           (c)   Kevin Wade Bothwell.
     (3)   James Alvin Bothwell married 1960 Geraldine Reichwaldt; children:
           (a)   Susan Margaret Bothwell.
           (b)   Sharon Jo Bothwell.
     (4)   John Glenn Bothwell married 1965 Greta Hink; child:
           (a)   Douglas Lee Bothwell.
     (5)   Judith Ann Bothwell married 1969 Oliver Merlyn Sonju; children:
           (a)   Sandra Dyann Sonju.
           (b)   Jared Oliver Sonju.
     (6)   Linda Lee Bothwell.
b.   Murriel Viola Noell married 1935 James Bernie Abbett; lived in Gree-
     ley, Colorado; children:
     (1)   Patricia Ann Abbett married (1) 1957 James Martin Kadlecek (2)
           Arvin Clarence Cropp; children:
           (by first marriage):
           (a)   James Joseph Kadlecek.
           (b)   Kathryn Ann Kadlecek.
           (by second marriage):
           (c)   Nancy Noell Cropp.
     (2)   Roberta Rae Abbett married 1960 Robert Lee Hite; children:
           (a)   Steven Lee Hite.
           (b)   Allan Ray Hite.
c.   Willard Lyle Noell married Gertrude Marie Roos; child:
     (1)   Billie Marie Noell.

***

17.   James Monroe McPherson was born about 1848 in Guthrie County, Iowa,
and lived in Stuart, Iowa. He married (1) October 5, 1876, Priscilla
A. Miller, died August 18, 1895; (2) November 1, 1896, Mrs. Lilly (Bohrer)
Barnett; his children were as follows:[33]

(by first marriage):
25. a.   Forrest S. McPherson; born July 3, 1881.
     b.   Maude McPherson married Wilbur Hume; lived in Mason City, Nebraska;
          child:
          (1)   (Dr.) Wayne S. Hume, born November 12, 1907; died 1973; married
                July 12, 1936, Esther A. Crow; lived in Walnut Creek, Califor-
                nia; children:
                (a)   Patricia J. Hume, born August 3, 1937; lived in Alexandria,
                      Virginia.
                (b)   Merril W. Hume, born April 30, 1939; married October 12,
                      1963, Nancy E. Johnson; children:
                      /1/   David A. Hume.
                      /2/   James E. Hume.
                      /3/   Ellen M. Hume.
                (c)   James S. Hume, born February 5, 1941; married June 19,
                      1965, Claudia E. Barclay; children:
                      /1/   Samuel W. Hume.
                      /2/   Christine P. Hume.

83

(by second marriage):
c. Matilda R. McPherson, born September 18, 1898; married December 31, 1918, George C. Lyall; child:
   (1) Robert V. Lyall, born June 20, 1920; married June 21, 1947, Marcella H. Krause; children:
      (a) Robert G. Lyall, born February 14, 1949.
      (b) Glen E. Lyall, born October 11, 1950.
      (c) Mary I. Lyall, born April 23, 1952.
d. Harold McPherson, born July 3, 1903; married May 31, 1924, Lenora A. Ripley; children:
   (1) Marcelyn G. McPherson, born February 1, 1925; married Kurt J. Urban; lived in Des Moines, Iowa; children:
      (a) Kurt J. Urban, born September 3, 1952.
      (b) Marilee Urban, born October 25, 1954.
   (2) Virgil E. McPherson, born October 21, 1926; married Carmelita P. Veach; children:
      (a) Michael E. McPherson, born April 17, 1950; married Pamela M. Siver.
      (b) Mark R. McPherson, born September 22, 1953.
      (c) Matthew J. McPherson, born April 11, 1955.
      (d) Melanie K. McPherson, born December 10, 1957.
   (3) Lois Elaine McPherson, born September 24, 1929; married John E. Walters; children:
      (a) Thomas C. Walters, born November 3, 1953.
      (b) John S. Walters, born February 14, 1955.
      (c) Bradley P. Walters, born November 1, 1958.
   (4) Bernard I. McPherson, born March 18, 1935; married Roberta K. Yates; children:
      (a) Robert H. McPherson, born January 23, 1959.
      (b) Beth A. McPherson, born October 11, 1963.
      (c) Randy O. McPherson, born October 10, 1966.
e. James M. McPherson married (1) Noreen Lydon (2) Helen F. Templeton; children (both by first marriage):
   (1) James Jon McPherson (adopted surname Kuester).
   (2) Thomas Joe McPherson (adopted surname Kuester).

***

25.   Forrest S. McPherson was born July 3, 1881; married Ida J. Mount; their children were as follows:[34]

a. Chase R. McPherson married Anna M. Talbott; lived in Damascus, Ohio; children:
   (1) Joseph D. McPherson married Margaret E. Maylor; children:
      (a) Joseph P. McPherson.
      (b) Philip D. McPherson.
      (c) Marsh Fletcher McPherson.
   (2) Talbott C. McPherson married Joan E. Jackson; children:
      (a) Ronald L. McPherson.
      (b) Beth A. McPherson.
      (c) Allen Gene McPherson.
   (3) Carolyn F. McPherson married Omar L. Shreve; children:
      (a) Dennis L. Shreve.
      (b) Daryl L. Shreve.
   (4) William M. McPherson married Marilyn A. McHugh; children:
      (a) Robert L. McPherson.
      (b) Timothy E. McPherson.
      (c) Daniel S. McPherson.
   (5) Margaret A. McPherson married John B. Durfee; children:

            (a) Jeanne A. Durfee.
            (b) Jonathan C. Durfee.
    b. Priscilla A. McPherson married Austin G. McCoig; lived in Newport
        News, Virginia; child:
        (1) Forrest D. McCoig married Katherine C. Renshaw; children:
            (a) James A. McCoig.
            (b) Amy K. McCoig.
            (c) Laura J. McCoig.
    c. Inez Maude McPherson married (1) George A. Yost (2) Franklin E. Win-
        slow; lived in Detroit, Michigan; child (by first marriage):
        (1) David A. Yost (adopted surname Winslow) married Frances L.
            Edwards.

                            ***

18.   Eunice Exaline McPherson was born May 9, 1856, in Guthrie County,
    Iowa, and died December 10, 1911, in Johnstown, Nebraska; married May 3,
    1877, to George Burgan, born May 15, 1845; died October 24, 1928. They
    had the following children:35

    a. Raymond Guy Burgan, born February 17, 1878; died January 24, 1959,
        in Norfolk, Nebraska; married Susan Freeman; children:
        (1) George Andrew Burgan, born February 21, 1933.
        (2) Louis Fenton Burgan, born January 28, 1935; married Izitta Fer-
            guson; lived in Fremont, Nebraska.
        (3) Olive E. Burgan, born January 23, 1936; married Charles Fergu-
            son; lived in Fremont, Nebraska.
        (4) Ivan Newton Burgan, born June 8, 1937.
        (5) Lottie May Burgan, born September 4, 1938; married Karl Herring;
            lived in Torrence, California.
        (6) Raymond Guy Burgan, born June 19, 1942.
        (7) Exa Irene Burgan, born July 14, 1945.
    b. Blanche Irene Burgan, born March 12, 1881; died March 30, 1968, in
        Chadron, Nebraska; married June 8, 1907, James W. Pace; child:
        (1) Estelline Pace, born March 24, 1915; married Len Augustson;
            lived in Los Angeles, California.
    c. Evans F. Burgan, born May 18, 1883; dsp August 28, 1883.
    d. Linda Sarah Burgan, born April 20, 1888; died April 29, 1968, in
        Bassett, Nebraska; married Almer Griffith; children:
        (1) Marlin Griffith married Hazel _____; lived in Norwalk, California.
        (2) Garold Griffith; lived in Lincoln, Nebraska.
    e. Horace Joseph Burgan, born November 15, 1896; married December 24,
        1920, Mary Etta Ruth Dorsett; lived in Norfolk, Nebraska; children:
        (1) Robert Horace Burgan, born March 25, 1922; married January 1,
            1948, Margaret Ogilvy; children:
            (a) David Burgan, born February 16, 1950; married September 9,
                1972, Bonnie Kucera; lived in Midland, Michigan.
            (b) Paul Burgan, born August 31, 19??.
        (2) William George Burgan, born April 19, 1925; married (1) April 12,
            1951, Donna Custer (2) June, 1968, Ann Martin; children (all by
            first marriage):
            (a) Randall Burgan, born June 14, 1952.
            (b) Douglas Burgan, born March 1, 1955.
            (c) Darla Joy Burgan, born December 6, 1959.
        (3) Edward Charles Burgan, born March 21, 1927; married September
            25, 1953, Phyllis Andrews; lived in Calgary, Canada; children:
            (a) Kara Lynn Burgan, born September 25, 1957.
            (b) Leah Lorraine Burgan, born May 7, 1959.

                            85

(c) Holly Ruth Burgan, born October 11, 1960.
(d) Kelly Sue Burgan, born June 30, 1962.
(e) Joseph Andrews Burgan, born November 14, 1963.

***

14.   John Locke McPherson was born October 30, 1818, in Cincinnati, Ohio,
and died November 30, 1898, in Palestine, Indiana; married (1) December
31, 1840, Juliann Bailey, born January 1, 1822; died March 29, 1856; (2)
October 27, 1856, Martha Shirey, born January 29, 1833; died January 26,
1874, daughter of William Shirey and Silence Turner. His children were
as follows:[36]

(by first marriage):
a. Austin L. McPherson, born c1843; dsp December 4, 1863, in Jefferson
    Barracks, Missouri.
b. Louisa Jane McPherson, born c1845; died 1928; married William Gochen-
    our; children:
    (1) Grace Gochenour, born April 5, 1883; died February 8, 1963; mar-
        ried January 4, 1903, William O. Singrey, died April 13, 1928;
        child:
        (a) Gertrude Singrey married _____ Williams; lived in Misha-
            waka, Indiana; children:
            /1/ (daughter) married Donald Cubbison; lived in South
                Bend, Indiana.
            /2/ (daughter) married Harold Graf; lived in South Bend,
                Indiana.
    (2) Irene Gochenour, born c1885; married Claude Glingle; dsp; lived
        in Bourbon, Indiana.
19. c. Martha Ann McPherson, born November 9, 1847.
    d. Sarah McPherson, died young.
(by second marriage):
    e. Jesse Hiram McPherson, born c1857; dsp c1880.
    f. Milton Henry McPherson, born July 6, 1858; died February 2, 1941, in
        Seattle, Washington; married November 5, 1890, Mrs. Mary Ella (Snavely)
        Kitson, born March 28, 1867; died January 19, 1950, daughter of John
        A. Snavely and Elizabeth A. Wagner; children:
        (1) Hugh Courtland McPherson, born October 16, 1892; dsp October,
            1963, in Syracuse, Indiana; married Bertha Crawford.
        (2) Dewey A. McPherson, born March 30, 1898; married March 20, 1923,
            Frances S. Craft, born September 16, 1897, daughter of Frank
            Craft and Cora Farr; child:
            (a) Robert Dewey McPherson, born July 18, 1924; dsp; lived in
                Wabash, Indiana.
20. g. Malinda Evelyn McPherson, born c1860.
21. h. Charity Elizabeth McPherson, born June 18, 1862.
22. i. Silence Emma McPherson, born May 2, 1864.
    j. Victoria E. McPherson, born January 14, 1867; dsp October 10, 1868.
    k. Cora Elzira McPherson, born c1869; married John A. Butt; children:
        (1) Eston Butt, born c1887; married Jessie _____; lived in Elkhart,
            Indiana; children:
            (a) Lawrence Butt.
            (b) Vernon Butt married Louise _____; children:
                /1/ Allen Butt.
                /2/ Kathleen Butt.
        (2) Edgar Butt, born September 8, 1889; lived in Syracuse, Indiana.
    l. Madison Herman McPherson, born c1871; dsp c1944 in Syracuse, Indiana;
        married Sarah Ott, born c1867; died 1947.

***

19.   Martha Ann McPherson was born November 9, 1847, in Wayne County, Indiana; died c1940 in Mentone, Indiana; married December 12, 1867, to John Sell, born September 27, 1846; died c1919. Their children were as follows:[37]

23. a. Victoria Ellen Sell, born June 5, 1869.
      b. Catherine Jane Sell, born July 25, 1872; died June 26, 1953; married February 9, 1889, Theodore W. Jenks; children:
         (1) Etta Blanche Jenks, born May 24, 1891; married September, 1919, Jay C. Kellogg, born December 15, 1924; lived in Columbus, Ohio.
         (2) Estella May Jenks, born December 10, 1892; married (1) January 17, 1917, Raymond Hoover (2) c1940 H. E. Wright; lived in Mukilteo, Washington; children (all by first marriage):
            (a) Richard Raymond Hoover, born April 26, 1918; lived in San Leandro, California.
            (b) James Jenks Hoover, born September 30, 1919; lived in Seattle, Washington.
            (c) Mary Jane Hoover, born August 2, 1923; married _____ Shields; lived in Everett, Washington.
      c. Jessie Sell, born c1875; died young.
      d. Rose May Sell, born c1877; died young.
      e. Rosetta Sell, born c1877; died c1964; married _____ McCullough; lived in Riverside, California; children:
         (1) Ruth McCullough, born c1900; married Oliver Shilling; dsp.
         (2) Francis McCullough, born c1905; dsp c1946.
      f. Ben Sell, born c1879; died c1959; married Alma Abbott; child:
         (1) Mary Jane Sell married Paul Straight; lived in Lansing, Michigan; child:
            (a) Charles Straight.
      g. William Sell, born 1882; dsp 1907.

***

23.   Victoria Ellen Sell was born June 5, 1869, in Wayne County, Indiana, and died July 31, 1941, in Mentone, Indiana; married February 25, 1895, to Morgan Ward, born June 5, 1863; died December 29, 1931. Their children were as follows:[38]

  a. Rea H. Ward, born April 10, 1896; married December 30, 1916, to Zoa Celeste Davis, born September 1, 1897; children:
      (1) Rea Davis Ward, born April 23, 1918; married (1) June 15, 1941, Ruth Callander, born May 2, 1918; (2) May 9, 1962, Patricia Scalf, born November 29, 1924; children (all by first marriage):
         (a) Tana Rebecca Ward, born March 3, 1943.
         (b) Rena Marie Ward, born September 15, 1951.
      (2) Margaret Ann Ward, born February 7, 1920; married February 6, 1943, to Raymond M. Dodson, born July 8, 1920; children:
         (a) Karen Louise Dodson, born November 15, 1945; married January 19, 1968, to Terry C. Bloom, born June 27, 1945.
         (b) Steven Richard Dodson, born March 27, 1949; married December 27, 1969, to Tanya Leigh Jacobs, born January 16, 1948.
         (c) Debra Lee Dodson, born April 29, 1952; married October 10, 1969, to Anthony Choquette, born September 10, 1949; child:
            /1/ Sean Lee Choquette, born May 20, 1970.
         (d) Rebecca Diane Dodson, born June 2, 1955.
      (3) Lois Genevieve Ward, born September 30, 1922; married March 16, 1943, to Paul O. Fritz, born March 11, 1919; children:
         (a) Kerry Ward Fritz, born June 11, 1950; married July 19, 1968

87

to Jerry Ann Klinkle, born June 20, 1949; child:
/1/ Michael Lynn Fritz, born October 10, 1969.
- (b) Janene Marie Fritz, born June 29, 1954.
- (c) Keith Lindsey Fritz, born January 24, 1956.
- (d) Kevin Wayne Fritz, born April 5, 1958.

b. Coy Ward, born February 21, 1899; married (1) Ruth Brant, born April 10, 1899; (2) Jeanette _____; children (all by first marriage):
- (1) (Dr.) Berl Brant Ward married Beryl _____; children:
  - (a) Mark Ward, born April 5, 1950.
  - (b) Michelle Ward, born April 5, 1950.
- (2) Jerry Wade Ward married Eunice _____; two adopted children.
- (3) Max Eugene Ward married June _____; children:
  - (a) John Ward died young.
  - (b) James Ward.

c. Martha Jane Ward, born September 4, 1904; married Dewey O. Kesler; lived in South Bend, Indiana; children:
- (1) Fred Lewis Kesler, dsp.
- (2) Robert Ward Kesler married Grace _____; children:
  - (a) Kathy Kesler.
  - (b) Kari Kesler.
  - (c) Kristeen Kesler.
- (3) Willodean Kesler, born December 21, 1931; married Joe C. McFarland; children:
  - (a) Georgia Jane McFarland.
  - (b) Dewey McFarland.
  - (c) Patsy McFarland.
  - (d) Joy McFarland.
  - (e) Cathleen McFarland.
  - (f) Donald Robert McFarland.
- (4) Edwin Dale Kesler married Blanche _____; children:
  - (a) Dennis Kesler.
  - (b) Wanda Kesler.
  - (c) Danny Kesler.
- (5) Lorraine Kesler.
- (6) Sharon Sue Kesler.

***

20.   Malinda Evelyn McPherson was born May 2, 1860, in Wayne County, Indiana, and died about 1935 in Hersey, Michigan; married Socrates Doremire and had the following children:[39]

a. Jacob E. Doremire, born c1886; dsp 1967 in Atwood, Indiana.
b. John S. Doremire; lived in Chalmers, Indiana.
c. Iva Christine Doremire, born October 14, 1889; died July 3, 1970, in Corvallis, Oregon; married October 12, 1912, to Clyde S. Brown; children:
- (1) Eleanor Brown married _____ Moore; lived in Ellensburg, Washington.
- (2) Hester Brown married _____ Deplazes; lived in Towner, North Dakota.
- (3) Edith Brown married _____ Slabaugh; lived in Wolford, North Dakota.
- (4) Virginia Brown married _____ Ten Eyck; lived in Sommerdale, New Jersey.
- (5) Lois Brown married W. D. Greig; lived in Corvallis, Oregon.
d. Anna Doremire, born March 28, 1891; married February 25, 1920, to _____ Gingrich; lived in Bay City, Michigan; children:
- (1) Grover M. Gingrich, born November 17, 1920; lived in Bay City,

Michigan.

    (2) Harvey W. Gingrich, born September 10, 1923; lived in Beaver-
ton, Michigan.

    (3) Ruth E. Gingrich, born November 20, 1924; married _____ Bryce;
lived in Pinconning, Michigan.

    (4) Kenneth D. Gingrich, born February 14, 1926; lived in Sanford,
Michigan.

e. Ira N. Doremire, born June 21, 1895; lived in Otsego, Michigan; child:

    (1) Pauline Doremire, dsp.

f. Atlee E. Doremire, born c1897; died c1968 in Hersey, Michigan; child:

    (1) Adria Doremire married _____ Scharmen; lived in Rochester, Mich-
igan; children:

        (a) Gary Scharmen married Karen Sue Hicks; lived in Pensacola,
Florida; children:

            /1/ Sara Scharmen.

            /2/ Pam Scharmen.

            /3/ Jackie Sue Scharmen.

        (b) Loralee Scharmen married Robert Putman; children:

            /1/ Edith Putman.

            /2/ Dale Putman.

        (c) Larry Scharmen.

        (d) Lynne Scharmen.

g. Sidney Doremire, died young.

h. Harry Doremire married Ruth M. Hoyt; lived in Honor, Michigan; children:

    (1) Avis F. Doremire married Louis Ando; children:

        (a) Judy L. Ando married Richard Smith; children:

            /1/ Laura A. Smith.

            /2/ Lisa M. Smith.

        (b) Cathy Jo Ando married Donald Soderlund.

    (2) Evelyn L. Doremire married Edward A. Sorge; children:

        (a) Mark E. Sorge.

        (b) Lynn E. Sorge.

    (3) Virginia L. Doremire married Harry G. Turner; children:

        (a) Scott S. Turner.

        (b) Douglas H. Turner.

***

21.   Charity Elizabeth McPherson was born June 18, 1862, in Wayne County,
Indiana, and died January 20, 1948, in Mentone, Indiana; married Eugene
Flory and had the following children:[40]

24. a. Cora Adeline Flory, born October 7, 1883.

     b. Ora Adelia Flory, born June 30, 1885; dsp January 12, 1945; married
Fred Ott, died January 11, 1933.

     c. Frank Flory, born January 9, 1888; died December 10, 1966, in Zephyr
Hills, Florida; married (1) March 21, 1910, Bernice Brosius, born
April 26, 1890; died April 12, 1940; (2) February 14, 1944, Marie
Stone Moore, born October 29, 1899; children (all by first marriage):

        (1) Frank Flory; lived in Lakeville, Indiana.

        (2) Arnold Flory; lived in Tippecanoe, Indiana.

        (3) Marion Flory; lived in South Bend, Indiana.

        (4) Harold B. Flory; lived in South Bend, Indiana.

        (5) Elsie Flory married Vern Coleman; lived in Niles, Michigan.

        (6) Margaret Flory married Ken Rose; lived in Niles, Michigan.

        (7) Eldonna Flory married Robert Blue; lived in Niles, Michigan.

25. d. Lawrence P. Flory, born January 25, 1890.

e. Ruth Ann Flory, born May 9, 1892; dsp October 23, 1919.
f. Eugene Flory, died young.
g. Lewis Flory, born May 26, 1899; dsp November 22, 1961, in Bourbon, Indiana; married Eva Hanes, born October 15, 1891.
h. Nellie Jane Flory, born August 16, 1901; dsp October 28, 1959; married March 4, 1918, Harold Heckman.

***

24.   Cora Adeline Flory was born October 7, 1883, and died October 8, 1918; married Clyde Ward, born August 6, 1882; died November 4, 1954; their children were as follows:[41]

a. Don Leo Ward, born October 7, 1902; married Harriet _____.
b. Ethel Lois Ward, born December 8, 1905; married Glenn Snyder; children:
    (1) Phyllis Snyder.
    (2) Bettie Snyder married _____ Baer.
c. Edith Marguerite Ward, born February 25, 1907; married Wilfred King; lived in Bremen, Indiana.
d. Melvin DeVon Ward, born May 28, 1909; married Zora _____; children:
    (1) Gene Ward.
    (2) Marilyn Ward married _____ Korthel.
e. Ralph C. Ward, born October 25, 1912; married Vadis _____; children:
    (1) Ted Ward.
    (2) Jackie Ward.
    (3) Ronnie Ward.
f. Harold Edgar Ward, born September 29, 1914; married Kate _____; child:
    (1) Susie Ward.
g. Ruth Annabell Ward, born July 9, 1916; married Delbert Bowles; children:
    (1) Dannie Bowles.
    (2) Vivian Bowles.
h. Marcella Jeanette Ward, born August 11, 1918; married Howard Griffin; children:
    (1) Gary Griffin.
    (2) Janice Griffin.

***

25.   Lawrence P. Flory was born January 25, 1890, and died August 6, 1966, in Largo, Florida; married February 4, 1911, Maude R. Davidson, born August 30, 1892; their children were as follows:[42]

a. Doris Flory, born October 21, 1914; married October 3, 1942, Frank Nocera; lived in Largo, Florida; children:
    (1) Thomas E. Nocera, born September 26, 1948.
    (2) Frank Lawrence Nocera, born February 10, 1950.
    (3) Vicki Maudell Nocera, born February 25, 1953.
    (4) Dixie Lea Nocera, born January 13, 1956.
b. Willis E. Flory, born October 19, 1917; married February 3, 1940, Hazel Stephens; lived in Largo, Florida; children:
    (1) Larry Harley Flory, born May 30, 1942; married August 11, 1965, Tamara Baum; lived in Jacksonville, Florida; child:
        (a) Cinthy Michelle Flory, born January 15, 1968.
    (2) Sharen Sue Flory, born October 23, 1949; married March 25, 1969, David Harbaugh.
c. Alma Fawn Flory, born May 12, 1920; married (1) George Ballinger (2)

October 19, 1944, Loren von Riesen; lived in S. Merrit Island, Florida; children:
(by first marriage):
(1) George Barry Flory (adopted by grandparents), born November 29, 1939; married November 5, 1962, Suzanne Dorsey; children:
    (a) Lawrence Paul Flory, born October 10, 1963.
    (b) Mark Alan Flory, born July 22, 1966.
    (c) Robin Rene Flory, born July 28, 1968.
(by second marriage):
(2) Alan von Riesen, born August 26, 1948.
(3) Clark von Riesen, born January 25, 1950.
(4) Terri K. von Riesen, born September 5, 1952.
(5) Doris Jan von Riesen, born August 26, 1956.

***

22.   Silence Emma McPherson was born May 2, 1864, in Indiana, and died June 16, 1936, in Barron, Wisconsin; married January 16, 1887, to Hiram John Hover, born April 17, 1861, in Cass County, Missouri, and died March 29, 1927, in Barron, Wisconsin. Their children were as follows:[43]

26. a. Stella Hover, born April 4, 1888.
     b. Ira Hover, born June 23, 1889; married (1) June 10, 1922, Ella Becker, born September 18, 1895; died December 23, 1943; (2) October, 1950, Myrtle Bixby; children (all by first marriage):
(1) Warren G. Hover, born April 29, 1923; married March 26, 1948, Laura Etta Gyger; lived in Springfield, Missouri; children:
    (a) Darrell Warren Hover, born February 5, 1949.
    (b) Terrance Dale Hover, born September 13, 1950.
    (c) Thomas Oscar Hover, born October 10, 1958.
(2) Hazel Fern Hover, born August 25, 1926; married June 23, 1945, Edward Jutila; lived in Barron, Wisconsin; children:
    (a) Ronald Jutila, born October 6, 1946.
    (b) Marvin Jutila, born August 11, 1948.
    (c) Harlyn Jutila, born October 13, 1951.
     c. Jay John Hover, born September 5, 1891; married (1) April 23, 1916, Florence Dawson, born August, 1898; died February 19, 1918; (2) December 21, 1932, Bertha Klefstad; child (by first marriage):
(1) Edwin Hover, born July 14, 1917; married Lois Campbell; children
    (a) Gary Allen Hover, born April 17, 1942.
    (b) Jayne Florence Hover, born November 29, 1946; married September 21, 1968, Richard Frants.
    (c) Donald Edwin Hover, born May 13, 1951.
    (d) Jean Marie Hover, born February 22, 1959.
     d. Ray Ronald Hover, born January 7, 1894; married April 15, 1920, Edna Gertrude Silvius, born September 27, 1900; lived in Barron, Wisconsin; children:
(1) Evelyn Doris Hover, born March 11, 1923; dsp March 18, 1923.
(2) Douglas Gene Hover, born June 20, 1926; dsp.
(3) Norma Rae Hover, born April 23, 1931; married October 24, 1953, Wayne A. Barrett; lived in Barron, Wisconsin; children:
    (a) Marilyn Kay Barrett, born September 4, 1954.
    (b) Nancy Jean Barrett, born March 2, 1958.
    (c) Julie Rae Barrett, born May 16, 1963.
27. e. Minnie Jemima Hover, born February 28, 1902.
     f. Hugh Hover, born November 26, 1904; dsp March 13, 1905.
28. g. Len Locke Hover, born January 27, 1907.

***

26.   Stella Hover was born April 4, 1888; married April 20, 1916, to
Martin Rockman; they lived in Barron, Wisconsin, and had the following
children:[44]

a. Niles Rockman, born May 14, 1918; dsp June 25, 1919.
b. Mae Rockman, born 1920; married Vernon L. Henricks; children:
    (1) Jerry Henricks, born 1942.
    (2) Joel Henricks, born 1945.
    (3) Stella Henricks, born 1948; married James Switala.
    (4) Steven Henricks, born 1950.
c. Bernard Rockman, born 1922; married June _____; children:
    (1) Roslyn Rockman, born 1951.
    (2) Luann Rockman, born 1955.
    (3) Nancy Rockman, born 1959.
d. Martha Rockman, born 1924; married Willis W. Sander; children:
    (1) Sandra Sander, born 1948.
    (2) Dianne Sander, born 1951.
    (3) Richard Sander, born 1960.
    (4) Terry Sander, born 1963.
e. John Rockman, born 1927; married Bernice _____; children:
    (1) Mary Rockman, born 1962.
    (2) Fred Rockman, born 1963.
    (3) Adelia Rockman, born 1965.
    (4) Nicholas Rockman.
f. Mary Rockman, born 1928; married Alvin J. Weidner; children (also
    have five adopted children):
    (1) Margie Weidner, born 1959.
    (2) David Weidner, born 1961.
    (3) Bruce Weidner, born 1964.

***

27.   Minnie Jemima Hover was born February 28, 1902; married (1) March
28, 1918, Elmer Elsworth Snider, died February 24, 1961; (2) Griffen
Vesper. Her children (all by first marriage) were as follows:[45]

a. Eleanora Snider, born October 16, 1918; dsp November 9, 1918.
b. Clifford Snider, born August 11, 1919; married April 26, 1940,
    Eleanore _____; children:
    (1) Carol Snider, born May, 1942; married January, 1960, to Byron
         Eicklehart; child:
         (a) Paul Eicklehart, born September, 1965.
    (2) Robert Snider, born December 25, 1946; married December, 1964,
         to Kathy Anderson; children:
         (a) Michael Snider, born May, 1965.
         (b) Amy Jo Snider, born June, 1966.
    (3) Roger Snider, born May 9, 1948.
c. Gearald Snider, born December 22, 1922; married (1) July 4, 1944, to
    Elizabeth _____ (2) 1953 Anna New; children:
    (by first marriage):
    (1) Sharon Snider, born May 29, 1945; married 1961 Robert Flowers;
         child:
         (a) Robert Flowers.
    (by second marriage):
    (2) Glen Snider, born September 19, 1954.
    (3) Gearald Snider, born February 4, 1959.
    (4) Kelly Snider, born May 14, 1960.
d. Beulah Snider, born December 22, 1924; dsp December, 1931.
e. Ilene Snider, born May 3, 1926; married (1) June 16, 1946, William

Nichols (2) January, 1953, Everett Garner; children:
(by first marriage):
(1) David Nichols, born June 19, 1947; married December 3, 1968,
      Helen Weber; child:
      (a) David Nichols, born March, 1969.
(2) Darlene Lois Nichols, born August 19, 1948; married June, 1967,
      Richard Kirshinsky; child:
      (a) Melany Kay Kirshinsky, born February 16, 1968.
(by second marriage):
(3) Douglas Garner, born April 4, 1954.
(4) Dale Garner, born July 20, 1955.
  f. Donna Snider, born March 22, 1928; married (1) October, 1950, to
    Donald Allen; (2) August 8, 1953, Wayne Marshall; children:
    (by first marriage):
    (1) Terri Lynn Allen, born December 26, 1951.
    (by second marriage):
    (2) Deborah Lynn Marshall, born February 28, 1955.
  g. Virgil Snider, born November 30, 1935; married June 7, 1958, Sharon
    Slack; children:
    (1) Kim Ellen Snider, born March 3, 1959.
    (2) Troy Clifton Snider, born January 26, 1961.
  h. Catherine Rae Snider, born June 4, 1937; dsp.

***

28.   Len Locke Hover was born January 27, 1907, in Barron, Wisconsin,
     and married (1) c1931 Beatrice Fay Chapman, born November 6, 1906, and
     died October 29, 1955; (2) May 8, 1958, Mata Isabelle Raven. His chil-
     dren (all by first marriage) were as follows:[46]

  a. Allen Leonard Hover, born November 11, 1932; married Shirley Ormson;
    lived in Minneapolis, Minnesota; children:
    (1) Cameron Joel Hover, born March 22, 1958.
    (2) Lance Daniel Hover, born April 23, 1959.
    (3) Darcey Lynn Hover, born March 14, 1963.
  b. Harley Jay Hover, born April 4, 1937; dsp.
  c. Carolyn Emma Hover, born April 10, 1940; married May 26, 1962; Jack
    Seitz; lived in Minneapolis, Minnesota; children:
    (1) Sherry Dee Seitz, born February 10, 1963.
    (2) Troy Anthony Seitz, born October 7, 1965.
  d. Lois Judy Hover, born October 26, 1943; married August 31, 1963,
    Virgil Olson; lived in Minneapolis, Minnesota; child:
    (1) Mark Alan Olson, born February 20, 1969.

***

7.   Jehu McPherson was born February 24, 1756, in Chester County, Penn-
    sylvania, and moved to Orange (now Chatham) County, North Carolina, in
    1765. He moved to Union County, South Carolina, and lived with his bro-
    ther John, and about 1788 he married Margery Nicholls (see p. 246) in
    Spartanburg County, South Carolina. On April 9, 1789, he bought 167
    acres on the waters of Dutchman's Creek in Union County from John and
    Mary Bennett for Ŀ6. On May 13, 1798, he bought an adjoining 48 acres
    from Mills Sumner for 12 shillings.[47]

    On June 28, 1790, Jehu McPherson was appointed one of the adminis-
    trators of the estate of his brother John McPherson, and he bought goods
    at the estate sale in July. In 1802 he was an administrator of the es-
    tate of Thomas Blasingame, and he served on juries several times between

93

1802 and 1804. On January 12, 1805, he and his wife Margery sold their plantation of 130 acres on the waters of Dutchman's Creek to Daniel Palmer for $100.00.[48]

Jehu McPherson then moved to Spartanburg County, South Carolina, where on June 7, 1805, he bought 200 acres south of the Tyger River from Simpson and Susanna Newman for $250.00. After the death of his mother-in-law, he sold the land to Benjamin Hooker for $300.00 on September 20, 1807.[49]

McPherson then moved to Barren (now Monroe) County, Kentucky, in the winter of 1807, although the destruction of the Monroe County records hinders the location of further information. On December 20, 1812, he bought 88 acres on the East Fork of Barren River from Curtis and Mary Wood for $100.00; he built and operated a mill and cultivated a plantation on the site. On March 23, 1824, he bought an adjoining 24 acres from Joseph G. Hardin for $24.00.[50]

Jehu McPherson made his will on January 17, 1819, dividing his property among his children, and he probably died in 1841. The children of Jehu and Margery McPherson were as follows:[51]

29. a. George McPherson, born November 25, 1789.
30. b. Mary McPherson, born c1791.
     c. Rachel McPherson, born c1793; married March 1, 1814, in Barren (now Monroe) County, Kentucky, to Hugh Marshall; he died about 1819; they had a son and a daughter.
31. d. Sarah McPherson, born c1796.
32. e. Eleanor McPherson, born July 18, 1798.
     f. Jehu H. McPherson, born c1800; married c1826 Minerva Hardin, daughter of David Hardin and Sarah Gist, and granddaughter of Joseph Gist and Hannah Breed (see p. 39); U. S. Census Marshal for Monroe County, Kentucky, 1830; moved to Marshall County, Mississippi, before 1838; there are many land transactions recorded for him; in 1856 he lived in DeSoto County, Mississippi; children:
     (1) (daughter), born c1827.
     (2) Mary McPherson, born c1829.
     (3) Elizabeth McPherson, born c1831.
     (4) William E. McPherson, born c1834.
     (5) Joseph B. McPherson, born c1836.
     g. Margery McPherson, born c1802 in Union County, South Carolina; died May 6, 1882, in Tulare County, California; married c1823 in Monroe County, Kentucky, to Hiram Gist (see p. 40).
     h. Joseph G. McPherson, born c1805 in Spartanburg County, South Carolina.
     i. Ruth McPherson, born November 3, 1807; died April 17, 1884, in Clay County, Tennessee; married c1827 in Monroe County, Kentucky, to Levi Gist (see p. 40).
33. j. Benjamin Nicholls McPherson, born June 18, 1810.

***

29.   George McPherson was born November 25, 1789, in Union County, South Carolina, and moved to Barren (now Monroe) County, Kentucky, in 1807. He married March 7, 1815, to Mary Harrison, who was born March 10, 1799, and died October 20, 1880. He died August 19, 1852, in Monroe County, Kentucky, leaving the following children:[52]

34. a. Sarah McPherson, born February 17, 1817.

94

b. John Harrison McPherson, born July 8, 1819; died September 4, 1854,
    in Barren County, Kentucky; married 1841 Letitia Young Peden, born
    March 8, 1826; died July 22, 1871, daughter of Benjamin Peden and
    Letitia Young; children:
    (1) Batley S. McPherson, born c1842; dsp February 25, 1864.
    (2) George Nicholls McPherson, born June 28, 1844; dsp February 15,
         1864.
    (3) Martha Jane McPherson, born c1846; married William Allen Bullock,
         born December 18, 1838; died March 18, 1915, son of John Waller
         Bullock and Minerva Glover; lived in Barren County, Kentucky.
    (4) Benjamin P. McPherson, born c1848; married Lovie Ellen Hayes;
         lived in Texas.
    (5) Owen Jehu McPherson, born July 30, 1850; dsp December 19, 1872.
    (6) Christopher T. McPherson, born March 14, 1854; married 1881
         Virginia T. Bellamy, daughter of Samuel D. Bellamy and Mary
         Elizabeth Huffman; dsp; lived in Barren County, Kentucky.
c. George Nicholls McPherson, born May 23, 1821; dsp April 9, 1836.
35. d. Samuel McPherson, born August 5, 1823.
36. e. Jehu McPherson, born January 7, 1826.
f. Mary McPherson, born March 14, 1828; died September 25, 1858; married
    Alexander Campbell Glover, born November 15, 1819; died March 15,
    1861; lived in Monroe County, Kentucky; children:
    (1) Kate Glover, born April 19, 1855; died June 3, 1916; married
         March 21, 1879, Smith Barlow Howard, born March 14, 1847; died
         July 12, 1925; children:
         (a) Hattie Howard, born February 16, 1880; dsp October 13, 1881.
         (b) Campbell Howard, born December 21, 1881; lived in Greenville,
              Kentucky.
         (c) Frank Howard, born February 27, 1884.
         (d) Nellie Mae Howard, born May 17, 1886.
         (e) Amy Barlow Howard, born May 23, 1893; dsp August 6, 1893.
         (f) Ava Glover Howard, born May 23, 1893.
         (g) Creed Howard, born May 20, 1901.
    (2) George Prentice Glover, born December 30, 1857; died April 4,
         1944; married June 9, 1881, to Martha Ann Bowles, died April
         19, 1942, daughter of Thomas Bowles and Rachel Ann Johnson;
         lived in Indiana; children:
         (a) Kate Glover, born August 23, 1883; dsp.
         (b) Annie Glover, born March 23, 1888; dsp February 6, 1963.
         (c) Orrin Glover, born April 4, 1890; married December 29,
              1915, to Urnal Eulalia Myler; dsp; lived in New Richmond,
              Indiana.
         (d) Avery Glover, born December 5, 1892; died April 4, 1951;
              married March 26, 1919, to Sarah Merle Waugh.
g. Malinda McPherson, born April 23, 1832; dsp November 10, 1856; mar-
    ried January 15, 1856, to A. J. Howard.

                              ***

34.   Sarah McPherson was born February 17, 1817, in Barren (now Monroe)
   County, Kentucky, and died June 2, 1887, in Barren County, Kentucky;
   married August 20, 1835, to Lewis Wilkinson, born April 12, 1809; died
   July 29, 1895, son of William Wilkinson and Lucy Bryan. They had the
   following children:53

   a. James N. Wilkinson, born March 5, 1837; dsp August 7, 1864.
   b. Mary Elizabeth Wilkinson, born January 17, 1840; dsp 1918; married
       August, 1880, to Schuyler M. Renfro.

                               95

37. c. Julia Grissom Wilkinson, born March 23, 1843.
    d. Lucy Ann Wilkinson, born January 23, 1845; dsp February 28, 1864.
    e. George McPherson Wilkinson, born May 3, 1848; dsp August 19, 1852.
    f. Samuel W. Wilkinson, born May 6, 1849.
    g. Batley B. Wilkinson, born October 11, 1851; married 1874 Ora D. Ellis.
    h. Franklin P. Wilkinson, born September 4 1855; dsp October 11, 1856.
    i. Jehu T. Wilkinson, born March 10, 1857.

                                   ***

37.   Julia Grissom Wilkinson was born March 23, 1843, and died December
    7, 1926; married December 12, 1868, to Evermond Johnson Sanders, born
    March 11, 1828; died October 15, 1882, son of Nelson A. Sanders and Sarah
    W. Hughes. They lived in Barren County, Kentucky, and had the following
    children:[54]

    a. Samuel Bryan Sanders, born October 29, 1871; died January 10, 1943;
       married 1894 Hattie Word, died 1895, daughter of William and Jane
       Word; child:
       (1) Clarence Lee Sanders, born July 27, 1895; died November 12,
           1946; married August 15, 1922, Mary Elizabeth Myler, born April
           1, 1892, daughter of Samuel Myler and Elizabeth Evans; child:
           (a) Lee Samuel Sanders, born September 13, 1923; married May
               19, 1945, Ruth Virginia Barnes; children:
               /1/ Douglas Lee Sanders, born June 20, 1946.
               /2/ Michael John Sanders, born February 15, 1949.
               /3/ Stephen James Sanders, born September 3, 1953.
               /4/ Jeffery Lynn Sanders, born October 13, 1957.
38. b. Annie Reid Sanders, born April 3, 1873.
    c. Lewis Nelson Sanders, born April 12, 1875; dsp April 12, 1933; mar-
       ried Lula _____; lived in Lindsay, California.

                                   ***

38.   Annie Reid Sanders was born April 3, 1873, and died November 16,
    1963; married May 8, 1889, to Schuyler Grooms, born July 10, 1863, died
    December 22, 1943, son of Thomas Grooms and Elizabeth Harrison. They
    lived in Barren County, Kentucky, and their children were as follows:[55]

39. a. Evermond Thomas Grooms, born January 18, 1891.
    b. Nellie Mary Grooms, born August 11, 1893; married June 1, 1927, to
       Paul Myddelton; born February 17, 1886; died August 23 1942, in Val-
       dosta, Georgia, son of Robert Thomas Myddelton and Uphremia Smith;
       child:
       (1) Paul Grooms Myddelton, born December 10, 1929; married November
           27, 1952, to Rena Mae Register, born December 21, 1933, daughter
           of Troy Register and Clyde Stallings.
    c. Delma Curtis Grooms, born November 12, 1899; married March 26, 1926,
       to Myrtle Marie Lindstrom; born August 21, 1906, daughter of Oscar
       Fredrick Lindstrom and Nannie Marie Broberg; lived in Rockwell City,
       Iowa; children:
       (1) Elnora Marie Grooms, born February 11, 1927; married Dale McDough;
           child:
           (a) Nene Elizabeth McDough.
       (2) Marjorie Ruth Grooms, born May 8, 1929; married June 2, 1950,
           to Herbert Lyle Larsen; children:
           (a) Curtis Albert Larsen, born May 18, 1952.
           (b) Laura Luanne Larsen, born November 18, 1953.

(c) Karen Sue Larsen, born August 16, 1956.
(d) George John Larsen, born November 10, 1958.
(3) Doris Louise Grooms, born March 24, 1931; married August 26, 1950, to Dean Richard Wilkinson; children:
(a) Nancy Jo Wilkinson, born January 16, 1952.
(b) Rand Alan Wilkinson, born October 22, 1953.
(4) Peggy Nan Grooms, born March 24, 1933; married June 5, 1954, to Rev. Calvin Lawrence Peterson; children:
(a) Lynette Jean Peterson, born May 7, 1955.
(b) Lance Eugene Peterson, born July 18, 1957.
(c) Larisa Marie Peterson, born January 26, 1959.
(d) Lincoln Curtis Peterson, born October 5, 1961.
(5) Martha Sue Grooms, born August 24, 1941.
(6) Mary Lou Grooms, born August 24, 1941.
d. Charles Bryan Grooms, born February 23, 1902; married Lillian Brown; dsp.
e. Ruby Sanders Grooms, born November 14, 1905; married December 23, 1922, to James Allen Bradshaw, born September 22, 1902, son of James and Ophelia Bradshaw; lived in Glasgow, Kentucky; children:
(1) Charles Allen Bradshaw, born September 18, 1924; married March 5, 1945, to Audrey Maxine Pedigo, born February 23, 1923, daughter of Oscar A. Pedigo and Nora Smith; children:
(a) Charles Pedigo Bradshaw, born April 16, 1946.
(b) Elizabeth Ann Bradshaw, born December 5, 1950.
(2) Ruby Nell Bradshaw, born November 26, 1926; married January 11, 1947, to Bruce Wilson Trabue, born July 18, 1926, son of Joe Rogers Trabue and Ada Wilson; children:
(a) Bruce Allen Trabue, born August 5, 1950.
(b) Robert David Trabue, born October 18, 1953.
f. Beulah Ruth Grooms, born January 23, 1912; dsp.
g. Claude Reid Grooms, born October 24, 1913; dsp November 23, 1914.
h. Clyde Lewis Grooms, born January 21, 1916; married July 17, 1941, to Marjorie Elenore Wagner; dsp.

***

39.   Evermond Thomas Grooms was born January 18, 1891; married February 28, 1922, to Daisy Marie Carlson, born March 24, 1904, daughter of Samuel Carlson and Johannah Broberg. Their children were as follows:

a. Nellie Reid Grooms, born January 4, 1923; married Lester Mosier; children:
(1) Virginia Carol Mosier, born September 30, 1944.
(2) Connie Mosier, born February 10, 1947.
(3) Darrel Mosier, born January 16, 1949.
(4) Brenda Mosier.
(5) Jerry Mosier.
(6) Marsha Mosier.
(7) Leslie Mosier.
(8) Angela Mosier, born April, 1962.
b. Annie Jewell Grooms, born August 10, 1924; married May 18, 1944, to Benton Harlan Wood, born October 25, 1919, son of Jonathan Wood and Roxie Harlan; children:
(1) Margaret Ann Wood, born October 8, 1947.
(2) Patricia Harline Wood, born December 25, 1948.
(3) Gwendolyn Wood, born March 24, 1950.
(4) Nancy Jewell Wood, born February 3, 1952.
c. Johannah Dell Grooms, born October 10, 1925; married (1) August 17, 1946, to Hayden Turner Smith (2) Allen Vincent; children (all by

97

first marriage):
(1) Hayden Turner Smith, born December 25, 1947.
(2) Philip Darrel Smith, born April 14, 1949.
(3) Thomas Allen Smith, born May 14, 1951.
(4) Cynthia Jo Smith, born December 27, 1952.
d. Edith May Grooms, born September 30, 1926; married 1946 James Guy Norman, born August 15, 1924; child:
(1) James Guy Norman, born October 3, 1946.
e. Beulah Jean Grooms, born January 1, 1928; married (1) Charles Dean (2) _____ Ratliff; children:
(by first marriage):
(1) Charlotte Jean Dean, born June 14, 1947; married 1963 Donald Ray Bunch.
(by second marriage):
(2) Lynn Ratliff, born December 20, 1956.
f. Virginia Lee Grooms, born February 8, 1929; married February 28, 1948, to William Paul Thomas, born December 8, 1921, son of Gilbert Reed Thomas and Myrtie Frances Jones; child:
(1) William Gayle Thomas, born September 23, 1951.
g. Paul Lewis Grooms, born March 3, 1932; married January 28, 1955, to Rosie Elizabeth Coulter, born February 14, 1929, daughter of Lonnie Coulter and Mary Jane Wood; children:
(1) Elizabeth Ann Grooms, born November 28, 1955.
(2) Nina Gay Grooms, born August 3, 1960.
(3) Lisa Gayle Grooms, born August 3, 1960.
h. Samuel Woodford Grooms, born October 24, 1933; married August 21, 1954, to Mildred Ann Konop, born December 24, 1932, daughter of Joseph Konop and Angeline Svejda; children:
(1) Marcia Dale Grooms, born March 3, 1955.
(2) Glen Curtis Grooms, born February 7, 1956.
(3) Patricia Ann Grooms, born March 8, 1957.
(4) Gregory Thomas Grooms, born January 21, 1959.
i. Betty Jane Grooms, born October 28, 1935.
j. Linda Grooms, born June 3, 1940; married March 27, 1959, to Wayne Baxter, born April 18, 1940, son of Bazz Hamilton Baxter and Della Kirk Harlan; children:
(1) Tammie Sue Baxter, born February 27, 1960.
(2) Jason Barlow Baxter, born June 4, 1962.

***

35.   Samuel McPherson was born August 5, 1823, and died September 19, 1892; married Margaret Walker, daughter of Jefferson Walker and Hannah Hale. Their children were as follows:[57]

a. Campbell Glover McPherson, born c1861; married Lucy Cox; lived in St. Louis, Missouri; children:
(1) Samuel Hunter McPherson, born September 10, 1888; dsp May 11, 1889.
(2) Baker Blaine McPherson; married Lucy Twente; dsp; lived in Cairo, Illinois.
(3) Campbell Wallace McPherson, born June 14 1892; died February 9, 1939; married Lovie Richardson; lived in Brentwood, Missouri; children:
(a) Mary McPherson, born June 20, 1921; married George Rothweiler; lived in St. Louis, Missouri; children:
/1/ Michael Rothweiler.
/2/ James Rothweiler.
/3/ Nancy Jane Rothweiler.

        (b) Martha McPherson, born April 27, 1923; married David Taylor;
            lived in St. Louis, Missouri; children:
            /1/ Denny Mack Taylor.
            /2/ Robert Merrill Taylor.
            /3/ Charles Wallace Taylor, died young.
        (c) Campbell Wallace McPherson, born November 3, 1929; married
            Marian Lee Burnett; lived in St. Louis, Missouri; children:
            /1/ Debra Sue McPherson, born March 12, 1955.
            /2/ Campbell Wallace McPherson, born May 20, 1956.
    (4) Denny McPherson; dsp; lived in St. Louis, Missouri.
    (5) William McPherson married (1) Arrel McGowan (2) Fern _____; dsp;
        lived in St. Louis, Missouri.
    (6) Lucy Mae McPherson married (1) Middleton Caruthers (2) Glenn
        Taylor; lived in Mobile, Alabama; children (all by first mar-
        riage):
        (a) Middleton Caruthers.
        (b) Ellen Caruthers married _____ Dixon.
        (c) Minnie Caruthers married _____ Habighorst.
    b. Mary McPherson, born c1864; married 1887 Cal Cox; children:
        (1) Ethel Cox.
        (2) Samuel Cox.
        (3) Nannie Mae Cox.
    c. Victoria McPherson, born c1866; married (1) 1891 George W. Payne (2)
       Cal Cox; dsp.
    d. Frances D. McPherson, born c1868; dsp.

                                 ***

36.   Jehu McPherson was born January 7, 1826, and died October 5, 1883,
    in Monroe County, Kentucky; married (1) Donna Martha Thomas, born January
    25, 1835; died October 23, 1867; (2) Ella Jones, born March 10, 1840; died
    November 31, 1881. His children were as follows:[58]

    (by first marriage):
    a. Willie M. McPherson, born November 8, 1855; dsp March 17, 1864.
    b. Sarah W. McPherson, born November 14, 1859; dsp April 3, 1875.
    c. Harrison P. McPherson, born June 7, 1861; dsp November 15, 1863.
40. d. James Batley McPherson, born November 29, 1863.
    e. Edward T. McPherson, born January 12, 1867; dsp April 20, 1867.
    (by second marriage):
    f. (Dr.) Uberto Wright McPherson, born January 28, 1871; died December
       11, 1926; married Elizabeth Wood Parrish, born November 25, 1873;
       died March, 1964, daughter of Fleming Parrish and Sarah Anderson;
       lived in Louisville, Kentucky; children:
        (1) Eugenia McPherson, born November 21, 1900; married Fielding H.
            Dickey; dsp; lived in Louisville, Kentucky.
        (2) Creal McPherson, born December 23, 1904; dsp; lived in Louis-
            ville, Kentucky.
        (3) Uberto Lynn McPherson, born December 17, 1912; married Rosalia
            Blum; lived in Louisville, Kentucky; children:
            (a) Patricia McPherson, born August 26, 1940.
            (b) Charles McPherson, born December 4, 1943.
            (c) Margaret Eugenia McPherson, born January 10, 1946.
            (d) Mary Elizabeth McPherson, born October 28, 1952.
    g. George W. McPherson, born c1873; married Sarah Shipley; children:
        (1) Wendell McPherson; lived in Louisville, Kentucky.
        (2) William Herbert McPherson married Ruby Katzman; lived in Louis-
            ville, Kentucky; child:
            (a) Almira McPherson.
                                 99

h. Mary Louise McPherson, born c1875; married 1895 Hiram P. Bowles; lived in Indiana; children:
    (1) Addie Bowles married _____ Lucas; children:
        (a) Minerva Lucas; lived in Lafayette, Indiana.
        (b) Truman Lucas.
    (2) Bryan Bowles.
    (3) Raymond Bowles; lived in Frankfort, Indiana.
    (4) Marie Bowles.
    (5) Virgil Bowles.
    (6) Loren Bowles.
    (7) Mayme Bowles.
    (8) Rosemary Bowles married Harley Kinder; lived in Rossville, Indiana.
i. Campbell B. McPherson, born June 2, 1877; died September 19, 1906; married Ida Mary Wathen, born July 7, 1884; died August 13, 1953, daughter of Edgar W. Wathen and Sarah Spalding; child:
    (1) Joseph Estell McPherson, born November 8, 1905; dsp; lived in Louisville, Kentucky.
j. Jehu B. McPherson, born May, 1879; dsp c1915.

***

40.   James Batley McPherson was born November 29, 1863, and died July 20, 1906, in Monroe County, Kentucky; married 1888 Bercha Olivia White, born October 18, 1871; died February 10, 1937, daughter of Asbury White and Permelia Bushong. Their children were as follows:[59]

a. Cecil McPherson, born October 27, 1889; married (1) December 29, 1912, to Kate Lyons, died April 14, 1955; (2) July 7, 1956, to Elva Ferguson; dsp; lived in Tompkinsville, Kentucky.
b. Donnie McPherson, born October 2, 1891; dsp January 14, 1912.
41. c. Acie McPherson, born March 3, 1895.
d. Homer McPherson, born May 24, 1897; married November 10, 1921, to Nellie Parrish; child:
    (1) Ruenell McPherson, born September 22, 1922; married March 9, 1940, to Travis Hamilton; children:
        (a) Lillian Hamilton, born March 1, 1942; married April 11, 1958, to Avalon Russell; children:
            /1/ Teresa Gail Russell, born August 14, 1959.
            /2/ Jimmy Wayne Russell, born August 30, 1961.
        (b) Judy Carol Hamilton, born August 16, 1948.
        (c) Ronnie Darrell Hamilton, born December 4, 1956.
e. Lee McPherson, born February 18, 1899; married December 21, 1922, to Nellie Hamilton; child:
    (1) Terrell Gene McPherson, born May 23, 1935; married April 17, 1956, to Frances Kathleen Price; lived in Monroe County, Kentucky.
f. Neva McPherson, born February 6, 1900; married March 4, 1918, to Frank Hope; lived in Tompkinsville, Kentucky; child:
    (1) Wilma Doris Hope, born February 5, 1923; married November 18, 1945, to Albert Hickman; lived in Ottawa, Kansas.
g. Harvey McPherson, born September 28, 1902; dsp October 12, 1902.
h. Verla Brince McPherson, born November 5, 1904; dsp December 13, 1905.
i. Rule McPherson, born September 30, 190?; married February 5, 1921, to Jack Hayes; children:
    (1) Cletra Olivia Hayes, born November 30, 1921; married January 23, 1944, to Stanley Head; lived in Tompkinsville, Kentucky; children:

100

             (a) Jacqueline Head, born March 26, 1945.
             (b) Sherry June Head, born July 24, 1947.
        (2) Joseph Marshall Hayes, born October 6, 1923; married April 29,
             1951, to Naomi Billingsley; lived in Edmonton, Kentucky; child:
             (a) Lou Ann Hayes, born September 20, 1953.
        (3) Julius Glen Hayes, born October 26, 1925; married November 10,
             1956, to Johannah Marie Price; lived in Sulphur Lick, Kentucky;
             child:
             (a) Jack Glen Hayes, born February 26, 1959.
        (4) James Harmon Hayes, born August 15, 1928; married August 8, 1953;
             to Dorothy Jane Wimpey; lived in Tompkinsville, Kentucky; chil-
             dren:
             (a) Emily Ruth Hayes, born November 20, 1954.
             (b) Patricia Helen Hayes, born February 2, 1957.

                                    ***

41.   Acie McPherson was born March 3, 1895; married November 25, 1916, to
    Amanda Ellen Hope; lived in Monroe County, Kentucky; their children were
    as follows:[60]

    a. Wallace McPherson, born September 22, 1917; married August 12, 1945,
        to Ruby Jewel McPherson (see p. 114); child:
        (1) Caroline Hope McPherson, born November 8, 1947.
    b. Marshall McPherson, born March 2, 1920; married July 4, 1946, to
        Rita Crowe; children:
        (1) Brenda Gail McPherson, born November 19, 1947.
        (2) Michael Glenn McPherson, born November 25, 1949.
        (3) Tommie Lynn McPherson, dsp December 7, 1951.
    c. Warren Denton McPherson, born February 22, 1922; married June 1,
        1940, to Ruth Jones; lived in Mt. Herman, Kentucky; children:
        (1) Jerry Douglas McPherson, born April 27, 1941; married August
             28, 1960, to Rebekah Hagan.
        (2) Janet Creal McPherson, born February 14, 1943.
    d. James Thomas McPherson, born May 7, 1925; married December 15, 1950,
        to Jean Grey; lived in Monroe County, Kentucky; children:
        (1) Pamela Joan McPherson, born November 24, 1953.
        (2) Paula Jean McPherson, born September 10, 1956.
    e. Royce Bronston McPherson, born March 12, 1929; married April 6, 1956,
        to Glaydene Martin; lived in Tompkinsville, Kentucky; children:
        (1) Terry Lucas McPherson, born January 5, 1957.
        (2) Sherry Martin McPherson, born December 27, 1961.

                                    ***

30.   Mary McPherson was born about 1791 in Union County, South Carolina,
    and died about 1871 in Barren County, Kentucky; married August 11, 1812,
    in Barren (now Monroe) County, Kentucky, to Cephas Dickerson; their chil-
    dren were as follows:[61]

    a. Elizabeth Dickerson married Henry Parker; children (perhaps among
        others):
        (1) (Dr.) George Thomas Parker married Emma Dishman.
        (2) William Parker married Lucy Wilson.
        (3) Lucetta Parker married Robert Puckett.
        (4) Cephas Parker, dsp.
    b. Jehu Dickerson, born c1815.
    c. John McPherson Dickerson, born February 17, 1818; died May 2, 1893;

                                    101

married June 18, 1844, Nancy Hatchett, born December 22, 1825; died August 24, 1899, daughter of Archibald Hatchett and Elizabeth Love; children:

(1) Cephas Bruce Dickerson, born April 6, 1845; dsp March, 1867.
(2) Mary Elizabeth Dickerson, born November 19, 1847; dsp August 24, 1895, in Memphis, Tennessee; married September 15, 1870, Herbert T. Hill.
(3) George Thomas Dickerson, born August 31, 1850; died September 12, 1921, in Houston, Texas; married December 5, 1878, Eliza Jane Dean, daughter of Allen Burkett Carlton Dean and Dorcas Jane Alexander.
(4) Susan Frances Dickerson, born December 4, 1853; died May 8, 1944; married February 28, 1883, Ideria Massey Crapps, son of Lemuel Crapps and Elvina Massey; lived in Wimberley, Texas; children:
    (a) Adella Crapps, dsp.
    (b) Alberta Crapps, dsp.
    (c) Alta Crapps married Wood Ada Leath.
    (d) Bruce Crapps.
    (e) Edwin L. Crapps married Dovie _____; lived in San Antonio, Texas; child:
        /1/ Joan Crapps married _____ Petros.
    (f) Wilma Crapps married R. E. New; lived in Wimberley, Texas.
(5) James Marshall Dickerson, born July 15, 1857; dsp June 19, 1887.
(6) Kate Love Dickerson, born September 16, 1860; died October 26, 1958, in San Antonio, Texas; married April 18, 1893, to Thomas Sheehan; children:
    (a) Thomas A. Sheehan; dsp; lived in San Antonio, Texas.
    (b) Walter B. Sheehan; dsp; lived in San Antonio, Texas.
    (c) Kathryn Sheehan married _____ Miller; lived in Seattle, Washington; child:
        /1/ Kathryn Miller married _____ Jones; lived in Ft. Lewis, Washington; child:
            /a/ Michael Thomas Jones.
(7) John Dickerson, born February 17, 1864; dsp.
(8) Edwin Dickerson, born April 6, 1866; died January 2, 1945; married Susie Alice Bolling; lived in Abilene, Texas.

  d. Sarah McPherson Dickerson, born c1820; dsp.
42. e. George Nicholls Dickerson, born February 10, 1821.
  f. Solomon Holland Dickerson, born February 18, 1824; died December 13, 1902; married Martha Jane Glover, daughter of William Glover and Charity Wilson; lived in Barren County, Kentucky.
  g. William Ripley Dickerson, dsp.

***

42.   George Nicholls Dickerson was born February 10, 1821, in Barren County, Kentucky, and died in December, 1893, in Conway, Arkansas; he married Tabitha Fowler, daughter of Levi Fowler and Mary Hill, and their children were as follows:[62]

  a. (Dr.) George Douglass Dickerson, born August 5, 1854; died January 23, 1914; married Sallie L. Richardson; children:
    (1) (Dr.) Cecil Harrod Dickerson.
    (2) Gladyse Nason Dickerson married Harry Little.
    (3) George Douglass Dickerson.
    (4) Foster Rod Dickerson, born August 14, 1903; died May 30, 1955.
  b. (Dr.) Prentiss Dickerson lived in Sulphur Springs, Texas.
  c. Arthur Bell Dickerson married Kittie Rowlett; lived in Rockdale,

Texas.
d. Rod Cephas Dickerson died February, 1932; lived in Conway, Arkansas.
e. William Haskell Dickerson married Lucinda Parker; lived in Sulphur
Springs, Texas; children:
(1) Verona Dickerson married Herbert Averitt; lived in Saltillo.
(2) Samuel Dickerson lived in Dallas, Texas.
(3) Morris Dickerson lived in Orange, Texas.
(4) Benjamin Dickerson lived in Sulphur Springs, Texas.
(5) A. B. Dickerson lived in Dallas, Texas.
(6) George Dickerson lived in Dallas, Texas.
(7) Margaret Dickerson lived in Dallas, Texas.
(8) Ann Lu Dickerson lived in Dallas, Texas.
(9) Douglass Dickerson, dsp.
f. Mary Dickerson, died young.

***

31.   Sarah McPherson was born about 1796 in Union County, South Carolina;
married March 16, 1817, in Barren (now Monroe) County, Kentucky, to
Robert Johnston, born c1787 in South Carolina; served in Capt. Thomas
Griffin's Company of Kentucky Militia in the War of 1812. He died about
1836 in Monroe County, Indiana, and his widow moved to Jefferson County,
Iowa, where she was living in 1856. Their children were as follows:[63]

a. Ruth Johnston, born March 16, 1818; died October 22, 1906; married
Joseph McLaughlin; children:
(1) John McLaughlin married Lucinda Zike.
(2) Robert McLaughlin married Mary Ann Johnston.
(3) Thomas McLaughlin married Evelyn Bridwell.
(4) Nancy Jane McLaughlin married John Donaldson; dsp.
(5) William McLaughlin married Martha Zike.
(6) Margaret McLaughlin married Jonathan Bougher.
(7) Mary McLaughlin married John Turner.
b. Nancy Johnston, born c1819; died 1898; married 1843 Nicholas Shipman,
born c1814; died 1893; children:
(1) Ruth Ellen Shipman married Eli Woodward.
(2) Sarah Elizabeth Shipman, born 1842; died 1919; married West
Bedwell.
(3) Robert Shipman, born 1851; died 1927; married Mary Jane Alsman.
(4) James Shipman, born 1857; married Malinda Gavard.
(5) George Shipman, born 1864; married Cora Murphy.
(6) John V. Shipman, born 1864; married Ann Walters.
43. c. John Green Johnston, born November 18, 1821.
d. Mary Johnston, born c1824; married August 18, 1841; to Alexander
Buchanan; lived in Iowa.
e. Rachel Johnston, born c1826; married December 6, 1852, to Job Shrout;
lived in Greene County, Indiana.
f. Margery Johnston, born December 14, 1827; died March 10, 1854; married April 14, 1848, to James Buchanan; children:
(1) Mary Jane Buchanan, born November 9, 1849.
(2) Jehu McPherson Buchanan, born January 24, 1854; died March 8,
1922; married 1878 Margaret Zike, born February 2, 1857; children:
(a) Charles Edward Buchanan, born 1878; married Lola Blackwell;
children:
1/ Ruth Buchanan married Horace Rankin.
2/ Mildred Buchanan married Oscar Whitlow.
3/ James Buchanan.
(b) Frederick Buchanan married Pearl Walker; child:

/1/ Margery Buchanan married 1933 Paul William Tanner.
- g. Sarah Johnston, born January 28, 1830; dsp July 22, 1902; married 1891 Alfred Storm.
- h. Susanna Johnston, born c1832; married _____ Holmes; lived in Iowa.
- i. Jehu Johnston, born c1834; lived in Iowa.

***

43.   John Green Johnston was born November 18, 1821, in Barren (now Monroe) County, Kentucky, and died February 2, 18??, in Indiana; married August 7, 1843, to Lucinda Sipes, born February 28, 1820; died June 7, 1904, daughter of William Sipes and Mary Meadows. Their children were as follows:[64]

44. a. William Henry Johnston, born October 26, 1844.
45. b. Rhoda Johnston, born May 24, 1846.
    c. George W. Johnston, born September 31, 1847; dsp June 9, 1864.
46. d. Robert Johnston, born October 13, 1849.
    e. Levi Johnston, born October 15, 1850; married (1) October 28, 1869, to Martha Emma Harrell (2) Sarah _____; child (by first marriage):
       (1) Viola Johnston, born December 25, 1874; dsp January 20, 1875.
    f. Marion Green Johnston, born 1853; died 1893; married April, 1875, Nancy Elizabeth Clay; children:
       (1) Effie Johnston married April 22, 1897, to Thomas Harold.
       (2) May Johnston married March 24, 1901, to William Burket.
       (3) Nettie Johnston married _____ Hill.
       (4) Rettie Johnston, born 1890; died 1938.
       (5) Carl Clay Johnston, born 1892; dsp 1893.
    g. Alfred Homer Johnston married April 2, 1879, to Deborah J. Morgan; children:
       (1) Amos L. Johnston, born March 29, 1882; dsp December 28, 1898.
       (2) Clarus Johnston married Lula Cobb; lived in Bedford, Indiana.
       (3) Romney Johnston.
       (4) Gertrude Johnston.
       (5) Goldie Johnston.
       (6) Bessie Johnston.
       (7) Truely Johnston.
       (8) Kathryn Johnston.
       (9) Avey Johnston.
    h. Mary Johnston, born May 1, 1857; dsp February 1, 1902; married December 2, 1880, Leicester McConnell.
    i. Lora Alice Johnston, born September 18, 1861; died August 11, 1888; married January 4, 1883, to Charles Johnson; children:
       (1) Claudius Johnson, born September 6, 1887; dsp November 7, 1887.
       (2) John C. Johnson; lived in Seattle, Washington.

***

44.   William Henry Johnston was born October 26, 1844, and died in 1926; married (1) March 3, 1861, to Sarah Hazel (2) Madelin Smith; his children were as follows:[65]

(by first marriage):
- a. Etta Rosetta Johnston, born 1861; dsp 1881.
- b. Lucinda May Johnston married January 17, 1889, John Robert Fulton Tate; child:
       (1) Joseph Robert Tate, born 1889; married 1907 Ethel Walls; children:
          (a) Ethel Marie Tate, born 1907.

        (b)   Loretta Tate, born 1909; married 1926 Lavere Gullett;
              children:
              /1/   Clara Lou Gullett, born 1928; dsp 1932.
              /2/   Lyman Robert Gullett, born 1931.
   c.   Josephine Johnston, born 1868; married May 5, 1889, Thomas Hayes;
        children:
        (1)   Bruce Hayes.
        (2)   Gladys Hayes.
        (3)   Thomas Hayes.
        (4)   Glen Hayes.
   d.   John Edward Johnston, born 1870; died September 30, 1956; married
        (1) Sarah Norton (2) October 21, 1894, Mary Etta Tyrell, born July
        29, 1862; died August 3, 1963; children:
        (by first marriage):
        (1)   Ervin Johnston, born July 4, 1892; married Agnes _____ ; chil-
              dren:
              (a)   Jack Johnston, born July 4, 1914.
              (b)   Virginia Johnston, born July 25, 19??.
        (by second marriage):
        (2)   LaVerne F. Johnston, born July 17, 1895; married February 28,
              1914, Clayton Earl Byrket; children:
              (a)   Rosemary Jane Byrket, born February 17, 1915; married
                    August 2, 1941, Robert F. Kors; children:
                    /1/   Robert F. Kors, born October 21, 1942; married 1964
                          Sally Yenko.
                    /2/   Susan Louise Kors, born April 21, 19??.
                    /3/   John E. Kors, born October 17, 1949.
                    /4/   Donald Kors, born March 8, 1951.
              (b)   William E. Byrket, born August 29, 1920; dsp March 27, 1943.
   (by second marriage):
   e.   Walter Johnston.
   f.   Amy Johnston married _____ Davis.

                              ***

45.   Rhoda Johnston was born May 24, 1846, and died March 18, 1916;
      married November 6, 1862, to Albert Perry, born May 23, 1840; died Dec-
      ember 1, 1928. Their children were as follows:[66]

   a.   Mary Elizabeth Perry, born August 21, 1863; died August 28, 1893;
        married April 3, 1889, to Charles Johnson.
   b.   John Perry, born 1864; died 1930; married Molly Mason; children:
        (1)   Charles Perry.
        (2)   Mamie Perry.
        (3)   Harry Perry.
        (4)   Artina Perry.
   c.   George Perry, born November 11, 1867; dsp August 12, 1888.
   d.   Sarah Perry, born 187?; married (1) 1898 George Scoville (2) _____
        McConnell (3) _____ Goodwin; children (all by first marriage):
        (1)   Stella Scoville married _____ Bigelow.
        (2)   Perry Scoville.
        (3)   Harold Scoville.
        (4)   Cecil Scoville.
        (5)   Clarence Scoville.
        (6)   Eugene Scoville.
   e.   Lora Ida Perry, born December 28, 1872; dsp February 28, 1873.
   f.   Cora Perry, born 1874; married January 19, 1899, to H. V. Underwood;
        children:
        (1)   Neva Underwood married Ray Kennedy.

                              105

```
        (2)   Gladys Underwood married (1)  Eulas Peterson (2) Ott Jones.
        (3)   Robert Underwood.
    g.  William L. Perry, born December 21, 187?; dsp January 20, 1889.
    h.  Edward Perry, born May 25, 1876; dsp March 28, 1893.
    i.  Homer Perry, born 1878; died February 13, 1962; married December 25,
        1904, to Mary Fossett; children:
        (1)   Leland F. Perry married Marie Cardwell.
        (2)   Blanche E. Perry married Ralph Sylvester.
        (3)   Dorothy Perry married (1) Claud Sylvester (2) William Hardy.
        (4)   Ida Perry married Clarence Veiglhchild.
        (5)   Ethyl Perry married Jack Veiglhchild.
        (6)   Chester F. Perry.
        (7)   Marjory Perry, dsp.
        (8)   John Perry married Gayle McGlothin.
        (9)   Wayne Perry married Naomi Southern.
        (10)  Jean Perry married Leithel Blackwell.
    j.  Walter Perry, born 1880; dsp 1882.
    k.  Lucille Perry, born 1885; married October 3, 1908, to Fred Brinegar;
        children:
        (1)   Henry Brinegar.
        (2)   Joseph Brinegar.
        (3)   Earnest Brinegar.
        (4)   George Brinegar.
        (5)   Edward Brinegar.
        (6)   Wayne Brinegar.
    l.  Lilly Perry, born 1887; married (1) November 25, 1908, to Charles
        Beyers (2) William Pickel; children (all by first marriage):
        (1)   Clinton Beyers.
        (2)   Mildred Beyers.
        (3)   Charles Beyers.
    m.  Lola Perry, born 1889; married November 25, 1908, to Otis Beyers;
        children:
        (1)   Virginia Beyers.
        (2)   Maxine Beyers.
        (3)   Lloyd Beyers.
        (4)   Anita Beyers.

                                    ***

46.       Robert Johnston was born October 13, 1849, and died April 27, 1931;
    married January 17, 1867, to Sarah A. Bennett, born March 31, 1851; died
    November 8, 1926.  Their children were as follows:[67]

47. a.  Emma Alice Johnston, born 1868.
    b.  Alfred Homer Johnson, born 1870; died 1957; married 1890 Margaret
        Helms; children:
        (1)   Clovis Johnson, born 1891; married (1) June 3, 1910, Goldie
              Boltenhouse (2) December 24, 1913, to Mrs. Myrtle Dunihue.
        (2)   Cletis Johnson, born 1894; married October 13, 1913, Nellie May
              Neill.
        (3)   Cecil Johnson, born 1897; married September 22, 1917, Mary Living-
              ston.
        (4)   Ralph Johnson, born 1901; married Margaret Madaris; dsp.
        (5)   Ramon Johnson, born 1901; married (1) Verna Burton (2) Gladys
              Goble.
        (6)   Hoy Johnson, born 1907; married 1926 Laura Headley.
        (7)   Hazel Johnson, born 1911.
        (8)   Ruby Johnson, born 1913; married 1936 Frederick Hancock.
    c.  Mary Lucinda Johnston, born January 19, 1873; dsp January 18, 1880.
```

d. Edith Edna Johnston, born 1875; died 1913; married 1893 Alvah Mc-
    Connell; children:
    (1) Eva Estell McConnell, born 1894; married James Daniel Beruff.
    (2) Virgil Elrod McConnell, born 1897; married 1918 Ruth Naomi
         Graves.
    (3) Oliva Eliece McConnell, born 1902; married Robert Russell Loesch.
    (4) Effa Maudeline McConnell, born 1904; dsp.
    (5) Christa Lola McConnell, born 1910; dsp 1911.
    (6) Ona Leola McConnell, born 1912; married 1930 Lester Lee Moore.
e. Frederick Johnston, born September 20, 1877; died March 21, 1961;
    married 1902 Mabel Wells; children:
    (1) Lila Pearl Johnston, born 1903; married 1925 William Spoonmore;
         children:
         (a) Robert Dean Spoonmore, born 1929.
         (b) Willa Jean Spoonmore, born 1930.
    (2) Leslie Dent Johnston, born 1907; married 1933 Ruth Edna Horney.
    (3) Russell Lowell Johnston, born 1909; married 1937 Dorothy Wag-
         goner; child:
         (a) Kenneth Johnston, born 1948.
f. Osmond Johnston, born March 4, 1883; dsp January 14, 1900.
48. g. Ona Zella Johnston, born 1887.

***

47.   Emma Alice Johnston was born in 1868 and died in 1952; married 1890
Sylvanus Jackson; their children were as follows:[68]

a. Aldyce Mymal Jackson, born 1891; married (1) Blanche Moore (2) Lola
    Sullivan (3) Leatha Haley; children (all by first marriage):
    (1) Twilah Jackson married (1) James Trissler (2) William Cockrell;
         children (by first marriage):
         (a) Marylu Trissler married Russell Blackburn.
         (b) John Trissler.
         (c) William Trissler.
    (2) Josephine Jackson married Lowell Mood.
    (3) Kathleen Jackson.
    (4) Malin Jackson.
    (5) William Jackson married Jeanette Barns.
    (6) Delores Jackson married Ames Hays.
    (7) Robert Jackson.
    (8) Roberta Jackson.
    (9) Margaret Jackson married _____ Knoop.
b. Opal Isom Jackson, born 1892; married (1) 1917 Mary Ruth McFaddin
    (2) Margaret _____ ; child (by first marriage):
    (1) Betty June Jackson.
c. Nettie Faye Jackson, born 1895; married Gilbert Kern; child:
    (1) Doris Mae Kern, born 1929.

***

48.   Ona Zella Johnston was born in 1887 and married Fred O. Storm in
1906; their children were as follows:[69]

a. Landis Reece Storm, born 1907; married 1931 Ruth Sparks; child:
    (1) Judith Ann Storm.
b. Blanche Marie Storm, born 1909; married 1934 Dale Armstrong; child:
    (1) Stanley Armstrong.
c. Wyoma Berniece Storm, born 1911; married 1929 Albert Roberts; chil-
    dren:

107

```
                    (1)  Joseph Roberts.
                    (2)  Thomas Roberts.
               d.  Mary Faye Ola Storm, born 1919; married William McCurry; children:
                    (1)  William McCurry.
                    (2)  Robert McCurry.
                    (3)  Milly McCurry.
                    (4)  Steven McCurry.
                    (5)  Michael McCurry.
```

***

32.   Eleanor McPherson was born July 18, 1798, in Union County, South
       Carolina, and died May 10, 1856, in Coryell County, Texas; married Oct-
       ober 23, 1821, in Monroe County, Kentucky, to George W. Chism, born Jan-
       uary 25, 1798; died January 23, 1863. Their children were as follows:[70]

```
49.    a.  Julia Ann Chism, born August 15, 1822.
50.    b.  Jehu McPherson Chism, born March 22, 1824.
       c.  George Chism, born October 2, 1825; dsp October 9, 1825.
       d.  Elizabeth Chism, born October 10, 1826; married October 11, 1856, to
            J. Edward Alsop.
       e.  Mary G. Chism, born October 25, 1828; married June 15, 1857, Arthur
            M. Alsop, who died June 10, 1864; children:
            (1)  Lucie E. Alsop, born October 15, 1858; married _____ Lusk; lived
                  in Breckinridge, Texas.
            (2)  Mollie B. Alsop, born May 8, 1860; married December 19, 1877,
                  J. M. Peevey; lived in Lott, Texas; children:
                  (a)  (daughter) married Bruce Storey.
                  (b)  Bonner Peevey.
                  (c)  Lottie Peevey, dsp.
                  (d)  Arthur Peevey lived in Woodson, Texas.
                  (e)  Nelle Peevey married J. D. Marrs; lived in Santa Monica,
                        California.
            (3)  Alice A. Alsop, born January 17, 1862.
       f.  Hiram Chism, born September 2, 1830; dsp May 18, 1864.
       g.  Margery V. Chism, born December 15, 1832; married June 17, 1858, to
            John F. Davidson; children (perhaps among others):
            (1)  Mark W. Davidson, born April 5, 1859.
            (2)  Sina A. Davidson, born January 8, 1861.
            (3)  Aaron C. Davidson, born February 7, 1863.
            (4)  Francis A. Davidson, born September 3, 1865.
            (5)  Mary E. Davidson, born September 17, 1867.
            (6)  Ira G. Davidson, born February 22, 1870.
       h.  Rachel Chism, born June 11, 1835; married January 24, 1869, to Robert
            Kidd.
       i.  Rebecca Chism, born May 13, 1838; married April 21, 1864, to Ira B.
            Sadler.
       j.  Ellen Chism, born February 27, 1841; married January 8, 1861, to John
            M. Webster.
       k.  Benjamin Chism, born October 10, 1842; dsp February 28, 1856.
```

***

49.   Julia Ann Chism was born August 15, 1822, and died May, 1909; mar-
       ried October 14, 1841, to Nicholas Nathaniel Dawson, who was born April
       28, 1819, and died March 26, 1897; their children were as follows:[71]

```
       a.  James H. Dawson, born July 8, 1842; died October 17, 1921; married
            February 6, 1866, to America A. Sparks.
```

b. John W. Dawson, born March 15, 1844; died April 12, 1910.
c. William M. Dawson, born February 23, 1846; died October 11, 1869.
d. Mollie M. Dawson, born December 29, 1847; died August 21, 1873; married February 4, 1869, to William H. Glenn; children:
    (1) Willie J. Glenn, born February 9, 1870.
    (2) Annie F. Glenn, born March 30, 1872; dsp July 24, 1873.
e. George C. Dawson, born January 28, 1850; died November 5, 1880; married December 1, 1878, to Fannie Kerr.
f. Thomas N. Dawson, born January 1, 1852; died 1923; married December 11, 1879, to Laura Cogdell.
g. Pleasant Hiram Dawson, born March 23, 1854; died September, 1939; married February 13, 1877, to Clara Brous; children (perhaps among others):
    (1) Jimmie Hallie Dawson, born December 4, 1877; dsp; lived in Ft. Worth, Texas.
    (2) Nettie Leigh Dawson, born August 2, 1879.
    (3) Annie Dawson, born October 16, 1881; married Leonard Mitchell; lived in Ft. Worth, Texas.
    (4) Edwin Hanneford Dawson, born May 19, 1883.
h. Kemper J. Dawson, born July 2, 1857.
51. i. Rebecca Belle Dawson, born April 14, 1861.
j. Joseph A. Dawson, born October 21, 1868; married December, 1895, Una Cryer.

***

51.   Rebecca Belle Dawson was born April 14, 1861, and died December 3, 1944, in Houston, Texas; married November 6, 1878, to James Lunsford Wheeless, who was born April 30, 1855, and died November 13, 1896; their children were as follows:

52. a. Justin Lorenzo Wheeless, born January 6, 1881.
b. Silvester Vivian Wheeless, born May 18, 1883; dsp.
c. Silveetus John Wheeless, born January 24, 1885; dsp 1906, at Welborne, Texas.
d. Bertha Belle Wheeless, born April 25, 1888; died February 15, 1967; married 1909 Percy Foster Knight, who died May 30, 1930; children:
    (1) Alice Agnes Knight, born November 22, 1910; married July, 1928, Maynor Thompson; child:
        (a) Charles Lynn Thompson married December 21, 1957, to Janice Louise Warncke; children:
            /1/ Jeffrey Thompson.
            /2/ Stephen Thompson, born September, 1963.
    (2) Alan Lunsford Knight, born January 1, 1914; married Daisy Lee Shepherd; child:
        (a) Shepherd Foster Knight, born February 21, 1949.
    (3) Bertha Julia Knight, born January 21, 1917; married (1) March 2, 1942, to Harris H. Morvant (2) May, 1955, Pete Bernard.
e. Annie Rebecca Wheeless, born May 9, 1890; married (1) December 23, 1918, to Rosemond Berard, who died September 9, 1937; (2) July 8, 1947, to John T. King.
f. Lunsford James Wheeless, born July 21, 1893; died February 4, 1962; married November 25, 1913, to Julia Terry; children:
    (1) Lucile Ann Wheeless, born December 30, 1915; married May 4, 1940, to Lewis William Knowles, who died September, 1964; dsp.
    (2) Mildred Mary Wheeless, born September 9, 1917; dsp.
    (3) Helen Ruth Wheeless, born September 15, 1919; dsp.
    (4) James Terry Wheeless, born December 2, 1931; married Lois Ferree; children:

                    (a) James Terry Wheeless, born December 9, 1955.
                    (b) Kim Ann Wheeless, born June 27, 1957.
          g. Jessie Dawson Wheeless, born February 25, 1895; married (1) David
              Gore (2) November 28, 1928, to Roy Brunt; lived in Houston, Texas;
              children:
              (by first marriage):
              (1) Jessie Ruth Gore, born November 6, 1916; married (1) Gordon
                   White (2) Robert Kirkwood; children:
                   (by first marriage):
                   (a) Patricia Ann White, born July, 1938.
                   (b) David White, born November 1, 1941.
                   (by second marriage):
                   (c) Robert Roy Kirkwood.
              (by second marriage):
              (2) Royce Ann Brunt, born February 2, 1934; married August 28, 1952,
                   to Albert Eugene Woodard; children:
                   (a) Cathy May Woodard, born 1954.
                   (b) Susan Woodard.
                   (c) Daniel Woodard.

                                      ***

52.   Justin Lorenzo Wheeless was born January 6, 1881, at Granbury, Texas,
        and died August 12, 1941, in El Campo, Texas; married January 18, 1903,
        to Willie Emma Heaver; their children were as follows:[73]

53. a. Ruth Aylene Wheeless, born November 3, 1903.
     b. Valta Ellafare Wheeless, born February 7, 1907; married September 10,
         1927, Albert Rich; children:
         (1) Geraldine Rich, born June 1, 1928; married November 1, 1947,
              Dempsey Dearman; children:
              (a) John Charles Dearman, born October 20, 1948.
              (b) Sherry Lynn Dearman, born October 22, 1949; married February
                   1, 1967, Jerry Jordan.
              (c) Gary Mac Dearman, born January 27, 1951.
         (2) George Clinton Rich, born March 10, 1933.
         (3) Hallie Joan Rich, born May 17, 1939; married December 26, 1961,
              Roy Pete Gunter; child:
              (a) Randall Pete Gunter, born October 31, 1963.
     c. Joseph Alfred Wheeless, born March 3, 1909; dsp September 18, 1926.
     d. Annie Belle Wheeless, born August 7, 1912; married (1) _____ DeFoor
         (2) January 10, 1945, James Flowers; children:
         (by first marriage):
         (1) Karen Joyce DeFoor, born June 6, 1936; married (1) June, 1954,
              Fred Jones (2) July 4, 1957, Lewis Moore; children (both by
              second marriage):
              (a) Dianna Lee Moore, born December 30, 1959; dsp August 2, 1960.
              (b) Kari Clayton Moore, born August 6, 1961.
         (by second marriage):
         (2) Dianna Merle Flowers, born January 29, 1946; married March 18,
              1966, Thomas Mancuso.
         (3) Janice Lee Flowers, born March 21, 1948.
54. e. Jesse Gore Wheeless, born October 8, 1914.
     f. Alba Joyce Wheeless, born October 4, 1917; married October 30, 1937,
         Michael Hunt Ardre, born June 13, 1913; children:
         (1) Betty Ruth Ardre, born August 11, 1938; married February 5, 1960,
              Paul Stephen Gupton; child:
              (a) Stephen Todd Gupton, born September 30, 1966.
         (2) Michael Hunt Amdre, born December 11, 1941.

                                      110

g. George Henry Wheeless, born January 27, 1920; married December 5, 1945, Mary Adams; children:
    (1) Grace Marie Wheeless, born September 29, 1946; married 1963 Richard DeHart.
    (2) Mary Louise Wheeless, born February 8, 1948.
    (3) George Henry Wheeless, born May 15, 1949.
    (4) Willie Emma Wheeless, born August 8, 1950.
    (5) Paul David Wheeless, born October 30, 1951.
h. Young Barnett Wheeless, born May 5, 1922; married August 27, 1945, to Norma Faye Gollnick; lived in Houston, Texas; children:
    (1) William Richard Wheeless, born October 5, 1952.
    (2) Katherine Elizabeth Wheeless, born September 20, 1956.
    (3) Nora Faye Wheeless, born December, 1957.
i. Emma Nelle Wheeless, born March 31, 1926; married December 18, 1943, to Homer Carl Roades; lived in El Campo, Texas; children:
    (1) Billie Ruth Roades, born August 5, 1945; married February 5, 1965, to Charles Ervin Richter.
    (2) Margaret Faye Roades, born May 8, 1947.
    (3) Carla Ann Roades, born October 22, 1955.
    (4) Homer Carl Roades, born August 8, 1962.

***

53.   Ruth Aylene Wheeless was born November 3, 1903; married December 31, 1923, to Elmer Ned Byers, who was born May 19, 1897, in Birmingham, Iowa, and died March 17, 1965, in Houston, Texas; their children were as follows:[74]

a. Elmer Ross Byers, born March 4, 1925; married April 21, 1952, to Mrs. Hilda Adelaide (San Martin) Maas; child:
    (1) Cheryl Ann Byers, born December 10, 1952.
b. Billy Deane Byers, born November 17, 1928; married April 4, 1953, to Marie Isabelle San Martin; lived in Houston, Texas; children:
    (1) Debra Deane Byers, born January 18, 1954.
    (2) David Ross Byers, born September 6, 1955.
    (3) Susan Marie Byers, born February 1, 1957.
    (4) Priscilla Kay Byers, born April 13, 1959.
c. Robert Earl Byers, born March 5, 1941; married April 27, 1962, to Florence Elizabeth Williams; lived in Houston, Texas; child:
    (1) Joel Wayne Byers, born March 13, 1963.

***

54.   Jesse Gore Wheeless was born October 8, 1914; married October 13, 1934, to Elvie Rowe; their children were as follows:[75]

a. Jesse Lorenzo Wheeless, born July 24, 1935; married May 6, 1956, to Lois Miller Greer; child:
    (1) Sharon Annette Wheeless, born November 7, 1959.
b. Sam Wayne Wheeless, born October 29, 1936; married (1) April, 1953, Patricia Mae Harvey (2) Dixie Toni Haddash; children:
    (by first marriage):
    (1) Mark Prentiss Wheeless, born November 23, 1953.
    (2) Carol Yvette Wheeless, born December 6, 1955.
    (by second marriage):
    (3) Janet Lynn Wheeless.

***

111

50.   Jehu McPherson Chism was born March 22, 1824; married August 4, 1850, to Sarah A. Hackworth; their children were as follows:[76]

a. James Marshall Chism, born October 10, 1851; married (1) Mary Jane Richardson (2) Almeda V. McCready; children:
    (by first marriage):
    (1) Frank Key Chism, born January 2, 1876; lived in Escondido, California.
    (2) Sallie Kate Chism, born March 6, 1878; died January 14, 1961; married _____ Jones; lived in Throckmorton, Texas.
    (3) Jehu Thomas Chism, born November 25, 1879; died November 25, 1950; lived in Hamlin, Texas.
    (by second marriage):
    (4) Viola Chism.
    (5) McPherson Chism.
    (6) Eliza Chism.
    (7) Edward Alsop Chism, born January 21, 1889.
    (8) Almeda Chism.
    (9) John Chism.
    (10) Ida Chism.
    (11) Willborn Chism.
b. Dr. Matthew Hackworth Chism, born March 18, 1854, in Tippah County, Mississippi; died February 23, 1952, in Huntsville, Texas; married September 2, 1883, to Mary Kirk Brown, who was born July 8, 1864, and died March 3, 1918; children:
    (1) Sarah Frances Chism, born July 13, 1884; died January 18, 1961, in Huntsville, Texas; married August 28, 1913, to Joseph Lynn Clark, who was born July 27, 1881, and died September 13, 1969.
    (2) Kester Kirk Chism, born March 24, 1888; dsp July 24, 1893.
    (3) Aytchie Hermine Chism, born June 3, 1890; married June 18, 1923, to Francis Augustus McCray, who was born August 28, 1888, and died September 14, 1960; lived in Huntsville, Texas.
c. Katherine Chism married Benjamin Williams.
d. George W. Chism married Addie M. Boles.
e. Oscar Johnson Chism, died 1940.
f. Jehu Willborn Chism.

***

33.   Benjamin Nicholls McPherson was born June 18, 1810, in Barren (now Monroe) County, Kentucky, where he died in October, 1883. He was sheriff of Monroe County in 1850; he had the following children:[77]

(by an unknown woman):
a. James Harrison McPherson, born December 11, 1844; died June 19, 1922, in Monroe County, Kentucky; married (1) America Allee, born January 11, 1855; died January 23, 1887; (2) Fanny Ferguson (3) 1899, Mrs. Mary E. (Padgett) Smith; children (all by first marriage):
    (1) Flora Belle McPherson, born October 1, 1877; dsp March 20, 1943.
    (2) Benjamin Chester McPherson, born February 7, 1881; died 1964; married (1) Nettie J. Billingsley (2) Mary Maines; children:
        (by first marriage):
        (a) James S. McPherson, born February 28, 1918; dsp October 25, 1924.
        (b) Philip McPherson, married Thelma Crowe; lived in Louisville, Kentucky.
        (c) Ruth McPherson married William Benedict; lived in Fowler, Indiana.

112

(by second marriage):
    (d) Marilyn McPherson.
  (3) Clara Wayne McPherson, born September 2, 1883; died September 27, 1921; married August 20, 1902, to Archie Nathaniel Gentry, born December 22, 1876; died December 9, 1960; son of Turner Gentry and Lou White; children:
    (a) Myrtle Margaret Gentry, born September 7, 1903; dsp; lived in Tompkinsville, Kentucky.
    (b) Emma Gladys Gentry, born February 20, 1908; married Marlin G. Howard; lived in Tompkinsville, Kentucky; children:
      /1/ James Wayne Howard.
      /2/ William G. Howard.
      /3/ Wilson Cleo Howard.
      /4/ Clinton Howard.
      /5/ Rosemary Howard.
    (c) Ilma Florine Gentry, born August 24, 1909; married Oakley Dugard; dsp; lived in Mt. Herman, Kentucky.
    (d) Glen Max Gentry, born November 8, 1915; married Betty Lester; child:
      /1/ Glen Max Gentry.
    (e) James Archie Gentry, born November 22, 1922; married Mary Jo Merriweather; children:
      /1/ Betty Jo Gentry married William Patton.
      /2/ James Archie Gentry.
      /3/ Georgette Gentry.
      /4/ Jamie Gentry.

(by Eliza Goodman):
55. b. Rufus Morgan McPherson, born March 25, 1853.
56. c. Lou Ella McPherson, born May 17, 1867.
57. d. Benjamin Nicholls McPherson, born October 5, 1868.
    e. Molly McPherson, born April 9, 1870; died young.
    f. Margery McPherson, born April 9, 1870; died young.

                    ***

55.   Rufus Morgan McPherson was born March 25, 1853, in Monroe County, Kentucky, and died there March 20, 1935. He married (1) Anna Belle Hayes daughter of Jefferson Hayes and Mary Meadows; (2) September 23, 1893, to Marcellus Hagan, born June 7, 1866; died March 23, 1946. Among others, he had the following children:[78]

(by first marriage):
a. Nora McPherson, born May 19, 1877; dsp April 12, 1960; married April 12, 1902, to J. Wood Denham, born October 30, 1872; died February 8, 1957.
b. Laura McPherson, born June 30, 1879; died March, 1926; married 1903 Moton C. Denham, born March, 1876; died October, 1951; children:
  (1) Leonard Guy Denham, born November 17, 1903; married Mary Eliza Humes; lived in Illinois; child:
    (a) Clinton Denham, born November 23, 1926.
  (2) Anna Ellen Denham, born 1907; married Nim Myatt; children:
    (a) Edith Myatt, born 1931; dsp 1932.
    (b) Dane Myatt.
    (c) Robert Myatt.
c. Luda McPherson, born June 30, 1879; died November 20, 1950; married November 29, 1916, to Roma Jackson; children:
  (1) Hattie Jackson, born November 6, 1917; dsp December 28, 1944.
  (2) Hettie Jackson, born November 6, 1917; married Marvin Holman.
  (3) Clara Jackson, married Joseph Stone.

        (4) Anna Lois Jackson, born May 5, 1923; dsp September 28, 1948.
    d. Oscar McPherson, born November 8, 1881; dsp September 12, 1928.
    (by second marriage):

58. e. Edd McPherson, born December 17, 1893.
59. f. Ada McPherson, born March 31, 1895.
    g. Brent McPherson, born September 20, 1899; married Emma Pedigo; lived
       in Tompkinsville, Kentucky; children:
       (1) Neva Nell McPherson married Dade High.
       (2) Wallace McPherson married Ruth Emmert.
       (3) Jack McPherson married Willadean Sprowls.
       (4) Ruth Ann McPherson.
       (5) Jean McPherson married Fred Bartley.
       (6) Jeanette McPherson married Gene Harlin.
    h. Ben McPherson, born April 15, 1902; married January 16, 1923, to
       Beatrice Rush; children:
       (1) Richard McPherson.
       (2) Alma Dean McPherson.
    i. Jack McPherson, born October 4, 1904; married July 9, 1926, to Velma
       Frodge; child:
       (1) Randall McPherson, born April 1, 1928; married Beatrice Brown;
           lived in Burkesville, Kentucky; children:
           (a) Venita McPherson, born September 4, 1948.
           (b) Sherrill McPherson, born March 31, 1950.
           (c) Ricky McPherson, born April 2, 1957.
           (d) Mark McPherson, born April 3, 1960.
    g. Jesse McPherson, born October 4, 1904; died young.

***

58.   Edd McPherson was born in 1893; married April 12, 1920, to Pearl
Harlan. They lived in Monroe County, Kentucky, and their children were
as follows:[79]

    a. Rufus Reed McPherson married Olene Wade; lived in Tompkinsville, Ken-
       tucky.
    b. Ruby Jewel McPherson married August 12, 1945, to Wallace McPherson
       (see p. 101).
    c. Delma Lee McPherson, born June 21, 1924; dsp September 27, 1946.
    d. Mary Ruth McPherson married Hoyt Clark.
    e. Rex Elmer McPherson married Edith Brown.
    f. Robert Edd McPherson married Jean Ferguson.
    g. Roger McPherson married Juanita Hedrick.
    h. Royce McPherson married Dean Woods.
    i. Rachel McPherson married Adrian Crowe.
    j. Robbie Dane McPherson, born November 11, 1938; dsp November 19, 1938.
    k. Phyllis McPherson married Roger Turner.
    l. Reggie McPherson.

***

59.   Ada McPherson was born March 31, 1895, in Monroe County, Kentucky,
and died January 30, 1961, in Chatsworth, Illinois; married June 13, 1915,
to J. E. Curtis; their children were as follows:[80]

    a. Harlan Lynwood Curtis married Janette Beck; children:
       (1) John Arthur Curtis.
       (2) Nora Lynn Curtis.
       (3) James Beck Curtis.
       (4) Thomas Dale Curtis.

     (5) Marilyn Joann Curtis.
b. Lovell Dale Curtis, dsp.
c. Rufus Jacob Curtis died November, 1950; married Nellie Weaver; children:
     (1) Katherine Ann Curtis.
     (2) Robert Dale Curtis.
d. Marilyn Runell Curtis married Robert Grant Fields; children:
     (1) Roger Bruce Fields.
     (2) Brian Mark Fields.
     (3) Randall Todd Fields.

***

56.   Lou Ella McPherson was born May 17, 1867; died September 26, 1949, in Monroe County, Kentucky; married December 28, 1883, to Samuel Turner Ferguson, born January 15, 1865; died July 14, 1927, son of Sparrel Ferguson and Charlotte Harris. Their children were as follows:[81]

a. Maud Ferguson, born October 27, 1884; married November 26, 1911, to Charles Monroe Thomas, born April 30, 1877, son of Joseph Thomas and Martha Geralds; dsp.
60. b. Buford Ferguson, born May 23, 1887.
61. c. Millard Ferguson, born December 7, 1890.
d. Clarence Ferguson, born May 11, 1892; married January 9, 1921, to Ivie Bowles; dsp; lived in Atterbury, Illinois.
e. Annie Ferguson, born November 16, 1894; married February 22, 1914, to Ovil T. Bybee, born January 29, 1893, son of William Owen Bybee and Ann Toy Bartley; lived in Freedom, Kentucky; children:
     (1) Cloteel Bybee, born February 5, 1917; married February 24, 1934, to Ernest Moore (see Trimble, Hiestand Family of Page County, Virginia).
     (2) Lunelle Bybee, born May 20, 1921; married December 15, 1943, to John H. Moore (see Trimble, Hiestand Family of Page County, Virginia).
     (3) Glen Mac Bybee, born November 11, 1929; married May 7, 1954, to Mrs. Marxie (Jeffrey) Billingsley.
f. Cecil Ferguson, born April 8, 1901; married December 29, 1925, to Ocie Hamilton, daughter of James Thomas Hamilton and Evie Lane; children:
     (1) Glenn Edward Ferguson, born September 26, 1926; married Patricia Fruits; children:
        (a) Glenda Ferguson.
        (b) Candace Ferguson.
        (c) Michael Ferguson.
     (2) Kenneth Ferguson, born January, 1930; dsp May 30, 1950.

***

60.   Buford Ferguson was born May 23, 1887; married January 3, 1908, to Quintella Kingrey, born December 6, 1884, daughter of Elijah Kingrey and Sarah Grimsley; lived in Illinois; their children were as follows:[82]

a. Sarah Ferguson, born September 26, 1908; married December 27, 1930, to Delmar Lake, born July 1, 1912; children:
     (1) Vernon Lake.
     (2) Patricia Lake.
     (3) Ella Mae Lake.
b. Mary Ferguson, born April 8, 1910; married March 10, 1940, to Henry Warsow, born February 28, 1908; child:

115

(1) Linda Warsow, born April 25, 1950.
c. Sam Ferguson, born August 26, 1911; married Erma Powell, born January 25, 1918; child:
(1) Glenda Ferguson, born January 18, 1946.
d. Blondine Ferguson, born April 18, 1913; married June 29, 1937, to John Bradford; child:
(1) Deanne Bradford married Richard Kreig.
e. Ora Ferguson, born May 3, 1918; married September, 1940, Christian Boyd; child:
(1) Tracey Leray Boyd, born December 28, 19??.
f. Voit Ferguson, born July 20, 1920; married Betty Burgess; children:
(1) Melody Ferguson.
(2) Sandra Ferguson.
g. Faye Ferguson, born August 5, 1922; married William Boyd; children:
(1) Kay Boyd.
(2) Donna Boyd.
h. Verman Ferguson, born December 12, 1924; married Luetta Cline; children:
(1) Dana Ferguson.
(2) Debbie Ferguson.
(3) Dwayne Ferguson.
i. Paul Ferguson, born May 24, 1927; married November 19, 1954, to Charlotte Myer.

**

61.   Millard Ferguson was born December 7, 1890; married January 20, 1920, to Lillie Walker, born January 30, 1899; they lived in Illinois and their children were as follows:[83]

a. Conley Ferguson, born May 28, 1920; married Willodee Bromlee; children:
(1) Stephen Ferguson.
(2) Marshie Ferguson.
(3) Debbie Ferguson.
(4) Christie Ferguson.
(5) Roger Ferguson.
b. Imogene Ferguson, born October 29, 1922; married John Lovley; children:
(1) Keith Lovley.
(2) Ronnie Lovley.
(3) Genie Lovley.
c. Geraldine Ferguson, born December 14, 1924; married Victor Reyniers; child:
(1) Pamela Gay Reyniers.
d. Millard Ferguson, born April 24, 1926; married Norma Degraodt; children:
(1) Kathie Ferguson.
(2) Donna Ferguson.
e. Wilma Ferguson, born January 10, 1928; married Lyle Dehm; children:
(1) Angie Dehm.
(2) Jeff Dehm.
(3) Eric Dehm.
f. Mary Ruth Ferguson, born June 24, 1929; married Leonard Therien; children:
(1) Linda Therien.
(2) Greg Therien.
(3) Sherry Therien.

116

  (4) Mark Therien.
g. Edith Ann Ferguson, born January 27, 1931; married Earl Robbins, born
  December 29, 1919; children:
  (1) Lynn Ann Robbins.
  (2) Charles Robbins.
  (3) Pam Robbins.
h. Clarence Dudley Ferguson, born November 18, 1932; married Karen Mies,
  born April 27, 1938; children:
  (1) Susan Ferguson.
  (2) Richard Ferguson.
i. Patricia Louise Ferguson, born July 15, 1936; married Neil Hornickle;
  children:
  (1) Cindy Hornickle.
  (2) Vicki Hornickle.
  (3) Lori Hornickle.
  (4) Richard Hornickle.
j. Larry Ferguson, born April 24, 1937; dsp 1960.
k. Rodney Joe Ferguson, born February 1, 1940; married Karen McCormick;
  child:
  (1) Chris Ferguson.
l. Marjory Lynn Ferguson, born March 26, 1944.

***

57.   Benjamin Nicholls McPherson was born October 5, 1868, in Monroe
County, Kentucky, and died there on November 17, 1948; married (1) November 1, 1888, to Angie Pitcock, born March 15, 1867; died October 18,
1898; (2) February 26, 1902, to Eunice Bray, born July 5, 1870; died
December 27, 1903; (3) 1912 to Mrs. Evie (Wax) Page, born October 19,
1877; died November 29, 1956. His children were as follows:[84]

(by first marriage):
a. Donna McPherson, born September 6, 1889; died June 17, 1952; married
  February 24, 1917, J. Groves McCreary, born May 24, 1881; died September 20, 1949; child:
  (1) Darrell McCreary lived in Indiana.
b. Bronner McPherson, born March 18, 1891; married (1) Ida Rhoten (2)
  Ada Gosnell; children (all by first marriage):
  (1) Virginia McPherson married Melvin Hinthorn.
  (2) Jim Bonner McPherson lived in Illinois.
  (3) Nelle Mitchell McPherson married Acie Droll; lived in Decatur,
    Illinois.
  (4) George McPherson lived in Bloomington, Illinois.
  (5) Harry Allen McPherson married Ann Ridenour.
  (6) Jerry Fred McPherson lived in Maine.
  (7) Mary Jo McPherson married Charles Carter; lived in Illinois.
c. Fred McPherson, born December 13, 1892; dsp October 2, 1919.
d. Dewey McPherson, born February 3, 1895; died October 21, 1966; married
  February 5, 1920, Silvia McCaughey; lived in Cullom, Illinois; children:
  (1) Gerald McPherson.
  (2) Kenneth McPherson.
  (3) Irma McPherson married _____ Palmer.
  (4) Peggy McPherson married _____ Reiniche.
  (5) Phyllis McPherson married _____ McDermott.
e. Betty M. McPherson, born February 9, 1897; married Basil Hammer; child:
  (1) Randall Hammer.
(by third marriage):
f. Clarice McPherson, born May 16, 1913; married Findlay Proffitt; lived
  in Monroe County, Kentucky.

117

g. Jessie Marrs McPherson, born April 10, 1916.
h. Hughie N. McPherson, born October 5, 1917; married Olene McMillin.
i. Ruth McPherson, born February 26, 1919.

***

2.   Daniel McPherson was born about 1722 in Chester County, Pennsylvania, and moved to Berkeley (now Jefferson) County, (West) Virginia,
where he was a member of Hopewell Friends Meeting. He made his will on
June 21, 1786; the estate was probated April 22, 1789. He married Mary
Richardson in Chester County, Pennsylvania, and their children were as
follows:[85]

a. William McPherson, born c1749; married Jane Chamberlain.
b. Ruth McPherson, born November 27, 1751; died September 15, 1821;
   married May 12, 1785, to Aquilla Janney, born October 16, 1758; died
   1805.
c. John McPherson, born c1753; married Hannah Bond.
d. Daniel McPherson married January 7, 1790, Martha Beeson, daughter of
   Edward and Jane Beeson; lived in Fairfax County, Virginia.
e. Mary McPherson /married Nathan Haines?7.
f. Isaac McPherson.
g. Rebecca McPherson married April 7, 1790, Joseph Neill.
h. Ann McPherson.

***

3.   William McPherson was born about 1726 in Chester County, Pennsylvania, and married (1) July 6, 1747, Margaret Trego; (2) about 1753 Phoebe
Passmore. He moved to Orange (now Chatham) County, North Carolina, in
1755, and died there about 1817, leaving the following children:[86]

(by first marriage):
a. Mary McPherson, born October 14, 1749; married Thomas Braxton, born
   June 10, 1744; died September 26, 1815.
b. Othneil McPherson, born c1751; married Christian _____.
(by second marriage):
c. Ruth McPherson /married David Johnson?7.
62.   d. William McPherson, born October 4, 1758.
e. Daniel McPherson married Mary /Evans?7.
f. Margaret McPherson married Jesse Pierce.
63.   g. John McPherson.
h. Phoebe McPherson married Aaron Lindley, born January 30, 1768; died
   August 10, 1845, son of Thomas Lindley and Sarah Evans; children:
   (1) Thomas Lindley married Mary Long.
   (2) William Lindley married Sarah Long.
   (3) Joshua Lindley married Judith M. Henley.
   (4) Sarah Lindley married Joshua Hadley.
   (5) David Lindley married Mary Hadley.
   (6) Aaron Lindley married (1) Ann Justice (2) Elizabeth B. Cary.
   (7) James Lindley married Ruth Hadley.
   (8) Ruth Lindley married Robert McCracken.
   (9) John Lindley married Camela Meachem.
   (10) Owen Lindley married (1) Temperance Meachem (2) Basha Elliott.
   (11) Phoebe Lindley married Abner Sanborn.
   (12) Edward Lindley.
i. Mary McPherson married Edward Stuart.
j. Ann McPherson married John Crutchfield.
k. Edith McPherson married Mark Morgan.

118

1. Enoch McPherson died 1837 in Chatham County, North Carolina; married
   Paray Neal; children:
   (1) Mary McPherson married Willis Dark.
   (2) William Enoch McPherson married January 22, 1839, Nancy Dark;
       children:
       (a) William McPherson.
       (b) Samuel McPherson.
       (c) Gray McPherson.
       (d) John D. McPherson married Sarah Dixon; children (perhaps
           among others):
           /1/ Caleb McPherson married Deborah McPherson (see p. 121);
               children:
               /a/ Dora McPherson married Robert Whitesell.
               /b/ Wade McPherson married Elsie Boggs.
               /c/ Beatrice McPherson married (1) Simon Teague (2)
                   Wiley Hathcock.
               /d/ Mabel McPherson married (1) Samuel Bivens (2)
                   Thomas Coleman.
           /2/ Lawrence McPherson married Maud McPherson (see p. 121);
               children:
               /a/ Nannie McPherson.
               /b/ Beryl McPherson married Troy Moser.
               /c/ Grace McPherson.
               /d/ Leonard McPherson.
       (e) Susan McPherson married David Dixon.
       (f) Nancy McPherson.
   (3) Eli McPherson.
   (4) Sarah McPherson married Abner Perry.

                              ***

62.   William McPherson was born October 4, 1758, in Orange (now Chatham)
   County, North Carolina; he moved to Anderson County, South Carolina, where
   he died August 8, 1832. He married Elizabeth Gillilan, born April 12,
   1766; died May 30, 1848, daughter of John and Sarah Gillilan. Their
   children were as follows:[87]

   a. Elisha McPherson married Dorcas _____.
   b. William McPherson, born April 24, 1786; died July 7, 1870, in Ran-
      dolph County, Alabama; married Eleanor McGee, born c1800; died Sept-
      ember 7, 1855; children:
      (1) Ruth Ann McPherson, born January 8, 1820; died August 14, 1872,
          in Randolph County, Alabama; married May 20, 1841, to Samuel
          Madison Cole, born May 5, 1818; died March 24, 1889, son of
          Samuel Madison Cole and Charlotte Blanche Harper; children:
          (a) Melissa Ann Cole, born April 7, 1842; died October 2, 1913,
              in Rusk County, Texas; married Joseph Clifford Demerval
              Rushton, son of Joseph Rushton and Martha Lorance.
          (b) William Samuel Cole, born November 6, 1843; died January
              14, 1941, in Lindale, Texas; married (1) Elizabeth Speights
              (2) Virginia Curry.
          (c) Augustus Magee Cole, born April 13, 1846; died August 29,
              1923, in Randolph County, Alabama; married Emily Jordan.
          (d) Claudius Harper Cole, born February 11, 1848; died August
              12, 1936, in Randolph County, Alabama; married Louisa
              Delilah Gaunt.
          (e) Benjamin Cole, dsp.
          (f) Demetrius Cole, dsp.

                              119

(g) Charlotte Cole, born July 19, 1856; died March 10, 1937, in Houston, Texas; married _____ Randall.
(h) Eleanor Cole, born July 19, 1856; died January 4, 1939, in Elgin, Texas; married _____ Lane.
(2) John McPherson, dsp March, 1830.
(3) Rebecca McPherson, dsp.
(4) Benjamin F. McPherson, born September 12, 1825; died July 17, 1909; married November 14, 1944, to Emily Prothro.
(5) Cyrus McPherson, dsp March, 1830.
c. John McPherson married Elizabeth Prothro.
d. Elijah McPherson.
e. Mary McPherson, born November 8, 1792; died September 30, 1839; married James Gunnin.
f. Salina McPherson married Matthew Earp, born July 12, 1797; lived in Cherokee County, Alabama.
g. Sarah McPherson married Elijah Browne.
h. Phoebe McPherson married Arthur McFall.
i. Malinda McPherson married Samuel McGee.
j. Louisiana McPherson married Joshua Fields; lived in Atlanta, Georgia.
k. Nancy McPherson married Darius Brown, born 1790; died 1849; lived in Coffee County, Tennessee.
l. Eleanor McPherson married Dennis Stell; lived in Gwinnett County, Georgia.
m. Elizabeth McPherson married _____ Stevenson.

***

63.   John McPherson died in Chatham County, North Carolina; he married Hannah _____ and left the following children (perhaps among others):[88]

a. William McPherson, born 1789; died 1871 in Alamance County, North Carolina; married Sarah Hadley, born 1788; died 1854; children:
(1) John McPherson married March 17, 1834, Mary Lindley.
(2) William McPherson married (1) Caroline Brower (2) Celia Hill.
(3) Hannah McPherson married Buck Hadley.
(4) Anna McPherson married Balaam Hornaday.
(5) Oliver McPherson, born July 20, 1823; died 1902 in Alamance County, North Carolina; married (1) Deborah Newlin, born November 23, 1823; died 1851; daughter of John Newlin and Rebecca Long; (2) April 27, 1852, Malinda Lamb, born 1824; died 1898; children: (by first marriage):
(a) John Will McPherson, born 1843; dsp 1862.
(b) Thomas Newlin McPherson, born 1846; married Cornelia Workman; children:
/1/ Minter McPherson married Georgia Allen.
/2/ Edward McPherson.
/3/ Charles McPherson.
/4/ Oliver McPherson.
/5/ Elzie McPherson.
/6/ Florrie McPherson.
/7/ Debbie McPherson married Rufus Mann.
64.   (c) James M. McPherson, born 1849.
(d) Addison V. McPherson, born February 23, 1851; died August, 1909, in Indiana; married August 18, 1874, Louisa Jane Gurley, born August 15, 1856; died February 20, 1916; children:
/1/ Dora Ione McPherson, born October 23, 1877; dsp November 20, 1965; married October 7, 1907, William H.

Henley, born December 5, 1882; died October 18, 1967.

/2/ Carrie Elma McPherson, born July 29, 1887; died April
20, 1963; married August 25, 1908, George Alpha Farmer,
born January 29, 1887; died April 20, 1963; child:
/a/ Dorothy Irene Farmer, born November 12, 1909; married June 2, 1930, Owen L. Prescott, born September 5, 1911; dsp; lived in Mooresville, Indiana.
/3/ Chester Arthur McPherson, born January 21, 1890; dsp
April 2, 1943; married (1) Mary Trusler, born 1893;
died 1927; (2) Bess Sink Hadley.

(by second marriage):
(e) Leanna McPherson, born 1856; dsp 1925; married John Thompson.
(f) Oliver Orren McPherson, born 1862; died 1925; married Victoria Russell; children:
/1/ Broadie McPherson married Swannie Payne.
/2/ Bessie McPherson married Odis Robertson.
/3/ Leslie McPherson married Emma Johnson.
/4/ Mary McPherson married Julius Payne.

b. James McPherson married Mary Conklin; children (perhaps among others):
(1) William McPherson married Mary Patterson.
(2) Ingram McPherson married (1) Lucinda York, daughter of Braxton
York and Mary Elliott; (2) Luena Edwards; child (perhaps among
others):
(a) Lizzie McPherson, born 1855; died 1878; married James M.
McPherson (see below).

***

64.   James M. McPherson was born in 1849 and died 1927 in Alamance County,
North Carolina; married (1) Lizzie McPherson (see above);   (2) Nancy
Clark; his children were as follows:[89]

(by first marriage):
a. Minnie McPherson, born September 29, 1874; married Albert L. Foust
(see p. 151).
b. Lonnie McPherson, born January, 1878; dsp May, 1878.
(by second marriage):
c. Thomas Webber McPherson, born March 31, 1880; married Virgie Allen;
children:
(1) Pauline McPherson married Garland Crutchfield.
(2) Guy McPherson.
(3) Billy McPherson.
(4) Harlan McPherson.
(5) Ruth McPherson married Charles Little.
(6) Hazel McPherson.
d. Deborah McPherson, born February 6, 1883; married Caleb McPherson
(see p. 119).
e. Maud McPherson, born April 8, 1885; married Lawrence McPherson (see
p. 119).
f. Robert Lee McPherson, born October 14, 1887; married Etta Cheek.
g. Oliver Roscoe McPherson, born November 26, 1890; married Sadie Thompson; children:
(1) Oliver Roscoe McPherson.
(2) Peggy McPherson.

***

4.   Stephen McPherson was born about 1728 in Chester County, Pennsylvania; married Ann ____ ; moved to Loudoun County, Virginia, where on October 5, 1773, he bought 285 acres on the road from Ashby's Gap to Alexandria from Josias Suttle. He made his will on February 2, 1799, and the estate was probated on October 14, 1799. He had the following children:[90]

    a. John McPherson.
    b. Stephen McPherson.
    c. Rachel McPherson married ____ Boyce.
    d. Joseph McPherson.
    e. Daniel McPherson.
    f. Ruth McPherson married ____ Merrill.
    g. William McPherson.
    h. Jesse McPherson.
    i. James McPherson.

***

REFERENCES

[1]Family records and traditions collected by John Calvin McPherson, born 1846; owned by Chester County Historical Society, West Chester, Pennsylvania; William S. Powell, James K. Huhta, and Thomas J. Farnham (editors), The Regulators in North Carolina (Raleigh: State Department of Archives and History, 1971).

[2]Chester County, Pennsylvania Deeds B, 66; Lancaster County, Pennsylvania, Wills B1, 104.

[3]Family records and traditions collected by John Calvin McPherson.

[4]Alpheus Hibben Harlan, History and Genealogy of the Harlan Family (Baltimore: The Lord Baltimore Press, 1914).

[5]Family records and traditions collected by John Calvin McPherson.

[6]Ibid.; John Green was probably the son of Thomas Green who died in 1712 in Chester County, Pennsylvania, and his wife Sarah; Thomas Green (son of Thomas and Margaret Green) arrived in Pennsylvania in the ship Delaware on May 11, 1686, from Bristol, England. Abigail Green was one of two sisters of Yorkshire, England, who were kidnapped and sent to America by their step-father to prevent their receiving an inheritance from their father.

[7-9]Family records and traditions collected by John Calvin McPherson; Otho Leon McPherson and John Marion Lewis, "Family Records of Early Oregon Pioneers," D.A.R. Library, Washington, D. C.

[10]Ida Brooks Kellam, Brooks and Kindred Families (Wilmington, N.C.: n.p., 1950).

[11]Family records and traditions collected by John Calvin McPherson; "Family Record of Early Oregon Pioneers;" Harlan, op. cit.; Union County, South Carolina, Deeds A, 164, 172, B, 15, Estates Box 1, Package 22, Census of 1790.

[12]Records belonging to Mrs. Alice O. Vitus.

[13]Union County, South Carolina, Wills.

[14-17]Records beloning to Mrs. Alice O. Vitus.

[18]Family records and traditions collected by John Calvin McPherson; Powell, Huhta, and Farnham, pp. 564-571.

[19-20]Family records and traditions collected by John Calvin McPherson.

[21]Ibid.; records belonging to Mattie Washburn Campbell.

[22]Records belonging to Frances Tarvin.

[23-26]Records belonging to Robert D. McPherson; History of Guthrie and Adair Counties (Iowa, 1884), p. 515.

[27-32]Records belonging to Alberta Wollen Velthoen.
[33-34]Records belonging to Robert D. McPherson.
[35]Records belonging to Mrs. Horace Burgan.
[36-46]Records belonging to Robert D. McPherson.
[47]Family records and traditions collected by John Calvin McPherson; statement of marriage by Allie Morrow Crowder; Union County, South Carolina, Deeds B, 426, E, 238.
[48]Union County, South Carolina, Deeds I, 83, Estates Box 1, Package 22, miscellaneous record books.
[49]Spartanburg County, South Carolina, Deeds K, 308, L, 234; "Family Record of Early Oregon Pioneers."
[50]Barren County, Kentucky, Deeds C, 415; Monroe County, Kentucky, Deeds, B, 157 (original owned by David B. Trimble).
[51]Jehu McPherson's will record, copied by Benjamin Nicholls McPherson in November, 1841 (original owned by Jack McPherson); Monroe County, Kentucky, census of 1840; Barren County, Kentucky, estate settlement of Hugh Marshall, census of 1820; Marshall County, Mississippi, census of 1850.
[52]Bible record belonging (1946) to Mrs. Mary Louise Bowles; records belonging to Mrs. James Allen Bradshaw.
[53-60]Records belonging to Mrs. James Allen Bradshaw.
[61-62]Records belonging to Mrs. Virginia Burgess.
[63-69]Records belonging to Leslie Dent Johnston.
[70-71]Records belonging to Miss Hallie Dawson.
[72-75]Records belonging to Mrs. Elmer Ned Byers.
[76]Records belonging to Joseph L. Clark.
[77-84]Records belonging to Mrs. Lunell Bybee Moore.
[85]Berkeley County, (West) Virginia, Will Bk. 2, p. 24.
[86]Orange County, North Carolina, Wills D, 517; Powell, Huhta, and Farnham, p. 240; records belonging to Miss Marcia Foust.
[87]Anderson County, South Carolina, Wills 2B, 232; records belonging to Mrs. Mary F. Dunn.
[88-89]Records belonging to Miss Marcia Foust.
[90]Loudoun County, Virginia, Deeds I, 395, Wills F, 121.

***

MARRIOTT and WARREN of Surry County, Virginia

Thomas Warren was born about 1722 in England and came to Virginia before 1640 with Daniel Gookin, who was probably his cousin. On February 3, 1640, he was granted 450 acres on Smith Fort Creek in James City (now Surry) County, Virginia, and was regranted 290 acres of the land on July 3, 1648.[1] He established Smith's Fort plantation and about 1651 he built a brick house there which was his home the remainder of his life.[2] After the death of his first wife, whose name is unknown, Warren in 1654 married Mrs. Elizabeth (Spencer) Shepherd, daughter of William and Alice Spencer. Warren was caretaker of the estate of Major Robert Shepherd and guardians of his orphans (Warren's step-children). About 1658 he married Mrs. Jane King, who survived him and later married Samuel Plaw.[3]

In May, 1661, Warren was a vestryman of Southwark Parish, and on December 22, 1668, he was appointed a commissioner of Surry County by Governor William Berkeley.[4] He made his will on March 16, 1669, and died shortly afterwards, leaving the following children:[5]

(by first marriage):
1. a. Alice Warren, born c1645.
   b. William Warren, born c1648; dsp 1670 in Surry County, Virginia.
   (by second marriage):
   c. Elizabeth Warren, born 1654; married 1671 to John Hunnicutt.
   (by third marriage):
   d. Thomas Warren, born January 9, 1659/60; died 1721 in Surry County, Virginia; married Elizabeth _____, died 1724; children:
      (1) William Warren.
      (2) John Warren.
      (3) Joseph Warren.
      (4) Robert Warren.
      (5) Elizabeth Warren married James Davis, died 1746; children:
          (a) Thomas Davis, died 1748.
          (b) Jane Davis married _____ Warren.
          (c) John Davis.
          (d) Henry Davis died 1767; married Mary Marriott (see p. 125); children:
              /1/ William Davis died 1772 in Brunswick County, Virginia.
              /2/ Ann Davis.
              /3/ Hannah Davis.
              /4/ Benjamin Davis died 1817 in Autauga County, Alabama; married Tabitha Rose.
              /5/ Isham Davis.
              /6/ Randolph Davis married Hannah Marriott (see p. 127).
              /7/ Elizabeth Davis married John Rose.
              /8/ Henry Davis.
              /9/ Keziah Davis.
              /10/ Marriott Davis.
              /11/ Sylvia Davis.
              /12/ James Davis.
          (e) James Davis died 1783; married Elizabeth Baldwin.
          (f) Robert Davis died 1749.
          (g) Nathaniel Davis.
          (h) Anne Davis married James Nicholson.
   e. Allen Warren, born c1663; died c1738 in Surry County, Virginia.
   f. Robert Warren, born c1666; died 1721 in Surry County, Virginia.

g. William Warren, born 1669; died 1702 in Surry County, Virginia.

***

1.   Alice Warren was born about 1645 in Surry County, Virginia; about 1665 she married Matthias Marriott,[6] who on September 24, 1670, received his share of the estates of Thomas and William Warren; on March 20, 1670/1, he gave the other heirs their shares. On October 13, 1671, Marriott sold a slave to George Watkins, and on August 14, 1672, he and Thomas Hart received a grant of 338 acres from the Virginia government. On July 23, 1673, Matthias and Alice Marriott sold the Warren house and 400 acres called Smith's Fort, inherited from her father, to John Salway.[7]

        Matthias Marriott made his will on June 12, 1707, leaving his property to his wife and children; the estate was probated on September 2, 1707; his children were as follows:[8]

a. Margaret Marriott married Robert Flake.
b. Elizabeth Marriott married Sion Hill.
c. Marian Marriott married _____ Cryar.
2. d. William Marriott, born c1685.

***

2.   William Marriott, who was born about 1685, was a planter in Surry County, Virginia, his entire life. About 1715 he married Sarah Collier of Surry County, who was born about 1695 (see p.   4). On March 9, 1722, he sold 200 acres adjoining Ware Neck to Michael Harris for five shillings; on June 19, 1723, he sold 343 acres in Southwark Parish to Abraham, Jacob, and Nicholas Faucon for five shillings; on October 27, 1724, he sold 35 acres near Mill Swamp to James Nicholson for ₤16; and on November 16, 1725, he sold 100 acres on Warrior's Swamp adjoining James Davis to William Westhue for ₤16.15. On November 1, 1731, he sold 60 acres adjoining the Southwark Parish Church to Thomas Bage for five shillings; on October 22, 1732, he sold 135 acres to William Gray, Jr., for five shillings; and on May 16, 1735, he sold 235 acres to John Johnson for five shillings.[9]

        On May 4, 1735, William Marriott bought 630 acres on the south side of Meherrin River and Avent's Creek in Brunswick County, Virginia, from Thomas Avent for ₤40; his son Thomas Marriott farmed the land and received it by his father's will, made on September 20, 1765, and probated January 20, 1767, in Surry County. William and Sarah Marriott had the following children:[10]

a. William Marriott, born c1716; dsp 1755 in Surry County, Virginia.
3. b. Thomas Marriott, born c1720.
c. Matthias Marriott, born c1722; died 1774 in Surry County, Virginia; married Elizabeth Gray.
d. Benjamin Marriott, born c1725.
e. Mary Marriott, born c1728; married Henry Davis (see p. 124).

***

3.   Thomas Marriott, who was born about 1720 in Surry County, Virginia, married Elizabeth _____ about 1745 and moved to his father's 630-acre tract on the south side of Meherrin River and Avent's Creek in Brunswick County, Virginia. On November 3, 1750, he acquired an adjoining 476 acres from the colony of Virginia, and on May 11, 1754, he bought an

125

adjoining 130 acres on Avent's Creek from William McKnight for £47.[11]

Marriott may have been a merchant as well as a planter, as in September, 1753, Thomas Marriott and Company sued the estate of Edward Gowing for debt. He sold his 130-acre tract to Sylvanus Stokes, Jr., for £70 on June 28, 1757, and on the same date he sold 270 acres of his plantation to John Knight for £55. On June 25, 1764, he sold 100 acres to William Davis for £55, and on February 17, 1770, he sold 130 acres to his son-in-law, Nathaniel Robertson, for £70. He made his will on October 21, 1785, leaving his property to his four children and his daughter Sarah's children; the estate was probated on August 24, 1789. His children were as follows:[12]

a. Sarah Marriott, born c1750; married (1) 1768 to John Warren, died October 31, 1779; (2) June 15, 1782, to William Holmes; children: (by first marriage):[13]
    (1) Elizabeth Warren, born c1771.
    (2) Marriott Warren, born c1773; died December, 1798, in Mecklenburg County, Virginia; married 1794 Mary Holmes, daughter of Samuel Holmes; children:
        (a) Samuel Holmes Warren; married December 12, 1820, Elizabeth Rebecca Delony; lived in Mecklenburg County, Virginia, in 1829.
        (b) Jane Warren married February 16, 1824, David H. Abernathy; lived in Mecklenburg County, Virginia, in 1829.
        (c) Marriott Warren lived in Richmond County, Georgia, in 1829.
    (3) John Warren, born c1775.
    (4) William Warren, born c1777.
    (5) Thomas Warren, born c1779.
    (by second marriage) (perhaps among others):
    (6) Warren Holmes, born c1783.
b. Elizabeth Marriott, born c1752; died c1790 in Brunswick County, Virginia; married October 23, 1769, to Nathaniel Robertson (see p. 178).
c. Hannah Marriott, born c1755; married c1772 to Randolph Davis (see p. 124).
d. Thomas Marriott, born c1760; married December 14, 1785, to Elizabeth Suggett, born c1769, daughter of Edgecomb Suggett and Constant Edmundson. He probably moved to Roane County, Tennessee, about 1807, and died there; his widow lived in Morgan County, Missouri, in 1850; his children, among others, were probably as follows:[14]
    (1) Constant Marriott, born c1786; married March 3, 1806, John Allen.
    (2) Edgecomb Marriott, born c1788; lived in Morgan County, Missouri.
    (3) Benjamin Marriott, born c1797; lived in Morgan County, Missouri.
    (4) Thomas Marriott lived in Tennessee.
    (5) John Marriott, born c1809; lived in Morgan County, Missouri.
    (6) Prudence Marriott, born c1812; married Martin Silvey; lived in Morgan County, Missouri.

***

REFERENCES

[1]Thomas Warren was probably the person by that name who was baptised on January 30, 1624, at Ripple, Kent, England, the son of William Warren and Catherine Gookin; John Bennett Boddie, Historical Virginia Genealogies (Redwood City, California: Pacific Coast Publishers, 1954); Virginia Patent Book 1, p. 146, State Archives, Richmond, Virginia.
[2]Surry County, Virginia, Deed Bk. 2, p. 166; the house was bought by the Rockefeller Foundation, restored, and given to the Society for

the Preservation of Virginia Antiquities, which now operates it.

[3]Surry County, Virginia, Deed Bk. 1, pp. 56, 169.

[4]Ibid., Bk. 1, pp. 56, 168, 338.

[5]Ibid., Bk. 1, pp. 377, 389, Will Bk. 9, p. 488; records belonging to John B. Boddie.

[6]Matthias Marriott was probably a close relative but not a son of Major William Marriott, who was in Surry County, Virginia, prior to 1660.

[7]Surry County, Virginia, Deed Bk. 1, pp. 374, 377, 389, Bk. 2, p. 30; Virginia Land Grant Book 6, p. 413, State Archives, Richmond, Virginia.

[8]Surry County, Virginia, Deed Bk. 5, p. 374.

[9]Ibid., Bk. 7, pp. 795, 473, 451, 568, 627, Bk. 8, pp. 281, 279, 493.

[10]Brunswick County, Virginia, Deed Bk. 1, p. 220; Surry County, Virginia, Wills.

[11]Surry County, Virginia, Wills; Virginia Land Grant Book 29, p. 363, State Archives, Richmond, Virginia; Brunswick County, Virginia, Deed Bk. 5, p. 615.

[12]Brunswick County, Virginia, Order Book 12, p. 80; Deed Bk. 6, pp. 191, 194, Bk. 7, p. 492, Bk. 9, p. 603, Will Bk. 5, p. 316.

[13]Ibid., Marriages; Mecklenburg County, Virginia, Marriages, Will Bk. 4, p. 85.

[14]Records belonging to Mrs. Ernest L. Merriott.

***

NEVILL of Orange County, North Carolina,

and Coffee County, Tennessee

William Nevill, who lived in Isle of Wight County, Virginia, as early as March, 1642/3, was probably the first of this family in America. He died before 1665, and his widow probably married Arthur Skinner, since on April 25, 1665, his son Roger Nevill sold his interest in William's lands to his "father-in-law," Arthur Skinner. On May 16, 1665, John Nevill and his wife Elizabeth of Nansemond County, Virginia, sold Arthur Skinner 125 acres granted to Nevill.[1]

The above John Nevill, a planter in Nansemond County, bought 400 acres from Henry Bradley on February 2, 1663/4, and sold the land to John Marshall of Isle of Wight in 1665. In 1684, he received a grant of 92 acres and in 1686 a grant of 246 acres, both in Isle of Wight County. In 1689, John and Elizabeth Nevill gave land to Benjamin Beale and his wife Martha and mentioned John's son Benjamin Nevill; the deed was witnessed by John Nevill, Jr. John Nevill, Sr., sold 100 acres in Isle of Wight County to John Johnson in 1698, and probably died shortly afterwards. The following were perhaps his children, probably among others:[2]

a. John Nevill paid quit rents on 430 acres in Isle of Wight County, Virginia, in 1704; died in 1730 leaving the following children:[3]
   (1) Penelope Nevill.
   (2) Elizabeth Nevill.
   (3) Martha Nevill.
   (4) Eleanor Nevill.
   (5) Florence Nevill.
   (6) Mary Nevill.
   (7) Patience Nevill.
   (8) Anne Nevill.
   (9) John Nevill died in 1740 in Isle of Wight County, Virginia; children:
      (a) John Nevill.
      (b) Thomas Nevill.
      (c) Joseph Nevill died in 1782 in Isle of Wight County, Virginia.
      (d) Penelope Nevill.
b. Martha Nevill married Benjamin Beale.
c. Benjamin Nevill paid quit rents on 475 acres in Nansemond County, Virginia, in 1704; further information is difficult to obtain because of the destruction of the Nansemond County records, but he was probably the father of the Benjamin Nevill, discussed below, who lived in Edgecombe County, North Carolina.

***

Benjamin Nevill was born about 1705, probably in Nansemond County, Virginia. He lived in Edgecombe (now Halifax) County, North Carolina, on February 11, 1746/7, when he bought 300 acres on Fishing Creek from John Hubbard for £21; on February 15, 1746/7, he bought 90 acres on the west side of Elk Marsh from Thomas Smith for £4.10; on June 13, 1748, he bought 200 acres on the west side of Elk Marsh from William Pace for £20. On March 25, 1752, he received a grant of 302 acres near Taylor's Creek in Granville County from Earl Granville, and on May 12, 1755, he received a 634 acre grant on the west side of Elk Marsh in Halifax County from Earl Granville.[4]

Benjamin Nevill sold 300 acres on the east side of Beaverdam Swamp to Thomas Nevill for £80 on December 29, 1753. On June 30, 1755, he sold part of his 634 acre grant on Elk March - 127 acres to Alexander McCulloch, 126 acres to Charles Drury, 126 acres to John Parks, and 126 acres to John Marshall; each paid £2.3.2. He made his will in Halifax County in 1759, giving his lands in Halifax to his son Benjamin and his lands in Edgecombe and Granville to his son Jesse; he left personal property to his wife Elizabeth and daughter Elizabeth; the estate was probated the same year.[5]

The children of Benjamin and Elizabeth Nevill were, probably among others, as follows:[6]

a. Thomas Nevill, born c1732; on July 4, 1760, received a grant of 491 acres on Bear Branch in Halifax County, North Carolina; children, probably among others:[7]
   (1) Goodman Nevill, born c1765; living in Halifax County, North Carolina, in 1830.
   (2) Benjamin Nevill, born c1768; living in Halifax County, North Carolina, in 1830.
   (3) John Nevill.
   (4) William Nevill.
   (5) Jesse Nevill.
   (6) Edmund Nevill.
b. Benjamin Nevill, born c1742; died in 1832 in Halifax County, North Carolina; children, perhaps among others:[8]
   (1) Thomas Nevill.
   (2) Bathsheba Nevill married _____ Whitaker.
c. Elizabeth Nevill.
1. d. Jesse Nevill, born September 24, 1746.

***

1.   Jesse Nevill was born September 24, 1746, in Edgecombe (now Halifax) County, North Carolina; in 1759 he inherited land in Edgecombe and Granville counties from his father, and on June 13, 1760, he acquired 390 acres in Edgecombe Parish, Halifax County, on the west side of Elk Marsh, from Earl Granville. On April 21, 1770, he sold 50 acres of the grant to Ephraim Knight, and on October 1, 1771, he sold the 302 acre grant in Granville County, inherited from his father, to Thomas Person for £100.[9]

Nevill moved to Orange County, North Carolina, about four miles west of Chapel Hill, about 1769, and on January 29, 1770, he bought 337 acres on Mark's Creek in St. Matthew's Parish from Samuel Parker for £140. On August 17, 1778, he received 300 acres on Meadow Fork and other branches of Morgan's Creek, including Round Mountain and land bought from John Hunnicutt, and on December 6, 1779, he received 400 acres on New Hope Creek adjoining his plantation, both grants from the state of North Carolina.[10]

Jesse Nevill married Elizabeth Parke, who was born September 8, 1752, in Orange County on November 8, 1770. In 1777, he was appointed by the county court to judge the best way to lay out a road from the Chatham County line over Haw River at Morgan's Mill to Hillsboro; he was in charge of repairing the road from Hillsboro to James Williams' mill in 1778; he was the tax assessor for St. Thomas' District in 1778; and he served on juries several times during those years. In 1777 he owned property valued at £7,316, and in 1780 he owned 10 slaves, 23 cattle, four horses, and 937 acres of land, all valued at £9,691.12.1.[11]

Jesse Nevill continued to buy land; on October 16, 1784, he bought 100 acres adjoining Nevill's Meeting House from Hugh Edwards, and on November 9, 1784, he received 370 acres on Morgan's Creek from the state of North Carolina. He sold 150 acres to Mark Cooper on March 21, 1785. On June 15, 1786, he bought 200 acres on the Chatham County line from Thomas Connally, and on June 10, 1786, he bought a town lot in Chatham County from Matthew Jones for £3.10; on October 25, 1785, he bought 149 acres on the Headwaters of Pokeberry Branch in Chatham County from William Hatley for £100, and sold it to Jesse Fann for the same price on June 14, 1787. He bought 140 acres on Bird's Branch in Orange County from Mark Cooper on December 12, 1788, 56 acres on Phil's Creek near Nevill's mill from James Blackwood on January 24, 1790, and 262 acres on Caswell's Creek, a branch of Morgan's Creek, from Robert Trotter on December 15, 1795. On October 14, 1793, he bought lot 13 on Franklin Street in Chapel Hill from the trustees of the University of North Carolina and sold it on August 22, 1796, to John Taylor. On August 13, 1800, he sold John Wilson 75 acres on Morgan's and Bird's Creeks near Nevill's home, and on January 31, 1801, he sold Daniel Stephens 110 acres on Bird's Branch.[12]

Jesse Nevill subscribed $100.00 in 1792 for the creation of the University of North Carolina, and according to family tradition, he hired out his slaves to build the first university buildings. He also kept a store and a mill on his plantation, and in 1797 he helped organize the Damascus Congregational Christian Church near Chapel Hill.[13]

In 1801, Nevill began giving his property to his sons as they came of age; on May 2, 1801, he gave his son Solomon 300 acres. He gave 300 acres to Benjamin and 350 acres to Jesse, Jr., on January 25, 1803, and he gave his son Goodman 300 acres on December 15, 1804. On February 20, 1809, he gave his son Wiley 248 acres in Chatham County which he had bought from Nathaniel Husketh for £186 on October 4, 1800. He made his will on September 8, 1809, giving the remainder of his estate to his children, and it was probated in 1810.[14]

The children of Jesse Nevill and Elizabeth Parke were as follows:[15]

   a. Goodwin Nevill, born January 13, 1771; married December 12, 1785, to James Kirk.
   b. Cynthia Nevill, born October 18, 1772; dsp c1775.
2. c. Elizabeth Nevill, born January 28, 1775.
3. d. Solomon Nevill, born April 3, 1777.
4. e. Benjamin Nevill, born July 8, 1779.
5. f. Jesse Nevill, born December 29, 1781.
6. g. Goodman Nevill, born January 9, 1784.
   h. Cynthia Aris Nevill, born March 16, 1786; lived in Dallas County, Alabama, in 1850; married September 13, 1804, to William Robertson (see p. 178).
   i. Wiley Whitley Nevill, born December 16, 1787; dsp.
7. j. Samuel Parke Nevill, born March 23, 1790.
   k. Selah Nevill, born April 18, 1792; married January 29, 1810, to Wiley Kirby.

***

2.   Elizabeth Nevill was born January 28, 1775, in Orange County, North Carolina, and married Francis Barbee on February 8, 1794; their children were as follows:[16]

    a. Elizabeth Barbee married John Craig.
8. b. Christopher Barbee, born June 23, 1796.
    c. William Barbee, born 1798; died 1880; married 1819 to Mary Norwood; lived in Hays County, Texas; children:
        (1) Sarah Barbee, born 1820; married Philip Walker.
        (2) William Francis Barbee, born 1822; dsp.
        (3) Howard Barbee, born 1824; dsp c1850.
        (4) David Allen Barbee, born 1826; married Helen Hubbard.
        (5) Edward Norwood Barbee, born 1828; married Willow Malone.
        (6) John Jones Barbee, born 1831; died 1912; married 1866 Cornelia Rachel Dailey.
        (7) James Gaston Barbee, born 1833; married Sarah _____.
        (8) Mary Frances Barbee, born 1835; married Addison Stanfield.
    d. Mary Barbee married Hyder Lindsey (see p. 175); lived in Arkansas.
    e. Allen Jones Barbee, born 1803; died 1878; married June 5, 1830, to Susan Young Taylor; lived in Tennessee.
    f. Susan Barbee married Sidney Lloyd; lived in Tennessee.
    g. Jones Barbee lived in Erath County, Texas.
    h. Nevill Barbee lived in Hollywood, Mississippi.

                              ***

8.   Christopher Barbee was born June 23, 1796, in Orange County, North Carolina, and died July 27, 1862; on January 20, 1820, he married Sarah Patterson, born February 15, 1798; died March 11, 1859, daughter of Chesley Page Patterson and Nancy Morgan, lived in Murray, Kentucky; and their children were as follows:[17]

9. a. Chesley Page Patterson Barbee, born January 24, 1821.
    b. Mary Adeline Jane Barbee, born March 13, 1822; dsp March 8, 1835.
    c. Emma Victoria Barbee, born February 28, 1839; died May 27, 1877, in Calloway County, Kentucky; married November 11, 1855, to Dr. Josiah Thompson Mathis, born August 18, 1827; died 1886; children:
        (1) William Herschel Mathis, born April 21, 1857; dsp October 20, 1857.
        (2) John Lenord Mathis, born December 1, 1859; married May 12, 1878, to Elizabeth Hope.
        (3) Chesley Page Mathis, born November 29, 1860; dsp September 24, 1868.
        (4) Ida Belle Mathis, born September 29, 1865; married February 21, 1884, to William Henry Firebaugh; lived in Redlands, California; children:
            (a) William Henry Firebaugh, born August 16, 1885; dsp.
            (b) Albert Mathis Firebaugh, born February 1, 1887; married December 9, 1908, to Fannie Walker; children:
                /1/ Mattie Belle Firebaugh, born February 8, 1910; married July 9, 1931, to J. L. Barber; dsp.
                /2/ Albert Mathis Firebaugh, born January 5, 1912; married June 13, 1939, to Patricia Hewett; children:
                    /a/ Albert Mathis Firebaugh, born March 29, 1942.
                    /b/ Mary Frances Firebaugh, born December 25, 1943.
                    /c/ Shirley Ann Firebaugh, born August 1, 1945.
                /3/ Frances Louise Firebaugh, born April 25, 1913; married September 19, 1935, to William C. Hale; children:
                    /a/ Jean Sylvia Hale, born December 2, 1936.

                              131

        /b/ Earl Jay Hale, born July 16, 1940.
        /c/ Charles Albert Hale, born March 18, 1949.
    /4/ Mary Josephine Firebaugh, born December 10, 1915;
    married March 25, 1944, to Joe Ellis; children:
        /a/ Emery John Ellis, born March 22, 1946.
        /b/ Judith Kay Ellis, born June 5, 1948.
    /5/ Julia Firebaugh, born December 11, 1920; married
    November 22, 1945, to Gordon M. Sundman; child:
        /a/ Susan Sundman, born January 5, 1947.
    /6/ Ruth Firebaugh, born September 11, 1924; married
    November 26, 1947, to Dan Law; child:
        /a/ Diana Lee Law, born and dsp February 11, 1949.
    /7/ John Madison Firebaugh, born November 7, 1928; mar-
    ried August 10, 1948, to Dorothy Harkness; children:
        /a/ Donald Gary Firebaugh, born June 9, 1949.
        /b/ John Christopher Firebaugh, born December 22, 1951.
(c) David Chester Firebaugh, born October 31, 1888; dsp
     October 30, 1893.
(d) Frederic L. Firebaugh, born January, 1893; married April
     30, 1922, to Christine Hesseler; dsp; lived in San Fran-
     cisco, California.

***

9.   Chesley Page Patterson Barbee was born January 24, 1821, in Orange
County, North Carolina, and died October 10, 1851, in Dallas County,
Arkansas. He married Elizabeth Keziah Smith on January 28, 1847, and
their children were as follows:[18]

a. Clara Coleman Barbee, born March 18, 1849; married October 5, 1870,
    to William Nathaniel Smith, born January 13, 1836, son of Samuel
    Harrison Smith and Frances Alston Martin; lived in Malvern, Arkansas;
    children:
    (1) Chesley Smith, born 1872; dsp 1873.
    (2) William Nathaniel Smith, born January, 1875; dsp December, 1875.
    (3) Natalie Smith, born January 23, 1878; died January 19, 1918;
        married April 6, 1904, to Samuel Ewell Henry; children:
        (a) Cala Sue Henry, born February 1, 1905; married Robert
            Wiley Thompson; lived in Gulfport, Mississippi; children:
            /1/ Natalie Thompson, born May 21, 1929.
            /2/ Barbara Thompson, born February 4, 1932.
        (b) Natalie Smith Henry, born January 4, 1907; dsp.
        (c) Samuel Ewell Henry, born July 24, 1909; dsp October 6,
            1938.
        (d) William Nathaniel Henry, born February 12, 1911; dsp.
        (e) Betty Barbee Henry, born November 9, 1914; dsp.
    (4) Herschel Smith, born January 10, 1880; dsp May 2, 1921; lived in
        Hot Springs, Arkansas.
    (5) Samuel Kennon Smith, born May 4, 1882; died December 16, 1950;
        married January 17, 1914, to Joe Henry Moffitt, born June 28,
        1895; lived in McKenzie, Tennessee; children:
        (a) Herschel Kennon Smith, born February 5, 1915; married
            December 25, 1936, to Dorothy Mae McGrady; lived in Mc-
            Kenzie, Tennessee; children:
            /1/ Herschel Kennon Smith, born May 8, 1939.
            /2/ Lucinda Sue Smith, born December 7, 1942.
        (b) Joe Ann Smith, born July 4, 1926; married June 12, 1944,
            to George Ellis Gibson; lived in Decatur, Alabama; chil-
            dren:

    /1/ George Ann Gibson, born March 3, 1945.
    /2/ Cala Carol Gibson, born July 15, 1947.
    /3/ Susan Jane Gibson, born July 2, 1948.
    /4/ Natalie Kennon Gibson, born and dsp July 23, 1950.
 (6) Frank Alston Smith, born May 31, 1884; died March 9, 195?, in
   Billings, Montana; married February 21, 1909, to Nannie May
   Jones; children:
   (a) Frank Alston Smith, born September 11, 1914; married July
     13, 1933, to Josephine Hunter; lived in Alamogordo, New
     Mexico; children:
     /1/ Barbara Ann Smith, born October 23, 1939; married
       William Adams; lived in Alamogordo, New Mexico.
     /2/ Frank Alston Smith, born April 7, 1942; lived in
       California.
   (b) Robert Maurice Smith, born March 19, 1917; married March
     29, 1946, to Geraldine Wall, born May 2, 1917, daughter of
     Frank Sewell Wall and Nancy Foey; lived in San Antonio,
     Texas; children:
     /1/ Cala Barbee Smith, born March 5, 1947; married Decem-
       ber 23, 1967, to George Albert Hesse, III; child:
       /a/ Diana Lynn Hesse, born December 23, 1968.
     /2/ Maidee Ann Smith, born March 5, 1951.
 (7) Frances Elizabeth Smith, born October 23, 1886; married October
   5, 1910, to James Douglas Wallace; lived in San Francisco, California; children:
   (a) Frances Elizabeth Wallace, born September 3, 1911; married
     August 30, 1942, to Donald K. Stark; child:
     /1/ David James Stark, born August 30, 1943.
   (b) James Douglas Wallace, born December 25, 1912; married
     September 1, 1942, to Ethel Granunks; child:
     /1/ Bruce James Wallace, born May 8, 1946.
   (c) Virginia Wallace, born February 25, 1916; married September
     21, 1946, to Perry Divine; child:
     /1/ Janice Lynn Divine, born August 24, 1953.
   (d) Clara Wallace, born August 31, 1920; dsp.
 (8) Sallie Will Smith, born August 11, 1889; married November 18,
   1912, to Oscar Blair Adams; children:
   (a) Cala Smith Adams, born November 26, 1916; dsp.
   (b) Ann Strain Adams, born October 11, 1919; married 1949 to
     Nathan Van Boddie; child:
     /1/ Cala Marie Boddie, born 1951.
10. b. Sallie Page Barbee, born August 26, 1851.

***

10.   Sallie Page Barbee was born August 26, 1851, and died April 3, 1906;
   married December 9, 1872, to Dr. Luther Lynnville Alexander; lived in
   Paris, Tennessee; their children were as follows:[19]

  a. Chesley Alexander, born December 7, 1873; married (1) October 15,
    1900, to Daisy Lemonds (2) November 7, 1907, to Kate Walters; lived
    in Paris, Tennessee; children:
    (by first marriage):
    (1) Maurice Alexander, born March 29, 1901; died January 6, 1955;
     married (1) 1922 to Thelma Dailey (2) 1935 to Elizabeth Mobley;
     children:
     (by first marriage):
     (a) Maurice Alexander.
     (by second marriage):

133

            (b) Betty Alexander, born June 9, 1938; lived in Salinas, Cal-
                 ifornia.
         (by second marriage):
         (2) Katherine Alexander, born October 22, 1914; married Joe B.
              Gaddy; lived in Paris, Tennessee; child:
              (a) Ann Gaddy, born May 12, 1938.
11.   b. Elizabeth Alexander, born May 16, 1875.
      c. Lynn Alexander, born October 20, 1876; married July 5, 1904, to
          Annie Laura Maxwell; dsp.
      d. Page Alexander, born March 10, 1878; married Lilly Jordan; dsp.
12.   e. Clara Herber Alexander, born May, 1881.
      f. Samuel Barbee Alexander, born June 15, 1884; died December 31, 1955;
          married April 17, 1910, to Myrtle Jane Haggard; lived in Phoenix,
          Arizona; children:
          (1) Cala Barbee Alexander, born February, 1911; dsp August, 1911.
          (2) Mary Ann Alexander, born August 26, 1913; died October 21, 1939;
               married December 26, 1928, to Frank Lee Adams; child:
               (a) Sally Ann Adams, born January 24, 1936; married 1951, to
                    Joe Durant; child:
                    /1/ Debra Joe Durant, born July 12, 1952.
          (3) Luther Olin Alexander, born June 15, 1915; married Maxine Olive;
               children:
               (a) Diana Alexander.
               (b) Shirley Alexander.
          (4) Samuel Barbee Alexander, born October 7, 1917; dsp.
          (5) Betty Gene Alexander, born August 10, 1922; married (1) April
               8, 1940, to Gail Arther Rowland (2) March 23, 1953, to Henry
               B. Hatch; children (by first marriage):
               (a) Jenna Lynn Rowland, born June 7, 1941.
               (b) Sharron Gail Rowland, born September 1, 1942.
               (c) James Barbee Rowland, born May 1, 1949.
      g. Roy Alexander, born September 6, 1887; died September 16, 1940; mar-
          ried September 12, 1912, to Thelma Tharp; child:
          (1) Beulah Tharp Alexander, born October 23, 1913; died April 30,
               1953; married Clarence Melton; child:
               (a) Carol Lynn Melton, born July 29, 1932; married (1) _____
                    _____ (2) Myron Linder Hultmark; child:
                    /1/ Lynn Hultmark, born 1954.
      h. Luther Alexander, born August 8, 1890; married Camille Jolly; chil-
          dren:
          (1) Patricia Alexander, born October 10, 1921; married Jurdine Car-
               ter Perkins; child:
               (a) Patricia Perkins, born July 28, 1940.
          (2) Angelynn Alexander, born June 4, 1927; married 1950 to Charles
               Ben Hall; children:
               (a) Angelynn Camille Hall, born January 10, 1951.
               (b) Charles Ben Hall, born October 11, 1952.

                                    ***

11.   Elizabeth Alexander was born May 16, 1875, and died January 30,
      1936; married November 14, 1895, to Rev. Reuben Clark Douglas; their
      children were as follows:[20]

      a. Sarah Douglas, born 1896; married June 24, 1919, to Benjamin Frank-
          lin Briggs; children:
          (1) Richard Douglas Briggs, born 1922; married 1950 to Elsie Somers;
               child:
               (a) Douglas Briggs, born May 23, 1951.

                                    134

(2) Ben Burrus Briggs, born November 10, 1927; married Margaret Thompson; children:
    (a) Cynthia Briggs, born 1951.
    (b) Kathryne Briggs, born December 14, 1952.
(3) Lynn Thomas Briggs, born 1932.
b. Lula Mary Douglas, born October 1, 1897; married June 24, 1919, to William E. Hastings; children:
  (1) Betty Hastings, born June 14, 1925; married Ray Sanders; child:
    (a) Rita Ray Sanders.
  (2) Dixie Ann Hastings, born October 4, 1926; married 1945 to Dr. Joseph de Gasperi; child:
    (a) Dixie Ann de Gasperi.
c. Emma Barbee Douglas, born April 6, 1899; married November 11, 1920, to Charles Roy Kenney; children:
  (1) Dorothy Douglas Kinney, born February 5, 1923; married November 3, 1941, to James Edward Smith; children:
    (a) James Edward Smith, born August 3, 1947.
    (b) Dorothy Barbee Smith, born May 25, 1950.
  (2) Elizabeth Kinney, born November 18, 1928; married August 5, 1948, to Paul Moody Windrow; children:
    (a) John Luther Windrow, born September 24, 1949.
    (b) Nancy Brown Windrow, born May 25, 1953.
d. Bessie Gene Douglas, born September 22, 1902; married September 12, 1927, to Stuart Felix McFarland; child:
  (1) Gene Douglas McFarland, born December 14, 1932; married September 1, 1956, to Benjamin Porteous Moore.
e. Reuben Chesley Douglas, born July 31, 1905; married October 30, 1932, to Mildred Ratcliffe; child:
  (1) Reuben Chesley Douglas, born March 15, 1942.
f. Dorothy Douglas, born February 23, 1912; married September, 1939, to Milton Carter; dsp.

***

12.   Clara Herber Alexander was born in May, 1881, and died January 6, 1956; married April 30, 1903, to James Lafayette Martin; lived in Puryear, Tennessee. Their children were as follows:[21]

a. Alexander Polk Martin, born January 31, 1904; married December, 1936, to Margaret Ann Howard; child:
  (1) Marilyn Ann Martin, born December 20, 1941.
b. James Lafayette Martin, born December 27, 1904; dsp August, 1906.
c. Sallie Barbee Martin, born May 8, 1906; dsp December, 1910.
d. Ida Katherine Martin, born December 29, 1907; dsp.
e. Bessie Martin, born November 12, 1909; married August, 1932, to William Rice Lain; children:
  (1) Chesley Martin Lain, born January 18, 1937.
  (2) Richard Barnett Lain, born April 12, 1939.
f. Addie Virginia Martin, born September 13, 1911; married August, 1933, to Mitchel Paschal; children:
  (1) Betty Lane Paschal, born August 13, 1935; married Roald Starks.
  (2) Sherill Paschal, born August 3, 1946.
g. Luther Lynnville Martin, born August 6, 1913; dsp.
h. Cala Lucille Martin, born July 25, 1915; dsp.
i. Robert Page Martin, born January 17, 1918; dsp July 4, 1923.
j. Dollie Ruth Martin, born July 1, 1920; dsp 1940.
k. Jennie Lynn Martin, born April 28, 1922; married April, 1945, to John C. Buchanan; children:
  (1) Donald Wayne Buchanan, born October 20, 1947.

(2) Diane Buchanan, born June 17, 1951.
1. Adolphus Farris Martin, born January 24, 1924; married December 1,
   1944, to Viola Mary Gaeta; children:
   (1) James Martin.
   (2) Nicholas Martin.
   (3) Janice Martin.

***

3.   Solomon Nevill was born April 3, 1777, in Orange County, North Carolina, and died January 20, 1848, in Montgomery County, Tennessee; married March 17, 1795, in Chatham County, North Carolina, to Susanna Walton, born December 15, 1775; died September 5, 1841. Their children
were as follows:[22]

a. Edward Walton Nevill, born April 5, 1798.
b. Jesse Parke Nevill, born November 7, 1799.
c. John Sims Nevill, born August 27, 1801.
d. Barbara Heston Nevill, born October 23, 1803; married _____ Farrier.
e. Edwin Walton Nevill, born January 24, 1806; died November 5, 1891;
   married December 22, 1840, to Elizabeth Ann Peebles.
13. f. Solomon Corbin Nevill, born February 1, 1808.
g. Elizabeth Whitley Nevill, born November 2, 1809; married Granderson
   Vaughn.
h. Granderson Dandridge Nevill, born August 21, 1812; died 1878 in Texas;
   married Annette Travis; children:
   (1) Josiah Hoskins Nevill, born March 4, 1847; married Molly
       Highsmith; children:
       (a) Edwin Ross Nevill.
       (b) Effie Nevill married Benjamin Strange.
       (c) Elizabeth Nevill married _____ Porter.
       (d) Eula Mae Nevill married _____ Boggett.
       (e) James Nevill.
       (f) Irma Nevill.
   (2) Edwin Jarrett Nevill, born June 10, 1849; married Mary Mildred
       Yates; children:
       (a) Pearl Annette Nevill married E. S. McAllister; child:
           /1/ Edward Nevill McAllister married Annabelle Cox; lived
               in Houston, Texas.
       (b) Ruby Margaret Nevill married R. F. Isbell; child:
           /1/ Robert Nevill Isbell married Katherine Burns.
i. Susanna Orange Nevill, born November 30, 1814.

***

13.   Solomon Corbin Nevill was born February 1, 1808, in Orange County,
North Carolina, and died October 19, 1881; married December 9, 1829, to
Frances Slaughter Bell Long, born May 20, 1811; died June 28, 1889, in
Allen County, Kentucky. Their children were as follows:[23]

a. Nimrod Nevill, born 1830; dsp 1832.
b. Eugenia Nevill, born 1832; died 1871; married James L. Alexander.
c. Barbara Ann Nevill, born March 18, 1834, in Clarksville, Tennessee;
   died November 28, 1908, in Corydon, Indiana; married July 1, 1851,
   to John A. Miller, born February 18, 1824; died April 27, 1874; children:
   (1) Neville Miller, born 1853; dsp.
   (2) Shackleford Miller, born 1856; married Mary Welman.

136

        (3) Mattie Miller, born 1859; married William Roberts.
        (4) Eugenia Miller, born 1861; married Adelbert Webster.
        (5) Robert Miller, dsp.
        (6) Cassandra Miller, dsp.
        (7) John Belle Miller, born April 2, 1868; died April 29, 1942, in
            Maysville, Kentucky; married January 28, 1891, to Christopher
            Wayne Cook, born April 1, 1853; died July 22, 1922; children:
            (a) Mary Barbara Cook, born January 23, 1892; married November
                25, 1916, to Henry Means Walker, born December 9, 1891;
                lived in Maysville, Kentucky; children:
                /1/ Harris Collins Walker, born September 7, 1917; mar-
                    ried October 2, 1946, to Louise Breslin; children:
                    /a/ Harris Collins Walker, born July 25, 1947.
                    /b/ Martha Barbara Walker, born January 8, 1950.
                /2/ Henry Means Walker, born September 26, 1920; married
                    September 12, 1946, to Mrs. Frances (Poe) Groce; child:
                    /a/ John Means Walker, born July 24, 1948.
            (b) Betty Lee Cook, born August 19, 1893; married Claude Sharp.
            (c) Lucy Neville Cook, born May 27, 1896; married Chester Tuell.
            (d) Dorothy Wayne Cook, born January 14, 1901; married Maxwell
                Chisholm.
        (8) Betty Taylor Miller, born 1870; married Dr. Eugene Shutterly.
    d. Indiana Nevill, born 1835; dsp 1836.
    e. Rosella Nevill, born 1837; dsp 1838.
    f. Martha Cash Nevill, born 1838.
    g. Frances Nevill, born 1840; dsp 1842.
    h. Adaline Nevill, born 1842; dsp 1851.
    i. Richard Slaughter Nevill, born 1847.
    j. Elizabeth Vaughn Nevill, born 1850; died 1877; married Dr. B. B.
       Nesbit.

                            ***

4.   Benjamin Nevill was born July 8, 1779, in Orange County, North
Carolina, and on October 16, 1800, married Nancy Robertson (see p. 178).
In 1801, he owned one slave, and on January 25, 1803, his father, Jesse
Nevill, gave him 300 acres of land; he also acquired 17 acres on Morgan's
Creek from the state of North Carolina on July 19, 1803. He deeded
58.2 acres on Collin's Creek to Athanasius Lindsey on January 10, 1803,
and on August 29, 1808, he sold 213 acres acquired from his father to
his brother Solomon.[24]

        Ben Nevill moved to McGowan's Creek on Elk River in Franklin (now
Coffee) County, Tennessee, where he became one of the wealthiest planters
in the vicinity. On June 26, 1811, he bought 200 acres on Elk River from
David Davis for $1,025.00; on May 20, 1813, he bought 25 acres from James
Hunt; on December 18, 1820, he bought 41 acres on the north side of Elk
River from Thomas Stone for $250.00; on April 15, 1822, he bought 121
acres on Elk River from John McGowan. He also bought 47 acres on Elk
River from Elizabeth Greenlee for $164.50 on February 14, 1824, and on
July 1 and September 14 of the same year he acquired grants of 50 and
60 acres on McGowan's Creek from the state of Tennessee. He also bought
64 acres from Robert Lackey for $400.00 on November 8, 1825, 77 acres
from Davis King for $462.00 on February 3, 1827, and 80 acres from John
McGowan for $200.00 on February 9, 1827, these lands being located on
Elk River.[25]

        After the death of Nancy Nevill on May 5, 1814, Ben Nevill on Feb-
ruary 4, 1816, married Susan Hearod, who died October 31, 1824; he then

married Mary Elizabeth Stiles on November 23, 1826. She was born July 11, 1791, and died October 24, 1873, of the effects of the bite of a rabid dog; her step-grandchildren remembered her as an unpleasant woman whom they did not like.[26]

Ben Nevill gave land to his three oldest sons on January 22, 1830; 105 acres on Elk River to Robertson, 77 acres to Hardin and 127 acres on McGowan's or Prairie Creek to Pleasant. Pleasant Nevill sold 80 acres to his father for $400.00 on October 23, 1830, and Hardin Nevill sold his 77 acres back to his father on December 15, 1831. Ben Nevill also bought 42½ acres from T. A. Moore and G. W. Thompson for $215.00 on April 22, 1830, and 157 acres on the north side of Elk River from Hutcheson Murphy and John M. Bennett for $315.00 on May 22, 1830. He bought 63 acres on Elk River from Willis Tilman on February 14, 1833.[27]

Benjamin Nevill weighed 400 pounds and had special furniture built for him; he supervised his plantation from the second story porch of his house. He died February 28, 1838, in Coffee County, Tennessee, leaving a large estate valued at $18,232.00, including 20 slaves, land, and personal property. His children were as follows:[28]

(by first marriage):
a. Elizabeth Nevill, born March 10, 1802; married Joel Cross; lived in Alabama in 1838.
14. b. Robertson Nevill, born September 1, 1803.
15. c. Hardin Nevill, born February 20, 1805.
16. d. Pleasant Nevill, born September 5, 1806.
17. e. Benjamin Oswin Nevill, born December 5, 1807.
f. Nancy Whitley Nevill, born July 23, 1810; married Isaac Reed; children (probably among others):
(1) Samuel Reed.
(2) Benjamin Reed lived in Decherd, Tennessee.
(3) Isaac Reed lived in Decherd, Tennessee.
(4) Nancy Reed married Bert Spalding.
g. Julia Franklin Nevill, born August 2, 1813; dsp c1840 in Coffee County, Tennessee; married c1839 to _____ Guinn.
(by second marriage):
h. Jesse Park Nevill, born December 30, 1816.
i. Thomas Edwin Nevill, born October 18, 1818.
j. Solomon Nevill, born May 26, 1820; dsp November 28, 1839.
k. Caroline Nevill, born October 2, 1821; married c1838 to William Hardin Milam.
l. Susan Nevill, born January 30, 1823; married 1838 to Benton C. Stonestreet; lived in Grundy County, Tennessee, in 1850; children (among others):
(1) Elizabeth Stonestreet, born c1842.
(2) Matilda Stonestreet, born c1844.
(3) Abner Stonestreet, born c1846.
(4) Martha Stonestreet, born c1847.
(5) Benjamin Stonestreet, born c1849.
(by third marriage):
m. Amelia Ann Nevill, born June 2, 1829; dsp c1832.
18. n. Martha Jane Nevill, born October 19, 1831.

***

14.   Robertson Nevill was born September 1, 1803, near Chapel Hill, North Carolina, and moved about 1808 to near Pelham in Franklin (now Coffee)

County, Tennessee. On November 8, 1828, he entered 50 acres on the
waters of Elk River for a cent an acre and received his grant on February 12, 1833. On April 30, 1829, he bought 34 acres from Henry M. Rutledge for $136.00 and made it his home. On January 22, 1830, his father,
Benjamin Nevill, gave him an additional 105 acres on Elk River. On
October 14, 1830, he married Lucy Stroud (see p. 191) in Warren County,
Tennessee.[29]

On April 26, 1831, Nevill exchanged with Henry M. Rutledge the 139
acres recently acquired for 129 acres on Bradley's Creek, where he then
moved; on August 11, 1834, he sold his 50 acre land grant to Rutledge for
$50.00. On July 5, 1838, he bought 62½ acres on Bradley's Creek from
Rutledge for $276.69, and on March 18, 1848, he bought land from George
Miller and Daniel H. Call.[30]

Robertson Nevill also acquired several slaves to work the plantation; on January 26, 1839, he bought from his father-in-law, William
Stroud, a boy named King for $300.00 and sold him to William G. Guinn
on February 15, 1842, for $800.00. On April 10, 1839, he bought a man
named Caesar from George Miller for $1,205.00; on September 5, 1843, a
girl named Sarah from L. D. Lynch for $230.00, and a man named Alfred
on June 28, 1847, from the estate of William Stroud, Sr.[31]

Nevill raised cotton and corn as the principal crops on his plantation. In 1829 and 1830 he sold his cotton to Richardson and Arnold
of Franklin County at $2.00 per hundred weight, and the sale of the corn
whisky from his still brought in several hundred dollars per year. On
September 2, 1844, he bought James Gordon's cotton and corn crop for
$24.60.[32]

In addition, Nevill loaned money to his neighbors and managed their
business affairs; in January, 1834, he bought Anderson F. Willis' personal property to prevent its seizure for debt; in 1842 he became attorney for William B. Willis to handle all his affairs; he also took mort-
gages on Nancy Wildman's and Hiram Smith's lands for their debts. In
1838, he was overseer of roads, and in 1845 he was school commissioner
for the 12th District of Coffee County.[33]

In March Court, 1838, Robertson Nevill and his brother Oswin asked
to be made administrators of the estate of their father, Benjamin Nevill,
and in October, Robertson posted a bond for $10,000.00 as guardian of
his half-sister, Martha Nevill. As administrator and guardian, he was
sued by James Wilkinson for the debts of his brother, Jesse Nevill, and
on October 31, 1842, he bought Benton C. Stonestreet's interest in the
estates of Solomon Nevill and Julia Nevill Guinn from Robert L. Singleton.
Benjamin Nevill's estate was still unsettled when Robertson Nevill died,
and Oswin Nevill sued his brother's administrators, George Stroud and
David Ramsey, in Chancery Court in Coffee County for an accounting, since
Robertson had been the better scholar of the two and usually kept the
papers belonging to the estate.[34]

Robertson Nevill died on March 21, 1848, and his widow continued to
manage the plantation ably; she kept her home very much as her husband
left it. On November 8, 1864, the U. S. Provost Marshall at Tullahoma
protected her property from molestation after she proved her loyalty to
the union. After the Civil War, she operated the plantation with several
of the former slaves who remained and with tenant farmers. After his
first wife died, her son Houston returned from Texas to help her manage
the farm. On December 11, 1895, Lucy Nevill sold William M. Brannan,

who farmed her land, 53 acres of it for $200.00, and on December 11, 1897, she gave him 14½ acres worth $140.00 for his services. Lucy Nevill died on April 23, 1904, in Coffee County, Tennessee; the children of Robertson and Lucy Nevill were as follows:[35]

    a. William Benjamin Nevill, born November 25, 1831; dsp March 10, 1863, in Coffee County, Tennessee; married February 12, 1856, to Mary Withrow.

    b. Nancy C. Nevill, born August 2, 1833; dsp January 9, 1850, in Coffee County, Tennessee; married November 15, 1849, to Hamilton L. Reynolds.

    c. Hardin Nevill, born February 14, 1835; dsp November 24, 1863, at Chickamauga, Tennessee; married January 3, 1861, to Mrs. Mary Ann Elizabeth (Chapman) Harris.

    d. Elizabeth Nevill, born April 23, 1837; died June 3, 1855, in Coffee County, Tennessee; married Philip Hawkins; child:
        (1) Samuel H. Hawkins, born 1855; lived in California.

    e. George Robertson Nevill, born July 18, 1839; dsp January 26, 1843.

19.   f. John Lafever Nevill, born August 7, 1841.

20.   g. Mary Ann Aris Nevill, born September 3, 1843.

    h. Lucy Jayne Nevill, born June 10, 1846; died April 19, 1884, in Tulare County, California; married January 10, 1872, to Levi Hinds Gist (see p. 41).

21.   i. Samuel Houston Nevill, born July 30, 1848.

***

19.   John Lafever Nevill was born August 7, 1841, in Coffee County, Tennessee. On August 24, 1861, he enlisted at Camp Trousdale as a private in Company G, 24th Infantry Regiment, Cleburne's Brigade, Cheatham's Division, Army of Tennessee. In 1861, he marched from Bowling Green, Kentucky, to Corinth, Mississippi, then fought in the battle of Shiloh. His unit then marched to Corinth, Chattanooga, and Perryville; after the battle of Perryville, he returned to the Chattanooga area. He suffered greatly from privation and on one occasion was believed dead and place in a pesthouse.[36]

        After the Civil War, he helped operate his mother's farm; on August 19, 1875, his brothers and sisters sold him their four-fifths interest in 112 acres of the farm for $1,200.00, and on January 1, 1876, he sold the land to W. H. Harris for $2,000.00.[37]

        In November, 1876, Johnny Nevill moved to Johnson County, Texas, with the Hestand family; on February 23, 1877, he and D. B. Hestand bought 160 acres from Robert P. Roby for $1,200.00, and on November 23, 1878, Hestand sold him his half for $750.00. On August 9, 1877, he married Barzillia Hestand (see Trimble, Hiestand Family of Page County, Virginia). He sold his farm to Samuel Kirkland in 1881 for $3,000.00[38] and moved several miles away to Hill County, where on September 16, 1881, he bought land on the waters of Nolan River about 20 miles northwest of Hillsboro from A. S. Chisman for $450.00. On October 17, 1883, he bought 52 acres in the same area from D. B. Hestand for $625.00, and on September 30, 1886, he bought additional land in that area from A. S. Chisman for $660.00. Also in 1886, he and Hestand bought 33 acres on the waters of Aquilla Creek in the Cross Timbers from Henry Beaver for $134.00. On April 25, 1889, he sold 55 acres of his farm to R. H. Fleming for $700.00, and on December 20, 1890, he sold other land to Rowland West for $600.00.[39]

140

Nevill moved to Jones County, Texas, about 1890, and for several years operated a furniture and undertaking business in Anson. He owned several lots in Anson as well as a farm near town. He made trips to Tennessee in 1879 and 1904, when he divided his mother's personal property with his brother Houston. About 1900 he and his sons acquired several sections of land in Pecos County, Texas, near Girvin, and he sometimes spent part of the year on the ranch which his son Virgil operated on his land; he sold several oil leases for enough money to live comfortably. As he grew older, he spent most of his time in Anson, where he died on February 24, 1932.[46]

Barzillia Nevill continued to live in Anson until 1941, when she moved to her ranch in Pecos County, operated by her son Virgil. She died on December 12, 1947, in Culberson County, Texas. The children of John and Barzillia Nevill were as follows:[41]

a. Effie Nevill, born May 12, 1878; died July 31, 1929, in Stephens County, Texas; married May 16, 1899, in Anson, Texas, to Benjamin Soule Davidson (see p. 16).

b. Virgil Gist Nevill, born November 2, 1880; died June 15, 1973, in Pecos County, Texas; married July 12, 1910, in Midland, Texas, to Laura Lou Bullock, born August 7, 1892; died November, 1970; children:
  (1) Marshall Gist Nevill, born 1912; married Preble Adams; lived in McCamey, Texas; child:
    (a) Marsha Louise Nevill, born September 17, 1947.
  (2) Ruby Ethene Nevill, born 1914; married (1) Thomas Barnsley (2) Jiggs Plummer; lived in Crane, Texas; children (all by first marriage):
    (a) William Abner Barnsley, born 1932.
    (b) Peggy Joyce Barnsley, born 1934.
    (c) Tommie Ethene Barnsley, born 1936.
  (3) Harrel Reginald Nevill, born 1917; married Willie Mae Shelton; lived in McCamey, Texas; child:
    (a) Ladonna Lou Nevill, born 1941.

c. Elzia John Nevill, born February 3, 1883; died September 5, 1958, in Jones County, Texas; married (1) December 12, 1904, in Haskell, Texas, to Ida Williams (2) March 16, 1930, in Carlsbad, New Mexico, to Mrs. Carrie L. (Jackson) Hastie; child (by first marriage):
  (1) Avnell Nevill, born 1906; married Henry Wardell Coker; lived in Midland, Texas; children:
    (a) Lyndell Nevill Coker, born August 16, 1930; married June 12, 1953, to Jean Barclay; child:
      /1/ Jeanie Lynette Coker, born April 30, 1954.
    (b) Stanley Dee Coker, born April 27, 1934.

d. Mirt Stroud Nevill, born August 7, 1885; died September 25, 1938, in Levelland, Texas; married September 26, 1915, in Dawson County, Texas, to Annie May Mullins; children:
  (1) John Lafever Nevill, born 1916; married Goldie Ticer; lived in Levelland, Texas; children:
    (a) Ella Mae Nevill, born March 2, 1937; died November 27, 1971; married James D. Lott; children:
      /1/ John Edwin Lott, born c1959; dsp November 27, 1971.
      /2/ Ricky Wayne Lott, born c1963; dsp November 27, 1971.
      /3/ Kimberly Ann Lott, born c1969.
    (b) Mirt Stroud Nevill, born September 25, 1939; lived in Anchorage, Alaska.
    (c) Katherine Nevill, born April, 1942; married _____ Rogers; lived in Portales, New Mexico.

141

        (2) Roberta Nevill, born 1921; married Paul Gilmer; lived in Lamesa,
             Texas; children:
             (a) Jerry Wayne Gilmer, born 1940.
             (b) Gary Ed Gilmer, born 1942.
        (3) Effie Doris Nevill, born 1924; married Ralph Burleson; lived
             in Lamesa, Texas; child:
             (a) Sandra Kay Burleson.

                                      ***

20.   Mary Ann Aris Nevill was born September 3, 1843, in Coffee County,
     Tennessee, and died January 28, 1914, in Bakersfield, California; mar-
     ried March 5, 1859, to Albert Washington Hess. Their children were as
     follows:[42]

     a. Josephine Hess, born c1861; died 1882; married Robert Green; child:
         (1) John Green, born c1882.
     b. Margaret E. Hess, born January 12, 1864; dsp March 2, 1864.
     c. Robertson Hess, born c1865; dsp.
     d. James Hess, born c1867; married Essie _____; child:
         (1) Frank Hess.
     e. Henrietta Hess, born c1869; married Pete Murray; children:
         (1) Mamie Murray, born January 4, 1890; married Emmett Hayes; lived
              in Bakersfield, California; children:
              (a) Thelma Hayes.
              (b) Jack Hayes.
         (2) William H. Murray, born July 27, 1895.
     f. Frances Hess, born July 18, 1871; died May 23, 1934; married (1)
         James Murray (2) 1906, _____ Grimm (3) _____ Cooper; children:
         (by first marriage):
         (1) Albert Washington Murray, born July 4, 1890; dsp.
         (2) Hazel Murray, born February 7, 1893; married Jack de Mello; dsp;
              lived in Larkspur, California.
         (by second marriage):
         (3) Frances Grimm, born 1908; married Duffy J. Little; dsp; lived
              in San Francisco, California.
     g. John Hess, born c1873; dsp.
     h. Laura Hess, born October 14, 1877; married October 11, 1896, to W.
         C. Gallagher; dsp.

                                      ***

21.   Samuel Houston Nevill was born July 30, 1848, in Coffee County,
     Tennessee, and died August 18, 1936, in Coffee County, Tennessee; mar-
     ried (1) January 10, 1872, to Mary Ann Levens (2) December 20, 1905, to
     Frances Brannan. His children were as follows:[43]

     (by first marriage):
     a. Lucy Nevill, born February 10, 1874; dsp c1900; married J. L. Stratt.
     b. Sarah Nevill, born November 2, 1876; died September, 1958; married
         G. Quitman Walling; children:
         (1) Vernon Walling, dsp.
         (2) Ruby Walling.
         (3) Elmer D. Walling.
         (4) Houston Walling.
         (5) Cecil Walling.
     c. Thurza Nevill, born c1878; died May, 1958; married Earl Akin; chil-
         dren:
         (1) W. E. Akin, dsp.

            (2) Euel Akin married Grace _____; dsp.
    d. Cora Lee Nevill, born October 19, 1881; dsp August 29, 1899.
    e. Maud Nevill, born c1883; married Russell C. Lott; children:
            (1) Hugh Lott.
            (2) Lois Lott married _____ Crayton; child:
                    (a) Bill Don Crayton.
            (3) Russell C. Lott; lived in Lamesa, Texas.
            (4) Billie Jim Lott married _____ Brown.
    f. Gibb Nevill, born c1885; died 1947; married Jewel McClain; lived in
        Wascum, Texas; children:
            (1) Jackie Nevill.
            (2) Fred Nevill.
            (3) Gibb Nevill.
    g. Benjamin Nevill, born c1887; dsp 1921.
    (by second marriage):
    h. Wilma Nevill, born February 2, 1907; married June 17, 1934, to Leo
        Huddleston; lived in Coffee County, Tennessee; child:
            (1) Robert Leo Huddleston, born 1949.
    i. Stroud Nevill, born November 10, 1909; dsp.

                            ***

15.   Hardin Nevill was born February 20, 1805, in Orange County, North
    Carolina, and died after 1880 in Brazos County, Texas; married (1)
    c1827, _____   (2) September 19, 1847, to Mrs. Susan (Farquhar)
    Young. His children (among others) were as follows:[44]

    (by first marriage):
    a. Mary E. Nevill, born c1828; married February 20, 1848, to William
        W. Hill.
    b. Minerva Nevill, born c1830; dsp.
    c. Sarah Ann Nevill, born c1833; married June 22, 1854, to John Crosley.
    d. David C. Nevill, born c1840.
    e. William W. Nevill, born c1843.
    f. Nancy Nevill, born c1846.
    (by second marriage):
22. g. Caroline Nevill, born c1848.
    h. James H. Nevill, born c1853; married c1879 Eva C. _____; child
        (among others):
            (1) Clarence C. Nevill, born 1880.

                            ***

22.   Caroline C. Nevill was born about 1848 in Brazos County, Texas,
    and married November 27, 1867, to James William Zimmerman; their children
    were as follows:[45]

23. a. William Zimmerman.
    b. James Hardin Zimmerman married Georgia Morris; children:
            (1) Hardin Morris Zimmerman lived in Monahans, Texas.
            (2) James Addison Zimmerman lived in Pecos, Texas.
            (3) Gladys Zimmerman, dsp.
            (4) Mattie Zimmerman married Ellison Tom; lived in Midland, Texas.
    c. Mary Susan Zimmerman married Ed Moore; children:
            (1) Charles Moore.
            (2) Rachel Moore married Rudolph Butler; lived in Hope, Arkansas.
            (3) Milton Moore.
            (4) Mary Lee Moore married Samuel Ingram; lived in Austin, Texas;
                 child:

                            143

                    (a) Edsam M. Ingram.
    d. Paul Zimmerman, dsp.
    e. John Zimmerman, dsp.
    f. Oscar Burch Zimmerman, born January 19, 1882; died August 15, 1946;
        married Clemmie Bodenhamer; child:
        (1) O. B. Zimmerman, born June 8, 1914; married June 2, 1946, to
             Evelyn Marie Weaver; lived in San Antonio, Texas; child:
             (a) Diane Zimmerman, born May 10, 1949; married August 14, 1971,
                  James B. Tedford; lived in San Antonio, Texas.
    g. Walter Ellis Zimmerman married Ella Newton; lived in Burnet, Texas;
        children:
        (1) Ellis Zimmerman married Ada Duncan; lived in Burnet, Texas.
        (2) Eleanor Merle Zimmerman married Howard Yeary; lived in Cleburne,
             Texas; children:
             (a) Howard Ellis Yeary.
             (b) Betty Yeary.
    h. Lydia Blanche Zimmerman married W. Claud Brown; lived in Lampasas,
        Texas; children:
        (1) Dorothy Lee Brown married _____ Parker; lived in Houston, Texas;
             child:
             (a) Sandra Parker.
        (2) W. Claud Brown married Jane _____ ; lived in Lampasas, Texas.
    i. Matt B. Zimmerman married Emma Myra Bodenhamer; children:
        (1) Winifred Lee Zimmerman married Iris Higgins; lived in Burnet,
             Texas; children:
             (a) Terry Lee Zimmerman.
             (b) Kerry Zimmerman.
        (2) Matt B. Zimmerman; lived in Austin, Texas.

                                  ***

23.   William Zimmerman married Ada Lee Wilson; their children were as
    follows:[46]

    a. James Guy Zimmerman married Mabel Fariss; lived in Burnet, Texas;
        children:
        (1) Billy Fariss Zimmerman married Clarice Walker; lived in Snyder,
             Texas; child:
             (a) Connie Zimmerman.
        (2) James Thomas Zimmerman lived in Burnet, Texas.
    b. Ruby Caroline Zimmerman married T. Van Coupland; lived in Taylor,
        Texas; children:
        (1) Katherine Coupland married John Smock; lived in San Antonio,
             Texas; children:
             (a) Debbie Smock.
             (b) John Smock.
        (2) Margaret Coupland married Lemuel Joiner; lived in San Antonio,
             Texas; child:
             (a) Jerry Joiner.
    c. Benjamin Hardin Zimmerman, died young.
    d. William Alfred Zimmerman married Dora Griffin; lived in Keller,
        Texas; children:
        (1) James Bryan Zimmerman, died young.
        (2) Alfred Ronald Zimmerman.
    e. Susan Ann Zimmerman married W. C. Cagle; lived in Austin, Texas.
    f. Sally Lee Zimmerman married A. R. Johnson; lived in Austin, Texas;
        child:
        (1) James William Johnson.
    g. Walter Edward Zimmerman married Viva Watson; lived in El Campo,

Texas; child:
(1) Mary Suzanne Zimmerman.
- h. Ada Virginia Zimmerman married W. A. Burrage; lived in Austin, Texas;
children:
(1) June Ann Burrage.
(2) Rebecca Carol Burrage.
i. Henry Rudolph Zimmerman married June Smith; lived in Burnet, Texas;
children:
(1) Mary Ada Zimmerman.
(2) Henry Rudolph Zimmerman.
j. Jeff Wilson Zimmerman married Clorene Wimpy; lived in Dell City,
Texas; children:
(1) Thomas Wilson Zimmerman.
(2) William Richard Zimmerman.

***

16.   Pleasant Nevill was born September 5, 1806, in Orange County, North
Carolina, and died about 1865 in Coffee County, Tennessee; married c1828
in Franklin (now Coffee) County, Tennessee, to Mary _____; their children
were (probably among others) as follows:[47]

a. Benjamin Nevill, born c1834; dsp.
b. Anderson Nevill, born c1839; dsp.
c. Henderson Nevill, born October 20, 1843; married February 10, 1867,
to Madora P. Corn; children:
(1) Emma Alice Nevill, born December 11, 1867; died November 4, 1908;
married _____ Waggoner; children:
(a) William Waggoner; lived in Dothan, Alabama.
(b) Dora Waggoner married Earl R. Harer; lived in Myrtle Beach,
South Carolina.
(2) Sallie B. Nevill, born November 22, 1869; dsp December 20, 1871.
(3) Ora Pinkney Nevill, born March 15, 1872; dsp 1956; married
Thomas Lasater; child:
(a) Ora Lasater lived in Cincinnati, Ohio.
(4) Pleasant O. H. Nevill, born April 29, 1874; died May 9, 1902;
married Lee Gotcher; children:
(a) Cornie Nevill, born c1897; lived in Fayetteville, Tennessee.
(b) Clyde Nevill, born c1899; lived in Fayetteville, Tennessee.
(5) John O. Nevill, born April 24, 1876; dsp December 18, 1883.
d. William Pleasant Nevill, born May 28, 1846; married (1) August 30,
1866, to Nancy Anderson (2) August 13, 1876, to Elizabeth Ann Finney
(3) October 12, 1892, to Eva Bryant; children:
(by first marriage):
(1) Willie Ann Nevill, born July 2, 1867.
(2) Ella Franklin Nevill, born May 8, 1869.
(3) Mary Louise Nevill, born January 19, 1871.
(4) Eliza Nevill, born April 10, 1872.
(5) G. M. Nevill, born May 24, 1874.
(by second marriage):
(6) James Madison Nevill, born June 16, 1877; lived in Fayetteville,
Tennessee.
(7) G. F. Nevill, born December 4, 1878; died young.
(8) Martha Line Nevill, born April 22, 1880.
(9) Susan Nevill, born September 22, 1881.
(10) Araia Nevill, born February 1, 1884; died 1955.
(by third marriage):
(11) Alexander Henderson Nevill, born October 25, 1893.

(12) Dora Kathleen Nevill, born December 21, 1894.
(13) Sarah Ophelia Nevill, born August 21, 1896.
(14) Daisy Bryant Nevill, born October 22, 1898; married Walter
     W. Lehr; lived in Niles, Michigan.
(15) Clara Addie Nevill, born November 1, 1901.
(16) Alice Nevill, born October 7, 1903.
(17) John Lemuel Nevill, born May 29, 1905; lived in Niles, Michigan.
e. Elizabeth Ann Nevill, born c1848; married 1867 to Benjamin F. Ander-
    son; children (among others):
(1) Cannon Anderson; lived in Texas.
(2) James Anderson; lived in Texas.
(3) Pleasant Anderson; lived in Texas.
(4) Frank Anderson; lived in Texas.

***

17.   Benjamin Oswin Nevill was born December 5, 1807, in Orange County,
North Carolina, and died October 14, 1851, in Coffee County, Tennessee;
married c1837 to Polexyna Coulson, born December 22, 1818; died May 12,
1880. Their children were as follows:[48]

a. David Benjamin Nevill, born August 1, 1838; dsp June 27, 1862.
b. Sarah Lucinda Nevill, born September 22, 1840; died February 8,
   1934; married March 12, 1866, to John Gilliland Howard, born October
   28, 1823; died January 30, 1914.
c. Nancy Ann Nevill, born December 7, 1842; died August 13, 1911; married Robert G. White, born December 16, 1837; died February 12, 1899.
d. Lucy Nevill, born May 29, 1845; dsp March 23, 1867; married December
   11, 1866, to William B. Pattie.
e. Mary Elender Nevill, born February 9, 1848; died February 20, 1943;
   married February 16, 1871, to William Polk Sims, born July 1, 1846;
   died December 31, 1932.
f. Martha Katherine Nevill, born December 14, 1850; married December 16,
   1867, to L. M. Baird.

***

18.   Martha Jane Nevill was born October 19, 1831, in Franklin (now Coffee) County, Tennessee, and died May 10, 1861, in Coffee County, Tennessee; married January 22, 1852, to William Bluford Buckner; their children were as follows:[49]

24. a. Mary Malinda Buckner, born November 5, 1852.
      b. Amelia Ann Buckner, born March 31, 1854; dsp June 18, 1855.
25. c. James Wilson Buckner, born November 26, 1855.
      d. Nancy Cora Buckner, born February 9, 1858; died August 5, 1909;
     married Robert Jordan Poole; children:
(1) Walter Acker Poole, born July 22, 1881; married Minnie _____;
    lived in Texline, Texas.
(2) Ola Esther Poole, born August 30, 1882; dsp.
(3) Myrtle May Poole, born April 21, 1884; died June 18, 1958;
    married (1) October 12, 1912, to Arthur Crawford (2) Emil
    Kellerhaus; child (by first marriage):
    (a) Merlyne Ethelyn Crawford, born July 26, 1913; married
       March 5, 1931, to Lewis William Penrod; lived in Port
       Arthur, Texas; children:
       /1/ Betty Penrod.
       /2/ Dale Penrod.
       /3/ Nancy Penrod.

      (4) Frederick Bluford Poole, born June 27, 1887; married Euna
                _____; lived in Houston, Texas.
      (5) Milton Jordan Poole, born September 23, 1893; lived in New
             Mexico.
  e. Polexyna Allen Buckner, born May 20, 1860; dsp July 17, 1864.

***

24.   Mary Malinda Buckner was born November 5, 1852, in Coffee County,
Tennessee, and died June 10, 1922, in Ft. Worth, Texas; married November 5, 1867, to Thomas Payne Elkins; their children were as follows:[50]

  a. Musa Emma Elkins, born March 4, 1869; married December 14, 1893, to
      James Paschal Yager; children:
      (1) Raymond Lee Yager, born September 3, 1900; married (1) July 3,
           1920, to Virginia Estella Miller; (2) June 19, 1926, to Myrtle
           Marie Kaler; children:
           (by first marriage):
          (a) Raymond Lee Yager, born October 10, 1921; dsp March 8,
              1923.
          (b) Harry Paschal Yager, born January 23, 1923; married June
              6, 1942, to Betty Ann Jones; child:
              /1/ Katherine Virginia Yager, born December 30, 1944.
          (by second marriage):
          (c) Margaret Yager, born January 23, 1927; married May 4, 1944,
              to Claude Lee Hamilton; child:
              /1/ Janet Rae Hamilton, born March 28, 1945.
      (2) Royal Milton Yager, born August 18, 1902; married December 24,
           1922, to Norah Isabella Blocker; children:
          (a) Mary Alice Yager, born February 15, 1925; married (1)
              July 24, 1944, to Billy Joe Kennedy (2) June 24, 1952,
              to Frederick E. Leaman; children:
              (by first marriage):
              /1/ Barbara Joanna (took surname Leaman), born May 10,
                  1945.
              (by second marriage):
              /2/ Catherine E. Leaman, born December 28, 1954.
              /3/ Deborah Alice Leaman, born May 18, 1959.
          (b) Dorothy Gertrude Yager, born August 8, 1927.
          (c) Roy Wesley Yager, born September 9, 1929.
      (3) Mayme Gertrude Yager, born May 10, 1906; married (1) February
           1, 1933, to William Craven Moy (2) April 3, 1949, to John Ike
           Corley; dsp; lived in Ft. Worth, Texas.
      (4) Clint William Yager, born October 9, 1909; married August 6,
           1937, to Frances Ann Oppe; dsp; lived in Dallas, Texas.
      (5) Clyde Thomas Yager, born October 9, 1909; married (1) March 31,
           1933, to Louise Teague (2) February 6, 1946, to Mrs. Mary
           (Vaughan) Harris; child (by first marriage):
          (a) Karen Sue Yager, born October 30, 1943.
  b. Elizabeth Elkins, born September 18, 1872; married (1) Robert Henry
      Cubley (2) Dr. Z. T. Hodge; children:
      (by first marriage):
      (1) Mable Cubley, born December 16, 1889; married Hugh Wilson; lived
           in Oklahoma; child:
          (a) Hugh Wilson.
      (2) Corinne May Cubley, born April 13, 1892; married (1) Jack Caton
           (2) Frank M. Anderson; lived in Corpus Christi, Texas.
      (by second marriage):

(3) Arnold Hodge, born August 21, 1900; married Madeline _____;
lived in California.
c. Charles Elkins, born c1884; dsp c1889.

***

25.   James Wilson Buckner was born November 26, 1855, in Coffee County,
Tennessee, and died September 26, 1930, in Bertram, Texas; married May
15, 1881, to Martha Lou Ellen Gardner, born March 1, 1858; died October
21, 1921. Their children were as follows:[31]

a. Armour Gertrude Buckner, born April 16, 1884; married (1) Joseph
   Howell (2) _____ Roberts; child (by first marriage):
   (1) Everett Howell married (1) _____ (2) Oleta Thompson;
       lived in Austin, Texas; child (by second marriage):
       (a) Joseph Howell.
b. Ira Arthur Buckner, born June 11, 1886; married Vonnie Ross; lived
   in Bertram, Texas.
c. Emory Albert Buckner, born May 10, 1888; dsp 1915.
d. Walter Henry Buckner, born April 13, 1890; married Dixie Ray; children:
   (1) Walter Weldon Buckner, born December 3, 1915; married Gladys
       Edwards; lived in Corpus Christi, Texas.
   (2) Ruth Lou Buckner, born May 29, 1923; married (1) _____ Bishop
       (2) Marlin Tatum; lived in Spicewood, Texas; children:
       (by first marriage):
       (a) James Weldon Bishop, born March 28, 1941.
       (by second marriage):
       (b) Mary Ruth Tatum, born October 14, 1945.
       (c) Karen Sue Tatum, born August 5, 19??.
       (d) Dickie Ann Tatum, born March 3, 1954.
       (e) Marlene Tatum, born August 26, 1957.
e. Isabel Almira Buckner, born November 14, 1891; married Jess McNabb;
   child:
   (1) Edward McNabb.
f. Milly Fern Buckner, born December 31, 1893; married March 13, 1919,
   to Edward Rudolph McNabb; lived in Bertram, Texas; children:
   (1) Edward Richard McNabb, born January 8, 1921; married December
       15, 1945, to Agnes Murphy; lived in San Antonio, Texas; chil-
       dren:
       (a) Edward Richard McNabb, born May 4, 1949.
       (b) James Wilson McNabb, born April 4, 1950.
       (c) Mary Ellen McNabb, born July 18, 1953.
       (d) Dennis Michael McNabb, born July 18, 1953.
       (e) John Timothy McNabb, born February 7, 1956.
       (f) Ollie Lynn McNabb, born February 15, 1961.
       (g) June Alane McNabb, born July 8, 1963.
   (2) Clinton Buckner McNabb, born November 6, 1923; married Jean
       Marie White; lived in Dallas, Texas; child:
       (a) Clinton Edward McNabb, born October 13, 1949.
   (3) Mary Lou McNabb, born November 15, 1931; married December 19,
       1953, to Joseph Nicholas Steingasser; child:
       (a) Joseph Nicholas Steingasser, born December 25, 1955.
g. Martha Jane Buckner, born August 10, 1895; dsp August 16, 1895.
h. Zuda Ollie Buckner, born February 26, 1897; married Dennis M. Poe;
   dsp; lived in San Antonio, Texas.
i. Fay Wilson Buckner, born June 14, 1900; married Vera Cox; lived in
   Austin, Texas; children:
   (1) Layton Ray Buckner.

(2) Margaret Buckner.

***

5.   Jesse Nevill was born December 29, 1781, in Orange County, North Carolina, and died April 11, 1859, in Marshall County, Mississippi; married May 6, 1802, in Chatham County, North Carolina, to Winifred Norwood, born August 1, 1786, died 1854, daughter of William Norwood and Ruth Wyche. Their children were as follows:[52]

a. Rebecca Nevill, born June 24, 1803; died August, 1847; married February 15, 1821, to Willie Hopson.
b. Martha Nevill, born March 14, 1805.
c. Selah Nevill, born January 20, 1807; died March 25, 1850; married May 13, 1824, to Yonge Snipes; children:
  (1) William Chester Snipes, born December 10, 1825; died August 5, 1910; married (1) Susan Brooks (2) January 30, 1867, to Margaret Ann Eliza Smith; children:
    (by second marriage):
    (a) Ophelia Snipes, born November 4, 1867; dsp August 30, 1886.
    (b) Eva Blanche Snipes, born April 29, 1870; married J. D. Cole.
    (c) Arthur Pratt Snipes, born January 24, 1878; married November 27, 1901, to Mary Virginia Cain; children:
       /1/ Edna Rivers Snipes, dsp; lived in Memphis, Tennessee.
       /2/ Lucile Snipes married M. J. Crane.
    (d) Brack Snipes, born January 13, 1881; married Mary Tackett.
  (2) Elbert Snipes, born August 30, 1827; married Nancy C. Harmon.
  (3) Fanny Snipes, born April 4, 1837; married (1) W. H. Harmon (2) W. R. Howell.
  (4) John A. Jones Snipes, born May 12, 1844; married Mary P. Cain.
  (5) Letitia Ann Snipes married Jesse Hopson.
  (6) Winfield Scott Snipes, born December 26, 1848; married Elizabeth Harmon.
  (7) Bellefield Taylor Snipes, born December 26, 1848; married Lucy Sanders.
d. Laneter Nevill, born May 16, 1809; dsp March, 1830.
e. Whitley Wich Nevill, born December 9, 1810; married December 9, 18??, to Frances _____.
f. William Nevill, born January 10, 1813; lived in Marshall County, Mississippi.
g. Jesse Nevill, born December 21, 1814; married March 22, 1837, to Nancy Crump.
h. Winifred Nevill, born March 9, 1817; married October 7, 1840, to Robert Harris.
i. Isaac Nevill, born February 1, 1819.
j. Norwood Nevill, born March 24, 1821; dsp May 24, 1821.
k. Nancy Elizabeth Nevill, born July 13, 1822; married November 25, 1841, to Rufus Carter.
l. Turley Nevill, born June, 1824; dsp September 1, 1824.

***

6.   Goodman Nevill was born January 9, 1784, in Orange County, North Carolina, and married September 15, 1804, to Jane McCauley, daughter of Matthew McCauley and Martha Johnston. Their children were as follows:[53]

26. a. Martha Nevill, born November 11, 1805.
27. b. Matthew Nevill, born April 14, 1808.

149

c. Jane Nevill, born 1810.
d. Elizabeth Nevill, born c1813; married October 6, 1834, to Thomas Shef-
   field Lindsey (see p. 175).
e. Charles Nevill, born c1815; died 1886 in Orange County, North Carolina; married Susan Snipes; children:
   (1) Alfred Nevill married Sarah Morgan.
   (2) John G. Nevill married April 24, 1863, to Frances S. Stanford.
   (3) William Nevill married Martha Frances Snipes.
f. Mary Nevill, born c1817; married December 18, 1854, to Isaac Morgan.

***

26.   Martha Nevill was born November 11, 1805, in Orange County, North
Carolina, and died June 13, 1886. She married December 16, 1824, to Manley E. Snipes, born June 30, 1803; died June 18, 1862, son of John Snipes
and Sarah Lindsey. Their children were as follows:[54]

a. Presley John Snipes, born 1825; died 1880; married Permelia Ward.
b. Marion Snipes, born 1827; married Tabitha Bowers.
c. Miranda Snipes, born 1829; died 1861; married Jesse O'Daniel.
d. Frances J. Snipes, born 1830; married Wesley Couch.

28.
e. Angeline E. Snipes, born December 8, 1832.
f. William G. Snipes, born May 22, 1835; dsp September 9, 1846.
g. Charles Manley Snipes, born August 5, 1837; died July 2, 1905; married Margaret Lamb.
h. Matthew J. Snipes, born July 1, 1839; died April 14, 1884; married
   Mary Laura Stanford.
i. Alfred G. Snipes, born September 9, 1841; dsp December, 1862.
j. Mary H. Snipes, born January 10, 1844; died November 28, 1935; married (1) John Ward (2) Bryant Durham.
k. Sarah Ann Snipes, born July 30, 1846; died June 17, 1922, in Durham,
   North Carolina; married January 14, 1869, Allison Justice Roberson,
   born January 15, 1835; died June 9, 1900, son of Stephen Roberson and
   Elizabeth Edwards; children:
   (1) Woodson Lee Roberson, born February 15, 1870; dsp August 24, 1871.
   (2) Eliar Foust Roberson, born February 19, 1872; died February 19,
       1960; married March 17, 1897, to Leonidas Sparrow, born March
       18, 1869; died February 4, 1949; children:
       (a) Buren Smith Sparrow, born March 23, 1898; married Jake Mc-
           Cracken Smith.
       (b) Roberta Justice Sparrow, born August 11, 1901; married Dec-
           ember 4, 1922, to Herman Hooker Brown; lived in Tucson,
           Arizona; children:
           /1/ Herman Hooker Brown, born February 4, 1930; died Sep-
               tember 28, 1962.
           /2/ Joyce Brown, born October 30, 1933.
       (c) Ralph Lee Sparrow, born December 24, 1902; married Jessie
           Dennis; child:
           /1/ William Allison Sparrow.
   (3) Arlula Elizabeth Roberson, born May 7, 1873, died January 13,
       1962; married January 29, 1896, to John P. Cate, born November
       25, 1861; died February 13, 1938; lived in Mebane, North Caro-
       lina.
   (4) Bazel Manley Roberson, born February 2, 1875; died March 4, 1954;
       married Fannie Ray, born June 7, 1865, died February 8, 1928.
   (5) Jennie N. Roberson, born September 23, 1877, died March 29, 1959;
       married October 16, 1901, to Edward J. Roberson, born March 14,
       1874; died March 29, 1934.
   (6) Stephen Wilson Roberson, born December 2, 1879; died February

5, 1954; married (1) Rhoda Parrish (2) November 1, 1903, to Lillie Barbee, died December 10, 1910.
- (7) Ola Morrow Roberson, born January 22, 1882; died June 7, 1951; married December 28, 1904, to William David Blackwood, born June 9, 1870; died June 24, 1944.
- (8) Mary J. Roberson, born August 18, 1884; died June 25, 1906; married November 30, 1904, to Luther J. Holloman.
- (9) Rosa Belle Roberson, born September 27, 1888; married October 17, 1906, to William Millard Todd, born October 2, 1886; lived in Greensboro, North Carolina.
1. Albert H. Snipes, born July 14, 1849; died March 23, 1931; married Sarah E. Wilson, born July 26, 1856; died November 19, 1946.

***

28.   Angeline E. Snipes was born December 8, 1832, in Orange County, North Carolina, and died February 10, 1908; married August 7, 1855, to John Foust, born January 16, 1828; died January 31, 1907, son of John Foust and Susan Hornaday. Their children were as follows:[55]

- a. William Arlendo Foust, born September 24, 1856; died December 23, 1946; married August 7, 1879, to Cornelia Moore, born June 3, 1856; died June 20, 1927.
- b. Martha Eleanor Foust, born April 24, 1861; died January 5, 1944; married September 2, 1880, to Robert S. Thompson, born August 18, 1859; died December 30, 1936.
- c. Mary Elizabeth Foust, born April 29, 1866; married March 23, 1887, to George Washington Holmes, born February 11, 1856; died December 11, 1937; children:
  - (1) James Eugene Holmes, born March 26, 1888; married September 11, 1917, to Bessie Shelton, born February 15, 1897.
  - (2) John Albert Holmes, born February 15, 1890; married December 23, 1919, to Willie McDonald Barrett, born October 17, 1895; died January 1, 1954; lived in Edenton, North Carolina; children:
    - (a) John Albert Holmes, born December 11, 1925; married November 3, 1951, to Doris Marie Baynes, born November 23, 1924; lived in Raleigh, North Carolina; child:
      - /1/ Jane Elizabeth Holmes, born November 17, 1954.
    - (b) Mary McDonald Holmes, born November 9, 1928; lived in Chapel Hill, North Carolina.
  - (3) Ralph Wendell Holmes, born March 15, 1893; dsp.
  - (4) Minnie Mae Holmes, born May 6, 1895; dsp.
  - (5) George Washington Holmes, born January 1, 1898; married Frances Thompson.
  - (6) Bessie Louise Holmes, born August 22, 1900; married January 10, 1942, to George Branson Robbins, born June 6, 1899; dsp.
  - (7) Joseph William Holmes, born January 21, 1904; married August 19, 1931, to Dorothy Lamb; dsp.
  - (8) Mary Elizabeth Holmes, born July 16, 1908; dsp March 26, 1911.
- d. John Manly Foust, born September 25, 1868; died June 19, 1941; married (1) Ellen Stafford, died May 22, 1894; (2) June 21, 1899, to Inez Wood, born September 4, 1872.
- e. Albert Lee Foust, born December 15, 1870; died January 24, 1956; married May 20, 1894, to Minnie McPherson, born September 29, 1874, (see p. 121).
- f. Ida Viola Foust, born November 27, 1874; died September 9, 1932; married Samuel McPherson, died September 9, 1932.

***

27.   Matthew Nevill was born April 14, 1808; died 1888; married October
        6, 1828, to Mahala Kirby; lived in Shelby County, Tennessee; their chil-
        dren were as follows:[56]

a. Jane Nevill married William J. Aitken.
b. Elizabeth Nevill, dsp.
c. Mary Rebecca Nevill married Henry Brewster; children:
    (1) Sarah T. Brewster married William Canada.
    (2) (son)
d. Weschina Ann Nevill, born October 24, 1838; died August 21, 1913,
    in Memphis, Tennessee; married November 28, 1861, to Jacob Joyner,
    born September 21, 1817; died January 6, 1901, in De Soto County,
    Mississippi; children:
    (1) Elizabeth Josephine Joyner, born February 20, 1863; dsp March
         26, 1913; lived in Bolivar, Tennessee.
    (2) Mahala Kirby Joyner, born January 1, 1865; married June 12, 1919,
         to Richard W. Kellar; dsp.
    (3) Matthew Nevill Joyner, born November 5, 1868; died December 5,
         1952, in Silver Spring, Maryland; married October 1, 1896, to
         Mrs. Elizabeth (McCaa) Mitchell; children:
         (a) Quintard Joyner, born 1897; married 1941 to Georgia Duncan
              McCague; children:
              /1/ Katherine Marie Joyner.
              /2/ John Nevill Joyner.
         (b) Nevill McCaa Joyner, born 1899; married Jean Blish; child:
              /1/ William Blish Joyner.
         (c) Mary Elizabeth Joyner, born 1900; married 1946 to Frederick
              Lawson; dsp.
    (4) Rebecca Harris Joyner, born March 3, 1871; died April 15, 1945,
         in Tupelo, Mississippi; married February 20, 1896, Benjamin
         Edgar Brigance, born October 11, 1873; children:
         (a) William Norwood Brigance, born November 17, 1896; married
              August 9, 1922, to Jane Martin; children:
              /1/ Virginia Joyce Brigance, born July 10, 1924; dsp.
              /2/ Shirley Jane Brigance, born October 24, 1926; married
                   August 11, 1950, to John Roger Oest; children:
                   /a/ John Norwood Oest, born September 28, 1952.
                   /b/ Thomas Nevill Oest, born June 15, 1955.
         (b) Julia Grey Brigance, born January 17, 1899; dsp September
              24, 1899.
         (c) Rebecca Olivia Brigance, born October 18, 1900; died
              October 13, 1948; married July 20, 1935, to Norman J.
              Brockley; lived in Long Beach, California.
         (d) Edgar Brigance, born September 23, 1904; married May 24,
              1927, to James Mial Tidwell; lived in Amarillo, Texas.
e. William Norwood Nevill, born April 9, 1840; died December 17, 1932;
    married Jennie Tubbeville; children:
    (1) Emma Nevill, dsp.
    (2) Mary Nevill, dsp.
f. Antoinette Nevill married David Dunlap.

***

7.   Samuel Parke Nevill was born March 23, 1790, in Orange County,
        North Carolina, and died November 14, 1854, in Orange County, North Caro-
        lina; married January 18, 1810, to Elizabeth McCauley; their children
        were as follows:[57]

a. Cynthia Nevill, born September 19, 1812; married January 4, 1830,

to Benjamin McCauley.
b. George Johnson Nevill(e), born September 15, 1814; died March 1, 1892.
c. Esperan Nevill, born September 12, 1816; died October 12, 1909; married September 27, 1847, to Orren Lloyd; children:
    (1) George Lloyd.
    (2) Elizabeth Lloyd married Thaddeus Lloyd.
    (3) Ruffin Lloyd married Nancy Robinson.
    (4) Annie Aiken Lloyd married William B. Andrews.
    (5) Samuel Parke Lloyd married Ella Blackwood,
    (6) Kate Lloyd married Columbus King.
d. James Nevill(e), born August 24, 1818; died December 3, 1885; married December 15, 1836, to Caroline Strowd; children:
    (1) Samuel Johnson Neville married July 28, 1861, to Margaret Adeline Tilley.
    (2) Esperan Neville married August 17, 1865, to William D. King.
    (3) Bryant Neville married Julia Lloyd.
    (4) Julia Neville, married Zachariah Lloyd.
    (5) Delia Neville married Dolphus Dollar.
e. Ruffin Nevill(e), born February 4, 1821; died January 7, 1861; married October 27, 1859, to Nancy Blackwood; child:
    (1) Perian Neville married Thomas Myrick.
f. Samuel Nevill(e), born August 19, 1824; lived in Texas.
g. Matthew Nevill(e), born June 5, 1829; married June 13, 1847, to Tabitha Bowers; lived in Mississippi.
h. John Nevill(e), born April 28, 1831; died October 3, 1881; married October 23, 1850, to Emily Lloyd; children:
    (1) William David Neville married December 7, 1873, to Sarah E. Pritchard; lived in Chapel Hill, North Carolina.
    (2) Martha Neville married Samuel J. McCauley.

***

REFERENCES

[1]Isle of Wight County, Virginia, Deeds.
[2]Ibid.; Virginia Land Grant Book 7, pp. 378, 545.
[3]Virginia Quitrents of 1704; Isle of Wight County, Virginia, Wills.
[4]Halifax County, North Carolina, Deed Bk. 3, p. 88, Bk. 5, p. 466, Bk. 3, p. 317, Bk. 6, p. 31; North Carolina Land Grant Bk. 11, p. 237, State Land Office, Raleigh, North Carolina.
[5]Halifax County, North Carolina, Deed Bk. 4, p. 537, Bk. 2, p. 281, Bk. 6, pp. 6, 20, Bk. 14, p. 474; J. Bryan Grimes, Abstract of North Carolina Wills (Raleigh: Uzzell, 1910), p. 262.
[6]Thomas Nevill(e) was not mentioned in Benjamin Nevill's will, but because of association and similarity of children's names was probably a son.
[7]Halifax County, North Carolina, Deed Bk. 7, p. 290, Bk. 17, pp. 24, 52, 135, 277, 377, 502.
[8]Ibid., Wills.
[9]Bible record belonging (1956) to Mrs. Louise Ivey; Halifax County, North Carolina, Deed Bk. 9, p. 48, Bk. 12, p. 53; Granville County, North Carolina, Deeds J, 424.
[10]Orange County, North Carolina, Deed Bk. 3, p. 607, Land Entries #282, #1043.
[11]Bible record belonging (1956) to Mrs. Louise Ivey; Orange County, North Carolina, Court Minutes, Tax lists, State Archives, Raleigh, North Carolina.

[12]Orange County, North Carolina, Deed Bk. 2, p. 167, Bk. 3, p. 104, Bk. 2, p. 185, Bk. 4, p. 683; Chatham County, North Carolina, Deed Bk. 4, pp. 277, 444, Bk. 6, p. 406, Bk. 5, pp. 209, 590, Bk. 9, pp. 257, 315.

[13]Hugh Lefler and Paul Wager, History of Orange County (Chapel Hill: The Orange Print Shop, 1953), pp. 78, 303; statement of Everette Neville.

[14]Orange County, North Carolina, Deed Bk. 9, p. 314, Bk. 10, pp. 377, 255, Bk. 11, p. 341; Chatham County, North Carolina, Deeds P, 410, M, 136; Orange County, North Carolina, Wills D, 263.

[15]Bible record belonging (1956) to Mrs. Louise Ivey.

[16-21]Records of Herschel Kennon Smith.

[22-23]Records of Mrs. Henry Means Walker.

[24]Bible record belonging (1960) to Mrs. Milly B. McNabb; St. Thomas District, Orange County, North Carolina, tax list, 1801, Deed Bk. 10, p. 377, Bk. 17, p. 329, Bk. 13, p. 511, Entry Book 118, p. 395.

[25]Franklin County, Tennessee, Deeds B, 134, 151, D, 148, 223, J, 519, Land Entry Book 1, pp. 26, 76, #110, #343, Deeds J, 606, L, 392, 390.

[26]Bible record belonging (1960) to Mrs. Milly B. McNabb; statement of Mrs. Frances Brannan Nevill.

[27]Ibid., Deeds M, 90, 91, 89, 327, 325, 328, 323, N, 474.

[28]Statement of Mary Nevill Sims; Bible record belonging (1960) to Mrs. Mildred B. McNabb; Bill of Complaint, Benjamin O. Nevill against administrators of Robertson Nevill, Chancery Court, Coffee County, Tennessee; Bill of Complaint by James Wilkinson against heirs of Benjamin Nevill, Chancery Court, Franklin County, Tennessee, originals owned by David B. Trimble.

[29]Bible record belonging (1960) to Stroud Nevill; Land Grant #2920, Tennessee State Archives, Nashville, Tennessee; Franklin County, Tennessee, Deeds M, 92, 90.

[30]Franklin County, Tennessee, Deeds M, 253, 220; Coffee County, Tennessee, Deeds B, 467, A, 276; Grundy County, Tennessee, Deeds A, 197, 198 (boundary changes placed this land in Coffee County later).

[31]Coffee County, Tennessee, Deeds A, 392, B, 410, A, 395, C, 148, D, 379.

[32]Original contracts and receipts for sales owned by David B. Trimble.

[33]Franklin County, Tennessee, Deeds N, 404; Coffee County, Tennessee, Deeds B, 429, 468, 481, Court Minutes, p. 157; Original receipt owned by David B. Trimble.

[34]Coffee County, Tennessee, Court Minutes, 1838, Chancery Court cases (original bill of complaint owned by David B. Trimble), Deeds B, 641.

[35]Bible record owned (1960) by Stroud Nevill; statement of Mrs. Frances Brannan Nevill; original order owned by David B. Trimble; Coffee County, Tennessee, Deed Bk. 3, p. 53, Bk. 12, p. 344.

[36]Bible record belonging (1960) to Virgil G. Nevill; Pension record, State Archives, Austin, Texas; statement of Barzillia H. Nevill.

[37]Coffee County, Tennessee, Deeds, P, 204, S, 50.

[38]Johnson County, Texas, Deeds N, 338, 579, Bk. 31, p. 604.

[39]Hill County, Texas, Deed Bk. 3, p. 365, Bk. 10, p. 590, Bk. 20, pp. 163, 162, Bk. 41, p. 180, Bk. 31, p. 116.

[40]Statement of Barzillia H. Nevill; Jones County, Texas, records have not been examined.

[41]Statement of Zella D. Trimble; Bible record belonging (1960) to Virgil G. Nevill; statements of Virgil G. Nevill, Mrs. Avnell N. Coker, and J. L. Nevill.

[42]Records of Mrs. Frances Grimm Little.

[43]Records of Mrs. Wilma Nevill Huddleston.

[44-46]Records of Mrs. Ada Zimmerman.

[47]Records of Mrs. Dora W. Harer and Alexander H. Nevill.

[48]Records of David Oswin Sims.

[49-50]Records of Mrs. Mayme Y. Corley.

[51]Records of Mrs. Milly B. McNabb.
[52]Records of Edna Rivers Snipes.
[53-55]Records of John Albert Holmes.
[56]Records of William N. Brigance.
[57]Records of Everette Nevill.

***

PENNINGTON and BOONE of Monroe County, Kentucky

George Boone was born in 1666 at Stoak, Devonshire, England, the son of George Boone, a blacksmith, and his wife, Sarah Uppey. About 1689 he married Mary Maugridge, who was born in 1669 at Bradninch, Devonshire, the daughter of John Maugridge and Mary Milton. After his marriage, George Boone was a weaver at Bradninch, and a member of Callumpton Monthly Meeting of Friends. On August 17, 1717, he and his family took ship at Bristol for America, landing at Philadelphia, Pennsylvania, on September 29, 1717. He later moved to Abington, and then to North Wales, Pennsylvania, for about two years; he then settled at Oley in Exeter Township, Philadelphia (now Berks) County, Pennsylvania, where he had joined Oley Monthly Meeting of Friends on October 31, 1717. George Boone died on July 27, 1744, in Berks County, and his wife Mary Boone died on February 2, 1740/1.[1] Their children were as follows:[2]

a. **George Boone, born July 13, 1690;** died November 20, 1753, in Berks County, Pennsylvania; married July 27, 1713, to Deborah Howell.
b. Sarah Boone, born February 18, 1691/2; married March 15, 1715, to Jacob Stover.
1. c. Squire Boone, born November 25, 1696.
d. Mary Boone, born September 23, 1699; died January 16, 1774; married September 13, 1720, to John Webb.
e. John Boone, born January 3, 1701/2; dsp October 10, 1785, in Berks County, Pennsylvania.
f. Joseph Boone, born April 5, 1704; died January 30, 1776, in Berks County, Pennsylvania; married Catherine _____ .
g. Benjamin Boone, born July 16, 1706; died October 14, 1762, in Berks County, Pennsylvania; married (1) Ann Farmer (2) Susannah _____ .
h. James Boone, born July 7, 1709; died September 1, 1785, in Berks County, Pennsylvania; married (1) May 15, 1735, to Mary Foulke (2) October 20, 1757, to Anne Griffith.
i. Samuel Boone, born 1711; died August 6, 1745, in Philadelphia (now Berks) County, Pennsylvania; married October 29, 1734, to Elizabeth Cassel.

***

1.   Squire Boone was born November 25, 1696, in Bradninch, Devonshire, England, and lived there until about 1712, when he accompanied his older brother and sister to America, settling in Philadelphia (now Berks) County, Pennsylvania. After his marriage on September 23, 1720, in Philadelphia (now Montgomery) County, Pennsylvania, to Sarah Morgan, he was a weaver at Oley. He bought 147 acres in New Britain Township, Bucks County, Pennsylvania, on December 3, 1728, and on December 27, 1730, he bought 250 acres at Oley in Berks County, where he was a member of Oley Monthly Meeting of Friends and active in church affairs. In 1744, he bought an additional 25 acres for grazing cattle.[3]

****

Edward Morgan was a tailor in Gwynedd, Philadelphia (now Montgomery) County, Pennsylvania, as early as 1704, probably having moved from Wales shortly before. In February, 1708, he bought 300 acres in Towamencin from Griffith Jones and in 1714 he bought 500 acres there from George Claypool.[4] He was the father of, perhaps among others, the following children:[4]

a. Morgan Morgan died in 1727 in Philadelphia (now Montgomery) County, Pennsylvania; married Dorothy _____.
b. Edward Morgan.
c. William Morgan, born c1692; married August 27, 1713, to Elizabeth Roberts.
d. Margaret Morgan, born c1694; married March 1, 1713, to Samuel Thomas.
e. Daniel Morgan, born c1696; married September 2, 1718, to Elizabeth Roberts.
f. John Morgan, born c1698; married September 8, 1718, to Sarah Lloyd.
g. Sarah Morgan, born 1700; died 1770 in Rowan (now Davie) County, North Carolina; married September 23, 1720, to Squire Boone.
h. Joseph Morgan, born c1702; married September 8, 1728, to Elizabeth Lloyd.

****

On April 11, 1750, Squire Boone sold his 158 acre farm to William Maugridge, and on May 1, 1750, the family moved to the Shenandoah Valley in Virginia. In 1752, they moved to Dutchman Creek at Buffalo Lick in Rowan (now Davie) County, North Carolina, where on April 30, 1753, he bought 640 acres on Grant's Creek from Earl Granville for three shillings; on December 29, 1753, he bought another 640 acres on Bear Creek from Granville for three shillings. In 1753, Boone was a justice of the Rowan County Court.[5]

On October 12, 1759, Squire and Sarah Boone sold the 640 acre tract on Bear Creek to their son Daniel for ₤50, and the 640 acres on Grant's Creek to their son Squire, and because of Indian troubles moved back to Virginia; in 1762, they returned to Dutchman Creek. Squire Boone died there on January 2, 1765, and his wife Sarah died in 1770.[6] Their children were as follows:[7]

a. Sarah Boone, born June 7, 1724; died in 1815 in Estill County, Kentucky; married 1742 to John Wilcoxen.
b. Israel Boone, born May 9, 1726; died June 26, 1756, in Rowan (now Davie) County, North Carolina.
c. Samuel Boone, born May 20, 1728; died in Fayette County, Kentucky; married Sarah Day.
d. Jonathan Boone, born December 6, 1730; died c1808 in Wabash County, Illinois; married Mary Carter.
e. Elizabeth Boone, born February 5, 1732; died February 25, 1825, in Fayette County, Kentucky; married William Grant, born February 22, 1726; died June 22, 1804.
f. Daniel Boone, born October 22, 1734; died September 26, 1820, in St. Charles County, Missouri; married August 14, 1756, to Rebecca Bryan.
g. Mary Boone, born November 3, 1736; died 1819 in Kentucky; married William Bryan, born March 6, 1733; died May 30, 1780.
h. George Boone, born January 2, 1739; died November 11, 1820, in Shelby County, Kentucky; married c1764 to Ann Linville.
i. Edward Boone, born November 19, 1740; died October 15, 1780, in Kentucky; married Martha Bryan.
j. Squire Boone, born October 5, 1744; died August, 1815, in Harrison County, Indiana; married August 8, 1765, to Jane Van Cleve.
2. k. Hannah Boone, born August 24, 1746.

***

2.   Hannah Boone was born August 24, 1746, in Philadelphia (now Berks) County, Pennsylvania, and on May 1, 1750, moved with her parents to the

Shenandoah Valley in Virginia, living on a farm in Augusta (now Rockingham) County until 1752, when the family moved to Dutchman Creek at Buffalo Lick in Rowan (now Davie) County, North Carolina. Because of Indian trouble, the Boones moved back to Virginia in 1759 but returned to Dutchman Creek in 1762.[8]

On February 14, 1765, Hannah Boone married John Stewart, who was later described by Joshua Pennington as being 5'11" tall, well-proportioned, with an excellent countenance, fair complexion, and pleasing smile; he was reserved in conversation, seldom jested, and was a remarkable hunter and woodsman.[9]

In the late summer of 1765, John Stewart accompanied Hannah's brother, Daniel Boone, on an expedition from St. Augustine to Pensacola, Florida; Stewart was separated from the party at one time and almost starved before finding it. In 1766 he accompanied Benjamin Cutbird on a trip westward to the Mississippi River. On May 1, 1769, with John Finley, Daniel Boone, and others, he started for Kentucky. The party crossed Cumberland Gap and then spent several months hunting and collecting furs at their camp on Station Camp Creek, a tributary of the Red Lick Fork of the Kentucky River. On December 22, 1769, Stewart and Boone were captured by Shawnee Indians, who robbed the camp of all furs, supplies, and horses. Stewart and Boone followed the Indians, were re-captured, and escaped about January 4, 1770. Shortly afterwards, while hunting along the Red River, Stewart was evidently killed by Indians.[10]

Hannah (Boone) Stewart re-married about 1777 to Richard Pennington, who was born in 1752 in Pennsylvania. Shortly afterwards they moved to the North Fork of the New River in Wilkes (now Ashe) County, North Carolina, where during the American Revolution, Richard Pennington served under Captain Enoch Osborn at Osborn's Fort in Montgomery (now Grayson) County, Virginia. He entered 156 acres in Morgan District of Wilkes (now Ashe) County, North Carolina, on July 25, 1794, and received the land from the state on January 1, 1798. On May 15, 1797, he sold the farm to Alexander Johnston for £60, and on August 7, 1797, he moved to Fayette County, Kentucky, settling nine miles from Lexington on the Little North Elkhorn River.[11]

In September, 1798, Richard and Hannah Pennington moved to Barren (now Monroe) County, Kentucky, where he acquired a 100 acre farm which he later enlarged. On March 9, 1799, Hannah joined the Mill Creek Baptist Church near Tompkinsville by letter, and she later joined a Campbellite group that seceded from Mill Creek.[12]

About 1811, Richard and Hannah Pennington moved to White County, Tennessee, with their son Joshua; Richard died there on December 21, 1813, and Hannah returned to Monroe County, Kentucky, and lived in the home of her son Daniel Pennington, where she died on April 9, 1828. The children of Hannah Boone Stewart Pennington were as follows:[13]

(by first marriage):
3. a. Sarah Stewart, born 1766.
4. b. Mary Stewart, born 1768.
5. c. Elizabeth Stewart, born February 25, 1770.
     (by unknown father):
     d. Rachel (surname unknown), born 1775; married James King.
     (by second marriage):
6. e. Joshua Pennington, born February 23, 1778.
7. f. Daniel Pennington, born December 3, 1781.

8. g. Stewart Pennington, born June 10, 1784.
    h. Abigail Pennington, born January 24, 1787; died c1835 in Jackson
        County, Alabama; married December 20, 1804, to William Gist.

***

3.   Sarah Stewart was born in 1766 in Rowan (now Davie) County, North
Carolina, and moved to Wilkes (now Ashe) County, North Carolina, about
1778. About 1784, she married John Osborn, who was born April 16, 1763,
in Shenandoah County, Virginia; the family later moved to Smith (now
Macon) County, Tennessee, where Sarah died in September, 1815. John
Osborn, who received a pension from his services in the American Revolution, moved to Harrison and then Fountain Counties, Indiana, and finally
to Linn County, Iowa, where he died in 1854. The children of John and
Sarah Osborn were as follows:[14]

    a. Nancy Osborn married /Thomas?/ Gist.
    b. Mary Osborn married _____ Ray.
    c. John Osborn.
    d. Samuel Osborn, born c1792; died October 21, 1851, in McDonough County,
        Illinois; married December 17, 1816, to Lydia Maxwell.
    e. Stephen Osborn lived in Linn County, Iowa.
    f. Ephraim Osborn.
    g. Hannah Osborn married James Starr.
    h. Aaron Osborn lived in Platte County, Missouri.
    i. Rachel Osborn married Stephen Cochran; lived in Illinois and Iowa.
    j. Robert Osborn, born August 1, 1809; died March 6, 1880, in Center
        Point, Iowa; married February 27, 1829, to Elizabeth Scott.

***

4.   Mary Stewart was born in 1768 in Rowan (now Davie) County, North
Carolina, and died in 1832 in Vermilion County, Illinois; married about
1787 in Wilkes (now Ashe) County, North Carolina, to Solomon Osborn;
their children were as follows:[15]

    a. (daughter) married William McCall; lived in Dennison, Iowa.
    b. John Osborn.
    c. Richard Osborn, born January 23, 1798; died in 1876 in Fulton County,
        Illinois; married in 1821 to Mary Shaw.
    d. Samuel M. Osborn, born c1802; died c1855 in Louisville, Kentucky;
        married Cynthia _____.
    e. William Osborn, born c1804; married Elizabeth Humphreys.
    f. Tabitha Osborn, born c1806; died May 13, 1862, in Mahomet, Illinois;
        married in 1824 to John Stone Robinson.
    g. James Osborn married Ruth _____.
    h. Sarah Osborn.
    i. Noah Osborn.

***

5.   Elizabeth Stewart was born February 25, 1770, in Rowan (now Davie)
County, North Carolina; married about 1786 in Wilkes (now Ashe) County,
North Carolina, to James Lewis, who was born September 6, 1767, in Gran-
ville County, North Carolina. They moved to Barren County, Kentucky,
Crawford County, Indiana, and St. Charles, Boone, Jackson, and Platte
Counties, Missouri, where they died; their children were as follows:[16]

    a. William Lewis, born September 27, 1787; died 1856 in Stockton, Cali-

159

fornia; married c1814 to Elvira Sloan.

   b. Jesse Lewis, born April 9, 1790; died December 28, 1884, in Atchison,
       Kansas; married c1812 to Miranda Sloan; lived in Barren (now Monroe)
       County, Kentucky, where he served as a private in Capt. Henry Yakey's
       Company, 3rd Regiment, Kentucky Militia, in the War of 1812; moved
       to Jackson, Platte, and Holt Counties, Missouri.
   c. Ann Lewis, born February 27, 1792.
   d. Gideon Lewis, born September 27, 1795.
   e. Joshua Lewis, born November 26, 1797; married Margaret Kelsey.
   f. John Stewart Lewis, born May 24, 1800; died September 29, 1843, in
       Jackson County, Missouri; married Mary Jane Fulgerson.
   g. Daniel Pennington Lewis, born January 20, 1802; died 1873; married
       Mary Paine; lived in Platte and Jackson Counties, Missouri.
   h. Byrum Lewis, born August 13, 1804; died 1886; married Mrs. Violet
       Wilson (Jones) Hand; lived in Kelseyville, California.
   i. Mary Grant Lewis, born November 16, 1806; died January 16, 1874, in
       Vacaville, California; married Jedidiah Williams.
   j. James Lewis, born November 12, 1808.
   k. Isaac T. Lewis, born January 29, 1811; died November 23, 1902, in
       Coyle, Oklahoma; married (1) Mary Alice Wigham (2) Mary J. White.

                                  ***

6.   Joshua Pennington was born February 23, 1778, in Wilkes (now Ashe)
   County, North Carolina. On November 24, 1804, he received a grant of 100
   acres on Line Creek in Barren (now Monroe) County, Kentucky; also in 1804
   he bought 100 acres on Line Creek from Welcome Ussery which he sold to
   John Casteel in 1811. On February 20, 1806, in Barren (now Monroe) County, Kentucky, he married Mary Gist, who was born October 13, 1786, in
   Greene County, Tennessee, and died October 10, 1839. About 1811, he
   moved to White County, Tennessee, where, after the death of his first
   wife, he married Sarah Howard on August 24, 1844. He died in Warren
   County, Tennessee, about 1868; his children (all by his first marriage)
   were as follows:[17]

   a. William Pennington, born c1807; lived in Schuyler County, Missouri,
       in 1872.
9. b. Richard Pennington, born April 11, 1809.
   c. Granderson Pennington, born April 22, 1811; died 1873 in Warren County,
       Tennessee; married c1833 to Sarah _____; children:
       (1) Mary J. Pennington, born c1834.
       (2) Caleb M. Pennington, born c1835; married August 25, 1857, Nancy
            Webb.
       (3) Joshua Pennington, born c1837.
       (4) William P. Pennington, born c1839.
       (5) Elizabeth Pennington, born c1844.
       (6) Samuel F. Pennington, born c1846.
       (7) Sarah A. Pennington, born c1849.
       (8) Charles Pennington, born c1852.
   d. John Pennington, born c1813; married Martha _____; lived in Houston
       County, Texas; children (among others):
       (1) William Pennington, born c1843.
       (2) Thomas Pennington, born c1845.
       (3) Richard Pennington, born c1847; married Sarah _____.
       (4) Joshua Pennington, born c1849.
       (5) Allen Pennington, born c1850.
       (6) Martha Pennington, born c1852; married _____ Parker; children:
            (a) Ira Parker, born c1868.

                                  160

        (b) William Parker, born c1870.
        (c) Caledonia Parker, born c1871.
        (d) John Parker, born c1873.
        (e) Miles Parker, born c1875.
        (f) Benjamin Parker, born c1876.
    (7) Lucinda Pennington, born c1854.
    (8) Margaret Pennington, born c1859.
    (9) Charity Pennington, born c1862.
e. Joseph Pennington, born c1815.
f. Altamira Pennington, born c1817; married January 3, 1839, to James
    Walling.
g. Elizabeth Pennington, born c1819; married January 2, 1840, to James
    W. Denton.
h. Rhoda Ann Pennington, born c1821; married February 16, 1841, to Ozias
    Walling.
i. Jane Pennington, born c1823; married February 6, 1842, to Timothy
    Couch.
j. Joshua Pennington, born c1826; married April 6, 1843, to Eliza J.
    Couch; lived in Warren County, Tennessee, in 1860; children (among
    others):
    (1) Joseph Pennington, born c1845.
    (2) Malinda J. Pennington, born c1847.
    (3) Timothy C. Pennington, born c1848; died young.
    (4) Sarah Pennington, born c1851.
    (5) Thomas Pennington, born c1855.
    (6) Nancy Pennington, born c1858.

                                    ***

9.   Richard Pennington was born April 11, 1809, in Barren (now Monroe)
    County, Kentucky, and died November 11, 1891, in Houston County, Texas;
    married c1829 in White County, Tennessee, to Mary Walling; their chil-
    dren were as follows:[18]

a. Catherine Pennington, born c1835; married ____ Beasley.
b. Edmund Gaines Pennington, born January 1, 1837; married c1858 to
    Nancy Jane Renfro; children (among others):
    (1) John Pennington, born c1859.
    (2) Susan Pennington, born c1861.
    (3) Mary Pennington, born c1865.
    (4) James H. Pennington, born c1869.
    (5) Lucy Pennington, born c1872.
    (6) Emily Pennington, born c1874.
    (7) Ida Pennington, born c1876.
    (8) Patty Pennington, born c1879.
c. Lawson James Pennington, born May 20, 1846; died October 4, 1925;
    married Lou Baker.
d. Jane Pennington, born February 22, 1848; died May 22, 1933; married
    Solomon J. Baker.
e. Susan Pennington, born 1850; died 1901; married Zadock Baker.
f. Henry Allen Pennington, born June 22, 1852; died 1925 in Grapeland,
    Texas; married 1873 to Mary Annalena Beeson, born July, 1850; died
    1937, daughter of Samuel Beeson; children:
    (1) Daniel Boone Pennington, born November 9, 1873; died December
         9, 1960; married (1) November 16, 1898, Alice Adelia Crow, born
         June 12, 1882; died 1907, daughter of Martin Inman Crow and
         Fannie Fitzsimmons; (2) Ada Ward; children:
         (by first marriage):
         (a) Fannie Mae Pennington, born January 5, 1902; married (1)

                                    161

January 24, 1922, Elmer Lee Brimberry; (2) February 5, 1923, Thomas J. Mitchell; lived in Hollis, Oklahoma.
- (b) Sam Henry Pennington.
- (by second marriage):
- (c) Dan Ward Pennington lived in Grapeland, Texas.
- (d) Mary Etta Pennington married Troy Lewis.
- (e) Jack Walter Pennington.
- (f) Hugh Allen Pennington.
- (g) Ava June Pennington married L. W. Bush; lived in Grapeland, Texas.
- (h) Wade Louise Pennington.
- (2) Samuel Henry Pennington, born c1875; dsp 1900.
- (3) James Richard Pennington, born October 5, 1877; died April 21, 19??; married Flora Brown.
- (4) Bertha Pearl Pennington, born February 3, 1880; died November 28, 19??; married Jack Beasley.
- (5) Addie Pennington married April 12, 1908, Robert Wherry.
- (6) Hardin Pennington, born April 1, 1884; died March 23, 1966; married Flora Lively.
- (7) Walter Pennington, born 1888; died January 26, 1956; married Susie Lee Brown.
- (8) Mary Anna Lena Pennington, born January 1, 18??; died August 7, 1909; married Jack Spence.
- (9) Earl Pennington married Alma Warner.
- (10) Florence Pennington, born January 23, 1896; married December 13, 1921, Robert Smith Dailey.
- g. Caledonia Pennington, born c1855; married (1) _____ Mabley (2) Hamp Huff.

***

7.   Daniel Pennington was born December 3, 1781, in Wilkes (now Ashe) County, North Carolina, and moved to near Lexington, Kentucky, in 1797. In September, 1798, he moved to Barren (now Monroe) County, Kentucky, where he spent the remainder of his life. On August 20, 1805, he married Esther Freiley (see p.   33). He enlisted as a private in Captain Henry Yakey's Company, 3rd Regiment, Kentucky Militia, in May, 1812; he was discharged at Hardinsburg, Kentucky, on December 25, 1812, later receiving 40 acres of bounty land for his services.[19]

Pennington received grants from the state of Kentucky; on May 23, 1804, he received 100 acres on Line Creek; on April 1, 1825, 50 acres on Lynn's Creek; on November 16, 1827, 100 acres on Mill Creek; and on February 20, 1841, 10 acres on Line Creek. He also bought 70 acres from John Casteel in 1812 and 100 acres from Joshua Pennington in 1813; he sold 100 acres to Stewart Pennington in 1812, all of this land being on Line Creek in what is now Monroe County.[20]

After the death of his wife, Esther Pennington, on April 30, 1854, his daughter and son-in-law, Esther and Benjamin Marshall, lived with him until his death on February 1, 1865. It is difficult to trace his career because of the destruction of the Monroe County records. He had the following children:[21]

a. S. Boone Pennington, born September 20, 1806; married January 12, 1832, to Martha _____; lived in Monroe County, Kentucky, in 1860, and had, perhaps among others, the following children:
- (1) B. S. Pennington, born c1833.
- (2) Nicholas Pennington, born c1835.

162

         (3) William Pennington, born c1837.
         (4) Elizabeth H. Pennington, born c1840.
         (5) Daniel Boone Pennington, born c1843.
         (6) Christopher H. Pennington, born c1846.
         (7) Martha Pennington, born c1849.
         (8) Joseph Pennington, born c1852.
         (9) Samuel P. Pennington, born c1855.
        (10) John C. Pennington, born c1858.
    b. Elizabeth Pennington, born February 24, 1808; died July 4, 1900, in
        Clay County, Tennessee; married January 17, 1826, in Monroe County,
        Kentucky, to Abraham M. Hestand (see Trimble, Hiestand Family of Page
        County, Virginia).
    c. Mary Pennington, born February 7, 1810; dsp April 31, 1870, in Monroe
        County, Kentucky.
    d. Freiley Pennington, born December 15, 1811; married March 29, 1832,
        to Elizabeth Fawbush; lived in Monroe County, Kentucky, in 1850.
    e. Stewart Pennington, born March 12, 1814.
    f. Lavesta Pennington, born February 26, 1816; married ____ Smith.
    g. Abigail Pennington, born April 24, 1818; married September 29, 1839,
        to Jonathan Moore.
    h. Esther Pennington, born July 4, 1820; dsp May 29, 1905, in Monroe
        County, Kentucky; married February 1, 1854, to Benjamin Marshall.
    i. Amanda Melvina Pennington, born October 30, 1822; married ____
        Ferguson.
10. j. Isaiah Crouch Pennington, born April 3, 1825.
11. k. Nancy Pennington, born September 15, 1827.

                                  ***

10.   Isaiah Crouch Pennington was born April 3, 1825, in Monroe County,
    Kentucky, and died there on February 5, 1892; married March 25, 1846, to
    Louisa Minerva Cherry; their children were as follows:[22]

    a. Prudence E. Pennington, born September 7, 1848; married Robert Beavers.
    b. Elkanah Dulaney Pennington, born December 22, 1849; died April 3, 1921;
        married Clementina Leanna Dunham; lived in Wise County, Texas; chil-
        dren:
        (1) Lavesta Pennington married ____ Clay.
        (2) Sanford Pennington.
        (3) Elzie Austin Pennington, born January 12, 1881; died November 27,
             1966, in Ontario, Oregon; married July 16, 1905, to Lora May
             Swaim, born March 25, 1883; died October 8, 1957; children:
             (a) Carroll William Pennington, born October 28, 1908; dsp Sept-
                  ember 18, 1943.
             (b) Mamie Jean Pennington, born July 21, 1910; married July 5,
                  1953, to William Robert Garrett; dsp; lived in Ontario,
                  Oregon.
             (c) Evadean Hildreth Pennington, born April 2, 1919; dsp Octo-
                  ber 19, 1919.
             (d) Alfred Austin Pennington, born November 19, 1920; married
                  June 26, 1956, to Frances Taylor; dsp.
             (e) Calvin Donald Pennington, born September 26, 1923; died Feb-
                  ruary 25, 1954; married July 16, 1947, to Darline Heaton;
                  children:
                  /1/ Steven Craig Pennington, born January 25, 1950.
                  /2/ Calvin Donald Pennington, born May 21, 1954.
        (4) Lorenzo Dow Pennington; children:
             (a) Vera Lee Pennington married Ralph Fillmore; lived in David-

                                  163

son, Oklahoma.
```
              (b)  Chester P. Pennington lived in San Marcos, Texas.
         (5)  Nora Pennington married _____ Webb.
         (6)  Ida Pennington married _____ Reid; children:
              (a)  Malcolm Reid lived in Phoenix, Arizona.
              (b)  Kenneth Reid.
              (c)  Melba Reid.
         (7)  Ada Pennington married _____ Dobbs; children:
              (a)  Walter Dobbs.
              (b)  Clyde Dobbs.
         (8)  John Pennington.
         (9)  Minnie Pennington married _____ Morris; children:
              (a)  Wendell Morris.
              (b)  Bennie Murrel Morris.
              (c)  Dorothy Morris.
        (10)  Lola Pennington married _____ Dobbs; lived in Helena, Montana;
              children:
              (a)  Yvonne Dobbs.
              (b)  Douglas Dobbs.
        (11)  Walter Pennington; child:
              (a)  Daymond Pennington lived in Alvord, Texas.
        (12)  Ray Pennington.
        (13)  Virgie Pennington married _____ Gee.
    c.  Lavesta Jane Pennington, born February 3, 1852; married William H.
        Rush; lived in Monroe County, Kentucky.
    d.  Carroll Austin Pennington, born February 2, 1854; married Eliza Tol-
        man; lived in Texas.
    e.  Esther A. Pennington, born August 1, 1857; dsp.
    f.  Tolbert Pirtle Pennington, born March 6, 1859; married Frances Keith.
    g.  Daniel Rufus Pennington, born March 23, 1861; married Leah Wood;
        lived in Monroe County, Kentucky.
```

***

```
11.        Nancy Pennington was born September 15, 1827, in Monroe County,
     Kentucky, and died there on August 2, 1896; married about 1849 to Isaac
     C. Hix, who was born January 1, 1824, and died January 17, 1910.  Their
     children were as follows:

     a.  William T. Hix, born January 24, 1851; lived in Texas.
     b.  Daniel Boone Hix, born December 15, 1852; dsp March 7, 1924, in Ken-
         tucky; married Jennie Jackson.
12.  c.  Mary Elizabeth Hix, born November 29, 1854.
     d.  Thomas Hix, born December 22, 1856; married Elizabeth Lakins; lived in
         Texas; children, among others:
         (1)  Oliver Hix.
         (2)  Orville Hix.
         (3)  Otis Hix.
         (4)  Oscar Hix.
     e.  Martha Hix, born February 14, 1859; had child by Isaac Rush:
         (1)  Virgil Hicks, born July 28, 1879; married (1) Dollie Poindexter
              (2) Billie Daniel; child (by first marriage):
              (a)  Nina Hicks married Frederick Logan; lived in Detroit, Mich-
                   igan.
         Martha Hix married Duncan Smith; lived in Texas; children:
         (2)  Porter Smith.
         (3)  Florence Smith.
         (4)  Homer Smith.
     f.  Reuben Fraley Hix, born February 21, 1864; married Belle Gentry; lived
```

164

in Holland, Kentucky.

g. Nancy Jane Hix, born March 2, 1867; married Thomas B. Hestand (see Trimble, Hiestand Family of Page County, Virginia).

h. John C. Hix, born March 1, 1871; dsp March 2, 1884.

***

12. Mary Elizabeth Hix was born November 29, 1854, in Monroe County, Kentucky, and died February 7, 1937, in Delaware County, Oklahoma; she had the following children by Isaac Rush:[34]

a. Hugh Victor Hicks, born June 25, 1885; married Mary Florence Bryant, born March 19, 1890; died 1940, daughter of William Thomas Bryant and Nancy Lavina Ray; children:
  (1) Blanche Olene Hicks, born October 7, 1909; married July 26, 1925, David Franklin Crumrine, born March 14, 1900; children:
     (a) Ruth Elizabeth Crumrine, born July 5, 1926; married W. T. Parcell; children:
        /1/ Patricia June Parcell, born June 17, 1944.
        /2/ Mary Jane Parcell, born September 7, 1945.
        /3/ Shirley Jean Parcell, born March 3, 1947.
        /4/ Roy Franklin Parcell, born May 3, 1948.
        /5/ Judy Kay Parcell, born February 11, 1950.
     (b) Mary Lee Crumrine, born July 13, 1930; married Robert Roomsburg; child:
        /1/ Steven Ray Roomsburg, born January 18, 1953.
     (c) Nina Fay Crumrine, born March 22, 1936; married Glenn Pierce; children:
        /1/ Glenda Faye Pierce, born October 2, 1952.
        /2/ Cynthia Kay Pierce, born March 10, 1954.
        /3/ David Glenn Pierce, born August 2, 1955.
     (d) Patricia Ann Crumrine, born July 2, 1937; married (1) Joseph Mauk (2) Ronald Baldwin; children (by first marriage):
        /1/ Mary Beth Mauk, born June 2, 1954.
        /2/ Keith Allen Mauk, born August 2, 1955.
  (2) Nina Virginia Hicks, born March 12, 1917; married November 26, 1949, to Josiah Tidwell Alspaugh; born May 11, 1911; dsp.
  (3) Tim Mitchell Hicks, born December 24, 1921; married February 9, 1945, to Ferne Kotlar; child:
     (a) Constance Eve Hicks, born December 14, 1946.
  (4) Jewel Virgil Hicks, born February 28, 1926; married March 5, 1947, to Billie Harper; children:
     (a) Nina Lee Hicks, born September 11, 1950.
     (b) Christopher Hicks, born December 8, 1954.
b. Herbert Hestand Hicks, born July 4, 1887; married (1) Minnie Tate (2) Vera Johnson; children:
  (by first marriage):
  (1) Mary Annis Hicks, died young.
  (by second marriage):
  (2) Wanda Irene Hicks lived in Columbia, Missouri.

***

8. Stewart Pennington was born June 10, 1784, in Wilkes (now Ashe) County, North Carolina, and died September 20, 1859, in McDonough County, Illinois. He married March 24, 1807, in Barren (now Monroe) County, Kentucky, to Jemima Houser, who was born February 24, 1788, and died September 22, 1852, the daughter of Nicholas and Jane Houser. In 1830, they settled in New Salem Township, McDonough County, Illinois; their children

165

were as follows:[25]

a. Nicholas Houser Pennington, born March 1, 1808; died October 13, 1834, in Kentucky.
13. b. Thomas Jefferson Pennington, born March 10, 1810.
c. Nancy Pennington, born February 19, 1812; died October 26, 1887, in McDonough County, Illinois; married James E. D. Hammer, who was born April 28, 1809.
14. d. Richard Pennington, born January 29, 1814.
e. Abigail Pennington, born April 1, 1816.
f. Warner Pennington, born May 17, 1818; married ____ Shannon.
g. Hannah Boone Pennington, born August 5, 1820; died September 29, 1885; married William Bird Pile.
15. h. Elizabeth Jane Pennington, born February 12, 1823.
i. Stewart McHenry Pennington, born August 4, 1825; married February 28, 1850, Linn County, Oregon, Abigail E. ____.
j. Joshua Jordan Pennington, born January 6, 1828; dsp September 8, 1838.
k. Mary Malinda Pennington, born May 16, 1830.
l. Leander W. Pennington, born January 5, 1834.
m. William Tandy Pennington, born March 16, 1836; died January 26, 1913, in Page County, Iowa; married January 30, 1856, to Sarah Amanda Nebergall.

***

13.   Thomas Jefferson Pennington was born March 10, 1810, and died September 27, 1875, in McDonough County, Illinois; he served in the Blackhawk War. He married (1) November 29, 1827, Mary H. Vail, born December 14, 1807, died August 3, 1840; (2) April 15, 1841, Mrs. Mary J. (Smithers) Rogers. His children were as follows:[26]

(by first marriage):
a. John L. Pennington, born June 6, 1828; dsp February, 1843.
b. William B. Pennington, born July 30, 1929.
c. Grannell M. Pennington, born January 16, 1831; dsp February 16, 1831.
d. James J. Pennington, born February 24, 1836.
e. Allen J. Pennington, born July 3, 1837; died October 11, 1928.
(by second marriage):
f. Thomas Jefferson Pennington, born February 12, 1842; died January 3, 1933, at Macomb, Illinois; married October 25, 1866, to Duanna Henry; children:
   (1) Frank Pennington.
   (2) Melvin Pennington.
   (3) Elmer Pennington.
   (4) Lambert Pennington.
g. Stewart M. Pennington, born December 30, 1843; died January 10, 1919, at Industry, Illinois; married May 30, 1874, to Susannah Tomberlin.
h. Nancy Jane Pennington, born February 10, 1847.
i. Jemima Pennington, born June 11, 1849.
16. j. Stephen A. Douglas Pennington, born August 19, 1852.
k. Charles Pennington, born November 9, 1854; dsp June 10, 1855.
l. Alonzo Pennington, born November 8, 1858.
m. James Morris Pennington, born April 11, 1860; dsp 1864.
n. Ulysses S. Pennington, born January, 1864; dsp August 25, 1864.

***

16.   Stephen A. Douglas Pennington was born August 19, 1852; died March 31, 1938; married October 12, 1886, to Mary Farrington, who was born

February 26, 1865, and died August 11, 1940, daughter of Osamus Farrington and Nancy Hogatt; their children were as follows:[27]

17. a. Elmer N. Pennington, born June 18, 1887.
    b. Francis Frederick Pennington, born April 25, 1889; married _____ Bolinger; lived in Tullis, Saskatchiwan, Canada; children:
       (1) Fred Pennington.
       (2) Ina Pennington.
       (3) Billie Pennington.
       (4) Hope Pennington.
       (5) Dixie Pennington.
       (6) Red Pennington.
       (7) Rex Pennington.
       (8) Pat Pennington.
       (9) Peg Pennington.
    c. Alice L. Pennington, born April 17, 1891; married Ira J. McFarland; lived in Vaslon, Washington.
    d. Earl M. Pennington, born October 2, 1893; died 1936 in Colfax, North Dakota; married Gladys Moffit.
18. e. Florine F. Pennington, born September 8, 1897.
    f. Florence T. Pennington, born September 8, 1897; married Alvin Torgerson; lived in Wyndmere, North Dakota; children:
       (1) Harold Torgerson.
       (2) Arthur Torgerson.
       (3) Harvey Torgerson.
       (4) Opal Torgerson.
       (5) Kenneth Torgerson.
       (6) Roger Torgerson.
       (7) Milton Torgerson.
    g. Avis L. Pennington, born March 14, 1908; married Darwin Lisk; lived in Yakima, Washington.

***

17.   Elmer N. Pennington was born June 18, 1887; married December 11, 1906, to Leona Bolinger, who was born September 1, 1888; they lived in McAllen, Texas, and had the following children:[28]

    a. Leonard A. Pennington, born December 27, 1907; lived in Colfax, North Dakota; children:
       (1) Virgil Pennington, born 1933.
       (2) Marcene Pennington, born 1935.
       (3) Marvin Pennington, born 1938.
       (4) Carmen Pennington, born 1940.
       (5) Bryan Pennington, born 1947.
    b. Harry Pennington, born August 18, 1909; children:
       (1) Gladys Pennington, born 1938; dsp 1941.
       (2) Janet Pennington, born 1941.
    c. Roy Pennington, born September 27, 1911; children:
       (1) Mary Pennington, born 1944.
       (2) David Pennington, born 1946.
       (3) Alice Pennington, born 1953.
    d. Eva M. Pennington, born October 27, 1914; married _____ Tarr; lived in Colfax, North Dakota; children:
       (1) Donna Tarr, born 1938.
       (2) Jerome Tarr, born 1940.
       (3) Frank Tarr, born 1942.
    e. Paul Pennington, born January 9, 1923; lived in Minnesota; children:
       (1) Richard Pennington, born 1949.

167

(2) Meredith Pennington, born 1951.
(3) Stephen Pennington, born 1953.
(4) Kathie Pennington, born 1955.
f. Ruth Pennington, born 1925; married _____ Carhart; lived in Minneapolis, Minnesota; child:
(1) Alden Carhart, born 1949.

***

18.   Florine F. Pennington was born September 8, 1897, in McDonough County, Illinois; died March, 1932, in Mooreton, North Dakota; married Vincent L. Jones and had the following children:[29]

a. Howard Jones, born May 4, 1922; married Betty Miller; lived in Escondido, California; children:
(1) Bobbi Jo Jones.
(2) Jeffery Jones.
(3) Rachel Jones.
b. Delbert A. Jones, born August 31, 1923; married July 3, 1947, to Luvorn Berg; lived in Wyndmere, North Dakota; children:
(1) Judy Jones.
(.2) Timothy Jones.
(3) Kathy Jones.
(4) Beverly Jones.
c. Marvin T. Jones, born May 13, 1925; married December 27, 1959, to Luvern Johnson; lived in Devil's Lake, North Dakota; children:
(1) Thomas Ray Jones, born October 29, 1960.
(2) Carol Florine Jones, born June 28, 1962.
d. Virginia Jones, born May 16, 1927; married December, 1946, to Lloyd L. Erickson; lived in Fargo, North Dakota; children:
(1) Pamela Erickson.
(2) David Erickson.
(3) Patti Erickson.
e. Colleen Jones, born April 3, 1929; married 1950 to Norman Schoethal; lived in Billings, Montana; children:
(1) Terry Schoethal.
(2) Shelly Schoethal.
(3) Galeon Schoethal.
(4) Stewart Schoethal.
f. Juanita Jones, born September 20, 1930; married 1950 to LaVern Neff; lived in Williston, North Dakota; children:
(1) Donna Neff.
(2) Barbara Neff.
(3) Charles Neff.

***

14.   Richard Pennington was born January 29, 1814, in Barren (now Monroe) County, Kentucky, and died October 26, 1891, in McDonough County, Illinois; married January 30, 1834, to Delila Shannon, who was born September 27, 1816, and died December 4, 1898, the daughter of Charles and Rachel Shannon. Their children were as follows:[30]

a. Elizabeth Pennington, born January 15, 1835; died October 25, 1913, in Scioto, Illinois; married Abyah Thomas Marrs, born February 12, 1831, and died January 29, 1900; children:
(1) (Dr.) Richard Franklin Marrs; married Eva Clarke; lived in Macomb, Illinois; children:
(a) Mildred A. Marrs; married _____ Young; lived in Macomb,

168

Illinois.
(b) Junia Marrs; married ____ Loy; lived in Macomb, Illinois.
(2) Alfred T. Marrs, born November 21, 1857; dsp April 2, 1860.
(3) Lovella B. Marrs, born December 1, 1859; died April 3, 1943, in Springfield, Illinois; married Rev. W. B. Shoop, born July 31, 1858.
(4) Ora A. Marrs, born September 16, 1864; dsp January 28, 1879.
b. Charles W. Pennington, born September 1, 1837; died May 5, 1875, in Warren County, Illinois.
c. Jane C. Pennington, born c1839; married C. A. Jones.
d. Mary C. Pennington, born c1840; married Elias W. Beghtol; lived in Fremont County, Iowa.
e. Albert S. Pennington, born March 14, 1842; dsp August 11, 1852.
f. Richard Warren Pennington, born March 3, 1844; dsp December 31, 1862, at battle of Stone River.
g. Sarilda Agnes Pennington, born c1846; married A. B. Metzel.
h. Elmora Frances Pennington, dsp October 3, 1852.
i. John Alfred Pennington, died young.
j. Ella Margaret Pennington.
k. Edward E. Pennington.

***

15.   Elizabeth Jane Pennington was born February 12, 1823, in Monroe County, Kentucky, and died February 7, 1901; married September 21, 1843, to James Marshall Vail, born July 4, 1820; their children were as follows:[31]

a. Perry Vail, born July 8, 1844; dsp February 10, 1845.
b. Ebenezer Vail, born December 14, 1845; died March 17, 1904.
19. c. Sarah A. Vail, born November 5, 1847.
d. Mary Elizabeth Vail, born September 18, 1849; died August 21, 1921; married February 21, 1875, to John Webster Kirkbride, born April 13, 1851, and died September 15, 1930; children:
(1) J. Chester Kirkbride, born February 20, 1877; married December 15, 1935, to Nancy Schullen, born March 23, 1894.
(2) Mary Especia Kirkbride, born May 16, 1879; dsp.
(3) Bishop Burdette Kirkbride, born November 10, 1880; died June 19, 1954.
(4) Audery Karl Kirkbride, born February 2, 1884.
(5) Roxie Vail Kirkbride, born December 27, 1886; married June 25, 1908, to Charles William Ross, born January 16, 1887; children:
(a) Especia Lucy Ross, born August 11, 1909; married September 27, 1934, John Herbert Gage, born July 23, 1908; children:
/1/ John Marshall Gage, born January 11, 1936.
/2/ William Ross Gage, born July 30, 1940; dsp May 12, 1944.
/3/ Stansifer Robert Gage, born August 6, 1945.
(b) Harold Kirkbride Ross, born February 17, 1912; married September 4, 1938, Mary Helen McMurtry, born May 26, 1914; children:
/1/ Edith Carolyn Ross, born August 10, 1942.
/2/ William Thomas Ross, born December 10, 1946.
(c) Albert Stansifer Ross, born December 6, 1914; married June 16, 1945, Eleanor Roth North, born October 22, 1921; children:
/1/ Anna Kerr Ross, born December 26, 1949.
/2/ Alan North Ross, born August 15, 1952.
(6) Emerson Glover Kirkbride, born June 9, 1890; dsp August 28, 1890.
20. e. Amelia Caroline Vail, born November 4, 1851.
f. John Silas Vail, born March 9, 1854; dsp February 20, 1870.

g. Thomas Pulaski Vail, born May 8, 1856.

***

19.   Sarah A. Vail was born November 5, 1847; died May, 1881; married
December 23, 1865, to William James Beaty; their children were as follows:[32]

    a. Lewis William Beaty, born November 1, 1866; died June 4, 1947; mar-
ried Christin Anna Sedestrum, born May 18, 1872, and died February,
1914; child:
      (1) Alice Beaty, born June 1, 1891; married May 28, 1911, William
Bridges, born July 17, 1889; children:
        (a) Orville Beaty Bridges, born and died April 19, 1912.
        (b) Evelyn Bridges, born May 10, 1913; married October 7, 1933,
Harold Adams, born September 3, 1912; child:
          /1/ Marsha Kay Adams, born October 28, 1941.
        (c) Ordelta Bridges, born February 24, 1915; married April 9,
1934, William Baker, born January 8, 1915; children:
          /1/ Mary Catherine Baker, born September 20, 1934; mar-
ried March, 1955, Sidney Allen, born November 26,
1935; children:
            /a/ Cynthia Sue Allen, born July 20, 1955.
            /b/ Jerold Wayne Allen, born December 29, 1957.
          /2/ Juanita Kathleen Baker, born March 11, 1937; married
May 19, 1956, Glenn Torrance, born February 18, 1934.
          /3/ Beverly Ann Baker, born July 15, 1942.
        (d) Mildred Bridges, born December 3, 1916; married December
12, 1936, James V. Roberts, born January 12, 1916; child:
          /1/ Janet Ann Roberts, born October 24, 1942.
        (e) Opal Bridges, born October 2, 1921; married Charles Zettle,
born August 6, 1917; children:
          /1/ Mary Leane Zettle, born November 10, 1942; dsp Janu-
ary 14, 1945.
          /2/ Thomas Edward Zettle, born November 26, 1945.
          /3/ Donna Jeanne Zettle, born January 1, 1948.
        (f) Jay Clifford Bridges, born July 1, 1924; married August
13, 1955, Delores Ufheil, born September 2, 1930; child:
          /1/ Alan Jay Bridges, born September 19, 1957.
21. b. William Leslie Beaty, born June 1, 1869.
    c. Lawrence Elmer Beaty, born August 13, 1874; died May 23, 1924; mar-
ried Eva _____; child:
      (1) Richard Beaty, born c1907; lived in Omaha, Nebraska.
    d. Alice Bertha Beaty, born May 13, 1877; married William Prugh; chil-
dren:
      (1) Ruth Prugh married H. E. Coffman; lived in Mt. Morris, Illinois.
      (2) Pridmore Prugh.
      (3) Thornton Prugh.
      (4) Katherine Prugh.
    e. Edwin Pulaski Beaty, born December 10, 1879.
    f. Etna May Beaty, born March 10, 1881; dsp March 11, 1881.
    g. Edith Blanch Beaty, born March 10, 1881; dsp May 4, 1881.

***

21.   William Leslie Beaty was born June 1, 1869; married July 4, 1889,
to Emma Eunice Andrews; their children were as follows:[33]

    a. Blanch Bertha Beaty, born April 15, 1890; married March 28, 1914,

170

James Gesler Cook; children:
(1) Thomas Herschel Cook, born May 26, 1915; married March 14, 1940,
    Rowena Pulley; child:
    (a) Carolyn Ann Cook, born September 16, 1942.
(2) Gerald Anderson Cook, born September 1, 1916; married April 6,
    1940, Theresa Katherine Marmino; children:
    (a) Margaret Anna Cook, born May 12, 1941; married November 8,
        1955, Henry Howard Cooper.
    (b) Mary Catherine Cook, born October 29, 1942.
    (c) Virginia Pearl Cook, born July 25, 1944.
    (d) Betty Jo Cook, born June 27, 1946.
    (e) James Gerald Cook, born September 30, 1947.
    (f) Linda Antoinette Cook, born December 7, 1950.
(3) Mildred Ellen Cook, born December 5, 1918; married January 15,
    1940, Lee Thomas Winn; child:
    (a) David Lee Winn, born August 31, 1941.
(4) Mary Evelyn Cook, born March 20, 1923; married March 25, 1944,
    Swithen Leo Roy Treadway; children:
    (a) Monica Elizabeth Treadway, born June 1, 1952.
    (b) Cynthia Denise Treadway, born August 26, 1953.
    (c) Deborah Marie Treadway, born September 10, 1956.
b. Anna Lois Beaty, born July 11, 1893; married October 25, 1946, Alma
   Clarence Hess; dsp; lived in Boonville, California.
c. Ronald Beaty, born February 24, 1898; dsp July 27, 1900.
d. Dorothy Carol Beaty, born August 31, 1901; married August 27, 1923,
   Henry Knute Lund; children:
   (1) Albert Howard Lund, born September 11, 1924; married October
       23, 1953, Ethel Joyce Maycroft; child:
       (a) Brian Leslie Lund, born March 23, 1956.
   (2) Charles Edward Lund, born April 4, 1946.
e. Helen Louise Beaty, born August 23, 1905; married February 4, 1929,
   Clarence Ernest Hoermann; two adopted children.

***

20.   Amelia Caroline Vail was born November 4, 1851; died January 28,
1921; married January 18, 1877, to George G. Laughlin, who died October
10, 1888; their children were as follows:[34]

a. Oscar T. Laughlin, born February 16, 1878; died December 3, 1953;
   married December 25, 1905, Nova _____, who died February 9, 1927;
   children:
   (1) D. Ruth Laughlin, born February 11, 1909; married January 12,
       1933, Otto Billeter.
   (2) Bessie M. Laughlin, born November 19, 1910; married June 2,
       1934, Francis Billeter.
b. Bernice B. Laughlin, born November 2, 1879; died June 6, 1953; married September 5, 1906, Ross Provine; children:
   (1) Carl G. Provine, born February 11, 1909; married August 25,
       1931, Vena Dewitt.
   (2) William G. Provine, born February 10, 1910; died August 20, 1955;
       married March 15, 1937, Zolla Sims.
c. Forrest V. Laughlin, born and died July 4, 1882.
d. Florence G. Laughlin, born July 4, 1882; married June 25, 1915,
   Louis Snyder.
e. Mary G. Laughlin, born March 15, 1885; married February 19, 1905,
   Melvin Wilson; children:
   (1) Alice M. Wilson, born December 28, 1909.
   (2) Doris J. Wilson, born December 29, 1912.

171

f. Ruth Laughlin, born December 2, 1887; married February 10, 1910, Roy Butcher; children:
    (1) Gertie B. Butcher, born December 18, 1910; married February 10, 1940, Leroy Williams.
    (2) Eugene R. Butcher, born September 19, 1912; married August 29, 1934, Kathryn M. Williams.
    (3) Alleyne C. Butcher, born October 18, 1914; married October 10, 1940, James Foster.
    (4) Mary E. Butcher, born February 8, 1917; married June 11, 1936, Harold F. Carman.
    (5) Ervin L. Butcher, born August 3, 1919; married April 29, 1944, Betty Barnes.
    (6) Dorothy R. Butcher, born February 13, 1922; married June 8, 1940, Fred L. Norton.
    (7) Marjorie N. Butcher, born May 12, 1924; married August 18, 1950, Kenneth W. Wolf.
    (8) Pauline Butcher, born November 6, 1927; married August 25, 1956, Robert F. Hacher.

***

REFERENCES

[1]James Boone, mss. history of the Boone family, in Wisconsin Historical Society Collections, Madison, Wisconsin; Oley Monthly Meeting Minutes, Pennsylvania Historical Society, Philadelphia, Pennsylvania.
[2]Ibid.; since descendants of the Boone family have been traced and published at various times, none are included here other than descendants of Squire Boone through his daughter Hannah (Boone) Stewart Pennington.
[3]James Boone, mss. history ... ; Gwynedd and Oley Monthly Meeting Minutes ... ; Bucks County, Pennsylvania, Deed Book 23; Berks County, Pennsylvania, Deeds A-VI, 1.
[4]Philadelphia County, Pennsylvania, Deeds, Marriages; Gwynedd Monthly Meeting Minutes.
[5]Berks County, Pennsylvania, Deeds; Draper Mss. 23C42, 23C41, 22C22, Wisconsin Historical Society Collections; Rowan County, North Carolina, Deed Bk. 3, pp. 137, 164, Court Minutes Bk. 1, p. 7.
[6]Rowan County, North Carolina, Deed Bk. 4, pp. 195, 196; Draper Mss. 23C42, 23C41; tombstone record, Davie County, North Carolina.
[7]Hazel Atterbury Spraker, The Boone Family (Rutland, Vermont: The Tuttle Company, 1922), pp. 56-72; only descendants of Hannah (Boone) Stewart Pennington are included here.
[8]Draper Mss. 23C27, 23C41, 23C42.
[9]Ibid., 8C64, 23C42.
[10]Ibid., 23C41, 23C39; W. H. Bogart, Daniel Boone and the Hunters of Kentucky (New York, 1876), pp. 52-54, prints Boone's account of the expedition as told to John Filson.
[11]Bible record belonging (1960) to Mrs. Nina Hicks Alspaugh; Draper Mss. 23C27, 23C37; Atlas Map of McDonough County, Illinois (Davenport, Iowa: Andreas, Lyter, & Co., 1871), p. 27; Fincastle and Montgomery Counties, Virginia, Revolutionary War Records, vol. 66, p. 3183, Virginia State Archives, Richmond, Virginia; North Carolina Land Entries #1423, Grant #1587, Entry 540, book 96, p. 225, State Land Office, Raleigh, North Carolina; Ashe County, North Carolina, Deeds A, 428; Draper Mss. 23C37, 23C41.
[12]Draper Mss. 23C41; Barren County, Kentucky, Order Book 1, p. 102; Mill Creek Church Minutes, Tompkinsville, Kentucky, p. 10; statement of Randolph Rush.
[13]Draper Mss. 23C41, 23C37, 23C42.

[14]Ibid., 23C42, Pension #32324, National Archives, Washington, D. C.; Material collected by Israel Clem (1905); for descendants, see Bess L. Hawthorne, Hannah Boone (Burlington, Vermont: Chedwato Service, 1960).

[15]Draper Mss. 23C37, 23C42; records of Willard Osborn and Mrs. Lydia Evans Walsh; for descendants, see Hawthorne, Hannah Boone.

[16]Records of P. Loyd Lewis; for descendants, see Hawthorne, Hannah Boone.

[17]Draper Mss. 23C37; Willard Rouse Jillson, The Kentucky Land Grants (Louisville: The Standard Printing Company, 1925), p. 383; Barren County, Kentucky, Deeds AA, 77, C, 363; Warren County, Tennessee, Will Bk. 4, p. 416, Marriages; Bethlehem Church cemetery, White County, Tennessee; Houston County, Texas, census of 1850, 1860; Warren County, Tennessee, census of 1850, 1860.

[18]Records belonging to Mrs. L. W. Bush.

[19]Bible record belonging (1960) to Mrs. Nina Hicks Alspaugh; Draper Mss. 23C41; Bounty Land Warrants, National Archives, Washington, D.C.

[20]Jillson, The Kentucky Land Grants, pp. 383, 679, 1588; Barren County, Kentucky, Deeds C, 353, B, 514.

[21]Bible record belonging (1960) to Mrs. Nina Hicks Alspaugh; Monroe County, Kentucky, census of 1850, 1860.

[22]Bible record belonging (1940) to Randolph Rush; records belonging to Mrs. William R. Garrett.

[23-24]Records belonging to Mrs. Nina Hicks Alspaugh.

[25]Bible record belonging (1960) to Mary Especia Kirkbride; Genealogical Material in Oregon Donation Land Claims (Genealogical Forum of Portland, Oregon, 1957), I, 89.

[26-27]Records belonging to Marvin T. Jones.

[28]Records belonging to Elmer N. Pennington.

[29]Records belonging to Marvin T. Jones.

[30]Records belonging to Mrs. Junia M. Loy.

[31-34]Records belonging to Mary Especia Kirkbride.

***

ROBERTSON and PHENIX of Brunswick County, Virginia

Abraham Phenix lived in St. Paul's Parish, Hanover County, Virginia, in 1731; on September 15, 1744, he bought 110 acres in Brunswick County, Virginia, on the south side of the Nottaway River below the mouth of Stonehouse Branch from his son-in-law, Athanasius Robertson for £15. He made his will on January 17, 1749, leaving one shilling each to his three children and the bulk of his property to Mary Harris, Jr; the estate was probated on June 26, 1750. His children, perhaps among others, were as follows:[1]

1. a. Cordelia Phenix, born c1720.
    b. Barbara Phenix.
    c. John Phenix.

***

1.   Cordelia Phenix was born about 1720 and married Athanasius Robertson about 1740; they lived in St. Andrew's Parish, Brunswick County, Virginia, as early as 1741 when they sued Richard and Ann Smith for slander. On June 25, 1743, Athanasius Robertson bought 219 acres on the Nottaway River from Richard Parr for £30; he sold 110 acres of it to his father-in-law, Abraham Phenix, on September 15, 1744. He bought 100 acres on the south side of Red Oak Creek from Moses Smith for £10 on March 3, 1747, and he sold the remaining 100 acres bought from Parr to Samuel Sentall for £25 on January 12, 1748. He sold his land on Red Oak Run to Thomas Harvey on August 2, 1764, and on August 22, 1764, he bought a Negro slave girl from William Matthews.[2]

Sometime after this, Athanasius and Cordelia Robertson moved to Caswell District, Orange County, North Carolina, where he was taxed on £1,615 in property in 1777. He entered a claim to 300 acres on both sides of Collins Creek and received it from the colony of North Carolina in 1779. In May, 1785, he gave slaves to his granddaughter Sarah Lindsey, his daughter Mary Lindsey, and his son Nathaniel. His will was probated in November, 1795, and the undivided part of his estate was sold on October 4, 1800. His children, perhaps among others, were as follows:[3]

2. a. Mary Robertson, born c1742.
3. b. Nathaniel Robertson, born c1745.

***

2.   Mary Robertson was born about 1742 in Brunswick County, Virginia, and married John Lindsey in Orange County, North Carolina, about 1760; he was the son of Caleb Lindsey and served in the American Revolution. On August 12, 1779, he was granted 600 acres on Collins Creek in Orange County, where he died in 1794, leaving, probably among others, the following children:[4]

    a. Elizabeth Lindsey, born c1764; married Henry Edwards, son of John Edwards; children:
       (1) Nathan Edwards married _____ Brewer.
       (2) John Edwards.
       (3) Henry H. Edwards married (1) Mary Willis Snipes (2) Henrietta Hardie.
       (4) Lindsey Edwards married _____ Marsh.

(5) Mary Edwards married Stephen Lloyd.
(6) Susan Edwards married (1) James Moore (2) Allen Roberson.
(7) Delilah Edwards married Thomas Lloyd.
(8) Elizabeth Edwards married (1) John Carruthers (2) John Cabe.
4. b. Athanasius Lindsey, born c1770.
   c. Sarah Lindsey.
   d. John Lindsey.
   e. Cordelia Lindsey.
   f. Dr. Caleb Lindsey, born 1785; married December 17, 1807, to Martha
      Brewer, daughter of Thomas Brewer; lived in Drew County, Arkansas;
      children:
      (1) Wadie Lindsey married 1827 to Nathaniel Robertson.
      (2) Hyder Lindsey married 1833 to Mary Barbee (see p. 131); lived
          in Arkansas.
      (3) Norris Lindsey married 1833 to Anna Price.
      (4) Thomas Sheffield Lindsey married October 6, 1834, to Elizabeth
          Nevill (see p. 150); children:
          (a) Jane Lindsey married Nathaniel Williams.
          (b) Matthew Lindsey married Martha Blake.
          (c) Thomas Lindsey married Martha Hutchins.
          (d) Manley Lindsey married Mrs. Adeline Judson (Kirby) McCallum,
              daughter of Ausburn Kirby and Biddy Ariel Riggsbee.
      (5) Caroline Lindsey, died young.
      (6) Cordelia Lindsey, died young.
      (7) Sarah Lindsey married (1) James Davis (2) James Tow.
      (8) Malissa Lindsey, born April 24, 1824; married November 16, 1837,
          to Joel Lee; lived in Drew County, Arkansas.
      (9) Emaline Lindsey married Rev. George Day.
      (10) Sophia Lindsey married Samuel Nelson.
      (11) Martha Lindsey, born March 2, 1831; married Daniel N. Cotner.

                              ***

4.   Athanasius Lindsey was born about 1770 and died in 1829; married
November 19, 1792, to Sarah Lloyd, daughter of Stephen Lloyd and Martha
Morris; their children were as follows:[5]

5. a. John Lindsey, born May 27, 1795.
   b. Stephen Lindsey married Sarah Snipes; children:
      (1) John Lindsey.
      (2) Candice Lindsey.
      (3) Eliza Lindsey.
   c. Sidney Lindsey.
   d. Martha Lindsey married August 5, 1829, to Peter F. Perry; children:
      (1) Sarah Ann Adeline Perry, born May 10, 1830; married Thomas S.
          Cate.
      (2) Manly Mebane Perry, born December 19, 1831.
      (3) Nancy Caroline Perry, born July 18, 1833; married Dr. Mansfield
          Durham, son of Archibald Durham.
      (4) Murphy Monroe Perry, born October 28, 1834.
      (5) Delilie Isabella Perry, born August 5, 1836; died September 15,
          1904; married September 9, 1866, to Saurin Malthus Lindsey (see
          p. 176).
      (6) Peter Carney Perry, born March 28, 1838.
      (7) John Athanatious Mangum Perry, born May 29, 1840.
      (8) Edward Norrice Perry, born January 9, 1842; lived in Indiana.
   e. Sarah Lindsey married _____ Johnson.

                              ***

                              175

5.   John Lindsey was born May 27, 1795, and died in 1847 in Orange
County, North Carolina; married August 24, 1820, to Elizabeth Craft,
born March 11, 1797, in Northern Ireland; their children were as follows:[6]

  a. Sarah Nash Lindsey, born April 30, 1821; died June 1, 1897; married
      August 19, 1842, to Richard Morris, born March 25, 1820; died Decem-
      ber 6, 1892, son of Isaac Morris and Nancy Cheek; children:
      (1) Anderson Morris married _____ Tripp.
      (2) John Lindsey Morris.
      (3) Isaac Bryant Morris married Cammie Morris.
      (4) Melissa Morris, born October 20, 1845; died December 16, 1918;
           married Winfield Williams.
      (5) Mary Eveline Morris married Henry Morris.
      (6) Elmina Morris married George Cook.
6. b. William Alvis Lindsey, born January 8, 1824.
  c. Levisa Eveline Lindsey, born October 30, 1826; married Pinkney
      Roberson.
  d. John Athanatious Lindsey, born May 1, 1829; died January, 1856, in
      Orange County, North Carolina; married December 26, 1853, to Louisa
      M. Roberson, born March 10, 1830; died March 27, 1910; children:
      (1) Adelaide Lindsey married Jesse Bailey.
      (2) Mary John Lindsey, born April 21, 1856; died November 1, 1946;
           married Thomas B. Rogers.
  e. Saurin Malthus Lindsey, born May 24, 1832; died May 26, 1888; mar-
      ried September 9, 1866, to Delilie Isabella Perry (see p. 175);
      children:
      (1) Deems Norris Lindsey, born January 18, 1867.
      (2) Willie Mead Lindsey, born July 21, 1868.
      (3) Murphy Bascom Lindsey, born October 3, 1870.
      (4) Numa Reid Lindsey, born November 2, 1873.
      (5) Marvin Theodore Lindsey, born November 15, 1877.
      (6) Mattie Belle Lindsey, born May 17, 1881.
  f. Martha Elmina Lindsey, born May 30, 1835; died January 20, 1892, in
      Orange County, North Carolina; married November 30, 1861, to Hugh
      Laughlin Edwards, born March 17, 1815; died March 21, 1903; son of
      Allen Edwards and Nancy Carruthers; children:
      (1) Sarah Frances Edwards, born July 22, 1863; dsp January 18, 1948.
      (2) Mary Elizabeth Edwards, born October 28, 1865; married May 19,
           1889, to William Pepper Phillips, born November 2, 1863; died
           December 3, 1930.
      (3) Celia Caroline Edwards, born March 28, 1867; died January 12,
           1900; married April 14, 1886, to Euclid Monroe Cooke, born Feb-
           ruary 1, 1843; died November 20, 1908.
      (4) Nancy Ann Edwards, born July 28, 1869; died June 15, 1944; mar-
           ried February 6, 1901, to Euclid Monroe Cooke.
      (5) Martha Levisa Edwards, born August 16, 1873; dsp April 16, 1949.
  g. Henry Minton Lindsey, born February 27, 1838.

                              ***

6.   William Alvis Lindsey was born January 8, 1824, and died February
6, 1859; married October 29, 1846, to Mary Lacy Lloyd, born November 24,
1825, and died September 8, 1906, daughter of John Lloyd and Nancy Hunter.
Their children were as follows:[7]

  a. John Monroe Lindsey, born July 20, 1848; died June 16, 1905, in Dur-
      ham, North Carolina; married December 14, 1869, to Nancy Catherine
      Morris, born November 2, 1849; died October 27, 1947; daughter of

Thomas Morris and Mary Ann Crutchfield; children:

7.
(1) Mary Valeria Lindsey, born c1870; dsp c1888.
(2) William Clarence Lindsey, born May 3, 1872.
(3) Robert Lee Lindsey, born March 16, 1874; married (1) Katie Terrell (2) Mrs. Sudie (Barbee) Perry; child (by first marriage):
    (a) Louise Lindsey married Edward Newton.
(4) Thomas Heber Lindsey, born March 9, 1876; dsp October 3, 1941; married (1) Lelia Clark, born May 16, 1878; dsp October 8, 1912; (2) Kate Tilghman, born March 18, 1890, daughter of James Tilghman.
(5) Eugene Lindsey, born July 22, 1878; dsp September 27, 1909; married 1903 to Grace Hutchinson.
(6) John Lindsey, died young.
(7) Edward Lindsey, died young.
(8) Samuel Excell Lindsey, born September 9, 1887; died December 27, 1911, in Durham, North Carolina; married Estelle Carden, born April 10, 1891; died in 1948; children:
    (a) Samuel Excell Lindsey, born August 30, 1909.
    (b) Edith Estelle Lindsey, born March 8, 1911; lived in Atlanta, Georgia.
(9) Annie Lindsey, born October 21, 1889; died November 12, 1919; married Oscar Pickett.
(10) Katie Lindsey, born January 11, 1892; dsp.
(11) Isaac Atha Lindsey, born August 17, 1895; married Lessie Weaver, born December 24, 1895; children:
    (a) Arthur Lindsey, born September 3, 1914; married Marion Massey.
    (b) James Lindsey, born August 29, 1915; married Hilda Dilling.
    (c) Gene Lindsey, born March 12, 1926; married Mildred Scoggin.
b. George Milton Lindsey, born August 20, 1850; dsp December 7, 1917.
c. Martha Elizabeth Lindsey, born April 4, 1853; dsp c1856.
d. William Henry Lindsey, born January 13, 1855; died January, 1923; married Lizzie Sellars.
e. Thomas Defonsas Lindsey, born October 8, 1856; died December, 1928; married Emma Fields.
f. Alvis Edward Saurin Lindsey, born September 4, 1858; died December 19, 1923, in Raleigh, North Carolina; married October 2, 1889, to Anna Eliza Taylor.

***

7.
    William Clarence Lindsey was born May 3, 1872; married November 15, 1899, to Annie Greason; lived in Durham, North Carolina; their children were as follows:[8]

a. Horace Byron Lindsey, born December 17, 1900; married (1) February 10, 1927, to Florence Koenig (2) July 10, 1943, to Mrs. Gladys (Jones) McCullen; children (by first marriage):
    (1) Horace Byron Lindsey, born December 19, 1927.
    (2) Dorothy Melba Lindsey, born November 30, 1934.
b. William Clarence Lindsey, born April 12, 1902; married March 12, 1931, to Thelma North.
c. Robert Eugene Lindsey, born May 29, 1904.
d. Annie Greason Lindsey, born September 4, 1906; married June 25, 1925, to Morry Martin; child:
    (1) Anne Martin, born August 27, 1926; married Bently Lynch.
e. Sarah Catherine Lindsey, born July 16, 1908; married February 14, 1948, to Walter Boettke, born January 26, 1904; child:

177

   (1) Sarah Louise Boettke, born February, 1949.
f. Mary Ellen Lindsey, born June 4, 1911; married January 14, 1936,
  Jack Beck, born August 30, 1900; children:
  (1) William Thomas Beck, born August 1, 1938.
  (2) George Robert Beck, born February 5, 1941.
g. John Thomas Lindsey, born January 3, 1914; married Helen Hopson, born
  September 3, 1915; children:
  (1) John Thomas Lindsey, born March 5, 1937.
  (2) Sidney Gerald Lindsey, born August 11, 1938.
h. Lelia Agnes Lindsey, born January 3, 1914; married August 15, 1937,
  to John Quincy Shaw, born August 21, 1909; children:
  (1) John Quincy Shaw, born August 13, 1941.
  (2) Mary Ann Shaw, born February 10, 1948.
i. Edna Redfern Lindsey, born May 29, 1916; married October 16, 1944,
  to John Vernice Shipp, born November 6, 1911; lived in Fresno, California.

***

3.   Nathaniel Robertson, who was a carpenter and builder and planter,
married Elizabeth Marriott on October 23, 1769 (see p. 126). He bought
130 acres on Avent's Creek in Brunswick County, Virginia, from his
father-in-law, Thomas Marriott, on February 17, 1770; on February 16, 1791,
he sold 162 acres on the south side of Meherrin River about two miles
above Pennington's Ford to Balaam Ezell.[9]

   Robertson then moved to Caswell District, Orange County, North
Carolina, where he owned no land until he inherited 311 acres from his
father. His estate, valued at $4,000.00, was probated in 1799 and his 12
slaves were divided among his children. Nathaniel and Elizabeth Robertson had the following children:[10]

a. Thomas Robertson, born c1771.
b. Nathaniel Robertson, born c1774; married Elizabeth Baldwin; lived in
  Coffee County, Tennessee, in 1840.
c. Sarah Robertson, born c1777; married December 10, 1795, in Orange
  County, North Carolina, to Mark Durham, born August 15, 1775, son of
  Matthew Durham and Susanna Lindsey.
d. Mary Robertson, born c1779; married March 27, 1798, in Orange County,
  North Carolina, to John Durham.
e. Nancy Robertson, born December 3, 1781; died May 5, 1814, in Franklin (now Coffee) County, Tennessee; married October 16, 1800, in
  Orange County, North Carolina, to Benjamin Nevill (see p. 137).
f. Hannah Robertson, born December 11, 1783; died September 7, 1850,
  in Warren County, Tennessee; married December 26, 1800, in Orange
  County, North Carolina, to Thomas Stroud (see p. 204).
8. g. William Robertson, born c1785.
h. Marriott Robertson, born c1787; married October 22, 1805, in Orange
  County, North Carolina, to Sarah Bailey.

***

8.   William Robertson was born about 1785 in Orange County, North Carolina; married September 13, 1804, to Cynthia Aris Nevill (see p. 130);
lived in Dallas County, Alabama, in 1839; their children, among others,
were probably as follows:[11]

a. Jesse Robertson, born c1806.
b. Elizabeth Merritt Robertson, born April 23, 1808; died March 6, 1853;

178

married December 11, 1828, to Thomas Johnson Carroll (see Trimble, American Beginnings).
- c. Thomas N. Robertson, born c1815; married February 20, 1850, to Martha Elder.
- d. Hannah Robertson, born c1817; married c1838 to John B. Carroll (see Trimble, American Beginnings).
9. e. William Robertson, born August 14, 1819.
- f. Sarah Robertson married January 11, 1844, to Benjamin Parnall.
- g. Harriet Robertson married February 8, 1844, to Elijah B. Moseley.
- h. Nancy Robertson.

***

9. William Robertson was born August 14, 1819, and died March 23, 1892, in De Soto Parish, Louisiana; married c1842 to Sarah Catherine Carroll (see Trimble, American Beginnings); their children were as follows:[12]

- a. Nancy Robertson, born July 19, 1847; died June 6, 1877; married Louis Williams.
- b. Angie Robertson married _____ Mayes.
- c. Mattie Robertson, born September 19, 1851; died December 27, 1894.
- d. Jane Robertson, born February 25, 1854; died November 30, 1910; married Benjamin Smith; children:
  - (1) Hoagie Smith married Eula Craig; children:
    - (a) Gladys Smith married Haudie Birdwell; lived in DeRidder, Louisiana.
    - (b) Craig Smith lived in DeRidder, Louisiana.
    - (c) Evelyn Smith married Weldon Love; lived in Mansfield, Louisiana.
    - (d) Mildred Smith married Joseph Mark Robinson; lived in Houma, Louisiana.
  - (2) Julia Smith married Joseph Fleniken.
  - (3) Ettie Smith married William Lord.
  - (4) Preston Smith.
  - (5) Blanche Smith married _____ Dees.
  - (6) Lessie Smith married George Webster; lived in Oxford, Louisiana; children:
    - (a) Burleson Webster, dsp.
    - (b) Lowry Webster married Annice Fincher; lived in Oxford, Louisiana.
    - (c) Lois Webster.
    - (d) Verna Webster.
    - (e) Warner Webster.
10. e. William John Thomas Robertson, born January 1, 1856.
- f. Margaret Robertson, born August 14, 1858; died May 6, 1906; married _____ Moore.
- g. Samuel H. Robertson, born 1860; died 1934; married (1) Nancy Bowden
  - (2) Mrs. Pearl Martin; children (by first marriage):
  - (1) Samuel Robertson.
  - (2) Berta Robertson married _____ DeSoto.
  - (3) Addie Robertson.
  - (4) (daughter) married _____ Stevenson.
- h. Ella Robertson, born October 24, 1863; died June 6, 1955; married Newton Breazealle; children:
  - (1) Ada Breazealle married _____ Rembert.
  - (2) Fred N. Breazealle married Thelma Joyner; lived in Pelican, Louisiana.
  - (3) Sallie C. Breazealle married Haven Howell; lived in Pelican, Louisiana.

179

(4) Guy Breazealle married Susan Goldsby; lived in Pelican, Louisiana.
i. James O. Robertson, born December 25, 1866; died August 19, 1945; married Minnie Craig; children:
(1) Percy Robertson, dsp.
(2) Eula Mae Robertson.
(3) William Henry Robertson married Exa Thigpen; lived in Mansfield, Louisiana.
(4) Eliza Robertson married _____ Fair.
j. Hattie Robertson married _____ Smith.

***

10.   William John Thomas Robertson was born January 1, 1856, and died December 4, 1917; married Minnie Breazealle, born May 8, 1859; died January 1, 1898; their children were as follows:[13]

a. William Newton Robertson, born March 28, 1876; dsp December 17, 1894.
b. George Marvin Robertson, born June 26, 1878; married Eva Craig; children:
(1) Ezelle Robertson.
(2) Fred Robertson.
c. James Leonard Robertson, born November 7, 1880; died December 16, 1964.
d. Ennis Breazealle Robertson, born October 31, 1882; married Ola Bloxom; children:
(1) Hazel Robertson married O. W. Neel; lived in Baton Rouge, Louisiana.
(2) Reba Robertson.
(3) Grace Robertson married _____ Midyett; lived in New Iberia, Louisiana.
e. Henry Clay Robertson, born June 12, 1885; married Ina Williams; children:
(1) Claudine Robertson married _____ Love; lived in Mansfield, Louisiana.
(2) Henry Robertson.
(3) Donald Robertson.
f. Dove Cecil Robertson, born December 27, 1887.
g. Wayne Eustus Robertson, born February 15, 1890; died October 14, 1940.
h. Herbert Robertson, born June 22, 1892; dsp July 7, 1897.
i. Mary Ima Robertson, born November 1, 1894; dsp.
j. Hugh Robertson, born June 21, 1898; married Bernice Jackson.

***

REFERENCES

[1]St. Paul's Parish, Hanover County, Virginia, Vestry Book, 1706-1786, p. 271; Brunswick County, Virginia, Deed Bk. 2, p. 497, Will Bk. 2, p. 181.
[2]Brunswick County, Virginia, Order Book, 1732-41, Deed Bk. 2, pp. 340, 497, Bk. 3, p. 478, Bk. 7, pp. 512, 525.
[3]Orange County, North Carolina, tax list, 1777, State Archives, Raleigh, North Carolina; North Carolina Land Entry #951, State Land Office, Raleigh, North Carolina; Orange County, North Carolina, Deeds A, 353, Wills C, 64, Inventories, 1800-1809.
[4]Orange County, North Carolina, Wills B, 265; North Carolina Revolutionary Army Accounts VII-49, folio 1, #459; North Carolina Grants,

File 1517, Entry 840; records of Robert Bruce Cooke.
    5-8Records of Robert Bruce Cooke.
    9Brunswick County, Virginia, Marriages, Deed Bk. 9, p. 603, Bk. 14,
p. 84.
    10Orange County, North Carolina, tax lists 1791, 1796, 1797; Court
Records 1795-1800, Inventories 1800-1809, pp. 21, 114; Marriages.
    11-13Orange County, North Carolina, Marriages; Dallas County, Alabama,
Census of 1805; records of Mrs. Hazel Robertson Neel.

***

STROUD of Orange County, North Carolina

John Stroud paid quitrents on 60 acres of land in Prince George County, Virginia, in 1704. He received a grant of 46 acres on the south side of Monoferock Creek adjoining his own land in Prince George (now Dinwiddie?) County on July 15, 1717; he and his wife Hannah sold this land to Richard Massey on November 9, 1724. He received another grant of 392 acres on both sides of Sturgeon Run in Brunswick County on September 28, 1728, and 104 acres on both sides of Sapponey Creek adjoining his plantation on September 28, 1730.[1] In 1732, he was exempted from paying the parish levy. He died about 1737, leaving a will which has been lost, and Hannah Stroud administered his estate, although the destruction of the Prince George County records makes further information difficult to locate. His children were, perhaps among others, probably as follows:[2]

a. Joseph Stroud had land surveyed on Sapponey Creek in Prince George County on October 19, 1715, and on Buckskin Creek in the same county on December 19, 1722. On November 9, 1724, he and his wife Sarah sold 80 acres on the south side of Mankesneck Creek to Richard Massey. He received a grant of 183 acres on the north side of Buckskin Creek in Prince George (now Dinwiddie) County on September 28, 1730. He evidently married again, since he and his wife Mary had at least two children born in Bristol Parish (Dinwiddie County):
   (1) William Stroud, born February 22, 1730/31.
   (2) David Stroud, born March 19, 1731/2; lived in Granville County, North Carolina, in 1754, and owned land on Mayo Creek in Orange County, North Carolina, in 1769.[3]
1. b. William Stroud, born c1700.
2. c. John Stroud, born c1703.
   d. Joshua Stroud deserted his wife and left Prince George County, Virginia, in 1739 after being sued for debt; his estate was attached by his creditors. He was in Brunswick County, Virginia, in 1740 when he was sued for adultery by the churchwardens of St. Andrew's Parish.[4]
   e. Thomas Stroud died in Brunswick County, Virginia, in 1739, leaving all his property to his wife, Christian Stroud; he probably had no children.[5]

***

1. William Stroud was born about 1700 and received a grant of 100 acres on the south side of Meherrin River in Surry (probably now Mecklenburg) County, Virginia, on November 13, 1721; he sold it to Arthur Kavenaugh on August 21, 1723. He lived in Bristol Parish (Dinwiddie County, Virginia) on November 29, 1726, when he and his wife Margaret recorded the birth of a child. He lived in St. Andrew's Parish, Brunswick County, Virginia, on August 1, 1739, when he bought 100 acres on the south side of Roanoke River from George King. He was sued for adultery by the churchwardens of the parish, for trespass and assault, and for debt; on August 7, 1740, it was reported that he was not in the county.[6]

On June 27, 1741, William Stroud sold Drury Stith the 196 acres on Sturgeon Run where he then lived, part of the 392 acres granted to John Stroud, Sr. He then moved to Edgecombe Precinct (now Warren County), North Carolina, where in 1741 he sold his 100 acres on the south side of the Roanoke River in Brunswick County, Virginia, to John Shearman for £20.[7]

On March 15, 1742/43, Stroud received a grant of 400 acres on Cabin Branch in Edgecombe County; he sold 100 acres of it to Ephraim Estridge on February 22, 1743/4. On March 25, 1749, he received a 500 acre grant on Cabin Branch, and on October 26, 1752, a 750 acre grant on Little Creek. He bought 536 acres on Smith's Creek from Robert and Jemima Caller for £35 in 1750; 100 acres on Smith's Creek from John Jones for £5 on February 1, 1752; and 420 acres on Little Creek from Henry King for £20 on September 4, 1754. He sold 150 acres on Cabin Branch to James Buchanan for £8 on August 8, 1750; he gave his son John 125 acres on Cabin Branch on June 3, 1751. On December 6, 1752, he sold 250 acres on Cabin Branch to Benjamin Harrison of Surry County, Virginia, for £60; on December 18, 1752, he and his wife Elizabeth sold 200 acres on Smith's Creek to John Jones for £25; on October 18, 1755, he sold 300 acres on Howell's Branch to Robert Caller for £100.[8]

In 1755, William Stroud, Sr., was imprisoned in Granville (now Warren) County, North Carolina, but escaped aided by Elizabeth Stroud, Sr., Elizabeth Stroud, Jr., William Stroud, and others. He then moved to Orange County, North Carolina, where he continued to sell land in Granville County; he sold 420 acres on Little Creek to John Abernathy for £30 on March 2, 1756; 300 acres on Little Creek to William Sprunt for £15 on June 1, 1756; and 150 acres on Smith's Creek to William Bullock for £10.15 on March 7, 1758. Also in March, 1758, he bought 315 acres in Orange County and immediately gave 157 acres of it to William Stroud, Jr., and 158 acres to Peter Stroud.[9]

In 1759, Stroud was living temporarily in Lunenburg County, Virginia, when he bought 100 acres on Dodson's Branch in Granville County, North Carolina, from William Woodward for £40; he then returned to Granville County, where he sold the land to John Garner for £30 on February 23, 1760. He bought 640 acres on Little Creek from Robert Caller for £40 on June 25, 1759; 50 acres on Smith's Creek from James Dozier for £15 on February 20, 1764; and 150 acres on Smith's Creek from John Dozier for £85 on February 21, 1764. He sold 153 acres on Smith's Creek to Joseph Allen for £12.4 on August 12, 1760; 190 acres on Little Creek to his son William for £20 on May 9, 1761; 200 acres on Little Creek to George Rose for £10 on May 11, 1761; 60 acres on Roberson's Mill Creek to Benjamin Parham for £6 on March 25, 1762; and 296 acres on Little Creek to Abraham Mayfield on December 6, 1762. He sold 200 acres on Smith's Creek, the last of his land in Warren County, to Leonard Henley Bullock for £75.15.9 on December 19, 1764, and evidently moved to Tryon (now Lincoln) County, North Carolina, with his son John.[10]

The last known mention of William Stroud was on February 1, 1783, when he acknowledged in Lincoln County that John Stroud of that county was his eldest son by his first wife.[11] He probably had the following children, among others, probably by his first wife, Margaret:

a. John Stroud, born November 29, 1726; probably died in Wilkes County, Georgia; married Martha (Dozier?). He had many land transactions in Granville (now Warren) County, North Carolina, between 1751 and 1765, when he moved to Mecklenburg (now Lincoln) County, North Carolina. He had many land records there between 1767 and 1784, when he probably moved to Wilkes County, Georgia, where he probably soon died. His widow, Martha Stroud, made her will there on October 21, 1816; the estate was probated on September 1, 1817, mentioning the following children:[12]
   (1) (daughter) married James Arnold.
   (2) Sarah Stroud married _____ Little.
   (3) Susan Stroud married _____ Carter.

(4) Sherod Stroud died December 17, 1838, in Cobb County, Georgia;
married Hannah ____.
3. b. William Stroud, born c1732.
   c. Peter Stroud married Rebecca ____; lived in Burke County, North Carolina, in 1790.[13]
   d. Thomas Stroud married Mrs. Sarah Moss in 1763 and dsp in 1783 in Wilkes County, Georgia.[14]
   e. Yearby Stroud probably died in Georgia.[15]

***

1.   William Stroud was born about 1732 on Sturgeon Run in Brunswick County, Virginia, and lived there until 1741, when he moved to Edgecombe Precinct (now Warren County), North Carolina. He evidently was the person indicted for helping William Stroud, Sr., escape jail in 1755 in Granville County, North Carolina, and went with him to Orange County, North Carolina, where William Stroud, Sr., gave or sold him and his brother, Peter Stroud, 157 and 158 acres respectively in March, 1758.[16]

        Stroud moved back to Granville County in 1760, and on May 9, 1761, William Stroud, Sr., sold him 190 acres on the west side of Little Creek for £20; he sold the land to John Fowler for £33.10 on December 1, 1763, and returned to Orange County. He served on a Superior Court jury at Hillsboro on September 22, 1768; he was appointed to determine the route for a road from the Chatham County line over Haw River at Morgan's Mill to Hillsboro in 1777; he was the tax assessor for St. Thomas' District in 1777; he served to repair the road from Hillsboro to James Williams' mill, and he was overseer of the road from the Chatham County line to 10-mile tree.[17]

        By 1777, William Stroud's plantation was valued at £6,547, and on August 9, 1779, he entered 640 acres on Terrill's Creek adjoining land entered by his brother, Peter Stroud; the land was issued to him on September 21, 1785. In 1780, he owned 892 acres of land, five slaves, 19 cattle, and six horses for a total value of £5,780.[18]

        About 1755, William Stroud married Elizabeth ____ in Granville (now Warren) County, North Carolina. He made his will on August 4, 1786, dividing his property among his children and his wife; the estate was probated the same month. Elizabeth Stroud continued to live on the plantation, and on August 23, 1788, she bought 100 acres on Phil's Creek where her son John lived; she sold 60 acres of it to Stephen Lloyd on August 25, 1788. In October, 1799, she and her children sued Peter Stroud to clear up their land titles. She made her will on September 25, 1800, dividing her property among her children, and the estate was probated in November. William and Elizabeth Stroud had the following children:[19]

2. a. Margaret Stroud, born c1756.
3. b. John Stroud, born October 1, 1758.
   c. Frances Stroud, born c1761; married Edward Howell, who died in 1800 in Sumner County, Tennessee.
4. d. Mary Stroud, born c1763.
5. e. Sarah Stroud, born c1765.
6. f. Anderson Stroud, born c1768.
7. g. William Stroud, born May 17, 1771.
   h. Elizabeth Stroud, born c1773; married October 20, 1792, to William Rand; lived in Cumberland County, North Carolina, in 1796.
   i. Marshall Stroud, born c1775; lived in Warren County, Tennessee, in 1830; children (perhaps among others):

184

      (1) Calvin Stroud, born c1807 in Warren County, Tennessee; died
           June 12, 1876, in Desha County, Arkansas; married (1) ____
               (2) November 20, 1851, Elizabeth Wolverton (3) September 22, 1869, Susan McBride.
      (2) William Stroud, born c1809 in Warren County, Tennessee; lived
           in Desha County, Arkansas, in 1850.
      (3) Alfred Stroud.
      (4) Marshall Stroud.
      (5) Sarah Stroud.
      (6) Mary Stroud.
      (7) Elizabeth Stroud.
8. j. Thomas Stroud, born March 15, 1778.
    k. Dixon Stroud, born c1780; lived in Jefferson County, Mississippi,
      in 1816.

***

2.   Margaret Stroud was born about 1756 in Orange County, North Carolina,
and died April 26, 1816, in Sumner County, Tennessee; married May 1,
1776, to William Douglass, who died August 3, 1814, in Sumner County,
Tennessee; their children, perhaps among others, were as follows:[20]

9. a. Sarah Douglass, born c1780.
    b. John Douglass married ____ Gregory.
    c. Elizabeth Douglass died April 16, 1817; married Matthew Scoby.
    d. Mary Douglass died November 3, 1817; married Abner Dement.
    e. James Douglass died July 27, 1812; married ____ Dobson.
    f. Margaret Douglass married ____ Howell.
    g. Alfred M. Douglass died 1822 in Sumner County, Tennessee; married
      May 1, 1817, Cherry Ferrell; children:
      (1) James H. Douglass, born April 22, 1818; married Margaret Rogers.
      (2) Louisa M. Douglass, born October 22, 1819; married September 9,
          1846, Rev. Burkett F. Ferrell; children:
          (a) William Ferrell married Sally Shaw.
          (b) Mona Ferrell married Dr. William Davis.
          (c) Alfred Douglass Ferrell died in 1919; married Loula C. Wolfe.
          (d) Lula Ferrell married Frank Blair.
          (e) John Cage Ferrell married (1) Etha Jennings (2) Clida
             McGlothlin.
      (3) Alfred William Douglass, born April 12, 1822; married Mourning
          H. Boddie; dsp.

***

9.   Sarah Douglass was born about 1780 in Orange County, North Carolina,
and died January 22, 1810; married James Mayes, born October 13, 1777;
died July 23, 1851; their children were as follows:[21]

    a. William Douglass Mayes, born October 8, 1800; died February 24, 1873,
      in San Antonio, Texas; married December 24, 1837, to Mary Ann Cotton,
      born April 25, 1821; died December 20, 1878; children:
      (1) Fernando Cotton Mayes, born February 24, 1839.
      (2) Alvarado Mayes, born May 19, 1842; married November 12, 1872,
          to Dora Mayes.
      (3) Florida Arabella Mayes, born April 20, 1846; died February 21,
          1927, in San Antonio, Texas; married Thomas Moore Paschal;
          children:
          (a) Mary Natalie Paschal married C. E. Hampton; children:
             /1/ Dorothy Hampton married H. T. Powell; lived in Kansas

185

City, Missouri.

/2/ Helen Hampton lived in Dallas, Texas.

/3/ Carmen Hampton lived in McAllen, Texas.

(b) Harold Addison Paschal,dsp; lived in Mexico.

(c) Lenore Paschal,dsp; lived in San Antonio, Texas.

(d) Pauline Paschal married Charles H. Benson; dsp; lived in Hong Kong, China.

(e) Thomas Elmore Paschal, dsp.

(4) Garland Leath Mayes, born April 25, 1849; died March 31, 1918.

(5) Ida Rosalie Mayes, born October 25, 1852; married G. M. Devereaux.

(6) Elmore Douglass Mayes, born September 9, 1855; died October 4, 1932; married February 23, 1887, to Mary H. Houston.

(7) Branch Bertrand Mayes, born December 13, 1858; died June 10, 1893; married December 18, 1884, to Annie Park.

(8) Nellie H. Mayes, born March 5, 1862; died January 27, 1952; married Hal Gosling; children:

(a) Lytle Gosling, dsp; lived in San Antonio, Texas.

(b) Harry Gosling.

(9) Robert Edward Lee Mayes, born March 16, 1866; dsp July 26, 1882.

b. Martha Mayes, born c1802; married June 13, 1820, to John A. Creswell.

c. (child) born c1804.

d. (child) born c1806.

10. e. Sarah W. Mayes, born c1808.

f. (child) born c1809.

**

10.   Sarah W. Mayes was born about 1808 and died July 13, 1875, in St. Landry Parish, Louisiana; married September 16, 1827, to Samuel Creswell, born about 1791; died December 25, 1837, in Wilkinson County, Mississippi; their children were as follows:[22]

a. Samuel R. H. Creswell, born July 7, 1828; dsp October 10, 1833.

b. Francis Marion Creswell, born March 27, 1830; married November 17, 1861, to Ann Elizabeth Creswell, daughter of John A. Creswell and Nancy Mayes; children:

(1) Henry Minor Creswell, born January 7, 1863; died young.

(2) Samuel Francis Creswell, born February 2, 1865; dsp.

(3) Mary Lilly Creswell, born December 4, 1867; dsp.

(4) Norval Douglass Creswell, born December 5, 1869; dsp November 3, 1950.

(5) Bessie B. Creswell, born April 9, 1872; dsp.

(6) Hinton Elmore Creswell, born April 8, 1874; died young.

(7) George Allison Creswell, born July 14, 1876; died May, 1928; married Lydia Mary St. Gaudens.

(8) James Herbert Creswell, born 1879; married Mrs. Jennie (Thompson) Compton; dsp.

(9) Mattie Mayes Creswell, born January 20, 1881; died July 5, 1940; married Raymond Davis Wolfe.

c. James H. Creswell, born July 4, 1832; dsp August 22, 1833.

d. Mary A. E. Creswell, born October 8, 1834; dsp July 19, 1843.

11. e. James Alfred Creswell, born April 17, 1837.

f. Henry Minor Creswell, born April 17, 1837; died August 29, 1902, in Pearl River County, Mississippi; married August 19, 1857, to Isabel J. Baxter, born c1842; died November 18, 1910; children:

(1) Sarah F. Creswell, born April 6, 1861; married Ernest Montague.

(2) Martha Amana Creswell, born July 24, 1862; married N. J. Williams.

(3) Mary Josephine Creswell, born March 14, 1868; dsp September 19,

1871.
- (4) Susan Amelia Creswell, born September 16, 1869; married J. H. Henley.
- (5) Paul Creswell, born September 22, 1871; died May 7, 1899; married Celeste Teutch.
- (6) Marian Allen Creswell, born May 10, 1874; married J. D. Ducharme.
- (7) Henry Pierce Creswell.
- (8) Frank R. Creswell.
- (9) Richard Clarence Creswell, born December 6, 1880; died December 8, 1925; married Lena LeBlanc.
- (10) George Baxter Creswell, born July 1, 1884; died December 8, 1955; married (1) Jeanne LeBlanc (2) Lula LeBlanc.

***

11.   James Alfred Creswell was born April 17, 1837, in Wilkinson County, Mississippi, and died April 12, 1914, in Canfield, Arkansas; married January 15, 1868, in New Orleans, Louisiana, to Susan Bridget Chinn, born September 11, 1842, and died March 24, 1925, daughter of Chichester Thornton Chinn and Martha Catherine Ferguson. Their children were as follows:[23]

- a. Cora Creswell, born January 4, 1869; dsp December 24, 1885, in Houston County, Texas.
- b. James Alfred Creswell, born May 14, 1871; dsp October 7, 1871.
- c. Alice Creswell, born November 7, 1872; died February 15, 1958, in Shreveport, Louisiana; married October 26, 1898, in Paris, Texas, to Canfield Colbert, born August 9, 1872; died December 20, 1941; son of John Augustus Colbert and Anne Haseltine Canfield; children:
  - (1) James Canfield Colbert, born September 2, 1899; married September 10, 1922, to Margaret Amelia Bates, born November 30, 1900; died November 8, 1961; lived in Norman, Oklahoma; child:
    - (a) Thomas Alfred Colbert, born August 20, 1925; married July 1, 1951, to Esther Mae Parker, born September 9, 1930; children:
      - 1/ Frederick James Colbert, born October 3, 1952.
      - 2/ Amelia Rose Colbert, born December 9, 1957.
  - (2) Katherine Chinn Colbert, born October 25, 1900; dsp; lived in Shreveport, Louisiana.
- d. Alfred Chichester Creswell, born October 10, 1874; dsp June 24, 1877.
- e. Edith Creswell, born September 6, 1878; died January 10, 1959, in Shreveport, Louisiana; married June 13, 1909, to Otto Longino, born April 8, 1877; died March 18, 1961; son of William Pulliam Longino and Priscilla Evelyn Traylor; child:
  - (1) Edna Longino, born August 11, 1910; married (1) February 13, 1932, to Shaler Charles Magaw, born November 22, 1902; died April 6, 1941; (2) August 9, 1949, to Robert W. Alexander, born January, 1890; died November 20, 1949; children (by first marriage):
    - (a) Edith Anne Magaw, born November 17, 1933; married April 14, 1963, to Elwood Williams.
    - (b) Barbara Louise Magaw, born April 14, 1935.
- f. Edna Creswell, born August 27, 1881; dsp January 21, 1905.

***

3.   John Stroud was born October 1, 1758, in Orange County, North Carolina, and died in 1831 in Orange County; married August 8, 1779, to Delilah Bryant, born August 14, 1762, daughter of William and Elizabeth Bryant. Their children were as follows:[24]

187

a. William Stroud, born September 15, 1780.
b. Bryant Stroud, born January 18, 1782; died 1872; married (1) 1804 to Ann Snipes; (2) April 9, 1829, to Martha Wilson.
c. Elizabeth Stroud, born May 18, 1784; married February 1, 1803, to Henry Lloyd.
d. Margaret Stroud, born April 16, 1787; married March 29, 1803, to Archibald Durham.
e. Fielding Stroud, born April 16, 1789; married January 2, 1813, to Elizabeth Blackwood.
f. Tabitha Stroud, born June 18, 1791.
g. Hawkins Stroud, born October 6, 1793; died October 13, 1854; married (1) July 18, 1818, to Frances Snipes; (2) January 3, 1831, to Mary Edwards.
h. Delilah Stroud, born September 5, 1795; married March 27, 1817, to John Powell.
i. Patsy Stroud, born August 20, 1798.
j. Nancy Stroud, born January 13, 1801; married January 22, 1820, to Alexander Cheek.
k. John Sumner Stroud, born October 5, 1804.

***

4.   Mary Stroud was born about 1763 in Orange County, North Carolina; married about 1780 to Isham Thrift, who died in Orange County, North Carolina, in 1812; their children were as follows:[25]

a. Elizabeth Thrift married _____ Snipes.
b. Susanna Thrift married _____ Booker.
c. Perry Thrift.
d. Sarah Thrift.
e. Delilah Thrift married _____ Perry.
f. Margaret Thrift.
g. William Thrift.
h. David Thrift, born November 17, 1794.
i. Drury Thrift.
j. Isham Thrift.
k. Mary Thrift.
l. Nancy Thrift.
m. Levisa Thrist.

***

5.   Sarah Stroud was born about 1765 and was living in Orange County, North Carolina, in 1839; married October 25, 1781, to William King, who died February 14, 1820; their children were as follows:[26]

a. Patsy King, born March 19, 1782.
b. Senea King.
c. Frances King.
d. Elizabeth King.
e. Margaret King.
f. Sarah King.
g. John King.
h. William D. King.
i. Marshall King.
j. Pleasant King.

***

6.   Anderson Stroud was born about 1768 in Orange County, North Carolina, and was living in Warren County, Tennessee, in 1830; married Levisa Rand; their children were as follows:[27]

a. Wade H. Stroud married Nancy Stubblefield (see p.   213); lived in Lawrence County, Missouri; children (perhaps among others):
    (1) John Stroud, born c1832.
    (2) Columbus Stroud, born c1835.
    (3) Sarah Stroud, born c1837.
    (4) Leonidas Stroud, born c1841.
    (5) Louisa Stroud, born c1843.
    (6) Anderson Stroud, born c1845.
b. Abraham Stroud married _____ Rains.
c. Walter Stroud, born c1806; married Sarah Stubblefield (see p. 227); children (perhaps among others):
    (1) Anderson Stroud, born c1831; married December 3, 1854, to Sarah Ann Sparks.
    (2) Mary Stroud, born c1833; married April 28, 1856, to George Roach.
    (3) George Stroud, born c1836.
    (4) Jane Stroud, born c1838; married November 16, 1854, to Moses L. Banks.
    (5) Louisa Stroud, born c1839; married October 17, 1857, to George Hoodenpile.
    (6) Nancy Stroud, born c1841.
    (7) Martha Stroud, born c1844.
    (8) Walter Stroud, born c1846.
    (9) Sarah Stroud, born c1848.
d. Margaret Stroud married William Sutliff.
e. Eliza Stroud married _____ Broils.
f. Elizabeth Stroud married _____ McGee.
g. Sophia Stroud, born c1812; married Zadock Duncan; children (probably among others):
    (1) Frances Duncan, born c1828.
    (2) William Duncan, born c1829.
    (3) Patrick Duncan, born c1831.
    (4) Louisa Duncan, born c1833.
    (5) Zadock Duncan, born c1835.
    (6) Mary Duncan, born c1837.
    (7) Isham Duncan, born c1840.
    (8) Wade Duncan, born c1842.
    (9) Jane Duncan, born c1844.
    (10) Deuna Duncan, born c1847.

***

7.   William Stroud was born May 17, 1771, in Orange County, North Carolina, until on October 20, 1792, he sold his brother Anderson Stroud his interest in their father's estate. He then moved to Hawkins County, Tennessee, where about 1793, he married Nancy Stubblefield (see p. 212). He returned to Orange County in 1794, where he lived until 1797, when he moved to Grainger (now Claiborne) County, Tennessee.[28]

He received a grant of 200 acres in Hawkins County and bought 300 acres on the Clinch River in Claiborne County on October 16, 1797, from John Walling for $433.33. He bought 30 acres from James Chism for $100.00 on November 5, 1803, and held 300 acres for Thomas Jeffers on October 2, 1803. He sold 16 acres to Silas Clark for $40.00 on November 1, 1803. He served on the first Claiborne County grand jury in 1801. He sold his 330 acre plantation on the north side of the Clinch River to Thomas Hurst on October 29, 1807.[29]

William Stroud moved to Warren County, Tennessee, in the winter of
1807/8 and settled on Hickory Creek near Viola; he received a grant of
40 acres in 1810 and on August 22, 1811, he bought 74 acres on the West
Fork of Hickory Creek from John Doak for $150.00. On October 17, 1812,
he bought 150 acres on the West Hickory from Mordecai Boone and another
17 acres there from Boone for $20.00 on October 31, 1813. On August 26,
1813, he bought 108 acres on Hickory from William P. Anderson for $216.00,
and he and Boone divided the lands that they had bought from Doak and
Anderson with Stroud getting more than half because Boone got the mill-
site.[30]

By 1820, Stroud was a prosperous planter with 15 slaves. On March
29, 1823, as administrator of the estate of Jenkin Reynolds, whose widow
Margaret he married about 1820, Stroud sold land to Shadrack Tribble.
In 1824 he received grants to 10 acres on the East Fork of Stone's River
and 100 acres on Hickory Creek, and with John B. Rodgers, 300 acres on
Hickory Creek and Collins' River. On August 22, 1826, he and Elisha
Reynolds received 21½ acres on Hickory Creek, and on January 17, 1827, he
received 150 acres on Horse Spring Fork of Stone's River and 50 acres
adjoining his sugar camp. On June 3, 1828, he received 75 acres on Horse
Spring Fork. He also bought 200 acres on Bean's Creek from John Farrar
for $1,890.00 on October 8, 1835, and 51 acres on Bean's Creek from
Hosea Stamps for $200.00 on December 27, 1837. He sold land on Hickory
Creek to Houston Hammons for $53.75 on December 11, 1839, and he sold
a slave boy named King to Robertson Nevill for $300.00 on January 26,
1839.[31]

. William Stroud was a Tennessee elector for Andrew Jackson in 1828
and was a Warren County commissioner for several years. He was a moder-
ator of the Blue Springs Separate Baptist Church for 30 years and was
evidently known for his many kindnesses. On March 13, 1829, he gave
Joshua Dial's five children all the personal property he bought at their
father's sale, and in 1836 he gave the 186 acres of land he bought at
the estate sale of Jenkin Reynolds to the heirs. On April 5, 1839, he
gave John Whitlock 200 acres on the Barren Fork of Collins' River because
of respect and regard and because his family was large and helpless.
On May 20, 1839, he gave his son Thomas 157 acres on Hickory Creek, and
on June 11, 1839, he gave his son-in-law, Davis Darnell, 233 acres on
Hickory Creek.[32]

William Stroud made his will on March 26, 1839, devising his remaining property to his 13 children, although he had already given them
cash and slaves. His estate was probated in August, 1841. On December
28, 1843, after all debts were paid, the executors had $5,277.61 in cash,
and on January 8, 1852, they sold 440 acres of the plantation, which
had been surveyed in 1807 and 1808 on Hickory Creek, to William Ramsey
for $3,680.00. William Stroud's children were as follows:[33]

(by first marriage):
12. a. Thomas Stroud, born September 11, 1794.
13. b. Elizabeth Stroud, born December 6, 1795.
    c. Sarah Stroud, born May 9, 1798; married Charles Coulson; lived in
       Coffee County, Tennessee, in 1850.
    d. William Stroud, born June 24, 1800; married Charlotte Powell.
14. e. George Stroud, born February 10, 1802.
15. f. Mary Stroud, born December 23, 1803.
    g. Nancy Stroud, born April 20, 1806; dsp before 1839; married Dennis
       Cox.
16. h. Anna Stroud, born May 30, 1808.

i. Lucy Stroud, born November 27, 1810; died April 23, 1904, in Coffee County, Tennessee; married October 14, 1830, to Robertson Nevill (see p. 139).

17. j. Frances Stroud, born February 9, 1813.
k. John Doak Stroud, born January 16, 1816; dsp before 1839 in Warren County, Tennessee.

18. l. Margaret Stroud, born March 12, 1818.
(by second marriage):
m. Martha Jane Stroud, born March 15, 1822; died June 2, 1847, in Coffee County, Tennessee; married Robert Hines.

19. n. Bartlett Smith Stroud, born December 16, 1823.
o. Preston Anderson Stroud, born January 19, 1827; dsp.

***

12.   Thomas Stroud was born September 11, 1794, in Orange County, North Carolina, and died about 1872 in Warren County, Tennessee; served in War of 1812; married 1813 to Lucy Jarvis. Their children were as follows:[34]

a. Sarah Stroud married William McSpain.
b. George Stroud.
c. Elizabeth Stroud married John McAfee.
20. d. Albert G. Stroud, born c1819.
21. e. Oliver Hazard Perry Stroud, born August 10, 1820.
f. Nancy Stroud married _____ Quarles.
g. Lucy Stroud married _____ Harmon.
h. Thomas J. Stroud, born c1825.
i. Reziah Stroud, born c1828; married November 9, 1856, to Nancy Walling.
j. John A. Stroud, born c1830.
k. Marcus L. Stroud, born c1832; married December 4,1855, to Harriet Powell.
l. Hettie Mabel Stroud, born c1834.
m. Frances C. Stroud, born c1836; married August 1, 1853, to William Sapp.
n. Minerva Stroud, born c1838; married October 28, 1860, to Robert Henderson.

***

20.   Albert G. Stroud was born about 1819 in Warren County, Tennessee, and died in Izard County, Arkansas; married (1) Elizabeth Bernette _____ (2) c1877 to Matilda Frances _____; his children were as follows:[35]

(by first marriage):
a. James M. Stroud, born c1842.
b. Jane Arsnoe Stroud, born February 14, 1842; died December 2, 1895; married James Andrew Jackson; children:
  (1) Sarah Ann Jackson.
  (2) Marah Frances Jackson.
  (3) Thomas Jefferson Jackson.
  (4) James Madison Jackson.
  (5) Charles Eldon Jackson.
  (6) Phronissa Lee Jackson.
  (7) Cassie Jackson.
  (8) Bernette Jackson.
c. John S. Stroud, born c1845; married Sarah C. _____; children (perhaps among others):
  (1) Martha J. Stroud, born c1867.

191

            (2) Mary B. Stroud, born c1869.
            (3) William B. Stroud, born c1872.
            (4) Minerva E. Stroud, born c1873.
            (5) Columbus G. Stroud, born c1874.
        d. Henderson Stroud, born 1847.
22.   e. Bartlett Smith Stroud, born September 14, 1850.
        f. Harrington Stroud, born c1853; married Frances N. _____; lived in
            Mt. Pleasant, Arkansas; children:
            (1) Leonidas Stroud, born c1879.
            (2) Herschell M. Stroud, born 1880.
            (3) Maggie Stroud.
            (4) Josie Stroud.
            (5) Elam Stroud.
            (6) Ed Stroud.
            (7) Mystice Stroud.
23.   g. (Dr.) William Jefferson Stroud, born March 11, 1855.
        h. Frances M. Stroud, born c1858; married Thomas Seay.
        i. A. Madison Stroud, born c1860.
        (by second marriage):
        j. Cora Stroud, born c1878.
        k. George A. Stroud, born c1879.
        l. Viola Stroud.

                              ***

22.   Bartlett Smith Stroud was born September 14, 1850, and died Decem-
        ber 4, 1912, in Arkansas. He married (1) Martha E. Johnson (2) Laura E.
        Screws; his children were as follows:[36]

        (by first marriage):
        a. Nancy Bernette Stroud, born c1876.
        b. Amelia E. Stroud, died young.
        (by second marriage):
        c. Allie Nora Stroud, born 1880.
        d. George Albert Stroud.
        e. Arthur Bartlett Stroud.
        f. Inez Stroud.
        g. Genarah Stroud married William Walls; lived in Mt. Pleasant, Arkansas.
        h. Annie Maybell Stroud.
        i. James Maxwell Stroud, died young.
        j. Ninah Arsnoe Stroud, died young.

                              ***

23.   (Dr.) William Jefferson Stroud was born March 11, 1855, and died
        April 1, 1939, in Izard County, Arkansas; married Martha Jane Cornealus
        and their children were as follows:[37]

        a. Effie Stroud.
        b. Espy Madson Stroud, born October 31, 1887; died December 6, 1956, in
            Yuma, Arizona; married February 23, 1916, to Laura Madglena Hightower,
            born October 28, 1895; children:
            (1) Grace Elizabeth Stroud, born December 26, 1916; married August
                 21, 1937, to Thomas Dee Farthing; child:
                 (a) Virginia Ann Farthing, born January 7, 1943; married (1)
                      June 15, 1962, Skip Alender (2) October 15, 1965, Jack
                      Graffham.
            (2) Medrith Lois Stroud, born January 24, 1919; married July, 1938,
                 to Richard Slade; lived in Izard County, Arkansas; children:

                              192

     (a) Lois Marie Slade, born July 13, 1940; married December 25,
         1962, to Jerry Rassmussen; children:
         /1/ Sherryl Rassmussen, born c1963.
         /2/ Dana Rassmussen, born December 18, 1969.
     (b) William Royce Slade, born September 16, 1941; married
         Barbara Nealey.
  (3) Homer Allison Stroud, born May 22, 1922; married June 17, 1944,
     to Jean Ross; lived in Yuma, Arizona; children:
     (a) Martha Jane Stroud, born March 27, 1948; married December
         21, 1967, to John Kubiak.
     (b) Edward Clyde Stroud, born March 5, 1953.
  (4) Martha Irene Stroud, born November 28, 1923; married (1) Feb-
     ruary 19, 1944, Raymond Hendricks (2) 1962 Glenn Goode; lived
     in Yuma, Arizona; children (by first marriage):
     (a) Dennis Lynn Hendricks, born August 25, 1950.
     (b) Linda Joyce Hendricks, born April 18, 1955.
  (5) Max Henry Stroud, born and died October 18, 1927.
  (6) Jonnie Marie Stroud, born November 10, 1935; married (1) April
     13, 1957, William Houston (2) April 3, 1960, Dale Sattley; lived
     in Yuma, Arizona; children (by second marriage):
     (a) Jackie Marie Sattley, born October 4, 1961.
     (b) Talbert Lee Sattley, born May 13, 1963.
     (c) Lawrence Pick Sattley, born November 8, 1964.
  (7) Claudia Lanell Stroud, born April 14, 1937; married February 4,
     1956, to James F. Borst; lived in Yuma, Arizona; children:
     (a) Debra Lynn Borst, born November 4, 1956.
     (b) Claudette Ann Borst, born June 12, 1958.
     (c) Laura Kin Borst, born April 19, 1960.
     (d) James Allison Borst, born February 8, 1965.

***

21.   Oliver Hazard Perry Stroud was born August 10, 1820, in Warren
County, Tennessee; died July 4, 1902, in Izard County, Arkansas; married
in 1844 to Martha Jourdan, born February 17, 1827; died August 19, 1899,
daughter of John Jourdan and Edith Alexander. His children were as
follows:[38]

a. Minerva Stroud, born c1845; dsp.
b. John A. Stroud, born 1846; married 1874 to Euphemia Guest, daughter
    of Morgan Guest and Eliza Dennison; lived in Izard County, Arkansas;
    children:
    (1) Jeff A. Stroud.
    (2) Lillie B. Stroud.
    (3) Dorothea N. Stroud.
    (4) Perry L. Stroud.
    (5) Fannie C. Stroud.
c. William L. Stroud, born c1849.
d. George R. Stroud, born January 1, 1851; died February 12, 1904, at
    Union, Arkansas; married Sarah E. _____.
e. James M. Stroud, born c1855.
24. f. Martha Elizabeth Stroud, born 1857.
g. Lawson P. Stroud, born c1862.
h. Oliver Hazard Stroud, born c1864.
i. Mary F. Stroud, born c1867.
j. Richard A. Stroud, born c1869.
k. Robert H. Stroud, born c1871.
l. Taylor M. Stroud, born c1873.

***

193

24.   Martha Elizabeth Stroud, born 1857; died March 8, 1915, at Bradford,
Arkansas; married 1877 to Francis Wesley Pearson, born September 30, 1855;
died May 13, 1922, son of Emerson Summerfield Pearson and Ellen Morris.
Their children were as follows:[39]

    a. Shelby Marvin Pearson, born September 21, 1877; died December 27,
        1947, in Little Rock, Arkansas; married June 11, 1908, to May Barron,
        born March 16, 1877; died September 22, 1951, daughter of Thomas
        Edward Barron and Maria Frances Ballou; children:
        (1) Frances Elizabeth Pearson, born November 15, 1909, married August,
            31, 1928, to Dale Claude Loyd, born December 9, 1907, son of
            William Berry Loyd and Ida Jane Nicholson; children:
            (a) (Dr.) Marvin Dale Loyd, born December 3, 1932; married
                June 7, 1953, Marilynn Nisler, born February 23, 1934,
                daughter of William Cargile Nisler and Mildred Martin;
                children:
                /1/ Gregory Marvin Loyd, born April 9, 1957.
                /2/ Nancy Lynn Loyd, born December 3, 1959.
            (b) Jane Suzanne Loyd, born May 7, 1937; married June 7, 1959,
                to James William Chesshir, born March 5, 1937, son of W. J.
                Chesshir and Ruth McClure; children:
                /1/ Deborah Jane Chesshir, born July 7, 1961.
                /2/ James William Chesshir, born March 7, 1963.
                /3/ Bryan Loyd Chesshir, born October 24, 1964.
            (c) William Pearson Loyd, born August 10, 1945; married Jan-
                uary 28, 1966, to Marsha Ann McKennon, born February 17,
                1946, daughter of Archibald Monroe McKennon and Mary
                Cotton.
        (2) Oramae Barron Pearson, born May 23, 1911; married February 6,
            1936, to Rev. John Lewis Cannon, born May 13, 1908; died Novem-
            ber 11, 1955, in Greggton, Texas, son of Rev. John Lewis Cannon
            and Annie Elizabeth Turrentine; children:
            (a) John Lewis Cannon, born January 23, 1937; married August
                23, 1959, to Effie Caffall Ogden, born December 11, 1940,
                daughter of Robert Vincent Ogden and Kate Crocker McFerrin;
                children:
                /1/ John Lewis Cannon, born November 27, 1963.
                /2/ Stephanie Lynn Cannon, born December 15, 1966.
            (b) Margaret Lynn Cannon, born February 23, 1939; married
                November 25, 1965, to Philip Ronald Spencer, born February
                18, 1943, son of William Edwin Spencer and Mildred Elizabeth
                Tucker.

    b. (Dr.) William H. M. Pearson, born January, 1880.
    c. Bertha O. Pearson married 1908 J. W. Churchwell; lived in Indepen-
        dence County, Arkansas.
    d. Martha E. Pearson, dsp 1910.
    e. Robert W. Pearson, died February 13, 1968, in Clarendon, Arkansas.
    f. Thad O. Pearson.
    g. Malissa Pearson, died young.
    h. Emery P. Pearson, died young.
    i. Minerva Frances Pearson, died March 28, 1965, in Little Rock, Arkan-
        sas; married William F. Hurt.
    j. Cleveland Pearson.

                    ***

13.   Elizabeth Stroud was born December 6, 1795, in Orange County, North

Carolina, and died September 5, 1880, in Warren County, Tennessee; married in 1815 to William Ramsey, born January 8, 1795, and died August 9, 1865, son of David Ramsey and Jane McCaslin. Their children were as follows:[40]

a. Nancy Ramsey, born 1816; died 1889; married 1838 Robert B. Biles, died 1873; children (perhaps among others):
   (1) Thomas B. Biles, born c1840.
   (2) Elizabeth Biles, born c1842.
   (3) James C. Biles, born c1844.
   (4) William Biles, born c1845.
   (5) John Biles, born c1847.
   (6) Robert P. Biles.
   (7) Joseph R. Biles.
b. David Ramsey, born January 6, 1818; died November 22, 1901; married (1) Sarah Tilford, born December 30, 1817; died September 5, 1877; (2) Rebecca Custer, born April 5, 1833; died October 2, 1906; children (all by first marriage) (perhaps among others):
   (1) Charles C. Ramsey.
   (2) Lytle Ramsey.
   (3) William Ramsey, died young.
   (4) Drucilla Ramsey.
   (5) Nancy Ramsey.
   (6) Gula Ramsey.
25. c. Frances Ramsey, born c1819.
d. James C. Ramsey, born c1823; married Susan Colville; children (perhaps among others):
   (1) Ella Ramsey married _____ Hickerson.
   (2) Laura Ramsey married _____ Ivie.
   (3) James C. Ramsey.
   (4) William Ramsey.
e. John Ramsey, born c1825; married Cynthia J. Colville; children (perhaps among others):
   (1) Fulton Ramsey, died young.
   (2) (Dr.) A. B. Ramsey.
   (3) Elizabeth Ramsey married _____ Womack.
   (4) Callie Ramsey married _____ Baldwin.
   (5) Mary Ramsey married _____ Duncan.
f. Jane Ramsey, born c1828; married O. F. Brewster; children (perhaps among others):
   (1) William Brewster.
   (2) Ed Brewster; lived in Texas.
   (3) Finley Brewster; lived in Texas.
   (4) Samuel Brewster; lived in McMinnville, Tennessee.
   (5) Frank Brewster; lived in McMinnville, Tennessee.
   (6) Evelyn Brewster married Joseph C. Smartt.
   (7) (daughter) married K. B. Fleming; lived in McMinnville, Tennessee.
   (8) Frances Brewster married _____ Moseley; lived in Chattanooga, Tennessee.
26. g. William R. Ramsey, born March 9, 1832.

***

25.   Frances Ramsey was born about 1819 in Warren County, Tennessee; married Thomas Jefferson King, born about 1805; their children (perhaps among others) were as follows:[41]

a. Sarah Elizabeth King, born c1839; married George W. Ramsey; children

195

(perhaps among others):
(1) George S. Ramsey married Evelyn Young.
(2) Foster Ramsey married Berta Hines; lived in Winchester, Tennessee.
(3) Mollie Ramsey married Horace Burger; children (perhaps among
others):
(a) Laura Burger married _____ Covington.
(b) George Burger.
(c) Sada Burger.
(d) Louise Burger.
b. William W. King, born c1841; married Queen Thomas.
c. Laura A. King, born c1843.
d. Philip T. King, born c1845.

***

26.   William R. Ramsey was born March 9, 1832, and died April 20, 1908;
married Mary Taylor, born February 22, 1841; died May 6, 1913; their
children (perhaps among others) were as follows:[42]

a. James R. Ramsey.
b. John Ramsey.
c. Frank Ramsey.
d. William Thomas Ramsey married July 8, 1894, Ann Waterhouse Smartt,
born November 6, 1870, daughter of Euclid Ramsey Smartt and Nancy
Esther Davis.
e. Floyd Ramsey.
f. Belle Ramsey.
g. Elizabeth Ramsey married H. B. Evans.

***

14.   George Stroud was born February 10, 1802, in Claiborne County, Tennessee, and died about 1862 in Warren County, Tennessee; married (1)
Isabel Ramsey (2) c1859 Mrs. Angelina (Smartt) Nelson, born January 2,
1823; died June 23, 1908, daughter of George Smartt and Athelia Randolph.
His child (by second marriage) was as follows:[43]

a. George Smartt Stroud, born April 10, 1861; died October 26, 1926;
married (1) October 29, 1883, to Vesta Ann Smartt (2) April 27, 1898,
to Allie R. Holman (3) December 27, 1900, to Ellie Womack; children:
(by first marriage):
(1) Harry Stroud, born August 30, 1884; dsp July 15, 1888.
(2) Eugene Stroud, born December 24, 1887; dsp September 9, 1892.
(3) Frank Stroud, born July 9, 1891; married January 27, 1923, to
Elizabeth Burton Purcell; children:
(a) James Madison Stroud, born March 7, 1925.
(b) David Hannah Stroud, born September 13, 1931.
(4) Belle Stroud, born July 9, 1891; married October 14, 1913, to
Carl West Flemister; children:
(a) Carl West Flemister, born July 8, 1915.
(b) George Stroud Flemister, born September 13, 1920.
(by third marriage):
(5) George Smartt Stroud, born May 6, 1902; married June 2, 1928,
to Louise Chase Holsten; children:
(a) Michael Holsten Stroud, born September 19, 1929.
(b) George Smartt Stroud, born June 13, 1934.
(6) Robert Womack Stroud, born March 2, 1911; married May 18, 1935,
to Rosalind Elizabeth Veatch.

***

15.   Mary Stroud was born December 23, 1803, in Claiborne County, Tennessee, and died September 1, 1877, in Warren County, Tennessee; married Samuel Ramsey, born April 23, 1798, and died August 28, 1870, son of David Ramsey and Jane McCaslin. Their children were as follows:[44]

a.   William Ramsey, born 1822; died 1914.
b.   Andrew Jackson Ramsey, born c1826; married (1) January 13, 1857, to Mrs. Nancy (Winton) Stroud (2) Lou Austell; children (perhaps among others):
    (by first marriage):
    (1) Betty Ramsey married November 24, 1878, to William H. Sain.
    (2) Hence Ramsey.
    (3) Mary Sue Ramsey married _____ Etter.
    (by second marriage):
    (4) Dora Ramsey married I. B. Smartt.
    (5) Flora Ramsey.
    (6) Andrew Ramsey.
c.   David Ramsey, born c1828.
d.   Joseph Ramsey.
e.   George W. Ramsey, born c1834.
f.   Martha Ann Ramsey, born 1838; died 1906; married December 8, 1855, to John Macon; children:
    (1) Eugene LaMalmon Macon, born 1857; married (1) Margaret Drake (2) Ann Wharton.
    (2) Eliza Lou Macon, born 1859; married William Edgecomb.
    (3) Elizabeth Laura Macon, born 1861; married Charles Eddins.
    (4) Emory John Macon, born 1863; dsp 1908.
    (5) Samuel Ramsey Macon, born 1865; dsp 1905.
    (6) Sallie Caroline Macon, born 1867; died 1907; married Harry Nichols.
    (7) Martha Ann Macon, born 1868; married (1) 1884 to W. P. Walling (2) 1898 to Dr. William E. Youree.
    (8) David Harrison Macon, born 1870; married 1899 to Mathilda Richardson.
    (9) George Manasseh Macon, born 1872; dsp 1874.
   (10) Robert Gideon Macon, born 1874; married Nancy Wayne; lived in Bentonville, Arkansas.
   (11) Mary Margaret Pearl Macon, born 1876; married (1) Burford Holden (2) LeVert Harrison.

***

16.   Anna Stroud was born May 30, 1808, in Warren County, Tennessee, and died March 7, 1898, in Warren County, Tennessee; married (1) c1828 to Philip Dial (2) c1835 to David McD. Darnell; her children were as follows:[45]

(by first marriage):
a.   (Dr.) Joseph Newton Dial, born c1829; lived in Mississippi.
b.   Nancy Emaline Dial, born January 15, 1831; died May 3, 1917; married June 26, 1855, to George Washington Stroud (see p. 204).
(by second marriage):
c.   James J. Darnell, born c1836; lived in Coleman, Texas.
d.   Mary Isabella Darnell, born October 5, 1838; died March 22, 1920, in Archer County, Texas; married Newsome Richard Wolf, born August 14, 1834; died 1909 in Austin, Texas; children:
    (1) Davis Levi Wolf, born January 24, 1862; died January 5, 1953; married Esther Maria Hutton.
    (2) Della Wolf married Charles Welch.
    (3) Florence Wolfe married _____ Browning.

(4) El Wolfe married (1) Isola Shackleford (2) Mary _____.
(5) Martha Wolf married Jerry Harbour.
(6) Beulah Wolf married Frank M. _____.
(7) Lena Wolf.
(8) Grace Wolf married Ernest McDaniel; child:
   (a) Mary Ellen McDaniel.

e. Esther Jane Darnell, born c1844; dsp.

27. f. Ann Elizabeth Darnell, born c1846.

g. William Thomas Darnell, born c1848; died 1925; married (1) Margaret Bryan, daughter of Joseph Wilson Bryan and Rebecca Hawks; (2) Elizabeth Custer, born December 8, 1844, daughter of Abraham Custer and Margaret Bowers; children:
(by first marriage):
(1) William Darnell.
(2) Cleo Darnell married Ed Elder; children:
   (a) Jesse Elder.
   (b) James Elder.
   (c) Polk Elder.
   (d) Coleman Elder.
   (e) Porter Elder.
(3) Joseph Newton Darnell; children:
   (a) Paul Darnell.
   (b) Thomas Darnell.
   (c) (daughter).
(4) Dora Darnell.
(5) George Darnell.

***

27.   Ann Elizabeth Darnell was born about 1846 and married James Thomas Darnell; their children were as follows:[46]

a. Myra Darnell married John C. Smoot; children:
(1) James Smoot.
(2) William Smoot; lived in Morrison, Tennessee.
(3) Mabel Smoot.
(4) Jennie Smoot.
(5) Myra Smoot.
(6) John Smoot; lived in Morrison, Tennessee.
(7) Sutton Smoot.

b. May Darnell married Matthew Smoot; children:
(1) Mathilda Smoot married _____ Burkes; lived in McMinnville, Tennessee.
(2) Maggie Smoot.
(3) Willie Matt Smoot, died young.
(4) J. T. Smoot.

c. Belle Darnell married William Cunningham; children:
(1) Robert Cunningham married Amanda Rayburn; lived in Detroit, Michigan.
(2) George Cunningham.

d. James Jackson Darnell married Arie Brickey; children:
(1) Dr. Clarence Darnell married Kate Shelton; lived in Hollywood, California.
(2) Serena Elizabeth Darnell married James Robert Dearman; lived in Morrison, Tennessee.
(3) James Darnell, dsp; lived in Grand Junction, Colorado.

e. Robert Darnell, died young.

f. Jesse Darnell, died young.

g. Bessie Darnell married _____ Denton; children:

        (1) James Denton.
        (2) Lorena Denton married _____ Gregory.
        (3) Ruth Denton married _____ Stroud.
        (4) Faye Denton married _____ Tolbert.

                                    ***

17.   Frances Stroud was born February 9, 1813, in Warren County, Ten-
        nessee, and died about 1892 in Coffee County, Tennessee; married about
        1829 to Matthew Bucie Bryan, born October 23, 1805, and died November
        13, 1870; son of John Bryan and Sarah Elizabeth Bucie. Their children
        were as follows:[47]

        a. Sarah Jane Bryan, born November 28, 1830; married John Cunningham.
        b. John Doak Bryan, born April 19, 1832; died young.
        c. William Gaines Bryan, born December 13, 1833; died 1862.
        d. Nancy Elizabeth Bryan, born March 4, 1836; married Jackson Bonner.
        e. Mary Ann Bryan, born October 24, 1848; died November 8, 1925; mar-
            ried October, 1867, to John Custer, born September 6, 1829; died
            March 8, 1912; son of Abraham Custer and Margaret Bowers; children:
            (1) Fanny Margaret Custer, born November 6, 1870; died 1964; mar-
                 ried May 6, 1896, to Charles Brookover, born March 11, 1870;
                 died March 17, 1922, son of Robert Chunn Brookover and Ruth
                 Pence.
            (2) Emma Cora Custer, born September 10, 1874; married George
                 Edwards; children:
                 (a) Lucile Edwards, born August 6, 1894; married Herbert Cha-
                      fin; child:
                      /1/ Betty Chafin, born 1922.
                 (b) John Arthur Edwards, born April, 1901; died 1955; married
                      (1) Grace _____ (2) Ann _____; child (by first marriage):
                      /1/ John Arthur Edwards.
        f. George Abner Bryan, born April 25, 1850; died May 25, 1912; married
            Sarah Ann Isabel Braley (see below).

                                    ***

18.   Margaret Stroud was born March 12, 1818, in Warren County, Tennes-
        see, and died May 23, 1862, in Warren County, Tennessee; married (1)
        c1835 to George Mumford Sain, born April 30, 1811; died about 1841, son
        of Daniel Sain and Martha Davis (2) c1850 to Columbus C. Braley. Her
        children were as follows:[48]

        (by first marriage):
        a. James Bailey Sain, born 1836; dsp 1862; married November 4,1858, to
            Margaret Garner.
        b. William McDonald Sain, born 1838; dsp 1862; married February 21,
            1860, to Sarah J. Bryan.
28.   c. George Thomas Sain, born February 16, 1840.
        (by second marriage):
        d. Alfred Josephus Braley, born April 14, 1851; died October 5, 1930.
        e. Mary Frances Braley, born August 25, 1852; married Merritt Stroud.
        f. Nancy Elizabeth Braley, born October 12, 1853; dsp July 3, 1927.
        g. Sarah Ann Isabel Braley, born November 30, 1854; died October 2,
            1922; married George Abner Bryan (see above).
        h. Lucy Romaline Braley, born February 16, 1856; died May 6, 1927; mar-
            ried Paul Vaughn Johns, born August 31, 1855, son of Paul Vaughn
            Johns and America C. Smith; children:
            (1) George Johns, born September 30, 1880; married (1) Anna Snell

                                    199

         (2) Freeda Brown; lived in Kansas; children (by first marriage):
         (a) Cecil Johns.
         (b) Viola Johns.
     (2) Cliff Johns, born January 23, 1882; married Blanch Taylor;
         lived in Los Angeles, California.
     (3) Burr Paty Johns, born February 21, 1884; married Nellie Jones.
     (4) Minnie Geneva Johns, born July 8, 1886; married Charles Snell;
         lived in Kansas.
     (5) Lulu Johns, born September 25, 1888; died young.
     (6) Zulu Johns, born September 25, 1888; married William Oliver
         Burke.
     (7) Gennie V. Johns, born October 24, 1890; married Arthur Lester;
         lived in Nashville, Tennessee; children:
         (a) Margaret L. Lester, born February 8, 1908; married Walter
            West.
         (b) Burwell Lester, born September 9, 1910.
         (c) Vera Ruth Lester, born c1913.
         (d) Ethel Pauline Lester, born November, 1917.
         (e) Lucy Geneva Lester, born October 22, 1926.
     (8) Horace Josephus Johns, born January 9, 1894; married Frankie
         Sweet; lived in Kansas.
     (9) Myrtle Johns, born April 18, 1896; married Ralph Moore; chil-
         dren:
         (a) Ralph Moore.
         (b) Paul Moore.
         (c) Frank Moore, died young.
         (d) Annie Lois Moore, born February 13, 1927.
   (10) Paul Vaughn Johns, born March 9, 1898; married Maurice Hewett.
   (11) Lucille Johns, born May 10, 1900; married Forrest Tucker; chil-
         dren:
         (a) Wayne Tucker.
         (b) Lucy Tucker.
i. Eliza Jane Braley, born November 8, 1857; married September 7, 1876,
    to Joseph Lafayette Bryan, born October 15, 1854.

***

28.   George Thomas Sain was born February 16, 1840, and died October 12,
1930, in Chattanooga, Tennessee; married (1) February 13, 1861, to Ann
Eliza Jane Paty, born August 28, 1844; died May 8, 1871; (2) April 9,
1872, to Cinderella Paty, born January 30, 1850; died January 13, 1931,
both daughters of John W. Paty and Frances Asbury Parker. His children
were as follows:[49]

(by first marriage):
29. a. William Thomas Sain, born January 21, 1863.
    b. John W. Sain, born September 1, 1866; dsp May 27, 1885.
    c. James Paty Sain, born August 28, 1868; died February 15, 1909; mar-
       ried Bessie Watson.
    d. Pearl Sain, born March 13, 1871; dsp April, 1871.
    (by second marriage):
    e. Lorenzo Burr Sain, born December 31, 1872; died November 11, 1961,
       in Chattanooga, Tennessee; married Belle Russell; children:
       (1) Lillian Sain married Braxton A. Damewood.
       (2) Hyman Sain, dsp.
    f. Jennie Frances Sain, born June 10, 1874; dsp November 30, 1964, in
       Chattanooga, Tennessee; married Ed L. Swick.
30. g. Charles Gwynn Sain, born October 14, 1875.
    h. George Comer Sain, born March 10, 1877; dsp November 10, 1953, in

Miami, Florida; married (1) Pearl Garrett (2) December 31, 1918, Dosha Wilson (one adopted daughter).

    i. Lucy Lavina Sain, born September 6, 1878; died May 17, 1903; married Herbert Powers.

31.   j. Willie Ethel Sain, born April 19, 1880.

    k. Robert Fite Sain, born January 4, 1882; dsp November 13, 1966, in Chattanooga, Tennessee; married Annie Lemmons.

    l. Stroud Lillard Sain, born June 14, 1884; dsp April 2, 1868, in Chattanooga, Tennessee; married (1) Henrietta Funk (2) Emma Duda (3) Maud _____ .

    m. Porter Fall Sain, born April 10, 1886; died June 18, 1968, in Chattanooga, Tennessee; married (1) Marian Black (2) Martha _____ ; child (by second marriage):
      (1) Porter Fall Sain.

    n. May Rilla Sain, born April 12, 1889; married (1) January 24, 1906, Everrett E. Pitsinger, born January 15, 1888; died August 1, 1935; (2) December 21, 1918, Harvey D. Porter, died May 26, 1958; (3) Leland Earl May; lived in Chattanooga, Tennessee; children:
      (by first marriage):
      (1) Edwin Earl Pitsinger, born May 28, 1908; married November 6, 1928, Doris Mae Loeber.
      (2) Barnes Pitsinger, born June 10, 1915; married (1) Laura M. Booth (2) Pauline Shelton.
      (by second marriage):
      (3) Harvey David Porter, born July 15, 1920; married July 15, 1940, Mary E. Duncan.
      (4) Carl Slater Porter, born September 24, 1929; married September 23, 1952, Anne E. Bogart.

    o. Myrtle Alma Sain, born July 13, 1891; dsp June 12, 1936; married Carl Slater.

***

29.   William Thomas Sain was born January 21, 1863, in Warren County, Tennessee, and died September 13, 1929, in Nashville, Tennessee; married January 12, 1881, to Emma Sue Jones, born March 11, 1865, and died October, 1923, daughter of William Ewing Jones and Elizabeth Wade. Their children were as follows:[50]

    a. Finis Ewing Sain, born February 17, 1882; died June 27, 1956, in Chattanooga, Tennessee; married January 22, 1902, to Myrtle Shead, born September 17, 1880; child:
      (1) Anna Louise Sain, born December 28, 1903; married June 25, 1924, to Marvin Kirkland Barry, born December 20, 1896, son of James B. Barry and Emma Barnes; children:
        (a) Richard Harwood Barry, born October 8, 1942; married July 11, 1964, Barbara Buist.
        (b) Ann Kirkland Barry, born September 11, 1945; married March 31, 1964, Frank Newsom; child:
          /1/ Cynthia Ann Newsom, born February 10, 1965.

    b. Ervin Jones Sain, born May 12, 1884; died October 22, 1962, in Nashville, Tennessee; married September 19, 1906, Frances Hill, born December 23, 1887; died August 10, 1961, daughter of George Mathias Hill and Huldah Rogers; child:
      (1) George Thomas Sain, born January 26, 1908; married March 16, 1931, Grace McMillan, born March 24, 1911, daughter of Fred McMillan and Mary Clark Black; lived in Nashville, Tennessee; children:
        (a) Ervin Thomas Sain.

(b) Mary Gennette Sain married (1) _____ _____ (2) October 10,
     1958, Seth Norman; children:
     (by first marriage):
     /1/ Thomas Jay Norman, born November 28, 1955 (adopted
          by his step-father).
     (by second marriage):
     /2/ Frances Gennette Norman, born August 27, 1959.
     /3/ Jack Norman, born February 20, 1961.
   (c) Susan Grace Sain married September 23, 1967, Ben Ervin Ward.
c. William Thearle Sain, born November 23, 1886; died March 23, 1966,
    in San Antonio, Texas; married 1919 Grace Evans; child:
    (1) Gloria Sain, dsp.
d. James Leon Sain, born November 2, 1889; dsp April 6, 1917.
e. George Thomas Sain, born December 25, 1891.
f. Wade Sain, born August 27, 1894; married July 5, 1922, Eva Patterson,
    born September 3, 1897; lived in Nashville, Tennessee; child:
    (1) Frances Sain, born March 26, 1923; married June 25, 1945, Hel-
         mer Carl Kristofferson, born January 11, 1915; died July 29,
         1952; child:
         (a) Anne Kristofferson, born September 2, 1948.
g. Mary Belle Sain, born June 16, 1897; married April 12, 1916, Edward
    M. Bush, born July 12, 1896; died 1925 in Nashville, Tennessee; chil-
    dren:
    (1) Walter Thomas Bush, born March 8, 1918; married June 14, 1952,
         Norma Lee Koelling; children:
         (a) Danny Bush, born April 25, 1953.
         (b) Carolyn Bush, born August 24, 1955.
         (c) Elizabeth Ann Bush, born December 18, 1960.
    (2) Harold Sain Bush, born August 30, 1921.
    (3) Emmalene Bush, born April 17, 1923.
    (4) Mary Belle Bush, born December 11, 1924; married January 4,
         1946, James Billingsley; child:
         (a) Nancy Sue Billingsley, born November 14, 1948.
h. Charles Jackson Sain, born May 5, 1901; married April 12, 1930,
    Celestine Fitz, born November 24, 1906; lived in Gallatin, Tennessee
    (one adopted son).

                              ***

32.   George Thomas Sain was born December 25, 1891, in Marietta, Georgia,
    and died April 5, 1968, in Nashville, Tennessee; married October 7, 1922,
    to Anne Margaret Johnson, born May 30, 1901, daughter of James Patrick
    Johnson and Margaret Alice Fowler. Their children were as follows:[51]

    a. George Thomas Sain, born November 26, 1923; married January 14, 1949,
        Elizabeth Loretta Buttrey, born January 13, 1922, in Hills Station,
        Pennsylvania, daughter of Louis Lawrence Buttrey and Anna Gertrude
        McKavick; children:
        (1) Margaret Anne Sain, born January 4, 1950.
        (2) William Louis Sain, born December 29, 1950.
        (3) George Lawrence Sain, born April 5, 1952.
        (4) Stephen Thomas Sain, born July 20, 1954.
        (5) Wade Johnson Sain, born May 8, 1956.
        (6) Elizabeth Louise Sain, born July 13, 1960.
        (7) Philip Robert Sain, born March 4, 1963.
    b. Robert Johnson Sain, born April 29, 1927; married Lois Overby; child:
        (1) Robert Lee Sain, born July 9, 1954.

                              ***

30.   Charles Gwynn Sain was born October 14, 1875, in Rutherford County, Tennessee, and died December 20, 1907; married Mary Lou Lawing, born July 22, 1877; died February 20, 1968. Their child was as follows:[52]

a. Grace Paty Sain, born April 22, 1902; married May 20, 1920, Braxton Robert Spearman, born November 17, 1899, son of Solomon J. Spearman and Mary Bradley; children:
    (1) Grace Paty Spearman, born March 2, 1921; married March 23, 1946, John Hartford Boyle, born July 6, 1918, son of Hartford Desmoine Boyle and Clementine Zimmerman; lived in Dallas, Texas; children:
        (a) John Michael Boyle, born May 6, 1947.
        (b) Robert Hartford Boyle, born January 25, 1949.
        (c) Patrick Joseph Boyle, born July 12, 1954.
        (d) Timothy Richard Boyle, born November 23, 1957.
        (e) Sharon Paty Boyle, born August 20, 1962.
    (2) Joe Ernest Spearman, born February 8, 1924; married December 26, 1948, Virginia Jo Irwin, born September 9, 1929, daughter of Clayton C. Irwin and Frennie Needham; children:
        (a) Jo Lynn Spearman, born November 22, 1949.
        (b) Robert Irwin Spearman, born October 15, 1955.
        (c) Paty Virginia Spearman, born March 13, 1957.
        (d) Mary Louise Spearman, born February 21, 1962.

***

31.   Willie Ethel Sain was born April 19, 1880, in Rutherford County, Tennessee, and died January 17, 1967, in Chattanooga, Tennessee; married July 28, 1901, to Kendred W. Hudgins, born July 22, 1878; died December 19, 1962, son of Henry E. Hudgins and Rebecca Muse. Their children were as follows:[53]

a. Kendred W. Hudgins, born July 30, 1903; married Frances Rutledge, born October 26, 1901, daughter of Garland M. Rutledge and Martha Stokes; lived in Chattanooga, Tennesse; children:
    (1) Kendred Miller Hudgins, born November 8, 1925; married March 16, 1946, Martha Joe Hogue, lived in Nashville, Tennessee; children:
        (a) Kendred Miller Hudgins, born February 7, 1950.
        (b) Joseph Edward Hudgins, born February 7, 1950.
        (c) Martha Joy Hudgins, born March 27, 1953.
    (2) Evelyn Frances Hudgins, born June 16, 1930; married July 8, 1951, Thomas Manning Cate, born August 6, 1930, son of John Moffitt Cate and Claudia Crowe; children:
        (a) Cynthia Frances Cate, born December 11, 1955.
        (b) Thomas Douglas Cate, born December 3, 1958.
        (c) Susan Ann Cate, born September 22, 1964.
b. Frank Sain Hudgins, born September 11, 1908; died December 31, 1951; married Jean Thweat; child:
    (1) Frank Sain Hudgins.

***

19.   Bartlett Smith Stroud was born December 16, 1823, in Warren County, Tennessee, and died October 12, 1853, in Coffee County, Tennessee; married about 1845 to Nancy Winton, daughter of Stephen Winton. Their children were as follows:[54]

a. George W. Stroud, born c1847; died c1900; lived in Texas.

b. Hester Juliette Stroud, born April 6, 1849; dsp August, 1862.
c. William Stroud, born c1852; died c1925; lived in Texas.
d. Bartlett Smith Stroud, born February 14, 1854; died March 4, 1939;
    married (1) December 17, 1879, to Fannie Powers, born September 13,
    1860; (2) November 20, 1901, to Jennie Taylor; children:
    (by first marriage):
    (1) Horace Bartlett Stroud, born March 20, 1881; lived in Missouri.
    (2) Hence Albert Stroud, born February 1, 1894; lived in Washington,
         D. C.
    (3) John Maxwell Stroud, born January 6, 1897.
    (by second marriage):
    (4) Beulah Mae Stroud, born May 21, 1904; married _____ Scudder.
    (5) George W. Stroud, born August 5, 1907; married February 27,
         1927, to Mary Sue Jackson; children:
         (a) Jeanne Jackson Stroud, born June 3, 1928; married _____
              Shieffler.
         (b) Pamela Sue Stroud, born January 29, 1942.
    (6) Hester Jane Stroud, born January 27, 1915; married _____
         Chattin.

***

8.   Thomas Stroud was born March 15, 1778, in Orange County, North
    Carolina, and died April 14, 1838, in Warren County, Tennessee; married
    December 26, 1800, to Hannah Robertson (see p. 178); their children were
    as follows:[55]

a. Elizabeth Merritt Stroud, born February 14, 1802; dsp March 3, 1802.
b. Lucinda Stroud, born April 15, 1803; dsp August 17, 1806.
c. Sarah Stroud, born March 5, 1805; dsp June 20, 1879; married Alex-
    ander Powell.
d. William Stroud, born June 15, 1807; married Rachel Jarvis.
e. Nancy Stroud, born February 5, 1810; married Ephraim Cates.
f. Robertson M. Stroud, born November 28, 1812; married Hester Hammer;
    child:
    (1) Lonn K. Stroud, born c1852.
33. g. Thomas B. Stroud, born March 31, 1814.
h. Dickson A. Stroud, born December 17, 1815; died October 27, 1871;
    married (1) Jane Keele (2) Lucetta Matthews, born May 3, 1836; died
    March 22, 1908.
i. Love Stroud, born February 17, 1818; married Bilbery Bonner, born
    January 3, 1816; child:
    (1) Redding Bonner, born September 18, 1838.
j. Benjamin Franklin Stroud, born March 31, 1820; married Martha Wright.
k. Pleasant H. Stroud, born March 31, 1822; married Mary Hammonds.
l. Hannah Stroud, born May 12, 1824; married D. S. McAfee; children
    (probably among others):
    (1) Thomas W. McAfee, born February 13, 1844; died young.
    (2) Hughes McAfee, born February 13, 1844.
    (3) John Bilbery McAfee, born February 4, 1846.
    (4) Sarah McAfee, born c1848.
m. George Washington Stroud, born November 10, 1827; died January 10,
    1862; married June 26, 1855, to Nancy Emaline Dial (see p. 197);
    children:
    (1) Kate Stroud, born c1859; married Jesse Bonner; dsp.
    (2) George Washington Stroud, born c1861; died 1926; married
         Margaret Brown; children:
         (a) Alice Stroud married _____ Seneker.
         (b) Philip Stroud, died 1937.

    (c) Howard Stroud, died 1926.
    (d) Grady Stroud.
    (e) Linnie Stroud, born 1892; married Elmer Davis; children:
       /1/ Kenneth Davis.
       /2/ George Davis.
       /3/ James Davis.
       /4/ Noel Davis.
       /5/ Paul Davis.
       /6/ Franklin Davis.
       /7/ Leo Davis.
    (f) Luther Stroud, born May 12, 1895; dsp November 28, 1898.
    (g) Emmett Sutton Stroud, born September 12, 1897; dsp April
        10, 1898.

***

33.   Thomas B. Stroud was born March 31, 1814, and died February 16,
1898; married Eleanor Elizabeth Wright, born January 5, 1828, and died
July 2, 1890. Their children were as follows:[56]

a. Martha Jane Stroud, born January 18, 1848; dsp January 30, 1850.
b. Hannah Isabel Stroud, born December 28, 1849.
c. Mary Ann Stroud, born July 28, 1851.
d. George Norton Stroud, born September 27, 1853; died November 30,
    1926; married Mary Caroline _____, born September 2, 1859; children:
    (1) Ida Cleo Stroud, born December 7, 1879.
    (2) George Henry Stroud, born February 14, 1882.
    (3) John Thomas Stroud, born April 9, 1884; died January 1, 1949.
    (4) William Isaac Stroud, born December 7, 1886; died January 26,
        1941.
    (5) Josie Beulah Stroud, born December 23, 1888; married Robert
        Taylor Parker, born November 3, 1886.
    (6) Sarah Elizabeth Stroud, born March 2, 1890.
    (7) Harry Brown Stroud, born June 7, 1892.
    (8) Oscar Avony Stroud, born August 17, 1894.
    (9) Mattie Lee Stroud, born March 20, 1896.
e. Andrew Eichbaum Stroud, born October 10, 1856.
f. Thomas Benjamin Stroud, born October 4, 1859.
g. Robert Washington Stroud, born May 23, 1863.
h. William Dixon Stroud, born August 8, 1866.
i. Nancy Emma Stroud, born February 3, 1869.

***

2.   John Stroud was born about 1703 and lived in Bristol Parish, Dinwiddie County, Virginia, where on February 17, 1726/7, he and his wife Jane
recorded the birth of a child. He was in St. Andrew's Parish, Brunswick
County, Virginia, on March 5, 1740, when he and Jane sold Drury Stith 196
acres on Sturgeon Run, which had been granted to John Stroud, Sr., and
given by him to his son John by will. He was living in Orange County,
North Carolina, by 1755, and on July 25, 1760, he received a grant from
Earl Granville of 240 acres on both sides of New Hope Creek in Orange
County. In 1763 he sold 100 acres of the grant to Joshua Stroud, and
on December 4, 1770, he sold the remaining 140 acres to Thomas Kirkland,
evidently leaving Orange County at that time. He was probably father of
the following, among others:[57]

a. William Stroud, born c1725, of St. Andrew's Parish, Brunswick County,
    Virginia, when he bought 130 acres on the south side of Sturgeon Run

205

from Drury Stith on January 4, 1748; this is probably the same land
he sold the same day to John Stroud, Jr., of St. Andrew's. William
Stroud also sold 100 acres on the north side of Sturgeon Run, part of a
322 acre grant to John Stroud, Sr., to Drury Stith on March 1, 1748.[58]
On June 1, 1750, he received a grant of 187 acres on Genayhominy Creek
in Lunenburg County, Virginia, which he and his wife Rosamund, then
living in Orange County, North Carolina, sold to Alexander Roberts on
May 2, 1764. On October 22, 1760, he and his wife Rose and his brother John and his wife Sarah, all of New Hope in Orange County, sold
226 acres on Sturgeon Run in Brunswick County to James Hardyman.[59]
  b. Olive Stroud, born February 17, 1726/27.
  c. Mary Stroud, born April 29, 1730.
  d. John Stroud, born 1732; died 1806 in Clarke County, Georgia; had
      several land transactions in Orange County, North Carolina, between
      1754 and 1787; married Sarah Connally; children:[60]
      (1) Margaret Stroud, born June 11, 1757; married Stephen Crow.
      (2) William Stroud, born January 10, 1761.
      (3) Mark Stroud, born February 27, 1763; died July 2, 1798; married
           Mrs. Martha (Strother) Thompson.
      (4) John Stroud, born February 8, 1765; married Sarah Phillips.
      (5) Betty Stroud, born July 18, 1767; married Isaac Crow.
      (6) Hannah Stroud, born March 3, 1770; married October 12, 1786, to
           John Strother.
      (7) Tabitha Stroud, born April 1, 1772; married Jonathan Melton.
      (8) Sally Stroud, born April 29, 1777; married William Bankston.
      (9) James Stroud, born May 18, 1779; married Nancy Durbin.
  e. Joshua Stroud, born c1735; sold James Thackston 100 acres on the
      north side of Cain Creek in Orange County, North Carolina, on May 1,
      1770, which he had bought from John Stroud in 1763.[61]
  f. Matthew Stroud, born 1747; lived in Shelby County, Alabama, in 1832.[62]

***

REFERENCES

[1]Virginia Quitrents of 1704, Virginia Land Grant Bk. 10, p. 335,
Bk. 13, p. 529, Bk. 14, p. 78, Virginia State Archives, Richmond, Virginia;
Prince George County, Virginia, Deeds 1713-28, p. 768.
[2]Bristol Parish (Prince George - Dinwiddie Counties, Virginia) Re-
gister, p. 62; Prince George County, Virginia, Minute Book, 1737-40,
pp. 120, 358.
[3]Prince George County, Virginia, Deeds 1713-28, pp. 752, 762, 767;
Virginia Land Grant Bk. 13, p. 503; Bristol Parish Register; Granville
County, North Carolina, tax list, 1754; Orange County, North Carolina,
Deed Bk. 3, p. 235. Joseph Stroud was perhaps also the father of the
John Stroud who died in Mecklenburg County, Virginia, 1776; Mecklenburg
County, Virginia, Will Bk. 1, p. 218.
[4]Prince George County, Virginia, Minute Book, 1737-40, pp. 211, 218,
236, 260, 276, 289, 293, 353; Brunswick County, Virginia, Order Book 1.
Further research might indicate that the Elizabeth Stroud who died in
1786 in Marlboro County, South Carolina, was his widow; Marlboro County,
South Carolina, Wills A, 13.
[5]Brunswick County, Virginia, Will Bk. 2, p. 1.
[6]Virginia Land Grant Bk. 11, p. 70; Surry County, Virginia, Deeds,
1715-30, p. 474; Bristol Parish Register; Brunswick County, Virginia,
Deed Bk. 1, p. 139, Order Book 1, 1732-41.
[7]Brunswick County, Virginia, Deed Bk. 2, pp. 125, 107/109.
[8]North Carolina Land Grants, State Land Office, Raleigh, North Carolina; Halifax County, North Carolina, Deed Bk. 5, p. 211; Granville County,

North Carolina, Deeds A, 288, C, 59, B, 131, 31, 401, A, 533, B, 56, 113, 166, 499, 83.

[9]Granville County, North Carolina, Equity Cases, 1755; Orange County, North Carolina, Registration of Deeds, 1758; Granville County, North Carolina, Deeds B, 513, C, 72, 434.

[10]Granville County, North Carolina, Deeds C, 465, D, 25, 3, G, 231, 232, C, 703, D, 227, 338, E, 310, F, 81; Warren County, North Carolina, Deed Bk. 1, p. 104.

[11]Lincoln County, North Carolina, Deed Bk. 2, p. 595.

[12]Granville County, North Carolina, Deeds B, 56, C, 239, 536, E, 388, F, 160, 407; Warren County, North Carolina, Deed Bk. 4, p. 112, A, 92, Bk. 5, p. 35; Mecklenburg County, North Carolina, Deed Bk. 3, p. 64, Bk. 4, p. 886; Lincoln County, North Carolina, Deed Bk. 1, pp. 512, 658, Bk. 2, pp. 13, 318, 710, 481, 520, 567, 582, 761; Wilkes County, Georgia, Wills, 1792-1819, p. 84.

[13]Orange County, North Carolina, Deed Bk. 4, p. 299; Burke County, North Carolina, census of 1790.

[14]Warren County, North Carolina, Deeds A, 50; Wilkes County, Georgia, Inventories.

[15]Granville County, North Carolina, tax lists, 1754, 1760, 1764; Warren County, North Carolina, tax list, 1771; Jasper County, Georgia, census of 1820.

[16]Granville County, North Carolina, Equity Cases, 1755; Orange County, North Carolina, Registration of Deeds, 1758.

[17]Granville County, North Carolina, Deeds D, 227, G, 206; Walter Clark (ed.), The State Records of North Carolina (Goldsboro, N.C.: Nash Brothers, 1886-1907), VII, 842; Orange County, North Carolina, Court Minutes, 1777-84.

[18]Orange County, North Carolina, tax lists, 1777, 1780; North Carolina Land Grants #846, entry 804, book 59, page 36.

[19]Orange County, North Carolina, Wills B, 6, D, 9, Deed Bk. 4, pp. 570, 135, Equity Cases, October, 1799.

[20-23]Records of Katherine Chinn Colbert.

[24]Revolutionary Pension #W9675; Orange County, North Carolina, Marriages.

[25]Orange County, North Carolina, Wills D, 344.

[26]Ibid.; Revolutionary Pension #W20332.

[27]Records of Dr. David Bryan; Warren County, Tennessee, census of 1850, Marriages.

[28]Bible record belonging (1920) to William Ramsey; Orange County, North Carolina, Deed Bk. 9, p. 190, Bk. 13, p. 295; Hawkins County was the residence of Nancy Stubblefield.

[29]Tennessee Land Grants, C, 199, State Archives, Nashville, Tennessee; Grainger County, Tennessee, Deeds A, 39; Claiborne County, Tennessee, Deeds A, 103, 107, 128, B, 69, Court Minutes.

[30]Tennessee Land Grants C, 170; Warren County, Tennessee, Deeds A, 397, B, 37, 38, A, 366.

[31]Warren County, Tennessee, census of 1820, Plat Book 1, pp. 4, 5, 122, 325, 236, Plat Book 2, pp. 278, 157, Deeds E, 206, P, 85, Q, 418, O, 386; Coffee County, Tennessee, Deeds A, 392.

[32]Statement of William Ramsey; Minutes of Blue Springs Baptist Church; Warren County, Tennessee, Deeds L, 212, F, 462, M, 31, 33, L, 177, 252, 254.

[33]Warren County, Tennessee, Will Bk. 1, p. 375, Bk. 2, p. 20, Deeds S, 252; Bible record belonging (1920) to William Ramsey; statement of William Ramsey.

[34-36]Records of Milton L. Jackson.

[37]Records of Claudia Stroud Borst.

[38-39]Records of Mrs. Dale C. Loyd.

[40-42]Records of William Ramsey.
[43]Records of Frank Stroud.
[44]Records of Mrs. William E. Youree.
[45-46]Records of Joseph Newton Darnell.
[47]Records of Mary Ruth Brookover.
[48-53]Records of Charles J. Sain.
[54]Records of George W. Stroud.
[55]Records of Mrs. Elmer Davis.
[56]Records of Mrs. Robert T. Parker.
[57]Bristol Parish Register; Brunswick County, Virginia, Deed Bk. 2, p. 51; Orange County, North Carolina, tax list, 1755, Deed Bk. 3, pp. 542, 452.
[58]Brunswick County, Virginia, Deed Bk. 3, pp. 528, 529, 545.
[59]Virginia Land Grant Book 29, p. 166; Brunswick County, Virginia, Deed Bk. 8, p. 225, Bk. 7, p. 221.
[60]Orange County, North Carolina, Deed Bk. 1, p. 41, Bk. 2, p. 172, Bk. 3, p. 10; John Stroud Bible record.
[61]Orange County, North Carolina, Deed Bk. 3, p. 275, tax lists, 1755, 1777, 1780.
[62]Ibid., 1777, 1781, 1782; Revolutionary Pension #S3980, National Archives, Washington, D.C.

***

STUBBLEFIELD of Virginia and Warren County, Tennessee

Simon Stubblefield was probably born in England about 1640 and lived in Virginia as early as March 27, 1672, when "a matter of difference between Ed. Cheesman and Thomas Cheesman and Symon Stubblefield" was referred to "judgment in England." On April 23, 1688, he was granted 288 acres in Gloucester County, Virginia, for transporting four persons into the colony; the land was near the courthouse and adjacent to the land of William Ross. In 1704, he paid quit rents on 200 acres in Ware Parish, Gloucester County.[1] While there is no proof, he was probably the father of Edward Stubblefield and the Stubblefield families of Gloucester and Charles City County and of the following:

George Stubblefield was probably born about 1675 in Virginia and probably died in Gloucester County. In 1704 he paid quit rents on 400 acres in King William County, Virginia, but lived in Gloucester County; married Ann _____.[2] While there is no proof, they were probably the parents of the following:

1. a. Robert Stubblefield, born c1702.
   b. George Stubblefield, born c1705; died 1752 in Spotsylvania County, Virginia; married Catherine Beverly, born December 17, 1708; died 1778, daughter of Henry Beverley; children:[3]
      (1) George Stubblefield married Sarah Morrison.
      (2) Henry Stubblefield married Frances Smith.
      (3) Beverley Stubblefield, born 1742; died December 25, 1823; married (1) _____ (2) Mary Shelton.
      (4) Robert Stubblefield married Susannah Parker; moved to Kentucky.
      (5) Peter Stubblefield married Margaret Apperson; dsp in Georgia.
   c. John Stubblefield, born 1709; probably lived in Spotsylvania County, Virginia, in 1734, and in Lunenburg County, later Charlotte County, Virginia, in 1764.[4]
   d. Thomas Stubblefield, born c1712; died 1758 in Culpeper County, Virginia; married Ellen Hackley; children:[5]
      (1) George Stubblefield.
      (2) James Stubblefield died 1777; married Ann Slaughter, daughter of John Slaughter and Mildred Coleman; child:
         (a) Thomas Stubblefield.
      (3) Anna Stubblefield married Hezekiah Brown.
      (4) Mary Stubblefield.
      (5) Elizabeth Stubblefield married Gabriel Long.
   e. Edward Stubblefield, born c1715; died 1750 in Culpeper County, Virginia; married Eleanor Yancey; child:[6]
      (1) Ann Stubblefield.

***

1.   Robert Stubblefield was probably born about 1702 in Gloucester County, Virginia. On May 15, 1723, he presented a petition to the General Court, and on August 22, 1726, he sold two tracts of land in King and Queen County, Virginia, to John Collier, Jr., of Stratton Major Parish; in return he received 800 acres in St. George Parish, Spotsylvania County, Virginia, from John Collier, Jr., on October 5, 1730. The land, which was located on branches of South River, was mortgaged to Collier for £65 on October 16, 1730. Robert and Anne Stubblefield sold 200 acres of the land to Benjamin Matthews for 4090 pounds of tobacco on May 7, 1734, and on June 29, 1734, they sold another 200 acres to Ralph Williams for 2500 pounds of tobacco. On November 1, 1748, they sold the remaining 400 acres

to Richard Baylor for £100.[7]

Stubblefield then moved to Amelia (now Prince Edward) County, Virginia, although he bought no land there. In September, 1755, Robert Stubblefield and George Walton brought suit against John, Richard, and Joel Stubblefield, and Abraham Womack, but failed to prosecute the suit.[8]

About 1756, the family moved to Hogan's Creek in Orange (now Rockingham) County, North Carolina. In March, 1758, Robert Stubblefield requested permission to build a public grist mill on his land; between 1763 and 1769 he gave or sold land to Wyatt, Richard, and Thomas Stubblefield and Abraham Womack. He probably died in Guilford (now Rockingham) County, North Carolina, about 1775.[9]

On March 1, 1780, Anne Stubblefield, who was probably the widow of Robert, bought 30 acres on Bugaboo creek in Wilkes County, North Carolina, from Edmond Boaz for £200; she sold the land to George Parks for £200 on March 1, 1787; she probably died shortly afterwards.[10]

While there is no proof, Robert and Anne Stubblefield probably had, among others, the following children:

2. a. George Stubblefield, born c1728.
   b. John Stubblefield, born c1730; married Elizabeth _____; lived in Amelia (now Prince Edward) County, Virginia, in 1750-55; in 1758 sued Isaiah Watkins in Orange County, North Carolina; on August 23, 1762, received a grant of 452 acres on Hogan's Creek in Orange County; on August 15, 1775, he bought 164 acres in Guilford and Orange Counties from Wyatt Stubblefield for £90, and sold it to Archibald Yarborough for £553 in 1783 after moving to Surry County, North Carolina. He sold three slaves to Jacob Nichols in 1783.[11]
3. c. Richard Stubblefield, born 1732.
   d. Joel Stubblefield, born c1734; lived in Amelia (now Prince Edward) County, Virginia, 1750-52; served as a guard in 1754; on April 9, 1765, sold his personal property in Amelia County, Virginia, to Daniel Jones.[12]
   e. Elizabeth Stubblefield, born c1736; died March, 1780, in Caswell County, North Carolina; married c1752 Abraham Womack, born c1726; died May 6, 1800; children:[13]
      (1) William Womack, born November 11, 1753.
      (2) Mary Womack, born March 22, 1756; married _____ Benton.
      (3) Ann Womack, born September 21, 1758; married _____ Engram.
      (4) Lucy Womack, born June 16, 1761; married _____ Engram.
      (5) Jeremiah Womack, born August 16, 1763.
      (6) Sina Womack, born January 4, 1766; married _____ Brackin.
      (7) Jehu Womack, born July 19, 1768.
      (8) Josiah Womack, born March 26, 1771; married February 17, 1803, Mary Massey.
      (9) Elizabeth Womack, born September 19, 1773.
      (10) Levi Womack, born December 7, 1775.
   f. Wyatt Stubblefield, born c1744; died 1824 in Caswell County, North Carolina; married Ann Challis, daughter of Hugh Challis; children (perhaps among others):[14]
      (1) Martha Stubblefield, born c1778; married July 26, 1797, Thomas Mullins; child:
         (a) Robert Mullins.
      (2) Hugh Challis Stubblefield, born c1785; died 1821; married November 29, 1809, Frances Lindsey; children:

        (a) John Wyatt Stubblefield died October 15, 1841.
        (b) Malinda Ann Vernum Stubblefield.
        (c) Catherine Stubblefield.
    (3) Peter Beverly Stubblefield, born 1792, died 1842; married (1)
         March 30, 1816, Sarah Worsham; (2) December 2, 1833, Nancy Wynne.
    (4) George W. Stubblefield married August 12, 1817, Sarah Lawson.
    (5) Catherine Stubblefield married May 23, 1817, Elijah Withers;
         children:
        (a) John A. Withers.
        (b) Albert G. Withers.
        (c) James Withers.
        (d) Lewis W. Withers.
        (e) Elizabeth Withers.
    (6) Nancy Stubblefield married July 1, 1819, William B. Pemberton.
4. g. Thomas Stubblefield, born c1746.

                                    ***

2.   George Stubblefield was born about 1728 in Virginia and married
    Keziah _____ about 1750; he lived in Spotsylvania County, Virginia, un-
    til 1748, when the family moved to Amelia (now Prince Edward) County,
    Virginia, where in 1755, he was appointed a county constable. He was in
    Halifax County, Virginia, in 1761, when he sued the firm of Buchanan,
    Bowman, and Company, and in March and December, 1762, he was a county
    road surveyor. In 1765, he recorded his cattle brand, and he was later
    exempted from county taxes. On January 15, 1765, he bought 214 acres in
    Antrim Parish, Halifax County, four acres to be used as a meeting house,
    from William Echols for ₤7, and on November 15, 1790, he sold the land
    to George Wood for ₤75. His later residence has not been determined;
    his children were as follows:[15]

5. a. Robert Loxley Stubblefield, born June 8, 1751.
    b. James Stubblefield, born December, 1755.
    c. William Stubblefield, born May 19, 1758.
    d. Mary Stubblefield, born January 1, 1763; married January 4, 1788, in
        Halifax County, Virginia, to Frederick Colquitt.
    e. Elizabeth Stubblefield, born December 22, 1764.
    f. Martin Stubblefield, born May 18, 1767; died December 10, 1838, in
        Cincinnati, Ohio; married October 27, 1788, in Halifax County, Vir-
        ginia, to Sarah Moore; children:
        (1) Nancy Stubblefield, born July 3, 1794; married _____ Poindexter.
        (2) Rebecca Stubblefield, born November 20, 1798; married _____
             Wilson.
        (3) James Stubblefield, born May 20, 1803; married December 10, 1821,
             to Phoebe Riggs.
        (4) Mary Stubblefield, born April 19, 1806; died August 26, 1888;
             married January 25, 1820, to Henry Counts.
        (5) Elizabeth Stubblefield, born December 25, 1807; married Septem-
             ber 29, 1825, to _____.
        (6) Wesley Stubblefield married May 14, 1830, to Matilda Millikan.
        (7) Robert W. Stubblefield, born August 5, 1812; married May 20,
             1836, to _____.
    g. Sarah Stubblefield, born February 20, 1770; married October 26, 1789,
        in Halifax County, Virginia, to Beverly Mays.
    h. Joseph R. Stubblefield, born April 15, 1772; married Rebecca Sullins.
    i. Ann Stubblefield, born April 20, 1774.
    j. Keziah Stubblefield, born June 14, 1778.

                                    ***

5.   Robert Loxley Stubblefield was born June 8, 1751, in Amelia (now
Prince Edward) County, Virginia, and lived in Antrim Parish, Halifax
County, Virginia, as early as 1761. On July 15, 1772, he married Sarah
Easley (see p.   26), and on May 20, 1773, his father-in-law, Stephen
Easley, gave Sarah Easley Stubblefield 200 acres where "Lock" and Sarah
then made their home. On June 15, 1780, they sold the land to George
Wood for ₤5,000.[16]

        Lock Stubblefield then moved to a plantation near the border between
Hawkins and Grainger Counties, Tennessee. North Carolina granted him 100
acres on Gammon's Branch in Sullivan County, Tenneseee, on August 7, 1787,
which he sold to Sarah Chase for ₤100 on July 24, 1789, and 100 acres on
Sinking Creek in Sullivan County in 1788 which he sold to Sarah Chase for
₤30 in 1791. He received a grant of 300 acres on the north side of the
Holston River in Hawkins County on January 14, 1793, and another 300 acres
in the same area, adjoining William Cocke and Wyatt Stubblefield, on April
23, 1794.[17]

        Stubblefield signed a petition in 1787 to separate Tennessee from
North Carolina. On June 10, 1795, he bought 300 acres on the north side
of the Holston River in Hawkins County, adjoining his plantation, from
Robert King for ₤100; on June 30, 1806, he bought an adjacent 215 acres
from William Cocke; on November 27, 1811, he bought an adjacent 250 acres
from Thomas Cocke for $1,000.[18]

        Stubblefield gave his son Thomas 200 acres of land in Hawkins County
on August 23, 1813, and another 215 acres on March 4, 1817, and made his
will on the same date, dividing the remainder of his property among his
children, who were as follows:[19]

6.   a. William Stubblefield, born June 4, 1773.
     b. Nancy Stubblefield, born May 27, 1775; died c1819 in Warren County,
         Tennessee; married c1793 in Hawkins County, Tennessee, to William
         Stroud (see p. 189).
     c. Thomas Stubblefield, born December 18, 1776; died c1833 in Hawkins
         County, Tennessee; married June 12, 1806, in Hawkins County, Tennes-
         see, to Martha Bond, born February 13, 1791; children:[20]
         (1) Nancy Stubblefield, born January 27, 1808; married March 9, 1826,
              Fleming Mays.
         (2) Mary Stubblefield, born April 20, 1810; married Samuel Haywood.
         (3) Sarah Stubblefield, born January 4 1812; married James Long.
         (4) Wilmuth Stubblefield, born May 28, 1814; dsp.
         (5) Susan Stubblefield, born c1816; married January 20, 1834, Henry
              Bridgewaters.
         (6) Orlianna Stubblefield, born c1818.
         (7) Martha Stubblefield, born c1820.
         (8) William Stubblefield, born c1824.
         (9) Robert Loxley Stubblefield, born c1826.
        (10) America Stubblefield, born c1828.
        (11) Thomas Stubblefield, born c1831.
     d. Mary Stubblefield, born June 29, 1778.
7.   e. George Stubblefield, born July 6, 1780.
     f. Keziah Stubblefield, born July 30, 1782.
     g. Anna Stubblefield, born January 7, 1785.
     h. Sarah Stubblefield, born December 18, 1787.
8.   i. Stephen Stubblefield, born January 6, 1789.
     j. Susannah Stubblefield, born January 28, 1792.
     k. Elizabeth Stubblefield, born June 28, 1793.

1. Winifred Stubblefield, born November 11, 1797.

***

6.   William Stubblefield was born June 4, 1773, in Halifax County, Virginia, and moved to Hawkins County, Tennessee, about 1780; on March 5, 1800, he married Wilmuth Bond. They moved to Warren County, Tennessee, where she died January 11, 1850, and he died December 25, 1858. Their children were as follows:[21]

9. a. Sarah Stubblefield, born May 11, 1803.
    b. Mary Stubblefield, born January 26, 1805; died c1838; married Thomas Middleton.
    c. Nancy Stubblefield, born December 27, 1806; married Wade H. Stroud (see p. 189).
10. d. William Stubblefield, born March 1, 1809.
    e. Martha Stubblefield, born March 8, 1812; married Wyatt Hitson.
11. f. Elizabeth Stubblefield, born December 14, 1814.
    g. Frances Stubblefield, born June 8, 1817; married Jacob Rogers.
    h. Wilmoth Stubblefield, born June 19, 1819; dsp August 10, 1900.
    i. George Stubblefield, born December 21, 1821; died August 11, 1847; married Cyrena Rogers; children:
        (1) Sarah Stubblefield, born c1841; married October 18, 1855, to Ellsberry Fults.
        (2) Thomas Stubblefield, born c1843.
        (3) Catherine Stubblefield, born c1845; married January 12, 1864, to James Newton Clendenen.
        (4) George Stubblefield, born c1847.
12. j. Robert Loxley Stubblefield, born February 18, 1824.
    k. Louisa Stubblefield, born October 30, 1827; dsp January 22, 1849.

***

9.   Sarah Stubblefield was born May 11, 1803, in Hawkins County, Tennessee, and died October 16, 1864, in Rusk County, Texas; married about 1820 to Larkin Caison, who was born May 16, 1795, and died December 22, 1863. Their children were as follows:[22]

    a. Mary Caison, born January 22, 1822; died February 18, 1874; married 1838 to Thomas J. Heath, born November 7, 1817; lived in Rusk County, Texas.
    b. Nancy Caison married _____ O'Hair.
    c. Martha Caison married December 2, 1847, to John Scott; lived in Rusk County, Texas.
    d. Lucinda Caison married January 8, 1849, to A. K. Sandlin.
    e. Sarah Jane Caison married July 2, 1850, to Little Berry Davis Sain, born December 19, 1805; died October 1, 1882, son of Daniel Sain and Martha Davis; children:
        (1) Sarah Wilmuth Sain, born May 13, 1851; died August 7, 1928, in Troup, Texas; married August 12, 1869, to Francis Duty Fitch, born December 3, 1843, in Caswell County, North Carolina, and died November 21, 1914, in Troup, Texas, son of Empson Fitch and Delilah Hightower; children:
            (a) William Francis Fitch, born September 7, 1872, in New Salem, Texas; died February 24, 1918, in Gould, Texas; married November 11, 1893, Ida Vivian McMichael, born November 7, 1874, and died August 26, 1943, in San Angelo, Texas; child:
                /1/ Lois Fitch, born September 11, 1907, in Griffin, Texas;

213

married June 5, 1932, to Dr. Frank Ray Black, born
August 19, 1904; lived in Huntsville, Texas; children:
  /a/ Frank Ray Black, born February 3, 1937.
  /b/ (Dr.) Robert Michael Black, born May 1, 1939.
  /c/ (Dr.) Roland Eugene Black, born March 10, 1940.
(b) Elmina Fitch married (1) _____ Kelley (2) _____ Duty.
(c) John T. Fitch.
(d) Leota Fitch married Wiley Shaw; lived in Troup, Texas.
(e) Oran Edward Fitch married Helen Taylor.
(f) Fannie D. Fitch married Ed Smith; lived in Jacksonville,
     Texas.
(g) Gertrude Fitch, dsp.
(h) Travis T. Fitch, dsp.
(2) George K. Sain, born c1853; dsp c1864.
(3) James M. Sain.
(4) Mary Sain married John T. Norwood.
(5) William Larkin Edward Sain, born May 20, 1861; died February 16,
     1950, in Hereford, Texas.
f. Wilmuth Caison married July 11, 1854, to John E. Pennington; lived
   in Justin, Texas; child:
   (1) (Dr.) William H. Pennington, born September 27, 1855; married
        in 1878 to Martha L. Donald, daughter of Hon. R. H. Donald; lived
        at Drop, Texas.
g. William C. Caison, born c1840; married (1) Catherine Martin (2) September 19, 1865, to Elmina S. Foreman; children (by second marriage):
   (1) Laura E. Caison, born c1872; married Thomas Heath.
   (2) Monnie M. Caison, born c1877; married Scott Arnwine.

                                    ***

10.   William Stubblefield was born March 1, 1809, and died April 30,
    1898; married Minerva Reynolds, born April 1, 1816, and died December 19,
    1867, daughter of Jenkin and Margaret Reynolds. Their children were as
    follows:[23]

       a. Margaret E. Stubblefield, born January 16, 1833; dsp November 2, 1894.
13.   b. Elisha J. Stubblefield, born September 22, 1834.
       c. Sarah B. Stubblefield, born February 5, 1836; dsp December 18, 1866.
       d. James Madison Stubblefield, born October 29, 1837; dsp May 15, 1857.
       e. William Harrison Stubblefield, born August 1, 1840; died March 17,
          1906; married Mary A. Colville, daughter of Samuel Colville; children:
          (1) Sarah Stubblefield married Robert Roddy.
          (2) Susan Stubblefield married Robert Parker.
          (3) May Stubblefield married John Sain.
          (4) W. Fulton Stubblefield, born March 14, 1865; died March 15, 1905;
               married Belle Morrow.
          (5) Lou Stubblefield married _____ Thaxton.
          (6) Lusk Stubblefield married Susan _____.

                                    ***

13.   Elisha J. Stubblefield was born September 22, 1834, and died August
    29, 1882; married January 5, 1867, to Elizabeth Martin, born July 4, 1833,
    and died March 23, 1918, daughter of H. Patterson Martin and Rhoda Holt.
    Their children were as follows:[24]

       a. George Thomas Stubblefield, born and died May 5, 1866.
14.   b. Asa Faulkner Stubblefield, born September 22, 1869.
       c. William Ransom Stubblefield, born November 17, 1872; died July 6,
          1927; married Georgia Reynolds; children:

                                    214

(1) Ernest Elisha Stubblefield, born April 23, 1894; married (1) November 30, 1904, to Mary Alice Nunley, died August, 1951; (2) August 26, 1952, to Mrs. Marie (Gander) Campbell; dsp.
(2) Nellie Rue Stubblefield, born May 5, 1899; married May 16, 1942, to Thomas Rumbley; dsp.
(3) Hence Winfred Stubblefield, born July 14, 1902; married February 12, 1927, to Clara Josephine Davis, born January 10, 1910; child:
    (a) Dalores Nell Stubblefield, born April 15, 1931; married September 2, 1950, to Benjamin Horace Wright; children:
       /1/ Rodney Hense Wright, born July 26, 1951.
       /2/ Karen Jo Wright, born November 16, 1955.
       /3/ Belinda Nell Wright, born September 28, 1963.
(4) Hermy Brown Stubblefield, born February 28, 1905; died June 19, 1959; married June 25, 1930, to Daisy Josephine Butcher; child:
    (a) Barbara Jo Stubblefield, born July 12, 1931; married (1) July 31, 1947, to Billy Stroud Mullican (2) July 20, 1962, to Lonnie Benton Capshaw; children (all by first marriage):
       /1/ Teresa Ann Mullican, born December 8, 1949; married June 1, 1968, to Grover Lee Hennessee.
       /2/ Terry Lee Mullican, born November 13, 1951.
       /3/ Marcia Lou Mullican, born October 29, 1953; married January 25, 1969, to Hugh Wayne Stubblefield; child:
         /a/ Lisa Carol Stubblefield, born August 9, 1969.
(5) Dillard Ransom Stubblefield, born August 16, 1907; married December 31, 1932, to Violet Lackey, born April 20, 1901.
(6) Frances Irene Stubblefield, born December 1, 1909; married Eugene Thomas Pride.
(7) Lucille Murry Stubblefield, born August 1, 1913; married (1) March 6, 1934, to David Jackson Willis, born June 8, 1915, son of Farmer Willis and Lily Taylor; (2) May 1, 1942, to James Smith Flanders, born December 23, 1911; died February 13, 1943; (3) September 8, 1954, to Ross Sims, born April 1, 1915; child (by first marriage):
    (a) Elynor Lucille Willis married (1) July 3, 1954, to Billy Welch Douglas (2) May 24, 1960, to Seth Madison Smith, born September 27, 1931; children:
    (by first marriage):
       /1/ Eric Kenin Douglas, born June 25, 1956.
       /2/ Alan Keith Douglas, born March 14, 1958.
    (by second marriage):
       /3/ Ida Elynor Marie Smith, born February 20, 1961.

15. d. Edgar Patterson Stubblefield, born May 24, 1874.
16. e. Margaret Ella Stubblefield, born May 7, 1876.
17. f. Samuel Madison Stubblefield, born September 4, 1878.

***

14.   Asa Faulkner Stubblefield was born September 22, 1869, and died May 23, 1948; married Mary Ellen Hix, born December 4, 1871, and died November 9, 1954, daughter of William Taylor Hix. They lived in Warren County, Tennessee, and had the following children:[25]

18. a. Hugh Thomas Stubblefield, born January 5, 1892.
    b. Flora Ella Stubblefield, born December 12, 1893; dsp February 24, 1894.
19. c. Ruby Irene Stubblefield, born April 3, 1895.
    d. Jessie May Stubblefield, born January 31, 1898; married September 4, 1927, to Charles Mabry Brown; children:
    (1) Mary Anne Brown, born June 16, 1928; married John Hart Krickel; children:

```
                    (a)  John Hart Krickel.
                    (b)  Martha Ellen Krickel.
               (2)  Charles Mabry Brown, born November 14, 1932; dsp September 4,
                    1949.
          e.  Clara Belle Stubblefield, born October 3, 1890; married December 19,
               1913, to Eli Clarence Shelton; children:
               (1)  Betty Jean Shelton, died young.
               (2)  Margaret Juanita Shelton, born May 21, 1921; married Howard L.
                    Ward; children:
                    (a)  David Howard Ward married Eleanor Spicer.
                    (b)  Marilyn Diane Ward.
          f.  Ora Lee Stubblefield, born June 19, 1903; married January 6, 1934,
               to Rex Elton Stribling; child:
               (1)  Patricia Anne Stribling, born February 22, 1935; married Charles
                    Norman Alley; children:
                    (a)  Suzanne Alley, born January 4, 1956.
                    (b)  Charles Michael Alley, born May 11, 1959.
                    (c)  Mark Elton Alley, born August 20, 1963.
          g.  Fred Hix Stubblefield, born November 20, 1905; married September 4,
               1937, to Patsy Carhart Moorehead; children:
               (1)  Fred Hix Stubblefield, born December 27, 1941; married Nancy
                    Etta Kirby.
               (2)  Nancy Ellen Stubblefield, born May 5, 1944; married Danny Pres-
                    ton Davis.
```

***

18.   Hugh Thomas Stubblefield was born January 5, 1892; married December
     24, 1923, to Mary Lizzie Hancock; their children were as follows:[26]

```
          a.  Carl Thomas Stubblefield, born October 11, 1924; married Dorothy
               Troxler; children:
               (1)  Carla Sue Stubblefield married Robert Hall.
               (2)  Mark Thomas Stubblefield.
               (3)  Amy Lee Stubblefield.
          b.  Leslie Jay Stubblefield, born July 20, 1926; married Betty Baxter;
               children:
               (1)  Steve Baxter Stubblefield.
               (2)  Leslie Anne Stubblefield.
               (3)  Lisa Rhea Stubblefield.
               (4)  Lydia Kay Stubblefield.
          c.  Mary Christine Stubblefield, born April 9, 1929; married June 21,
               1953, to Walter H. Searcy; children:
               (1)  Walter Keith Searcy.
               (2)  Rebecca Elizabeth Searcy.
               (3)  Susan Clay Searcy.
          d.  Hugh Hix Stubblefield married July 25, 1959, to Elizabeth Ann Blair,
               daughter of Cleatus Blair; children:
               (1)  Katie Elizabeth Stubblefield.
               (2)  Jon David Stubblefield.
```

***

19.   Ruby Irene Stubblefield was born April 3, 1895; married June 1, 1917,
     to Fred Wesley Sain; their children were as follows:[27]

```
          a.  Mary Elizabeth Sain, born March 12, 1918; married John Orel Bailey;
               children:
```

        (1) Wanda Bailey married Dr. David James.
        (2) Lynn Bailey married Denis Rambo; children:
             (a) Donna Rambo.
             (b) Justin Rambo.
             (c) Chad Rambo.
        (3) Bruce Bailey.
    b. Fred Wesley Sain, born December 7, 1919; married Kathleen Martin;
        children:
        (1) Linda Sain married John T. Mason; children:
             (a) Malissa Mason.
             (b) John T. Mason.
        (2) Norman Sain married Barbara Gaut.
    c. Frances Lillian Sain, born May 25, 1921; married Cecil D. Prater;
        children:
        (1) Larry C. Prater.
        (2) Nick A. Prater.
    d. Mildred Irene Sain, born August 31, 1922; married Fredric Riffle Mc-
        Giboney; children:
        (1) Fredric McGiboney.
        (2) Tana R. McGiboney married Barry Gipson.
        (3) Amy McGiboney married Clifford Reynolds.
       ·(4) James McGiboney.
        (5) Jane McGiboney.
        (6) Jean McGiboney.
    e. Raymond Leon Sain, born January 1, 1932; died June 6, 1963; married
        Collene Akers; children:
        (1) John R. Sain.
        (2) Mary Cheryl Sain.
        (3) Kathy Darlen Sain.

                                 ***

15.   Edgar Patterson Stubblefield was born May 24, 1874, and died July 4,
    1929, in Morrison, Tennessee; on October 1, 1893, he married Sarah Ophelia
    Maddux, who was born October 6, 1875, and died August 8, 1969, the daugh-
    ter of James William Maddux and Clarissa Drue Locke. Their children were
    as follows:[28]

    a. William Locke Stubblefield, born December 25, 1894; married December
        8, 1921, to Anna Clara Gessler, born December 13, 1897; died December
        15, 1970, daughter of John Gessler and Mary Lohberger; children:
        (1) Mary Frances Stubblefield, born August 12, 1925.
        (2) William Maddox Stubblefield, born November 26, 1933; married
             December 28, 1957, to Nancy Gibbs Dillon, born November 20, 1937,
             daughter of Hubert Allen Dillon and Frances Marguerite Crick;
             children:
             (a) Mary Dillon Stubblefield, born November 7, 1958.
             (b) William David Stubblefield, born September 26, 1961.
    b. Druella Stubblefield, born October 17, 1896; died December 14, 1943;
        married August 14, 1926, to Arthur Weir Crouch, born November 17,
        1898; lived in Nashville, Tennessee; children:
        (1) Edward Weir Crouch, born February 20, 1929; married December
             12, 1952, to Mary Charlesie Gentry.
        (2) Margaret Ann Crouch, born April 2, 1932; married March 19, 1953,
             to James Addison Nimmo.
        (3) William Arthur Crouch, born April 2, 1932; married June 13, 1959,
             to Mrs. Helen (Cameron) Heller.
    c. Jay Eugene Stubblefield, born December 23, 1898; died September 24,
        1966; married January 18, 1922, to Nellie Elizabeth Smith, born June

                                   217

27, 1901; died September 29, 1959, daughter of Walter Lee Smith and
Hugh Elliott Mabry; child:
(1) Sarah Jean Stubblefield, born December 20, 1924.
d. Mabel Belle Stubblefield, born March 20, 1901; married August 24, 1924,
to Elmer Neal Walling, born January 19, 1900; died September 23, 1953,
son of James Monroe Walling and Emma Worthington; dsp.
e. Elizabeth Ina Stubblefield, born February 17, 1903; died July 20, 1943;
married May 29, 1926, Euclid Smartt Ramsey, born June 23, 1901, son
of William Thomas Ramsey and Ann Waterhouse Smartt (see p. 196);
children:
(1) Dorothy Heloise Ramsey, born December 25, 1926; married June 23,
1950, to James Robert Dearman, born July 10, 1925; died February
8, 1966, son of Robert Avant Dearman and Serena Elizabeth Darnell;
children:
(a) Jan Elizabeth Dearman, born November 25, 1954.
(b) James Robert Dearman, born September 12, 1959.
(2) Sarah Elizabeth Ramsey, born August 6, 1928; married June 17,
1960, to Oliver Myers Donnell, born June 19, 1930, son of James
Luther Donnell and Lucy Stuman Ware; child:
(a) Sarah Elizabeth Donnell, born July 16, 1966.
f. James Cortelyou Stubblefield, born March 21, 1905; married August
22, 1926, to Alma Adelaide Jacobs, born January 23, 1907; children:
(1) Charles Edgar Stubblefield, born December 8, 1930; married November 4, 1954, to Bertie Lee Beasley, born September 3, 1933,
daughter of Charles Dennis Beasley and Lucy Marie Martin; children:
(a) Michael Lee Stubblefield, born October 24, 1957.
(b) James Steven Stubblefield, born September 27, 1960.
(2) Martha Carolyn Stubblefield, born March 23, 1933; dsp February
17, 1953; married June 9, 1951, to Andrew Hardy Jacobs.
g. Edward Maddux Stubblefield, born December 14, 1914; died June 4, 1962;
married October 21, 1939, to Jeanie Katherine Fontaine, daughter of
James Francis Fontaine and Teen Syme Ratliff; child:
(1) James F. Stubblefield.

***

16.   Margaret Ella Stubblefield was born May 7, 1876, and died August
20, 1964; married (1) December 11, 1892, to David Foster Wagner, born
August 22, 1871; died May 6, 1896; (2) December 24, 1901, to William
Charles Locke, born January 15, 1877; died July 27, 1957, son of Jesse
Burton Locke and Hannah Narcissus Magnus; her children were as follows:[29]

(by first marriage):
a. Carrie Louise Wagner, born September 10, 1893; married December 5,
1908, to George Cleveland Womack; children:
(1) Morris Wagner Womack, born October 7, 1909.
(2) Pauline Womack, born October 21, 1911; dsp December 23, 1932.
(3) George Everett Womack, born August 9, 1916.
(4) Irene Womack, born February 6, 1919.
(5) Dorothy Jean Womack, born July 2, 1927.
b. Charles Atlee Wagner, born December 6, 1894; dsp March 27, 1895.
(by second marriage):
c. Samuel McMillan Locke, born August 24, 1902; married April 19, 1925,
to Bessie May Dearman; children:
(1) June Locke, born June 26, 1926.
(2) Samuel McMillan Locke, born September 9, 1931.
(3) Nancy Petter Locke, born May 11, 1946.
d. Herman Burger Locke, born June 9, 1904; married June 30, 1929, to

Anita Smartt; children:
(1) William Locke.
(2) Mary Ellen Locke.
(3) Jon Thomas Locke.
e. Fairy Elizabeth Locke, born September 24, 1905; married November 28, 1929, to Poindexter Allison, born June 18, 1885; died January 8, 1949; dsp.
f. Charles Burford Locke, born September 17, 1907; married November 14, 1932, to Bonnie Rhea; children:
(1) Betty Frances Locke, born July 4, 1934.
(2) William Buford Locke, born December 29, 1936; dsp May 30, 1938.
(3) Charles Thomas Locke, born March 8, 1940.
(4) Howard Rance Locke, born February 24, 1943.
(5) James Edward Locke, born September 8, 1946.
g. Catherine Locke, born January 13, 1910; married June 7, 1936, to Willard Talley; children:
(1) Mary Sandra Talley, born July 30, 1941.
(2) Larry Collin Talley, born September 30, 1944.
h. Mary Frances Locke, born September 16, 1911; married September 16, 1932, to George Edley Newman; children:
(1) George Edley Newman, born September 25, 1935.
(2) Robert Wesley Newman, born June 15, 1951.
i. Evelyn Locke, born October 14, 1913; married October 17, 1931, to William Glenn Phifer, born November 20, 1904; died August 4, 1959, son of James Phifer and Margaret Crain; children:
(1) Marilyn Joy Phifer, born October 4, 1936; married Thomas Coppedge.
(2) William Glenn Phifer, born November 10, 1941.

***

17,   Samuel Madison Stubblefield was born September 4, 1878, and died June 1, 1919; married April 25, 1906, to Sally Parker, born October, 1878, and died May 11, 1966, daughter of William Thomas Parker and Mary Esta Lea Berry. Their children were as follows:[30]

a. Paul Stubblefield, born June 28, 1907; dsp May 27, 1933.
b. Robert Edward Stubblefield, born July 12, 1908; died December 23, 1944; married September 25, 1933, to Margaret Sadler; children:
(1) Robert Edward Stubblefield, born June 18, 1934.
(2) Wanda June Stubblefield, born February 11, 1936.
c. Thomas Jay Stubblefield, born December 12, 1909; married June 24, 1934, to Elizabeth Ramsey, daughter of Horace Ramsey; children:
(1) Buena Vista Stubblefield, born June 22, 1935; married June 14, 1953, to Barry Valentine; children:
(a) Susan Valentine, born January 31, 1960.
(b) Nancy Lynn Valentine, born January 26, 1962.
(2) Paul Ramsey Stubblefield, born January 12, 1938; married Barbara Slack; children:
(a) Mark Ramsey Stubblefield, born December 7, 1959.
(b) Stacy Lynn Stubblefield.
(c) Ann Morley Stubblefield, born 1969.
(3) Thomas Michael Stubblefield, born October, 1944; married August 5, 1965, to Maxine Quesenberry; children:
(a) Brian Scott Stubblefield, born November 20, 1966.
(b) Laura Kay Stubblefield, born August 5, 1970.
(4) Jerry Erskin Stubblefield, born January 18, 1950.
d. William Royce Stubblefield, born December 9, 1914; died March 8, 1970; married December 16, 1938, to Alene Hoover; child:

219

(1) Donna Jean Stubblefield, born February 9, 1950.
e. Mary Elizabeth Stubblefield, born April 28, 1916; married February 16, 1943, to Frank Carpenter, born June 6, 1915; dsp.
f. Samuel Madison Stubblefield, born April 8, 1919; married December 28, 1941, to Frances Weiland; children:
    (1) Samuel Madison Stubblefield, born July 17, 1942.
    (2) Frank Weiland Stubblefield, born July 1, 1943.
    (3) Royce Edward Stubblefield, born May 12, 1947.
    (4) Katherine Stubblefield, born February 16, 1949.
    (5) Emma Sue Stubblefield, born December 28, 1951.

***

11.   Elizabeth Stubblefield was born December 14, 1814, in Warren County, Tennessee, and died December 27, 1862; married c1833 Basil Gaither Sain, son of Daniel Sain and Martha Davis. Their children were as follows:[31]

a. B. F. Sain, born c1834; married Sarah _____; children:
    (1) Ada C. Sain, born c1856.
    (2) Joseph Sain, born c1860.
    (3) Bettie B. Sain, born c1866.
b. Martha Sain, born c1836.
c. Wilmuth Sain, born c1838.
d. Nancy Sain, born c1840.
e. Mary E. Sain, born c1842; married December 19, 1867, to A. M. Horton.
f. George M. Sain, born c1844; dsp July, 1861.
g. James C. Sain, born May 15, 1847; died September 5, 1923; married July 21, 1867, to Elizabeth Summers; children:
    (1) William Sain, born c1871.
    (2) Lillie Sain, born c1875.
    (3) Alfred Forbes Sain, born c1879.
    (4) Ellis B. Sain, born August 25, 1881; died September 18, 1964; married J. Barkley Mathews, born February 12, 1869; died October 4, 1959; children:
        (a) James E. Mathews, born January 13, 1901.
        (b) Florence Belle Mathews, born May 4, 1904; married Dorris E. Jackson.
        (c) William Summers Mathews, born October 5, 1906.
        (d) Elizabeth Ione Mathews, born November 8, 1910; married Coy St. John.
        (e) John Roberts Mathews, born January 5, 1916; dsp January 28, 1918.
h. Louisa Sain, born c1849.
20. i. William Hampton Sain, born August 24, 1852.
j. Sarah Sain, born c1854.
k. Alice Sain, born c1858.

***

20.   William Hampton Sain was born August 24, 1852, and died in 1935 in Coffee County, Tennessee; married c1876 to Mary Lou Ferguson, born January 29, 1856, and died May 24, 1903, daughter of Dr. Henry P. Ferguson and Lucy Francie Parker. Their children were as follows:[32]

a. Edward Sain, born July 24, 1877; died July 23, 1949, in San Antonio, Texas; married Nannie Thacker, born April 10, 1878, daughter of Jesse Ellis Thacker and Josie Elizabeth Gentry; children:
    (1) Earl Sain, born 1903; married Blanche Mann.
    (2) James E. Sain, born 1906; married Fay McCoy.

(3) Wade Sain, born 1909; died 1951; married Louise Walker.
(4) Carl Sain, born 1911.
(5) Mary E. Sain, born 1914; married Harold B. Moss.
(6) Dorothy Bell Sain, born 1918; married James C. Cunningham.
b. Thomas Edgar Sain, born December 19, 1880; married January 19, 1918, to Vera Fullerton.
c. Henry Pearl Sain, born May 13, 1883; dsp.
d. Bessie Sain, born August 10, 1886; married September, 1916, to Albro Norvell.
e. Daniel Parker Sain, born August 27, 1888; died January 12, 1938, in Manchester, Tennessee; married January, 1908, to Alice Eugene Burrow, born June 22, 1893; died August 29, 1963; children:
(1) Mary Lou Sain, born November 3, 1908; married December 6, 1925, to Lonnie C. Haley.
(2) James William Sain, born January 14, 1911; died May 20, 1961; married August 18, 1934, to Carolyn Ruehl.
(3) Henry Pearl Sain, born May 27, 1913; died December, 1968; married November 26, 1938, to Virginia Hunt Wright, born November 7, 1919, daughter of Ernest Bowlin Wright and Tappie Hunt Moore; children:
(a) Henry Parker Sain, born September 30, 1940; married August 12, 1960, to Lynne A. Burkhart.
(b) Elizabeth Fay Sain, born November 20, 1942.
(4) Naomi Ruth Sain, born March 20, 1916; married March 22, 1936; to Charles R. Kell.
(5) Willie Novella Sain, born February 18, 1919; married August 11, 1942, to Jack W. Walter.
f. James Sain, born 1892; married September 27, 1917, to Bertha Burrow.
g. George M. Sain, born June 17, 1897; married May 23, 1915, to Gladys Carden.

***

12.   Robert Loxley Stubblefield was born February 18, 1824, and died November 20, 1909, in Warren County, Tennessee; married September 6, 1851, to Mary Jane Catherine Stout, born January 1, 1830; died March 5, 1926; daughter of Jacob Van Dyke Stout and Anna Maria Berry Anthony; their children were as follows:[33]

a. Annie Laura Stubblefield, born July 6, 1852; dsp March 8, 1943, in Franklin County, Tennessee; married April 29, 1896, to John Lipscomb.
b. Martha Jane Stubblefield, born September 29, 1853; died in 1941 in Dallas, Texas; married December 10, 1879, to Alvin J. Reagan, born 1853; died 1916 in San Angelo, Texas; child:
(1) Robert Carl Reagan, born September 29, 1880; dsp 1944 in Dallas, Texas; married Mollie Dabney.
c. Mary Louisa Stubblefield, born August 17, 1855; died April 14, 1887, in Viola, Tennessee; married October 8, 1879, to Andrew Hycen Bonner, born March 25, 1856, and died June 24, 1911, son of Redding Bonner and Elizabeth Rutledge; children:
(1) Millie Pearl Bonner, born July 16, 1880; married October 2, 1929, to Dr. Herman Reynolds, born April 26, 1878; died July 7, 1911, in McMinnville, Tennessee, son of Thomas Monroe Reynolds and Mary Tittsworth; dsp.
(2) Ernest Kirkendall Bonner, born February 14, 1882; died November 8, 1959, in Nashville, Tennessee; married July 7, 1907, to Emma Lee Craven, born June 23, 1887, daughter of Peter Craven; child:
(a) Cicero Harold Bonner, born March 31, 1910; dsp April 21, 1910.
21. d. William Thomas Haskell Stubblefield, born March 15, 1857.

22. e. George Horace Stubblefield, born February 8, 1859.
23. f. James Robert Stubblefield, born March 8, 1861.
24. g. Emma Adelaide Stubblefield, born February 14, 1866.

***

21.   William Thomas Haskell Stubblefield was born March 15, 1857, and died April 13, 1958, in Temple, Texas; married October 12, 1887, to Pernita Elizabeth Jones, born September 8, 1869, and died November 24, 1934, daughter of Ebenezer Jones and Sciotha Elizabeth England. Their children were as follows:[34]

    a. Ruby Stubblefield, born July 12, 1888; married May 10, 1911, to Robert Franklin Crum, born November 3, 1888; son of Robert Price Crum and Margaret Elizabeth Magby; lived in Santa Anna, Texas; dsp.

    b. Lorita Stubblefield, born December 28, 1893; married May 31, 1917, to Dr. Roy Green Giles, born August 30, 1888; son of Samuel Green Giles and Martha Belle Nichols; lived in Marlin, Texas; child:
      (1) Kathryn Glenna Giles, born October 13, 1925; married July 11, 1952, to Luther Don Loughridge, born August 2, 1916; lived in Houston, Texas; dsp.

    c. William Haskell Stubblefield, born October 7, 1895; died August 25, 1969; married May 27, 1920, to Nina Viola Macy Moore Dickenson, born August 10, 1899; daughter of Rufus Bracken Dickenson and Macy Charles Moore; lived in San Antonio, Texas; children:
      (1) Marilyn Stubblefield, born August 17, 1921; married August 30, 1943, to Philip LaFrance Willis, born August 2, 1918; son of Alvin Samuel Willis and Eliza Phillips; lived in Dallas, Texas; children:
         (a) Linda Kay Willis, born July 29, 1949.
         (b) Rosemary Willis, born May 3, 1953.
      (2) Warren Loxley Stubblefield, born January 24, 1924; married March 3, 1949, to Louise Haughton Manning, born April 13, 1923; daughter of Charles William Manning and Gladys Olliff; lived in San Antonio, Texas; children:
         (a) Marilyn Kathleen Stubblefield, born October 27, 1950.
         (b) William Warren Stubblefield, born January 30, 1955.

    d. Maude Elizabeth Stubblefield, born September 16, 1900; married March 20, 1920, to Charles Franklin McDonald, born November 12, 1902; son of Albert Franklin McDonald and Julia Evelyn Taylor; lived in Belton, Texas; child:
      (1) Jean Evelyn McDonald, born January 19, 1922; married July 3, 1941, to William Leroy Bell, born July 13, 1917; son of Leroy Pender Bell and Nancy Council; lived in Austin, Texas; child:
         (a) Vicky Bell, born December 25, 1944; married June 7, 1963, to Robert Carter Whitfield, born January 24, 1941; son of Robert Lee Whitfield and Lillian Belle Peters; lived in Washington, D. C.

    e. Mary Kathryn Stubblefield, born October 17, 1905; married April 14, 1939, to Harry Harrison Morrow, born March 4, 1901; died August 25, 1961; son of James Luther Morrow and Cora Amanda Rooker; dsp; lived in Abilene, Texas.

***

22.   George Horace Stubblefield was born February 8, 1859, and died November 1, 1948, in Viola, Tennessee; married October 26, 1899, to Dessie Dean Ramsey, born August 31, 1876; daughter of David Armstrong Ramsey and Hattie Strickler. Their children were as follows:[35]

222

a. Inez Catherine Stubblefield, born September 20, 1902; died September
    5, 1955, in Maplesville, Alabama; married May 10, 1929, to Pierson H.
    Barnes, born June 9, 1888, in Dallas County, Alabama; son of Michael
    H. Barnes and Sarah Friday; child:
    (1) Betty Annette Barnes, born September 1, 1938; married December
        2, 1960, to Jack Harley King, born October 17, 1930, in Green-
        wood, South Dakota; son of Joseph Vincent King and Blanche Rans;
        lived in Murfreesboro, Arkansas; children:
        (a) William Ray King, born August 14, 1961.
        (b) Joseph Harrison King, born November 20, 1963.
b. Raymond Ramsey Stubblefield, born August 22, 1905; married November
    16, 1936, to Evelyn Lucille Kimsey, born February 17, 1909, in Sparta,
    Tennessee; daughter of Thomas Norris Kimsey and Eva Lucille Story;
    lived in Viola, Tennessee; child:
    (1) Anne Ramsey Stubblefield, born October 16, 1937; married May
        24, 1962, to Ronald Arthur Rathert, born September 7, 1937, in
        Randolph County, Illinois; son of Edwin C. Rathert and Emma
        Middendort; lived in Viola, Tennessee; child:
        (a) Dianna Raye Rathert, born October 28, 1964.
c. George Horace Stubblefield, born June 15, 1908; married Evelyn _____;
    lived in Birmingham, Alabama; child:
    (1) Johnnie Louise Stubblefield.
d. Hattie Louise Stubblefield, born July 30, 1911; married June 23, 1934,
    to Edgemond Parker Callahan, born December 16, 1907, in Blount County,
    Tennessee; son of Hugh Lawson Callahan and Eva Cornelia Coltharp; lived
    in Hyattsville, Maryland; children:
    (1) David Edgemond Callahan, born July 14, 1938; married June 25,
        1960, to Virginia Ann Conley, born June 18, 1938, daughter of
        John Edward Conley and Virginia Woodworth; lived in Baltimore,
        Maryland; children:
        (a) Katherine Lynn Callahan, born November 15, 1962.
        (b) Elizabeth Susan Callahan, born September 21, 1965.
    (2) Caroline Louise Callahan, born December 16, 1946.
e. Dessie Dean Stubblefield, born September 28, 1916; married November
    6, 1938, to Benjamin Edward Dodd, born September 14, 1915; son of
    Clarence Holman Dodd and Lula Travis; lived in Nashville, Tennessee;
    dsp.

***

23.   James Robert Stubblefield was born March 8, 1861, and died March
21, 1950, in Viola, Tennessee; married October 30, 1890, to Sarah Surrelda
Campbell, born July 21, 1862, and died February 1, 1925. Their children
were as follows:[36]

a. Royce Landon Stubblefield, born March 30, 1892; married (1) Dolly
    Holder, born April 25, 1900; died October 8, 1922; (2) December 12,
    1925, to Ruth Givens, daughter of Herman Ford Givens and Sallie Maude
    Inman; lived in Viola, Tennessee; dsp.
25. b. Herman Powell Stubblefield, born April 19, 1894.
c. Howard Gowan Stubblefield, born June 14, 1896; married March 9, 1918,
    to Annie Hughes, born February 22, 1900; lived in Nashville, Tennessee;
    children:
    (1) Elizabeth Ward Stubblefield, born January 13, 1919; married April
        25, 1942, to William Henry Pirtle, born August 9, 1912; son of
        William Lee Pirtle and Melinda Lappin; lived in Nashville, Ten-
        nessee; children:
        (a) Elizabeth Caroll Pirtle, born June 28, 1943; married June
             8, 1965, to Robert Dean Berry.

223

    (b) William Larry Pirtle, born February 21, 1948.
  (2) Alethea Stubblefield, born February 27, 1920; married June 7,
    1945, to Clarence Virgil Booth, born June 21, 1911; son of John
    William Booth and Minnie Wiener; dsp.
  (3) Howard Hughes Stubblefield, born April 18, 1923; married September 16, 1947, to Peggy Louise Lewis, born June 16, 1926; daughter
    of Edward Earl Lewis and Louise Campbell; lived in Nashville,
    Tennessee; children:
    (a) Howard Lewis Stubblefield, born July 27, 1955.
    (b) Melinda Ann Stubblefield, born April 29, 1957.
  (4) Annie LaNelle Stubblefield, born July 23, 1927; married December
    1, 1945, to Robert Marvin Bufford, born September 3, 1923; son
    of Warren Bufford and Myrtle Outlaw; lived in Nashville, Tennessee; children:
    (a) John Roland Bufford, born January 26, 1952.
    (b) Vickie Lee Bufford, born May 7, 1955.
    (c) Howard Douglas Bufford, born January 1, 1957.
  (5) Jack Glenn Stubblefield, born November 24, 1931; married August
    27, 1955, to Betty Ann Rucker, born November 5, 1936; daughter
    of John Bumpas Rucker and Pearl Mayo; lived in Nashville, Tennessee; children:
    (a) John Dwayne Stubblefield, born July 10, 1962.
    (b) Glenna Deanne Stubblefield, born June 27, 1966.
  d. Lota Elizabeth Stubblefield, born November 20, 1899; dsp.
26. e. James Grant Stubblefield, born December 10, 1901.

***

25.   Herman Powell Stubblefield was born April 19, 1894; married August
10, 1919, to Mamie Hall, born July 6, 1897; daughter of Jeff Davis Hall
and Mollie Elkins; lived in Morrison, Tennessee; their children were as
follows:[37]

  a. Herman Hall Stubblefield, born January 21, 1921; married October 6,
    1944, to Rebecca Watson, born July 27, 1923; daughter of Jerre Watson
    and Myrtle Garrett; lived in Maryville, Tennessee; children:
    (1) Murna Ann Stubblefield, born June 21, 1945; married March 20,
      1965, to Gerald W. Napier.
    (2) Locksley Stuart Stubblefield, born September 21, 1947.
    (3) Lota Antoinette Stubblefield, born February 8, 1955.
  b. Sarah Elkins Stubblefield, born March 1, 1923; married May 31, 1945,
    to Loyd Collier, born August 2, 1920; son of Floyd Collier and Etta
    Ballard; lived in Essen-Kupferdreh, Germany; children:
    (1) Connie Theresa Collier, born October 3, 1948.
    (2) James Dale Collier, born October 27, 1950.
    (3) Linda Jean Collier, born October 22, 1956.
    (4) David Loyd Collier, born April 20, 1958.
  c. Robert Davis Stubblefield, born January 4, 1925; married April 1, 1955,
    to Maxine Marshall, born August 6, 1929; daughter of Clarence Dillon
    Marshall and Willie Cassidy; lived in Manchester, Tennessee; children:
    (1) Mary Sharon Stubblefield, born December 5, 1958.
    (2) Bradley Davis Stubblefield, born January 29, 1962.
  d. Edwin Powell Stubblefield, born November 23, 1926; married December
    23, 1951, to Mildred Antham Chambers, born June 22, 1927; daughter
    of William Hugh Chambers and Vela Mae Ora Riggs; lived in Luxora, Arkansas; children:
    (1) Stephen Charles Stubblefield, born November 17, 1956.
    (2) William Scott Stubblefield, born June 6, 1960.
    (3) Robert Kent Stubblefield, born September 16, 1963.

224

e. James Gray Stubblefield, born July 27, 1929; married Carmella Patricia Lirosi, born December 24, 1923; daughter of Peter Lirosi and Louise Stephens; lived in Poughkeepsie, New York; child:
    (1) Sandra Stubblefield, born October 31, 1957.
f. Charles Bryan Stubblefield, born September 14, 1931; married September 1, 1960, to Margaret Carolyn White, born November 17, 1938; daughter of Willis Clay White and Belva Rose DeLozier; lived in Corpus Christi, Texas; children:
    (1) James Jeffrey Stubblefield, born October 18, 1961.
    (2) Jane Clark Stubblefield, born August 17, 1965.

***

26.   James Grant Stubblefield was born December 10, 1901, and married June 3, 1926, to Hazel Woodson King, born April 19, 1906; daughter of P. W. King and Susan St. John; lived in Tullahoma, Tennessee; their children were as follows:[38]

a. Sarah Susanna Stubblefield, born February 27, 1927; married February 23, 1945, to Joseph Carden McMillan, born December 9, 1926; son of William Orrill McMillan and Thelma Lee Keeling; lived in Manchester, Tennessee; children:
    (1) Joseph Carden McMillan, born March 23, 1947.
    (2) Isaac Grant McMillan, born November 14, 1948.
    (3) Susan King McMillan, born September 21, 1951.
    (4) William Mark McMillan, born August 30, 1954.
    (5) Jonathan Luke McMillan, born December 23, 1958.
b. Mary Catherine Stubblefield, born April 9, 1929; married August 25, 1950, to Alvin Foster Moudy, born January 12, 1929; son of Robert Thomas Moudy and Lella Virginia Foster; lived in Happy, Texas; children:
    (1) Alvin Foster Moudy, born July 28, 1951.
    (2) Janet Kaye Moudy, born July 10, 1953.
    (3) James Robert Moudy, born May 6, 1956.
    (4) Carolyn King Moudy, born November 29, 1960.
c. James Grant Stubblefield, born February 15, 1933; married March 8, 1952, to Shirley Patsy Melson, born December 23, 1935; daughter of Allen Clark Melson and Rose Sutton; lived in Shelbyville, Tennessee; children:
    (1) James Grant Stubblefield, born November 8, 1952.
    (2) Allen Clark Stubblefield, born November 19, 1954.
    (3) Lisa Rosann Stubblefield, born September 4, 1956.
d. Carol Jeanne Stubblefield, born February 16, 1936; married December 20, 1955, to Carl Ray Russell, born January 12, 1934; son of E. Glenn Russell and Gwendolyn Tucker; lived in Hillsboro, Tennessee; children:
    (1) Carl Ray Russell, born March 23, 1957.
    (2) Jeanne Lee Russell, born February 22, 1960.

***

24.   Emma Adelaide Stubblefield was born February 14, 1866, in Warren County, Tennessee, and died March 21, 1898, in Redlands, California; married December 25, 1892, to Noel Jackson Wilson. Their children were as follows:[39]

a. Mary Abbott Wilson, born February 7, 1894, married June 20, 1915, to Curtis Pierce O'Banion, born May 5, 1895; died July 10, 1962, in Yerington, Nevada; son of John William O'Banion and Charlotte Arline Pierce; children:
    (1) John Marcus O'Banion, born April 6, 1916; died December 12, 1958, in San Bernardino, California; married September, 1938, to

225

Lilian Hammer, born August 29, 1920, in Winnepeg, Canada, daughter
of Heinrich Hammer and Lilian Milovich; children:
    (a) Gary Norman O'Banion, born January 6, 1943; married February
        14, 1964, to Rebecca Kaylor, born July 17, 1945.
    (b) Susan Patricia O'Banion, born March 9, 1952.
    (c) Constance Elizabeth O'Banion, born April 6, 1957.

27.   (2) Hulda Marguerite O'Banion, born May 29, 1917.
    (3) Mary Elaine O'Banion, born August 24, 1918; married November 26,
        1939, to Benjamin Woodrow Hobson, born July 26, 1916; lived in
        San Diego, California; children:
        (a) Carrie Lee Hobson, born December 23, 1940; married January
            25, 1964, to Robert James Mullin, born July 6, 1937; son of
            Thomas Martin Mullin and Florence Marie O'Neill; lived in
            Chula Vista, California.
        (b) Benjamin C. Hobson, born March 12, 1945.
        (c) Bruce William Hobson, born August 31, 1949.
        (d) Ella Grace Hobson, born March 25, 1952.
    (4) Julia Elizabeth O'Banion, born July 7, 1920; married September
        22, 1940, to Bruce Francis Smith, born October 30, 1915; dsp.
    (5) Barbara Ann O'Banion, born January 14, 1925; married March, 1943,
        to Lloyd George Alm; children:
        (a) Richard Allen Alm, born December 28, 1943; married September
            4, 1966, to Sharon Troup.
        (b) Sherry Arline Alm, born February 28, 1948; married June 4,
            1966, to Donald Belcourt.
    (6) James Robert O'Banion, born January 9, 1928; married September
        11, 1949, to Carol Ruth Sheldon, born May 14, 1930; daughter of
        Allan Vroman Sheldon and Helen Fulmore Bowers; lived in Welling-
        ton, Nevada; children:
        (a) James Lance O'Banion, born August 1, 1951.
        (b) David Scott O'Banion, born September 23, 1952.
    (7) William Curtis O'Banion, born December 8, 1932; married November
        9, 1957, to Carryl Phyllis Kersting; daughter of Carl Kersting
        and Irma Mae Jamison; lived in Santa Maria, California; children:
        (a) David Lynn O'Banion, born July 1, 1959.
        (b) Marcus Allen O'Banion, born August 13, 1961.
b. Romyn Sylvester Wilson, born June 12, 1896; dsp July 22, 1897.

***

27.   Hulda Marguerite O'Banion was born May 29, 1917, and married June 25,
1937, to Cyrus Archibald Lyon, born March 22, 1907; son of Steven Douglas
Lyon and Martha M. Graves; lived in Chula Vista, California; their children were as follows:[40]

a. Lloyd Curtis Lyon, born March 10, 1938; married June 13, 1959, to
    Barbara Jean Turner, born January 15, 1942; daughter of Jesse Turner
    and Grace Lauderdale; lived in San Diego, California; child:
    (1) Shirley Jean Lyon, born January 29, 1963.
b. Richard Douglas Lyon, born July 1, 1939; married June 18, 1960, to
    Caroline Pearl Holder, born April 19, 1941; daughter of Walter Albert
    Holder and Dorothy McClure; lived in National City, California; chil-
    dren:
    (1) Richard Dee Lyon, born April 8, 1962.
    (2) Charles Ray Lyon, born March 14, 1963.
c. Martha Jane Lyon, born August 15, 1940; married October 8, 1960, to
    Richard Marion Heifner, born October 15, 1938; lived in National City,
    California; children:
    (1) Elizabeth Ann Heifner, born May 8, 1961.

226

(2) Deborah Lynn Heifner, born May 26, 1962.
(3) Marilyn Sue Heifner, born March 6, 1964.

***

7.   George Stubblefield was born July 6, 1780, in Halifax County, Virginia, and moved to Hawkins County, Tennessee, in infancy; moved to Warren County, Tennessee, about 1810, and died there on October 15, 1866. He married January 16, 1800, to Mary Jeffries, born January 17, 1783; died April 18, 1857; their children were as follows:[41]

28.   a. Robert Loxley Stubblefield, born May 19, 1801.
      b. Thomas Stubblefield, born April 5, 1803.
      c. William J. Stubblefield, born April 10, 1805; died October 9, 1890; married c1832 Rebecca Reynolds, born August 2, 1813; died March 22, 1906, daughter of Jenkin and Margaret Reynolds; children (among others):
          (1) Lycurgus J. Stubblefield, born May 27, 1833; died January 23, 1859.
          (2) Leonidas Stubblefield, born c1836; married October 5, 1858, to Nancy Hoodenpile.
          (3) Roma Stubblefield, born c1837; married Robert Safley.
          (4) Hannibal Stubblefield, born c1839; died November 11, 1901; married Sarah S. Smith, born c1842; died December 9, 1912, in Warren County, Tennessee; children:
               (a) Jonathan Smith Stubblefield lived in Aurelia, Iowa.
               (b) Henry Percy Stubblefield, born November 28, 1871.
               (c) William J. Stubblefield lived in San Francisco, California.
          (5) Napoleon Stubblefield, born c1844; married Nancy Jane Hayes, born February 9, 1844.
          (6) Thaddeus Stubblefield, born c1846.
          (7) Lucretia Stubblefield, born c1849.
      d. Martha Stubblefield, born April 27, 1808; married Nicholas P. Dodson; lived in Smith County, Texas, in 1850.
      e. Sarah Stubblefield, born July 28, 1810; married Walter Stroud (see p. 189).
      f. John L. Stubblefield, born April 21, 1812; died December 13, 1859; married Ann Elizabeth Wooldridge.
      g. (Dr.) Hiram B. Stubblefield, born September 25, 1814; dsp June 17, 1861; married June 22, 1843, to Mary Sullivan Cain.
      h. George Jeffries Stubblefield, born December 3, 1817; died September 9, 1894; married November 15, 1849, to Mary Ann Rankin, born March 4, 1831; died April 18, 1914; children:
          (1) John Lafayette Robertson Stubblefield, born October 26, 1851; dsp September 12, 1921.
          (2) Hiram Boone Stubblefield, born October 16, 1853; died July 6, 1924; married February 29, 1888, to Genevieve Beatrice Smith, born December 4, 1866; child:
               (a) Louise Stubblefield married Dr. Duncan Eve; children:
                    /1/ Genevieve Eve married Dudley Bransford.
                    /2/ Duncan Eve.
          (3) David Rankin Stubblefield, born June 16, 1856; died March 12, 1913; married December 24, 1884, to Betty Kennedy Wilkins; children:
               (a) David Rankin Stubblefield.
               (b) Kitty Stubblefield married Harding Jackson; dsp.
               (c) Daniel Wilkins Stubblefield, born November 29, 1890.
               (d) John McWilliams Stubblefield.
          (4) James Robertson Stubblefield, born February 3, 1859; dsp January 8, 1865.

227

(5) Mary Aline Stubblefield, born February 3, 1862; died May 20, 1958; married April 26, 1888, to George W. Stahlman, born May 7, 1854; died September 22, 1932; children:
    (a) Margaret Ann Stahlman married Littell Rust.
    (b) Carolyn Stahlman.
    (c) George W. Stahlman, born November 11, 1899; died June 3, 1945; married Josephine Gaskill; child:
       /1/ Sylvia Stahlman.
(6) George Jeffries Stubblefield, born April 20, 1867; dsp July 10, 1935; married October 16, 1895, to Virginia Mayes Watkins, born August 27, 1871.
i. James C. Stubblefield, born February 10, 1819; died April 8, 1847.

***

28.   Robert Loxley Stubblefield was born May 19, 1801, in Hawkins County, Tennessee, and died February 3, 1858, in Bell County, Texas; married 1821 to Elizabeth Dodson, born December 30, 1804; died February 10, 1871, daughter of Elisha Dodson and Mary Matlock. Their children were as follows:[42]

a. George W. Stubblefield, born August 8, 1822; died May 8, 1905; married 1847 to Jane Susan Shamblin.
b. Lavona Stubblefield, born December 6, 1823; died November 15, 1904, in Lawrence County, Missouri; married Thomas Taylor.
c. Elisha Dodson Stubblefield, born February 8, 1825; died February 20, 1875, in Barry County, Missouri; married May 2, 1861, to Eliza Earl, born in 1837 and died January 4, 1920, in Claremore, Oklahoma.
29. d. Isaac Newton Stubblefield, born November 13, 1826.
e. Mary Stubblefield, born March 31, 1828; dsp November 4, 1903.
f. Malissa Victoria Stubblefield, born July 7, 1829; died April 28, 1911; married Marion Francis Taylor.
g. Mahala Jane Stubblefield, born January 19, 1831; died January 17, 1914, in Barry County, Missouri; married Monroe Lucky, born January 15, 1829, and died August 15, 1866.
h. Amanda Caroline Stubblefield, born December 8, 1832; died May 1, 1916, in Marionville, Missouri; married _____ Frost.
i. James McCoy Stubblefield, born December 12, 1834; died February 17, 1906, in Monument, Oregon; married 1858 to Mary Burnham.
j. Arthur Toll Stubblefield, born August 4, 1836; dsp November 16, 1905, in Kansas City, Missouri.
k. Jefferson Park Stubblefield, born November 13, 1844; died April 25, 1880; married Elizabeth Houchins.
l. Martha Cleopatra Sutbblefield, born February 13, 1846; died December 31, 1877, in Bethany, Missouri; married Cyrus Roberts.

***

29.   Isaac Newton Stubblefield was born November 13, 1826, and died June 27, 1905, in Exeter, Missouri; married September 15, 1854, to Nancy Jane Scott, born August 23, 1835, and died December 29, 1924, in Barry County, Missouri; daughter of John Wesley Scott and Alzira Johnson. Their children were as follows:[43]

30. a. Clay Stubblefield, born March 27, 1856.
b. John Loxley Stubblefield, born September 25, 1858; dsp July 29, 1926, in Kansas City, Missouri.
31. c. Alzira Elizabeth Stubblefield, born August 22, 1861.
32. d. William Penn Stubblefield, born March 18, 1864.
e. James Scott Stubblefield, born August 24, 1866; died January 15, 1931,

in Merced, California; married (1) September 11, 1895, to Mattie Carver Lacey, born November 16, 1870; died October 22, 1909; (2) April 15, 1912, to Verna Ann Weaver, born June 1, 1879; children (by first marriage):

 (1) Ethel Stubblefield, born October 31, 1897; dsp; lived in Fresno, California.
 (2) Frank Wilbur Stubblefield, born February 8, 1899; dsp October 1, 1900.
 (3) Gertrude Stubblefield, born November 2, 1903; dsp; lived in Fresno, California.

33. f. Albert George Stubblefield, born December 10, 1868.
  g. Ed Arthur Stubblefield, born October 13, 1870; dsp August 17, 1947, in Bend, Oregon; married May 27, 1909, to Bess Robinson, born April 24, 1883; died December 31, 1943, in Vinita, Oklahoma.
  h. Frank Stubblefield, born November 3, 1872; dsp October 17, 1948, in Los Angeles, California; married October 10, 1906, to Ollie Bell Paxon, born March 12, 1881.
  i. Demie Tee Stubblefield, born November 3, 1874; dsp October 17, 1932, in Pueblo, Colorado.
  j. Garfield Stubblefield, born July 18, 1878; died November 14, 1964, in Sacramento, California; married February 14, 1916, to Minnie Bell Smith, born August 29, 1880; died December 17, 1961; children:
  (1) Robert Scott Stubblefield, born January 17, 1917; dsp.
  (2) William Maxwell Stubblefield, born March 31, 1918; married August 6, 1949, to Mrs. Billie L. (Yaws) Nutt, born March 25, 1922; children:
   (a) Robert Glenn Stubblefield, born May 17, 1950.
   (b) Bradley Owen Stubblefield, born June 28, 1957.
  (3) Amy Elizabeth Stubblefield, born February 4, 1921; married (1) 1944 Harold Gamble (2) April 1, 1954, to William Hofflinger; lived in Stockton, California; children:
   (by first marriage):
   (a) David Lawrence Gamble, born December 16, 1944.
   (by second marriage):
   (b) Patricia Ilona Hofflinger, born August 11, 1955.

***

30. Clay Stubblefield was born March 27, 1856, and died March 29, 1928, in Premont, Texas; married June 1, 1884, to Martha Skellen Henbest, born January 17, 1858, in Marshall, Illinois; died January 14, 1933, in Barry County, Missouri; daughter of Albert Henbest and Octavia Matthews. Their children were as follows:

  a. Etalee Stubblefield, born March 22, 1885; dsp July 5, 1921, in Black Oak, Arkansas; married December 28, 1911, to Reuben M. Barrett, born September 9, 1883; died December 26, 1948.
34. b. Victoria Stubblefield, born September 13, 1886.
35. c. Claud Blaine Stubblefield, born April 9, 1888.
  d. Allen Leslie Stubblefield, born February 24, 1891; died March 20, 1949; married January 3, 1923, to Mae Hunt, born September 5, 1902; lived in Monette, Arkansas; children:
  (1) Etalee Stubblefield, born January 22, 1924; dsp July 2, 1924.
  (2) Royce Benzil Stubblefield, born April 19, 1925; married December 22, 1951 to Betty Comer, born April 24, 1928; lived in Caraway, Arkansas; child:
   (a) Lee Ann Stubblefield, born January 20, 1960.
  (3) Reuben Leon Stubblefield, born July 24, 1929; married April 4, 1954, to Leslie Fae Haag, born December 6, 1933; lived in Cara-

229

way, Arkansas; children:
    (a) Mark Allen Stubblefield, born March 7, 1957.
    (b) David Anthony Stubblefield, born May 21, 1959.
e. Park Leroy Stubblefield, born October 4, 1892; married December 8, 1925, to Lennie Dickerson, born March 25, 1904; lived in Premont, Texas; child:
    (1) Margarette Winnona Stubblefield, born September 20, 1930; married February 18, 1952, to Joseph Vincent Maranto, born August 27, 1926; lived in Stamford, Connecticut; children:
        (a) Gina Lisa Maranto, born February 7, 1953.
        (b) Marcus Scott Maranto, born July 15, 1957.
f. Emma Octavia Stubblefield, born September 22, 1894; married May 25, 1921, to John Edwin Stewart, born March 8, 1888; died October 11, 1951; lived in Monette, Arkansas; child:
    (1) Robert Spencer Stewart, born September 2, 1923; married September 9, 1951, to Donna L. Erickson, born April 26, 1929, daughter of Reuben Lester Erickson and Gerturde Wilhelmina Jennings; children:
        (a) Scott Neil Stewart, born June 4, 1953.
        (b) Sarah Ann Stewart, born December 19, 1955.
36. g. Leona Louzietta Stubblefield, born September 2, 1898.
h. Albert Newton Stubblefield, born May 7, 1901; married December 7, 1931, to Ruby Raymond Anderson, born September 12, 1905, daughter of Noah P. Anderson and Lennie K. Arnhart; lived in Cassville, Missouri; children:
    (1) Allen Leo Stubblefield, born August 7, 1934; married November 22, 1959, to Marian Ellis, born May 25, 1939, daughter of Curtis Ellis and Mary Patterson; lived in Cassville, Missouri; child:
        (a) Jeffrey Allen Stubblefield, born April 17, 1963.
    (2) Allene Cleo Stubblefield, born August 7, 1934.
    (3) Gilbert Clay Stubblefield, born July 19, 1941.

***

34.   Victoria Stubblefield was born September 13, 1886; died March 20, 1957, in Mercedes, Texas; married December 20, 1908, to Emmett Ellsworth Freeze, born June 26, 1886, in Cassville, Missouri; died January 15, 1945, in Los Angeles, California; their children were as follows:[45]

a. Wilma B. Freeze, born June 28, 1913; married June 28, 1931, to John Nickols, born January 5, 1911; lived in Purdy, Missouri; children:
    (1) Jimmie Lee Nickols, born July 31, 1933; married October 14, 1950, to Venita June Ogle, born January 1, 1932; lived in South Gate, California; children:
        (a) Deborah Lee Nickols, born February 12, 1951.
        (b) Barbara Ellen Nickols, born November 5, 1952.
        (c) William Wesley Nickols, born June 29, 1954.
    (2) Lila Joyce Nickols, born February 9, 1935; married 1955 to Bill Winfield, born March 15, 1932; lived in Maywood, California; children:
        (a) Sandra Joyce Winfield, born January 6, 1956.
        (b) April Denise Winfield, born April 26, 1958.
        (c) Cheryl Ann Winfield, born April 3, 1959.
b. Alberta Freeze, born December 19, 1914; dsp February 2, 1915.
c. Elbert Emmett Freeze, born June 9, 1916; died October 7, 1959; married July 16, 1939, to Winfred Poteet, born August 6, 1920; lived in Mercedes, Texas; children:
    (1) Sandra Kay Freeze, born December 19, 1943.
    (2) Suzanne Freeze, born December 19, 1944.

      (3) Larry Elbert Freeze, born August 29, 1952.
  d. H. Clay Freeze, born November 10, 1920; dsp.

***

35.   Claud Blaine Stubblefield was born April 9, 1888, and died June 21, 1955, in Monett, Missouri; married November 23, 1910, to Eliza Jane Varner, born December 28, 1889, daughter of John Shipley Varner and Margaret Josephine Felker. Their children were as follows:[46]

  a. Verdayne Blaine Stubblefield, born December 12, 1911; **married March 14, 1934,** to Lela Mae Long, born August 24, 1911, daughter of Edward Long and Mollie Jackson; lived in Monett, Missouri; child:
      (1) Earl Blaine Stubblefield, born July 16, 1947.
  b. Agnes Leola Stubblefield, born April 22, 1913; married April 5, 1942, to John L. Fairchild, born December 4, 1910; dsp.
  c. Lyle Leolyn Stubblefield, born November 22, 1914; married July 16, 1936, to Lena Kennedy, born August 13, 1915, daughter of Curtis Kennedy and Bertha Harbut; lived in Monett, Missouri; children:
      (1) James Lyle Stubblefield, born May 24, 1937; married December 3, 1955, to Mary Bliss Elrod, born May 23, 1940; lived in Merced, California; child:
         (a) Rena Stubblefield, born August 1, 1957.
      (2) Richard Ray Stubblefield, born September 18, 1938; married August 2, 1957, to Lois Turner, born August 4, 1937; lived in Republic, Missouri; children:
         (a) Robert Ray Stubblefield, born March 17, 1958.
         (b) Russel Brian Stubblefield, born March 7, 1960.
  d. Leland Airel Stubblefield, born May 22, 1917; married September 24, 1947, to Cleo Hartness; dsp; lived in Monett, Missouri.
  e. Lowell Rayburn Stubblefield, born April 13, 1921; married April 24, 1943, to Ethel Jean Newcum, born August 18, 1922, daughter of Charles E. Newcum and Martha Paralee Jennings; lived in Aurora, Missouri; children:
      (1) Gary Dewayne Stubblefield, born July 31, 1944.
      (2) Gale Lynn Stubblefield, born July 10, 1948.
      (3) Dennis Dale Stubblefield, born February 17, 1952.
  f. Dolores Etalee Stubblefield, born March 6, 1924; married March 4, 1944, to Chester Pennel, born January 3, 1922, son of Frank Pennel and Lillie Todd; lived in Monett, Missouri; children:
      (1) Roger Lee Pennel, born May 11, 1947.
      (2) Donna Kay Pennel, born April 29, 1950.

***

36.   Leona Louzietta Stubblefield was born September 2, 1898, and married (1) February 20, 1923, to Archie Nolan Davis; (2) March 20, 1927, to Lewis Harper; lived in Neosho, Missouri; their children were as follows:[47]

(by first marriage):
  a. Archie Lavoy Davis, born September 24, 1924; married September 15, 1946, to Margaret Young, born April 26, 1926, daughter of Austin Young and Lois Van Hoozer; lived in Kansas City, Missouri; children:
      (1) Nancy Lynn Davis, born June 23, 1947.
      (2) Gary Wayne Davis, born September 9, 1952.
(by second marriage):
  b. Carroll Harper, born February 27, 1928; married May 7, 1952, to Joyce Garrett, born November 2, 1934, daughter of Ray Garrett and Halene Picketts; lived in Spearman, Texas; children:

231

      (1) Park Anthony Harper, born March 18, 1953.
      (2) Timothy Lee Harper, born January 21, 1957.
      (3) Carla Kay Harper, born June 26, 1959.
      (4) Kelly Jo Harper, born August 15, 1961.

***

31.   Alzira Elizabeth Stubblefield was born August 22, 1861, and died June 30, 1948, in Norman, Oklahoma; married January 29, 1880, to John Franklin Webb, born August 2, 1849, in Bellbuckle, Tennessee, and died December 19, 1919, in Tipton, Oklahoma; son of Steven Bedford Webb and Eliza Prudence Murphree. Their children were as follows:[48]

a. Horace Webb, born December 10, 1880; dsp September 16, 1962, in Altus, Oklahoma; married February 1, 1910, to Sadie Woodworth, born February 1, 1878; died August 10, 1959, daughter of Hiram C. Woodworth and Hattie Scott.

b. Alice Webb, born July 14, 1882; dsp February 5, 1900.

c. Hugh Webb, born March 14, 1884; dsp April 24, 1899.

d. Ulys Webb, born February 26, 1886; died July 20, 1957, in Skiatook, Oklahoma; married October 30, 1920, to Berthe Louise Bourgain, born November 25, 1895, daughter of Philippe Bourgain and Marie Marohain; child:
    (1) Jacqueline Elizabeth Webb, born July 28, 1921; married December 28, 1945, to Keegan Carter, born March 4, 1915, son of Mark Carter and Jimmie Laura Cook; lived in Kilgore, Texas; children:
       (a) John Mark Carter, born August 20, 1954.
       (b) James Keegan Carter, born October 21, 1955.
       (c) Paul Webb Carter, born March 19, 1958.

e. Nix Webb, born December 20, 1888; married July 27, 1919, to Clara Esther Van Slyke, born July 8, 1895, daughter of E. E. Van Slyke and Elizabeth Keyes; lived in Wichita, Kansas; child:
    (1) Robert John Webb, born October 28, 1925; married November 30, 1953, to Shirley Armstrong, born March 18, 1934, daughter of Orval J. Armstrong and Verla June Waggoner; lived in Wichita, Kansas; children:
       (a) Roberta Jo Ann Webb, born December 30, 1954.
       (b) Dorothy Jean Webb, born November 1, 1956.

37. f. Inez Webb, born November 27, 1890.

g. Iva Jayne Webb, born January 6, 1893; married April 16, 1919, to Stanford Lee Owens, born December 8, 1892, son of John W. Owens and Ophelia Blann; lived in Tahoka, Texas; children:
    (1) John Lee Owens, born February 16, 1920; married June 9, 1944, to Jack Dunn, born December 26, 1921, son of Oliver Buck Dunn and Lalla Beeman Rancier; lived in Victoria, Texas; children:
       (a) Sue Owens, born March 26, 1945.
       (b) John Rancier Owens, born December 2, 1946.
       (c) Thomas Dunn Owens, born April 18, 1952.
    (2) Frank Talbert Owens, born January 24, 1921; married June 8, 1944, to Margaret Ruth Ridley, born June 1, 1926; lived in Albuquerque, New Mexico; children:
       (a) John Ralph Owens, born July 21, 1946.
       (b) Kent Lee Owens, born June 2, 1949.
       (c) Mary Ann Owens, born March 1, 1951.
    (3) Mary Jayne Owens, born January 24, 1923; married January 1, 1942, to Frank Lawrence Butler; dsp; lived in Augusta, Georgia.

h. Mary E. Webb, born April 16, 1895; married June 23, 1931, to Robert W. Hurd, born November 5, 1897; lived in Tampa, Florida; child:
    (1) Helen M. Hurd, born December 4, 1932; married June 28, 1952, to

Leonard M. Vineg, born February 11, 1932; lived in Madison, Wisconsin; child:
    (a) Robert L. Vineg, born June 13, 1953.
  i. Frank Webb, born August 28, 1897; dsp July 19, 1909.
38. j. Xoe Webb, born October 28, 1900.
  k. Faye Webb, born April 6, 1903; married September 16, 1946, to Roland Vincent Kapeller, born October 17, 1901; died January 17, 1962; dsp; lived in Norman, Oklahoma.
  l. Doris Tee Webb, born October 15, 1906; married June 3, 1939, to Joseph Noel Lee, born October 23, 1905, son of Robert L. Lee and Laura Wheeler; lived in Bartlesville, Oklahoma; children:
    (1) Charles Edward Lee, born December 29, 1940.
    (2) Doris Jo Lee, born June 25, 1945; dsp June 26, 1945.
    (3) John Robert Lee, born October 11, 1946.
    (4) Noeleta Ann Lee, born October 11, 1946.

***

37.   Inez Webb was born November 27, 1890; married March 6, 1919, to Joseph Isom Gober, born December 31, 1887, son of Isom A. Gober and Louise Ring. They lived in Farwell, Texas, and their children were as follows:[49]

  a. Frank Louise Gober, born January 2, 1917; married September 20, 1942, to David Hugh Carson, son of Fred Lee Carson and Anna Lowery; lived in Friona, Texas; children:
    (1) David Lee Carson, born January 3, 1946.
    (2) Linda Kay Carson, born December 19, 1950.
    (3) John Scott Carson, born March 20, 1960.
  b. Ashberry Webb Gober, born August 17, 1918; married November 29, 1942, to Irene Lucile Sachs, born January 7, 1916, daughter of George Sachs and Clara Bultmeir; lived in Farwell, Texas; children:
    (1) Gerald Robert Gober, born July 28, 1943.
    (2) Dale Eugene Gober, born April 1, 1947.
    (3) Katherine Ann Gober, born May 7, 1949.
    (4) Alan Jack Gober, born April 18, 1954.
  c. Claud Isom Gober, born August 3, 1920; dsp November 25, 1943.
  d. Berneil Gober, born and dsp January 11, 1924.
  e. Horace Lloyd Gober, born December 19, 1924; married February 19, 1946, to Frances Maureen Roach, born November 17, 1924, daughter of James Oran Roach and Nellie Viola Joyner; lived in Bovina, Texas; children:
    (1) Lloyd Lane Gober, born October 3, 1946.
    (2) Kimberly Gober, born June 15, 1954.
  f. Leroy Scott Gober, born November 19, 1928; married August 11, 1952, to Clara Etha Derrick, born May 30, 1934, daughter of Earl Abraham Derrick and Annie Lorena McPherson; lived in Bovina, Texas; children:
    (1) Rebbie Rene Gover, born November 18, 1953.
    (2) Gary Scott Gober, born February 7, 1956.
    (3) Ginger Denise Gober, born October 10, 1957.
  g. Jaquetta Gober, born August 22, 1930; dsp August 8, 1938.
  h. Dorris Marie Gober, born February 22, 1935; married March 5, 1954, to Charles Ansell Roark, born July 18, 1933, son of Charles Everett Roark and Louise Nichols; lived in Amarillo, Texas; children:
    (1) Susan Marie Roark, born December 15, 1954.
    (2) Richard Lynn Roark, born May 17, 1958.

***

38.   Xoe Webb was born October 28, 1900; married June 11, 1925, to Louis Albert Schrickram, born February 10, 1900, son of Louis A. Schrickram and

233

Minnie Massey. They lived in Santa Barbara, California, and their children were as follows:[50]

a. Horace John Schrickram, born December 30, 1926; married August 4, 1952, to Jean Bynum, born July 16, 1931, daughter of Thomas William Bynum and Doris Ladena Ridley; lived in Dayton, Ohio; child:
(1) Scott Lowell Schrickram, born September 23, 1953.
b. Arthur Louis Schrickram, born February 17, 1929; married June 27, 1954, to Earlene Gittrick, born September 7, 1929, daughter of Henry H. Gittrick and Elsa Lane McFadden; lived in Lompoc, California; children:
(1) Ann Patricia Schrickram, born April 13, 1955.
(2) Karen Louis Schrickram, born January 13, 1960.
(3) Charles Alan Schrickram, born March 26, 1961.
c. Rita Marie Schrickram, born October 10, 1931; married December 24, 1950, to Curtis Edmund Bray, born December 30, 1931, son of Curtis B. Bray and Maxine Lamont Gerdes; lived in Lubbock, Texas; children:
(1) Katherine Marie Bray, born February 10, 1952.
(2) Jeffrey Bruce Bray, born July 19, 1953.
(3) Thomas Edmund Bray, born April 6, 1956.
d. Martha Xoe Schrickram, born March 12, 1936; married July 16, 1955, to Monte Sheppard, born November 1, 1934; lived in Vernon, Texas.

***

32.   William Penn Stubblefield was born March 18, 1864, and died July 27, 1932, in Premont, Texas; married May 28, 1882, to Octavia Lavina Henbest, born December 27, 1864, and died September 27, 1937, in Tipton, Oklahoma, daughter of Albert Henbest and Octavia Matthews. Their children were as follows:[51]

a. Alfred Charles Stubblefield, born March 9, 1883; died December 26, 1953, in Sacramento, California; married (1) June 26, 1905, to Lottie Bell Graham, born July 8, 1880; died July 27, 1927; (2) October 5, 1929, to Pearl Scotten; child (by first marriage):
(1) Glenn Elmo Stubblefield, born February 1, 1908; married 1940 to Lillian Nevada Hall, born October 7, 1911; dsp; lived in Wichita, Kansas.
b. Oscar Frank Stubblefield, born December 27, 1884; died May 12, 1962, in Burlingame, California; married March 3, 1907, to Emma Livingston; children:
(1) George Stubblefield, born 1908.
(2) Jessie Stubblefield, born June 19, 1910; married April 4, 1931, to Frank Beveridge, who died May 17, 1960; dsp; lived in Chicago, Illinois.
c. Nora Stubblefield, born February 23, 1886; married April 3, 1913, to Thomas Powell Jackson, born February 15, 1881; died March 11, 1951; children:
(1) W. Stanley Jackson, born November 7, 1914; married December 14, 1942, to Marie Lingle, born October 4, 1917, daughter of Lee Anthony Lingle and Frances Dozier; lived in San Antonio, Texas; children:
(a) Karen Marie Jackson, born May 9, 1946.
(b) William Stanley Jackson, born January 10, 1949.
(c) Thomas Lingle Jackson, born December 27, 1951.
(2) Tom Webb Jackson, born 1917; dsp November 26, 1945.
d. John O. Stubblefield, born August 12, 1888; dsp August 25, 1962, in Dallas, Texas; married (1) September 20, 1908, to Ollie Wiley, born April 19, 1880; (2) May 13, 1946, to Maud M. Harrison, born October 24, 1898.

234

39.   e. Alva Blanch Stubblefield, born January 28, 1891.
40.   f. Beulah Stubblefield, born May 30, 1893.
      g. Hazel Mae Stubblefield, born May 12, 1897; married October 11, 1913,
          to George M. Shaw, born August 25, 1896; died August 2, 1925; lived
          in Richmond, California; children:
          (1) Pearl L. Shaw, born December 27, 1915; married (1) November 16,
               1931, to Ernest T. Whitaker, born March 1, 1913; died February,
               1958; child:
               (a) Jimmie Whitaker, born May 2, 1934; married April, 1952, to
                    Janet Nona Barker, born March 29, 1935; children:
                    /1/ Galor Jo Whitaker, born July 10, 1954.
                    /2/ Karen L. Whitaker, born May 22, 1956.
          (2) Don Marley Shaw, born March 9, 1921; married August 5, 1945, to
               Aileen Doty, born August 21, 1923; lived in Grand Prairie, Texas;
               child:
               (a) Alan Marley Shaw, born November 27, 1947.
          (3) Alice Faye Shaw, born December 14, 1923; married September 15,
               1944, to Neil Joyce Horstman, born April 24, 1923; lived in Rich-
               mond, California; child:
               (a) Larry N. Horstman, born May 21, 1947.
41.   h. Norris James Stubblefield, born January 1, 1900.
      i. Don Tex Stubblefield, born November 15, 1902; married (1) Jay Shrop-
          shire (2) Isabel Saloza Garcia; dsp; lived in Belen, New Mexico.
      j. King Albert Stubblefield, born May 22, 1905; married November 23,
          1924, to Beatrice Elliott; lived in Phoenix, Arizona; child:
          (1) Keith Allen Stubblefield, born October 29, 1931; married June
               20, 1959, to Ramona Marie Van Sant, born April 19, 1935, daugh-
               ter of Clifford Van Sant and Leola Cairiens; lived in Sacramento,
               California.
42.   k. Robert Cecil Stubblefield, born May 7, 1907.

                                        ***

39.   Alva Blanch Stubblefield was born January 28, 1891; married July 3,
      1908, to Elza Nash, born August 31, 1889; died April 30, 1946; their chil-
      dren were as follows:52

      a. Marvin Nash, born May 19, 1909; married November 22, 1935, to Vera
          Mae Jackson, born April 27, 1905; lived in El Paso, Texas; child:
          (1) Mary Jean Nash, born November 1, 1936.
      b. Mable Nash, born July 27, 1911; married October 3, 1931, to Virgil
          Adams, born May 31, 1903, son of Isaac Adams and Fannie Palmer; lived
          in Forgan, Oklahoma; children:
          (1) Clinton Adams, born November 11, 1934; dsp February 19, 1936.
          (2) Barbara Ann Adams, born March 31, 1937; married August 26, 1955,
               to Everett Clapp, born January 11, 1937; lived in Forgan, Okla-
               homa; children:
               (a) Rodney Ray Clapp, born July 30, 1957.
               (b) Kary Don Clapp, born June 13, 1959.
      c. Cheston A. Nash, born July 12, 1914; married August 23, 1942, to
          Gladys Brooks, born July 13, 1914, daughter of Samuel Brooks and Ida
          Belle Glossup; lived in Oklahoma City, Oklahoma; child:
          (1) Reford Nash, born June 17, 1944.
      d. Eva Nash, born November 1, 1922; married May 24, 1940, to Alex Satter-
          white, born April 15, 1917, son of T. B. Satterwhite and Beulah Jane
          Berry; lived in Forgan, Oklahoma; children:
          (1) Patricia Ann Satterwhite, born June 28, 1942; married February
               19, 1960, to Ardyce Sanders, born October 14, 1939; lived in
               Electra, Texas; child:

                                        235

        (a) Terri Charles Sanders, born March 16, 1961.
    (2) Joe Donald Satterwhite, born April 15, 1946.
  e. Veta C. Nash, born February 8, 1924; married June 10, 1943, to Edward
      Minderman, born December 24, 1916; lived in Oklahoma City, Oklahoma;
      children:
    (1) Carol Ann Minderman, born October 21, 1948.
    (2) Kenneth Ray Minderman, born August 17, 1953; dsp February 9, 1955.

                                    ***

40.   Beulah Stubblefield was born May 30, 1893, and died October 22, 1930,
    in Clovis, New Mexico; married February 14, 1908, to Walter William Smith,
    born November 6, 1887, died December 11, 1947; their children were as
    follows:[53]

  a. Jesse Lee Smith, born June 30, 1909; married June 1, 1939, to Lucille
      Jones, born April 11, 1922; lived in Capitan, New Mexico; children:
    (1) Jo Lee Smith, born April 3, 1942.
    (2) Judith Irene Smith, born October 24, 1944; married June 3, 1962,
         to Jimmie Kerr.
    (3) Joy Kay Smith, born March 16, 1948.
  b. Albert Smith, born March 2, 1911; dsp March 18, 1911.
  c. Beatrice Omiga Smith, born May 17, 1912; married February 28, 1932,
      to John Wesley Stephens, born February 11, 1910; lived in Clovis, New
      Mexico; children:
    (1) Beulah Ann Stephens, born December 11, 1932.
    (2) Cordie Mae Stephens, born January 25, 1934.
    (3) Peggy Patricia Stephens, born May 19, 1935.
    (4) William Hale Stephens, born June 3, 1937.
    (5) Wesley Wayne Stephens, born November 9, 1947.
  d. Viola Agatha Smith, born January 8, 1914; married March 2, 1932, to
      Walter Rowe Cherry, born June 30, 1907; lived in Clovis, New Mexico;
      children:
    (1) Cleijo Josephine Cherry, born June 19, 1933.
    (2) Della Marie Cherry, born January 11, 1935.
    (3) Jesse Ross Cherry, born November 20, 1936.
    (4) Clare Jean Cherry, born March 29, 1939.
  e. Alfred Charles Smith, born November 29, 1915; married Irene Cantrell,
      born November 5, 1920; lived in Amarillo, Texas; children:
    (1) Terry Clarence Smith, born November 19, 1933.
    (2) Joseph Daniel Smith, born September 12, 1948.
  f. Walter William Smith, born October 16, 1917; married August 5, 1958,
      to Mrs. Betty Louise (Jennings) Hurt; lived in Salinas, California.
  g. Francise Christine Smith, born January 4, 1921; married May 30, 1942,
      to Horace Guy McLean, born February 23, 1923; lived in Bovina, Texas;
      children:
    (1) Betty Jo McLean, born February 5, 1944; married September 11,
         1960, to Douglas McLaughlin; child:
        (a) Brian Patrick McLaughlan, born April 8, 1961.
    (2) Kristina McLean, born April 22, 1947.
    (3) John Walter McLean, born January 22, 1953.
  h. Lorena Alice Smith, born March 29, 1923; married December 25, 1937,
      to Joe Felty, born August 5, 1918; lived in Clovis, New Mexico; chil-
      dren:
    (1) Betty Ruth Felty, born July 31, 1939; married May 3, 1958, to
         James A. Brady, born February 19, 1937.
    (2) Yvonne Josephine Felty, born November 10, 1940; married January
         30, 1960, to John C. Edwards; child:

                                    236

(a) John C. Edwards, born September 12, 1960.
(3) Ida Lou Felty, born June 3, 1942; married August 20, 1960, to
     Herschell Bowser.
i. Benjamin Franklin Smith, born March 27, 1925; married August 14, 1945,
    to Mary Bell Jones, born August 27, 1929; lived in Clovis, New Mexico;
    children:
    (1) Donna Sue Smith, born September 2, 1947.
    (2) Danny William Smith, born April 8, 1952.
j. Vina Luetta Smith, born November 3, 1929; married December 6, 1944,
    to Roy Dee Wise, born July 17, 1925; lived in Belen, New Mexico; chil-
    dren:
    (1) Freda Nell Wise, born March 30, 1946.
    (2) Barbara Ann Wise, born March 20, 1948.
    (3) Peggy Lee Wise, born February 10, 1950.
    (4) Roy Dee Wise, born June 3, 1953.

                              ***

41.   Norris James Stubblefield was born January 1, 1900; married September
     21, 1919, to Dessie Mae Clark, born December 28, 1900, daughter of John
     Columbus Clark and Emma Mae Adcock. They lived in Dumas, Texas, and their
     children were as follows:[54]

     a. Patricia Fay Stubblefield, born August 8, 1924; married May 31, 1941,
         to Alden Royce Fowler, born May 28, 1920; lived in Midland, Texas;
         children:
         (1) Barbara K. Fowler, born May 1, 1942.
         (2) Diana Dale Fowler, born October 18, 1946.
         (3) Donald Royce Fowler, born August 2, 1953.
         (4) Steve Fowler, born January 10, 1957.
     b. James Earl Stubblefield, born July 25, 1928; married December 16, 1955,
         to Guadalupe Terragas, born February 8, 1930, daughter of Miguel Ter-
         ragas and Eloisa Taboda; lived in Amarillo, Texas; child:
         (1) James Earl Stubblefield, born September 18, 1956.

                              ***

42.   Robert Cecil Stubblefield was born May 7, 1907; married September 7,
     1930, to Lillian Empson, born August 6, 1908, daughter of George J. Empson
     and Lillian Drucker. They lived in Minneapolis, Minnesota, and their
     children were as follows:[55]

     a. Richard Dave Stubblefield, born April 4, 1932; married September 25,
         1954, to Colleen Barry, born September 6, 1932; lived in Arvada, Colo-
         rado; children:
         (1) Denise Stubblefield, born August 30, 1955.
         (2) Barry Stubblefield, born August 17, 1956.
         (3) Ricky Stubblefield, born September 2, 1957.
         (4) Gregory Stubblefield, born April 9, 1959.
     b. Jerry Jean Stubblefield, born October 16, 1936; married December 7,
         1955, to William Cook, born August 21, 1934; lived in St Louis Park,
         Minnesota; children:
         (1) Kimberly Cook, born September 7, 1956.
         (2) Lisa Cook, born September 7, 1958.

                              ***

33.   Albert George Stubblefield was born December 10, 1868, and died Sep-

                              237

tember 5, 1941, in Pueblo, Colorado; married August 23, 1905, to Mabel
Louise Harris, born January 1, 1879; died September 27, 1929; their children were as follows:[56]

a. Ruth Mabel Stubblefield, born June 12, 1906; married June 1, 1934,
    to Hubert Ambrose Buchanan, born August 5, 1905, son of Fulton Wylie
    Buchanan and Josephine Smith; dsp; lived in Santa Clara, California.
b. Evelyn Jane Stubblefield, born October 21, 1909; married May 7, 1933,
    to Dr. Ed. E. Cass, born August 3, 1906; lived in Denver, Colorado;
    children:
    (1) Mary Louise Cass, born April 13, 1935; married April 13, 1958,
         to Robert W. Tice, born March 13, 1928, son of Ralph Jesse Tice
         and Vivian Marie Asplund; lived in Alamosa, Colorado; children:
         (a) Neil William Tice, born February 10, 1959.
         (b) Roberta Susan Tice, born May 9, 1960.
    (2) William G. Cass, born July 21, 1936; married June 21, 1959, to
         Margaret Elaine Schlichtmeir, born October 21, 1935, daughter of
         Paul Schlichtmeir and Ruth Evelyn Marshall; lived in Long Beach,
         California; children:
         (a) Jeffrey William Cass, born February 21, 1961.
         (b) Jennifer Lynn Cass, born April 12, 1963.
c. Jean Alberta Stubblefield, born September 25, 1911; married January
    20, 1934, to Robert Emmett Barnard, born May 8, 1904, son of Charles
    Letcher Barnard and Ellen Melinda Mooney; children:
    (1) Lee Ann Barnard, born August 5, 1936; married September 7, 1957,
         to Howard Duane Funk, born April 11, 1933, son of Albert Ernest
         Funk and Lillian Mae Johnson; lived in Fort Collins, Colorado;
         children:
         (a) Kristin Carol Funk, born August 6, 1958.
         (b) Melissa Ann Funk, born September 5, 1960.
    (2) Jean Kathleen Barnard, born March 3, 1939; married June 23, 1962,
         to Sherwyn Maurice Heckt; lived in Boulder, Colorado.
    (3) Judith Ellen Barnard, born January 9, 1941.
d. Albert George Stubblefield, born July 10, 1914; married May 5, 1944,
    to Sally Ann Anthony, born March 8, 1922, daughter of David Anthony
    and Lucile Barfield; lived in Seattle, Washington; children:
    (1) Scott E. Stubblefield, born February 20, 1951.
    (2) Susan L. Stubblefield, born January 19, 1956.
e. Marjorie Ann Stubblefield, born September 26, 1922; married 1942 to
    Jack Raymond Dunlap, born December 31, 1921; children:
    (1) Beth Ann Dunlap, born February 26, 1943.
    (2) Jerry Lynn Dunlap, born September 17, 1944.
    (3) Nancy Jane Dunlap, born November 9, 1946.
    (4) Jackie Ruth Dunlap, born May 18, 1951.
    (5) Jean Louise Dunlap, born April 18, 1953.

***

8.   Stephen Stubblefield was born January 6, 1789, in Hawkins County,
Tennessee, and married July 30, 1808, in Grainger County, Tennessee, to
Elizabeth Moore, died c1862. He served in the War of 1812 and received
bounty land for his services; moved to Rusk County, Texas, about 1844,
and to Houston County, Texas, about 1856; he died there on July 14, 1860.
His children, probably among others, were as follows:[57]

43. a. William H. Stubblefield, born c1812.
    b. Anderson Stubblefield, born c1815; died c1855; married Martha Eliza-
        beth _____; children:
        (1) Julius Mc. Stubblefield, born c1840.
        (2) Mary E. Stubblefield, born c1842; dsp.

    (3) Thomas J. Stubblefield, born c1846.
    (4) James Mark Stubblefield, born c1848.
    (5) Martha Ann Stubblefield, born c1849; dsp.
    (6) Marcena Stubblefield, born c1851.
    (7) Jethro Elisha Stubblefield, born c1853.
c. Dixon Stubblefield, born c1819; married October 3, 1847, Eliza Webb.
d. Robert Loxley Stubblefield, born c1821; lived in Houston County, Texas,
    in 1880; married Susan A. _____ ; children:
    (1) Joel Stubblefield, born c1846.
    (2) Stephen A. Stubblefield, born c1848.
    (3) Wyatt Stubblefield, born c1850.
    (4) Mary Stubblefield, born c1853.
    (5) Clark C. Stubblefield, born c1859.
    (6) Margaret Stubblefield, born c1866.
e. Wilson M. Stubblefield, born c1825; died c1863; married November 19,
    1850, Lucy Ann Murchison; children:
    (a) D. W. Stubblefield, born c1854.
    (b) Walter Stubblefield, born c1857.
    (c) M. Elizabeth Stubblefield, born c1859.
    (d) M. J. Stubblefield, born c1862.
f. Nancy Stubblefield, born c1827; dsp.
g. Sarah Stubblefield, born c1829; married June 9, 1848, James V. Holland.
h. Thomas J. Stubblefield, born c1831; married Lucy Jane _____ ; lived in
    Houston County, Texas, in 1880; children (among others):
    (a) Fannie Stubblefield, born c1864.
    (b) Eunice Stubblefield, born c1874.
    (c) Georgia Stubblefield, born c1876.
i. Stephen Stubblefield, born c1833; dsp.

***

43.   William H. Stubblefield was born about 1812 in Grainger County, Ten-
    nessee, and died about 1866 in Trinity County, Texas; married (1) August
    6, 1831, in Davidson County, Tennessee, to Melissa Martin, died January
    22, 1851; (2) Basel _____ . His children were as follows:[58]

a. John H. Stubblefield, born c1833; married Sarah _____ ; lived in Hous-
    ton County, Texas, in 1860.
b. Betsy Ann Stubblefield, born c1836.
c. Wyatt M. Stubblefield, born c1838; married Eliza A. _____ ; lived in
    Houston County, Texas, in 1880; children (among others):
    (1) William H. Stubblefield, born c1868.
    (2) Stephen R. Stubblefield, born c1870; lived in Groveton, Texas.
    (3) Ida Stubblefield, born c1877.
    (4) Irene Stubblefield, born c1879.
d. Martha Jane Stubblefield, born c1839.
e. Polly Ann Stubblefield, born c1841; married Cushman Johnston; lived
    in Trinity County, Texas; children (among others):
    (1) Theodosia Johnston, born c1861; married John Bowman.
    (2) Lilla Johnston, born c1868.
    (3) Wilson Johnston, born c1869.
    (4) Udora Johnston, born c1870.
    (5) Wyatt Johnston, born c1872.
    (6) William Johnston, born c1874.
    (7) John Johnston, born c1876.
    (8) Sevoya Johnston, born c1878.
f. Samuel Stubblefield, born c1842; lived in Nacogdoches, Texas.
g. Betsy Jane Stubblefield, born c1844.
h. Thomas Stubblefield, born c1845; married Martha _____ ; lived in Croc-
    kett, Texas; children (among others):

239

        (1) Martha J. Stubblefield, born c1870.
        (2) James A. Stubblefield, born c1872.
        (3) Margaret L. Stubblefield, born c1874.
        (4) Thomas M. Stubblefield, born c1876.
        (5) Henry Stubblefield, born c1879.
    i. Stephen Stubblefield, born c1846.
    j. Willie T. Stubblefield, born c1848; married Jack Provost.
44. k. William Robert Stubblefield, born January 22, 1851.
    (by second marriage):
    l. N. O. Stubblefield, born c1852.
    m. Matilda Stubblefield, born c1855.

                            ***

44.   William Robert Stubblefield was born January 22, 1851, in Rusk County,
    Texas, and died February 13, 1937, in Lufkin, Texas; married January 11,
    1877, in Trinity County, Texas, to Terry Mary Ann Josephine Thompson, born
    February 13, 1861, in Covington County, Mississippi; died September 22,
    1935, daughter of Arthur James Thompson and Elizabeth Williams. Their
    children were as follows:[59]

    a. Minnie Lavolya Stubblefield, born October 31, 1878; died January 21,
        1934; married Nathan Dawson Wright; children:
        (1) Granville Wright.
        (2) Jessie Louise Wright married Leland T. Jordan; lived in Lufkin,
             Texas.
    b. William Arthur Stubblefield, born April 8, 1881; dsp September 18,
        1882.
    c. Dora Elen Stubblefield, born May 24, 1883; married W. Thomas Hutson;
        children:
        (1) Alpha Jo Hutson.
        (2) Kimble P. Hutson.
        (3) Robert Hutson.
        (4) Minnie Evelyn Hutson.
    d. Lula Bell Stubblefield, born September 22, 1885; dsp August 1, 1889.
    e. Kimmey Stubblefield, born March 2, 1888; dsp March 6, 1890.
    f. Rosa Ellen Stubblefield, born February 18, 1890; died May 20, 1966;
        married Fauchie B. Thompson; child:
        (1) Helen Marie Thompson.
    g. John Ollie Stubblefield, born January 19, 1892; died September 24, 1967;
        married Cleo Allbritton; children:
        (1) Roy Stubblefield.
        (2) Hubert Stubblefield.
        (3) Marie Stubblefield.
        (4) Jessie Nell Stubblefield.
    h. Sarah Fleater Stubblefield, born April 17, 1894; married (1) Mack C.
        Anderson, died 1935; (2) W. S. Moody, died 1949; children (all by first
        marriage):
        (1) Polly Anderson.
        (2) Elwood Anderson.
        (3) Mary L. Anderson.
        (4) Billy M. Anderson.
    I. Berta Lee Stubblefield, born September 21, 1898; married Robert L.
        Stanaland; children:
        (1) Irving Dawson Stanaland.
        (2) Mary Frances Stanaland.
        (3) Betty Jean Stanaland.
    j. Horace Gandy Stubblefield, born February 5, 1901; married Vivian Canon;
        children:

       (1) Horace Gandy Stubblefield.
       (2) Charles Ray Stubblefield.
    k. Dewey Praiter Stubblefield, born May 10, 1904; married (1) Bertie
        _____; (2) Gertrude _____, died 1965; dsp.

***

3.   Richard Stubblefield was born in 1732 in Spotsylvania County, Virginia, and moved to Amelia (now Prince Edward) County, Virginia, in 1748; in 1754 he received a land grant in Halifax County, Virginia, but never resided there. In August, 1765, he received land in Orange (now Rockingham) County, North Carolina, from Robert Stubblefield, and on March 1, 1780, he received a 71 acre grant on the north side of Hogan's Creek from the state of North Carolina. He died in 1817 in Rockingham County, North Carolina; he married Susannah Carter, daughter of Theodorick Carter; their children were as follows:[60]

    a. Theodorick Stubblefield, born c1757; married March 28, 1779, Frances Barton.
    b. Lucy Stubblefield, born November 17, 1759; died April 16, 1848, in White County, Illinois; married January, 1779, to Robert Harris, who died June 9, 1806; children:
       (1) Nancy Harris married _____ Trousdale.
       (2) Robert Harris.
       (3) Richard Harris.
       (4) Susanna Harris married _____ Taylor.
       (5) Frances Harris married _____ Taylor.
       (6) Sarah Harris married _____ Trousdale.
    c. Nancy Stubblefield married William Bethel.

45. d. Richard Stubblefield, born February 20, 1763.
    e. Carter Stubblefield died 1829 in Rockingham County, North Carolina; married Sarah Mills; children:[61]
       (1) Martha Stubblefield married Joseph Holderby.
       (2) Sarah Stubblefield.
       (3) Peyton Terry Stubblefield, born October 9, 1809; married (1) November 1, 1832, Mary Permelia Nunnally, born May 18, 1814; (2) February 8, 1872, Mary Venable; children (all by first marriage):
         (a) Sarah M. Stubblefield, born September 8, 1833.
         (b) James C. Stubblefield, born October 29, 1835.
         (c) William L. Stubblefield, born December 6, 1837; died February 8, 1917; married Lucy Samuel Green Thompson; children:
           /1/ Lee Stubblefield, died young.
           /2/ Mary Mavis Stubblefield.
           /3/ Kelly Stubblefield.
           /4/ Roy Irvin Stubblefield.
           /5/ Lou Stubblefield, died young.
           /6/ Annie Stubblefield.
           /7/ E. Page Stubblefield lived in Bloomington, Texas.
           /8/ Willie Stubblefield.
         (d) Rufus Watson Stubblefield, born January 17, 1841.
         (e) Victoria Ann Stubblefield, born December 7, 1842.
         (f) Dandridge Augustine Stubblefield, born October 9, 1844.
         (g) Louisa Elvira Stubblefield, born July 28, 1846.
         (h) Mary Permelia Stubblefield, born June 28, 1848.
         (i) Peyton Madison Stubblefield, born May 19, 1850.
         (j) Richard Jephtha Stubblefield, born February 21, 1852.
         (k) David A. W. Stubblefield, born May 22, 1854.
         (l) Edwin Henry Stubblefield, born February 4, 1857.
       (4) William Stubblefield.

241

f. Jeremiah Stubblefield lived in Sumner County, Tennessee, in 1820.
g. Robert Stubblefield.
h. Elizabeth Stubblefield married _____ Mitchell.
i. Nathan Stubblefield, born c1773; died c1800; married November 6, 1794, Elizabeth Todd; children:
   (1) Susanna Stubblefield, born c1796.
   (2) Nancy Stubblefield, born c1798.

***

45.   Richard Stubblefield was born February 20, 1763, in Orange (now Rockingham) County, North Carolina, and died in 1847 in Rockingham County, North Carolina; married Elizabeth Coleman; children:[62]

a. Tilman I. Stubblefield.
b. Robert C. Stubblefield married December 21, 1818, Mildred Walker; lived in Calloway County, Kentucky.
c. Susanna Stubblefield married May 26, 1817, Reason Waters; lived in Calloway County, Kentucky.
d. Martha Stubblefield married _____ Waters.
e. Beverley B. Stubblefield married Rebecca Willson; lived in New Concord, Kentucky.
f. William L. Stubblefield.
g. Theodorick Stubblefield.
h. Sarah Stubblefield married _____ Moore.
i. Elizabeth Stubblefield married _____ Harris.
j. Richard Carter Stubblefield, born March 6, 1806; died 1868; married June 14, 1832, Sarah Elizabeth Rice, died 1894; lived in Fulton, Kentucky.

***

4.   Thomas Stubblefield was born about 1746 in Spotslvania County, Virginia; married Nancy _____; in May, 1769, he was given land in Orange County, North Carolina, by Robert Stubblefield; he sold the land, then in Caswell County, North Carolina, to John Johnson in October, 1775, after moving to Surry (now Wilkes) County, North Carolina. On March 3, 1779, he received 200 acres on the north side of the Yadkin River from the state of North Carolina, and in 1780 he received 118 acres adjoining Thomas Parks from the state; on August 30, 1794, he bought 111 acres adjoining George Stubblefield, all in Wilkes County, North Carolina. On November 30, 1795, he sold the 118 acre tract for £100 and the 200 acre tract for £500, both to Benjamin Jones, and on August 23, 1798, he sold the 111 acre tract to Benjamin Jones for £50. He then moved to Sumner County, Tennessee, where he died about 1825; his will divided his property among the following children:[63]

a. Armstreet Stubblefield.
b. George Stubblefield.
c. Woodruff Stubblefield.
d. Frances Stubblefield married Edward Bradley.
e. Tilman Stubblefield.
f. Elizabeth Stubblefield married 1803 William Bradshaw.
g. Nancy Wand Stubblefield married _____ Walton.
h. Garrison Stubblefield.

***

REFERENCES

[1] Minutes of the Council and General Court, Virginia Quit Rent Rolls of 1704, Virginia Land Grants, Book 7, p. 637, State Archives, Richmond, Virginia.

[2] Virginia Quit Rent Rolls of 1704, baptismal record of son John, 1709, Gloucester County, Virginia.

[3] Spotsylvania County, Virginia, Wills; records belonging to John S. Stubblefield; George, Thomas, and Edward Stubblefield called each other "brother" in their wills.

[4] Spotsylvania County, Virginia, Deeds; Lunenburg County, Virginia, tithe lists, 1764.

[5-6] Culpeper County, Virginia, Wills; records belonging to John S. Stubblefield.

[7] Minutes of the Council and General Court; Spotsylvania County, Virginia, Deed Books B, C, and D.

[8] Amelia County, Virginia, tax lists, 1748-53; Prince Edward County, Virginia, Order Book 1, p. 63.

[9] Orange County, North Carolina, Minutes of the Court of Pleas and Quarter Sessions, Bk. 69, p. 138, Register of Deeds, 1752-93.

[10] Wilkes County, North Carolina, Deeds A1, 140, 538.

[11] Amelia County, Virginia, tax lists, 1748-53; Prince Edward County, Virginia, Order Book 1, p. 63; Orange County, North Carolina, Minutes of the Court of Pleas and Quarter Sessions, Bk. 2, p. 142; North Carolina Land Grants, State Land Office, Raleigh, North Carolina; Guilford County, North Carolina, Deed Bk. 1, pp. 360, 480; Wilkes County, North Carolina, Sales Bk. 1, p. 105.

[12] Amelia County, Virginia, tax lists, 1748-53, Deed Bk. 8, p. 800; Prince Edward County, Virginia, Order Bk. 1, p. 63.

[13] Prince Edward County, Virginia, Order Bk. 1, p. 63; Amelia County, Virginia, tax lists, 1748-53; Orange County, North Carolina, Register of Deeds, 1752-93; Bible record of Abraham Womack, D. A. R. Library, Washington, D. C.

[14] Caswell County, North Carolina, Wills, Marriages; records belonging to John S. Stubblefield.

[15] Amelia County, Virginia, tax lists, 1748-53; Prince Edward County, Virginia, Order Bk. 1, p. 391; Halifax County, Virginia, Order Bk. 3, pp. 325, 435, Bk. 7, p. 540, Bk. 5, p. 134, Bk. 13, p. 43, Deed Bk. 5, p. 358, Bk. 15, p. 138; Bible records belonging (1960) to Mrs. Walter A. George.

[16] Bible record belonging (1933) to Mrs. Duncan Eve; Halifax County, Virginia, Order Bk. 3, p. 325, Deed Bk. 9, p. 43, Bk. 12, p. 30.

[17] Sullivan County, Tennessee, Deed Bk. 2, pp. 389, 466, 477, 487; North Carolina Land Grant Bk. 64. p. 139, Bk. 73, p. 46, Bk. 78, p. 342, Bk. 82, p. 153.

[18] Original petition, North Carolina State Archives; Hawkins County, Tennessee, Deed Bk. 2, p. 248, Bk. 4, p. 181, Bk. 3, p. 447.

[19] Hawkins County, Tennessee, Deed Bk. 3, p. 241, Bk. 7, p. 108, Will Bk. 1, p. 434; Bible record belonging (1933) to Mrs. Duncan Eve.

[20] Hawkins County, Tennessee, Wills; Bible record belonging (1933) to Mrs. Duncan Eve.

[21] Records belonging to Mrs. Roy Green Giles.

[22] Records belonging to Mrs. Frank Ray Black.

[23-30] Records belonging to Arthur Weir Crouch.

[31-32] Records belonging to C. J. Sain.

[33-40] Records belonging to Mrs. Roy Green Giles.

[41] Records belonging to Mrs. Duncan Eve.

[42-56]Records belonging to Park Leroy Stubblefield.

[57-59]Records belonging to Mrs. Leland T. Jordan.

[60]Spotsylvania County, Virginia, Deeds; Amelia County, Virginia, tax lists, 1748-53; Halifax County, Virginia, Survey Book; Prince Edward County, Virginia, Order Bk. 1, p. 63; Orange County, North Carolina, Register of Deeds, 1752-93; Guilford County, North Carolina, Deed Bk. 2, p. 323; Rockingham County, North Carolina, Wills.

[61]Records belonging to Miss Lucy Marbury.

[62]Records belonging to Forrest W. Stubblefield.

[63]Orange County, North Carolina, Register of Deeds, 1752-93; Caswell County, North Carolina, Deeds; Wilkes County, North Carolina, Deeds A1, 19, 331, G&H, 23; Sumner County, Tennessee, Wills.

***

TRAIL of Montgomery County, Maryland

Charles Trail was probably born about 1685; he lived in Frederick (now Montgomery) County, Maryland, when he made his will on June 28, 1763, leaving his property to his wife Susanna and his children; the estate was probated on August 1, 1763. His children were as follows:[1]

    a. Thomas Trail.
1. b. James Trail, born c1715.
2. c. David Trail, born c1720.
    d. Charles Trail; probably the person of that name who lived in Amherst County, Virginia, in 1783.
    e. Jane Trail.

***

1.   James Trail was born about 1715 and lived in Prince Georges County, Maryland, in 1744, when he signed a petition to divide the county. On November 10, 1778, he bought 16½ acres, part of "Pleasant Valley" and part of "Pleasant Fields," from William Benson for £33; on October 24, 1788, he agreed to a settlement of the boundary of "Father's Good Will." On February 18, 1792, he bought 17¼ acres, part of "Resurvey on Mill Tract," from Henry Brooke for five shillings, and on April 23, 1792, he sold part of "Resurvey of the Younger Brother," conveyed to him by Joseph West, Sr., on October 1, 1765, to Henry Brooke for five shillings. On February 25, 1793, he sold 4½ acres, part of "Fertile Meadow," to John Yost for £14.18.4.[2]

James Trail made his will on March 11, 1783, leaving his property to his wife Rachel and his children; he died May 1, 1799, and his widow died on August 26, 1799. His estate was probated on March 18, 1800, after adjustments in land boundaries had been settled by his heirs; in addition to the land, the estate was valued at $1033.02. The children of James and Rachel Trail were as follows:[3]

    a. William Trail, born c1740; died c1779 in Montgomery County, Maryland; married Frances Northcroft; children:[4]
        (1) Elizabeth Trail, born June 3, 1765.
        (2) James Trail.
        (3) William Trail.
        (4) Edward Trail.
        (5) Nathan Trail.
3. b. Eleanor Trail, born c1742.
4. c. Jean Trail, born c1744.
    d. Sarah Trail, born c1746; married _____ Buxton.
5. e. James Trail, born c1748.
    f. Cassandra Trail, born c1750; married Zadok Ford; lived in Spartanburg County, South Carolina.
    g. Rachel Trail, born c1752; married _____ Cybert.
    h. Archibald Trail, born c1755; died c1814 in Montgomery County, Maryland; married Monica _____; children:[5]
        (1) Henry Trail, born c1795.
        (2) Elizabeth Trail, born c1797.
        (3) Ann Trail, born c1800.
        (4) David Trail, born c1803.
        (5) Archibald Trail, born c1805.
    i. Margery Trail, born March 20, 1757; married May 9, 1780, Walter Fryer,

born June 11, 1760; died April 20, 1821, in Pendleton County, Kentucky; children:[6]
(1) Richard Fryer, died young.
(2) James Fryer.
(3) Walter Fryer, born January 20, 1785; married Mary Payne Sharpe.
(4) William Fryer, born c1788; married Eliza Barker.
(5) Margery Fryer married James Kirby.
(6) David Fryer.
(7) Lloyd Fryer.
(8) Horace Fryer, born November 4, 1798.
(9) Sarah Fryer.
j. Osborn Trail, born c1759; died 1814 in Campbell County, Kentucky; married October 9, 1781, Frances Merrill Fryer; children (among others):[7]
(1) Wesley Trail, born May 9, 1799.
(2) William Tomson Trail, born September 7, 1800.
(3) Airy Trail, born March 31, 1803.
(4) Kinsey Trail, born February 5, 1806.

***

3.   Eleanor Trail was born about 1742 and married (1) about 1760, _____ Nicholls, who died about 1778; (2) about 1780, James Lee; they moved to Spartanburg County, South Carolina, where in October, 1786, James Lee served as administrator of George Nicholls. On March 18, 1789, James Lee bought the 137½ acres where he then lived from Thomas Clary for ₤50; on December 20, 1803, he and his wife Eleanor sold 150 acres on the South Fork of Mitchell's Creek to Amos Lee of Union District, South Carolina, for $400.00. On September 4 1805, James and Eleanor Lee gave Solomon West power of attorney to receive their share of the estate of James Trail. On December 10, 1807, after the death of his wife, James Lee sold 92½ acres on Dutchman's Creek to Nancy, wife of Abraham Poole. James Lee was a member of Friendship Baptist Church in Spartanburg County.[8]

While there is no proof, the children of Eleanor Trail Nicholls Lee (all by her first marriage) were probably, among others, as follows:[9]

a. George Nicholls, born c1762; dsp 1786 in Spartanburg County, South Carolina; received a posthumous grant of 50 acres on Tyger River.
b. Margery Nicholls, born c1768; married c1788 Jehu McPherson (see p.   93).
c. Nancy Nicholls married Abraham Poole, who in 1806 sold 113 acres on Enoree River to Matthew Crouch; children (among others):
(1) John Poole.
(2) Cassandra Poole.
(3) Margaret Poole.
d. Eleanor Nicholls.
6. e. Benjamin Nicholls, born c1775.

***

6.   Benjamin Nicholls was born about 1775 in Frederick (now Montgomery) County, Maryland, and moved to Spartanburg County, South Carolina, as a child. On August 30, 1788, he bought 33 acres on Sugar Creek from William and Mima Hamby, and on August 20, 1798, he sold 73 acres on Sugar Creek to Isaac Bogan. On November 6, 1800, he bought 70½ acres on the south side of Dutchman's Creek from Thomas Bearden for $151.00, which he sold to Samuel Morrow for $200.00 on February 12, 1806; he bought another 100 acres in the same area for $210.00, which he sold back to Bearden for the same price on December 24, 1805. Arthur Faulkner gave him 110 acres on Cain Creek on April 23, 1808, and he bought and sold other tracts later.[10]

246

Benjamin Nicholls married about 1800 Ann Howard, who was born in Maryland about 1781 and died in Spartanburg County, South Carolina, on January 7, 1852, the daughter of Thomas Howard. Nicholls evidently made a trip to Montgomery County, Maryland, where on December 13, 1810, he sold his mother's, Jean West's, and Cassandra Ford's interest in "Fertile Meadow," which had belonged to their father, James Trail, to James Trail, Jr., for $30.00. In 1824, Benjamin Nicholls received a grant from South Carolina of 798 acres on the north side of Tyger River, and in 1828 another grant of 150 acres in the same area.[11]

Nicholls made his will on March 22, 1823; the estate was probated on December 23, 1830. The children of Benjamin and Ann Nicholls were as follows:[12]

	a.	Cassandra Nicholls, born c1801; married John Miller.
	b.	Mary Nicholls, born c1803; married _____ Howard.
7.	c.	George Nicholls, born December 2, 1806.
	d.	Joseph Nicholls, born c1809.
	e.	Elizabeth Nicholls, born c1811; married _____ Young.
	f.	Eleanor Nicholls, born c1813; married _____ Bearden.
8.	g.	Benjamin Franklin Nicholls, born April 25, 1821.

***

7.   George Nicholls was born December 2, 1806, in Spartanburg County, South Carolina; County Sheriff; died there on August 10, 1849; married January 12, 1843, Catherine Malissa Crook, born April 4, 1817; died October 24, 1854, daughter of Jesse Crook and Catherine Barry. Their children were as follows:[13]

	a.	John Moore Nicholls, born December 4, 1843; sergeant, Company H, First South Carolina Volunteers, in Civil War; Sheriff of Spartanburg County; died January 18, 1918, in Eutaw, Alabama; married May, 1891, to Mrs. Ella (Bobo) Copeland, daughter of Hon. Simpson Bobo and widow of Capt. Alexander Copeland; child:
		(1) Catherine Nicholls lived in Georgia.
9.	b.	Andrew Barry Crook Nicholls, born June 10, 1845.
10.	c.	Benjamin Franklin Nicholls, born November 3, 1847.
	d.	George Williams Nicholls, born December 3, 1849; died October 17, 1926, in Spartanburg County, South Carolina, where he served as judge of the Probate Court; married May 29, 1884, Mary Lavinia Jones, born July 6, 1861; died January 1, 1946; children:

        (1) Samuel Jones Nicholls, born May 7, 1885; dsp November 23, 1937; U. S. Congressman from South Carolina; married 1914 Eloise Clark.
        (2) George Williams Nicholls, born January 19, 1887; dsp November 16, 1908.
        (3) Katherine Montague Nicholls, born April 28, 1889; married June 7, 1917, Thomas Samuel Perrin, born May 31, 1881; lived in Spartanburg, South Carolina; children:
            (a) Thomas Samuel Perrin, born August 11, 1918; married August 21, 1952, Jane Anderson; lived in Charlotte, North Carolina; children:
                /1/ Jane Emily Perrin, born August 23, 1953.
                /2/ Katherine Lenore Perrin, born August 17, 1955.
            (b) George Nicholls Perrin, born January 18, 1922; dsp.
        (4) William Montague Nicholls, born December 1, 1892; dsp September 26, 1915, in Loos, Belgium.
        (5) Lottie Lee Nicholls, born February 20, 1895; married April 20, 1918, Robert Purviance Hazlehurst, born January 15, 1896; died

February 17, 1958, in Short Hills, New Jersey; children:
- (a) Robert Purviance Hazlehurst, born January 7, 1919; married February 20, 1947, Mary Margarethe Kierulff, born March 27, 1917; lived in Short Hills, New Jersey; children:
  - /1/ Ellen Bonde Hazlehurst, born February 20, 1948.
  - /2/ Charlotte Nicholls Hazlehurst, born September 5, 1949.
  - /3/ Anne Purviance Hazlehurst, born August 14, 1952.
- (b) George Nicholls Hazlehurst, born August 29, 1922; married December 21, 1946, Edith Montfort Batcheller, born August 24, 1924; children:
  - /1/ Virginia Batcheller Hazlehurst, born December 28, 1947.
  - /2/ Elizabeth Hazlehurst, born April 9, 1950.
  - /3/ Katherine Nicholls Hazlehurst, born February 2, 1952.
  - /4/ Mary Montague Hazlehurst, born July 17, 1953.
  - /5/ Isobel Hazlehurst, born April 19, 1955.
  - /6/ William Montague Hazlehurst, born January 8, 1957.
  - /7/ Laurence Nicholls Hazlehurst, born April 23, 1959.
- (c) Franklin Hamilton Hazlehurst, born November 6, 1925; married August 26, 1950, Carol Foord, born April 3, 1928; children:
  - /1/ Franklin Hamilton Hazlehurst, born August 18, 1951.
  - /2/ Robert Purviance Hazlehurst, born November 15, 1952.

***

9.   Andrew Barry Crook Nicholls was born June 10, 1845, in Spartanburg County, South Carolina, and died August 10, 1919, in Tuscaloosa, Alabama, where he was a physician. He married December 31, 1871, Mary Ellen Foster, born September 22, 1849; died December 19, 1924, daughter of Rev. John Collier Foster and Georgia Ann _____; their children were as follows:[14]

11. a. George John Nicholls, born September 9, 1872.
  b. Jesse Crook Nicholls, born August 29, 1874; married September 26, 1906, Florence Zacharie Ellis, born July 11, 1879; died January 20, 1957; lived in Ithaca, New York; children:
  - (1) Jesse Crook Nicholls, born August 11, 1907; dsp; lived in Murphy, North Carolina.
  - (2) Florence Emma Nicholls, born August 28, 1908; married (1) February 4, 1934, Frank White Weitzmann, born 1907; died 1941; (2) July 24, 1948, Basil George Apostle, born December 30, 1902; dsp; lived in Richmond, Virginia.
  - (3) James Zacharie Nicholls, born December 29, 1909; married December 12, 1946, Clara Sheppard; dsp.
  - (4) Andrew Barry Crook Nicholls, born June 6, 1913; married December 4, 1943, Catherine Dymus, born October 22, 1918; lived in Watervliet, New York; children:
    - (a) Andrew Barry Crook Nicholls, born December 29, 1950.
    - (b) Gregory Dymus Nicholls, born April 28, 1954.
  - (5) George Nicholls, born March 8, 1916; dsp; lived in Ithaca, New York.
  - (6) Augustus Hoke Nicholls, born June 11, 1918; married June 22, 1946, Emma Jeannette Kiel, born October 29, 1922; lived in Manhattan Beach, California; children:
    - (a) Robin Kirstie Nicholls, born November 15, 1952.
    - (b) Barry Christopher Nicholls, born July 4, 1955.
  c. Augustus Hoke Nicholls, born March 22, 1877; dsp March 23, 1945.
  d. Catherine Mary Nicholls, born July 7, 1884; married November 26, 1912, Gen. James Kerr Crain, born August 28, 1879; member, British Order of Bath; lived in Washington, D. C.; children:
  - (1) Mary Gene Crain, born March 14, 1921; U.S. Consul, Johannesburg,

South Africa; dsp.
    (2) Catherine Barry Crain, born April 11, 1922; married August 21, 1943, Col. George Edward Glober, born July 18, 1915; lived in Washington, D. C.; children:
        (a) George Edward Glober, born August 10, 1944.
        (b) Catherine Barry Glober, born January 3, 1949.
        (c) Mary Louise Glober, born October 12, 1950.
        (d) James Kerr Crain Glober, born November 4, 1959.
12. e. Benjamin Franklin Nicholls, born January 16, 1888.

***

11.   George John Nicholls was born September 9, 1872, and died June 19, 1952, in Tuscaloosa, Alabama; married November 2, 1901, to Ellen Smith, born March 5, 1876; their children were as follows:[15]

a. John Barry Nicholls, born December 8, 1902; dsp October 4, 1905.
b. Mary Ellen Nicholls, born November 18, 1903; married November 19, 1922, William Harper Spencer, born June 23, 1898; lived in Eutaw, Alabama; children:
    (1) William Harper Spencer, born October 16, 1924; married September 1, 1948, Mabel Patricia Ruton, born September 29, 1928; lived in North Little Rock, Arkansas; children:
        (a) Barry Patricia Spencer, born June 6, 1950.
        (b) Gail Amelia Spencer, born January 11, 1953.
        (c) William Harper Spencer, born May 26, 1957.
    (2) Mary Josephine Spencer, born July 13, 1926; married September 3, 1952, Abner Francis Patton, born November 14, 1926; lived in Tuscaloosa, Alabama; child:
        (a) Abner Francis Patton, born October 16, 1956.
    (3) John Milton Spencer, born April 19, 1928; lived in Eutaw, Alabama.
    (4) Lillian Florence Spencer, born August 6, 1929; married August 16, 1951, William Dewey Campbell, born October 31, 1928; lived in Tuscaloosa, Alabama; children:
        (a) William Dewey Campbell, born June 20, 1956.
        (b) Susan Elizabeth Campbell, born March 17, 1958.
    (5) Susan Elizabeth Spencer, born February 1, 1935; married October 13, 1953, Oliver Ray Hitt, born May 24, 1930; lived in Bessemer, Alabama.
c. George Nicholls, born January 15, 1906; dsp August 4, 1928.
d. Frank Nicholls, born November 28, 1908; dsp April 15, 1921.
e. Andrew Barry Crook Nicholls, born August 26, 1910; died September 7, 1946; married July 8, 1940, Marjorie Elizabeth Davis, born July 26, 1919; children:
    (1) Marjorie Elizabeth Nicholls, born July 25, 1944.
    (2) Andrew Barry Crook Nicholls, born July 25, 1944.
f. William Warrior Nicholls, born December 28, 1912; married December 6, 1944, Helen Allison Jones, born July 18, 1921; lived in Atlanta, Georgia; children:
    (1) William Warrior Nicholls, born April 7, 1947.
    (2) Alison Catherine Nicholls, born January 22, 1949.
    (3) Claire Ellen Nicholls, born June 17, 1954.

***

12.   Benjamin Franklin Nicholls was born January 16, 1888; died November 14, 1939; married August 22, 1915, Doris Gage McMain, born November 27, 1895; their children were as follows:[16]

249

a. Doris Nicholls, born January 17, 1917; married December 26, 1940, Frank Crain Schleicher, born February 10, 1911; lived in Maracaibo, Venezuela; children:
(1) Frank Crain Schleicher, born December 18, 1943.
(2) Barry Michael Schleicher, born September 21, 1949.
b. Benjamin Frank Nicholls, born March 18, 1918; married June 3, 1948, Avalee Durham, born July 17, 1921; lived in Coronado, California; children:
(1) Avalee Nicholls, born June 26, 1950.
(2) Benjamin Frank Nicholls, born October 5, 1952.
(3) Lucy Virginia Nicholls, born October 5, 1955.
(4) Rebecca Ellen Nicholls, born April 22, 1958.
c. Andrew Barry Crook Nicholls, born June 24, 1919; married January 7, 1950, Sue Wright, born December 22, 1928; lived in Talladega, Alabama; children:
(1) Susan Lucille Nicholls, born February 27, 1952.
(2) Barry Graham Nicholls, born June 23, 1955.
(3) Brooke McMain Nicholls, born April 10, 1958.
d. John Collier Nicholls, born February 15, 1921; married April 15, 1944, Juanita Risdon, born January 16, 1923; lived in Bellevue, Washington; children:
(1) Janet Nicholls, born July 23, 1947.
(2) Nancy Nicholls, born October 27, 1949.
(3) John Craig Nicholls, born August 30, 1953.
(4) Jean Carol Nicholls, born December 17, 1955.
e. Hugh Nicholls, born July 24,1923; married August 6, 1949, Mary Moncure Dabney, born September 7, 1931; lived in Vicksburg, Mississippi; children:
(1) Mary Dabney Nicholls, born April 18, 1952.
(2) Kristin Nicholls, born October 18, 1953.
(3) Amy Lucille Nicholls, born October 3, 1956.
f. Richard McMain Nicholls, born August 31, 1925; married January 25, 1948, Patricia Eugenia Cook, born December 23, 1927; lived in Vicksburg, Mississippi; children:
(1) Martha Suzanne Nicholls, born July 11, 1951.
(2) Richard McMain Nicholls, born May 8, 1955.
g. James Albert Nicholls, born March 8, 1929; married March 6, 1949, Julia Elizabeth Helgason, born October 24, 1931; lived in Vicksburg, Mississippi; children:
(1) Pamela Ann Nicholls, born November 24, 1949.
(2) James Keith Nicholls, born August 30, 1951.
(3) Irene Ruth Nicholls, born August 20, 1953.
(4) Julia Lynn Nicholls, born January 5, 1955.
(5) Mary Nell Nicholls, born July 24, 1956.
(6) Doris Calloway Nicholls, born November 29, 1958.
h. Nancy Ann Nicholls, born July 20, 1931; married February 14, 1953, Charles Arthur McKesson, born December 20, 1922; lived in Maracaibo, Venezuela; children:
(1) Valerie Gage McKesson, born November 29, 1955.
(2) Warren Gage McKesson, born June 25, 1958.
i. Lucy Virginia Nicholls, born November 25, 1933; married April 18, 1954, Richard Emerson McCollum, born March 14, 1923; lived in Maracaibo, Venezuela; child:
(1) Richard Emerson McCollum, born January 20, 1955.

***

10. (Dr.) Benjamin Franklin Nicholls was born November 3, 1847, in Spartanburg County, South Carolina, and died February 15, 1895, in Philadelphia,

Pennsylvania; married November 4, 1875, Elizabeth Louise Klapp, born November 19, 1844; died May 21, 1915, daughter of Dr. Joseph Klapp and Anna Pauline _____. Their children were as follows:[17]

a. Joseph Klapp Nicholls, born December 25, 1876; dsp December 24, 1951; married November 24, 1917, Sarah _____.
b. George William Nicholls, born May 20, 1878; dsp June 7, 1889.
c. Benjamin Franklin Nicholls, born May 30, 1881; dsp February 12, 1891.
d. Andrew Barry Crook Nicholls, born August 4, 1883; died March 27, 1955; married March 21, 1907, Deborah Mills Figer, born May 27, 1885; died October 16, 1956; child:
  (1) Elizabeth Louise Nicholls, born January 26, 1908; married (1) Raymond E. Brewer; (2) July 8, 1948, Harold L. Odgers; lived in Malvern, Pennsylvania; children (all by first marriage):
    (a) Betty Lou Brewer, born September 29, 1926; married (1) October 21, 1944, Edward Cronrath; (2) May 6, 1948, Philip J. Remington, born December 22, 1925; lived in Prospect Park, Pennsylvania; children:
      (by first marriage):
      /1/ Victoria Jane Cronrath, born February 14, 1946.
      (by second marriage):
      /2/ Cynthia Remington, born December 18, 1949.
    (b) Raymond E. Brewer, born September 7, 1928; married Charlene Evans, born December 30, 1930; lived in Gloucester, New Jersey.
    (c) Dean Nicholls Brewer, born June 16, 1935; married Peggy Ann Wolfe, born March 18, 1933; lived in West Chester, Pennsylvania; child:
      /1/ Becky Lee Brewer, born July 26, 1958.
e. Katherine Louise Nicholls, born June 22, 1884; married June 3, 1914, John Hastings Landrum, born April 5, 1888; died March 27, 1937; lived in Augusta, Georgia; children:
  (1) Leurah Louise Landrum, born July 5, 1915; married October 26, 1946, John Joseph Murphey, born October 26, 1924; lived in Sardis, Georgia; children:
    (a) Dixie Lenore Murphey, born November 25, 1948.
    (b) Jacqueline Rose Murphey, born July 29, 1950.
    (c) Terry Duane Murphey, born April 11, 1954.
  (2) Benjamin Franklin Landrum, born March 6, 1921; married September 5, 1943, Anne Burnell Woodward, born June 8, 1921; lived in Warwick, Pennsylvania; children:
    (a) Robert Hastings Landrum, born November 5, 1947.
    (b) Benjamin Franklin Landrum, born May 14, 1949.
    (c) Joseph Andrew Landrum, born June 29, 1951.
    (d) Barbara Anne Landrum, born August 22, 1958.
  (3) Kathryn Milner Landrum, born May 15, 1932; married October 16, 1957, Floyd Ancel Diveley, born September 23, 1932; lived in Augusta, Georgia; child:
    (a) Mary Katherine Diveley, born December 5, 1958.

***

8.   (Dr.) Benjamin Franklin Nicholls was born April 25, 1821, in Spartanburg County, South Carolina, and died May 19, 1884, in Childersburg, Alabama; married (1) June 11, 1846, Eliza Eugenia Dickie, born July 27, 1829; died September 3, 1873, daughter of Willis Wyatt Dickie and Margaret Barry Crook; (2) October 28, 1874, Sallie Carrie Perry, born December 2, 1837, daughter of Jacob and Sallie Perry. His children were as follows:[18]

(by first marriage):
a. Tallulah Kate Nicholls, born May 17, 1847; died January 11, 1885; married October 5, 1865, Harden S. Hereford; lived in Texas; children (perhaps among others):
    (1) John Franklin Hereford, born January 18, 1867.
    (2) Hanford Hereford, born November 23, 1867.
b. Margaret Ann Nicholls, born February 21, 1849; dsp December 9, 1872.
c. George Willis Nicholls, born May 15, 1851; died November 7, 1881; married May 19, 1871, Nancy Perry; children:
    (1) Kate Nicholls, dsp.
    (2) Lena Nicholls married _____ McStay; lived in Birmingham, Alabama.
    (3) George Nicholls married Edna _____.
d. Benjamin Franklin Nicholls, born October 27, 1853; dsp March 23, 1859.
e. John Albert Nicholls, born December 6, 1855; died December 24, 1953; married January 27, 1881, Allie A. Simmons; children:
    (1) Alva Eugenia Nicholls, born April 15, 1882; married (1) Peyton Pitts (2) William T. Garlington; lived in Camp Hill, Alabama; child (by first marriage):
        (a) Allie May Pitts married Ison Johnson; child:
            /1/ Renny Johnson.
    (2) Benjamin Franklin Nicholls, born January 20, 1886; died c1943; married Victoria Howell; children:
        (a) Agnes Nicholls married Lucas Kidd; lived in Childersburg, Alabama.
        (b) Dorothy Nicholls married Edward Donahoo; lived in Childersburg, Alabama.
        (c) John Nicholls married (1) _____ _____ (2) Leona Jones; lived in Childersburg, Alabama.
f. Fannie Stella Nicholls, born September 1, 1858; died April 13, 1894; married February 2, 1882, William DeJournette Cosper, born January 29, 1856; died April 4, 1910; children:
    (1) Willie Albert Cosper, born December 26, 1882; lived in Birmingham, Alabama.
    (2) Annis Eugenia Cosper, born May 26, 1885; married Chalmos Thomas; lived in Alexander City, Alabama.
    (3) Jessie Belle Cosper, born September 18, 1888.
    (4) Ada May Cosper, born May 10, 1891.
    (5) Lidie Emma Cosper, born March 7, 1892; dsp September 28, 1898.
g. Jesse Dickie Nicholls, born December 19, 1860; dsp November 4, 1888.
h. Eolia Barry Nicholls, born June 3, 1864; dsp November 23, 1941; married J. A. Liner.
i. Oscar Nicholls, born January 7, 1867; dsp October 2, 1867.
j. Edward Nicholls, born January 7, 1867; dsp August 8, 1868.
k. Eliza Eugenia Nicholls, born January 10, 1870; married July 14, 1889, Charles H. Butler; children:
    (1) George Butler lived in Anniston, Alabama.
    (2) Edith Butler married John Morgan; lived in Charleston, West Virginia.
    (3) Margaret Butler, dsp.
(by second marriage):
l. (Dr.) Mary Paralee Nicholls, born August 4, 1876; dsp June, 1933.
m. (Dr.) Walter Lee Nicholls, born November 28, 1877; died March 31, 1942; had two daughters who left no issue.

*****

4.   Jean Trail was born about 1744 in Maryland and died about 1832 in Union County, South Carolina; married Benjamin West, born about 1742, murdered from ambush during the American Revolution, the son of William West

and Esther Duvall. Their children were as follows:[19]

a. Rachel West, born c1768; married _____ West.
b. James West, born c1770; died 1845; married Mary _____.
c. John West, born c1772; married _____ Lancaster.
13. d. George West, born c1776.
e. Benjamin West, born c1778; died 1815; children:
   (1) Levina West.
   (2) James West married Mary West; lived in Cherokee County, Georgia, in 1850.
   (3) Elizabeth West.
   (4) John West.
   (5) Jane West.
   (6) (child)
f. Solomon West, born c1780; married Eleanor _____; lived in Spartanburg, County, South Carolina.

***

13.   George West was born about 1776 in Spartanburg County, South Carolina; married Edith Calista McHanie; lived in Gilmer County, Georgia; their children were as follows:[20]

a. Perry West, born c1804; married (1) Rhoda Wofford (2) Nancy C. _____ (3) Harriet Shields.
b. Benjamin West, born c1806; married Elizabeth _____; lived in Gilmer County, Georgia; children:
   (1) Elmira West.
   (2) Pulaski West.
   (3) Susan A. West.
   (4) Adolphus West.
   (5) Amanda West.
   (6) Ferdinand West.
   (7) Frances West.
   (8) Tripena West.
c. Jennie West married _____ Hazelwood.
d. Mary West married _____ Greenberry.
e. Kendrick West.
f. Willis West, born c1815; married Jane _____; lived in Abilene, Texas; children:
   (1) Monroe West lived in Ft. Worth, Texas.
   (2) Javan West lived in Merkle, Texas.
   (3) Octavius West.
   (4) Harvey West.
   (5) Elinor West.
   (6) James M. West.
14. g. Eber West, born c1817.
h. Myrick H. West, born c1821; married Sarah _____; children:
   (1) Columbus West.
   (2) Hester A. West.
   (3) Louisa A. West.
   (4) Augustus West.
   (5) Thanotia West.

***

14.   Eber West was born about 1817; died in Pickens County, Georgia; married Elizabeth Rippy; their children were as follows:[21]

253

a. Rosella West, born c1842; married Joshua D. Dorsey.
b. Roxanna West married Robert Reed.
c. Julia Ann West, born November 10, 1848; died April 16, 1920; married
   Alfred N. Reed, born August 27, 1845; died November 23, 1927; children:
   (1) James Reed, born May 20, 1870.
   (2) David Reed, born January 12, 1876; died June, 1946.
   (3) Lizzie Reed, born 1879; died December, 1903.
   (4) Minnie Reed, born October 12, 1881; married Noah Halbert, born
       March 26, 1882.
   (5) Dicie Reed, born December 25, 1884; married _____ Nunnally.
   (6) N. A. Reed, born August 7, 1887.
   (7) Myrtle Reed, born May 28, 1890; married _____ Cupps.
   (8) Allie Reed, born May 9, 1893; dsp September 17, 1912.
d. Missouri West, born 1851; married Elias Andrew Moore.
e. Georgia Ann West, born 1854; married James Samuel Osborne.
f. Eber West, born 1855.
15. g. Sarah Calista West, born January 3, 1857.

***

15.   Sarah Calista West was born January 3, 1857, in Pickens County,
Georgia; died October 4, 1931, in Abilene, Texas; married January 2, 1877,
James Sampson Clayton, born July 20, 1850; died April 24, 1917; their
children were as follows:[22]

a. Kate Amelia Clayton, born February 29, 1880; dsp 1902.
16. b. Fannie Florence Clayton, born February 29, 1880.
c. Clara Etna Clayton, born March 4, 1883; married December 17, 1905,
   Emmett Stephen Swofford; children:
   (1) Lois Swofford, born September 25, 1906; married February 5, 1928,
       James Hill, born August 10, 1902.
   (2) Emmett Stephen Swofford, born February 9, 1913; married September
       10, 1937, Virgie Lee Smith, born August 7, 1915; children:
       (a) Stephanie Lois Swofford, born July 23, 1941.
       (b) William Emmett Swofford, born December 2, 1944.
d. Hattie Clovis Clayton, born February 14, 1885; married November 23,
   1909, William H. Dye; children:
   (1) Sterling William Dye, born December 2, 1910; married September
       26, 1935, Marguerite Eleanor LeMay, born January 7, 1914; child:
       (a) Donald William Dye, born November 15, 1938.
   (2) Etna Mae Dye, born April 20, 1912; married May 7, 1932, Offie
       Bayless, born August 1, 1908; children:
       (a) David Michael Bayless, born July 5, 1935.
       (b) Gary Lee Bayless, born August 11, 1941.
   (3) Jack Clayton Dye, born September 18, 1916; married September 27,
       1941, Frances Marie Cothrin, born November 7, 1920; child:
       (a) Jacklyn Marie Dye, born February 23, 1943.
   (4) William Henry Dye, born August 5, 1923; married December 4, 1948,
       Rozell Marie Medley, born May 23, 1926.
e. Edgar Clayton, born 1888; dsp 1916.
f. Byron L. Clayton, born December 22, 1889; married December 28, 1912,
   Maggie Phelps; child:
   (1) Clovis Marie Clayton, born September 22, 1917; married March 1,
       1941, William O. McCown, born April 10, 1918; child:
       (a) Sandra Jean McCown, born October 8, 1946.
g. Quay Clayton, born August 18, 1893; married Richard Coke Davis; children:
   (1) Sarah Frances Davis, born April 1, 1914; married July 13, 1935,
       E. O. Larkin, born March 22, 1907.

    (2) Richard Coke Davis, born June 14, 1916; married December 25, 1939,
        Fern Foster, born December 17, 1916; children:
        (a) Bitsy Lee Davis, born January 3, 1940.
        (b) Dixie Fern Davis, born September 23, 1942.
    (3) James McLemore Davis, born April 9, 1921; married June, 1943,
        Jean Ann Ellis, born February 19, 1923; child:
        (a) Marilyn Davis, born April 7, 1951.

***

16.   Fannie Florence Clayton was born February 29, 1880; married (1) July
25, 1899, Miles Artemus Holmes; (2) February 25, 1925, Brice C. Humphrey;
her children, all by her first marriage, were as follows:[23]

a. Ruth Holmes, born January 2, 1901; married Emis Edward Hollingshead,
    born February 7, 1893; children:
    (1) Gloria Hollingshead, born August 5, 1922; married December 12,
        1941, H. M. Ritchie, born April 10, 1920; children:
        (a) Rodney Charles Ritchie, born June 17, 1946.
        (b) Gregory Earl Ritchie, born May 21, 1948.
    (2) Bettye Edward Hollingshead, born November 11, 1925; married Sept-
        ember 2, 1944, William Guy Broyles, born March 21, 1913; child:
        (a) Bettye Katherine Broyles, born September 14, 1950.
b. Miles Clayton Holmes, born August 2, 1902; married 1925 Maud Maurine
    Hardy; child:
    (1) Miles Clayton Holmes, born June 19, 1926.
c. Kate Rhae Holmes, born November 24, 1907; married June 10, 1939, Hugh
    Matlock; dsp.

***

5.   James Trail was born about 1748 in Maryland; married Mary Ann ____ ;
on August 26, 1777, he bought 52 acres, part of "Buxton's Delight," from
John Buxton for five shillings; he moved to Kentucky and then returned to
Montgomery County, Maryland, where he made his will on February 1, 1823;
the estate was probated on April 8, 1823. He had the following children:[24]

a. Eleanor Trail married ____ Buxton.
b. Ashford Trail died December 8, 1863; married December 28, 1803, Anne
    Sanders.
c. Nathan Trail died November 29, 1825; married December 19, 1801, Sus-
    anna Buxton.
d. Mary Ann Trail married December 4, 1802, George Buxton.
e. James Trail.
f. Edward Northcroft Trail.
g. Rachel Trail married April 15, 1811, Nicholas Ricketts.
h. Gulielma Maria Trail, born October 10, 1794; died July 1, 1873; mar-
    ried February 12, 1817, Merchant Ricketts.
i. Susanna Trail married December 24, 1821, Clement Boswell.
j. Frances Trail, born December 11, 1798; married December 18, 1822, Wil-
    liam Ricketts.
k. Notley Trail married March 19, 1817, Virlinda Ricketts.

***

2.   David Trail was born about 1720; he lived in Montgomery County, Maryland, where he made his will on March 5, 1775, leaving his property to
his wife Margaret, who died in 1802 in South Carolina, and to his children;
the estate was probated on December 10, 1781. His children were as follows:[25]

a. David Trail, born c1750; sold 16½ acres to William Benson and bought
    the land back from him; on November 20, 1789, he sold 109¼ acres in
    Montgomery County, Maryland, to Alexander Catlett; he married c1776
    Elizabeth Fryer. He moved to Spartanburg County, South Carolina, where
    in 1808 he sold 150 acres on Dutchman's Creek to John Trail. He died
    there in 1831; children:
    (1) Frances Trail, born c1780; died November 25, 1861; married Wil-
         liam Posey, born c1774; died January 17, 1853; children:
         (a) Elizabeth Fryer Posey, born September 29, 1801; died October,
              1864, in Lowndes County, Alabama; married Thomas Joyce Under-
              wood.
         (b) David Trail Posey, born January 15, 1803; died November 28,
              1862, in Lowndes County, Alabama; married Wilmoth Underwood.
         (c) John Trail Posey, born February 8, 1805; died July 4, 1891,
              in Lowndes County, Alabama; married February 8, 1848, Deborah
              Howard.
         (d) Ann Posey, born c1807; married Peter Hamilton; lived in
              Lowndes County, Alabama.
         (e) William Posey lived in Texas.
         (f) Louise Posey, born c1811; died 1866 in Escambia County, Ala-
              bama; married June 21, 1849, James Loveless.
         (g) Andrew T. Posey, born November 15, 1813, died November 8,
              1857, in Sunflower, Alabama; married Eliza Munger.
         (h) Malinda Posey, born c1816; died May 29, 1893; married March
              23, 1839, McCormick Pruitt.
         (i) Elihu A. Posey, born February 15, 1820; dsp March 10, 1868,
              in Lowndes County, Alabama.
         (j) Frances C. Posey, born 1823; died April 28, 1852, in Lowndes
              County, Alabama; married June 21, 1849, Dr. Dana E. Monroe.
    (2) Eleanor Trail, born December 10, 1784; died October 22, 1824;
         married John Morrow.
    (3) John Trail, born December 14, 1786; died February 1, 1859.
    (4) Margaret Trail married John White.
    (5) Susanna Trail married _____ Posey.
    (6) Sarah Trail married Isaac Bearden.
    (7) Mary Trail married Zephaniah Posey.
    (8) Elizabeth Trail, born May 27, 1804; died March 3, 1883; married
         Ledson Bearden.
b. Basil Trail, born c1752; sold 54 acres to his brother, David Trail, on
    November 24, 1787, in order to clear his title to land inherited from
    their father; he then sold his land to Henry Brooke and moved to Spart-
    anburg County, South Carolina, where in 1789 he bought 240 acres on
    Dutchman's Creek from Sarah Sterling; in 1790 he bought 300 acres in
    the same area from Jean Heaney. He then moved to Sumner County, Tennes-
    see, where he died in 1812; in his will he gave his property to his
    wife Elizabeth and his children:
    (1) Solomon Trail.
    (2) David Trail.
    (3) John Trail.
    (4) Hamilton Trail.
    (5) Sarah Trail married _____ Moore.
    (6) Elizabeth Trail married _____ Smith.
c. Massa Trail, born c1755.
d. Cassandra Trail, born c1757; married December 14, 1779, Benjamin Peake.
e. Dorcas Trail, born December 14, 1759; died 1817; married November 17,
    1778, Osborn West; lived in Spartanburg County, South Carolina.

                                  ***

REFERENCES

[1]Frederick County, Maryland, Wills A, 190.

[2]Maryland "Black Books" #461; Montgomery County, Maryland, Deeds A, 191, D, 135, E, 94, 68, 385.

[3]Montgomery County, Maryland, Wills, D, 138, 254, Deeds I, 118, 173, M, 619, O, 290; Prince Georges Parish Register, Montgomery County, Maryland, in Maryland Historical Society Library, Baltimore, Maryland.

[4]Montgomery County, Maryland, Wills, D, 138, A, 324, B, 254; Prince Georges Parish Register.

[5]Montgomery County, Maryland, Deeds, D, 403, G, 248, 453, I, 173, K, 496, L, 171, M, 433, N, 156, 275; Equity Court Cases, Liber 1817-23, folio 519, July, 1820.

[6]Records belonging to Mrs. John R. Washam.

[7]Ibid., Deeds M, 619, 633, O, 291; Prince Georges Parish Register; Campbell County, Kentucky, Wills.

[8]96 District Estate Settlements, Box 70, package 1727; Spartanburg County, South Carolina, Deeds C, 73, K, 149, L, 146; Union County, South Carolina, Deeds H, 85; Leah Townsend, South Carolina Baptists, (1670-1805) (Florence, S. C.: The Florence Printing Company, 1935), p. 136.

[9]96 District Estate Settlements, Box 70, package 1727 (chief buyers were James Lee, and Margery, Nancy, and Eleanor Nicholls); South Carolina Post-Revolutionary plats 139:28, State Archives, Columbia, South Carolina; Spartanburg County, South Carolina, Deeds L, 146, 369.

[10]Union County, South Carolina, Deeds F, 3, 90; Spartanburg County, South Carolina, Deeds G, 172, K, 124, 265, 267, L, 329.

[11]Union County, South Carolina, Estates Box 22, package 16; Montgomery County, Maryland, Deeds P, 251; South Carolina Post-Revolutionary Plats 139:23, 24.

[12]Spartanburg County, South Carolina, Estates Box 22, package 6.

[13-18]Records belonging to Jesse Crook Nicholls.

[19-23]Records belonging to Mrs. E. C. Stone.

[24]Montgomery County, Maryland, Deeds A, 192, N, 103, Wills M, 314; Prince Georges Parish Register.

[25]Montgomery County, Maryland, Wills B, 64; Records belonging to Mrs. Reginald S. Hudson.

***

WEST of Harford County, Maryland

Robert West was probably born about 1670 in England and was in Baltimore (now Harford) County, Maryland, as early as 1692, living on the north
side of Gunpowder River on the land of John Hall. On November 10, 1695,
in St. George's Parish, he married Sarah Spinks, who was probably a sister
of Enoch Spinks of Baltimore County. In 1704, he patented 78 acres of
"Poor Man's Beginning;" on November 17, 1705, "Westwood," 500 acres on
Graveyard Branch, was laid out; it was patented in 1710. On June 10, 1721,
"Maiden's Mount, " 400 acres on the west side of Susquehanna River, was
laid out; it was patented in 1722; it was later known as Bald Friar and
was the site of a well-known ferry across the Susquehanna. In 1732 he
patented "Daniel's Neglect" of 75 acres and "Dear Bought and Nothing Got"
of 25 acres.[1]

In 1708, Robert West, a Baltimore County planter, sold "Poor Man's
Beginning," 78 acres, to John Hall, and 200 acres of "Westwood" to John
Edwards; in 1709 he sold 60 acres of "Westwood" to Gregory Farmer, and in
1713 he sold 100 acres of "Westwood" to Mark Whitaker; he bought 100 acres
of "Westwood" from Thomas Whitaker in 1740. In 1720 he bought 100 acres,
part of "Paradise" and "West's Addition," from John Hammond, Jr.[2]

Robert West gave "West's Addition" to his daughter Constant Barns in
1722; in 1733 he gave her "Paradise" and part of "Maiden's Mount." He
gave his sons John and Jonathan and his daughters Mary West and Sarah Cook
part of "Maiden's Mount" in 1727 and gave his son Robert part of "Westwood"
in 1729. He gave his son Enoch "Daniel's Neglect," 75 acres, in 1742. He
sold "Gash's Purchase" of 100 acres to Thomas Gash in 1740 and "Dear Bought
and Nothing Got" of 25 acres to Joseph Morgan in 1742.[3]

West made his will on April 9, 1747, leaving his property to his wife
Sarah; at her death it was to be equally divided among all their children;
the estate was probated on September 7, 1748.[4] Their children were as
follows:[5]

a. Sarah West, born October 24, 1701; married December 30, 1726, John
   Cook; children:
   (by unknown father):
   (1) Moses (Cook?), born March 28, 1721.
   (2) Daniel (Cook?), born December 17, 1723.
   (by marriage):
   (3) Mary Cook, born March 13, 1726/27.
   (4) Priscilla Cook, born March 27, 1730.
   (5) Robert Cook, born August 15, 1732.
   (6) John Cook, born December 8, 1734.
1. b. Constant West, born April 24, 1703.
2. c. Robert West, born November 6, 1706.
   d. Priscilla West, born March 28, 1709; dsp September 22, 1729; married
      April 15, 1729, to Joshua Wood.
3. e. John West, born December 29, 1711.
   f. Jonathan West, born June 26, 1714; married Eleanor ____.
   g. Mary West, born April 26, 1716; married November 23, 1729, to Daniel
      Gordon; child (probably among others):
      (1) John Gordon, born May 19, 1746.
   h. Susannah West, born March 6, 1717/8; married February 7, 1737/8, to
      Thomas Hilliard; child (probably among others):
      (1) Susannah Hilliard, born October 14, 1740.
   i. Enoch West, born May 17, 1721; married Elizabeth ____; lived in

Harford County, Maryland, in 1790; children:[6]
(1) Enoch West, born c1766.
(2) William West, born c1769.

***

1.   Constant West was born April 24, 1703, in Baltimore (now Harford) County, Maryland, and married (1) October 11, 1722, to Job Barns, who died November 11, 1739; (2) September, 1740, to Joseph Morgan; children:[7]

(by first marriage):
a. Job Barns, born December 20, 1723; married February 2, 1749/50, to Mary Crawford; children (probably among others):
    (1) Job Barns, born June 11, 1752.
    (2) Rachel Barns, born August 13, 1754.
    (3) Ezekial Barns, born July 4, 1758.
b. Margaret Barns, born July 30, 1725.
c. John Barns, born February 2, 1727/8.
d. Elizabeth Barns, born May 2, 1730; dsp August 23, 1734.
e. Cassiah Barns, born October 27, 1732.
f. Elizabeth Barns, born August 23, 1735.
g. Thomas Barns, born September 27, 1737.
h. Constance Barns, born September 30, 1739.
(by second marriage):
i. Joseph Morgan, born February 3, 1741/2.

***

2.   Robert West was born November 6, 1706, in Baltimore (now Harford) County, Maryland, and lived in Spesutia Hundred, where in 1729 his father gave him part of "Westwood." On January 22, 1732, he married Johannah Gash (see p.   34), and the same year he patented "West's Beginning" of 50 acres. In 1739 he patented "New Westwood" of 685 acres, and in 1743, "West's Long Acre" of 37½ acres. In 1757 he patented another 118 acres of "West's Long Acre," and in 1763, "West's Double Cost" of 110 acres; in 1761 he bought 10 acres of "Daniel's Neglect" from Enoch West. In 1740 West sold 40 acres of "Westwood" and 40 acres of "West's Beginning" and 385 acres of "New Westwood" to Josias Middlemore; in 1762 he sold five acres of "New Westwood" to Charles Gilbert, and in 1763 he sold part of "West's Long Acre," "Addition," and "West's Double Cost" to John Hall.[8]

         On April 4, 1764, Col. John Hall was appointed administrator of Robert West's estate with Walter Tolly his security.[9] The children of Robert and Johannah West, perhaps among others, were as follows:[10]

a. Thomas West, born June 13, 1732; married September 8, 1757, to Ann Pritchard; lived in Harford County, Maryland, in 1790; children (probably among others):
    (1) Elizabeth West, born March 2, 1758.
    (2) James West, born c1762.
    (3) Thomas West, born c1764.
    (4) Samuel West, born c1770.
    (5) Sarah West, born c1770.
    (6) Mary West, born c1773.
    (7) Isaac West, born c1775.
b. Robert West, born March 5, 1734/5; married c1760 Ann _____; lived in Harford County, Maryland, in 1790; children (probably among others):[12]
    (1) Elizabeth West, born c1761.
    (2) Benjamin West, born c1764.

259

    (3) Hannah West, born c1766.
    (4) John West, born c1768.
    (5) Mary West, born c1770.
    (6) Martha West, born c1772.
    (7) Michael West, born c1773.
    (8) Ephraim West, born c1774.
  c. Sarah West, born March 23, 1736/7; died young.
  d. Jonathan West, born July 14, 1740; died Anderson County, South Carolina; married March 31, 1758, to Sophia Kimball.
  e. Johannah West, born March 17, 1741/2.
  f. Sarah West, born April 5, 1743.
  g. John West, born February 18, 1746/7.
4. h. Michael West, born May 1, 1749.

***

4.   Michael West was born May 1, 1749, in Baltimore (now Harford) County, Maryland, where he married Nancy ____ about 1775. In 1783 he lived in Bush River Lower Hundred and had property valued at only £12 and owned no land. About 1793/4 he moved to Mason County, Kentucky, where on March 26, 1801, he sold furniture and livestock to Charles Evans for $136.00. About 1805 he moved to Bracken County, Kentucky, near Augusta, and died there about 1807/8; his widow died after 1810.[13] Although there is no proof, the children of Michael and Nancy West were probably, among others, as follows:[14]

5. a. Richard West, born c1776.
  b. Nancy West, born c1780; married January 4, 1800, to Elijah Galloway, who died in 1828 in Bracken County, Kentucky.[15]
  c. Charles West, born c1785; died May 19, 1857, in Bracken County, Kentucky; married (1) October 16, 1805, to Rebecca Carter; (2) June 16, 1835, to Mary Morford; children:[16]
    (by first marriage): not proven.
    (by second marriage):
    (1) Margaret West, born c1836.
    (2) Elizabeth West, born c1839.
  d. Mary West, born February, 1789; died 1867 in Cooke County, Texas; married June 17, 1810, to John Davidson (see p. 12).[17]
6. e. Michael West, born c1793.

***

5.   Richard West was born about 1776 in Harford County, Maryland, and moved with his family to Mason County, Kentucky, about 1794, and to Bracken County, Kentucky, about 1805. On July 15, 1810, he married Mary McCane, who was born about 1788 and who died October 17, 1852, the daughter of James McCane. On April 10, 1813, he bought 147½ acres on Little Bracken River from Michael and Mary Weaver for $350.00; on April 19, 1817, he bought 7½ acres on Little Bracken from Stephen and Sarah Taylor for $32.00. He made his will on May 27, 1864, dividing his property among his children; the estate was probated in July, 1864. The children of Richard and Mary West were as follows:[18]

  a. Nancy West, born c1810; married ____ Judd; child:
    (1) John Judd, born c1834.
  b. Elizabeth West, born c1812; married David Woods.
  c. Rebecca West, born c1816; died June 3, 1855; married George W. Case.
  d. America Ann West, born c1818; married August 24, 1846, Littleton Case.
7. e. Amanda T. West, born November 3, 1820.

f. Eliza West, born c1825; married David N. Louderback.
g. Innetia West, born c1827; dsp April 1, 1852.
h. Alfred P. West, born c1829.
i. Virginia E. West, born c1831; died June 1, 1861; married William P. Baston.

***

7.   Amanda T. West was born November 3, 1820, and died February 2, 1895, in Bracken County, Kentucky; married March 22, 1843, George Teegarden, born May 8, 1809, and died May 7, 1893, the son of Jeremiah Teegarden and Catherine Thomas. Their children were as follows:[19]

a. Alonzo Teegarden, born April 8, 1844; dsp.
b. William Tomlinson Teegarden, born January 22, 1846; dsp February 25, 1905.
8. c. Lucien Albert Teegarden, born November 2, 1847.
d. Laura Belle Teegarden, born December 25, 1849; married John J. Gebhardt.
e. Charles Pribble Teegarden, born September 20, 1854; dsp July 24, 1856.
f. Anderson Teegarden, born October 15, 1856; died April 2, 1933; married May 30, 1897, to Eva C. Bolender; child:
    (1) Penn Bolender Teegarden, born February 20, 1900; died 1936; married May 30, 1925, Stella Marie Jennings; child:
        (a) Maurice Penn Teegarden, born July 19, 1926.
g. Julia Teegarden, born and died 1859.

***

8.   Lucien Albert Teegarden was born November 2, 1847, and died November 9, 1925, in Bracken County, Kentucky; married March 26, 1875, to Laura Belle Hunter, born February 28, 1859; died 1942; their children were as follows:[20]

a. Minnie Maud Teegarden, born March 3, 1876; married December 8, 1897, Louis Schweitzer; lived in Augusta, Kentucky; children:
    (1) Howard Schweitzer, born September 14, 1898.
    (2) Raymond Schweitzer, born April 11, 1900.
    (3) Louis Schweitzer, born December, 1902.
b. Charles Stewart Teegarden, born December 17, 1877; married 1907 Bertha Remley, born April 1, 1887; children:
    (1) Lucien Mellor Teegarden, born January 5, 1908.
    (2) William Adrian Teegarden, born July 19, 1910.
    (3) Virginia Lawton Teegarden, born February 28, 1913.
    (4) Christine Teegarden, born January 28, 1916.
    (5) Charles Rice Teegarden, born November 28, 1919.
c. Fannie Bennett Teegarden, born November 29, 1879; married (1) November 16, 1898, to John Thomas Pollard, born May 3, 1867; died September 29, 1903; (2) November 22, 1906, Howard A. Thomas, born May 2, 1871; children:
    (by first marriage):
    (1) Pearlie May Pollard, born August 24, 1899; married June 27, 1917, Virgil B. Scott; children:
        (a) Rowena May Scott.
        (b) Wanda Earl Scott, born September 25, 1923.
    (2) Charles Thomas Pollard, born September 18, 1903; married September 19, 1926, Margaret Beckett; children:
        (a) Thomas Pollard, born August 25, 1927.
        (b) Jackie Beckett Pollard, born October 24, 1929.
    (by second marriage):

261

(3) Georgie Lillian Thomas, born August 19, 1907; married June 2, 1928, Walter Mohrsfield.
(4) Alexander Bradford Thomas, born May 20, 1909; married January 3, 1930, Cozette Best.
(5) Vivian Lee Thomas, born October 16, 1910; married September 4, 1929, Herbert Shafer.
(6) Albert Slack Thomas, born August 16, 1912.
(7) Stanley Howard Thomas, born August 2, 1914.
(8) James Foley Thomas, born June 10, 1916.
(9) Ileen Bennett Thomas, born April 5, 1919.
  d. Edna Pearl Teegarden, born September 14, 1881; married December 20, 1899, Charles T. Nash, born October 18, 1872; children:
(1) Henry Bowman Nash, born March 30, 1901; dsp May 23, 1902.
(2) Mabel Claire Nash, born March 30, 1903; married September 22, 1921, Ray Moore, born December 25, 18??; children:
  (a) Jewel Moore, born February 19, 1923.
  (b) Geraldine Moore, born April 28, 1924.
  (c) Ray Moore, born June 28, 1926.
  (d) Mory Charles Moore, born June 19, 1928.
(3) Edna Fay Nash, born January 29, 1906; married Jason Collins.
(4) Allen Graydon Nash, born June 16, 1910.
(5) Charles Albert Nash, born November 7, 1913.
(6) Alice Marcella Nash, born November 20, 1917.
  e. Lucy Price Teegarden, born March 26, 1884; married (1) James Harrison Nash (2) Martin Kuhlenburg; dsp.

***

6.   Michael West was born about 1793 in Harford County, Maryland, and moved in infancy to Mason County, Kentucky; he moved to Bracken County, Kentucky, about 1805. He married (1) June 18, 1823, to Sarah Woods; (2) September 4, 1832, to Mrs. Jane Woodward; (3) October 31, 1854, to Mrs. Elizabeth Wells. He made his will on February 1, 1875, leaving his property to his three children, and the estate was probated in August, 1875. His children were as follows:[21]

(by first marriage):
a. Sarah E. West, born c1823; married c1855 Edward J. Cooper; children:
(1) Joseph B. Cooper, born c1856.
(2) George Cooper, born July 19, 1858.
b. Samuel West, born c1825; died c1877 in Bracken County, Kentucky; married (1) November 24, 1852, Harriet Jane Day (2) Sarah Ellis; children:
(by first marriage):
(1) Emma West, born c1855.
(by second marriage):
(2) Lucy B. West, born September 26, 1860.
(3) Virginia M. West, born c1862.
(4) Mary West, born c1864.
(5) Francis A. West, born c1866.
(6) Caroline M. West, born c1871.
(by second marriage):
9. c. Caroline Matilda Thayer West, born March 6, 1836.
  d. Francis West, born c1837; died young.

***

9.   Caroline Matilda Thayer West was born March 6, 1836, and died January 18, 1898, in Bracken County, Kentucky; married October 6, 1859, to James William Staton, born May 27, 1835; died June 27, 1903, son of James Staton

262

and Jane Calvert; their children were as follows:[22]

a. Robert Edgar Staton, born June 30, 1860; died October 21, 1938; married January 19, 1887, Eva Corliss; children:
    (1) William Lynn Staton, born March 24, 1894; died August 20, 1973, in Lexington, Kentucky; child:
        (a) William Lynn Staton, lived in Wilmore, Kentucky.
    (2) John Staton married Audrey Young; children:
        (a) Gladys Lynn Staton, born September 11, 1915; married Rodney L. Harbour; lived in Tucson, Arizona; children:
            /1/ Lynn Staton Harbour, born September 8, 1942.
            /2/ John Lydick Harbour, born May 5, 1948.
            /3/ Robert Gregory Harbour, born January 30, 1952.
        (b) Dorothy Staton, born November 15, 1917; married John Gullermin; lived in Sacramento, California.
        (c) John Edgar Staton, born August 3, 1921; married Tina _____; lived in Sacramento, California; child:
            /1/ Allen Thomas Staton, born April 18, 1955.
    (3) Octa Jean Staton married Howard Jett; dsp; lived in Tucson, Arizona.
b. Halbert Wren Staton, born March 10, 1862; dsp 1907; married (1) Fanny R. Ginn, born 1866; died 1901; (2) Lou Struve, born 1859.
c. Joseph Francis Staton, born November 11, 1863; dsp January 16, 1935.
d. Carroll Augustus Staton, born July 19, 1866; died 1926; child:
    (1) (Dr.) Younger Staton; lived in West Palm Beach, Florida.
e. Caroline Jane Staton, born October 3, 1868; dsp November 17, 1934, in Brooksville, Kentucky; married W. H. Byron, died November 8, 1934.
10. f. James W. J. Staton, born February 25, 1871.

***

10.   James W. J. Staton was born February 25, 1871, and died January 16, 1932; married November 7, 1892, to Betty Wells, born March 6, 1876; died June 18, 1956. Their children were as follows:[23]

a. Garnet Gilbert Staton, born November 23, 1893; died November 6, 1959; married December 24, 1914, Zula F. Jolly; children:
    (1) Catherine Staton, died young.
    (2) James William Staton, born August 19, 1916; married (1) Margaret Hamilton; (2) Erma Bright; lived in Melbourne, Kentucky; child (by first marriage):
        (a) James William Staton, born January 7, 1947.
    (3) John Arthur Staton, born March 29, 1918; married Jean Whitehouse; children:
        (a) John Arthur Staton.
        (b) Jacklyn Staton.
11. b. Ruth Staton, born December 20, 1895.
c. Thayer Staton, born April 8, 1898; died July 27, 1947; married (1) July 26, 1930, Hilda Baker; (2) Beatrice (Ruth) Darrow; children: (by first marriage):
    (1) Joyce Staton, born May 16, 1931; married Charles Ratchford (one adopted son).
    (by second marriage):
    (2) Patricia Ann Staton, born February 6, 1935; married June 15, 1957, Gerald Wright.
    (3) Barbara Lee Staton, born October 2, 1937; married March 25, 1957, Charles Moniack.
d. Logan Marshall Staton, born March 31, 1901; died April 17, 1962; married (1) November, 1923, Dorothy Welte; (2) Lela Unrue; child (by first marriage):

263

        (1) Lowell Staton, born March, 1924.
- e. Carrie Jane Staton, born September 4, 1903; married January 16, 1921, Clarence D. Edgley, died October 21, 1953; children:
  - (1) Betty Jane Edgley, born June 9, 1922; married December 14, 1946, C. Raymond Brown; children:
    - (a) C. Raymond Brown, born September 7, 1947.
    - (b) Robert Grady Brown, born August 4, 1952.
  - (2) Jack Drennan Edgley, born September 4, 1926; married Joanna Mahaney; children:
    - (a) David Edgley, born August 21, 1948.
    - (b) Paul Edgley.
    - (c) Mark Edgley.
    - (d) Joseph Edgley.
    - (e) Andrew Scott Edgley, born May 16, 1957.
    - (f) Christine Edgley, born October 14, 1958.
  - (3) Ruth Joan Edgley, born February 6, 1931; married Norbert Reinert; children:
    - (a) Connie Reinert, born October 4, 1952.
    - (b) Charles Reinert.
    - (c) Carrie Reinert.
    - (d) Catherine Reinert, born October, 1958.
  - (4) Robert Gene Edgley, born July 13, 1939; married February 9, 1962, Shirley Spencer.
- f. Lettie Ware Staton, born March 10, 1907; married September 21, 1924, Raymond M. Borman, died January 25, 1966; children:
  - (1) Raymond M. Borman, born April 28, 1925; married September 21, 1947, Joyce Yost; children:
    - (a) Darlene Borman.
    - (b) Denise Borman.
  - (2) William Gilbert Borman, born October 28, 1927; married Louise Arwood; child:
    - (a) Michael Raymond Borman.

***

11.   Ruth Staton was born December 20, 1895, and died March 21, 1958; married August 2, 1913, Thomas Nelson Sansom, born March 18, 1889; died December 20, 1956. Their children were as follows:[24]

- a. Frances Byron Sansom, born November 4, 1914; married February 11, 1933, Heber Kenneth Wells; dsp; lived in Phoenix, Arizona.
- b. William Thayer Sansom, born June 1, 1916; dsp January 18, 1918.
- c. Carroll Thomas Sansom, born July 31, 1917; married June 9, 1938, Dorothy Farwick; lived in Alexandria, Kentucky; children:
  - (1) Leisla Joan Sansom, born April 2, 1939.
  - (2) Russell Owen Sansom, born April 24, 1943.
  - (3) Martha Nelle Sansom, born April 28, 1947.
- d. Robert Nelson Sansom, born January 7, 1921; dsp April 7, 1921.
- e. Richard Rae Sansom, born July 16, 1924; married January 26, 1944, Estelle Ruschell; children:
  - (1) Richard Thomas Sansom, born October 19, 1946.
  - (2) Alexis June Sansom, born August 19, 1949.
- f. Janet King Sansom, born January 13, 1927; married June 14, 1946, Ira Clarkson Anderson; children:
  - (1) Jennifer Anderson, born April 30, 1947.
  - (2) James Anderson, born April 30, 1949.
  - (3) Janette Anderson, born January 30, 1951.
  - (4) Janell Anderson, born August 12, 1954.

***

3.   John West was born December 29, 1711, in Baltimore (now Harford)
County, Maryland; married January 26, 1735/6, to Susanna Osborn; their
children were as follows:[25]

a. Margaret West, born March 24, 1735/6; died young.
b. John West, born March 26, 1737; married Susanna _____; children (pro-
    bably among others):
    (1) John West, born c1763.
    (2) James West, born c1765.
    (3) William West, born c1766.
    (4) Margaret West, born c1770.
    (5) Lydia West, born c1772.
    (6) Susanna West, born c1776.
    (7) Sarah West, born c1776.
c. Margaret West, born February 11, 1742/3.
d. David West, born June 8, 1745.
e. James West, born January 24, 1747/8.
f. Isaac West, born April 1, 1750.
g. Jacob West, born January 13, 1752/3.
h. Martha West, born November 11, 1754.
i. Susanna West, born August 8, 1756.
j. William West, born October 24, 1757.

***

REFERENCES

[1]Baltimore County, Maryland, tax lists, 1692 et seq.; St. George's
Parish Register, Harford County, Maryland, in the Maryland Historical Soc-
iety Library, Baltimore, Maryland; Maryland Land Patents CD#165, DD#5, 677,
IL#A, 48, AM#1, 228, 149.
    [2]Baltimore County, Maryland, Deeds RM#HS, 653, 619, TR#A, 48, 266,
HWS#IA, 382, TR#DS, 297.
    [3]Ibid., IS#G, 94, HWS#M, 9, IS#H, 393, 395, 397, IS#I, 264, TB#C, 93,
91, HWS#IA, 411.
    [4]Ibid., Will Bk. 25, p. 424.
    [5]St. George's Parish Register.
    [6]Harford County, Maryland, census of 1776.
    [7]St. George's Parish Register.
    [8]Ibid.; Baltimore County, Maryland, Deeds IS#I, 264, HWS#IA, 404, 387,
B#I, 468, B#K, 17, B#L, 106; Maryland Land Patents AM#1, 140, ES#5, 449,
LG#E, 228, BC&GS#9, 345, 348, BC&GS#21, 361, Certificate #1704, BC&GS#34,
295.
    [9]Baltimore County, Maryland, Testamentary Proceedings, Bk. 40, p. 265.
    [10]St. George's Parish Register.
    [11]Ibid., Harford County, Maryland, census of 1776, 1790.
    [12]Ibid.
    [13]Ibid., tax lists, 1783; Mason County, Kentucky, tax lists 1793 et
seq., Deeds F, 367; Bracken County, Kentucky, tax lists 1800 et seq.;
census of 1810.
    [14]Nancy West's marriage record proves her the daughter of Michael West;
the others were closely associated, all were of Maryland origin, and were
the only Wests in Bracken County, Kentucky, in 1810.
    [15]Mason County, Kentucky, Marriages; Bracken County, Kentucky, estate
settlements.
    [16]Bracken County, Kentucky, Marriages, Deaths, census of 1850.
    [17]Ibid., Marriages; Bible record owned by David B. Trimble; Portrait
and Biographical Album of Jefferson and VanBuren Counties for 1890 (Lake
Publishing Company, 1890), p. 405.

[18]Bracken County, Kentucky, Marriages, Deaths, census of 1850, Deeds D, 325, K, 3, E, 425, Wills.

[19-20]Jeanette Teegarden Jones, Ten Generations of Teegardens, n.d., n.p., p. 78.

[21]Bracken County, Kentucky, Marriages, Wills, census of 1850, 1860, 1870, 1880.

[22-24]John S. Stayton, Staton History (n.p., 1960), p. 22ff.; records belonging to Elizabeth Gibson.

[25]St. George's Parish Register; Harford County, Maryland, census of 1776.

***

WOLFE of Scott County, Virginia, and
Vermilion County, Illinois

Several members of the Wolfe family of Berkeley County, (West) Virginia, moved to the area along the border of Virginia and Tennessee, living
in Scott and Washington Counties, Virginia, and Sullivan and Hawkins (now
Hancock) Counties, Tennessee. Among these brothers and sisters were the
following:[1]

1. a. John Wolfe, born c1752.
2. b. Charles Wolfe, born c1755.
3. c. George Wolfe, born c1765.
   d. Barbara Wolfe married Adam Stoke; lived in Sullivan County, Tennessee.
   e. Mary Wolfe married (1) Valentine Pope (2) 1807 Robert Easley (see p.
      26); lived in Sullivan County, Tennessee.

***

1.   John Wolfe was born about 1752 and lived about 25 miles north of Winchester in Berkeley County, (West) Virginia, at the time of his marriage
about 1778 to Catherine Bare (see p. 1). He was known as a "genteel,
sober young man," although neither he nor his wife was educated; neither
could read or write. About four months after the marriage, he was present
when a murder was committed; the murderer was hanged, and although Wolfe
was only a witness, he fled in 1778 to South Carolina and Georgia for over
a year; he then returned and immediately took his wife and child to North
Carolina.[2]

        In the spring of 1788, the family moved to a farm on the south side
of the North Fork of the Holston River; they were extremely poor, but on
December 6, 1790, he bought 50 acres where he then lived from John Kearns,
and on November 14, 1796, 150 acres from Dennis Coudry.[3] The land was
located at the junction of the river with the Tennessee state line about
four miles from Gate City.

        John Wolfe was a strict, hard-working, and careful farmer and he ac-
cumulated a sizeable estate worth about $3,000.00 by 1806. He also ped-
dled whiskey in the Clinch River settlements and may have traded horses in
Kentucky. He also leased land to Robert Stubblefield. In 1792 his
brother-in-law, Peter Bare, lived with him for about four months.[4]

        After several years, Wolfe's mental condition began to deteriorate as
he became increasingly depressed about his part in the murder he had witnessed many years before. He sometimes realized when his fits of depres-
sion were coming on and would warn his family to stay away from him. However, according to Joseph Duncan, an employee, "sometimes he would immediately go to drinking and quarreling with his family and at other times he
would pass over the course of a night before he would break out so very
bad, during which times he and his wife would generally talk Dutch toge-
ther...and he would make all fly." He threatened his family with physical
violence and made many extravagant and scandalous statements about them.[5]

        His condition became worse after about 1803, when a blackmailer named
Stunn came to Wolfe, falsely claiming he had killed Stunn's father; he also
claimed to have a warrant for Wolfe's arrest but stated he would accept a
horse as the price for not prosecuting. Stunn was arrested but escaped,
and after this incident, Wolfe lost interest in his family and property as

he became more depressed. Life in the home became increasingly difficult, so that Caty Wolfe sent her daughter Hannah to live with her aunt Mary Pope in June, 1805, and her son Adam to live with his uncle Charles Wolfe in Tennessee. Wolfe threatened to desert his family, and after a severe emotional attack, he sold his 200 acre farm to John Weaver on February 13, 1806, for considerably less that it was worth. He then took his youngest son, Jacob, and went to the Moravian settlement near Winston-Salem, North Carolina, where he apprenticed the boy to a saddler and loaned his money out at interest.[6]

On April 12, 1806, after Wolfe had gone to North Carolina, his sons Henry and John forced John Weaver to return to them the 200 acre farm; Henry got a patent to the land in 1809. Then on September 15, 1806, they agreed to furnish their mother the house where she lived, and each year to provide her with a half acre of flax land, 50 bushels of Indian corn, 400 pounds of pork, a bushel of salt, eight bushels of wheat, hay or fodder, a half acre of cotton land, fruit, pasture, firewood, three pairs of shoes, and $4.00 cash.[7]

About a year later, John Wolfe returned to his family on the Holston and stayed with them about a year. He then lived in the home of Jacob Peters for about two years and then bought 250 acres on Copper Creek in Russell County, Virginia. He hanged himself there in January, 1811, and his personal debts were settled and his estate sold in 1816.[8]

The Wolfe family was involved in several lawsuits concerning the property, as Caty and her younger children sought a share in the land that Henry and John Wolfe had acquired from Weaver; it was eventually divided in 1821 among all the heirs. Henry Wolfe sold his mother 137 acres of the farm on January 25, 1814, for $500.00; she sold the land on June 27, 1828, to her son-in-law, Abraham Lane, with whom she subsequently made her home until her death about 1835 in Scott County, Virginia.[9]

The children of John and Caty Wolfe were as follows:[10]

4. a. Henry Wolfe, born January 14, 1779.
5. b. John Wolfe, born March 27, 1781.
6. c. Catherine Wolfe, born October 3, 1782.
7. d. Adam Wolfe, born September 3, 1784.
   e. George Wolfe, born October 18, 1786; married Elizabeth _____.
   f. Hannah Wolfe, born October 20, 1788; married c1808 in Sullivan County, Tennessee, to Stephen Easley.
8. g. Jonas Wolfe, born October 12, 1790.
   h. Mary Wolfe, born September 8, 1792; died c1820; married c1812 William LeForce; moved to Illinois; children:
      (1) Dionysius LeForce, born c1813.
      (2) John Steuben LeForce, born c1815.
      (3) Virginia LeForce, born c1817.
      (4) Benjamin Devault LeForce, born c1819.
   i. Margaret Wolfe, born July 8, 1794; died c1862 in Scott County, Virginia; married c1814 John Bounds, son of Jesse and Cassandra Bounds; their children, perhaps among others, were as follows:
      (1) George Washington Bounds.
      (2) William Bounds.
      (3) Addison Bounds.
      (4) Mary Bounds married B. A. Woodrum; lived in Sacramento County, California.
      (5) John Bounds, born c1834.
      (6) Jacob N. Bounds, born c1837; married December 3, 1857, to Mary Quillen.

9. j. Jacob Wolfe, born July 27, 1796.

***

4.   Henry Wolfe was born January 14, 1779, in Berkeley County, (West) Virginia, and moved in infancy to western North Carolina; in the spring of 1778 he moved to Washington (now Scott) County, Virginia. He married Anna Hickman (see p. 51) about 1806, and on April 12, 1806, he and his brother John forced John Weaver to return to them the land which he had acquired from their father before he deserted the family; Henry received a patent to the land in 1809. On September 15, 1806, Henry and his brother John agreed to furnish their mother the house where she lived and to support her in the future. On January 14, 1814, Henry made a final settlement with his mother when he sold her 137 acres on the south side of the North Fork of the Holston for $500.00. On September 10, 1814, he sold his brother John 60 acres in the same area for $100.00. In 1816 he was taxed on a 206 acre farm.[11]

      In 1814, Henry Wolfe moved about 20 miles away to Sullivan County, Tennessee, where on March 12, 1816, acting for his brothers and sisters, he sold Andrew McHenry 265 acres on the north side of the North Fork of the Holston, and he sold his brother John the remainder of their father's land.[12]

      In 1816 their younger brothers and sister sued Henry and John Wolfe for other assets and were awarded $443.55; Henry did not contest the suit, believing the estate should be divided fairly. On May 31, 1827, he bought 66 acres on the north side of the Holston from Jacob S. Sampson for $450.00; he sold the land to Henry Mauk for $264.00 on March 28, 1834. He also gave his interest in the personal estate of his father-in-law, Peter Hickman, to his wife's nephew, Peter Hickman, on July 2, 1834.[13] Henry was poorly educated and not physically strong.

      In 1834, Henry Wolfe moved to near Catlin in Vermilion County, Illinois, where he acquired 40 acres, the northeastern quarter of the southeastern quarter of Section 23, Township 19 north, Range 13 west, by U. S. patent, and bought other land from his brother-in-law, Jacob Hickman, in what was then almost a wilderness. The family suffered considerable hardship and missed the more comfortable life in East Tennessee. Henry Wolfe made his will on April 6, 1843, dividing his property among his children, and he died on December 24, 1843; Anna Wolfe, his widow, died on May 24, 1846.[14] They left the following children:[15]

<table>
<tr><td>10.</td><td>a.</td><td>Elizabeth Wolfe, born May 9, 1808.</td></tr>
<tr><td>11.</td><td>b.</td><td>John Wolfe, born October 16, 1810.</td></tr>
<tr><td>12.</td><td>c.</td><td>Mary Wolfe, born January 30, 1813.</td></tr>
<tr><td></td><td>d.</td><td>Margaret Wolfe, born April 29, 1816; dsp c1835.</td></tr>
<tr><td>13.</td><td>e.</td><td>Isaac C. Wolfe, born August 29, 1818.</td></tr>
<tr><td></td><td>f.</td><td>Susan Wolfe, born September 28, 1821; died June 28, 1901, in Anson, Texas; married December 18, 1840, to Benjamin Franklin Davidson (see p. 15).</td></tr>
<tr><td>14.</td><td>g.</td><td>William Alexander Wolfe, born January 16, 1824.</td></tr>
<tr><td>15.</td><td>h.</td><td>Sarah Ann Wolfe, born August 1, 1826.</td></tr>
<tr><td>16.</td><td>i.</td><td>Henry Wolfe, born October 31, 1828.</td></tr>
<tr><td>17.</td><td>j.</td><td>George Washington Wolfe, born February 22, 1832.</td></tr>
<tr><td></td><td>k.</td><td>Jacob Hickman Wolfe, born October 22, 1834; dsp December 22, 1861, in Jefferson Barracks, Missouri.</td></tr>
</table>

***

10.   Elizabeth Wolfe was born May 9, 1808, in Washington (now Scott) County, Virginia, and died in 1871 in Monroe County, Indiana; married 1828 in Sullivan County, Tennessee, to William E. Whisnand, born May 26, 1807, son of Jacob and Rebecca Whisnand. Their children were as follows:[16]

a. John C. Whisnand, born c1830.
b. Franklin Whisnand, born c1833; married _____ Reese.
c. Margaret Whisnand, born c1835; married January 27, 1856, to William Ridge, born January 8, 1821, son of Benjamin Ridge and Henrietta Staton; lived in Monroe County, Indiana; children:
    (1) Laura A. Ridge married _____ Akin.
    (2) Elizabeth Ellis Ridge.
d. Emanuel Whisnand, born c1837.
e. Elizabeth Whisnand, born c1839; married John Ridge; children:
    (1) Martha Ridge married Emsley Stanger.
    (2) (daughter)
    (3) William Ridge, died young.
f. Rebecca Whisnand, born c1841; married _____ Minett.
g. Sarah J. Whisnand, born c1843; married _____ Riddle.
h. Thomas Whisnand, born c1845.
i. Susan Whisnand, born c1849; married _____ Mayfield.
j. Laura C. Whisnand, born c1851; married _____ Parks.
k. Elihu Whisnand, born c1853.

                              ***

11)   John Wolfe was born October 16, 1810, in Washington (now Scott) County, Virginia, and died August 19, 1891, in Sullivan County, Tennessee; married about 1833 Priscilla Webb. Their children were as follows:[17]

a. Franklin M. Wolfe, born c1836; married Winifred Shell; children:
    (1) John Bunyan Wolfe, born 1857; died 1940; married Nora E. Hughes; lived in Piney Flats, Tennessee.
    (2) Addie Wolfe, dsp.
    (3) Effie Wolfe, dsp.
    (4) Ella Wolfe, dsp.
    (5) William E. Wolfe.
b. Ann Catherine Wolfe, born c1839; married October 18, 1866, to James M. Osborne; child:
    (1) Beulah Osborne, dsp.
c. Dorthula Wolfe, born c1841; married John Torbett; lived in Texas; children:
    (1) Eula Torbett married _____ Crow.
    (2) Robert Leonard Torbett.
    (3) Kate Torbett married _____ Snapp.
    (4) Etta Torbett married _____ Hatcher.
d. Thomas H. B. Wolfe, born c1843; married 1861 Lucretia S. Massengill; children:
    (1) Joseph Massengill Wolfe, born 1861; dsp 1863.
    (2) Thomas Creed Wolfe, born 1865; dsp 1884.
e. Creed T. Wolfe, born c1845; married (1) Kate Maxwell (2) Melissa White; children:
    (1) S. Merton Wolfe, died 1941.
    (2) Nellie Wolfe married _____ Warren.
    (3) William Wagner Wolfe.
f. Elbert S. Wolfe, born c1847; married Mary Akord; dsp.
g) John W. Robertson Wolfe, born c1855; died 1940; married c1877 Jane Webb; children:
    (1) Walter B. Wolfe, born c1878.

```
                (2)  Clark S. Wolfe, born September, 1880.
                (3)  Mary Wolfe.
                (4)  Beulah Wolfe.
                (5)  Joseph M. Wolfe, born c1886; lived in Umatilla, Florida.
                (6)  John Wolfe.
                (7)  Winifred Wolfe.
           h.   Loretta Wolfe, born c1857; dsp.
           i.   Penelope J. Wolfe, born c1861; married Landon Rader; lived in Texas;
                children:
                (1)  Ruby Rader.
                (2)  Frederick Rader; lived in Dallas, Texas.
                (3)  Don Rader.
```

                                    ***

12.   Mary Wolfe was born January 30, 1813, in Washington (now Scott) County,
      Virginia, and died November 30, 1897, in Vermilion County, Illinois; mar-
      ried about 1833 Samuel Cooper, born November 23, 1807, died March 1, 1859.
      Their children, probably among others, were as follows:[18]

```
      a.   Sarah A. Cooper, born c1834.
      b.   Isabel Cooper, born December 28, 1835; died November 7, 1863; married
           William Ginnison.
      c.   Nancy E. Cooper, born June 7, 183?; dsp August 7, 18??.
      d.   Margaret J. Cooper, born c1841.
      e.   Susan E. Cooper, born c1843.
      f.   Lucinda Cooper, born c1846.
      g.   Mary L. Cooper, born c1849.
      h.   John Edward Cooper, born March 12, 1856; dsp January 12, 1857.
```

                                    ***

13.   Isaac C. Wolfe was born August 29, 1818, in Sullivan County, Tennes-
      see, and died May 17, 1889, in Vermilion County, Illinois; married (1) Dec-
      ember 17, 1840, Eliza Ann O'Neal, born December 19, 1818; died March 20,
      1846; (2) September 7, 1848, Mary Pate (3) June 17, 1858, Elizabeth Pate.
      His children were as follows:[19]

```
      (by first marriage):
      a.   William F. Wolfe, born 1841; married (1) Cornelia A. Hickman (see p.
           54)  (2)  Mary Onley; children:
           (1)  Kate Wolfe married _____ Williams.
           (2)  Bert Wolfe.
      b.   Henry C. Wolfe, born 1843.
      c.   John Wolfe, born 1845.
      (by second marriage):
      d.   Catherine Wolfe, born 1850.
      e.   George W. Wolfe, born c1853; married (1) _____ _____ (2) Mathilda
           Martin; children:
           (by first marriage):
           (1)  Nell Wolfe married _____ Campbell; lived in Danville, Illinois.
           (by second marriage):
           (2)  Warren Wolfe, dsp.
           (3)  May Wolfe married _____ Lanter.
      f.   Anna Wolfe married John M. Shipps.
      (by third marriage):
      g.   Winfield Scott Wolfe married Emma McPherson; children:
           (1)  Lola Wolfe married (1) _____ Jones (2) _____ Fogle.
           (2)  Evert Wolfe married Kate Casteel; lived in Catlin, Illinois.
```

```
        (3)  Ethan Wolfe died November, 1944; married Inez Gavin.
        (4)  Lula Wolfe married James Blatteau; lived in Catlin, Illinois.
        (5)  Arthur Wolfe married Inez Pogue; lived in Catlin, Illinois.
        (6)  Angie Wolfe married _____ Moss.
        (7)  Virginia Wolfe, dsp.
        (8)  Irvin Wolfe married Madge Johnson; lived in Catlin, Illinois.
    h.  Clara Wolfe, dsp.
    i.  Adam Wolfe married (1) Ann Shipps (2) Martha Ellen Shaw; children:
        (by first marriage):
        (1)  Turner Wolfe married Bertha _____.
        (by second marriage):
        (2)  Ida Wolfe married William Colberg.
```

                                    ***

14.   William Alexander Wolfe was born January 16, 1824, in Sullivan County,
Tennessee, and died March 24, 1893, in Vermilion County, Illinois; married
about 1845 to Eliza Scroggin; their children were as follows:[20]

```
    a.  Henry Jefferson Wolfe died June 11, 1917; married Hannah Drusilla Bun-
        ker; children:
        (1)  Ethel M. Wolfe married _____ Neff; lived in Oakwood, Illinois.
        (2)  Jessie Wolfe married James Montgomery; lived in Oakwood, Illinois.
        (3)  Della Wolfe married _____ Musson; lived in Oakwood, Illinois.
    b.  Jacob Hickman Wolfe, born 1858; died 1928; married Ruth Ann Bunker;
        children:
        (1)  Ella Wolfe married Robert Bowles.
        (2)  Benjamin Franklin Wolfe married Cora A. Runyan; lived in Fairmount,
             Illinois.
        (3)  Bertha Wolfe married Bud Renfro.
        (4)  Ferman Wolfe married Ianthana See.
        (5)  Bessie Wolfe married Woodrow Poynter.
        (6)  Alice Wolfe married Oral Kinney.
    c.  Mary E. Wolfe married John R. Wilson.
    d.  John B. Wolfe married Ruvilla Yates.
    e.  Leonard Wolfe married Martha Bowmett.
    f.  Effie Wolfe married _____ Stinsey; dsp.
    g.  Alice Wolfe, dsp.
```

                                    ***

15.   Sarah Ann Wolfe was born August 1, 1826, in Sullivan County, Tennessee, and died March 9, 1899, in Vermilion County, Illinois; married April
21, 1844, to Philander Bennett; their children were as follows:[21]

```
    a.  Ann E. Bennett, born 1845; married William M. Jamison; lived in Cat-
        lin, Illinois; children:
        (1)  Charles Jamison.
        (2)  Kate Jamison.
        (3)  Mary Jamison.
        (4)  George Jamison.
        (5)  William Jamison.
        (6)  Bertie Jamison married _____ Linn; lived in Catlin, Illinois.
    b.  Henry J. Bennett, born February 16, 1847; married 1879 Malissa A.
        Stark; lived in Vermilion County, Illinois; children:
        (1)  Watella Bennett.
        (2)  Fra Bennett.
        (3)  Sarah Anna Bennett.
        (4)  Cora Bennett.
```

                                    272

        (5) Elma Bennett.
        (6) Ethel Bennett.
    c. DeWitt Clinton Bennett, born June 4, 1849; married 1877 Mrs. Nancy
        Jane (Fuller) Spellman; lived in Vermilion County, Illinois; children:
        (1) Sarah I. Bennett.
        (2) Charles Bennett.
        (3) Jacob Clark Bennett.
        (4) Bessie W. Bennett.
        (5) Luella Bennett.
    d. George Franklin Bennett married Rachel Trimble; lived in Dundee County,
        Nebraska; children:
        (1) Clinton Bennett.
        (2) Minnie Bennett.
        (3) Frank Bennett.
        (4) Grace Bennett.
        (5) Norma Bennett.
    e. Mary E. Bennett married Jonah Turner; child:
        (1) Louise Turner.
    f. William K. Bennett, died young.
    g. Ida B. Bennett married Esau Marsh; lived in Missouri; children:
        (1) Alice M. Marsh.
        (2) Anna Marsh.
        (3) Virgil Marsh.
    h. Alice M. Bennett married Wilson Glaze; lived in Kirkland, Washington;
        children:
        (1) Grover Glaze.
        (2) Zadel Glaze.
        (3) Mamie Glaze.
        (4) Frank Glaze.
        (5) Carvel Glaze.
        (6) Ruth Glaze.
        (7) Ralph Glaze.
        (8) Kenneth Glaze.
    i. Jacob Bennett married Emma Jones; children:
        (1) Hazel Bennett.
        (2) Lester Bennett.
        (3) Russell Bennett.
        (4) Sarah Bennett.
        (5) Wilbur Bennett.
        (6) Frances Bennett.
        (7) Thomas Bennett.
        (8) Robert Bennett.
        (9) Bessie Bennett.
        (10) Lena Bennett.

                            ***

16.   Henry Wolfe was born October 31, 1828, in Sullivan County, Tennessee,
    and died August 20, 1898, in Ulysses, Nebraska; married February 28, 1850,
    in Vermilion County, Illinois, to Mary Fielder, born March 3, 1833; died
    January 12, 1916, daughter of Enos Fielder and Fidelia Butler. Their chil-
    dren were as follows:[22]

18. a. John J. Wolfe, born November 5, 1850.
    b. Isaac Wolfe, born September 10, 1853; died young.
    c. Mary Ann Wolfe, born September 23, 1854; died young.
19. d. Susan Wolfe, born October 31, 1856.
    e. Eliza Jane Wolfe, born October 10, 1858; died October, 1932, in Coun-
        cil Bluffs, Iowa; married October, 1874, Ebenezer Vincent; children:

                   (1)   William Vincent.
                   (2)   Jesse J. Vincent.
                   (3)   Pleasant Vincent.
                   (4)   Emilie Vincent.
                   (5)   May Vincent.
                   (6)   Jimmie Vincent.
                   (7)   Virgie Vincent.
                   (8)   Ellwood Vincent.
                   (9)   Olive Vincent.
                   (10) Inez Vincent.
                   (11) Lee Vincent.
                   (12) Lucille Vincent.
                   (13) Pearl Vincent.
          f. Ellen Wolfe, born September 28, 1860; died young.
          g. Charles Wolfe, born September 28, 1860; died young.
          h. Julia Wolfe, born July 23, 1861; died young.
          i. William G. Wolfe, born March 12, 1863; married (1) 1886 Mary Wood (2)
              Ida Newberry; dsp (an adopted son).
          j. Elnora Wolfe, born September 23, 1865; died November, 1949; married
              (1) November, 1884, Charles Cook (2) Frank Thomas (3) _____ Bowen;
              children (all by first marriage):
                   (1)   Ralph Cook, died young.
                   (2)   Clem Cook, born March 29, 1888; married Lula Bruce; children:
                         (a)   Ruth Cook, born December 4, 1910.
                         (b)   Bruce Cook.
                   (3)   Faye Cook, born September 6, 1892; died March 8, 1952; married
                         (1) Henry Hern (2) Henry Morris Wolfe (see p. 275); children
                         (all by first marriage):
                         (a)   Eleanor Hern, born August 11, 1910; married Joseph Danaher;
                               dsp.
                         (b)   Clem H. Hern, born January 21, 1914; lived in Douglas,
                               Wyoming.
                   (4)   June Cook, died young.
          k. James D. Wolfe, born June 23, 1867; died January 3, 1956; married (1)
              1885 Flora Johnson (2) March 2, 1905, Ida Winton, died August 9, 1935;
              (3) August 6, 1936, Mrs. Amanda Morgan; lived in Green Forest, Arkan-
              sas; children (all by first marriage):
                   (1)   Hulda Wolfe.
                   (2)   Victoria Wolfe.
20.   l. George W. Wolfe, born January 10, 1870.
21.   m. Edwin Wolfe, born September 3, 1871.
22.   n. Henry Wolfe, born December 19, 1873.
          o. Walter Wolfe, born March 12, 1875; died young.
          p. Eva May Wolfe, born June 19, 1879; died young.
          q. Rose Wolfe, born July 18, 1880; died young.

                                    ***

18.   John J. Wolfe was born November 5, 1850, and died January 27, 1924,
     in Longmont, Colorado; married March 21, 1872, to Cornelia Marietta Wood,
     who was born September 20, 1853, and died April 8, 1923, daughter of Henry
     Morris Wood and Celestia Ward. They had the following children:[23]

          a. Julia Blanche Wolfe, born May 22, 1873; married Morris Milton Martin;
              lived in Grinnell, Kansas; children:
                   (1)   Lelia Grace Martin, died young.
                   (2)   Edna Lucy Martin, born February 16, 1905.
                   (3)   John Frederick Martin.
                   (4)   Morris Milton Martin, born November 11, 1911.
                   (5)   Hazel Blanche Martin.

                                    274

23. b. Lyman Clarke Wolfe, born January 26, 1875.
     c. Fred Ira Wolfe, born c1877; married Ethel Wrightsman; children:
         (1) Don Frederick Wolfe.
         (2) Roy Wolfe.
         (3) Dorothy Wolfe married Glen Miller; lived in Nappanee, Illinois.
         (4) Frances Wolfe.
     d. Ethel Olive Wolfe, born February 24, 1880; dsp November 17, 1902; mar-
         ried Otis L. Organ.
     e. George Guy Wolfe, born February 27, 1882; dsp March 29, 1890.
     f. Henry Morris Wolfe, born January 18, 1884; died August 22, 1959, in
         Lincoln, Nebraska; married (1) Susan Moreland (2) Mrs. Faye (Cook) Hern
         (see p. 274); child (by first marriage):
         (1) Clair Moreland Wolfe, born July 23, 1911; married (1) Dorothy
              Jackson (2) April 24, 1954, Elsiemae Johnsen; lived in Omaha,
              Nebraska; children (by first marriage):
              (a) Jacqueline Mae Wolfe, born December 16, 1943; married Ray-
                   mond Edwin Houdesheldt, born September 22, 1939; children:
                   /1/ Gary Guy Houdesheldt, born May 16, 1962.
                   /2/ Dean Edwin Houdesheldt, born October 4, 1968.
                   /3/ Neil Ray Houdesheldt, born January 31, 1970.
              (b) John Jackson Wolfe, born November 25, 1945; married August 29,
                   1968, Patricia Mary Widding, born January 20, 1950; child:
                   /1/ Teresa Ann Wolfe, born March 19, 1969.
24. g. Charles Adolph Wolfe, born August 29, 1886.
     h. Queenie Estelle Wolfe, born December 10, 1888; married February 1,
         1911, to James Harvey Truman, who died January 29, 1954; lived in
         Gonzales, California; children:
         (1) Ruth Dorothy Truman, born November 20, 1912; married (1) Ronald
              Wright (2) April 18, 1944, Joseph Rockford; children:
              (by first marriage):
              (a) Robert Leon Wright.
              (by second marriage):
              (b) Walter James Rockford.
         (2) Mary Rudore Truman, born September 10, 1914; died November 29,
              1951; married October 14, 1938, to Willard Leonard; children:
              (a) Karen Kay Leonard, born June 2, 1939.
              (b) Delton William Leonard, born April 21, 1940; dsp August, 1943.
              (c) Roy Lee Leonard, born March 21, 1944.
              (d) John Dennis Leonard, born March 25, 1951.
         (3) James Harvey Truman, born October 14, 1916; married April 20, 1944,
              to Betty Anna Dameron; lived in Longmont, Colorado; child:
              (a) Connie Sue Truman, born May 21, 1945.
     i. Grace Edna Wolfe, born October 28, 1892; dsp November 11, 1899.

                                   * * *

23.   Lyman Clarke Wolfe was born January 26, 1875; married June 22, 1903,
     to Maude Nora Lanham, born May 24, 1886, and died July 25, 1938; lived in
     Ft. Lupton, Colorado. Their children were as follows:[24]

     a. Ethel Grace Wolfe, born February 7, 1904; married 1906 Ray Mundy.
     b. Maryle Estella Wolfe, born August 13, 1906; married 1926 Yale Thayer.
     c. Edna Wolfe, born June 11, 1908; married December 2, 1933, Keith Carter.
     d. Cornelia Wolfe, born February 24, 1910; married June 26, 1930, Marvin
         Dull.
     e. Lela Wolfe, born November 25, 1911; married October 3, 1931, Loyd
         Elliot.
     f. Elmo Wolfe, born April 4, 1913; married January 26, 1936, Betty _____.
     g. Louella Wolfe, born March 3, 1917; married November 24, 1935, Roy

Davenport.
h. Vera Wolfe, born March 9, 1921; dsp May 31, 1934.
i. Patricia Wolfe, born March 15, 1929; married June 20, 1948, Donald Newman, born April 19, 1929.

***

24.   Charles Adolph Wolfe was born August 29, 1886, and married October 10, 1915, Fanny Pettit; lived in Newcastle, Wyoming; their children were as follows:[25]

a. Albert Eugene Wolfe, born August 23, 1916; married August 25, 1938, to Nellie _____, born May 28, 1918; lived in Roundup, Montana; children:
    (1) Charles Eugene Wolfe, born March 15, 1940.
    (2) David Lee Wolfe, born November 16, 1942.
    (3) Robert Wayne Wolfe, born April 19, 1945.
b. Charles Marvin Wolfe, born July 30, 1918; married June 30, 1949, to Kathryn _____; lived in Alamogordo, New Mexico; children:
    (1) Susan Bernice Wolfe, born c1950.
    (2) Kathryn Wolfe, born c1951.
    (3) Mary Ellen Wolfe, born c1952.
    (4) Timothy Charles Wolfe, born c1953.
    (5) James Daniel Wolfe, born c1954.
c. Clarence Wilbur Wolfe, born July 9, 1920; married December, 1942, to Albena _____, born June, 1921; lived in Newcastle, Wyoming; children:
    (1) Sherry Lorraine Wolfe, born March 15, 1946.
    (2) Eldon Francis Wolfe, born October, 1947.
d. Lyle Lorn Wolfe, born July 28, 1922; married February 27, 1946, to Dorothy _____, born February 27, 1920; lived in Rawlins, Wyoming; children:
    (1) Harold Wallace Wolfe, born December 4, 19??.
    (2) Lyla Lynn Wolfe, born November 16, 19??.
    (3) Doris Elizabeth Wolfe.
e. Harold Monroe Wolfe, born August 25, 1925; married July, 1946, to Janet _____, born May 6, 1930; lived in Anaconda, Montana; children:
    (1) Delores Ann Wolfe, born February 2, 1948.
    (2) Marrilan Wolfe, born December 11, 1951.
    (3) John Harold Wolfe, born November 21, 1952.
    (4) Diana Wolfe, born May 6, 1954.
    (5) Randall Thomas Wolfe, born January 3, 1958.
f. Ray Ernest Wolfe, born March 20, 1927; married June 1, 1949, to Helen _____, born April 6, 1930; lived in Newcastle, Wyoming; children:
    (1) Gary Ray Wolfe, born January 14, 1950.
    (2) Anita Helen Wolfe, born October, 1953.
g. Richard Urless Wolfe, born November 12, 1930; married (1) August 16, 1952, to Josephine Flossie _____, born November 8, 1932, (2) September 21, 1957, to Carol Naomi _____, born May 29, 1938; child (by first marriage):
    (1) Frederick Richard Wolfe, born April 18, 1953.

***

19.   Susan Wolfe was born October 31, 1856, and died after 1938 in David City, Nebraska; married March, 1874, Orrick D. Bunting; their children were as follows:[26]

a. Ora Edna Bunting, born December, 1876; married 1895 Edwin Wunderlich; lived in David City, Nebraska; children:
    (1) Bernice Wunderlich.
    (2) Ross Wunderlich.

276

b. Clara May Bunting, died young.
c. Walter Scott Bunting married Alta Moore.
d. Arthur Henry Bunting married Eleanor Moore.
e. Pearl Bunting, died young.
f. Esther Bunting, died young.
g. Ernest Elmer Bunting married Martha Gosney; lived in Fullerton, Nebraska.
h. Dolly Bunting, died young.
i. Vera Viola Bunting married September, 1912, John Barry Hall; lived in Gering, Nebraska; children:
   (1) Vera Lucille Hall married Willard Francis McGliff; lived in Gering, Nebraska.
   (2) John Elton Hall married Louise Oyler.
   (3) George Barry Hall married Elizabeth Odell.
   (4) Lavonne Viola Hall married Charlton M. Brown.
j. Fern Bunting married October, 1913, Paul Henry Lucas; lived in Denver, Colorado; children:
   (1) Pauline Vera Lucas, born October 30, 1914; married July, 1934, James R. Snyder; child:
       (a) Sandra Sue Snyder, born December 27, 1937; married September 30, 1955, Robert J. Call; lived in North Platte, Nebraska; children:
           /1/ Vanessa Lynn Call, born February 13, 1956.
           /2/ James Robert Call, born August 21, 1957.
           /3/ Melanie Sue Call, born January 23, 1963.
   (2) Donald Lucas, died young.

***

20.   George W. Wolfe was born January 10, 1870, and died May 14, 1952, in Sherman County, Nebraska; married September 7, 1892, to Josephine P. Shields, who died January 23, 1941; their children were as follows:[27]

a. Henry Thomas Wolfe, born December 20, 1894; died September 29, 1949, in Deadwood, South Dakota; married April 22, 1919, to Leona Melton; child:
   (1) Carlton Wolfe, born February 9, 1923; lived in Burlington, Iowa.
b. Mary Adeline Wolfe, born March 11, 1896; married March 11, 1915, to William Ray Estabrooks; lived in Colville, Washington:
   (1) Willis Wray Estabrooks, born September 16, 1925; married Betty Jane Thomas; lived in Colville, Washington; child:
       (a) Mark William Estabrooks, born October 8, 1960.
c. Leonard Wolfe, born May 4, 1898; married (1) June 4, 1919, to Edith Ann Cornford (2) September 16, 1944, to Della Shadd; lived in Grand Island, Nebraska; children (all by first marriage):
   (1) Louella Wolfe, born February 13, 1921; married Wilbur Hinrichs; children:
       (a) Willa Lou Hinrichs, born December 29, 1942.
       (b) Frederick L. Hinrichs, born February 20, 1947.
       (c) Phillip R. Hinrichs, born October 2, 1948.
       (d) Weldon S. Hinrichs, born May 10, 1952.
       (e) LeAnn R. Hinrichs, born May 19, 1955.
       (f) Carolina Hinrichs, born February 1, 1959.
   (2) George William Wolfe, born April 9, 1924; married Dorothy Kentta; lived in Lincoln, Nebraska; children:
       (a) Edith Wolfe, born November 17, 1951.
       (b) Judith Wolfe, born November 6, 1952.
       (c) Karen Wolfe, born November 26, 1954.
   (3) Eunice Wolfe, born May 16, 1930; dsp June 22, 1935.

277

(4) Genone Wolfe, born March 18, 1934; died June 23, 1935.

***

21.   Edwin Wolfe was born September 3, 1871, and died May 27, 1939, in
Seward, Nebraska; married February 28, 1892, to Rosella Rick, who was born
December 21, 1876, and died April 19, 1972; their children were as fol-
lows:[28]

    a. Merle A. Wolfe, born June 27, 1893; married February 12, 1913, to Carl
        C. Koch, who died September 14, 1946; lived in Casper, Wyoming; chil-
        dren:
        (1) Thelma R. Koch, born April 4, 1914; married March 22, 1935, to
             Claud L. Taylor; lived in Casper, Wyoming; child:
             (a) Patricia A. Taylor, born April 27, 1936; married June 5,
                  1954, Lyle E. Speer; children:
                  /1/ Michael E. Taylor, born March 8, 1955.
                  /2/ Karen J. Taylor, born January 8, 1958.
        (2) Dorothy L. Koch, born October 2, 1918; married February 20, 1949,
             to Gene D. Carson; lived in Casper, Wyoming; child:
             (a) Susan Dale Carson, born August 13, 1952.
        (3) Gerald L. Koch, born September 30, 1920; married November 6, 1948,
             to Dorothy R. Racich; lived in Casper, Wyoming; child:
             (a) Lynn M. Koch, born December 6, 1952.
25. b. Ray Edwin Wolfe, born January 24, 1895.
    c. Eugene O. Wolfe, born May 24, 1897; dsp November 11, 1918.
    d. Gladys L. Wolfe, born July 25, 1900; dsp January 4, 1971; married May
        20, 1938, to Charles B. Knapp.
    e. Francis Wolfe, born February 27, 1915; dsp March 4, 1915.

***

25.   Ray Edwin Wolfe was born January 24, 1895, and died February 6, 1958,
in Lincoln, Nebraska. He married February 11, 1920, to Ella M. Gunlack,
who was born November 3, 1900; their children were as follows:[29]

    a. Leslie L. Wolfe, born October 24, 1921; married Alice Cast; children:
        (1) Phillip L. Wolfe, born March 14, 1942.
        (2) Victor L. Wolfe, born February 2, 1944.
    b. Donald Ray Wolfe, born February 5, 1923; married Margie Oswald; lived
        in Lincoln, Nebraska, child (not including two adopted children):
        (1) David Wolfe, born September 9, 1952.
    c. Joanne Wolfe, born September 30, 1925; married William Kipf; lived in
        Beatrice, Nebraska; children:
        (1) Linda Jo Kipf, born July 23, 1952.
        (2) Billie Ray Kipf, born August 18, 1953.
        (3) Lorella K. Kipf, born January 20, 1955.
        (4) Lynelle J. Kipf, born June 1, 1956.
        (5) Loralee A. Kipf, born May 4, 1957.
        (6) Lecia Sue Kipf, born October 16, 1958.
        (7) Lorraine J. Kipf, born March 1, 1960.
    d. Harold C. Wolfe, born October 13, 1927; married Viola Brauer; lived in
        Lincoln, Nebraska; children:
        (1) Gail D. Wolfe, born June 21, 1948.
        (2) Michael G. Wolfe, born March 2, 1950.
        (3) Timothy J. Wolfe, born November 19, 1956.
        (4) Ranae Sue Wolfe, born January 22, 1960.
    e. Gene Edwin Wolfe, born November 1, 1929; married Mary Betzner; lived in
        Santa Susana, California; child (not including an adopted son):

        (1) Cheryl Sue Wolfe, born November 30, 1957.
    f. Dean J. Wolfe, born November 1, 1929; married Norma DeWolfe; lived in
        North Cambridge, Massachusetts; children:
        (1) George D. Wolfe, born October 23, 1949.
        (2) Richard Ray Wolfe, born November 21, 1950.
        (3) James J. Wolfe, born November 23, 1952.
        (4) Corrine M. Wolfe, born July 30, 1954.
        (5) Carol A. Wolfe, born December 20, 1956.
        (6) Deborah A. Wolfe, born September 26, 1961.
    g. Roger D. Wolfe, born April 21, 1942; married June 26, 1965, to LaDean
        Hraban; lived in Fullerton, California.

                                    ***

22.   Henry Wolfe was born December 19, 1873, and died August 30, 1952, in
    Fremont, Nebraska; married (1) 1895 Sadie Wood, who died July 5, 1951; (2)
    Mrs. Maggie Anderson. His children were as follows:[30]

    (by first marriage):
    a. Leigh Wolfe, born May 28, 1897; married July, 1925, Edna Bishop; lived
        in Casper, Wyoming; children:
        (1) Donald L. Wolfe, born March 13, 1926; married (1) DeLoris Daniels
             (2) Alberta Calder; lived in Canon City, Colorado; children:
             (by first marriage):
             (a) Laura Wolfe, born November 4, 1946.
             (by second marriage):
             (b) Wayne Wolfe, born August 25, 1950.
             (c) Connie Wolfe, born February 7, 1952.
             (d) Diane Wolfe, born June 18, 1953.
        (2) Wayne R. Wolfe, born May 25, 1928; married (1) Ellen Prior (2)
             Beruta Tigress; lived in Casper, Wyoming; child (by first mar-
             riage):
             (a) Tracy Wolfe, born August 27, 1929.
        (3) Donna M. Wolfe, born April 19, 1931; married Keith Ellerbruch;
             lived in Sunnyvale, California; children:
             (a) Terry Lea Ellerbruch, born December 30, 1955.
             (b) Timothy J. Ellerbruch, born February 2, 1958.
             (c) Jeffrey A. Ellerbruch, born March 5, 1960.
    b. Glenn Wolfe, born November 24, 1898; died 1971 in California.
    c. Harley Wolfe, born September 20, 1900; married Helen Thrasher; children:
        (1) Arnold Eugene Wolfe, born June 16, 1924; died young.
        (2) Geraldine Wolfe, born October 9, 1926; married Jack Collins; chil-
             dren:
             (a) Jackie Collins.
             (b) Deborah Collins.
             (c) James Collins.
        (3) Alvin Wolfe, born July 2, 19??; married Thylis _____.
        (4) Harold Wolfe, born January 27, 1935; married Joyce J. Grubtill;
             lived in Casper, Wyoming; children:
             (a) Kraig Wolfe, born May 3, 1955.
             (b) Karrie A. Wolfe, born April 20, 1956.
    (by second marriage):
    d. Ora Wolfe, born August, 1924.

                                    ***

17.   George Washington Wolfe was born February 22, 1832, in Sullivan County,
    Tennessee, and died January 23, 1913, in Catlin, Illinois; married October
    22, 1854, in Vermilion County, Illinois, to Ann Eliza Caraway. Their

children were as follows:[31]

a. Martha Belle Wolfe, born June 20, 1856; died August 26, 1893; married
Glenn S. Fleming; children:
   (1) Maude Fleming, born February 10, 1882; married Frank Bushong; dsp.
   (2) Mable Fleming, born October 27, 1885; married (1) _____ Johnson
       (2) _____ Folk.
   (3) Blanche Fleming, born May 5, 1888; married (1) Daniel Murphy (2)
       _____ Forbes.
   (4) Madge Fleming, born November 26, 1891; married Ross Nelson.
b. Charles Henry Wolfe, born July 27, 1858; died May 31, 1928; married
Mary Elizabeth Fleming; children:
   (1) Georgina Wolfe, born September 11, 1891; married Dayton Strickland.
   (2) Mary Fern Wolfe, born July 29, 1893; married _____ Miller.
   (3) Roscoe Charles Wolfe, born September 30, 1895; dsp.
c. John Milton Wolfe, born October 21, 1860; died August 18, 1887; married Clara Burkett; children:
   (1) Elmer Burkett Wolfe, born 1883; died 1926; married May Storm.
   (2) Winburn William Wolfe, born March 6, 1886; married Gertrude _____ .
d. Abraham Lincoln Wolfe, born December 24, 1862; died July 16, 1932;
married Louise M. Lloyd; children:
   (1) Edna Mabel Wolfe, born February 20, 1887; married Arthur Dix; dsp.
   (2) Howard Lloyd Wolfe, born May 17, 1889; married Ethel Jenkins;
       lived in Catlin, Illinois; children:
       (a) Arthur Lloyd Wolfe, born 1913; married Gretchen Drews; child:
           /1/ Charles Howard Wolfe, born December 1, 1944.
       (b) Anna Louise Wolfe, born December 7, 1923; dsp August 28,
           1942.
       (c) Bertha May Wolfe, born February 18, 1931.
e. Bertha C. Wolfe, born September 3, 1875; dsp July 16, 1942; married
James Sidell.

***

5.   John Wolfe was born March 27, 1781, in North Carolina, and died February 13, 1864, in Scott County, Virginia. He bought the interests of his
brothers and sisters in their father's estate and later acquired other
lands. He was a magistrate and sheriff of Scott County. About 1805 he
married Mary DeVault, born October 11, 1785; died December 29, 1868. They
had the following children:[32]

26. a. Elizabeth Wolfe, born c1806.
27. b. George Wolfe, born July 11, 1808.
28. c. Emmanuel Wolfe, born February 28, 1813.
29. d. Elvira Wolfe, born c1818.
30. e. Margaret Irene Wolfe, born October 24, 1820.
31. f. Lucinda Wolfe, born May 26, 1823.
32. g. Isaac Wolfe, born October 11, 1825.

***

26.   Elizabeth Wolfe was born about 1806 and married Stephen Epperson on
January 5, 1824; they had the following children:[33]

a. Mary A. Epperson.
b. William H. Epperson married Mary Delaney; children:
   (1) Lula Epperson married Joseph Butler; child:
       (a) Kelly Butler.
   (2) Minerva Epperson married Commodore Larkins; child:

    (a) Floyd Larkins.
  (3) Genette Epperson married Martin Caudill; child:
    (a) Floyd Caudill.
  (4) Elizabeth Epperson married Henderson Ford.
  (5) Eliza Epperson married William Dickerson.
  (6) John W. Epperson married Lou Francisco.
  (7) Stephen Floyd Epperson, born November 1, 1856; died March 23,
    1923; married Mary Virginia Lawson, born March 12, 1856; died
    February 2, 1937; child:
    (a) William F. Epperson, born June 12, 1882; married December
      15, 1909, Fena Ellen Reed, born November 1, 1884; children:
      /1/ Floyd B. Epperson married July 21, 1931, Beulah Swartz;
        children:
        /a/ Phyllis Ann Epperson, born January 28, 1932.
        /b/ Howard Lee Epperson, born September 11, 1935.
      /2/ William Henry Epperson, born June 12, 1913.
      /3/ Mary Elizabeth Epperson, born March 6, 1915; married
        March 12, 1938, Paul Kloster, born October 9, 1912;
        child:
        /a/ Paul Philip Kloster, born December 3, 1938.
 c. John W. Epperson.
 d. Elvira Epperson married David Haynes; children:
  (1) Lucinda Haynes.
  (2) William S. Haynes married Malinda P. Ladd, born August 7, 1850;
    died March 17, 1912; children:
    (a) George P. Haynes.
    (b) John Wiley Haynes.
    (c) David Gilmer Haynes.
    (d) Samuel Haynes.
    (e) Emory H. Haynes.
    (f) Orban P. Haynes.
    (g) Nannie Haynes, born June, 1888; dsp September, 1888.
    (h) James G. Haynes.
  (3) John W. Haynes.
  (4) Betty B. Haynes.
  (5) James J. Haynes.
  (6) Irene Haynes married (1) John Fletcher (2) Isaac Grigsby.
  (7) Samuel D. Haynes.
33. e. Irene Epperson, born April 1, 1840.
 f. Delphia Ann Epperson.
 g. Joseph Epperson.
 h. Isaac Epperson, died c1864.
 i. Sarah Epperson.

            ***

33.   Irene Epperson was born April 1, 1840, and died December 6, 1922;
married July 30, 1859, to David Shelton, born March 27, 1838; died July 5,
1897. Their children were as follows:[34]

34. a. William B. Shelton, born May 5, 1860.
 b. John Wolfe Shelton, born February 3, 1862; dsp December 30, 1886.
35. c. James Logan Shelton, born April 26, 1864.
 d. Bettie Ann Shelton, born September 16, 1869; died July 1, 1901; married Benjamin L. Russell; children:
  (1) Nannie Belle Russell, born September 20, 1889; married February 3,
    1907, to Ellis Ross, born June 9, 1879; lived near Fortuna, Cali-
    fornia; children:
    (a) Gertha Grace Ross.

```
                    (b)  Mattie Eulalia Ross.
                    (c)  Robert Cornelius Ross.
                    (d)  Nannie Belle Ross.
                    (e)  Lawrence Ellis Ross.
                    (f)  Elizabeth Irene Ross.
                    (g)  William Thomas Ross.
                    (h)  Marion Jean Ross.
                (2)  Benjamin Henry Russell.
                (3)  William J. Russell.
36.    e.  Stephen Martin Shelton, born December 6, 1872.
37.    f.  Robert A. D. Shelton, born August 14, 1876.
       g.  Henry Clinton Shelton, born March 11, 1881; married (1) February 18,
           1904, to Lockie L. Taylor, died August 26, 1907; (2) October 13, 1925,
           Ebbie Christian, born July 8, 1871; lived in Church Hill, Tennessee;
           children (all by first marriage):
                (1)  Bettie Shelton, born March 27, 1905; married December 29, 1925,
                     to James C. Robinette, born August 15, 1906; children:
                    (a)  U. L. Robinette, born April 28, 1926.
                    (b)  G. B. Robinette, born October 23, 1927.
                    (c)  W. L. Robinette, born July 13, 1930.
                    (d)  Ebbie Robineete, born March 25, 1932.
                    (e)  James C. Robinette, born January 13, 1934.
                (2)  Lockie L. Shelton, born February 25, 1907; married August 26,
                     1932, to Allen Christian, born May 26, 1913; children:
                    (a)  U. J. Christian, born August 20, 1933.
                    (b)  Charles C. Christian, born June 20, 1934.


                                    ***


34.         William B. Shelton was born May 5, 1860, and married January 7, 1880,
       to Rebecca Jane Hackney, born October 1, 1860; their children were as
       follows:35

       a.  Henry Flournoy Shelton, born December 28, 1880; dsp October 23, 1923;
           married August 1, 1909, to Hattie Moore, died June 23, 1914; lived in
           Merit, Texas.
       b.  John Wolfe Shelton, born January 11, 1882; married February 7, 1907,
           to Stella M. Clapp, born February 10, 1887; children:
                (1)  Eula Shelton, born October, 1909; married January 8, 1928, to
                     O. B. Henslee; lived in Blue Ridge, Texas; children:
                    (a)  John David Henslee, born March 6, 1930.
                    (b)  Almeta Henslee, born September 8, 1932.
                (2)  Luther Shelton, born February 10, 1911.
                (3)  Nell Shelton, born January 11, 1913; married December 28, 1933,
                     to J. L. Rhea; lived in Caddo Mills, Texas.
                (4)  Thomas Shelton, born July 17, 1915.
                (5)  Ralph Shelton, born February 24, 1917.
                (6)  Erma Ruth Shelton, born August 20, 1925.
       c.  Sallie Kate Shelton, born October 8, 1883.
       d.  Clauda Irene Shelton, born August 19, 1885; died April 23, 1918; mar-
           ried December 12, 1904, to Felix G. Ketron, born January 22, 1878;
           lived in Merit, Texas; children:
                (1)  Mary A. Ketron.
                (2)  William B. Ketron, born March 24,1907; married October 11, 1928,
                     to Daphne Coke; lived in Merit, Texas; children:
                    (a)  Kenneth Ketron, born December 19, 1929.
                    (b)  Billie Lou Ketron, born May 10, 1933.
                (3)  Christine Ketron.
                (4)  Frank Ketron.
```

e. Buena Ann Shelton, born February 9, 1888; married December 18, 1910,
   to H. A. Brotherton; born December 6, 1884; lived near Lockney, Texas;
   children:
   (1) Lawrence H. Brotherton, born September 10, 1911.
   (2) Maureta Brotherton, born June 9, 1913.
   (3) Wade H. Brotherton, born November 23, 1915; dsp October, 1919.
   (4) Henry F. Brotherton, born December 3, 1917.
   (5) Marvin G. Brotherton, born October 20, 1919.
   (6) H. A. Brotherton, born October 23, 1921.
   (7) R. B. Brotherton, born May 3, 1923.
   (8) Martha Joe Brotherton, born July 1, 1925.
   (9) Inell Brotherton, born February 7, 1928.
f. David Johnson Shelton, born June 26, 1893; dsp November 22, 1893.
g. Gussie May Shelton, born April 14, 1895; married April 14, 1928, to
   Gus A. Graham; lived near Floyd, Texas; children:
   (1) James Logan Graham, born June 30, 1930.
   (2) Billie Jean Graham, born October 30, 1931.
h. Fitzhugh Lee Shelton, born December 2, 1897; married Retha Brashear;
   children:
   (1) Avery Shelton, born April 23, 1918.
   (2) Winifred Shelton, born February 10, 1920.
i. Nell Shelton, born March 2, 1900; married August 11, 1918; to L. E.
   Griffin; lived in Henrietta, Oklahoma; children:
   (1) Eldon Griffin, born June 13, 1919.
   (2) Billie Elwana Griffin, born February 1, 1921.
   (3) John Fletcher Griffin, born October 15, 1922.
   (4) Nelda Christine Griffin, born December 27, 1928.
j. Willie Shelton, born May 13, 1902.
k. Sam Shelton, born May 18, 1904.

***

35.   James Logan Shelton was born April 26, 1864; married August 21, 1886,
to Pattie E. Adams, born September 13, 1863; died September 23, 1935.
Their children were as follows:[36]

a. Rebecca Irene Shelton, born December 16, 1886; married June 8, 1913,
   to William H. Jones.
b. Mary Belle Shelton, born October 10, 1888; died October 17, 1923; married January 22, 1911, to Grover C. Starnes, born December 23, 1884;
   lived near Kingsport, Tennessee; children:
   (1) Olie Starnes, born March 28, 1912; married Ruth Tate.
   (2) James M. Starnes, born August 15, 1915.
   (3) Mildred Starnes, born September 9, 1917; married December 21,
       1934, to William Carver.
   (4) Hobart Wilson Starnes.
c. Basil Bertrand Shelton, born July 8, 1890; dsp February 28, 1891.
d. Malcolm Leo Shelton, born March 30, 1892; married June 24, 1917, to
   Rachel Coley; children:
   (1) Nellie Lee Shelton.
   (2) Earl Shelton.
   (3) Malcolm Lee Shelton.
   (4) Joseph Shelton.
   (5) Grover Shelton.
e. Bernice Ray Shelton, born July 27, 1894; dsp December 28, 1896.
f. Ruth Ann Shelton, born November 17, 1896; married June 22, 1933, to
   Robert Knaffle; lived in Kingsport, Tennessee.
g. Lillian Grace Shelton, born November 13, 1898; married November 6, 1920,
   to Ezra E. Lane, born December 2, 1893; children:

283

      (1) Ellie Sue Lane, born September 2, 1921.
      (2) Mary Joe Lane, born October 14, 1922.
      (3) Edward Lane, born November 29, 1928; dsp December 24, 1928.
  h. Nannie Kate Shelton, born July 30, 1903; married June 23, 1920, to
      Conley T. McClellan; children:
      (1) June McClellan.
      (2) Vivian McClellan.
      (3) Anna Ruth McClellan.
      (4) Herman McClellan.
      (5) Conley T. McClellan.
  i. James Logan Shelton, born February 22, 1907; married February 18, 1925,
      to Bessie Watkins, born July 27, 1909; lived in Kingsport, Tennessee;
      children:
      (1) William Rhea Shelton, born October 10, 1926; dsp March 31, 1934.
      (2) Mary Sue Shelton, born May 16, 1928.
      (3) Betty Ann Shelton, born July 16, 1930.
      (4) Patty Ruth Shelton, born December 7, 1932.
      (5) Peggy Jane Shelton, born November 2, 1934.

***

36.   Stephen Martin Shelton was born December 6, 1862; married September
23, 1894, to Louxenia Winegar, born December 14, 1873. Their children
were as follows:[37]

  a. Lelia Edna Shelton, born March 16, 1898; married February 28, 1923,
      to James Wells, born February 28, 1902; lived in Lynch, Kentucky;
      child:
      (1) Dorothy Wells, born February 23, 1924.
  b. Beulah Ella Shelton.
  c. Trula Cleo Shelton, born February 26, 1903; married April 4, 1929, to
      Louis Reach, born July 5, 1906; child:
      (1) Christine Reach, born April 17, 1932.
  d. Ora Irene Shelton, born June 23, 1905; married July 14, 1923, to Theo-
      dore Robinette, born November 20, 1904; died September 9, 1937; lived
      in Big Stone Gap, Virginia; children:
      (1) Shelton Robinette, born October 13, 1928; dsp May 8, 1930.
      (2) Beulah V. Robinette, born September 8, 1930.
      (3) Georgia Lou Robinette, born January 27, 1932.
      (4) Shirley Jean Robinette, born October 14, 1934.
  e. Harry J. Shelton, born February 1, 1908; married Emma Rebar; lived
      in Omar, West Virginia; child:
      (1) Betty Gene Shelton.
  f. William C. Shelton.
  g. Georgia L. Shelton.
  h. Stephen C. Shelton.
  i. Ruby G. Shelton.

***

37.   Robert A. D. Shelton was born August 14, 1876; married (1) Ida Haynes
(2) Dora Noblin. He lived in Gate City, Virginia, and had the following
children (all by second marriage):[38]

  a. Augusta Mae Shelton, born January 10, 1903.
  b. Hubert Alley Shelton, born May 19, 1904; married Ola Frances Williams,
      born June 9, 1904; children:
      (1) Hubert Alley Shelton, born July 27, 1927.
      (2) Ola May Shelton, born May 3, 1929.
      (3) Richard Talmage Shelton, born June 3, 1932.

c. Monnie Elizabeth Shelton, born April 9, 1906; married November 23, 1933, to Floyd Odell Williams, born June 10, 1899; child:
(1) Monnie Lou Williams, born September 15, 1934.
d. Willard Gilmer Shelton, born August 21, 1908; married June 11, 1929, to Dona Virginia McMullen, born July 3, 1913; children:
(1) Willard Smith Shelton, born April 25, 1930.
(2) Bobby Delight Shelton, born March 13, 1932.
e. Lakie Shelton.
f. Laura Geneva Shelton, born March 2, 1913.
g. Alec N. Shelton, born May 8, 1916.
h. Glenna Sibyl Shelton, born November 12, 1919.

***

27.   George Wolfe was born July 11, 1808, and died February 26, 1890; married November 29, 1832, to Almira Davidson, born November 10, 1811; died October 5, 1880. Their children were as follows:[39]

a. Emaline Wolfe.
38. b. William Wolfe, born January 19, 1835.
c. Adaline Wolfe, born February 29, 1837; died October 24, 1880; married January 5, 1860, to William F. Hickam, born March 27, 1834; died July 21, 1894; lived near Gate City, Virginia; children:
(1) Ida Belle Hickam, born May 16, 1861; married William Peterson.
(2) Ephraim Hickam, born November 1, 1862; dsp November 17, 1862.
(3) Victoria Hickam, born September 18, 1863; dsp May 8, 1866.
(4) George Welton Hickam, born August 4, 1865; married Lillie Downs, born January 17, 1875; dsp.
(5) Kelley Hickam, born December 21, 1871; dsp December 7, 1926; married Mary Saunders, born May 1, 1873; died October 31, 1918.
(6) William F. Hickam, born August 23, 1875; died young.
(7) Marian Hickam, born August 23, 1875; married July 28, 1895, to W. G. Richmond, born April 28, 1871; died August 17, 1900; children:
(a) Gladstone Kenneth Richmond, born May 2, 1896; dsp September 16, 1935.
(b) Rebecca Adaline Richmond, born October 17, 1897; dsp April 20, 1899.
(c) Julian Robert Richmond, born September 3, 1899; dsp January 3, 1900.
d. Evaline Wolfe.
39. e. Mary Jeanette Wolfe, born April 9, 1841.
f. John Wolfe.
40. g. Hiram Wolfe, born October 20, 1844.
h. Isaac Wolfe, born June 5, 1845; dsp August 27, 1853.
41. i. Minerva Narcissus Wolfe, born July 5, 1848.
j. James Wolfe, born August 6, 1849; dsp August 22, 1849.
k. Nancy Wolfe, born August 6, 1849; dsp August 22, 1849.
l. Emmanuel Wolfe, born c1852; dsp May 30, 1934; married 1889 Dolly Shoemaker, born 1858; died March 7, 1911; lived in Soap Lake, Washington.
42. m. Lou A. Wolfe, born March 26, 1855.
43. n. Cordelia E. Wolfe, born March 26, 1855.

***

38.   William Wolfe was born January 19, 1835, and died January 22, 1903; married January 8, 1854, to Virginia Ann Vaughn, born November 17, 183?; died April 10, 1910; lived near Gate City, Virginia. Their children were as follows:[40]

a. Nancy Almyra Wolfe, born April 2, 1855; married Ezekial Kelly Catron;

285

children:
- (1) Mollie Catron.
- (2) James Catron.
- (3) Maude Catron.
- (4) William Catron.
- (5) Bessie Catron.
- (6) Charles Catron.
- (7) Virginia Belle Catron.
- (8) Katherine Catron.
- (9) Walter Catron.
- (10) Harry Catron.

44. b. Charles Herren Wolfe, born March 27, 1857.
45. c. Mary Evelyn Wolfe, born August 22, 1859.
    d. Emaline Elizabeth Wolfe, born February 17, 1863; died December 13, 1935; married November 22, 1888, to William T. Jayne, born September 15, 1864; lived near Gate City, Virginia; children:
- (1) Thomas H. Jayne, born October 16, 1894; married 1914 Lula Wilhelm; children:
  - (a) Thelma Lucile Jayne.
  - (b) Willie Catherine Jayne.
  - (c) Henry Thomas Jayne.
- (2) Elva May Jayne, born May 8, 1897; married September 15, 1921, to William J. McAuliff, born August 13, 1893; children:
  - (a) Margaret Elizabeth McAuliff, born February 9, 1923.
  - (b) Virginia Claire McAuliff, born July 27, 1926.
- (3) Nat Trigg Jayne, born January 28, 1900; married Nannie Frazier; child:
  - (a) Herschel Jayne, born February 3, 1923.
- (4) Maxwell W. Jayne, born August 20, 1901; married December 19, 1925, to Ethel McDavid, born December 9, 1907; lived near Gate City, Virginia.

    e. Fannie Louise Wolfe, born May 5, 1866; married May 25, 1890, to Edward Charles Thompson, born March 2, 1852; children:
- (1) Grace Frances Thompson, born October 30, 1891; married January 13, 1918, to William N. Jayne, born January 3, 1889; child:
  - (a) Roy Edmond Jayne, born April 14, 1920.
- (2) Nora Belle Thompson, born December 23, 1893; married December 23, 1914, to Mylus M. Malone, born April 4, 1892; lived in Blountville, Tennessee; children:
  - (a) Arlus Thompson Malone, born February 23, 1916; married July 28, 1935, to Thelma Lucile Houser, born August 10, 1919; lived near Blountville, Tennessee.
  - (b) Daphne Louise Malone, born September 10, 1917; dsp April 23, 1918.
- (3) Edward Thaddeus Thompson, born July 28, 1898; married Irene Pierce, born April 19, 1893; lived in Washington, D.C.

***

44.   Charles Herren Wolfe was born March 27, 1857, and died April 29, 1934; married August 9, 1881, to Margaret Ruth Parker, born July, 1849; died April 24, 1934; lived at Blountville, Tennessee. Their children were as follows:[41]

    a. Orin Alexander Wolfe, born May 3, 1882; dsp April 24, 1884.
    b. Ida Pearl Wolfe, born January 26, 1884; dsp October 30, 1885.
    c. Myrtle Ann Wolfe, born October 27, 1885; married Guy Elmer Tate, born November 14, 1888; died November 17, 1921; lived near Blountville, Tennessee; children:
- (1) Samuel Wilson Tate, born March 8, 1918.

286

       (2) Charles Elmer Tate, born March 28, 1921; dsp March 3, 1922.
d. Ina Gay Wolfe, born August 29, 1887; married September 1, 1904, Charles
    E. Carr, born May 17, 1875; lived in Blountville, Tennessee; children:
      (1) Emory Lee Carr, born July 8, 1905; married November 7, 1925,
          Altha Lee Shelby, born August 27, 1905; lived in Blountville, Ten-
          nessee; children:
          (a) Luther Evins Carr, born January 25, 1927.
          (b) Bobby Hobart Carr, born September 26, 1929.
          (c) Mary Ellen Carr, born February 29, 1932.
      (2) Anna Belle Carr, born October 25, 1907; married June 29, 1929,
          Andrew Houser, born October, 1902; child:
          (a) Paul Leland Houser, born April 30, 1930.
      (3) Carl Chester Carr, born April 17, 1910; married June 22, 1935,
          Mabel Gertrude Gott, born December, 1911.
      (4) Clarence Wolfe Carr, born December 30, 1912; married August 17,
          1935, to Monnie Pauline Rogers (see below).
      (5) Margaret Grace Carr, born February 28, 1916.
      (6) Charles William Carr, born August 1, 1919.
      (7) Aulden Wolfe Carr, born March 25, 1921.
      (8) Vestal Vaughn Carr, born June 10, 1924.
      (9) Mack Haynes Carr, born July 28, 1927.
e. Hazel Grace Wolfe, born March 26, 1890; dsp October 7, 1890.
f. Virginia Vaughn Wolfe, born February 10, 1896; dsp December 17, 1900.

***

45.   Mary Evaline Wolfe was born August 22, 1859, and died April 30, 1933;
married (1) September 23, 1883, to James B. Watkins, born February 5, 1862;
died June 28, 1890; (2) July 19, 1894, to Noah Frazier, born March 22, 1872.
She lived near Blountville, Tennessee; her children were as follows:[42]

(by first marriage):
a. Lula Virginia Watkins, born August 7, 1884; married John F. Moore,
    born June 6, 1877; lived in Kingsport, Tennessee; children:
    (1) Mary Anna Lee Moore.
    (2) Mabel Grace Moore.
    (3) Helen Elizabeth Moore.
    (4) John Coleman Moore.
b. William Leroy Watkins, born May 30, 1886; married September 7, 1913,
    Jeanette Esther Winegar, born November 11, 1895; children:
    (1) James Elroy Watkins, born September 22, 1914; died young.
    (2) Lula Frances Watkins, born March 29, 1916.
    (3) William Leroy Watkins, born January 21, 1919; dsp February 23, 1919.
    (4) Julia Mae Watkins, born August 17, 1920; dsp June 22, 1922.
    (5) Mabel Ruth Watkins, born February 23, 1923.
    (6) Mary Elizabeth Watkins, born March 5, 1926.
    (7) Robert Myles Watkins, born February 8, 1930.
(by second marriage):
c. Jennie Frazier, born May 27, 1895; married February 22, 1915, William
    A. Rogers, born July 11, 1893; lived near Blountville, Tennessee; chil-
    dren:
    (1) Jesse Kenneth Rogers, born February 27, 1916.
    (2) Monnie Pauline Rogers, born February 3, 1919; married August 17,
        1935, Clarence Wolfe Carr (see above).
d. Monnie Lee Frazier, born February 4, 1897; married 1926 John F. Moore;
    children:
    (1) Albert Marion Moore, born February 7, 1927.
    (2) Norma Jean Moore, born February 16, 1929.
    (3) Evelyn Jane Moore, born April 6, 1931.

e. Charles Gay Frazier, born April 12, 1899; married March 26, 1921, to
    Juanita Chappel, born April 16, 1897; lived near Blountville, Tennes-
    see; child:
    (1) Merle Ogelen Frazier, born September 5, 1923.
f. Joe Raymond Frazier, born September 12, 1903; dsp 1906.

***

39.   Mary Jeanette Wolfe was born April 9, 1841, and died July 8, 1917;
married July 13, 1869, to Jacob Gumm Fleenor, born January 13, 1841; died
June 23, 1911; lived at Freeman, Washington. Their children were as follows:[43]

a. John Fleenor, born June 8, 1870; dsp.
b. Kathryn Fleenor, born September 13, 1871; died January, 1896; married
    October 7, 1891, to W. J. Boy; child:
    (1) Beulah L. Boy, born April 11, 1893; married Guy C. Getz; child:
         (a) Gordon Sillman Getz, born May 29, 1920.
c. George P. Fleenor, born April 11, 1873; married Kathryn Langley.
d. Oscar Fleenor, born December 18, 1875; married Cora Browning; children:
    (1) Lucile Fleenor.
    (2) Florence Fleenor.
    (3) Helen Fleenor.
    (4) Audrey Fleenor.
e. Charles Fleenor, born August 1, 1877; married Mamie Knoable; children:
    (1) Ralph Fleenor, born May 8, 1906.
    (2) Blanche Fleenor, born November 7, 1907.
    (3) Arthur Fleenor, born August 5, 1910.
f. Minnie L. Fleenor, born September 8, 1875; married May 9, 1901, to
    W. J. Boy; children:
    (1) Irene Boy, born March 5, 1902.
    (2) Grace Boy, born September 17, 1903.
    (3) Gale Boy, born December 6, 1904.
    (4) Kenneth Boy, born April 15, 1907.
    (5) Kelly Boy, born April 15, 1907.
    (6) Glen Boy, born January 6, 1913.
    (7) Marjorie Boy, born January 1, 1921.
g. Susan Fleenor, born September 17, 1881; married January 25, 1900, to
    F. W. Langley; children:
    (1) Orbar Langley, born July 5, 1901.
    (2) Harold Langley, born May 27, 1904.
    (3) Clarence Langley, born December 12, 1905.
    (4) Percy Langley, born August 1, 1910.
h. Bessie Fleenor, born January 31, 1883; dsp July 2, 1900.

***

40.   Hiram Wolfe was born October 20, 1844, and died May 4, 1935; married
Mary Winegar; their children were as follows:[44]

a. Cornelius Wenten Wolfe, born November 3, 1872; married July 27, 1904,
    to Angela Pearl Morris, born July 27, 1886; children:
    (1) Myrtle Gertrude Wolfe, born July 10, 1905; dsp February, 1906.
    (2) Hazel Loretta Wolfe, born October 11, 1906; married October 22,
         1924, to Eldridge Victor Winegar; lived in Ontario, Oregon; chil-
         dren:
         (a) Dovie Jean Winegar, born April 12, 1926.
         (b) Eldridge Lee Winegar, born May 8, 1930.
         (c) Kenneth Gail Winegar, born December 15, 1937.

(3) Ida Lovenia Wolfe, born November 18, 1909; married May 24, 1934,
    to George Ellis Garner; dsp.
(4) Ruth Arlean Wolfe, born August 29, 1913; married August 14, 1934,
    to Russell Melvin Cooper; lived in Midvale, Idaho; child:
    (a) Virginia Mae Cooper, born January 30, 1936.
(5) Robert Cornelius Wolfe, born April 25, 1922.
b. Curtis Wolfe.
c. Emmanuel Wolfe.
d. Charles Wolfe, born April 23, 1877; married April 19, 1900, to Emma
   Yarber, born December 4, 1882; lived in Rockford, Washington; children:
   (1) Lottie Wolfe, born March 11, 1902; married 1921 John King; chil-
       dren:
       (a) Normandine King, born January 4, 1923.
       (b) Jacqueline King, born May 15, 1927.
   (2) James Wolfe, born February 10, 1903; married October 13, 1926,
       to Vivian Jones; children:
       (a) Lorraine Wolfe, born September 30, 1928.
       (b) James Wolfe, born September 3, 1929.
       (c) Richard Wolfe, born August 27, 1930.
   (3) Clyde Wolfe, born March 21, 1906.
   (4) Lorraine Wolfe, born February 28, 1908; married 1934 Harold Kle-
       vens.
   (5) Raymond Wolfe, born September 21, 1910; married _____ Potter;
       lived in Rockford, Washington; child:
       (a) Raymond Gene Wolfe, born April 22, 1935.
e. Nora Wolfe, born February, 1882; married April 19, 1900, to John Yarber, born October 31, 1874; children:
   (1) Iva Yarber, born November 18, 1901.
   (2) Fay Yarber, born October 23, 1904; married November 1, 1935, to
       Ernest Engstrom, born December 3, 1905.
   (3) Ralph Yarber, born December 5, 1908; married April 3, 1934, to
       Marina Marquandt, born February 1, 1910; child:
       (a) Janet Fay Yarber, born August 18, 1935.
   (4) Levi Yarber, born February 27, 1910.
   (5) Dorene Yarber, born May 26, 1917.
f. Vena Wolfe, born August 28, 1896; married November 27, 1918, to Charles
   Schultz, born February 28, 1893; lived near Ford, Washington; children:
   (1) Carl Schultz, born November 5, 1919.
   (2) Ernest Schultz, born October 16, 1921.
   (3) Lawrence Schultz, born September 8, 1934.
g. Edgar Wolfe.
h. Frank Wolfe.

***

41.   Minerva Narcissus Wolfe was born July 5, 1848, and died April 18, 1924;
married October 22, 1867, to Robert P. Stewart, born July 22, 1844; died
October 27, 1917; lived near Gate City, Virginia. Their children were as
follows:45

a. Ezekial Stewart, born July 17, 1868; dsp July 21, 1869.
b. Sarah Elizabeth Stewart, born August 22, 1870.
c. James Henry Stewart, born February 24, 1872; married Ella Smith.
d. Addie A. Stewart, born November 26, 1873; married October 1, 1889, to
   Sidney D. Case, born January 26, 1860; died December 30, 1920; lived in
   Gate City, Virginia; child:
   (1) Helen Virginia Case, born January 26, 1915.
e. Nannie L. Stewart, born February 8, 1875; dsp May 13, 1893.
f. George William Stewart.

g. Evelyn Virginia Stewart, born June 4, 1879; married November 20, 1901, to Nelson M. Horton, born January 23, 1871; died August 16, 1931; lived at Gate City Virginia; children:
   (1) Daphne Horton, born September 5, 1902; married April 11, 1928, to Berry P. Howard, born June 19, 1907; lived at Gate City, Virginia; child:
     (a) Virginia Howard, born September 28, 1931.
   (2) Robert M. Horton, born July 30, 1904; married November 25, 1925, to Irene Moers; child:
     (a) Robert M. Horton, born December 7, 1930.
   (3) Mary M. Horton, born September 2, 1907; married April 28, 1928, to Ross Hodges, born February 1, 1904.
h. Charles Robert Stewart, born December 21, 1880; married Alpha Stair, born December 17, 1873; lived near Gate City, Virginia; children:
   (1) Sidney L. Stewart, born February 19, 1902.
   (2) Eugene Stewart, born August 4, 1903.
   (3) John Stewart, born April 11, 1907.
   (4) Fred Stewart, born June 15, 1909.
   (5) Omer Stewart, born August 21, 1912.
   (6) Afton Stewart, born November 9, 1915; dsp January 9, 1933.
i. Mary Wood Stewart.
j. Josephine Stewart, born January 31, 1885; died young.
k. Margaret Stewart, born April 30, 1888; married Vernon Lane; children:
   (1) Wanda Lane, born December 26, 1912.
   (2) Edward Lane, born November 20, 1918.
   (3) John Frank Lane, born December 14, 1924.
   (4) Pat Lane, born March 17, 1930.
l. Frank E. Stewart, born January 11, 1890; married May 5, 1915, to Emma Fugate, born September 13, 1895; lived in Clinchport, Virginia; child:
   (1) Margaret Narcissus Stewart, born March 12, 1924.

***

42.   Lou A. Wolfe was born March 26, 1855, and died August 23, 1934; married August 25, 1881, to John F. Derting, born August 22, 1859; died January 14, 1929; lived near Hiltons, Virginia. Their children were as follows:[46]

a. Walker Stewart Derting, born June 15, 1882; married July 27, 1902, to Peggy Gardner, born February 18, 1884; children:
   (1) Cordia Derting, born June 1, 1903; dsp November 14, 1909.
   (2) Oliver Derting, born June 5, 1905; married October 22, 1924, to Dollie Jones, born September 20, 1905; lived near Hiltons, Virginia; children:
     (a) John Franklin Derting, born May 15, 1930.
     (b) Joseph William Derting, born October 20, 1933.
   (3) Velma Derting, born January 16, 1907; dsp November 8, 1909.
   (4) Blanch Derting, born January 16, 1907; dsp February 14, 1919.
   (5) Grace Derting, born July 16, 1909; married September 11, 1926, to W. M. Fleenor, born May 21, 1904; children:
     (a) Edsil Fleenor, born April 25, 1930.
     (b) Donald Fleenor, born July 12, 1932.
   (6) Maxie Derting, born June 26, 1911.
   (7) Charles Sidney Derting, born February 27, 1913; dsp July 16, 1913.
   (8) John Derting, born June 9, 1920; dsp January 14, 1921.
   (9) Joseph Derting, born April 12, 1924; dsp June 13, 1924.
  (10) Calvin Derting, born July 18, 1926.
b. Phebe Corda Derting, born December 24, 1884; married T. J. Carter; lived near Hiltons, Virginia; children:
   (1) Orlan Carter.

        (2) Violet Carter.
        (3) Nannie L. Carter.
        (4) Monnie Carter.
        (5) Bonnie Carter.
        (6) Maggie Carter.
        (7) Florida Carter.
        (8) J. W. Carter.
        (9) Claude W. Carter.
    c. Ida E. Derting, born September 26, 1890; married Walker Ramsey; born
        January 5, 1886; lived near Kingsport, Tennessee; children:
        (1) Daphne Ramsey, born October 20, 1911.
        (2) John Lester Ramsey, born May 20, 1913.
        (3) Claude Franklin Ramsey, born May 2, 1918.

                                    ***

43.   Cordelia E. Wolfe was born March 26, 1855, and died January 17, 1931,
    in Rockford, Washington; married April 11, 1875, to William F. Benham,
    born December 27, 1852; died February 20, 1936. Their children were as
    follows:[47]

    a. Almira L. Benham, born March 19, 1876; married September 10, 1893, to
        M. J. McClellan; children:
        (1) Bertha McClellan, born November 14, 1894; married December 23,
             1911, to Thomas Hubbard; children:
             (a) Deverne Hubbard, born August 8, 1913; married June 2, 1934,
                  to Hope Rivers.
             (b) Bernadine Hubbard, born October 27, 1916.
        (2) Howard P. McClellan, born November 25, 1895; married March 16,
             1915, to Sallie Burton, born June 10, 1892; lived near Dutton,
             Montana; children:
             (a) Madge L. McClellan, born December 23, 1915.
             (b) Betty M. McClellan, born April 2, 1917.
             (c) David B. McClellan, born June 26, 1925.
             (d) James E. McClellan, born September 28, 1929.
        (3) Irene McClellan, born January 15, 1898; married February 6, 1918,
             to Avery Sheldon; dsp; lived near Worley, Idaho.
    b. Bertha J. Benham, born September 18, 1877; married March 4, 1895, to
        Charles C. Setzer, born April 16, 1874; died November 1, 1931; chil-
        dren:
        (1) Violet Setzer, born January 1, 1896; married December 16, 1914,
             to Louis Thomlinson, born March 3, 1894; children:
             (a) Merle Dean Thomlinson, born March 24, 1916.
             (b) Edward R. Thomlinson, born August 10, 1922.
        (2) Emory D. Setzer, born April 2, 1898; married (1) September 8, 1916,
             to Goldie Howard, born January, 1898; (2) June 30, 1925, to Melva
             Schultz, born November 9, 1900; children:
             (by first marriage):
             (a) Barbara Setzer, born August 16, 1917.
             (by second marriage):
             (b) Marvin D. Setzer, born September 21, 1926.
             (c) William C. Setzer, born February 15, 1929.
        (3) Ralph R. Setzer, born February 1, 1900.
    c. Augusta M. Benham, born February 4, 1880; married August 10, 1904, to
        Carl C. Brown, born August 2, 1881; children:
        (1) Earl K. Brown, born June 28, 1905; married July 31, 1936, to
             Pauline Dahman, born February 9, 1916.
        (2) Glen F. Brown, born June 15, 1910; married June 20, 1936, to Elsie
             Jenner, born November 18, 1912.

                                    291

d. Julia J. Benham, born March 13, 1882; married December 23, 1911, to
    John Conner, died July 9, 1931; children:
    (1) Wayne B. Conner, born September 16, 1913.
    (2) Cordelia Jane Conner, born February 12, 1915.
e. Joel M. Benham, born March 1, 1884; married December 28, 1904, to Emma
    Crosley; children:
    (1) Ernest Benham, born January 11, 1906; married June 15, 1933, to
         Helen Cogley; child:
         (a) Pline Joy Benham, born September 21, 1934.
    (2) Robert Benham, born April 6, 1908; married 1929 Elsie Strong.
f. Cora C. Benham, born April 19, 1886; married February 26, 1913, to Otto
    Loeffler, born June 17, 1889; children:
    (1) Leroy Loeffler, born March 16, 1914.
    (2) Maxine Loeffler, born October 31, 1915.
    (3) William Loeffler, born May 18, 1920.
g. George W. Benham, born August 25, 1888; married 1914 Zeta Alexander;
    dsp.
h. Frances M. Benham, born October 24, 1894; married September 6, 1916,
    to Elmer Thomas, born May 6, 1891; children:
    (1) Nadine Thomas, born February 3, 1918.
    (2) Gene Thomas, born February 3, 1922.

***

28.   Emmanuel Wolfe was born February 28, 1813, and died May 26, 1851, in
    Osage County, Missouri; married October 2, 1834, to Sarah Martin Kerr, born
    July 1, 1817; died March 16, 1871. Their children were as follows:[48]

a. Mary Lucinda Wolfe, born April 6, 1836; dsp 1842.
b. Isabel Malinda Wolfe, born April 6, 1836; married March 8, 1870, to
    James S. Haynes; children:
    (1) Sallie C. Haynes, born March 1, 1871; married January 8, 1902,
         to Hiram H. Taylor, born October 4, 1879; children:
         (a) Rhea Taylor, born December 5, 1902.
         (b) Carl Clay Taylor, born January 1, 1905; dsp February 24, 1934;
              married Rusha B. Crowell, born May 29, 1907; lived in Gate
              City, Virginia.
         (c) Kent Wolfe Taylor, born June 1, 1907; dsp April 17, 1932.
         (d) Linnie Irene Taylor, born October 12, 1909.
         (e) Ruby Virginia Taylor, born April 20, 1912.
    (2) Hannah Minerva Haynes, born October 13, 1874; dsp March 6, 1876.
    (3) Albert P. Haynes, born February 14, 1879; dsp July 5, 1898.
46. c. Barbara Elizabeth Wolfe, born March 11, 1838.
d. Margaret Irene Wolfe, born January 4, 1840; died August 10, 1908; mar-
    ried (1) April 18, 1860, to Wesley Butler, died June 13, 1864; (2) Dec-
    ember 27, 1865, to William Gaines Butler, born March 2, 1836; lived at
    Milligan, Tennessee; children:
    (by first marriage):
    (1) Sarah Ruth Butler, born October 17, 1861; dsp February 8, 1863.
    (by second marriage):
    (2) Mollie E. Butler, born November 5, 1866.
    (3) Sallie M. Butler, born March 27, 1869.
    (4) William Bascom Butler, born March 13, 1872; dsp January 31, 1890.
    (5) Frazier Sullins Butler, born May 23, 1873; married February 23,
         1899, to Elizabeth M. Hawkins; children:
         (a) Gaines Hawkins Butler, born December 19, 1906.
         (b) William John Butler, born December 24, 1909.
         (c) Mary Irene Butler, born September 22, 1912.
         (d) Frazier Sullins Butler, born January 14, 1915.

       (e) Paul Bascom Butler, born September 1, 1918.
   e. William McDonald Wolfe.
47. f. John Melville Wolfe, born July 17, 1844.
   g. James Kerr Wolfe, born January 17, 1847; married Ella Sproles; children:
      (1) Linnie Kerr Wolfe.
      (2) Bessie Wolfe.
      (3) Gale Wolfe.
      (4) Hugh Wolfe.
   h. George Wiley Wolfe.

***

46.   Barbara Elizabeth Wolfe was born March 11, 1838, and died June 14, 1914; married January 22, 1857, to Joseph E. Tate, born June 16, 1831; died January 6, 1912; lived near Yuma, Virginia. Their children were as follows:[49]

   a. Emmanuel Philetus Tate, born March 31, 1858; died June 23, 1910; married November 15, 1883, to Venus Slemp, born March 11, 1863; died 1908; child:
      (1) Joseph Campbell Tate, born October 16, 1892; married February 12, 1913, to Martha Ann Dorton, born September 5, 1894; children:
         (a) Nancy Catherine Tate, born October 2, 1914.
         (b) Susan Jane Tate, born January 2, 1917; married August 9, 1934, to Jack Morelock.
         (c) Campbell Bascom Tate, born November 29, 1919.
   b. Nancy Virginia Tate, born January 22, 1860; dsp May, 1908.
   c. William D. Tate, born October 16, 1861; died September 21, 1923; married February 25, 1892, to Bendetta Clark.
   d. John Robert Tate, born February 25, 1867; died June 17, 1926; married January 1, 1898, to Elizabeth Harkleroad, born February 26, 1872; children:
      (1) William Andrew Tate, born October 28, 1899; married August 14, 1926, to Bessie Agnes Stewart, born January 15, 1908; children:
         (a) Joyce May Tate, born May 14, 1927.
         (b) Melba Elizabeth Tate, born November 27, 1934.
      (2) Nannie Manderl Tate, born February 4, 1901.
   e. George G. Tate, born March 14, 1868; died July 5, 1937.
   f. James Stephen Tate, born July 11, 1870; married June 8, 1898, to Myrtle E. Purcell, born February 8, 1877; dsp.
   g. Charles D. Tate, born April 18, 1872; died February 28, 1928; married August 27, 1912, to Carrie V. Starnes; children:
      (1) Charles D. Tate.
      (2) James Stephen Tate.
   h. Sarah I. Tate, born June 23, 1875; died April 10, 1914; married August 10, 1899, to Milligan W. Quillen; children:
      (1) Tate B. Quillen, born August 15, 1904; married June 10, 1929, to Bess Hillman, born July 28, 1904.
      (2) Vesta Elizabeth Quillen, born June 15, 1907; married Gilmer Easterly.
      (3) Livingston Quillen, born March 10, 1911; married Irene Bolson.
      (4) Juanita Quillen, born September 10, 1913.
   i. Maggie Ellen Tate, born October 29, 1877; married August 11, 1903, to Charles Wofford Wells, born August 30, 1872; children:
      (1) George Orr Wells, born September 7, 1907.
      (2) Morris Tate Wells, born March 30, 1909.
   j. Frances C. Tate, born March 21, 1880; dsp April 20, 1912.
   k. Carmine Summers Tate, born April 23, 1882; married Myrtle Arline Wil-

liams, born October 23, 1891; child:
(1) Virginia Elizabeth Tate, born October 9, 1915.

***

47.   John Melville Wolfe was born July 17, 1844, and died November 13,
1917, in Dryden, Virginia; married May 14, 1867, to Rebecca Heneger McMullen, born August 23, 1844; died October 8, 1937. Their children were as
follows:50

a. Jackson Bascom Wolfe, born July 14, 1868; married July 5, 1893, to
Nettie Lee Orr; children:
(1) Eugenia Priscilla Wolfe, born November 24, 1894; married June 25,
1923, to Charles Reasor.
(2) Rebecca Burr Wolfe, born July 26, 1896; married June 27, 1924, to
Claude Graham.
(3) Mary Lynn Wolfe, born May 26, 1900; married J. W. Gilbert; children:
(a) John Walter Gilbert, born February 21, 1927.
(b) Jack Elbert Gilbert, born March 9, 1930.
(c) Joe Lynn Gilbert, born December 21, 1934.
(4) Josephine Amanda Wolfe, born July 13, 1902.
(5) John Bascom Wolfe, born July 8, 1904.
(6) Wiley Herman Wolfe, born July 12, 1909.
b. Mollie Cordelia Wolfe, born July 22, 1870; married October 7, 1890, to
Charles Dougherty Orr; children:
(1) Charlie Reba Orr, born June 26, 1891; married July 8, 1918, to
Bayard Gilley; dsp.
(2) George Wolfe Orr, born February 25, 1894; married May 18, 1919,
to Waive Herndon.
(3) John David Orr, born August 26, 1898; married June 18, 1921, to
Beulah Tarver.
(4) Joe Steel Orr, born February 11, 1907.
c. Sallie Malinda Wolfe, born November 27, 1871; died February 14, 1914,
in Topeka, Kansas; married (1) May 23, 1893, to Orley M. Maples (2)
December 21, 1895, to Allen Bryan Saffel; children (all by second marriage):
(1) Fletcher Wolfe Saffel.
(2) Allen Bryan Saffel.
(3) Eugene Samuel Luttrell Saffel.
(4) Minerva Saffel.
d. Joseph Emmanuel Wolfe, born February 9, 1874; married September 30,
1903, to Pearl Gordon Stockton.
e. Josephine Elizabeth Wolfe, born February 9, 1874; married October 6,
1899, to Reece Victor Hicks; children:
(1) Reeselyn Hicks.
(2) Victor Melville Hicks.
(3) Charles Frazier Hicks.
(4) Katherine Rebecca Hicks.
f. Amelia Virginia Wolfe, born April 10, 1876; dsp July 11, 1876.
g. Cleo Margaret Wolfe, born June 22, 1877; married December 27, 1904,
to Ira Evans Hicks; children:
(1) Evans Hicks.
(2) Weimer Kerr Hicks.
h. John Lucian Wolfe, born May 25, 1879; dsp March 30, 1884.
i. Fannie Rebecca Wolfe, born September 20, 1881; dsp February 17, 1882.
j. Carrie Lou Wolfe, born August 3, 1883.
k. Eugene French Wolfe, born June 11, 1886; married November 27, 1912,
to Ella Thompson Love, born January 25, 1886; dsp.

***

29.   Elvira Wolfe was born about 1818 and married June 28, 1838, to John M. Dickerson; their children were as follows:[51]

a. Elizabeth Dickerson, born February 18, 1840; died October, 1909; married March 17, 1858, to David Tittsworth, born September 18, 1833; children:
  (1) John Tittsworth.
  (2) Sallie Tittsworth.
  (3) Elizabeth Tittsworth.
  (4) William K. Tittsworth, born December 8, 1868; married Nannie B. Perry, born June 26, 1871; lived near Gate City, Virginia; children:
    (a) Georgia Ethel Tittsworth, born April 23, 1895; married June 10, 1916, to Guy Hobart Culbertson, born December 31, 1895; children:
      /1/ Evelyn Jane Culbertson, born April 3, 1920.
      /2/ Elizabeth Ann Culbertson, born May, 1930.
      /3/ Edna Sue Culbertson, born June, 1932.
    (b) Ella Kate Tittsworth, born January 30, 1897; married December 20, 1919, to Arthur Horton, born September 8, 1896; lived in Speers Ferry, Virginia; child:
      /1/ John William Horton, born September 9, 1920.
    (c) Mary Vergie Tittsworth, born March 22, 1899; married October 20, 1920, to Thomas Blair Wolfe, born January 9, 1899; lived near Speers Ferry, Virginia; children:
      /1/ Nan Edna Wolfe, born January 25, 1923.
      /2/ Mary Jo Wolfe, born April 11, 1927.
    (d) Lois Fay Tittsworth, born November 14, 1900; married August 30, 1925, to Cloyd Byars Warren, born September 20, 1901; children:
      /1/ Eleanor Fay Warren, born September 26, 1926.
      /2/ William Jefferson Warren, born September 14, 1927.
    (e) William David Tittsworth, born December 14, 1902.
  (5) George A. Tittsworth.
  (6) Walter David Tittsworth.
  (7) Mary Kate Tittsworth.
  (8) Lula Tittsworth.
b. John William Dickerson married (1) May 31, 1864, to Frances E. Wilhelm (2) Nannie Wilhelm (3) Eliza Epperson; lived near Gate City, Virginia; children:
(by first marriage):
  (1) Ida Jo Dickerson.
  (2) Elvira Dickerson.
  (3) Geneva Dickerson.
(by second marriage):
  (4) John Dickerson, born May 28, 1877; died September 21, 1927; married Sallie Elizabeth Smith, born May 12, 1881; died December 24, 1906; child:
    (a) Nannie Lovada Dickerson, born December 2, 1906; married February 9, 1927, to Frank James Duncan, born September 19, 1907; lived in Norton, Virginia; child:
      /1/ Peggy J. Duncan, born July 27, 1931.
  (5) Charles R. Dickerson.
  (6) Elsie Dickerson.
(by third marriage):
  (7) Fannie Dickerson, born December 15, 1890; married October 10, 1909, to Neal P. Click, born December 4, 1880, lived near Gate City, Virginia; children:
    (a) Annie Lynn Click, born November 13, 1910.

        (b) Inez Click, born October 3, 1913.
        (c) Neal J. Click, born December 8, 1916.
        (d) Eva Click, born June 20, 1921.
        (e) Nancy Click, born July 24, 1926.
    (8) Lula Dickerson married Harry Click.

                                   ***

30.   Margaret Irene Wolfe was born October 24, 1820, and died January
    14, 1893; married October 27, 1840, to John Jett, born October 29, 1810;
    died February 20, 1876; lived near Mendota, Virginia. Their children were
    as follows:52

    a. Mary E. Jett, born December 10, 1841; died July 19, 1898; married Nov-
        ember 21, 1865, to Amos M. Fleenor; children:
        (1) Emma Fleenor.
        (2) Stephen Fleenor.
        (3) John Fleenor.
        (4) Katie Fleenor.
    b. Stephen Jett, born May 22, 1844; married October 2, 1873, to Margaret
        Snapp; child:
        (1) Samuel Jett.
    c. John W. Jett, born December 26, 1846; died May 7, 1906; married Octo-
        ber 19, 1875, to Louise R. Stoffel, born December 15, 1860; died March
        28, 1933; children:
        (1) Custis L. Jett, born August 10, 1876; died December 17, 1945;
             married April 28, 1902, to Charles F. Hagan, born March 31, 1866;
             children:
             (a) Pattie L. Hagan, born November, 1903; married October 4, 1930,
                  to Fred Andrews; lived in New York City.
             (b) Charles F. Hagan, born April 27, 1907.
             (c) Irene Hagan, born August 18, 1912; married August 6, 1932, to
                  Don Carico.
             (d) Hugh Hagan, born September 23, 1915.
        (2) Stewart Jett, born July 9, 1879; dsp February 7, 1880.
        (3) Irene Jett, born January 28, 1882; dsp January 14, 1904.
    d. Peter L. Jett, born July 27, 1849; died January 29, 1918; married Nov-
        ember 8, 1870, to Cornelia Oyler, born December 21, 1852; died February
        26, 1934; children:
        (1) Neva Jett, born November 20, 1871; married August 19, 1896, to
             Nathan E. Sutton, born March 23, 1866; children:
             (a) Luther J. Sutton, born July 26, 1897; married November 24,
                  1927, to Frances Osborne, born November 1, 1905; lived near
                  Hansonville, Virginia; children:
                  /1/ Betty Jo Sutton, born May 18, 1929.
                  /2/ Edith Ann Sutton, born September 6, 1934.
             (b) Fred Wood Sutton, born August 20, 1905; dsp August 6, 1907.
        (2) Curtis Oyler Jett, born November 8, 1877; married March 8, 1908,
             to Lelia May Kaylor, born November 2, 1879; lived near Carlock,
             Illinois; children:
             (a) Wilfred Lyle Jett, born May 31, 1909.
             (b) Roena Frances Jett, born May 9, 1912.
             (c) Merle L. Jett, born March 16, 1915; dsp October 15, 1915.
             (d) Virginia Vanda Jett, born May 17, 1920; died young.
        (3) Charles Jett.
        (4) James Jett.
        (5) Irene Jett, born July 25, 1885; married March 19, 1913, to John
             Henry Sourbeer, born March 27, 1883; child:
             (a) John Henry Sourbeer, born September 1, 1915; died young.
    e. Sarah Irene Jett, born August 2, 1851; married James Madison Wolfe

                                   296

(see p. 298).

f. William H. Jett.
g. Isaac F. Jett, born January 8, 1859; dsp March 13, 1859.

***

31.   Lucinda Wolfe was born May 26, 1823, and married September 26, 1843, to W. R. Grim, born November 16, 1821. Their children were as follows:[53]

a. C. L. Grim.
b. W. P. Grim.
c. Mary C. Grim, born October 30, 1848; died December 11, 1926; married March 14, 1868, to Joseph H. Wilhelm, born November 29, 1846; lived near Gate City, Virginia; children:
   (1) William Francis Wilhelm, born May 23, 1869; married Frances God-sey; children:
      (a) Dana Wilhelm married ____ Quillen.
      (b) Geneva Wilhelm, born April 11, 1897; married June 14, 1919, to Dewey H. Stallard, born April 15, 1898; children:
         /1/ Dewey H. Stallard, born July 16, 1920.
         /2/ James Carter Stallard, born January 18, 1922.
         /3/ Frank Wilhelm Stallard, born May 4, 1923.
         /4/ Don Elbert Stallard, born August 26, 1928.
      (c) William K. Wilhelm married (1) Bessie Gillenwater (2) Harriet Rollins; child (by second marriage):
         /1/ Ed Rollins Wilhelm.
   (2) Charles Robert Wilhelm.
   (3) Richmond Kemper Wilhelm.
d. Emily J. Grim.
48. e. Susan Elizabeth Grim.
f. Sarah E. Grim.
g. Ann R. Grim, born March 28, 1857; dsp c1872.
h. Caledonia Grim.
i. J. W. Grim, born October 6, 1861; dsp c1885.
j. Frank S. Grim.
k. D. C. Grim.
l. Cora Lee Grim.

***

48.   Susan Elizabeth Grim married Thomas Winegar; their child was as follows:[54]

a. Cora Geneva Winegar, born June 10, 1874; married July 20, 1890, to Charles Stewart Cole, born September 23, 1870; children:
   (1) Bertie May Cole, born May 26, 1892; married Kyle D. Dishner; child:
      (a) Charles B. Dishner, died young.
   (2) Thurman Roy Cole, born April 25, 1894; died August 15, 1931; married October 25, 1912, to Pearly Ethel Fields; children:
      (a) Kyle Elmer Cole, born September 24, 1913.
      (b) Estella Cole, born September 7, 1915.
      (c) Edith Cole, born 1918; dsp October 8, 1922.
      (d) James Cole.
      (e) Ethel Sue Cole, born September 14, 1923.
      (f) Dewey T. Cole, born May 7, 1926.
   (3) Edith Lou Cole, born February 14, 1896; married (1) August 11, 1913, to George A. Bailey (2) December 24, 1921, to Fleet Poston, born April 4, 1896; children:
   (by first marriage):

297

(a) George A. Bailey, born May 28, 1914.
(b) Charles Bailey, born July 25, 1916.
(c) James Bernard Bailey, born September 26, 1919; dsp October 24, 1919.
(by second marriage):
(d) Cora Geneva Poston, born March 26, 1924.
(e) Willie Ray Poston, born September 26, 1931.
(4) Campbell Clinton Cole, born June 13, 1898; married _____ Scott; child:
(a) Mattie Marie Cole.
(5) Iona Belle Cole, born April 9, 1900; married April 3, 1920, to Elmer N. Reed; child:
(a) Norma Talmadge Reed, born February 28, 1921.
(6) Charles Preston Cole, born September 19, 1902; married Thelma Hicks.
(7) Elva Sue Cole, born March 4, 1904; married Harry Grogan; child:
(a) Bert D. Grogan, born October 13, 1922.
(8) Joseph William Cole, born November 30, 1906; dsp January 10, 1908.
(9) James Robert Cole, born July 10, 1908; married Evelyn Bronist; child:
(a) Jacqueline Ann Cole, born August 16, 1931.
(10) Maggie Pearl Cole, born July 13, 1911; married January 8, 1928, to Roy Frazier, born February 26, 1906; children:
(a) Billy Wallace Frazier, born August 7, 1929.
(b) Bobby Gene Frazier, born June 13, 1931.
(11) Thomas Edward Cole, born September 8, 1913.
(12) Beatrice Lee Cole, born September 11, 1915.

***

32.   Isaac Wolfe was born October 11, 1825, and died May 25, 1891; married October 9, 1845, to Rebecca Jett, born December 25, 1828; died December 1, 1907. Their children were as follows:55

a. Hiram Wolfe, born March 25, 1847; dsp March 30, 1847.
49. b. John Jett Wolfe, born March 8, 1848.
c. James Madison Wolfe, born October 11, 1849; married Sarah Irene Jett (see p. 297); lived near Mendota, Virginia; children:
(1) Worley Wolfe.
(2) John Jett Wolfe.
(3) Garnett Wolfe.
(4) Katie Myrtle Wolfe.
50. d. George Winfield Scott Wolfe, born August 6, 1852.
e. William E. Wolfe, born July 9, 1854; married Lavena Francisco; lived in Churchill, Tennessee; children:
(1) Berta Wolfe.
(2) Lucian Isaac Wolfe.
f. Mary Livingston Wolfe, born May, 1856; married James Fleenor.
g. Stephen D. Wolfe, born May 1, 1858; dsp March 8, 1861.
h. Emmanuel Wolfe.
i. Sallie Irene Wolfe.
j. DeWitt Clinton Wolfe, born June 9, 1864; married May 3, 1891, to Lillian Miller, born March 16, 1869; children:
(1) Lena Gladys Wolfe, born April 9, 1892; married December 10, 1916, to George Roebuck, born July 23, 1892; died December 24, 1938; child:
(a) Gladys Eloise Roebuck, born September 19, 1920.
(2) Mary Myrtle Jett Wolfe, born July 6, 1893; married September 15, 1921, to Emmett Lee Ellmaker, born August 2, 1896; children:

        (a) Emmett Lee Ellmaker, born December 11, 1922.
        (b) William Elmer Ellmaker, born December 26, 1925.
    (3) Lillian Grace Wolfe, born January 1, 1895.
    (4) DeWitt Clinton Wolfe, born June 30, 1899; married May 17, 1924, to Ruth Mildred Irvin; child:
        (a) DeWitt Clinton Wolfe, born October 20, 1926.
    (5) Kenneth Ray Wolfe, born August 5, 1901; married Zelda Clendaniel; child:
        (a) Kenneth Ray Wolfe, born April 16, 1934.
    (6) Hazel Austin Wolfe, born March 23, 1906; dsp April 23, 1906.
    (7) Mildred Newland Wolfe, born February 24, 1909.
k. Samuel Gaines Wolfe, born June 14, 1866; died October 4, 1932; married March 15, 1900, to Laura Hensley, born January 17, 1878; children:
    (1) James Harry Wolfe, born December 16, 1900.
    (2) Ernest Roy Wolfe, born March 30, 1902.
l. Charles Draper Wolfe.
m. Walter Floyd Wolfe, born March 14, 1872; dsp October 4, 1890.

***

49.   John Jett Wolfe was born March 8, 1848; married March 18, 1868, to Nancy E. Courtney, born December 6, 1852, died November 4, 1918. Their children were as follows:[56]

a. Geneva Annette Wolfe, born February 1, 1869; died March 9, 1928; married February 18, 1900, to John Jacob Haynes, born October 4, 1869; died April 24, 1934; children:
    (1) Wilma Elizabeth Haynes, born June 25, 1904; married October 25, 1923, to Walter Brandt Peters, born April 4, 1893; children:
        (a) Robert Haynes Peters, born November 6, 1924.
        (b) Wayne Brandt Peters, born September 13, 1926.
        (c) Jeannine Annette Peters, born March 25, 1929.
    (2) Helen Virginia Haynes, born March 3, 1911; married December 16, 1933, to Homer Emmerson Whitman, born December 1, 1908; child:
        (a) Wilma Jeannine Whitman, born February 19, 1935.
b. William E. Wolfe, born September 9, 1870; dsp July 30, 1916.
c. Bert J. Wolfe, born December 24, 1871; married January 21, 1900, to Ionia Brock, born March 27, 1881; lived in Buffalo, Missouri; children:
    (1) Audrey I. Wolfe, born July 25, 1901; married October 28, 1925, to W. W. Van Gilder, born December 15, 1894; children:
        (a) W. W. Van Gilder, born February 24, 1929.
        (b) Dixie June Van Gilder, born February 20, 1934.
        (c) Shirley Jean Van Gilder, born December 2, 1935.
    (2) Reginald Wolfe, born January 23, 1908; married January 23, 1929, to Katherine D. Rodgers, born October 8, 1910; child:
        (a) Virginia Lee Wolfe, born December 2, 1932.
    (3) Berta E. Wolfe, born January 21, 1913.
    (4) Willard E. Wolfe, born December 16, 1917.
d. Effie L. Wolfe, born February 16, 1873; married December 23, 1900, to J. J. Van Horn; dsp.
51. e. John Ernest Wolfe, born March 18, 1875.
f. Sarah Etta Wolfe, born September 16, 1878; married April 19, 1905, to Henry Lafayette Francisco, born September 28, 1873; child:
    (1) Lyle DeWolfe Francisco, born April 23, 1906; married May 14, 1928, to Pearl Clement, born June 13, 1912; children:
        (a) Lyle Donald Francisco, born June 26, 1929.
        (b) Henry Lynn Francisco, born April 30, 1931.
g. Mark H. Wolfe, born April 28, 1880; died July 22, 1937; married May 31, 1909, to Ressie Bennett, born September 19, 1887; children:

(1) Dale Bennett Wolfe, born April 6, 1910.
(2) Darrell Woodward Wolfe, born February 3, 1914.

***

51.   John Ernest Wolfe was born March 18, 1875, and died March 7, 1922;
married February 14, 1900, to Edna L. Parrish, born March 9, 1876; lived
in Buffalo, Missouri; their children were as follows:[57]

a. Vivian Opal Wolfe, born August 15, 1902; married February 28, 1924, to
    Luther Glenn Gregg, born November 6, 1899; children:
    (1) Willa Jean Gregg, born February 18, 1925; died young.
    (2) Cleo Raye Gregg, born August 1, 1926.
b. Crystal Edith Wolfe, born July 5, 1904.
c. Courtney Armour Wolfe, born July 4, 1906; married October 8, 1930, to
    Lillie May Van Horn, born June 17, 1909; children:
    (1) Jervis Lee Wolfe, born October 25, 1931.
    (2) Dixie Josephine Wolfe, born January 26, 1933.
    (3) Helen May Wolfe, born April 1, 1934.
    (4) John Ellis Wolfe, born September 18, 1937.
d. Gayle Parrish Wolfe, born May 31, 1911; married January 20, 1935, to
    Drucilla Selena Bone, born April 17, 1918.
e. Illa Ionia Wolfe, born March 27, 1913; married May 13, 1931, to Roy
    Oliver Griffith, born March 5, 1910; children:
    (1) Richard D. Griffith, born May 20, 1932.
    (2) Joan Elizabeth Griffith, born February 26, 1934.
    (3) Robert Ernest Griffith, born December 26, 1936.
f. Josephine Elizabeth Wolfe, born December 19, 1915; married October 12,
    1936, to Arlie B. Franklin, born February 2, 1915; child:
    (1) Janice Louella Franklin, born February 19, 1938.

***

50.   George Winfield Scott Wolfe was born August 6, 1852, in Scott County,
Virginia, and died February 23, 1917, in Gate City, Virginia; married Oct-
ober 15, 1873, to Rebecca Vance Wilhelm, born September 13, 1857; died
August 16, 1934. Their children were as follows:[58]

a. Kelly Herron Wolfe, born February 24, 1875; died January 30, 1922;
    married (1) Martha Gardner (2) January 3, 1904, to Geneva A. Dickenson;
    children:
    (by first marriage):
    (1) Fain Wolfe, died young.
    (by second marriage):
    (2) George William Wolfe, born November 29, 1904.
    (3) Bert Patton Wolfe, born October 2, 1910; married August, 1934,
         to Marie Teague.
b. Evaline Wolfe, born July 4, 1879; married April 21, 1896, to George
    Patton Roller, born April 4, 1861; lived near Kingsport, Tennessee;
    children:
    (1) Gladys Roller, born June 19, 1897; married July 14, 1918, to Clyde
         Groseclose, born August 22, 1891; children:
         (a) Ruth Groseclose, born June 24, 1919.
         (b) Rita Groseclose, born June 5, 1921.
         (c) Mary Sue Groseclose, born February 25, 1925.
         (d) Clyde Groseclose, born April 21, 1929.
    (2) Scott Herron Roller, born January 13, 1899.
    (3) Lucile Roller, born January 31, 1906; married August 26, 1926, to
         Victor Freels, born July, 1895.

300

        (4) Clara Roller, born November 15, 1908; married January 3, 1932, to
             John Charles Slack, born November 16, 1905; children:
             (a) Clara Roller Slack, born March 19, 1933.
             (b) Ada Cox Slack, born March 16, 1936.
     c. Jodilee Wolfe, born August 28, 1886; married May 20, 1903, to John
         Jett, born January 2, 1882; children:
         (1) Vance Jett, born December 21, 1904.
         (2) Eileen Jett, born April 10, 1907.

                                    * * *

6.   Catherine Wolfe was born October 3, 1782, in North Carolina, and died
     before 1869 in Scott County, Virginia; married July 8, 1802, to Abraham
     Lane; their children were as follows:[59]

     a. Mary Lane married January 12, 1832, to William Peters.
     b. John R. Lane.
     c. Abraham Z. Lane married Barbara Lotts.
     d. Samuel W. Lane.
     e. Joseph T. Lane married Jane Shoemaker.
     f. Jacob E. Lane
     g. James H. Lane.
     h. Margaret Lane, born December 15, 1816; married October 10, 1839, to
         Robert Bailey.
     i. Jonas W. Lane
     j. Enoch P. Lane, born April 3, 1820; died July 24, 1877; married November
         20, 1840, to Jane Bailey.
     k. Katherine Lane, born November 4, 1821; died February 28, 1917; married
         September 3, 1856, to John C. Taylor.
     l. Frances Lane, born April 19, 1823; died October 25, 1889; married March
         29, 18??, to William F. Templeton.
     m. William D. Lane, born June 15, 1825; married June 14, 1846, to Nancy
         Lawson.
     n. Martha Lane, born June 25, 1827; died May 4, 1904; married December 20,
         1848, to Nelson G. Taylor, born December 21, 1827; died November 11,
         1896.

                                    * * *

7.   Adam Wolfe was born September 3, 1784, in North Carolina, and died
     September 28, 1862, in Grainger County, Tennessee; married about 1811 in
     Hawkins County, Tennessee, to Jemima McCoy, born November 27, 1792, and
     died July 1, 1873, the daughter of Archibald McCoy and Margaret Norton.
     Their children were as follows:[60]

     a. George Wolfe, born March 18, 1812; married Jane Allen; children (among
         others):
         (1) Manuel Wolfe, born c1833.
         (2) Gideon Wolfe, born May 6, 1835; Captain, Company B, 1st Tennessee
              Cavalry, U.S.A.; married May 5, 1861, Lidia Mills, born November
              26, 1838; lived in Hancock County, Tennessee; children:
              (a) J. Harrison Wolfe.
              (b) George W. Wolfe.
              (c) Thomas G. Wolfe.
         (3) Mila Wolfe, born c1838.
         (4) Nancy Wolfe, born c1841.
         (5) Wiley Wolfe, born c1848.
     b. Archibald Wolfe, born August 3, 1813; died August 16, 1854, in Grain-
         ger County, Tennessee; married Temperance McGinnis, born December 6,

                                    301

1820 (see p. 308); children (among others):
(1) Leroy Wolfe, born c1840.
(2) Amanda Wolfe, born c1842.
(3) Arthur Wolfe, born c1849.
c. Catherine Wolfe, born November 24, 1814; died February 4, 1856.
d. David Wolfe, born September 13, 1817; died June 30, 1886, in Hancock County, Tennessee; married Jane Greene; children:
(1) Ewell Wolfe, died young.
(2) Adam Wolfe married Sylvia Trent.
(3) Susan Wolfe married Robert Trent.
(4) Hannah Wolfe, born c1850; married Richard Drinnon.
(5) Serena Wolfe, born c1852; married Daniel Trent.
(6) Richard Wolfe, born c1854; married Margaret Trent.
(7) Martha Wolfe, born c1856; married Mack Trent.
(8) Claiborne Wolfe, born c1858; married Susan Trent.
(9) George Wolfe, born c1860; married Victoria Trent.
(10) Elizabeth Wolfe, born c1862; married John Lawson.
e. William Wolfe, born February 28, 1819.
f. Elizabeth Wolfe, born January 20, 1821.
g. Margaret Wolfe, born November 3, 1823.
h. Adam Wolfe, born July 21, 1824; married March 28, 1848, in Grainger County, Tennessee, to Rebecca Coffey.
i. Claiborne Wolfe, born April 22, 1826; married Hannah Mallicoat; children (among others):
(1) Simeon Wolfe, born c1856.
(2) James Wolfe, born c1857.
(3) Jesse Wolfe, born c1858.
(4) Daniel Wolfe, born c1860.
j. Mary Wolfe, born July 14, 1828.
k. Jane Wolfe, born September 29, 1830; married John Dalton.
l. John Wolfe, born August 25, 1832; died July 1, 1901, in Grainger County, Tennessee; married Amanda _____, born June 12, 1842; died November 4, 1924.
m. Henry Wolfe, born January 16, 1835; married Elvira Coffey, daughter of Ausbon Coffey and Matilda Dalton.
52. n. Lydia Wolfe, born December 5, 1836.

* * *

52.   Lydia Wolfe was born December 5, 1836, in Grainger County, Tennessee, and died November 30, 1930, in Rockcastle County, Kentucky; married March 8, 1857, James Madison Coffey, born November 20, 1834; died June 20, 1886, son of Ausbon Coffey and Matilda Dalton. Their children were as follows:[61]

a. Thomas Jefferson Coffey, born April 9, 1858; died October 4, 1934, in Madison County, Kentucky; married November 21, 1883, to Alice McGuire.
b. John Henry Coffey, born May 20, 1861; died April 10, 1951, in Rockcastle County, Kentucky; married February 5, 1891, to Margaret Langford.
c. Margaret Angeline Coffey, born August 16, 1863; dsp October 15, 1863.
d. Glathia Coffey, born October 20, 1864; died June 24, 1939, in Berea, Kentucky; married February 28, 1898, to Joseph Love Ramsey.
e. Mimia Coffey, born December 15, 1866; dsp March 1, 1967, in Rockcastle County, Kentucky.
f. Addie Coffey, born November 16, 1868; died February 24, 1953, in Ohio; married December 6, 1893, to John Dotson.
g. Hulda Coffey, born October 10, 1870; died November 3, 1951, in Indiana; married George Ketron.
h. William Ausbon Coffey, born February 22, 1873; died May 28, 1964, in

302

Wildie, Kentucky; married December 12, 1895, to Tee Reynolds.
i. Eliza B. Coffey, born July 23, 1875; dsp.
j. Cordelia Coffee, born September 14, 1877; died July 6, 1952, in Rockcastle County, Kentucky; married Freeman Ketron.

***

8. Jonas Wolfe was born October 12, 1790, in Washington (now Scott)
County, Virginia, and died September 26, 1857, in Scott County, Virginia;
married (1) March 7, 1816, to Elizabeth Perkins McKenzie, born May 30,
1796; died February 13, 1845; (2) April 27, 1847, to Isabella R. Kerr, born
December 12, 1819; died May 20, 1896. His children (all by first marriage)
were as follows:[62]

a. Malinda Wolfe, born February 20, 1817; dsp July 25, 1817.
b. Rebecca Wolfe, born August 26, 1818.
c. Isaac Willson Wolfe, born August 9, 1820; died September 9, 1907; married (1) April 8, 1846, to Mary Ann Ekin Kerr, born April 6, 1822; died
July 30, 1866; (2) March 2, 1868, to Rachel B. Orr, died April 13, 1903;
children:
(by first marriage):
(1) Thomas Montgomery Wolfe, born July 14, 1847; dsp September 1, 1856.
(2) Mary Elizabeth Wolfe, born June 4, 1849; dsp September 28, 1851.
(3) Sarah Isabella Wolfe, born September 10, 1853; dsp September 30,
1879; married Archelaus Craft.
(4) Jonas Henderson Wolfe, born August 6, 1855; married Amanda Powers;
children:
(a) Oliver Perry Wolfe, born January 8, 1880; dsp December 23,
1953; married Florence Morcom.
(b) Isaac Jefferson Wolfe, born June 23, 1881; married Martha
McClain; dsp.
(c) George Washington Wolfe, born March 30, 1883; dsp October
26, 1926.
(d) Julia Catherine Wolfe, born August 7, 1885; married March
29, 1922, to Charles N. Kelsey; dsp.
(e) Charles Martin Wolfe, born February 11, 1886; married March
27, 1922, to Edna Cox; dsp.
(5) Margaret Rebecca Wolfe, born July 31, 1857; dsp October 5, 1859.
(6) James Nicholas Vance Wolfe, born November 8, 1859; died February
12, 1913; married Alice Dishner.
(7) Louisa Catherine Wolfe, born November 26, 1861; married William
Hickam.
(8) Nancy Ann Wolfe, born March 8, 1865; dsp.
(by second marriage):
(9) Amanda Jane Wolfe, born January 26, 1869; dsp October 1, 1876.
(10) William Alexander Wolfe, born March 14, 1871; married Callie
Fickle.
(11) Oliver Mitchell Wolfe, born April 17, 1873; dsp September 26, 1876.
d. Nancy Wolfe, born October 28, 1822.
e. Greenberry G. M. Wolfe, born March 18, 1825.
f. Thomas Blair McKenzie Wolfe, born April 8, 1827.
g. Mary Wolfe, born October 11, 1829.
h. John Patton Wolfe, born June 2, 1832.
i. Oliver Miller Wolfe, born January 20, 1835; dsp July 24, 1862.
j. William Henderson Wolfe, born November 22, 1840; married Amanda Bell.

***

9. Jacob Wolfe was born July 27, 1796, in Washington (now Scott) County,

303

Virginia, and died May 30, 1863, in Scott County, Virginia; married about 1818 to Jalah Stallard, born March 29, 1802; died May 11, 1884. Their children were as follows:[63]

a. Nancy Wolfe, born 1820; dsp 1829.
b. John Steuben Wolfe, born May 15, 1822; died November 15, 1868; married Rosa Dingus.
53. c. Reuben Dewayne Wolfe, born April 24, 1824.
d. Mary Wolfe, born June 18, 1826; died August 27, 1903; married Thomas Easterling.
e. Dionysius Wolfe, born November 5, 1828; died December 20, 1897; married Mary Carter.
f. Merab E. Wolfe, born April 13, 1830; died May 3, 1909; married David Osborne.
g. Jasper Marion Wolfe, born February 10, 1832; died June 13, 1897; married Mary Davis.
h. Jalah C. Wolfe, born August 29, 1833; died January 11, 1877; married Edward D. Culbertson.
i. Lucy Wolfe, born June 12, 1836; died April 24, 1924; married John Riner.
j. Jacob McDaniel Wolfe, born June 13, 1838; died February 28, 1908; married Lydia Hackney.
k. Martin Van Buren Wolfe, born August 11, 1840; died April 1, 1906; married Elizabeth Addington.
l. Virginia Wolfe, born c1843; died January, 1877; married Creed Farmer.

***

53.   Reuben Dewayne Wolfe was born April 24, 1824, and died June 27, 1890; married (1) Louemma Easterling (2) Mrs. Mary E. (Fuller) Holt. He moved to Martin County, Kentucky, in 1857 and to Ray County, Missouri, after the Civil War; his children were as follows:[64]

(by first marriage):
a. James M. Wolfe, born June 20, 1848; dsp July 16, 1924; lived in Ray County, Missouri.
b. Jacob J. Wolfe, born June 31, 1851; lived in Houston, Texas.
c. Martha J. Wolfe, born July 26, 1853; died January 3, 1931; married July 29, 1875, to George W. Ward; lived in Offut, Kentucky.
d. Jalah Elizabeth Wolfe, born May 25, 1855; married William B. McMillan; lived in Missouri.
54. e. George Washington Wolfe, born December 26, 1856.
f. Mary Louemma Wolfe, born October 10, 1858; died April 5, 1934; married Wilson Perry Compton.
g. Virginia Victoria Wolfe, born December 4, 1860; married (1) Thomas P. Austin (2) c1930 George Turner.
(by second marriage):
h. Emily F. Wolfe, born August 18, 1866; died November, 1951; married (1) John W. Wackman (2) J. J. Henderson; lived in Missouri.
i. Sonora E. Wolfe, born May 27, 1868; married George Remington; lived in Missouri.
j. Albert E. Wolfe, born January 1, 1871; married Mattie E. McMillen; lived in Missouri.
k. John S. Wolfe, born December, 1872; married Laura McMillen; lived in Missouri.
l. Ruby D. Wolfe, born June 12, 1874; died 1918; married James Stone; lived in Missouri.

***

54.   George Washington Wolfe was born December 26, 1856, and died June 9, 1938; married (1) January 5, 1892, to Margaret Venters, died April 13, 1904; (2) June 11, 1906, to Rachel J. Goble, died February 2, 1958; lived in Martin County, Kentucky. His children were as follows:[65]

(by first marriage):
55. a. John Wheatley Wolfe, born November 25, 1892.
56. b. Mary Belle Wolfe, born November 26, 1894.
    c. Silas Dean Wolfe, born October 7, 1896; died May 19, 1942; married August 22, 1919, to Grace Williamson; lived in Big Rock, Virginia; children:
      (1) Silas Dean Wolfe, born October 24, 1924; married January 27, 1946, to Carole Dills; lived in Oxford, Mississippi; children:
        (a) Roderick Dean Wolfe, born October 20, 1948.
        (b) Patricia Lee Wolfe, born October 29, 1958.
      (2) Della Mae Wolfe, born April 30, 1926; married October 12, 1951, to Harvey Irwin; lived in Washington, D. C.; child:
        (a) Paula Dorene Irwin, born July 14, 1953.
      (3) Laurence Hubert Wolfe, born June 18, 1928; married August 13, 1949, to Virginia Helton; lived in Winchester, Kentucky; children:
        (a) Charles Dewey Wolfe, born November 13, 1950.
        (b) Rena Lou Wolfe, born January 29, 1952.
        (c) William Dean Wolfe, born May 11, 1954.
    d. Addie Wolfe, born and died February 11, 1898.
    e. Charles Adam Wolfe, born July 20, 1900; married December 13, 1929, to Ruby Pauline Willis; lived in Inez, Kentucky; children:
      (1) William Hal Wolfe, born October 27, 1930; lived in Orlando, Florida.
      (2) Wanda Ann Wolfe, born March 12, 1934; married Dr. Truman Mays; children:
        (a) Evert Truman Mays, born 1958.
        (b) Elizabeth Ann Mays, born 1959.
(by second marriage):
    f. William George Wolfe, born June 30, 1907; married Zella Goble; lived in Chicago, Illinois.
    g. Kermit Sheridan Wolfe, born September 20, 1910; dsp.
    h. Laban Theodore Wolfe, born December 3, 1911; dsp.
    i. Pearlie May Wolfe, born May 17, 1915; married Hancel Newsome.
    j. James Pershing Wolfe, born January 31, 1918; dsp; lived in Buffalo, New York.

                ***

55.   John Wheatley Wolfe was born November 25, 1892; married May 8, 1922, to Goldie Small; lived in McAndrews, Kentucky; their children were as follows:[66]

    a. Leon Ernest Wolfe, born May 4, 1923; married August 1, 1944, to Elizabeth Wilson; lived in Opus, Florida; children:
      (1) Sandra Lee Wolfe, born June 30, 1945; married August, 1961, to Stuart Duncan.
      (2) Jo Ann Wolfe, born July 26, 1946.
      (3) Leon Ernest Wolfe, born September 20, 1948.
    b. Harold Wheatley Wolfe, born May 26, 1925; died young.
    c. Margaret Geneva Wolfe, born September 10, 1926; married August 26, 1947, to Irving J. Murphy; lived in Hollywood, Florida; children:
      (1) Irving J. Murphy, born May 1, 1947.
      (2) John R. Murphy, born April 12, 1948.
    d. Charles Albert Wolfe, born June 10, 1928.

    e. Mildred Geraldine Wolfe, born June 22, 1930; married John C. Bennizi;
        lived in Detroit, Michigan; children:
        (1) Karen Sue Bennizi, born January 29, 1956.
        (2) Kathy Lou Bennizi, born September 21, 1957.
    f. George Clayton Wolfe, born January 29, 1933; married November 13, 1953,
        to Jane Curry; child:
        (1) George Michael Wolfe, born June 27, 1957.
    g. John Buchanan Wolfe, born April 27, 1936; dsp March 19, 1942.

* * *

56.   Mary Belle Wolfe was born November 26, 1894; married April 10, 1915,
to V. L. Harless; lived in Inez, Kentucky; their children are as follows:[67]

    a. Ramon Harless, born November 4, 1916; dsp June 6, 1918.
    b. Clarence Harless, born March 4, 1918; dsp.
    c. Dean Dewey Harless, born September 29, 1919; dsp July 19, 1944.
    d. Roger V. Harless, born November 21, 1921; married Marcella Goble;
        lived in Kopperston, West Virginia; child:
        (1) Roger Harless.
    e. Wheatley Charles Harless, born August 11, 1924; married Lucille Mead-
        ows; lived in Inez, Kentucky; child:
        (1) Geraldine Harless, born November 27, 1945.
    f. Frank J. Harless, born November 31, 1926; married Rebecca Cassady;
        lived in Churchville, New York.
    g. Leo Harless, born March 14, 1929; married 1954 Angie Delong; child:
        (1) Dewey Harless, born 1955.
    h. Myrtle Harless, born May 19, 1931; married J. C. Preece; lived in Inez,
        Kentucky; child:
        (1) Terry Lee Preece, born March 5, 1955.
    i. Shirley T. Harless, born May 19, 1931; married 1954 Rosie Smith; lived
        in Cleveland, Ohio.
    j. Lundy P. Harless, born May 25, 1933; lived in Inez, Kentucky.
    k. George Harless, born July 23, 1935; married Avinalle Muncy; lived in
        Columbus, Ohio; child:
        (1) Debbie Harless, born April 5, 1958.
    l. Robert T. Harless, born November 7, 1938; lived in Cleveland, Ohio.

* * *

2.   Charles Wolfe was born about 1755 and lived in Berkeley County, (West)
Virginia, while young. In 1792 he lived between Walker's and Henderson's
lines in the area disputed between Washington County, Virginia, and Sullivan County, Tennessee. About 1797 he moved to Hawkins (now Hancock) County,
Tennessee. On March 8, 1803, he sold his nephew Adam Wolfe, for $100.00, 50
acres on the north side of Clinch Mountain on the south side of Copper
Ridge adjoining his own land; on February 25, 1806, for $60.00 he bought
100 acres from Thomas Evans and sold it to Thomas Johnston for $150.00 on
September 25, 1810. On April 10, 1811, he and his son Jacob bought 75
acres between their farms on the north side of Clinch Mountain from Samuel
Nicholson; in 1811 he was taxed in Hawkins County on 200 acres of land.[68]

    Charles Wolfe made his will on March 17, 1813, and his estate was pro-
bated in May, 1819; he left his property to his wife Susanna, who was born
in Pennsylvania about 1759 and who was living in Hancock County in 1850,
and to his children. On September 30, 1840, Susanna Wolfe gave her daughter Mary McGinnis, for taking care of her in her old age, the use of the
127½ acres which Charles Wolfe had bought from Robert Kyle, and the 37½
acres which was Charles' half of the land bought from Samuel Nicholson.[69]

306.

The children of Charles and Susanna Wolfe were as follows:

a. Jacob Wolfe, born c1782 in North Carolina; lived in Hancock County, Tennessee; in 1850; married Mary _____.
b. Philip Wolfe, born c1784.
c. Peter Wolfe, born c1786 in Tennessee; lived in Hancock County, Tennessee, in 1870.
d. Catherine Wolfe, born c1788; married _____ Davis.
e. Elizabeth Wolfe, born c1790.

57. f. Hannah Wolfe, born c1793.
58. g. Mary Wolfe, born March 15, 1796.
h. Barbara Wolfe, born c1798; died October 10, 1882; married c1819 to John McCoy, born c1799; died July 10, 1875; son of Archibald McCoy and Phoebe Hill; lived in Christian County, Missouri; children:
   (1) Phoebe McCoy, born August 29, 1820; died April 10, 1910; married Jeff Wolfe.
   (2) Andrew McCoy, born November 3, 1822; died January 1, 1881; married (1) Ozina Smallin (2) Mary J. McGinnis.
   (3) Eliza McCoy, born December 18, 1824; dsp January 1, 1876.
   (4) William McCoy, born March 23, 1826; dsp September 9, 1908.
   (5) Charles McCoy, born July 9, 1828; died February 13, 1910; married Delphi McGinnis, born October 21, 184?; died June 23, 1934, daughter of James McGinnis and Sarah Dalton (see below).
   (6) Catherine McCoy, born November 8, 1832; died August 30, 1899; married James Taylor Tillman.

59. i. Charles Wolfe, born c1801.
j. George S. Wolfe, born December 27, 1803; died May 15, 1873, in Hancock County, Tennessee; married Margaret McCoy, born September 5, 1801; died June 6, 1882; children:
   (1) (daughter), born c1825.
   (2) Peter Wolfe, born c1827; died 1877 in Christian County, Missouri.
   (3) Edley Wolfe, born January 5, 1829; died June 26, 1889, in Christian County, Missouri.
   (4) Elizabeth Wolfe, born c1831.
   (5) Jemima Wolfe, born c1833.
   (6) Susanna Wolfe, born c1835.
   (7) Mary Wolfe, born c1837.
   (8) Melvina Wolfe, born c1839.
   (9) Emeline Wolfe, born c1842.
  (10) Martha Wolfe, born c1844.
  (11) William Wolfe, born c1846.

***

57.   Hannah Wolfe was born about 1793 and died June 8, 1853; married Aaron McGinnis, who died February 24, 1857, son of Edward and Nancy McGinnis. Their children were as follows:[71]

a. Edward McGinnis, born November 20, 1812; died November 9, 1888.
b. Charles McGinnis married Margaret Rucker.
c. James McGinnis married Sarah Dalton.
d. Noble McGinnis married Louisa Nash.
e. Peter McGinnis died May 22, 1864; married Susan Winkler.
f. Robert McGinnis, born November 17, 1821; died March 27, 1884; married November 14, 1854, to Martha A. Stone.
g. Andrew McGinnis.
h. Elizabeth McGinnis married Colby Dalton.
i. Barbara McGinnis married James Courtney.

***

58.   Mary Wolfe was born March 15, 1796, and died March 24, 1864; married
Moses McGinnis, born July 16, 1788; died December 16, 1873, son of Edward
and Nancy McGinnis; their children were as follows:[72]

a. Nancy McGinnis married Jack Payne.
b. John McGinnis.
c. Margaret McGinnis, born May 14, 1817; married John Hicks.
d. Barbara McGinnis, born December 10, 1818; died March 7, 1905; children:
    (1) William McGinnis.
    (2) Elizabeth McGinnis.
e. Temperance McGinnis, born December 6, 1820; married Archibald Wolfe
    (see p. 302).
f. James McGinnis, born March 30, 1822; married _____ Dunsmore.
g. Elizabeth McGinnis, born June 7, 1825; married _____ Anderson.
h. Mary McGinnis, born February 19, 1827; died October 25, 1900; married
    James Livesay.
i. Hannah McGinnis, born February 28, 1828; married James Greenlee.
j. A. B. McGinnis, born May 31, 1830; married _____ Stokes.
k. Charles McGinnis.
l. Allie McGinnis married A. J. Livesay.
m. Edward S. McGinnis, born February 16, 1836; died October 6, 1863; mar-
    ried _____ James.
n. Jane McGinnis, born January 16, 1839; married (1) Wiley Wolfe (2) Cole-
    man Hicks.
o. Eliza McGinnis, born February 23, 1842; married _____ Carpenter.

***

59.   Charles Wolfe was born about 1801 in Hawkins (now Hancock) County,
Tennessee, and lived there in 1850. He married Lydia McCoy about 1818 and
their children were as follows:[73]

a. (son), born c1819.
b. (son), born c1821.
c. (daughter), born c1823.
d. Mary Wolfe, born c1825.
e. Peter Wolfe, born c1827.
f. Elizabeth Wolfe, born c1829.
g. Susan Wolfe, born c1831.
h. Charles Wolfe, born c1833.
i. Jane Wolfe, born c1835.
j. Caroline Wolfe, born c1837.
k. Nancy Wolfe, born c1839.
l. Perlina Wolfe, born c1841.

***

3.   George Wolfe was born about 1765 and lived in Berkeley County, (West)
Virginia, while young; about 1790 he married Mary _____, who was born about
1770 and died after 1840. In 1796/7, he lived in Sullivan County, Tennessee, but moved to Hawkins (now Hancock) County, Tennessee, where on August
29, 1797, he bought 200 acres on the north side of Clinch Mountain from
Stephen Richards for $50.00; he was taxed on that land in 1811. On May 18,
1818, he bought 40 acres adjoining his farm from George and Hannah Moody
for $333.33, and on March 8, 1819, he bought 290 acres on the waters of
Big War Creek on the south side of Cooper Ridge from Thomas Johnson for
$213.00.[74]

     On December 30, 1828, George Wolfe gave his son Valentine 112 acres of
the land bought from Johnson for $10.00, and 100 acres of the same land

to his son John. He made his will on April 15, 1837, and the estate was probated in September, 1839. His children were as follows:75

a. Valentine Wolfe, born c1791; lived in Gasconade County, Missouri, in 1840.
60. b. Hannah Wolfe, born c1793.
c. Katherine Wolfe, born c1795.
61. d. John Wolfe, born c1797.
e. Elizabeth Wolfe, born c1799.
f. Barbara Wolfe, born c1801.
g. Sarah Wolfe, born c1803; married December 12, 1824, to William Elrod; children:
   (1) (son), born c1825.
   (2) (daughter), born c1827.
   (3) Mary Elrod, born c1829.
   (4) George Elrod, born c1831.
   (5) Peter Elrod, born c1832.
   (6) Sarah Elrod, born c1834.
   (7) James Elrod, born c1835.
   (8) Caroline Elrod, born c1837.
   (9) Susan Elrod, born c1840.
h. Mary Wolfe, born c1805; died June 2, 1896, in Owsley County, Kentucky; married September 3, 1838, to Howell Cobb Brewer.
i. Susannah Wolfe, born c1807.
j. George Wolfe, born c1809; lived in Hancock County, Tennessee, in 1850; married Louisa ____; children (probably among others):
   (1) Emeline Wolfe, born c1834.
   (2) Nicholas Wolfe, born c1836; married Ruth Greene; children:
      (a) George Wolfe, born c1855.
      (b) Melissa Wolfe, born c1859.
      (c) Martha Wolfe, born c1862.
      (d) Mary Wolfe, born c1862.
      (e) Jefferson Wolfe, born c1867.
      (f) Nancy Wolfe, born c1869.
   (3) Alois Wolfe, born c1839.
   (4) Susan Wolfe, born c1841.
   (5) John Wolfe, born c1843.
   (6) Mary Wolfe, born c1845.
   (7) Amanda Wolfe, born c1848.
   (8) Perry Wolfe, born 1850.
k. Nicholas Wolfe, born c1811; lived in Hancock County, Tennessee, in 1850, then moved to Missouri; married Nancy ____; children (probably among others):
   (1) George Wolfe, born c1837.
   (2) Joshua Wolfe, born c1839.
   (3) Eliza Wolfe, born c1841.
l. Margaret Wolfe, born c1813.
m. Allie Wolfe, born c1815.

**

60.   Hannah Wolfe was born about 1793 and married Peter Ogan, who was born February 16, 1799, and died January 4, 1881, son of John and Hannah Ogan. They lived in Hancock County, Tennessee, in 1860, and their children were as follows:76

a. John Ogan married Catherine ____; children:
   (1) Erwin Ogan.
   (2) Helen Ogan.

```
            (3)  George Ogan.
            (4)  Mary Ann Ogan.
            (5)  Margaret Ogan.
            (6)  Nancy Ogan.
            (7)  Hannah Ogan.
            (8)  William Ogan.
            (9)  Peter Ogan.
62.    b.  Elizabeth Ogan.
       c.  Barbara Ogan married John Elrod; children:
            (1)  Elizabeth Elrod.
            (2)  Susan Elrod.
            (3)  Peter Elrod.
            (4)  William Elrod.
            (5)  George Elrod.
            (6)  Mary L. Elrod.
            (7)  Millard Fillmore Elrod.
       d.  Mary Ogan married John Hayes; children:
            (1)  Elizabeth Hayes.
            (2)  Sarah Hayes.
            (3)  Hannah Hayes.
            (4)  Permelia Hayes.
            (5)  Florence Hayes.
       e.  Susan Ogan, dsp.
       f.  George E. Ogan, born February 14, 1832; died January 23, 1905, in Erath
           County, Texas; married Louisa Hunter, born October 10, 1834; died
           October 23, 1917; children:
            (1)  M. H. Burket Ogan, born December 24, 1858, in Calloway County,
                 Missouri; died February 18, 1939, in Erath County, Texas; married
                 March 16, 1892, to Gertrude Crissman, born December 29, 1866,
                 in Sinking Valley, Pennsylvania; died March 5, 1939.
            (2)  Martha Ogan.
            (3)  Robert Peter Ogan.
            (4)  Narcissus Ogan, dsp.
            (5)  Jane Ogan, dsp.
            (6)  Mary Frances Ogan, dsp.
            (7)  Henry Lee Ogan.
            (8)  Hannah Ogan, dsp.
            (9)  James Ogan, dsp.
       g.  Hannah Louise Ogan, born c1834; married William Cloud Mills;  children:
            (1)  Orville Mills.
            (2)  Govan Mills.
            (3)  Susan Mills.
            (4)  Frances Mills.
            (5)  Elizabeth Mills.
            (6)  Celia Mills.
            (7)  Peter Barnet Mills.
            (8)  Mary Mills.
            (9)  Barbara Mills.
           (10)  Josephine Mills married Alexander Barton.
       h.  Winnie Jane Ogan, born c1838; married _____ Lakin.
```

***

```
62.        Elizabeth Ogan, born c1823; married Thomas S. Hayes, born August 27,
       18??; died March 13, 1912, son of Thomas Hayes and Sarah Rucker; they had
       the following children:??

       a.  William Clifton Hayes.
       b.  Hester Ann Hayes.
       c.  Colbert Newton Hayes.
```

d. Zachary Taylor Hayes.
e. John Hasgue Hayes.
f. Colby Columbus Hayes.
g. Thomas Winfield Hayes.
h. Sarah Cornelia Hayes.
i. Hannah Angeline Hayes.
j. James Madison Hayes.
k. Luther Lafayette Hayes.
l. Albert Hayes.
m. Peter Hayes.

***

61.   John Wolfe was born about 1797 and lived near Treadway, Tennessee, in 1850; married Mary Holloway and had the following children:[78]

a. George Wolfe.
b. William Wolfe, born c1826.
c. Frances Wolfe, born c1828.
d. James Wolfe, born c1829.
e. John Wolfe, born c1831.
f. Woodson T. Wolfe, born October 8, 1833; married Catherine Mills; lived near Treadway, Tennessee.
g. Wiley Wolfe, born c1835.
h. Sarah Wolfe, born c1837.
i. Marion Wolfe, dsp.
j. Mary Wolfe, born c1841.
k. Eliza Wolfe, born c1843.
l. Hiram Wolfe, born June 3, 1846; died April 9, 1931, at Luttrell, Tennessee; married June 15, 1865, to Mary Jane Mynatt, born July 10, 1843; died January 3, 1911.
m. Jesse Wolfe, born c1848; dsp.

***

REFERENCES

[1]Adam Wolfe, son of John Wolfe, lived with his uncle Charles Wolfe; Charles Wolfe and George Wolfe were closely associated and undoubtedly brothers; Barbara Stoke was named as a sister of John Wolfe; Mary Pope was a sister of either John Wolfe or Catherine Bare (probably the former); depositions of Catherine Bare Wolfe and Barbara Stoke, Chancery Court Papers, Wythe County, Virginia; tax lists of Sullivan County, Tennessee, 1796/97; Hawkins County, Tennessee, Wills.
[2]Depositions of Adam Hickman, Peter Bare, John Berry, and Catherine Wolfe, Chancery Court Papers, Wythe County, Virginia.
[3]Depositions of Catherine Wolfe, et al., Chancery Court Papers, Wythe County, Virginia; Hawkins County, Tennessee, Deed Bk. 1, p. 79, Bk. 4, p. 506, Bk. 3, p. 147.
[4]Depositions of Charles Ison, Gideon Ison, George Morison, Catherine Wolfe, and Peter Bare, Chancery Court Papers, Wythe County, Virginia.
[5]Depositions of Charles Ison, John Berry, Joseph Duncan, and John England, Chancery Court Papers, Wythe County, Virginia.
[6]Ibid., deposition of Catherine Wolfe; Washington County, Virginia, Deeds.
[7]Washington County, Virginia, Deed Bk. 3, pp. 504, 573.
[8]Depositions of Gideon Ison, Jacob Peters, and Charles Ison, Chancery Court Papers, Wythe County, Virginia; Scott County, Virginia, Will Bk. 1, p. 8.

[9]Chancery Court Papers, Wythe County, Virginia; records belonging to Lillian Wolfe Wampler; Washington County, Virginia, Deed Bk. 6, p. 3; Scott County, Virginia, Deed Bk. 3, p. 434.

[10]Deposition of Catherine Wolfe, Chancery Court Papers, Wythe County, Virginia; records belonging to Lillian Wolfe Wampler.

[11]Washington County, Virginia, Deed Bk. 3, pp. 504, 573, Bk. 6, pp. 3, 4; Scott County, Virginia, tax lists, 1816.

[12]Scott County, Virginia, Deed Bk. 1, pp. 138, 153.

[13]Sullivan County, Tennessee, Deed Bk. 10, p. 323, Bk. 11, pp. 343, 358.

[14]Vermilion County, Illinois, Entry Book, Deeds, Wills; statement of Isaac C. Wolfe; tombstone record, Vermilion County, Illinois.

[15]Bible record belonging (1950) to Howard L. Wolfe.

[16]Charles Blanchard, History of Morgan, Monroe, and Brown Counties, Indiana (Chicago: F. A. Battey & Co., 1884).

[17]Records belonging to Miss Mary Wolfe.

[18]Records belonging to Wayne Hickman.

[19]Records belonging to Ethan Wolfe.

[20]Records belonging to Benjamin Franklin Wolfe.

[21]Records belonging to Bertie Linn.

[22-30]Records belonging to Merle Wolfe Koch.

[31]Records belonging to Howard L. Wolfe.

[32]Scott County, Virginia, Deed Bk. 1, p. 153, Bk. 2, pp. 253, 305, 368, 444.

[33-59]Records belonging to Lillian Wolfe Wampler.

[60-61]Records belonging to Alice Lake Ketron.

[62]Records belonging to Isaac Jefferson Wolfe.

[63-67]Records belonging to Silas Dean Wolfe.

[68]C. E. Carter (ed.), Territorial Papers of the U. S. (Washington, D. C., 1936), IV, 206; Sullivan County, Tennessee, tax lists; Hawkins County, Tennessee, Deed Bk. 3, p. 389, Bk. 4, p. 163, Bk. 6, p. 317, Bk. 20, p. 41, tax lists.

[69]Hawkins County, Tennessee, Will Bk. 1, p. 482, Deed Bk. 19, p. 381; Hancock County, Tennessee, census of 1850.

[70-73]Ibid.; records belonging to Mary Ruth Hansen.

[74]Sullivan County, Tennessee, tax lists; Hawkins County, Tennessee, Deed Bk. 1, p. 367, Bk. 9, p. 106, Bk. 12, p. 15, tax lists, census of 1840.

[75]Hawkins County, Tennessee, Deed Bk. 13, p. 273, Bk. 16, p. 559, Will Bk. 1, p. 491; Hancock County, Tennessee, census of 1850; records belonging to Mary Ruth Hansen.

[76-77]Records belonging to Cecilia Ogan Mann.

[78]Records belonging to Ferol Frost Hubbs.

***

INDEX

313

BALLARD, Etta, 224; BALLER, Adeline, 82; BALLINGER, George, 90; BALLOU, Maria F., 194; BANKS, Moses L., 189; BANKSTON, William, 206; BAR, George P., 1; BARBEE, Allen J., 131; Chesley P. P., 131, 132; Christopher, 131; Clara C., 132; David A., 131; Edward N., 131; Elizabeth, 131; Emma V., 131; Francis, 131; Howard, 131; James G., 131; John J., 131; Jones, 131; Lillie, 151; Mary, 131, 175; Mary A. J., 131; Mary F., 131; Nevill, 131; Sallie P., 133; Sarah, 131; Susan, 131; William, 131; William F., 131; BARBER, Belle, 64; J. L., 131; James, 64; BARCLAY, Claudia E., 83; Jean, 141; BARE, Barbara, 1, Catherine, 1, 267; Deborah, 1; George, 1; Henry, 1; Jacob, 1; James, 1; Matthias, 1; Michael, 1;

BARE, Nancy, 1; Peter, 1, 267; Susan, 1; BARFIELD, Lucile, 238; BARGER, E. B., 72; Montgomery C., 72; Philip, 40; BARKER, Eleanor, 46; Eliza, 246; Janet N., 235; BARNARD, Charles L., 238; Jean K., 238; Judith E., 238; Lee A., 238; Robert E., 238; BARNES, Alison L., 80; Betty, 172; Betty A., 223; Calvin, 80; Emma, 201; James, 28; John, 28; Leslie S., 80; Michael H., 223; Pierson H., 223; Ruth V., 96; Sarah R., 28; William, 28; BARNETT, Lilly B., 83; BARNS, Cassiah, 259; Constance, 259; Elizabeth, 259; Ezekial, 259; Jeanette, 107; Job, 259; John, 259; Margaret, 259; Rachel, 259; Thomas, 259; BARNSLEY, Peggy J., 141; Thomas, 141; Tommie E., 141; William A., 141; BARRETT, Julie R., 91; Marilyn K., 91;

BARRETT, Nancy J., 91; Reuben M., 229; Wayne A., 91; Willie M., 151; BARRON, May, 194; Thomas E., 194; BARROWS, Allen, 54; Fred, 54; Walter, 54; BARRY, Ann K., 201; Catherine, 247; Colleen, 237; James B., 201; Marvin K., 201; Peter, 53; Richard H., 201; BARTHOLOMEW, Chester G., 11, 12; Edwin H., 12; Homer G., 12; Inez, 12; Inez V., 11; Lesley, 12; Lorin C., 12; Lucy M., 12; Lula, 12; Marian, 12; Mildred, 12; Othneil A., 12; Randy L., 80; Robert K., 80; Russell R., 80; Samuel M., 12; Susan I., 12; Thomas, 12; Thomas B., 12; Virgil G., 12; William E., 12; Winnie, 12; BARTLETT, Julie R., 81; Lynne E., 81; BARTLEY, Ann T., 115; Fred, 114; BARTON, Alexander, 310; Beatrice, 43; Frances, 241; BASS, Will, 24;

BASTON, William P., 261; BATCHELLER, Edith M., 248; BATES, Charles, 43; Hannah, 28; John, 28; Margaret A., 187; BAUM, Tamara, 90; BAXTER, Bazz H., 98; Betty, 216; Grace, 27; Isabel J., 186; Jason B., 98; Tammie S., 98; Wayne, 98; BAYLESS, David M., 254; Gary L., 254; Offie, 254; BAYLOR, Richard, 210; BAYNES, Doris M., 151; BEAIRD, John, 65; BEALE, Benjamin, 128; BEALS, Charles, 43; BEAM, Eleanor, 9; BEAMER, J. P., 15; BEARDEN, Isaac, 256; Ledson, 256; Thomas, 246; BEASLEY, Bertie Lee, 218; Charles D., 218; Jack, 162; Leslie D., 19; Raoul B., 19; BEATY, Alice, 170; Alice B., 170; Anna L., 171; Blanch B., 170; Dorothy C., 171; Edith B., 170; Edwin P., 170; Etna M., 170; Helen L., 171; Lawrence E., 170;

BEATY, Lewis W., 170; Richard, 170; Ronald, 171; William J., 170; William L., 170; BEAVER, Henry, 140; BEAVERS, Robert, 163; BECK, George R., 178; Jack, 178; Janette, 114; William T., 178; BECKER, Ella, 91; BECKETT, Margaret, 261; BECKHAM, Herman R., 46; J. T., 46; Jackie L., 46; BEDWELL, West, 103; BEECHER, John, 36; BEEBS, Ernest, 53; BEESON, Edward, 118; Jane, 61, 62; Martha, 118; Mary A., 161; Samuel, 161; BEGHTOL, Elias W., 169; BELCOURT, Donald, 226; BELL, Amanda, 303; Leroy P., 222; Vicky, 222; William L., 222; BELLAMY, Cecil, 16; Samuel D., 95; Virginia T., 95; BENEDICT, William, 112; BENHAM, Almira L., 291; Augusta M., 291; Bertha J., 291; Cora C., 292; Ernest, 292; Frances M., 292;

BENHAM, George W., 292; Joel M., 292; Julia J., 292; Pline J., 292; Robert, 292; William F., 291; BENNETT, Alice M., 273; Ann E., 272; Bessie, 273; Bessie W., 273; Charles, 273; Clinton, 273; Cora, 272; Dewitt C., 273; Elma, 273; Ethel, 273; Fra, 272; Frances, 273; Frank, 273; George F., 273; Grace, 273; Hazel, 273; Henry J., 272; Homer W., 45; Ida B., 273; J. H., 18; Jacob, 273; Jacob C., 273; John, 93; John M., 138; Lena, 273; Lester, 273; Luella, 273; Mary E., 273; Minnie, 273; Norma, 273; Patsy R., 45; Philander, 272; Ressie, 299; Robert, 273; Russell, 273; Sarah, 273; Sarah A., 106, 272; Sarah I., 273; Thomas, 273;

BENNETT, Watella, 272; Wilbur, 273; William K., 273; BENNIZI, John C., 306; Karen S., 306; Kathy L., 306; BENSKIN, Jeremiah, 25; Mary, 25; BENSON, Catherine, 26; Charles H., 186; William, 245, 256; BENTON, Zula E., 77; BERARD, Rosemond, 109; BERG, Luvorn, 168; BERNARD, Pete, 109; BERRY, Beulah J., 235; Mary E. L., 219; Robert D., 223; BESCHERER, Jacob, 61; BEST, Cozette, 262; BETHEL, William, 241; BETZNER, Mary, 278; BEVERIDGE, Frank, 234; BEVERLEY, Catherine, 209; Henry, 209; BEYERS, Anita, 106; Charles, 106; Clinton, 106; Lloyd, 106; Maxine, 106; Mildred, 106; Otis, 106; Virginia, 106; BIGGERS, Gussie, 7; BILES, Elizabeth, 195; James C., 195; John, 195; Joseph R., 195; Robert B., 195; Robert P., 195;

BILES, Thomas B., 195; William, 195; BILLETER, Francis, 171; Otto, 171; BILLINGSLEY, David R., 66; James, 202; Marxie J., 115; Nancy S., 202; Naomi, 101; Nettie J., 112; BINGAMAN, John, 9, 10; BIRDWELL, Haudie, 179; Sam J., 41; Samuel J., 41; BISHOP, Edna, 279; James W., 148; BIVENS, Samuel, 119; BIXBY, Myrtle, 91; BLACK, Frank R., 214; Marian, 201; Mary C., 201; Robert M., 214; Roland E., 214; BLACKBURN, Mary, 52; Russell, 107; BLACKMON, Eliza J., 7; Henry C., 8; BLACKSHEAR, Frances, 45; BLACKWELL, Leithel, 106; Lola, 103; BLACKWOOD, Elizabeth, 188; Ella, 153; James, 130; Nancy, 153; William D., 151; BLAGG, Philip W., 53; BLAINE, Samuel, 20; BLAIR, Cleatus, 216; Elizabeth A., 216;

BLAIR, Frank, 185; BLAKE, Joseph, 28; Martha, 175; BLANKENSHIP, Katherine, 27; BLANN, Ophelia, 232; BLASINGAME, Thomas, 93; BLATTEAU, James, 272; BLAWS, Robert, 24; BLEDSOE, Anthony, 50; BLISH, Jean, 152; BLISS, Clara B., 64; BLOCK-ER, Norah I., 147; BLOOM, Terry C., 87; BLOOMER, Beatrice, 53; Daisy I., 53; David, 53; Jean, 53; Ransom, 53; Ruby N., 53; William D., 53; BLOXOM, Ola, 180; BLUE, Robert, 89; BLUM, Rosalia, 99; BOAZ, Edmond, 210; BOBBITT, Winifred, 68; BOBO, Simpson, 247; BODDIE, Cala M., 133; Mourning H., 185; Nathan V., 133; BODENHAMER, Clemmie, 144; Emma M., 144; BOETTGER, Mildred R., 82; BOETTKE, Sa-rah L., 178; Walter, 177; BOGAN, Isaac, 246; BOGART, Anne E., 201; BOGGS, Carol J., 44; David R., 44; Durwood, 44; Elsie, 119; Kenneth R., 44; BOGUE, Job, 30;

BOGUE, Jonathan, 30; BOLDING, William, 16; BOLEN, Absolem, 59; Annetta, 59; Calvin, 59; Hannah, 59; Hanson, 59; John, 59; Martha, 59; Mary J., 59; Robert W., 59; Sarah A., 59; William A., 59; BOLENDER, Eva C., 261; BOLES, Addie M., 112; BOLINGER, Leona, 167; BOLLING, John, 24, 25; Susie A., 102; BOLSON, Irene, 293; BOLTENHOUSE, Goldie, 106; BOND, Hannah, 118; Joel, 61; John, 61, 62; Joseph, 62; Martha, 212; William, 61; Wilmuth, 213; BONE, Drucilla S., 300; BONNER, Andrew H., 221; Bilbery, 204; Cicero H., 221; Ernest K., 221; Jackson, 199; Jesse, 204; Millie P., 221; Redding, 204, 221; BOOK, Susanna, 51, 52; BOONE, Benjamin, 156; Daniel, 157, 158; Edward, 157; Elizabeth, 157; George, 156, 157; Hannah, 157, 158; Israel, 157; James, 156; John, 156; Jonathan, 157; Joseph, 156;

BOONE, Mary, 156, 157; Mordecai, 190; Samuel, 156, 157; Sarah, 156, 157; Squire, 156, 157; BOOTH, Clarence V., 224; John W., 224; Laura M., 201; BOOZER, Billie, 17; BORMAN, Darlene, 264; Denise, 264; Michael R., 264; Raymond M., 264; William G., 264; BORST, Claudette A., 193; Debra L., 193; James A., 193; James F., 193; Laura K., 193; BORUFF, James D., 107; BOSTIC, Dorothy, 78; BOSWELL, Clement, 255; BOTHWELL, Arthur R., 83; Connie S., 83; Douglas L., 83; James A., 83; John G., 83; Judith A., 83; Keith R., 83; Keith T., 83; Kevin W., 83; Linda L., 83; Robert A., 83; Sharon J., 83; Susan M., 83; BOUGHER, Jonathan, 103; BOUNDS, Addison, 268; George W., 268; Jacob N., 268; Jesse, 268; John, 268;

BOUNDS, Mary, 268; William, 268; BOURGAIN, Berthe, 232; Philippe, 232; BOURLAND, Jack, 46; Robert, 46; Steven, 46; BOWDEN, Nancy, 179; BOWEN, John, 72; BOWERS, Helen F., 226; Margaret, 198, 199; Tabitha, 150, 153; BOWLES, Addie, 100; Bryan, 100; Dannie, 90; Delbert, 90; Elizabeth, 77; Hiram P., 100; Ivie, 115; Loren, 100; Marie, 100; Martha A., 95; Mayme, 100; Raymond, 100; Robert, 272; Rosemary, 100; Thomas, 95; Virgil, 100; Vivian, 90; BOWMAN, John, 239;

BOWMETT, Martha, 272; BOWSER, Herschell, 237; BOY, Beulah L., 288; Gale, 288; Glen, 288; Grace, 288; Irene, 288; Kelly, 288; Kenneth, 288; Marjorie, 288; W. J., 288; BOYD, Carl, 57; Christian, 116; Donna, 116; Kay, 116; Tracey L., 116; William, 116; BOYER, Daniel, 82; Shar L., 82; BOYLE, Hartford D., 203; John H., 203; John M., 203; Patrick J., 203; Robert H., 203; Sharon P., 203; Timothy R., 203; BRADFORD, Bruce, 18; Deanne, 116; John, 116; Johnson, 20, 21; Maria, 20; Pierce, 18; Stella, 18; Thomas, 21; BRADLEY, Edward, 242; George, 74; Mary, 203; BRADSHAW, Charles A., 97; Charles P., 97; Elizabeth A., 97; James, 97; James A., 97; Ruby N., 97; William, 242; BRADY, James A., 236; John, 65;

BRADLEY, Alfred J., 199; Columbus C., 199; Eliza J., 200; Lucy R., 199; Mary F., 199; Nancy E., 199; Sarah Ann I., 199; BRANCH, Matthew, 29; BRANNAN, Frances, 142; William M., 139; BRANSFORD, Dudley, 227; BRANT, Clark, 54; Ruth, 88; BRANTLEY, Parthenia, 8; BRASHEAR, Retha, 283; BRAUER, Viola, 278; BRAWNER, James H., 8; BRAXTON, Thomas, 118; BRAY, Curtis E., 234; Eunice, 117; Jeffrey B., 234; Katherine M., 234; Lucinda, 72; Thomas E., 234; BREAZEALLE, Ada, 179; Fred N., 179; Guy, 180; Minnie, 180; Newton, 179; Sallie C., 179; BREED, Hannah, 39, 94; BRESLIN, Louise, 137; BREWER, Becky L., 251; Betty L., 251; Dean N., 251; Howell C., 309; Martha, 175; Raymond E., 251; Thomas, 175; BREWSTER, Ed, 195; Evelyn, 195; Finley, 195; Frances, 195; Frank, 195; Henry, 152; O. F., 195;

BREWSTER, Samuel, 195; Sarah T., 152; William, 195; BRICKEY, Arie, 198; BRIDGES, Alan J., 170; Evelyn, 170, Jay C., 170; Mildred, 170; Opal, 170; Ordelta, 170; Orville B., 170; William, 170; BRIDGEWATERS, Henry, 212; BRIDWELL, Evelyn, 103; BRIGANCE, Benjamin E., 152; Edgar, 152; Julia G., 152; Rebecca O., 152; Shirley J., 152; Virginia J., 152; William N., 152; BRIGGS, Ben B., 135; Benjamin F., 134; Cynthia, 135; Douglas, 134; Kathryne, 135; Lynn T., 135; Richard D., 134; Samuel, 3; Sarah, 3; BRIGHT, Erma, 263; BRIMBERRY, Elmer L., 162; BRINEGAR, Earnest, 106; Edward, 106; Fred, 106; George, 106; Henry, 106;Joseph, 106; Wayne, 106; BROBERG, Johannah, 97; Nannie M., 96; BROCK, Ionia, 299; Violet, 97; BROCKLEY, Norman J., 152; BRODERICK, Donald, 82; BRODHEAD, Daniel,9;

BROMLEE, Willodee, 116; BRONIST, Evelyn, 298; BROOKBANK, Alva, 10; Bessie, 10; George E., 10; Henry, 11; John W., 10; Lois F., 10; Mary, 10; William, 11; BROOKE, Henry, 245, 256; BROOKOVER, Charles, 199; Robert C., 199; BROOKS, Gladys, 235; Isaac, 71, Job, 71; Samuel, 235; Susan, 149; BROSIUS, Bernice, 89; BROTHERTON, H. A., 283; Henry F., 283; Inell, 283; Lawrence H., 283; Martha J., 283; Marvin G., 283; Maureta, 283; R. B., 283; Wade H., 283; BROUS, Clara, 109; BROWER, Caroline, 120; BROWN, Allen H., 56; B. E., 15; Beatrice, 114; Carl C., 291; Caroline E., 56; Charles M., 215, 216; Charlton M., 277; Clark J., 56; Clyde S., 88; Cordell, 45; Darius, 120; Dorothy Lee, 144; Earl K., 291; Edith, 88, 114; Eleanor, 88; Ellen E., 17; Flora, 162; Florence, 56; Freeda, 200;

BROWN, George, 26; Glen F., 291; Herman H., 150; Hester, 88; Hezekiah, 209; Hiram, 13; James C., 56; Jane, 66; John, 9, 56; John H., 56; Joyce, 150; Ladene E., 17; Lillian, 97; Lois, 88; Margaret, 204; Martha, 56; Mary A., 56, 215; Mary K., 112; Natalie, 56; Raymond, 264; Robert G., 264; Sally, 81; Sarah J., 56; Sim R., 17; Susie L., 162; Vincent D., 56; Virginia, 88; W. Claud, 144; BROWNE, Elijah, 120; M. F., 14; BROWNING, Cora, 288; BROYLES, Bettye K., 255; William G., 255; BRUCE, Lula, 274; BRUMLEY, Archibald, 50; BRUNT, Roy, 110; Royce A., 110; BRYAN, George A., 199; John, 199; John D., 199; Joseph L., 200; Joseph W., 198; Lucy, 95; Margaret, 198; Martha, 157; Mary Ann, 199; Matthew B., 199; Nancy E.,199;

BRYAN, Rebecca, 157; Sarah J., 199; William, 157; William G., 199; BRYANT, Delilah, 187; Eva, 145; Mary F., 165; William, 187; William T., 165; BUCHANAN, Alexander, 103; Charles E., 103; Diane, 136; Donald W., 135; Frederick, 103; Fulton W., 238; Hubert A., 238; James, 103, 183; Jehu M., 103; John C., 135; Margery, 104; Mary J., 103; Mildred, 103; Ruth, 103; BUCIE, Sarah E., 199; BUCK, Lydia A., 30; BUCKNER, Amelia A., 146;

BUCKNER, Armour G., 148; Emory A., 148; Fay W., 148; Ira A., 148; Isabel A., 148; James W., 146, 148; Layton R., 148; Margaret, 149; Martha J., 148; Mary M., 146, 147; Milly F., 148; Nancy C., 146; Polexyna A., 147; Ruth L., 148; Walter H., 148; Walter W., 148; William B., 146; Zuda O., 148; BUFFORD, Howard D., 224; John R., 224; Robert M., 224; Vickie L., 224; Warren, 224; BUIST, Barbara, 201; BULLARD, Martha, 66; BULLINGTON, Robert, 24; BULLOCK, James, 79; Laura L., 141; Leonard H., 183; William, 50, 183; William A., 95; BULTMEIR, Clara, 233; BUNCH, Donald R., 98; BUNKER, Hannah D., 272; BUNTING, Arthur H., 277; Clara M., 277; Dolly, 277; Ernest E., 277; Esther, 277; Fern, 277; Ora E., 276; Orrick D., 276; Pearl, 277; Vera V., 277; Walter S., 277; BUOY, Mary, 57; BURCHFIELD, Aquilla, 34; Elizabeth, 34; Hannah, 34; Mary, 34; Sarah, 34; Thomas, 34;

BURGAN, Blanche I., 85; Darla J., 85; David, 85; Douglas, 85; Edward C., 85; Evans F., 85; Exa I., 85; George, 85; George A., 85; Holly R., 86; Horace J., 85; Ivan N., 85; Joseph A., 86; Kara L., 85; Kelly S., 86; Leah L., 85; Linda S., 85; Lottie M., 85; Louis F., 85; Olive E., 85; Paul, 85; Randall, 85; Raymond G., 85; Robert H., 85; William G., 85; BURGER, George, 196; Horace, 196; Laura, 196; Louise, 196; Sada, 196; BURGESS, Betty, 116; Sarah C., 11; BURKE, William O., 200; BURKET, William, 104; BURKETT, Clara, 280; BURKHART, Lynne A., 221; BURLESON, Ralph, 142; Sandra K., 142; BURNETT, Marian L., 99; BURNHAM, Mary, 228; BURNS, Katherine, 136; BURRAGE, June A., 145; Rebecca C., 145; W. A., 145;

BURRIS, John, 13; BURROW, Alice E., 221; Bertha, 221; Otis, 45; William B., 45; BURTON, Ann, 5, 26; Lewis, 5; Marianne D., 26; Sallie, 291; Samuel, 28; Verna, 106; William, 5, 24; BUSH, Carolyn, 202; Danny, 202; Edward M., 202; Elizabeth A., 202; Emmalene, 202; Harold S., 202; L. W., 162; Mary B., 202; Walter T., 202; BUSHONG, Frank, 280; Permelia, 100; BUTCHER, Alleyne C., 172; Daisy J., 215; Dorothy R., 172; Ervin L., 172; Eugene R., 172; Gertie B., 172; Marjorie N., 172; Mary E., 172; Pauline, 172; Roy, 172; BUTLER, Charles H., 252; Edith, 252; Elijah, 26; Fidelia, 273; Frank L., 232; Frazier S., 292; Gaines H., 292; George, 252; Joseph, 280; Kelly, 280; Margaret, 252; Mary I., 292; MollieE., 292;

BUTLER, Paul B., 293; Rudolph, 143; Sallie M., 292; Sarah R., 292; Wesley, 292; William B., 292; William G., 292; William J., 292; BUTT, Allen, 86; Edgar, 86; Eston, 86; John A., 86; Kathleen, 86; Lawrence, 86; Vernon, 86; BUTTREY, Elizabeth L., 202; Louis L., 202; BUXTON, George, 255; John, 255; Susanna, 255; BYBEE, Cloteel, 115; Glen M., 115; Lunelle, 115; Ovil T., 115; William D., 115; BYERS, Billy D., 111; Cheryl A., 111; David R., 111; Debra D., 111; Elmer N., 111; Elmer R., 111; Joel W., 111; Priscilla K., 111; Robert E., 111; Susan M., 111; BYNUM, Jean, 234; Thomas W., 234; BYRAM, Ebenezer, 62; Huldah, 62; BYRD, William, 24, 25; BYRKET, Clayton E., 105; Rosemary J., 105; William E., 105;

BYRON, W. H., 263; CABAN, Michael, 82; Michael D., 82; CABE, John, 175; CADWALLADER, Subina, 30; CAGLE, W. C., 144; CAIN, Mary P., 149; Mary S., 227; Mary V., 149; CAIRIENS, Leola, 235; CAISON, Larkin, 213; Laura E., 214; Lucinda, 213; Martha, 213; Mary, 213; Monnie M., 214; Nancy, 213; Sarah J., 213; William C., 214; Wilmuth, 214; CALDER, Alberta, 279; CALDWELL, Abraham, 62; CALL, Daniel H., 139; James R., 277; Melanie S., 277; Robert J., 277; Vanessa L., 277; CALLAHAN, Caroline L., 223; David E., 223; Edgemond P., 223; Elizabeth S., 223; Hugh L., 223; Katherine L., 223; CALLANDER, Ruth, 87; CALLER, Robert, 183; CALLIHAM, John, 68; CALVERT, Jane, 263; CAMERON, Gordon, 65; CAMPBELL, Andrew, 32; Lois, 91; Louise, 224; Marie, 215; Peter, 68; Sarah S., 223; Susan E., 249; Thomas, 76;

CAMPBELL, William D., 249; CANADA, William, 152; CANFIELD, Anne H., 187; CANNADY, Henry, 54; J. Rice, 54; James, 54; Joseph R., 54; Robert, 54; CANNON, John Lewis, 194; Margaret L., 194; Stephanie L., 194; CANON, Vivian, 240; CANTRELL, Irene, 236; CAPSHAW, Lonnie B., 215; CARAWAY, Ann E., 279; CARDEN, Estelle, 177; Gladys, 221; CARDWELL, Marie, 106; Thomas, 28; CARHART, Alden, 168;

CARICO, Don, 296; CARLILE, Robert, 61; CARLSON, Daisy M., 97; Samuel, 97; CARMAN, Harold F., 172; CARPENTER, Carl, 75; Frank, 220; Margaret, 75; Mildred, 75; CARR, Anna B., 287; Aulden W., 287; Bobby H., 287; Carl C., 287; Charles E., 287; Charles W., 287; Clarence W., 287; Emory L., 287; Hattie, 19; Luther E., 287; Mack H., 287; Margaret G., 287; Mary E., 287; Vestal V., 287; CARROLL, Daniel, 36; John B., 179; Sarah C., 179; Thomas J., 179; CARRUTHERS, John, 175; Nancy, 176; CARSON, David H., 233; David L., 233; Fred L., 233; Gene D., 278; John S., 233; Linda K., 233; Susan D., 278; CARTER, Bonnie, 291; Charles, 117; Claude W., 291; Edith, 70; Elizabeth, 70; Florida, 291; Hannah, 70; J. W., 291;

CARTER, James K., 232; John, 38, 39, 70; John M., 232; Keegan, 232; Keith, 275; Maggie, 291; Mark, 232; Mary, 26, 70, 157, 304; Milton, 135; Monnie, 291; Nannie L., 291; Nathaniel, 70; Orlan, 290; Paul W., 232; Rebecca, 260; Richard, 29; Rufus, 149; Ruth, 70; Susannah, 241; T. J., 290; Theodorick, 241; Violet, 291; William, 70; CARUTHERS, Ellen, 99; Middleton, 99; Minnie, 99; CARVER, William, 283; CARY, Elizabeth B., 118; Henry, 25; CASE, George W., 260; Helen V., 289; Littleton, 260; Sidney D., 289; CASS, Ed. E., 238; Jeffrey W., 238; Jennifer L., 238; Mary L., 238; William G., 238; CASSADY, Rebecca, 306; CASSEL, Elizabeth, 156; CASSIDY, Willie, 224; CAST, Alice, 278; CASTEEL, John, 162; Kate, 271;

CASTLE, Delano D., 45; Henry G., 45; CATE, Cynthia F., 203; John M., 203; John P., 150; Susan A., 203; Thomas D., 203; Thomas M., 203; Thomas S., 175; CATES, Ephraim, 204; CATLETT, Alexander, 256; CATON, Jack, 147; CATRON, Bessie, 286; Charles, 286; Ezekial K., 285; Harry, 286; James, 286; Katherine, 286; Maude, 286; Mollie, 286; Virginia B., 286; Walter, 286; William, 286; CAUDILL, Floyd, 281; Martin, 281; CEIBERT, Leroy, 55; CHADWICK, Bernice, 57; Donald, 57; Lois, 57; Marjorie, 57; Ray, 57; CHAFIN, Betty, 199; Herbert, 199; CHALLIS, Ann, 210; Hugh, 210; CHALMERS, John, 73; CHAMBERLAIN, Jane, 118; CHAMBERS, James, 32; Mildred A., 224; William H., 224; CHANCELLOR, Della, 16; CHANDLER, Joel, 25;

CHANDLER, Wuanita, 82; CHAPMAN, Beatrice F., 93; CHAPPEL, Juanita, 288; John, 26; Robert, 26; CHASE, Sarah, 212; CHASTAIN, John, 5; Judith, 5; CHEEK, Alexander, 188; Etta, 121; Nancy, 176; CHEESMAN, Ed., 209; Thomas, 209; CHERRY, Clare J., 236; Cleijo J., 236; Della M., 236; Jesse R., 236; Louisa M., 163; Walter R., 236; CHESSHIR, Bryan L., 194; Deborah J., 194; James W., 194; W. J., 194; CHEUVRONT, Mae, 58; CHEW, Lois, 58; CHILDRESS, Elizabeth, 62; John, 62; Mary, 62; William, 26; CHINN, Chichester T., 187; Susan B., 187; CHISHOLM, Maxwell, 137; CHISM, Almeda, 112; Aytchie H., 112; Benjamin, 108; Edward A., 112; Eliza, 112; Elizabeth, 108; Ellen, 108; Frank K., 112; George, 108; George W., 108, 112; Hiram, 108; Ida, 112; James, 189; James M., 112; Jehu M., 108, 112;

CHISM, Jehu T., 112; Jehu W., 112; John, 40, 112; Julia A., 108; Katherine, 112; Kester K., 112; Margery V., 108; Mary G., 108; Matthew H., 112; McPherson, 112; Michael, 40; Oscar J., 112; Rachel, 108; Rebecca, 108; Sallie K., 112; Sarah F., 112; Viola, 112; Willborn, 112; CHISMAN, A. S., 140; CHOQUETTE, Anthony, 87; Sean L., 87; CHRISTIAN, Allen, 282; Charles C., 282; Ebbie, 282; U. J., 282; CHURCHWELL, J. W., 194; CLAPP, Everett, 235; Kary D., 235; Rodney R., 235; Stella M., 282; CLARDY, John, 29; CLARK, Bendetta, 293; Charles, 27; Dessie M., 237; Eloise, 247; Hoyt, 114; John C., 237; Joseph L., 112; Josiah, 15; Kathy J., 47; Lelia, 177; Marnie, 47; Nancy, 121; Pamela A., 47; Richard, 47; Roxie, 43;

CLARK, Silas, 189; Vernon, 47; William, 12; CLARKE, Eva, 168; CLARKSON, Robert, 36; CLARY, Thomas, 246; CLAY, Henry, 52; Nancy E., 104; CLAYPOOL, George, 156; CLAYTON, Byron L., 254; Clara E., 254; Clovis M., 254; Edgar, 254; Fannie F., 254, 255; Hattie C., 254; James S., 254; Kate A., 254; Quay, 254; CLEMENT, J. W., 40; Pearl, 299; CLENDANIEL, Zelda, 299; CLENDENEN, James N., 213; CLIBOURN, John, 65; CLICK, Annie L., 295; Eva, 296; Harry, 296; Inez, 296; Nancy, 296; Neal J., 296; Neal P., 295; CLIFTON, Aury, 43; Shirley F., 43; CLINE, Luetta, 116; CLIVE, Robert, 64; CLOYD, James L., 40; COBB, Lula, 104;

318

COCHRAN, Stephen, 159; COCKE, Thomas, 212; William, 212; COCKEY, Susanna, 37; COCKRELL, William, 107; COFFEE, Cordelia, 303; COFFEY, Addie, 302; Ausbon, 302; Eliza B., 303; Elvira, 302; Glathia, 302; Hulda, 302; James M., 302; John H., 302; Margaret A., 302; Mimia, 302; Rebecca, 302; Thomas J., 302; William A., 302; COFFMAN, H. E., 170; COGDELL, Laura, 109; COGLEY, Helen, 292; COKE, Daphne, 282; COKER, Henry W., 141; Jeanie L., 141; Lyndell N., 141; Stanley D., 141; COLBERG, William, 272; COLBERT, Amelia R., 187; Canfield, 187; Frederick J., 187; James C., 187; John A., 187; Katherine C., 187; Thomas A., 187; COLE, Augustus, 119; Beatrice L., 298; Benjamin, 119; Bertie M., 297; Campbell C., 298;

COLE, Charles P., 298; Charles S., 297; Charlotte, 120; Claudius H., 119; Demetrius, 119; Dewey T., 297; Edith, 297; Edith L., 297; Eleanor,120;Elva S.298; Estella, 297; Ethel S., 297; Iona B., 298; J. D., 149; Jacqueline A., 298; James, 297; James R., 298; Joseph W., 298; Kyle E., 297; Maggie P., 298; Mattie M., 298; Melissa A., 119; Samuel M., 119; Thomas E., 298; Thurman R., 297; William S., 119; COLEMAN,Elizabeth, 26, 242; Mildred, 209; Thomas, 119; Vern, 89; COLEY, Rachel, 283; COLLIER, Benjamin, 3; Charles, 3; Connie T., 224; David L., 224; Edward, 3; Elizabeth, 3; Floyd, 224; Grace, 3; Henry, 3; James D., 224; Jean, 3; John, 3, 4, 209; Joseph, 3; Linda J., 224; Loyd, 224; Mary, 3; Sarah, 3, 4, 125;

COLLIER, Thomas, 3, 4; William, 3; COLLINS, Deborah, 279; Jack, 279; Jackie, 279; James, 279; Jane, 70; Ruth M., 67; COLLISTER, Devonne, 78; COLQUITT, Frederick, 211; COLTHARP, Eva C., 223; COLVILLE, Cynthia J., 195; Mary A., 214; Samuel, 214; Susan, 195; COMER, Betty, 229; COMPTON, Jennie, 186; Wilson P., 304; CONKLIN, Mary, 121; CONLEY, James, 79; John E., 223; Virginia A., 223; CONNALLY, Eliza M., 62; Sarah, 206; Thomas, 130; CONNEL, Aubrey, 46; Nollie N., 47; Odie C., 47; Van T., 47; Violet F., 46; CONNER, Cordelia J., 292; John, 292; Wayne B., 292; CONNOR, Catherine J., 57; COOK, Betty J., 171; Betty L., 137; Bruce, 274; Carolyn A., 171; Charles, 274; Christopher W., 137; Clem, 274;

COOK, Dorothy W., 137; Faye, 274; George, 176; Gerald A., 171; James G., 171; Jimmie L., 232; John, 258; June, 274; Kimberly, 237; Linda A., 171; Lisa, 237; Lucy N., 137; Margaret A., 171; Mary, 258; Mary B., 137; Mary C., 171; Mary E., 171; Mildred E., 171; Patricia E., 250; Priscilla, 258; Ralph, 274; Richard A., 30; Robert, 258; Ruth, 274; Thomas H., 171; Virginia P., 171; William, 237; COOKE, Euclid Monroe, 176; COOPER, Edward J., 262; George, 262; Henry H., 171; Isabel, 271; John E., 271; Joseph B., 262; Lucinda, 271; Margaret J., 271; Mark, 130; Mary L., 271; Nancy E., 271; Russell M., 289; Samuel, 271; Sarah A., 271; Susan E., 271; Virginia M., 289; COPASS, Charles W., 40; COPELAND, Alexander, 247; Ella B., 247; Ripley, 27; COPPEDGE, Thomas, 219;

CORLEY, John I., 147; CORLISS, Eva, 263; CORN, Madora P., 145; CORNEALUS, Martha J., 192; CORNFORD, Edith A., 277; COSPER, Ada M., 252; Annis E., 252; Jessie B., 252; Lidie E., 252; William D., 252; Willie A., 252; COTHRIN, Frances M., 254; COTNER, Daniel N., 175; COTTON, Mary, 194; Mary A., 185; COUCH, Eliza J., 161; Timothy, 161; Wesley, 150; COUDRY, Dennis, 267; COULSON, Charles, 190; Polexyna, 146; COULSTON, Fern, 45; COULTER, Lonnie, 98; Rosie E., 98; COUNCIL, Nancy, 222; COUNTRYMAN, Wilburn, 79; COUNTS, Henry, 211; COUPLAND, Katherine, 144; Margaret, 144; COURTNEY, James, 307; Nancy E., 299; COWES, Mabel, 65; COX, Annabelle, 136; Cal, 99; Carmelita, 79; David, 17; Dennis, 190; Edith, 43;

COX, Edna, 303; Ethel, 99; Lucy, 98; Nannie M., 99; Patricia, 79; Perry H., 17; Samuel, 99; Theodore X., 79; Vera, 148; Zachariah, 61; COZATT, Mary, 57; CRABTREE, David L., 45; Edward E., 45; Nannie, 43; CRAFT, Archelaus, 303; Elizabeth, 176; Frances S., 86; Frank, 86; CRAIG, Eula, 179; Eva, 180; John, 131; Minnie, 180; CRAIN, Catherine B., 249; James K., 248; Margaret, 219; Mary G., 248; CRAMER, William, 79; CRANE, M. J., 149; CRAPPS, Adella, 102; Alberta, 102; Alta, 102; Bruce, 102; Edwin L., 102; Ideria M., 102; Joan, 102; Lemuel, 102; Wilma, 102; CRAVEN, Emma L., 221; Peter, 221; CRAWFORD, Arthur, 146; Bertha, 86;

CRAWFORD, Mary, 259; Merlyne E., 146; CRAYTON, Bill D., 143; CRESWELL, Alfred C., 187; Alice, 187; Ann E., 186; Bessie B., 186; Cora, 187; Edith, 187; Edna, 187; Francis M., 186; Frank R., 187; George A., 186; George B., 187; Henry M., 186; Henry P., 187; Hinton E., 186; James A., 186, 187; James H., 186; John A., 186; Marian A., 187; Martha A., 186; Mary A. E., 186; Mary J., 186; Mary L., 186; Mattie M., 186; Norval D., 186; Paul, 187; Richard C., 187; Samuel, 186; Samuel F., 186; Samuel R. H., 186; Sarah F., 186; Susan A., 187; CRICK, Frances M., 217; CRISSMAN, Gertrude, 310; CROMWELL, Edith, 36; Richard, 36; William, 36; CRONRATH, Edward, 251; Victoria J., 251; CROOK, Catherine M., 247; Jesse, 247; Margaret B., 251; CHOPP, Arvin C., 83; Nancy N., 83; CROSLEY, Emma, 292;

CROSLEY, John, 143; CROSMAN, Joseph, 61; Robert, 61; Samuel, 61; CROSS, Joel, 138; CROUCH, Arthur W., 217; Edward W., 217; Margaret A., 217; Matthew, 246; William A., 217; CROW, Alice A., 161; Esther A., 83; Isaac, 206; J. W., 80; Laura, 80; Martin I., 161; Renee, 80; Robert, 80; Stephen, 206; CROWE, Adrian, 114; Claudia, 203; Rita, 101; Thelma, 112; CROWELL, Rusha B., 292; CRUM, Robert F., 222; Robert P., 222; CRUMP, Nancy, 149; CRUMRINE, David F., 165; Mary L., 165; Nina F., 165; Patricia A., 165; Ruth E., 165; CRUTCHFIELD, Garland, 121; John, 118; Mary A., 177; CRYER, Una, 109; CUBBISON, Donald, 86; CUBLEY, Corinne M., 147; Mable, 147; Robert H., 147; CUFFMAN, Chris, 43; CULBERTSON, Edna S., 295;

CULBERTSON, Edward D., 304; Elizabeth A., 295; Evelyn J., 295; Guy H., 295; CULP, Sophia, 62; CUNNINGHAM, George, 198; James C., 221; John, 199; Robert, 198; William, 198; CURRY, Jane, 306; Virginia, 119; CURTIS, Harlan L., 114; J. E., 114; James B., 114; John A., 114; Katherine A., 115; Lovell L., 115; Marilyn J., 115; Marilyn R., 115; Nora L., 114; Robert D., 115; Rufus J., 115; Thomas D., 114; CURZON, George N., 64; CUSTER, Abraham, 198, 199; Donna, 85; Elizabeth, 198; Emma C., 199; Fanny M., 199; John, 199; Rebecca, 195; CUTBIRD, Benjamin, 158; DABNEY, Mary M., 250; Mollie, 221; DAHMAN, Pauline, 291; DAILEY, Cornelia R., 131; Robert S., 162; Thelma, 133; DALTON, Colby, 307; John, 302; Matilda, 302; Sarah, 307; DAMERON, Betty A., 275; DAMEWOOD, Braxton A., 200;

DANAHER, Joseph, 274; DANIEL, Billie, 164; DANIELS, Deloris, 279; Mildred, 44; DARK, Nancy, 119; Willis, 119; DARNELL, Ann, 16; Ann E., 198; Belle, 198; Bessie, 198; Burrell, 16; Clarence, 198; Cleo, 198; Davis, 190, 197; Delura, 16; Dora, 198; Esther J., 198; George, 198; James, 198; James J., 197, 198; James T., 198; Jerusha, 16; Jesse, 198; John B., 15, 16; Joseph N., 198; Mary I., 197; Mattison D., 16; May, 198; Myra, 198; Paul, 198; Reese, 16; Robert, 198; Serena E., 198, 218; Thomas, 198; William, 16, 198; William T., 198; DARROW, Beatrice R., 263; DAVENPORT, Roy, 276; DAVID, Abraham, 6; Anne, 5, 29; Caroline, 7; Celia, 7; Charity, 7; Clementine, 8; Elizabeth, 5, 6, 7, 8; Francis C., 8; Henry, 7;

DAVID, Henry C., 7; Henry F., 30; Isaac, 5, 6, 7; Isaiah, 7; Jacob W., 7, 8; James A., 7; Jane A. M., 8; Jean, 6; John I., 7; John P., 6; Josephine A., 8; Judith, 6; Lavonia, 6; Locky H., 7; Lucy, 6; Magdalene, 6; Margaret L., 8; Marianne, 6; Mary, 6; Mildred, 7; Morriset, 6; Patience, 7; Peter, 5, 6; Phoebe, 6; Pierre, 5; Samuel, 6; Sarah, 6; Sarah A., 8; Susan, 6, 7; William, 6; William J., 8; DAVIDSON, Aaron C., 108; Almira, 285; Ann C., 11; Ann W., 15; Arnetty B., 16; Benjamin F., 13, 15, 16, 269; Benjamin S., 16, 141; Bessie N., 14; Betty J., 19; C. May, 18; Catherine W., 11; Cecil I., 17; Celestine J., 13, 14; Christopher C., 13; Corrina, 14; Corwin M., 14; Daisy L., 14; E. M., 14; Earl, 14; Eleanor, 10; Eliza, 13; Elizabeth, 10, 11, 18, 20; Ella, 11, 14, 18; Emmett, 19;

DAVIDSON, Esther, 14; Eugene V., 17; Frances, 10; Francis A., 108; George J., 17; George W., 13, 18; Georgeann, 18; Gertrude G., 19; Glen, 19; Grace E., 17; Harry N., 14; Henry, 10; Henry W., 16; Howard L., 19; Hurder, 19; Ira G., 108; Iza Mae, 19; James, 18; James D., 17; James I., 16; Johanna, 18; John, 10, 11, 12, 13, 14, 260; John A., 14; John F., 108; John W., 13, 14; Jonathan, 10; Joseph, 9, 10; Joshua, 9, 11; Joshua E., 16, 17; Julia, 11; Lewis E., 17;

DAVIDSON, Lila, 18; Lulu B., 19; Mariah, 18; Marion B., 17; Mark W., 108; Martha, 10, 13, 16; Mary, 10, 11, 18, 21; Mary A., 13; Mary E., 108; Mary S.,17; Mary Z., 16; Mathilda J., 14; Maude R., 90; Molly J., 17; Nancy, 10, 13, 16, 21; Nellie, 14; Nina C., 14; Oliver E., 13; Rachel, 10; Rosa M., 17; Rose M., 19; Ruth, 10; Sarah, 18; Sarah F., 11; Sarles T., 18; Sina A., 108; Susan, 14, 16, 19; Thomas, 11, Thomas P., 13; Thurman A., 19; Walter,11; William, 10, 13; William C., 17; William F., 16; William T., 17; Willie L., 17; DAVIS, Anita K., 44; Ann, 124; Anne, 124; Archie L., 231; Archie N., 231; Benjamin, 124; Benjamin M., 7; Bitsy L., 255; Charles, 74; Clara J., 215; Danny P., 216; David, 137; Dixie F., 255; Elizabeth, 124; Elmer, 205; Emma, 75; Etta, 74; Eva B., 44; Francis,75;

DAVIS, Franklin, 205; Gary W., 231; George, 205; George W., 44; Guy, 17; Hannah, 124; Henry, 124, 125; Isham, 124; Jack D., 44; Jack R., 44; James, 124, 125, 175, 205; James M., 44, 255; Jane, 124; Jean, 16; Jimmy R., 44; John, 124; Kenneth, 205; Keziah, 124; Lallie I., 17; Lee, 74; Leo, 205; Lois B., 44; Margie, 75; Marilyn, 255; Marjorie E., 249; Marriott, 124; Martha, 199, 213, 220; Mary, 304; Mary G., 44; Nancy E., 196; Nancy L., 231; Nathaniel, 124; Noel, 205; Paul, 205; Pearl M., 11; Randolph, 124, 126; Richard, 75; Richard C., 254, 255;Robert, 124; Samuel E., 16; Sarah, 75; Sarah F., 254; Shirley A., 44; Sylvia, 124; Thomas, 124; Walter, 44; Walter D., 44; William, 124, 126, 185; Zoa C., 87;

DAWSON, Annie, 109; Edwin H., 109; Florence, 91; George C., 109; James H., 108; Jimmie H., 109; John W., 109; Joseph A., 109; Kemper J., 109; Mollie M., 109; Nettie L., 109; Nicholas N., 108; Pleasant H., 109; Rebecca B., 109; Thomas N., 109; William M., 109; DAY, George, 175; Harriet J., 262; Sarah, 157; DeGASPERI, Dixie A., 135; Joseph, 135; DeMELLO, Jack, 142; DEAN, Allen B. C., 102; Charles, 98; Charlotte J., 98; Eliza J., 102; DEARMAN, Bessie M., 218; Dempsey, 110; Gary M., 110; James R., 198, 218; Jan E., 218; John C., 110; Robert A., 218; Sherry L., 110; DEATHERAGE, Mary C., 28; DEE, Kathleen, 80; DEERE, Nancy A., 76; DEFOOR, Karen J., 110; DEGRAODT, Norma, 116; DEHART, Richard, 111;

DEHM, Angie, 116; Eric, 116; Jeff, 116; Lyle, 116; DELANEY, Joseph, 57; Margaret A., 57; Mary, 280; DELONG, Angie, 306; DELONY, Elizabeth R., 126;DELOZIER, Belva R., 225; DEMENT, Abner, 185; DEMLER, Ruth, 80; DENHAM, Anna E., 113; Clinton, 113; J. Wood, 113; Leonard G., 113; Moton C., 113; DENNIS, F. N., 20; Jessie, 150; DENNISON, Eliza, 193; DENTON, Faye, 199; James, 199; James W., 161; Lorena, 199; Ruth, 199; DEROSIER, Valley, 19; DERRICK, Clara E., 233; Earl A., 233; DERTING, Blanch, 290; Calvin, 290; Charles S., 290; Cordia, 290; Grace, 290; Ida E., 291; John, 290; John F., 290; Joseph, 290; Joseph W., 290; Maxie, 290; Oliver, 290; Phebe C., 290; Velma, 290; Walker S., 290; DEVAULT, Mary, 280;

DEVEREAUX, G. M., 186; DEWEESE, Bernard, 12; DEWITT, Vena, 171; DEWOLFE, Norma, 279; DIAL, Joseph N., 197; Nancy E., 197, 204; Philip, 197; DIALS,Joshua, 190; DICKENSON, Geneva A., 300; Nina V., 222; Rufus B., 222; DICKERSON, A. B., 103; Ann L., 103; Arthur B., 102; Benjamin, 103; Cecil H., 102; Cephas, 101; Cephas B., 102; Charles R., 295; Douglas, 103; Edwin, 102; Elizabeth, 101, 295; Elsie, 295; Elvira, 295; Fannie, 295; Foster R., 102; Geneva, 295; George, 103; George D., 102; George N., 102; George T., 102; Gladyse N., 102; Ida J., 295; James M., 102; Jehu, 101; John, 102, 295; John M., 101, 295; John W., 295; Kate L., 102; Lennie, 230; Lula, 296; Margaret, 103; Mary, 103; Mary E., 102; Morris, 103; Nannie L., 295; Prentiss, 102; Richard C., 41; Rod C., 103; Samuel, 103;

DICKERSON, Sarah M., 102; Solomon H., 102; Susan F., 102; Verona, 103; William, 281; William C., 41; William H., 103; DICKEY, Fielding H., 99; DICKIE, Eliza E., 251; Willis W., 251; DICKSON, Daisy, 19; DILLING, Hilda, 177; DILLON, Hubert A., 217; Nancy G., 217; DILLS, Carole, 305; DIMMAUX, Catherine, 71; DINGUS, Rosa, 304; DISHMAN, Emma, 101; DISHNER, Alice, 303; Charles B., 297; Kyle D., 297; DIVELEY, Floyd A., 251; Mary K., 251; DIVINE, Janice L., 133; Perry, 133; DIX, Arthur, 280; DIXON, David, 119; Sarah, 119; Simon, 75; Solomon, 75;

DIXON, Winifred, 26; DOAK, John, 190; DOBBS, Clyde, 164; Douglas, 164; Walter, 164; Yvonne, 164; DODD, Benjamin E., 223; Clarence H., 223; DODDRIDGE, Bertha, 11; DODGE, Julia, 57; DODSON, Debra L., 87; Elisha, 228; Elizabeth, 228; Karen L., 87; Nicholas P., 227; Raymond M., 87; Rebecca D., 87; Steven R., 87; DOLLAR, Dolphus, 153; DONAHOO, Edward, 252; DONALD, Martha L., 214; R. H., 214; DONALDSON, Andrew, 12; John, 103; DONNELL, James L., 218; Oliver M., 218; Sarah E., 218; DONOHOE, Thomas, 29; DOREMIRE, Adria, 89; Anna, 88; Atlee E., 89; Avis F., 89; Evelyn L., 89; Harry, 89; Ira N., 89; Iva C., 88; Jacob E., 88; John S., 88; Pauline, 89; Sidney, 89; Socrates, 88; Virginia L., 89; DORSETT, Mary E. R., 85; DORSEY, Joshua D., 254; Suzanne, 91; DORTON, Martha A., 293;

DOTSON, John, 302; DOTY, Aileen, 235; DOUGHERTY, Beriah M., 52; Malinda A., 52; Margaret, 52; Sarah, 52; DOUGLAS, Alan K., 215; Bessie G., 135; Billy W., 215; Dorothy, 135; Emma B., 135; Eric K., 215; Joseph, 55; Lula M., 135; Reuben C., 134, 135; Sarah, 134; DOUGLASS, Alfred M., 185; Alfred W., 185; Elizabeth, 185; James, 185; James H., 185; John, 185; Louisa M., 185; Margaret, 185; Mary, 185; Sarah, 185; William, 185; DOWELL, Carl H., 42; Hugh M., 42; Polly E., 42; DOWERS, Harold, 58; DOWNS, Lillie, 285; DOZIER, Frances, 234; James, 183; John, 183; DRAKE, Margaret, 197; Matthias, 11; DRAPER, Lawrence, 34; DREWS, Gretchen, 280; DRINNON, Richard, 302; DRIVER, Walter, 74; DROLL, Acie, 117;

DRUCKER, Lillian, 237; DRURY, Charles, 129; DUCHARME, J. D., 187; DUDA, Emma, 201; DUDLEY, A., 65; DUGAN, Eliza, 64; DUGARD, Oakley, 113; DUGGAN, Alfred, 64; Hubert, 64; Marcella, 64; DULL, Marvin, 275; DUNCAN, Ada, 144; Arnett M., 43; Deuna, 189; Dixie D., 43; Frances, 189; Frank J., 295; Goldie, 41; Hugh M., 43; Isham, 189; J. J., 41; Jane, 189; Joseph, 267; Louisa, 189; Lucy, 41; Mary, 189; Mary E., 201; Pamela R., 43; Patrick, 189; Peggy J., 295; Roger L., 43; Stuart, 305; Wade, 189; Wanda L., 43; William, 189; William M., 43; Zadock, 189; DUNHAM, Clementina L., 163; DUNIHUE, Myrtle, 106; DUNLAP, Beth A., 238; David, 152; Jack R., 238; Jackie R., 238; Jean L., 238; Jerry L., 238; Nancy J., 238; DUNN, Jack, 232; Oliver B., 232; DUPRAY, Thomas, 24, 28; DURANT, Debra J., 134;

DURANT, Joe, 134; DURBIN, Nancy, 206; DURFEE, Jeanne A., 85; John B., 84; Jonathan C., 85; DURHAM, Archibald, 175; 188; Avalee, 250; Bryant, 150; John, 178; Mansfield, 175; Mark, 178; Matthew, 178; DUVALL, Esther, 253; DYE, Donald W., 254; Etna M., 254; Jack C., 254; Jacklyn M., 254; Sterling W., 254; William H., 254; DYMUS, Catherine, 248; EARL, Eliza, 228; EARP, Matthew, 120; EASLEY, Ann, 30; Anna, 27; Benjamin, 29; Benskin, 25; Daniel, 5, 26, 29, 30; Daniel W., 28; Ecleo, 27; Edward, 27; Elizabeth, 24, 27, 29, 30; Frances, 27; Isaac, 29,30; James, 28; James D., 27; John, 24, 25, 26, 27, 28, 29, 30; John S., 29; Joseph, 28; Judith, 25, 28, 29, 30; Margaret, 24; Marianne, 29; Martha, 29, 30; Mary, 27, 29; Mary A., 27, 30; Miller, 28; Millington, 26; Moses, 27; Nancy, 27, 30;

EASLEY, Peter, 26, 27; Phoebe, 29, 30; Phoebe D., 27; Pyrant, 29; Rachel, 30; Richard, 30; Robert, 24, 25, 26, 27, 28, 29, 267; Roderick, 28, 29; Ruth, 30; Samuel, 25, 29; Sarah, 26, 27, 30, 212; Stephen, 5, 25, 26, 27, 29, 30, 212,268; Susanna, 28; Thomas, 26, 29, 30; Thomas W., 27; Vincent, 27; Warham, 24, 25, 26, 27, 28, 29; William, 24, 25, 28, 29; William A., 29; William M., 27; Winifred, 27; EASTERLING, Louemma, 304; Thomas, 304; EASTERLY, Gilmer, 293; ECHOLS, Elizabeth, 29; William, 211; EDDINS, Charles, 197; EDGECOMB, William, 197; EDGLEY, Andrew S., 264; Betty J., 264; Christine, 264; David, 264; Jack D., 264; Joseph, 264; Mark, 264; Paul, 264; Robert G., 264; Ruth J., 264; EDLEY, Clarence D., 264;

EDMOND, Rachel, 6; EDMUNDS, George, 56; Hunter, 56; Margaret, 56; EDMUND-SON, Constant, 126; EDWARDS, Allen, 176; Celia C., 176; Delilah, 175; Elizabeth, 150, 175; Frances L., 85; George, 199; Gladys, 148; Henry, 174; Henry H., 174; Hugh, 130; Hugh L., 176; Jane, 70; John, 174, 258; John A., 199; John C., 236, 237; Lindsey, 174; Lucile, 199; Luena, 121; Martha L., 176; Mary, 74, 175, 188; Mary E., 176; Nancy A., 176; Nathan, 174; Sarah F., 176; Susan, 175;

EGY, David R., 53; Elizabeth, 53; Frank, 53; Homer H., 53, 55; Leo, 53; Mary E., 53; EHALT, Jacqueline A., 80; Janette K., 80; Jean M., 80; Joseph, 80; Pamela J., 80; Patricia J., 80; Penny J., 81; EICKLEHART, Byron, 92; Paul, 92; ELDER, Coleman, 198; Ed, 198; James, 198; Jesse, 198; Martha, 179; Polk, 198; Porter, 198; ELIASON, Beth A., 12; Carolyn R., 11; Donald D., 11; Donna J., 11; Doris P., 11; Douglas D., 12; Gaar G., 11; Inezetta, 11; Kathryn J., 11; Nina G., 12; Rebecca S., 12; Ronald, 11; Thomas C., 11; Thomas D., 11; Wood E., 11; Woodice E., 11; ELKINS, Charles, 148; Elizabeth, 147; Mollie, 224; Musa E., 147; Thomas P., 147; ELLERBRUCH, Jeffrey A., 279; Keith, 279; Terry L., 279;

ELLERBRUCH, Timothy J., 279; ELLIOT, Loyd, 275; ELLIOTT, Basha, 118; Beatrice, 235; Burleigh, 53; Grace, 53; James W., 53; Mary, 70, 121; ELLIS, Curtis, 230; Elizabeth, 29; Emery J., 132; Florence Z., 248; Jean A., 255; Joe, 132; Judith K., 132; Marian, 230; Ora D., 96; Sarah, 262; ELLMAKER, Emmett L., 298, 299; William E., 299; ELROD, Caroline, 309; Elizabeth, 310; George, 309, 310; James, 309; John, 310; Mary, 309; Mary B., 231; Mary L., 310; Millard F., 310; Peter, 309, 310; Ruth E., 44; Sarah, 309; Susan, 309, 310; William, 309, 310; EMERSON, James, 71; EMMERT, Ruth, 114; EMPSON, George J., 237; Lillian, 237; ENGLAND, Sciotha E., 222; ENGSTROM, Ernest, 289; EPPERSON, Delphia A., 281;

EPPERSON, Eliza, 281, 295; Elizabeth, 281; Elvira, 281; Floyd B., 281; Genette, 281; Howard L., 281; Irene, 281; Isaac, 281; John W., 281; Joseph, 281; Lula, 280; Mary A., 280; Mary E., 281; Minerva, 280; Phyllis A., 281; Sarah, 281; Stephen, 280; Stephen F., 281; William F., 281; William H., 280, 281; ERICKSON, David, 168; Donna L., 230; Lloyd L., 168; Pamela, 168; Patti, 168; Reuben L., 230; ERVIN, Esther, 14; ESTABROOKS, Mark W., 277; William R., 277; Willis W., 277; ESTRIDGE, Ephraim, 183; EVANS, Aaron, 71; Abigail, 71; Allene, 16; Charlene, 251; Charles, 260; Elizabeth, 96; Grace, 202; H. B., 196; John, 71; John W., 19; Mary, 71; Owen, 71; Rebecca, 71; Ruth, 71; Sarah, 71, 75, 118; Thomas, 71, 306; EVE, Duncan, 227; Genevieve, 227; EWING, John, 20; EZELL, Balaam, 178; FAIRCHILD, John L., 231; FANN, Jesse, 130; FARISS, Mabel, 144; FARLOW, Nathan,70;

FARMER, Ann, 156; Creed, 304; Dorothy I., 121; George A., 121; Gregory, 258; FARR, Cora, 86; FARRAR, John, 28, 190; FARRINGTON, Mary, 166; Osamus, 167; FARTHING, Thomas D., 192; Virginia A., 192; FARWICK, Dorothy, 264; FAUCON, Nicholas, 125; FAULKNER, Arthur, 246; FAWBUSH, Elizabeth, 163; FELKER, Margaret J., 231; FELTY, Betty R., 236; Ida L., 237; Joe, 236; Yvonne J., 236; FERGUSON, Annie, 115; Blondine, 116; Buford, 115; Candace, 115; Cecil, 115; Charles, 85; Chris, 117; Christie, 116; Clarence, 115; Clarence D., 117; Conley, 116; Dana, 116; Debbie, 116; Donna, 116; Dwayne, 116; Edith A., 117; Elva, 100; Fanny, 112; Faye, 116; Geraldine, 116; Glenda, 115, 116; Glenn E., 115; Henry P., 220; Imogene, 116; Izitta, 85; Jean, 114; Kathie, 116; Kenneth, 115; Larry, 117;

FERGUSON, Marjory L., 117; Marshie, 116; Martha C., 187; Mary, 115; Mary L., 220; Mary R., 116; Maud, 115; Melody, 116; Michael, 115; Millard, 115, 116; Ora, 116; Patricia L., 117; Paul, 116; Richard, 117; Rodney J., 117; Roger, 116; Sam, 116; Samuel T., 115; Sandra, 116; Sarah, 115; Sparrel, 115; Stephen, 116; Susan, 117; Verman, 116; Voit, 116; Wilma, 116; FERREE, Lois, 109; FERRELL, Alfred D., 185; Burkett F., 185; Cherry, 185; John C., 185; Lula, 185; Mona, 185; William, 185; FICKLE, Callie, 303; FIDLAR, Delbert C., 14; Robert L., 14; Robert O., 14; Ruth D., 14; FIELD, Thomas, 45; FIELDER, Enos, 273; Mary, 273; FIELDS, Brian M., 115; Emma, 177; Joshua, 120; Pearly E., 297; Randall T., 115; Robert G., 115;

FIELDS, Roger B., 115; FIGER, Deborah M., 251; FIGUERAS, Anita, 58; John,58; John W., 58; Julia, 58; Richard, 58; FILLMORE, Ralph, 163; FINCH, Elizabeth, 28; FINCHER, Annice, 179; FINLEY, John, 158; FINNEY, Elizabeth A., 145; William, 25; FIREBAUGH, Albert M., 131; David C., 132; Donald G., 132; Frances L., 131; Frederic L., 132; John C., 132; John M., 132; Julia, 132; Mary F., 131; Mary J., 132; Mattie B., 131; Ruth, 132; Shirley A., 131; William H., 131; FISHER, Asberry, 59;

FISHER, Lindy, 79; Ralph, 79; Raylyn, 79; Ronna, 79; FITCH, Elmina, 214; Empson, 213; Fannie D., 214; Francis D., 213; Gertrude, 214; John T., 214; Leota, 214; Lois, 213; Oran E., 214; Travis T., 214; William F., 213; FITZ, Celestine, 202; FITZSIMMONS, Fannie, 161; Nicholas, 37; FLAKE, Robert, 125; FLANDERS, James S., 215; FLATHERS, Clara M., 77; FLEENOR, Amos M., 296; Arthur, 288; Audrey, 288; Bessie, 288; Blanche, 288; Charles, 288; Donald, 290; Edsil, 290; Emma, 296; Florence, 288; George P., 288; Helen, 288; Jacob G., 288; James, 298; John, 288, 296; Kathryn, 288; Katie, 296; Lucile, 288; Minnie L., 288; Oscar, 288; Ralph, 288; Stephen, 296; Susan, 288; W. M., 290; FLEMING, Blanche, 280; Glenn S., 280;

FLEMING, K. B., 195; Mable, 280; Madge, 280; Mary E., 280; Maude, 280; R.H., 140; Susannah, 28; FLEMISTER, Carl W., 196; George S., 196; FLENIKEN, Joseph, 179; FLETCHER, John, 281; FLORY, Alma F., 90; Arnold, 89; Cinthy M., 90; Cora A., 89, 90; Doris, 90; Eldonna, 89; Elsie, 89; Eugene, 89, 90; Frank, 89; George B., 91; Harold B., 89; Larry H., 90; Lawrence, 89, 90, 91; Lewis, 90; Margaret, 89; Marion, 89; Mark A., 91; Nellie J., 90; Ora A., 89; Robin R., 91; Ruth A., 90; Sharon S., 90; Willis E., 90; FLOWERS, Dianna M., 110; James, 110; Janice L., 110, Robert, 92; FOEY, Nancy, 133; FOLKER, John, 13; FONTAINE, James F., 218; Jeanie K., 218; FOORD, Carol, 248; FOOSHEE, John, 67; FORD, Henderson, 281; Zadok, 245;

FOREMAN, Elmina S., 214; FOSSETT, Mary, 106; FOSTER, Fern, 255; James, 172; John C., 248; Lella V., 225; Mary E., 248; Milton, 46; FOULKE, Mary, 156; FOUST, Albert L., 121, 151; Ida Viola, 151; John, 151; John M., 151; Martha E., 151; Mary E., 151; William A., 151; FOWLER, Alden R., 237; Barbara K., 237; Diana D., 237; Donald R., 237; John, 77, 184; Levi, 102; Margaret A., 202; Mary, 12; Steve, 237; Tabitha, 102; FRAIM, William, 40; FRAME, Jack L., 11; FRANCIS, Joseph, 28; FRANCISCO, Henry L., 299; Lavena, 298; Lou, 281; Lyle D., 299; FRANKLIN, Arlie B., 300; Janice L., 300; FRANTS, Richard, 91; FRAZIER, Billy W., 298; Bobby G., 298; Charles G., 288; Jennie, 287; Joe R., 288; Merle O., 288; Monnie L., 287;

FRAZIER, Nannie, 286; Noah, 287; Roy, 298; FREE, Newman, 46; FREELS, Victor, 300; FREEMAN, Susan, 85; FREEZE, Alberta, 230; Elbert E., 230; Emmett E., 230; H. Clay, 231; Larry E., 231; Sandra K., 230; Suzanne, 230; Wilma B., 230; FREILEY, Adam, 33; Barbara, 32; Christian, 32; Edward, 33; Esther, 32, 162; Joanna, 32; John, 33; Jonathan, 33; Mary, 32, 33; Nicholas, 32, 33; Samuel, 33; Thomas, 33; FREY, Solomon, 62; FRIDAY, Sarah, 223; FRITZ, Janene M., 88; Keith L., 88; Kerry W., 87; Kevin W., 88; Michael L., 88; Paul O., 87; FRODGE, Velma, 114; FRUITS, Patricia, 115; FRYER, David, 246; Elizabeth, 256; Frances M., 246; Horace, 246; James, 246; Lloyd, 246; Margery, 246; Richard, 246; Sarah, 246;

FRYER, Walter, 245, 246; William, 246; FUGATE, Emma, 290; FULGERSON, Mary J., 160; FULLER, Andrew, 81; Mark, 81; Mary E., 7; FULLERTON, Vera, 221; FULTON, Mary, 14; FULTS, Ellsberry, 213; FUNK, Albert E., 238; Henrietta, 201; Howard D., 238; Kristin C., 238; Melissa A., 238; GADD, Catha, 54; Frank, 54; Fred W., 54; James H., 54; Laura, 54; Mae, 54; Myra, 54; Susanna, 54; GADDY, Ann, 134; Joe B., 134; GAETA, Viola M., 136; GAGE, John H., 169; John M., 169; Stansifer R., 169; William R., 169; GAINES, James S., 28; GALLAGHER, W. C., 142; GALLOWAY, Elijah, 260; GAMBLE, David L., 229; Harold, 229; GARCIA, Isabel S., 235; GARDENHIRE, Arminta, 20; Elmira, 19; Emma L., 20; Essie, 20; Eva, 20; Hannah, 20; Jacob, 19;

GARDENHIRE, Jesse J., 20; John D., 20; Lillie, 20; Mary B., 19; S. Jarvis, 20; Sarah J., 19; Tennessee A., 20; Thomas, 20; Thomas M., 19; GARDNER, David H., 42; Margaret, 63; Martha, 300; Martha L., 148; Peggy, 290; Warren H., 42; GARLINGTON, William T., 252; GARMAN, Mildred, 43; GARNER, Dale, 93; Douglas, 93; Everett, 93; George E., 289; John, 183; Margaret, 199; GARRETT, A. J. B., 15; Joyce, 231; Myrtle, 224; Pearl, 201; Ray, 231; William R., 163; GASH, Blanche, 34; Elizabeth, 34; Hannah, 34; Johannah, 34, 259; Martha, 34; Mary, 34; Michael, 34; Sarah, 34; Thomas, 34, 258; GASKILL, Josephine, 228; GASTON, Eva. M., 14; GAUNT, Louisa D., 119; GAUT, Barbara, 217; GAVARD, Malinda, 103; GAVIN, Inez, 272

324

GEARHART, James M., 72; GEBHARDT, John J., 261; GENTRY, Archie N., 113; Belle, 164; Betty J., 113; Emma G., 113; Georgette, 113; Glen M., 113; Ilma F., 113; James A., 113; Jamie, 113; Josie E., 220; Mary C., 217; Myrtle M., 113; Thelma, 14; Turner, 113; GERALDS, Martha, 115; GERDES, Maxine L., 234; GEREN, Lydia, 62; Simeon C., 66; Susan C., 66; William L., 67; GERON, Hiram, 65; GESS- LER, Anna C., 217; John, 217; GETZ, Gordon S., 288; Guy C., 288; GIBSON, CalaC., 133; George A., 133; George E., 132; Nathalie K., 133; Susan J., 133; GILBERT, Charles, 259; J. W., 294; Jack E., 294; Joe L., 294; Johannah, 34; John W., 294; Thomas, 34; GILES, Charlotte, 18; Earl B., 18; Eva L., 18; Josephine, 18; Kath- ryn G., 222; Maggie D., 18; Oran, 18; Presley, 18; Roy G., 222; Samuel G., 222;

GILES, Samuel S., 18; GILGAS, John, 12; GILKISON, Cena L., 58; Miriam L., 58; GILLENWATER, Bessie, 297; GILLEY, Bayard, 294; GILLILAN, Elizabeth, 119; John, 119; GILMER, Gary E., 142; Jerry W., 142; Paul, 142; GINGRICH, Grover M., 88; Harvey W., 89; Kenneth D., 89; Ruth E., 89; GINN, Fanny R., 263; GINNISON, William, 271; GIPSON, Barry, 217; GIST, Abigail, 40; Adeline, 40; Amy, 39; Ann, 39; Anthus C., 45, 46; Bayless, 40; Benjamin, 37, 38, 39, 66, 68; Betty M., 47; Beulah, 41; Byron L., 47; Christopher, 36, 37; Coleman C., 45; Debbie, 47; Della R., 46; Dollie, 45; Dollie F., 45; Doris M., 46; Dorothy J., 46; Edith, 37; Effie M., 46; Eleanor, 40; Elizabeth, 40; Frances E., 46; Frances L., 46; Fred G., 46; Fred M., 46; Gary, 47; Goldie E., 47; Guy, 47; Guy J., 47; Herman C., 46;

GIST, Hiram, 40, 41, 94; Huron F., 45, 46; Ida, 41; J. M., 46; Jack M., 47; James E., 46; James T., 46; Jehu M., 41, 45; Jemina, 37; John, 37, 39; Joseph, 39, 40, 94; Julia D., 46; Levi, 40, 94; Levi H., 41, 140; Lucinda, 40, 41; Lura, 45, 46; Mamie A., 47; Mary, 39, 40, 160; Merry M., 45; Nathaniel, 37; Ned, 45; Newman H., 47; Nollie H., 46; Olivia, 45; Olivia F., 46; Porter, 41; Rhoda, 40; Richard, 36, 37; Ruth, 37; Sanford C., 45; Sarah, 40, 94; Thomas, 37, 39; Ver- elda K., 47; Watson, 40; William, 37, 159; GITTRICK, Earlene, 234; Henry H., 234; GIVENS, Herman F., 223; Ruth, 223; GLAZE, Carvel, 273; Frank, 273; Grover, 273; Kenneth, 273; Mamie, 273; Ralph, 273; Ruth, 273; Wilson, 273; Zadel, 273;

GLEN, Nathan, 72; GLENN, Annie F., 109; William H., 109; Willie J., 109; GLINGLE, Claude, 86; GLOBER, Catherine B., 249; George E., 249; James K., 249; Mary L., 249; GLOCKLE, J. L., 14; GLOSSUP, Ida A., 235; GLOVER, Alexander C., 95; Annie, 95; Avery, 95; Bullock, 95; George P., 95; Kate, 95; Martha J., 102; Minerva, 95; Orrin, 95; William, 102; GOBER, Alan J., 233; Ashberry W., 233; Berneil, 233; Claud I., 233; Dale E., 233; Dorris M., 233; Frank L., 233; Gary S., 233; Gerald R., 233; Ginger D., 233; Horace L., 233; Isom A., 233; Jaquetta, 233; Joseph I., 233; Katherine A., 233; Kimberly, 233; Leroy S., 233; Lloyd L., 233; GOBLE, Gladys, 106; Marcella, 306; Rachel J., 305; Zella, 305; GOCHENOUR, Grace, 86; Irene, 86; William, 86; GODFREY, Edwin L., 11; Thomas W., 11;

GOLDSBY, Susan, 180; GOLLNICK, Norma F., 111; GOODE, Glenn, 193; GOODMAN, Eliza, 113; William, 3; GOOKIN, Daniel, 124; GORDON, Daniel, 258; James, 139; John, 258; GORE, David, 110; Jessie R., 110; GOSLING, Hal, 186; Harry, 186; Lytle, 186; GOSNELL, Ada, 117; GOSNEY, Martha, 277; GOTCHER, Lee, 145; GOTT, Mabel G., 287; GOUGH, Cornelius, 32; GOVER, Rebbie R., 233; GOWEN, Ann, 25; GOWING, Edward, 126; GRAF, Harold, 86; GRAFFHAM, Jack, 192; GRAHAM, Billie J., 283; Claude, 294; Gus A., 283; I. H., 57; James L., 283; Lottie B., 234; Velma I., 46; GRANADE, Martha A., 7; GRANT, G. W., 13; William, 157; GRANTHAM, Harold, 17; GRANUNKS, Ethel, 133; GRASTY, Mary, 72; GRAVES, Boston, 65; Martha M., 226;

GRAVES, Ruth N., 107; GRAY, Donald, 17; Elizabeth, 125; Jane, 16; John M., 17; Katie, 17; Roger W., 7; Ronald, 17; William, 125; GREASON, Annie, 177; GREEN, John, 142; Mary, 71; Peter H., 11; Raymond S., 16; Robert, 28, 142; Sammie S., 16; GREENE, Jane, 302; Ruth, 309; GREENLEE, Elizabeth, 137; James, 308; GREEN- LEY, Anna, 55; GREER, Lois M., 111; GREGG, Cleo R., 300; Luther G., 300; Willa J., 300; GREIG, W. D., 88; GREY, Jean, 101; GRIFFIN, Billie E., 283; Dora, 144;

GRIFFIN, Eldon, 283; Gary, 90; Howard, 90; Janice, 90; John F., 283; L. E., 283; Louis P., 64; Nelda C., 283; GRIFFITH, Almer, 85; Anne, 156; Garold, 85; Joan E., 300; Marlin, 85; Richard D., 300; Robert E., 300; Roy O., 300; GRIGSBY, Isaac, 281; GRIM, Ann R., 297; C. L., 297; Caledonia, 297; Cora L., 297; D. C., 297; Emily J., 297; Frank S., 297; J. W., 297; Mary C., 297; Sarah E., 297; Susan E., 297; W. P., 297; W. R., 297; GRIMM, Frances, 142; GRIMSLEY, Sarah, 115; GRINER, Martha, 54; GROCE, Frances, 137; GROGAN, Bert D., 298; Harry, 298; GROOMS, Annie J., 97; Betty J., 98; Beulah J., 98; Beulah R., 97; Charles B.,97; Claude R., 97; Clyde L., 97; Delma C., 96; Doris L., 97; Edith M., 98;

GROOMS, Elizabeth A., 98; Elnora M., 96; Evermond T., 96, 97; Glen C., 98; Gregory T., 98; Johannah D., 97; Linda, 98; Lisa G., 98; Marcia D., 98; Marjorie R., 96; Martha S., 97; Mary L., 97; Nellie M., 96; Nellie R., 97; Nina G., 98; Patricia A., 98; Paul L., 98; Peggy N., 97; Ruby S., 97; Samuel W., 98; Schuyler, 96; Thomas, 96; Virginia L., 98; GROSECLOSE, Clyde, 300; Mary S., 300; Rita, 300; Ruth, 300; GRUBTILL, Joyce J., 279; GUEST, Euphemia, 193; John, 70; Morgan, 193; GUINN, Julia N., 139; William G., 139; GULLERMIN, John, 263; GULLETT, Clara L., 105; Lavere, 105; Lyman R., 105; GUNLACK, Ella M., 278; GUNNIN, James, 120; GUNTER, Randall P., 110; Roy P., 110; GUPTON, Paul S., 110; Stephen T., 110; GURLEY, Louisa J., 120; GYGER, Laura E., 91; HAAG, Leslie F., 229;

HACHER, Robert F., 172; HACKLEY, Ellen, 209; HACKNEY, Lydia, 304; Rebecca J., 282; HACKWORTH, Sarah A., 112; HADDASH, Dixie T., 111; HADLEY, Bess S., 121; Buck, 120; Joshua, 118; Mary, 118; Ruth, 118; Sarah, 120; HAGAN, Charles F.,296; Hugh, 296; Irene, 296; Marcellus, 113; Mary, 33; Pattie L., 296; Rebekah, 101; HAGGARD, Myrtle J., 134; HAIN, Elizabeth S., 77; HALBERT, Noah, 254; HALE, Charles A., 132; Earl J., 132; Elizabeth, 6; Hannah, 98; Jean S., 131; William C., 131; HALEY, Leatha, 107; Lonnie C., 221; HALL, Angelynn C., 134; Charles B., 134; George B., 277; Jeff D., 224; John, 63, 258, 259; John B., 277; John E., 277; Joseph, 63; Lavonne V., 277; Lillian N., 234; Mamie, 224; Robert, 216;

HALL, Vera L., 277; HALSO, Jane, 3; William, 3; HAM, Dolores F., 47; Doria M., 47; Leroy, 46; HAMBY, William, 246; HAMILTON, Claude L., 147; James T., 115; Janet R., 147; Judy C., 100; Lillian, 100; Margaret, 263; Mary, 27; Nancy W., 27; Nellie, 100; Ocie, 115; Peter, 256; Ronnie D., 100; Travis, 100; HAMMER, Basil, 117; Heinrich, 226; Hester, 204; James E. D., 166; Lilian, 226; Randall, 117; HAMMOND, John, 258; Thomas, 36; HAMMONDS, Mary, 204; HAMMONS, Houston, 190; HAMPTON, Bessie, 57; C. E., 185; Carmen, 186; Charles, 57; Dorothy, 185; Helen, 186; John, 57; Mona, 57; HANCOCK, Frederick, 106; Mary L., 216; HAND, Gertrude, 7; Violet W., 160; HANES, Eva, 90; HANKINS, Absolem, 66; Susannah, 66; HARBAUGH, David, 90; HARBOUR, Jerry, 198; John L., 263; Lynn S., 263; Mary E., 77;

HARBOUR, Robert G., 263; Rodney L., 263; HARBUT, Bertha, 231; HARDIE, Henrietta, 174; HARDIN, David, 94; Joseph G., 94; Minerva, 94; HARDING, Elizabeth, 32; HARDY, Maud M., 255; William, 106; HARDYMAN, James, 206; HARER, Earl H.,145; HARKINS, Roland, 51; HARKLEROAD, Elizabeth, 293; HARKNESS, Dorothy, 132; HARLAN, Aaron, 71; Della K., 98; Enoch, 70; Mary, 71; Pearl, 114; Roxie, 97; Sarah, 71; Stephen, 70; HARLESS, Clarence, 306; Dean D., 306; Debbie, 306; Dewey, 306; Frank J., 306; George, 306; Geraldine, 306; Leo, 306; Lundy P., 306; Myrtle,306; Ramon, 306; Robert T., 306; Roger, 306; Roger V., 306; Shirley T., 306; V. L., 306; Wheatley C., 306; HARLIN, Benton R., 41; Gene, 114; Texie M., 42; HARMON, Elizabeth, 149; Nancy C., 149; W. H., 149; HARNER, Margaret, 66; Susan, 66;

HAROLD, Thomas, 104; HARPER, Billie, 165; Carla K., 232; Carroll, 231; Charlotte B., 119; John H., 81; Kathy, 81; Kelly J., 232; Lewis, 231; Park A., 232; Paul, 81; Robert L., 7; Susan, 81; Timothy L., 232; Victoria A., 81; HARRELL, Martha E., 104; HARRIS, Charlotte, 115; Frances, 241; Mabel L., 238; Mary A. E., 140; Mary, 174; Mary V., 147; Michael, 125; Nancy, 241; Rebecca, 32; Richard, 32, 241; Robert, 149, 241; Sarah, 241; Sterling, 62; Susanna, 241;

HARRIS, W. H. H., 140; HARRISON, Benjamin, 183; Elizabeth, 96; Levert, 197; Mary, 94; Maud M., 234; HART, Thomas, 125; William, 52; HARTNESS, Cleo, 231; HARTSOCK, Ann, 58; Anna, 59; Elisha B., 59; Ellen, 58; George, 59; Hannah J., 59; Ida, 59; James, 58, 59; John, 58; Joseph, 59; Laura B., 59; Rachel, 59; William H., 59; HARVEY, Patricia M., 111; Thomas, 174; William, 70; HARVILL, Sarah, 27; HASTIE, Carrie L., 141; HASTINGS, Betty, 135; Dixie A., 135; William E., 135; HATCH, Henry B., 134; HATCHETT, Archibald, 102; Nancy, 102; HATHCOCK, Wiley, 119; HATLEY, William, 130; HAWKINS, Elizabeth M., 292; Philip, 140; Samuel H., 140; HAWKS, Rebecca, 198; HAWLEY, Brad A., 80; Donald, 80; Herbert C., 80; Karen J., 80; Opal, 81; HAYES, Albert, 311; Anna B., 113; Bruce, 105; Cletra O., 100;

HAYES, Colbert N., 310; Colby C., 311; Elizabeth, 310; Emily R., 101; Emmett, 142; Florence, 310; Gladys, 105; Glen, 105; Hannah, 310; Hannah A., 311; Hester A., 310; Jack, 100, 142; Jack G., 101; James H., 101; James M., 311; Jefferson, 113; John, 40, 310; John H., 311; Joseph M., 101; Julius G., 101; Lou A., 101; Lovie E., 95; Luther L., 311; Nancy J., 227; Patricia H., 101; Permelia, 310; Peter, 311; Sarah, 310; Sarah A., 40; Sarah C., 311; Sarah J., 41; Thelma, 142; Thomas, 105, 310; Thomas S., 310; Thomas W., 311; William C., 310; Zachary T., 311; HAYNES, Albert P., 292; Betty B., 281; David, 281; David G., 281; Emory H., 281; George P., 281; Hannah M., 292; Helen V., 299; Ida, 284; Irene, 281;

HAYNES, James G., 281; James J., 281; James S., 292; John J., 299; John W., 281; Lucinda, 281; Nannie, 281; Orban P., 281; Sallie C., 292; Samuel, 281; Samuel D., 281; William S., 281; Wilma E., 299; HAYS, Ames, 107; HAYWOOD, Samuel, 212; HAZEL, Sarah, 104; HAZLEHURST, Anne P., 248; Charlotte N., 248; Elizabeth, 248; Ellen B., 248; Franklin H., 248; George N., 248; Isobel, 248; Katherine N., 248; Laurence N., 248; Mary M., 248; Robert P., 247, 248; Virginia B., 248; William M., 248; HEAD, Jacqueline, 101; Sherry J., 101; Stanley, 100; HEADLEY, Laura, 106; HEANEY, Jean, 256; HEAROD, Susan, 137; HEATH, Mary J., 45; Thomas, 214; Thomas J., 213; HEATON, Darline, 163; HEAVER, Willie E., 110; HECKMAN, Harold, 90; HECKT, Sherwyn M., 238; HEDMAN, Elma, 78; HEDRICK, Juanita, 114;

HEIFNER, Deborah L., 227; Elizabeth A., 226; Marilyn S., 227; Richard M., 226; HELGASON, Julia E., 250; HELLER, Helen, 217; HELMS, Margaret, 106; HELTON, Virginia, 305; HENBEST, Albert, 229, 234; Martha S., 229; Octavia L., 234; HENDERSON, J. J., 304; Robert, 191, HENDRICKS, Dennis L., 193; Linda J., 193; Lura, 56; Raymond, 193; HENDRICKSON, Donna, 82; HENLEY, J. H., 187; Judith M., 118; William H., 121; HENNESSEE, Grover L., 215; HENRICKS, Jerry, 92; Joel, 92; Stella, 92; Steven, 92; Vernon L., 92; HENRY, Betty B., 132; Cala S., 132; Duanna, 166; Mary, 57; Natalie S., 132; Samuel E., 132; William N., 132; HENSLEE, Almeta, 282; John D., 282; O. B., 282; HENSLEY, Laura, 299; HEREFORD, Hanford, 252; Harden S., 252; John F., 252; HERN, Clem H., 274; Eleanor, 274; Faye C., 275;

HERN, Henry, 274; HERNDON, Waive, 294; HERRING, Karl, 85; HESLER, Amanda, 13; Andrew J., 52; Elizabeth, 13; Francis, 13; George H., 52; Gibson, 13; Jane, 52; Mary A., 52; Samuel 13, 52; Sarah, 13; Sarah A., 52; William, 52; William H., 52; HESS, Albert W., 142; Alma C., 171; Frances, 142; Frank, 142; Henrietta, 142; James, 142; John, 142; Josephine, 142; Laura, 142; Margaret E., 142; Robertson, 142; HESSE, Diana L., 133; George A., 133; HESSELER, Christine, 132; HESTAND, Abraham M., 163; Barzillia, 140; D. B., 140; Daniel B., 41; James P., 46; Thomas B., 165; HEWETT, Maurice, 200; Patricia, 131; HICKAM, Ephraim, 285; George W., 285; Ida B., 285; Kelley, 285; Marian, 285; Victoria, 285;

HICKAM, William, 303; William F., 285; HICKEY, Carter, 67; Sarah A., 66; HICKMAN, Achsa, 57; Ada, 55; Adam, 50; Albert, 100; Alice, 57; Allen, 52; Allen R., 57, 58; Alva, 55; Andrew J., 52, 55; Ann, 51, 58; Anna, 51, 269; Asa, 55; Betty J., 58; Carol A., 58; Catherine, 51; Charles P., 57; Charles W., 58; Cornelia A., 54, 271; Dale, 55; Daniel, 50; David, 58; David K., 53; Delores A., 58; Edward, 57; Eliza, 55; Elizabeth, 51; Elizabeth M., 51; Fanny M., 54;

HICKMAN, Frances R., 57; Frank, 57; Frank A., 55; Frederick A., 57; Gene, 55; George E., 58; George R., 52; George W., 58; Gertrude, 57; Glenn, 58; Hannah, 51, 52, 56, 58; Hannah L., 53; Hardy, 54; Helen A., 58; Hila M., 57; Hiram, 52, 54; Howard H., 57; Isabel, 54; Isabel D., 55; Jacob, 50, 51, 52, 53; Jacob B., 52; James O., 58; James R., 57; Janet E., 58; John, 50, 51; John P., 50, 52; Joseph H., 51; Katherine 51, 53; Kenneth, 58; Laura A., 53; Loren M., 52; Lorinda, 54; Lou, 54; Louise A., 57; Lucian D., 57; Lura J., 53; Magdalene, 50; Margaret, 55; Margaret A., 53, 55; Margaret J., 51; Marian, 58; Martha, 55; Martha J., 54; Mary A., 50, 52, 56; Mary E., 54; Mary J., 55; Michael, 50, 51, 52;

HICKMAN, Morgan, 52, 55; Nancy, 52; Nettie, 57; Oscar C., 57; Paul, 58; Peggy A., 58; Peter, 50, 51, 58, 269; Peter P., 51; Philip S., 58; Richard C., 52, 57; Robert, 58; Ronald, 55; Rosanna, 51; Samuel H., 52, 55; Sarah, 52, 54; Sarah A., 55; Sarah O., 53; Serane, 53; Serilda, 53; Sidney M., 53; Susan, 53; Susannah, 51; Susannah H., 52, 53; Thelma, 55; Vernon, 58; Wayne, 58; Wilfred, 58; William C., 57; William M., 55; Wilma J., 58; HICKS, Blanche O., 165; Charles F., 294; Christopher, 165; Coleman, 308; Constance E., 165; Evans, 294; Herbert H., 165; Hugh V., 165; Ira E., 294; Jewel V., 165; John, 308; Karen S., 89; Katherine R., 294; Lucretia, 76; Mary A., 165; Nina, 164; Nina L., 165;

HICKS, Nina V., 165; Reece V., 294; Reeselyn, 294; Thelma, 298; Tim M., 165; Victor M., 294; Virgil, 164; Wanda I., 165; Weimer K., 294; HIGGINS, Iris, 144; HIGH, Dade, 114; HIGHSMITH, Molly, 136; HIGHTOWER, Delilah, 213; Laura M., 192; HILL, A. B., 19; Celia, 120; Frances, 201; George M., 201; Herbert T., 102; Mary, 102; Nancy, 68; Phoebe, 307; Sarah E., 13; Sion, 125; William W., 143; HILLIARD, Susannah, 258; Thomas, 258; HILLMAN, Bess, 293; HINDS, Abigail, 62,66; Ada A., 64; Adolphus L., 64; Albert, 65, 66; Albert M., 64; Amanda, 66; Anita, 65; Ann, 63; Anna, 67; Asa, 66; Asa F., 66; Benjamin, 61, 62; Byram, 62; Calvin, 62; Caroline, 63; Catherine, 54; Charity, 61, 62, 63; Charles E., 64;

HINDS, Charles L., 54; Charles M., 64; Chloe, 62; Claiborn, 63; Eleanor, 63; Eliza, 66; Elizabeth, 63; Emily E., 64; Ferris S., 64; Florence 54; Francis M., 63; Francis S., 64; Geneva M., 63; George, 61; George W., 67; Grace E., 64; Hannah, 61, 62, 65, 66; Henry, 66; James B., 64; James C., 63, 66; James R., 66; Jane, 61; Jenny, 62; Jerome J., 64; Joel, 62; John, 61, 63, 65, 66; John B., 64; John C., 63; Joseph, 61, 62, 63, 65, 66, 67; Joseph M., 64; Josephine, 65; Josiah, 62; Leslie, 65; Levi, 61, 62, 65, 66; Levi J., 66; Lucretia, 62; Lydia, 62; Mahala, 62; Margaret, 61; Mary, 61, 62, 63, 66; Mary E., 63; Milly, 62; Nancy, 62, 63; Phoebe, 62; Rhoda, 39, 66; Ruth, 62, 65; Ruth C., 66; Samuel, 62;

HINDS, Sarah, 62, 63, 65; Sarah A., 66, 67; Simeon, 61, 62, 63, 64, 66; Stephen, 62; Susan, 63, 67; Susannah, 66; Sylvanus, 66; Thyrza, 62; Trillia, 65; HINES, Berta, 196; Happy A., 6; Robert, 191; HINK, Greta, 83; HINKLE, Mary, 61; HINRICHS, Carolina, 277; Frederick L., 277; Leann R., 277; Phillip R., 277; Weldon S., 277; Wilbur, 277; Willa L., 277; HINTHORN, Melvin, 117; HINTON, Betty J., 19; Holly L., 19; Howard M., 19; Robert H., 19; Walter H., 19; HITE, Allan R., 83; Franklin P., 11; Robert L., 83; Steven L., 83; HITSON, Wyatt, 213; HITT, Oliver R., 249; HIX, Daniel B., 164; Isaac C., 164; John C., 165; Martha, 164; Mary E., 164, 165, 215; Nancy J., 165; Oliver, 164; Orville, 164; Oscar, 43,164;

HIX, Otis, 164; Reuben F., 164; Thomas, 164; William T., 164, 215; HOBSON, Benjamin C., 226; Benjamin W., 226; Bruce W., 226; Carrie L., 226; Ella G., 226; HODGE, Arnold, 148; Z. T., 147; HODGES, Ross, 290; HOERMANN, Clarence E., 171; HOFFLINGER, Patricia I., 229; William, 229; HOGATT, Nancy, 167; HOGUE, Martha J., 203; HOLDEN, Burford, 197; Elizabeth, 10; HOLDER, Caroline P., 226; Dolly, 223; Walter A., 226; HOLDERBY, Joseph, 241; HOLLAND, Francis, 34; James V., 239; HOLLINGSHEAD, Bettye E., 255; Emis E., 255; Gloria, 255; HOLLINGSWORTH, Sarah, 71; HOLLOMAN, Luther J., 151; HOLLOWAY, Mary, 311; HOLMAN, Allie R., 196; Marvin, 113; HOLMES, Bessie, 151; George W., 151; James E., 151; Jane E., 151;

HOLMES, John A., 151; Joseph W., 151; Kate R., 255; Mary, 126; Mary E., 151; Mary M., 151; Miles A., 255; Miles C., 255; Minnie M., 151; Ralph W., 151; Ruth, 255; Samuel, 126; Warren, 126; William, 126; HOLSTEN, Louise C., 196; HOLT, Mary E., 304; Rhoda, 214; HOODENPILE, George, 189; Nancy, 227; HOOKER, Benjamin, 94; HOOS, Orville,11; Robert, 11; HOOVER, Alene, 219; James J., 87; Mary J., 87; Richard R., 87; HOPE, Amanda E., 101; Elizabeth, 131; Frank, 100; Wilma D., 100; HOPPER, Sadie P., 58; HOPSON, Helen, 178; Willie, 149; HORN, Samuel, 12; HORNADAY, Balaam, 120; Susan, 151; HORNEY, Ruth E., 107; HORNICKLE, Cindy, 117; Lori, 117; Neil, 117; Richard, 117; Vicki, 117;

HORSTMAN, Larry N., 235; Neil J., 235; HORTON, A. M., 220; Arthur, 295; Daphne, 290; John W., 295; Mary M., 290; Nelson M., 290; Robert M., 290; HOS-KINS, Dollie, 29; HOUCHINS, Elizabeth, 228; HOUDESHELDT, Dean E., 275; Gary G., 275; Neil R., 275; Raymond E., 275; HOUSE, James, 70; HOUSER, Andrew, 287; Jemima, 165; Nicholas, 165; Paul L., 287; Thelma L., 286; HOUSTON, Mary H., 186; William, 193; HOVER, Allen L., 93; Cameron J., 93; Carolyn E., 93; Darcey L., 93; Darrell W., 91; Donald E., 91; Douglas G., 91; Edwin, 91; Evelyn D., 91; Gary A., 91; Harley J., 93; Hazel F., 91; Hiram J., 91; Hugh, 91; Ira, 91; Jay J., 91; Jayne F., 91; Jean M., 91; Lance D., 93; Len L., 91, 93; Lois J., 93;

HOVER, Minnie J., 91, 92; Norma R., 91; Ray R., 91; Stella, 91, 92; Ter-rance D., 91; Thomas O., 91; Warren, 91; HOWARD, A. J., 95; Amy B., 95; Ann, 247; Ava G., 95; Berry P., 290; Campbell, 95; Clinton, 113; Creed, 95; Deborah, 256; Frank, 95; Goldie, 291; Hattie, 95; James W.,113;John G., 146; Margaret A., 135; Marlin G., 113; Mary, 37; Nellie M., 95; Rosemary, 113; Sarah, 37, 160; Smith B., 95; Thomas, 247; Violetta, 37; Virginia, 290; William G., 113; Wilson C., 113; HOWELL, Deborah, 156; Edward, 184; Everett, 148; George, 54; Haven, 179; Joseph, 148; Victoria, 252; W. R., 149; HOWLAND, Sarah, 10; HOWSER, Thomas, 32; HOYT, Ruth M., 89; HRABAN, Ladean, 279; HUBBARD, Bernadine, 291; Deverne, 291; Helen, 131; Joel, 30; John, 128; Thomas, 291; HUDDLESTON, Leo, 143; Robert L., 143; HUDGINS, Evelyn F., 203; Frank S., 203; Henry E., 203; Joseph E., 203;

HUDGINS, Kendred M., 203; Kendred W., 203; Martha J., 203; HUFF, Hamp, 162; HUFFMAN, Mary E., 95; HUGHES, Annie, 223; Nora E., 270; Sarah W., 96; HULTMARK, Lynn, 134; Myron L., 134; HUME, Christine P., 83; David A., 83; Ellen M., 83; James E., 83; James S., 83; Merril W., 83; Patricia J., 83; Samuel W., 83; Wayne S., 83; Wilbur, 83; HUMES, Mary E., 113; HUMPHREY, Brice C., 255; HUMPHREYS, Elizabeth, 159; HUNNICUTT, Barbara, 17; John, 124, 129; Penelope, 17; William, 17; HUNSAKER, Viola, 57; HUNT, Ed, 56; James, 137; Mae, 229; HUNTER, Allie, 57; Carl, 56; Carrie, 56; Charles, 56; Edward E., 56; Essa, 57; Fanny, 56; Frank, 57; George W., 56; Gertie, 57; Hannah D., 55; Henry H., 56; Homer, 57;

HUNTER, James F., 57; Josephine, 56, 133; Laura A., 52; Laura B., 261; Louisa, 310; Lucy, 55, 57; Martha A., 57; Mary J., 56; Maude, 56; Nancy, 176; Narz W., 56; Nora, 55; Ollie, 57; Ona, 56; Richard, 57; Richard C., 56; Samuel D., 56; Sarah I., 56; Walter, 56; Wayde, 57; HURD, Helen M., 232; Robert W., 232; HURST, Thomas, 189; HURT, Betty L., 236; Daniel, 62; William F., 194; HUSKETH, Nathaniel, 130; HUSON, Andrew S., 10; Pamela, 10; Scott, 10; Shelley, 10; Stacey, 10; HUSSEY, Thomas, 75; HUTCHINS, Martha, 175; HUTCHINSON, Grace, 177; HUTSON, Alpha J., 240; Kimble P., 240; Minnie E., 240; Robert, 240; W. Thomas, 240; HUTTON, Esther M., 197; IMBLER, Abraham, 57; Claude, 57; INGRAM, Edsam M., 144;

INGRAM, Samuel, 143; INMAN, Sallie M., 223; IRVIN, Ruth M., 299; IRWIN, Alice B., 14; Clayton C., 203; Harvey, 305; Paula D., 305; Virginia J., 203; ISBELL, R. F., 136; Robert N., 136; JACKSON, Aldyce M., 107; Anna L., 114; Ber-nette, 191; Bernice, 180; Betty J., 107; Cassie, 191; Charles E., 191; Clara, 113; Delores, 107; Dorothy, 275; Dorris E., 220; Harding, 227; Hattie, 113; Hettie, 113; James A., 191; James M., 191; Jennie, 164; Joan E., 84; Josephine, 107; Karen M., 234; Kathleen, 107; Malin, 107; Marah F., 191; Margaret, 107;

JACKSON, Mary S., 204; Mollie, 231; Nettie F., 107; Opal I., 107; Phronissa L., 191; Robert, 107; Roberta, 107; Roma, 113; Sarah A., 191; Sylvanus, 107; Thomas J., 191; Thomas L., 234; Thomas P., 234; Tom W., 234; Twilah, 107; Vera M., 235; W. Stanley, 234; William, 107; William S., 234; JACOBS, Alma A., 218; Andrew H., 218; Tanya L., 87; JAMES, David, 217; Lavinda, 56; Mesech, 32; JAMISON, Bertie, 272; Charles, 272; George, 272; Irma M., 226; Kate, 272; Mary, 272; William, 272; William M., 272; JANNEY, Aquilla, 118; JARRATT, Adda, 68; Allen, 68; David, 68; Eleanor, 68; Gregory, 68; Lucy, 68; Mary, 38, 68; Nancy, 68; Peter, 68; Rebecca, 68; Thomas, 38, 68; William, 68; Wyatt, 68; Young, 68;

JARVIS, Lucy, 191; Rachel, 204; JAYNE, Elva M., 286; Henry T., 286; Herschel, 286; Maxwell W., 286; Nat T., 286; Roy E., 286; Thelma L., 286; Thomas H., 286; William N., 286; William T., 286; Willie C., 286; JEFFERS, Ewell, 52; Thomas, 189; JEFFERSON, Thomas, 24, 29; JEFFRIES, Mary, 227; Thomas, 65; JENKINS, Ethel, 280; JENKS, Estella M., 87; Etta B., 87; Theodore W., 87; JENNER, Elsie, 291; JENNINGS, Etha, 185; Gertrude W., 230; Martha P., 231; Stella M., 261; JETT, Charles, 296; Curtis O., 296; Custis L., 296; Eileen, 301; Howard, 263; Irene, 296; Isaac F., 297; James, 296; John, 296, 301; John W., 296; Mary E., 296; Mary M., 298; Merle L., 296; Neva, 296; Peter L., 296; Rebecca, 298; Roena F., 296; Samuel, 296; Sarah I., 296, 298; Stephen, 296; Stewart, 296; Vance, 301; Virginia V., 296; Wilfred L., 296; William H., 297; JOHNS, Burr P., 200; Cecil, 200;

JOHNS, Cliff, 200; Gennie, 200; George, 199; Horace J., 200; Lucille, 200; Lulu, 200; Minnie G., 200; Myrtle, 200; Paul V., 199, 200; Viola, 200; Zula, 200; JOHNSEN, Elsiemae, 275; JOHNSON, A. R., 144; Alfred H., 106; Alzira, 228; Anne M., 202; Cecil, 106; Charles, 104, 105; Claudius, 104; Cletis, 106; Clovis, 106; Emma, 121; Flora, 274; Hazel, 106; Hoy, 106; Ison, 252; James P., 202; James W., 144; John, 24, 125, 128, 242; John C., 104; Lillian M., 238; Lucy, 20; Luvern, 168; Madge, 272; Martha E., 192; Moses, 3; Nancy E., 83; Rachel A., 95; Ralph, 106; Ramon, 106; Renny, 252; Ruby, 106; Thomas, 308; Vera, 165; JOHNSTON, Alexander, 158; Alfred H., 104; Amos L., 104; Amy, 105; Avey, 104; Bessie, 104;

JOHNSTON, Carl C., 104; Clarus, 104; Cushman, 239; Edith E., 107; Effie, 104; Emma A., 106, 107; Ervin, 105; Etta R., 104; Frederick, 107; George W., 104; Gertrude, 104; Goldie, 104; Jack, 105; Jehu, 104; John, 239; John E., 105; John G., 103, 104; Josephine, 105; Kathryn, 104; Kenneth, 107; Laverne F., 105; Leslie D., 107; Levi, 104; Lila P., 107; Lilla, 239; Lora A., 104; Lucinda M., 104; Margery, 103; Marion G., 104; Martha, 149; Mary, 103, 104; Mary A., 103; Mary L., 106; May, 104; Nancy, 103; Nettie, 104; Ona Z., 107; Osmond, 107; Rachel, 103; Rettie, 104; Rhoda, 104, 105; Robert, 103, 104, 106; Romney, 104; Russell L., 107; Ruth, 103; Sarah, 104; Sevoya, 239; Susanna, 104; Theodosia, 239; Thomas, 306;

JOHNSTON, Truely, 104; Udora, 239; Viola, 104; Virginia, 105; Walter, 105; William, 104, 239; William H., 104; Wilson, 239; Wyatt, 239; JOINER, Jerry, 144; Lemuel, 144; JOLLY, Camille, 134; Zula F., 263; JONES, Benjamin, 242; Betty A., 147; Beverly, 168; Bobbi Jo, 168; C. A., 169; Carol F., 168; Colleen, 168; Daniel, 210; Delbert A., 168; Dollie, 290; Ebenezer, 222; Ella, 99; Emma, 273; Emma S., 201; Fred, 110; Griffith, 156; Helen A., 249; Howard, 168; James, 63; Jeffery, 168; John, 183; Juanita, 168; Judy, 168; Kathy, 168; Leona, 252; Lucille, 236; Marvin T., 168; Mary B., 237; Matthew, 130; Michael T., 102; Myrtie F., 98; Nancy M., 7; Nannie M., 133; Nellie, 200; Ott, 106; Pernita E., 222; Rachel, 168;

JONES, Ruth, 101; Sarah A., 8; Thomas R., 168; Timothy, 168; Vincent L., 168; Virginia, 168; Vivian, 289; William E., 201; William H., 283; JORDAN, Emily, 119; Jerry, 110; Leland T., 240; Lilly, 134; JOURDAN, John, 193; Martha, 193; JOYNER, Elizabeth J., 152; Jacob, 152; John N., 152; Katherine, 152; Mahala K., 152; Mary E., 152; Matthew N., 152; Nellie V., 233; Nevill M., 152; Quintard, 152; Rebecca H., 152; Thelma, 179; William B., 152; JUDD, John, 260; JUSTICE, Ann, 118; JUSTIS, Henry, 70; JUTILA, Edward, 91; Harlyn, 91; Marvin, 91;

JUTILA, Ronald, 91; KADLECEK, James J., 83; James M., 83; Kathryn A., 83; KAISER, Diane R., 42; Edward F., 42; Joan M., 42; Kenyon E., 42; KALER, Myrtle M., 147; KAMMERER, Rosalind, 78; KAPELLER, Roland V., 233; KARRELLS, Celeste, 78; KATZMAN, Ruby, 99; KAVENAUGH, Arthur, 182; KAYLOR, Lelia M., 296; Rebecca, 226; KEELE, Jane, 204; KEELING, Thelma L., 225; KEENE, B. B., 15; KEETHLER, Katherine, 21; KEFFELER, Charles, 78; Darleen, 78; Duane, 78; Kay, 78; Mable, 78; Roger, 78; KEITH, Frances, 164; KELL, Charles R., 221; KELLAR, Richard W., 152; KELLERHAUS, Emil, 146; KELLOGG, Jay C., 87; KELSEY, Charles N., 303; Margaret, 160; KENNEDY, Billy J., 147; Curtis, 231; Lena, 231; Ray, 105; KENNEY, Charles R., 135; KENTTA, Dorothy, 277; KERN, Doris M., 107; Gilbert, 107; KERR, Fannie, 109;

KERR, Isabella R., 303; Jimmie, 236; Mary A., 303; Sarah M., 292; KERSTING, Carl, 226; Carryl P., 226; KESLER, Danny, 88; Dennis, 88; Dewey O., 88; Edwin D., 88; Fred L., 88; Karl, 88; Kathy, 88; Kristeen, 88; Lorraine, 88; Robert W., 88; Sharon S., 88; Wanda, 88; Willodean, 88; KETRON, Billie L., 282; Christine, 282; Felix G., 282; Frank, 282; Freeman, 303; George, 302; Kenneth, 282; Mary A., 282; William B., 282; KEYES, Elizabeth, 232; KIDD, Lucas, 252; Robert, 108; KIEL, Emma J., 248; KIERULFF, Mary M., 248; KILPATRICK, Alexander, 28; Joseph, 53; KIMBALL, Sophia, 260; KIMSEY, Evelyn L., 223; Thomas N., 223; KINDER, Harley, 100; KING, Columbus, 153; Davis, 137; Elizabeth, 50, 188; Frances, 27, 188;

KING, George, 182; Hazel W., 225; Jack H., 223; Jacqueline, 289; James, 158; Jane, 124; John, 188, 289; John T., 109; Joseph H., 223; Joseph V., 223; Laura A., 196; Margaret, 188; Marshall, 188; Normandine, 289; P. W., 225; Patsy, 188; Philip T., 196; Pleasant, 188; Robert, 212; Sarah, 188; Sarah E., 195; Senea, 188; Thomas J., 195; Wilfred, 90; William, 188; William D., 153, 188; William R., 223; William W., 196; KINGREY, Elijah, 115; Quintella, 115; KINNEY, Dorothy D., 135; Elizabeth, 135; Oral, 272; KINSEY, Nancy, 30; KIPF, Billie R., 278; Lecia S., 278; Linda J., 278; Loralee A., 278; Lorelia K., 278; Lorraine J., 278; Lynelle J., 278; William, 278; KIRBY, Etta, 216; James, 246; Mahala, 152;

KIRBY, Wiley, 130; KIRK, James, 130; KIRKBRIDE, Audery K., 169; Bishop B., 169; Emerson G., 169; J. Chester, 169; John W., 169; Mary E., 169; Roxie V., 169; KIRKLAND, Samuel, 140; Thomas, 205; KIRKPATRICK, Ruth, 76; KIRKWOOD, Robert, 110; Robert R., 110; KIRSHINSKY, Melany K., 93; Richard, 93; KITSON, Mary E. S., 86; KITTEN, Bernice, 42; KLAPP, Elizabeth L., 251; Joseph, 251; KLEFSTAD, Bertha, 91; KLEVENS, Harold, 289; KLINKLE, Jerry A., 88; KLOSTER, Paul, 281; Paul P., 281; KNAFFLE, Robert, 283; KNAPP, Charles B., 278; KNAUS, Henry, 10; Susan, 10; KNIGHT, Alan L., 109; Alice A., 109; Bertha J., 109; Ephraim, 129; John, 63,126; Nancy C., 63; Percy F., 109; Shepherd F., 109; KNOABLE, Mamie, 288; KNOCK, Daniel, 30; KNOWLES, Lewis W., 109; KOCH, Carl C., 278; Dorothy L., 278;

KOCH, Gerald L., 278; Lynn M., 278; Thelma R., 278; KOELLING, Norma L., 202; KOENIG, Florence, 177; KOHLER, Hetwich, 57; KONOP, Joseph, 98; Mildred A., 98; KORS, Donald, 105; John E., 105; Robert F., 105; Susan L., 105; KOTLAR, Ferne, 165; KRAUSE, Marcella H., 84; KREIG, Richard, 116; KRICKEL, John H., 215, 216; Martha Ellen, 216; KRISTOFFERSON, Anne, 202; Helmer C., 202; KRUEGER, Margaret E., 19; Rubin L., 19; KUBIAK, John, 193; KUCERA, Bonnie, 85; KUHLENBURG, Martin, 262; KYLE, Robert, 306; LACEY, Mattie C., 229; LACKEY, Robert, 137; Violet, 215; LADD, Malinda P., 281; LAIN, Chesley M., 135; Richard B., 135; William R., 135; LAKE, Delmar, 115; Ella M., 115; Patricia, 115; Vernon, 115; LAKINS, Elizabeth, 164; LAMB, Dorothy, 151; Malinda, 120; Margaret, 150; LANDIS, Catherine, 74;

LANDRUM, Barbara A., 251; Benjamin F., 251; John H., 251; Joseph A., 251; Kathryn M., 251; Leurah L., 251; Robert H., 251; LANE, Abraham, 301; Abraham Z., 301; Edward, 284, 290; Ellie S., 284; Enoch P., 301; Evie, 115; Ezra E., 283; Frances, 301; Jacob E., 301; James H., 301; John F., 290; John R., 301; Jonas W., 301; Joseph T., 301; Katherine, 301; Margaret, 301; Martha, 301; Mary, 301; Mary J., 284; Pat, 290; Samuel W., 301; Vernon, 290; Wanda, 290; William D., 301;

LOCKE, William B., 219; William C., 218; LOEBER, Doris M., 201; LOEFFLER, Leroy, 292; Maxine, 292; Otto, 292; William, 292; LOESCH, Robert R., 107; LOEW, Barbara, 79; LOGAN, Frederick, 164; LOGBERGER, Mary, 217; LONG, Edith I., 77; Edward, 231; Frances S., 136; Gabriel, 209; James, 212; Lela M., 231; Mary, 118; Rebecca, 120; Sarah, 118; William, 66; LONGINO, Edna, 187; Otto, 187; William P., 187; LORANCE, Martha, 119; LORD, William, 179; LOTT, Billie J., 143; Hugh, 143; James D., 141; John E., 141; Kimberly A., 141; Lois, 143; Ricky W., 141; Russell C., 143; LOTTS, Barbara, 301; LOUDERBACK, David N., 261; Francis M., 21; Newton, 21; LOUGHRIDGE, Luther D., 222; LOVE, Elizabeth, 102; Ella T., 294; Weldon, 179;

LOVELESS, James, 256; LOVLEY, Genie, 116; John, 116; Keith, 116; Ronnie,116; LOWE, Eliza, 59; LOWERY, Alexander, 38, 39; Anna, 233; Charles, 38; LOYD, Dale C., 194; Gregory M., 194; Jane S., 194; Marvin D., 194; Nancy L., 194; William B., 194; William P., 194; LUCAS, Donald, 277; Minerva, 100; Paul H., 277; Pauline V., 277; Truman, 100; LUCE, Ethel M., 46; LUCKY, Monroe, 228; LUND, Albert H., 171; Brian L., 171; Charles E., 171; Henry K., 171; LYALL, George C., 84; Glen E., 84; Mary I., 84; Robert G., 84; Robert V., 84; LYDON, Noreen, 84; LYNCH, Bently, 177; L. D., 139; LYON, Charles R., 226; Cyrus A., 226; Lloyd C., 226; Martha J., 226; Mary, 28; Richard D., 226; Steven D., 226; LYONS, Kate, 100;

MAAS, Hilda A., 111; MABRY, Hugh E., 218; MACKEY, Aeneas, 9; MACON, David H., 197; Eliza L., 197; Elizabeth L., 197; Emory J., 197; Eugene L., 197; George M., 197; John, 197; Martha A., 197; Mary M., 197; Robert G., 197; Sallie C., 197; Samuel R., 197; MADARIS, Margaret, 106; MADDUX, James W., 217; Sarah O., 217; MAGAW, Barbara L., 187; Edith A., 187; Shaler C., 187; MAGBY, Margaret E., 222; MAGNUS, Hannah N., 218; MAHANEY, Joanna, 264; MAINES, Mary, 112; MALLET,Stephen, 5; MALLICOAT, Hannah, 302; MALONE, Arlus T., 286; Daphne L., 286; Mylus M., 286; Willow, 131; MALSON, Rena, 43; MANCUSO, Thomas, 110; MANN, Blanche, 220; Robert, 29; Rufus, 120; Sarah, 29; MANNING, Charles W., 222; Louise H., 222;

MAPEL, Audrey, 82; David H., 82; Deann M., 82; Donald, 82; Dorothy J., 82; Dwaine, 82; Goldie, 82; Harlan, 82; Howard, 82; Raymond, 82; Robert I., 82; Stanley, 82; Suzanne, 82; Vada R., 82; William M., 82; MAPLES, Orley M., 294; MARANTO, Gina L., 230; Joseph V., 230; Marcus S., 230; MARMINO, Theresa K., 171; MAROHAIN, Marie, 232; MARQUANDT, Marina, 289; MARRIOTT, Benjamin, 125, 126; Constant, 126; Edgecomb, 126; Elizabeth, 125, 126, 178; Hannah, 124, 126; John, 126; Margaret, 125; Marian, 125; Mary, 124, 125; Matthias, 125; Prudence, 126; Sarah, 126; Thomas, 125, 126, 178; William, 4, 125; MARRS, Abyah T., 168; Alfred T., 169; J. D., 108; Junia, 169; Lovella B., 169; Mildred A., 168; Ora A., 169;

MARRS, Richard F., 168; MARSH, Alice M., 273; Anna, 273; Esau, 273; Virgil, 273; MARSHALL, Benjamin, 162, 163; Bettie M., 43; Bliss G., 43; Charles L., 21; Clarence B., 224; Daisy B., 43; Deborah L., 93; Donnie, 42; Dorothy, 42; Doye K., 43; Elizabeth, 20; Fred E., 43; George C., 20; George M., 42; George W., 42; Georgia B., 43; Howard P., 43; Hugh, 94; Hugh G., 43; Ina P., 43; Iris, 42; Iva L., 43; James A., 42, 43; James C., 42; James E., 42; John, 128, 129; Lockie M., 42; Luther C., 43; Margaret P., 21; Martin P., 20; Mary C., 42; Mary E., 42; Mary T., 20; Matilda B., 20; Maxine, 224; Mildred, 42; Only H., 42; Otia E., 43; Pearl, 42; Philip H., 42; Robbie M., 42; Robert H., 42; Robert P., 20; Robert W., 42; Ruth, 42; Ruth E., 238; Sue E., 42; Wayne, 93; William C., 20;

MARSHALL, William T., 20; Witt, 43; MARTIN, Addie V., 135; Adolphus F., 136; Alexander P., 135; Ann, 85; Anne, 177; Bessie, 135; Cala L., 135; Catherine, 42, 214; Dollie R., 135; Edna L., 274; Elizabeth, 214; Elmer, 42; Frances A., 132; Glaydene, 101; H. Patterson, 214; Hazel B., 274; Ida K., 135; James, 73, 136; James L., 135; Jane, 152; Janice, 136; Jennie L., 135; John, 25; John F., 274; Kathleen, 217; Lelia G., 274; Lucy M., 218; Luther L., 135; Marilyn A., 135; Mathilda, 271; Maude A., 73; Melissa, 239; Mildred, 194; Morris M., 274; Morry, 177; Nicholas, 136; Pearl, 179; Robert P., 135; Sallie B., 135;

MARTINEZ, Frank, 81; Jerome, 81; Kathy, 81; MASON, John T., 217;Malissa,217;
Molly, 105; Ross, 52; MASSENGILL, Lucretia S., 270; MASSEY, Elvina, 102; Marion,
177; Mary, 210; Minnie, 234; Richard, 182; MASTERS, David, 63; Mary, 63; MATH-
EWS, Elizabeth I., 220; Florence B., 220; J. Barkley, 220; James E., 220; John
R., 220; K. T., 79; William S., 220; MATHIS, Chesley P., 131; Ida B., 131; John
L., 131; Josiah T., 131; William H., 131; MATLOCK, Hugh, 255; Mary, 228; MAT-
THEWS, Benjamin, 209; Lucetta, 204; Octavia, 229, 234; William, 174; MAUGRIDGE,
John, 156; Mary, 156; MAUK, Henry, 269; Joseph, 165; Keith A., 165; Mary B., 165;
MAXEY, Zouella, 44; MAXWELL, Annie L., 134; Kate, 270; Lydia, 159; MAY, Leland
E., 201; MAYCROFT, Ethel J. 171; MAYES, Alvarado, 185; Branch B., 186;

MAYES, Dora, 185; Elmore D., 186; Fernando C., 185; Florida A., 185; Gar-
land L., 186; Ida R., 186; James, 185; Martha, 186; Nancy, 186; Nellie H., 186;
Robert E., 186; Sarah W., 186; William D., 185; MAYFIELD, Abraham, 183; MAYLOR,
Margaret E., 84; MAYO, Joseph, 29; Pearl, 224; MAYS, Beverly, 211; Elizabeth A.,
305; Evert T., 305; Fleming, 212; Truman, 305; McAFEE, D. S., 204; Hughes, 204;
John, 191; John B., 204; Sarah, 204; Thomas W., 204; McALLISTER, E. S., 136;
Edwin N., 136; McARTHUR, Dee, 45; Douglas G., 45; Merry D., 45; McCAULIFF, Mar-
garet E., 286; Virginia C., 286; William J., 286; McBRIDE, Susan, 185; McCAGUE,
Georgia D., 152; McCALL, Charles, 55; Connie, 55; Marshall, 55; Morgan, 55;

McCALL, Nattie, 55; William, 159; McCALLUM, Adeline J., 175; McCANE, James,
260; Mary, 260; McCASLIN, Jane, 195, 197; McCAUGHEY, Silvia, 117; McCAULEY, Ben-
jamin, 153; Elizabeth, 152; Jane, 149; Matthew, 149; Samuel J., 153; McCLAIN,
James, 39; Jewel, 143; Martha, 303; McCLELLAN, Anna R., 284; Bertha, 291; Betty
M., 291; Conley T., 284; David B., 291; Herman, 284; Howard P., 291; Irene, 291;
James E., 291; June, 284; M. J., 291; Madge L., 291; Vivian, 284; McCLELLAND,
Irene, 14; McCLURE, Dorothy, 226; Ruth, 194; McCOIG, Amy K., 85; Austin G., 85;
Forrest D., 85; James A., 85; Laura J., 85; McCOLLUM, Richard E., 250; McCONNELL,
Alvah, 107; Christa L., 107; Effa M., 107; Eva E., 107; Leicester, 104; Oliva
E., 107; Ona L., 107; Virgil E., 107; McCORD, Gladys, 41; McCORKLE, James, 52;

McCORMICK, Karen, 117; McCOWN, Sandra J., 254; William O., 254; McCOY, Andrew, 307; Archibald, 301, 307; Catherine, 307; Charles, 307; Daniel, 14; Eliza,
307; Fay, 220; Jemima, 301; John, 307; Lydia, 308; Margaret, 307; Phoebe, 307;
William, 307; McCRACKEN, Robert, 118; McCRAY, Francis A., 112; McCREADY, Almeda
V., 112; McCREARY, Darrell, 119; Green, 8; J. Grove, 117; McCULLEN, Gladys J.,
177; McCULLOCH, Alexander, 129; McCULLOUGH, Francis, 87; Ruth, 87; McCURDY,
George W., 63; McCURRY, Michael, 108; Milly, 108; Robert, 108; Steven, 108; William, 108; McDADE, William E., 13, 15; McDANIEL, Ernest, 198; Mary E., 198;
McDAVID, Ethel, 286; McDONALD, Albert F., 222; Charles F., 222; Jean E., 222;

McDOUGH, Dale, 96; Nene E., 96; McFADDEN, Elsa L., 234; McFADDIN, Mary R.,
107; McFALL, Arthur, 120; McFARLAND, Cathleen, 88; Dewey, 88; Donald R., 88;
Gene D., 135; Georgia J., 88; Ira J., 167; Joe C., 88; Joy, 88; Patsy, 88;
Stuart F., 135; McFERRIN, Kate C., 194; McGEE, Eleanor, 119; Macajob, 71; Samuel, 120; McGIBONEY, Amy, 217; Fredric, 217; Fredric R., 217; James, 217; Jane,
217; Jean, 217; Tana R., 217; McGINNIS, A. B., 308; Aaron, 307; Allie, 308; Andrew, 307; Barbara, 307, 308; Charles, 307, 308; Delphi, 307; Edward, 307, 308;
Edward S., 308; Eliza, 308; Elizabeth, 307, 308; Hannah, 308; James, 307, 308;
Jane, 308; John, 308; Margaret, 308; Mary, 308; Mary J., 307; Moses, 308;

McGINNIS, Nancy, 308; Noble, 307; Peter, 307; Robert, 307; Temperance, 301,
308; William, 308; McGLIFF, Willard F., 277; McGLOTHIN, Gayle, 106; McGLOTHLIN,
Clida, 185; McGOWAN, Arrel, 99; John, 137; McGRADY, Dorothy M., 132; McGUIRE,
Alice, 302; McHANIE, Edith C., 253; McHENRY, Andrew, 269; John, 61; McHUGH, Mari-
lyn A., 84; McKAVICK, Anna G., 202; MaKAY, Karen S., 10; Patricia L., 10; Robert
R., 10; McKEE, Benjamin, 74; Benjamin F., 73; Clara, 74; Elizabeth, 73; Eva, 74;
James, 73; Martha, 73; Nettie, 73; Olive, 74; Rodney, 74; McKEEHAN, Emma L., 16;

McKENNON, Archibald M., 194; Marsha A., 194; McKENZIE, Elizabeth P., 303; Jennie A., 79; McKESSON, Charles A., 250; Valerie G., 250; Warren G., 250; McKINNEY, James, 12, 56; Raleigh, 56; Ruth, 56; McKINZIE, Barbara A., 21; McKNIGHT, William, 126; McLAUGHLAN, Brian P., 236; Douglas, 236; John, 103; Joseph, 103; Margaret, 103; Mary, 103; Nancy J., 103; Robert, 103; Thomas, 103; William, 103; McLEAN, Betty J., 236; Horace G., 236; John W., 236; Kristina, 236; McMAHAN, Letitia, 12; McMAIN, Doris G., 249; McMICHAEL, Ida V., 213; McMILLAN, Fred, 201; Grace, 201; Isaac G., 225; Jonathan L., 225; Joseph C., 225; Susan K., 225; William B., 304; William M., 225; William O., 225; McMILLEN, Laura, 304;

McMILLEN, Mattie E., 304; McMILLIN, Olene, 118; McMULLEN, Dona V., 285; Rebecca H., 294; McMURTRY, Mary H., 169; McNABB, Clinton B., 148; Clinton E., 148; Dennis M., 148; Edward, 148; Edward R., 148; James W., 148; Jess, 148; John T., 148; June A., 148; Mary E., 148; Mary L., 148; Ollie L., 148; McPHEETERS, Perry L., 56; McPHERSON, Aaron, 72; Aaron H., 72; Abigail, 71, 76; Abigail R., 76; Abraham L., 77; Acie, 100, 101; Ada, 114; Addison V., 120; Adell, 74; Allen G., 84; Alma D., 114; Almira, 99; Amy, 73; Andrew K., 75; Ann, 70, 73, 75, 118; Anna, 120; Annie L., 233; Arnold E., 78; Augustus W., 77; Austin L., 86; Baker B., 98; Batley S., 95; Beatrice, 119; Ben, 114; Benjamin, 74; Benjamin C., 112;

McPHERSON, Benjamin F., 120; Benjamin N., 112, 113, 117; Benjamin P., 95; Bernard I., 84; Bertha, 77; Beryl, 119; Bessie, 121; Beth A., 84; Betty M., 117; Billy, 121; Brenda G., 101; Brent, 114; Broadie, 121; Bronner, 117; Caleb, 119, 121; Campbell B., 100; Campbell G., 98; Campbell W., 98, 99; Caroline, 73; Caroline H., 101; Carolyn F., 84; Carrie E., 121; Cecil, 100; Chandos, 74; Charity E., 86, 89; Charles, 99, 120; Charles P., 77; Chase R., 84; Cheryl, 78; Chester A., 121; Christopher T., 95; Clara W., 113; Clarice, 117; Cora E., 86; Creal, 99; Cyrus, 120; Dale W., 78; Daniel, 70, 71, 118, 122; Daniel S., 84; David, 78; David H., 77; Debbie, 120; Deborah, 119, 121; Debra S., 99; Della, 77; Denny, 99;

McPHERSON, Dewey, 117; Dewey A., 86; Donald R., 78; Donna, 117; Donnie, 100; Dora, 119; Dora I., 120; Dorena, 74; Earl E., 78; Edd, 114; Edith, 118; Edna, 75, 78; Edward, 120; Edward S., 77; Edward T., 99; Eleanor, 94, 108, 120; Eli, 119; Elijah, 120; Elisha, 119; Elizabeth, 72, 73, 94, 120; Elizabeth J., 76; Elzie, 120; Emma, 271; Emma C., 77; Ennis L., 75; Enoch, 119; Ethel S., 77, 79; Eugene, 77, 78; Eugenia, 99; Eunice E., 77, 85; Evertt, 77; Flora B., 112; Florrie, 120; Forrest S., 83, 84; Frances D., 99; Frankie, 77; Fred, 78, 117; George, 94, 117; George B., 77; George D., 75, 76; George N., 95; George W., 99; Gerald, 117; Girren, 74; Glenn, 77; Glenn T., 78; Grace, 77, 119; Gray, 119; Guy, 121;

McPHERSON, Hannah, 75, 120; Hardin, 73; Harlan, 72, 74, 121; Harold, 84; Harrison P., 99; Harry A., 117; Harvey, 78, 100; Hazel, 121; Hester A., 72; Homer, 100; Hugh C., 86; Hugh R., 76; Hughie N., 118; Inez M., 85; Ingram, 121; Irma, 117; Isaac, 118; Jack, 114; James, 121, 122; James B., 99, 100; James C., 72, 74; James H., 112; James J., 84; James M., 75, 77, 83, 84, 120, 121; James S., 112; James T., 101; James W., 76; Jane, 75; Janet C., 101; Jay, 78; Jean, 114; Jeanette, 114; Jehu, 71, 76, 93, 94, 95, 99, 246; Jehu B., 100; Jehu H., 94; Jerry D., 101; Jerry F., 117; Jesse, 114, 122; Jesse H., 86; Jessie M., 118; Jim B., 117; John, 70, 71, 72, 73, 75, 76, 93, 118, 120, 122; John B., 77; John C., 76;

McPHERSON, John D., 119; John G., 72; John H., 95; John J., 76; John L., 76, 86; John W., 120; Joseph, 71, 72, 75, 76, 122; Joseph B., 72, 78, 94; Joseph D., 84; Joseph E., 100; Joseph G., 94; Joseph H., 75; Joseph P., 84; Joseph S., 76; Joseph W., 76, 77; Joshua, 72; Joshua R., 74; Judith, 78; Kathleen, 78; Kenneth, 117; Kevin, 78; Laura, 113; Lawrence, 78, 119, 121; Leanna, 121; Lee, 100; Lena, 74; Leonard, 119; Leslie, 121; Lewis F., 72; Lizzie, 121; Lois E., 84; Lonnie, 121; Lou E., 113, 115; Louisa J., 86; Louisiana, 120; Lucinda, 72; Lucinda J., 76; Lucretia H., 76; Lucy M., 99; Luda, 113; Lula, 74; Lydia, 76; Lydia E., 76; Lydia N., 76; Mabel, 119; Madison H., 86; Malinda, 95, 120; Malinda E., 86, 88;

McPHERSON, Malvina, 74; Marcelyn G., 84; Marcia, 78; Margaret, 118; Margaret A., 84; Margaret E., 99; Margaret I., 77; Margery, 40, 94, 113; Marilyn, 113; Mark, 114; Mark R., 84; Marsh F., 84; Marshall, 101; Martha, 99; Martha A., 76, 86, 87; Martha E., 75; Martha G., 76; Martha J., 95; Mary, 71, 75, 78, 94, 95, 98, 99, 101, 118, 119, 120, 121; Mary A., 75; Mary E., 99; Mary J., 77, 78, 117; Mary L., 78, 100; Mary R., 114; Matilda R., 84; Matthew J., 84; Maud, 119, 121; Maude, 83; Melanie K., 84; Michael E., 84; Michael G., 101; Milton H., 86; Minnie, 121, 151; Minter, 120; Molly, 113; Myrtle E., 77; Nancy, 72, 119, 120; Nannie, 119; Nelle M., 117; Neva, 100; Neva N., 114; Nora, 113; Oliver, 120; Oliver O., 121; Oliver R., 121; Oscar, 114; Othniel, 70, 118; Owen J., 95;

McPHERSON, Pamela J., 101; Patricia, 99; Paula J., 101; Pauline, 121; Peggy, 117, 121; Philip, 112; Philip D., 84; Phoebe, 72, 118, 120; Phyllis, 114, 117; Pierson M., 74; Preston J., 74; Priscilla A., 85; Rachel, 73, 94, 114, 122; Randall, 114; Randy O., 84; Ranswell B., 77; Rebecca, 73, 118, 120; Reggie, 114; Rex E., 114; Rhoda, 72; Richard, 114; Ricky, 114; Robbie D., 114; Robert D., 86; Robert E., 114; Robert H., 74, 84; Robert L., 84, 121; Rodney E., 75; Roger, 114; Ronald L., 84; Roscoe E., 77; Ross, 78; Royce, 114; Royce B., 101; Ruby E., 77; Ruby J., 101, 114; Ruenell, 100; Rufus K., 77; Rufus M., 113; Rufus R., 114; Ruie, 100; Ruth, 40, 71, 75, 94, 112, 118, 121, 122; Ruth A., 114, 119; Salina, 120; Samuel, 95, 98, 119, 151; Samuel H., 98; Sarah, 71, 72, 73, 75, 86, 94, 95, 103, 119, 120; Sarah D., 76; Sarah W., 99; Seth, 74; Sherrill, 114; Sherry M., 101; Silence E., 86, 91; Stephen, 70, 71, 72, 75, 122; Susan, 119; Talbott C., 84;

McPHERSON, Terrell G., 100; Terry, 78; Terry L., 101; Thomas J., 84; Thomas N., 120; Thomas W., 121; Timothy E., 84; Todd, 78; Tommie L., 101; Uberto L., 99; Uberto W., 99; Venita, 114; Vennie, 74; Verla B., 100; Victoria, 99; Victoria E., 86; Viola M., 77; Virgil E., 84; Virginia, 117; Wade, 74, 119; Wallace, 101, 114; Walter, 74; Warren D., 101; Wayne, 78; Wendell, 99; William, 70, 72, 75, 99, 118, 119, 120, 121, 122; William E., 94, 119; William H., 99; William M., 84; William Y., 76; Willie M., 99; McSPAIN, William, 191; McWILLIAMS, Elizabeth, 73; MEACHEM, Camela, 118; Temperance, 118; MEADOWS, Lucille, 306; Mary, 104, 113; MEANS, Thomas, 32, 33; MEDLEY, Rozell M., 254; MELETIO, Alex, 7;

MELLICK, Mae, 19; MELSON, Allen C., 225; Shirley P., 225; MELTON, Carol L., 134; Clarence, 134; Jonathan, 206; Leona, 277; MERRIWEATHER, Mary J., 113; METZEL, A. B., 169; MEYER, Clara, 82; MIDDENDORT, Emma, 223; MIDDLEMORE, Josias, 259; MIDDLETON, Thomas, 213; William C., 20; MIES, Karen, 117; MILAM, William H., 138; MILBURN, Donna L., 19; MILLER, Betty, 168; Betty T., 137; Bluford, 73; Cassandra, 137; Eugenia, 137; George, 139; Glen, 275; John, 247; John A., 136; John B., 137; Kathryn, 102; Lillian, 298; Mary, 27; Mattie, 137; Neville, 136; Priscilla A., 83; Robert, 137; Shackleford, 136; Thomas, 39; Virginia E., 147; MILLIKAN, Matilda, 211; MILLIKEN, H. A., 56; MILLS, Barbara, 310; Catherine, 311;

MILLS, Celia, 310; Elizabeth, 310; Frances, 310; Govan, 310; Josephine, 310; Lidia, 301; Mary, 310; Orville, 310; Peter B., 310; Rufus K., 76; Sarah, 241; Susan, 310; William C., 310; MILNER, John, 24; MILOVICH, Lilian, 226; MILTON, Mary, 156; MINDERMAN, Carol A., 236; Edward, 236; Kenneth R., 236; MITCHELL, Elizabeth, 152; Leonard, 109; Robert, 81; Thomas J., 162; Victor, 81; MIX, Elsa, 19; MIZE, James, 68; Judith, 68; MOBLEY, Elizabeth, 133; MOERS, Irene, 290; MOFFIT, Gladys, 167; MOFFITT, Joe H., 132; MOHRSFIELD, Walter, 262; MONIACK, Charles, 263; MONROE, Dana E., 256; MONTAGUE, Ernest, 186; MONTGOMERY, James, 9, 272; MOOD, Lowell, 107; MOODY, George, 308; W. S., 240; MOOKLER, William B., 11;

MOONEY, Ellen M., 238; MOORE, Albert M., 287; Alta, 277; Annie L., 200; Benjamin P., 135; Blanche, 107; Charles, 143; Cornelia, 151; Dianna L., 110; Ed, 143; Eleanor, 277; Elias A., 254; Elizabeth, 238; Ernest, 115; Evelyn J., 287; Frank, 200; Geraldine, 262; Hattie, 282; Helen E., 287; James, 175; Jewel, 262; John C., 287; John F., 287; John H., 115; Jonathan, 163; Kari C., 110;

MOORE, Lester L., 107; Lewis, 110; Mabel G., 287; Macy C., 222; Marie S., 89; Mary A. L., 287; Mary L., 143; Milton, 143; Mory C., 262; Norma J., 287; Paul, 200; Rachel, 143; Ralph, 200; Ray, 262; Richard, 27; Sarah, 211; T. A., 138; Tappie H., 221; MOOREHEAD, Patsy C., 216; MORCOM, Florence, 303; MORELAND, Susan, 275; MORELOCK, Jack, 293; MORFORD, Mary, 260; MORGAN, Amanda, 274; Daniel, 157; Deborah J., 104; Edward, 156, 157; Isaac, 150; Jacob, 1; Jane, 1; Jemima, 37; John, 157, 252; Joseph 157, 258, 259; Margaret, 157; Mark, 118; Morgan, 157; Nancy, 131; Sarah, 150, 156, 157; Thomas, 37; William, 157; MORRIS, Anderson, 176; Angela P., 288; Ann, 73; Bennie M., 164; Cammie, 176; Charles, 54; Dorothy, 164; Dwight, 54; Edward, 54; Eleanor, 73; Ellen, 194; Elmina, 176; Georgia, 143;

MORRIS, Henry, 176; Howard G., 73; Isaac, 62, 176; Isaac B., 176; John L., 176; Martha, 175; Mary E., 176; Melissa, 176; Nancy C., 176; Rachel, 73; Richard, 176; Robert, 73; Thomas, 177; Thomas B., 73; Wendell, 164; MORRISET, Elizabeth, 5; Pierre, 5; MORRISON, Sarah, 209; MORROW, Belle, 214; Harry H., 222; James L., 222; John, 256; Samuel, 246; MORVANT, Harris H., 109; MOSELEY, Elijah B., 179; MOSER, Troy, 119; MOSIER, Angela, 97; Brenda, 97; Connie, 97; Darrel, 97; Jerry, 97; Leslie, 97; Lester, 97; Marsha, 97; Virginia C., 97; MOSS, Harold B., 221; Sarah, 184; MOTLEY, Huron J., 46; W. Robert, 46; MOUDY, Alvin F., 225; Carolyn K., 225; James R., 225; Janet K., 225; Robert T., 225; MOULDER, Virginia, 42;

MOUNT, Ida J., 84; MOY, William C., 147; MULLICAN, Billy S., 215; Marcia L., 215; Teresa A., 215; Terry L., 215; MULLIN, Robert J., 226; Thomas M., 226; MULLINS, Annie May, 141; Robert, 210; Thomas, 210; MUMPOWER, Catherine, 51; Peter, 51; MUNCY, Avinalle, 306; MUNDY, Ray, 275; MUNGER, Eliza, 256; MURCHISON, Lucy A., 239; MURPHEY, Dixie L., 251; Jacqueline R., 251; John J., 251; Terry D., 251; MURPHREE, Eliza P., 232; MURPHY, Agnes, 148; Cora, 103; Daniel, 280; Hutcheson, 138; Irving J., 305; John R., 305; MURRAY, Albert W., 142; Hazel, 142; Jabez, 37; James, 37, 142; Josephus, 36, 37; Mamie, 142; Morgan, 37; Nicholas, 37; Pete, 142; William H., 142; Zipporah, 36, 37; MUSE, Rebecca, 203;

MYATT, Dane, 113; Edith, 113; Nim, 113; Robert, 113; MYDDELTON, Paul, 96; Paul G., 96; Robert T., 96; MYER, Charlotte, 116; MYERS, Alfred N., 21; Amanda, 20; Caroline, 20; Louisa C., 21; Lucy, 21; Susan, 20; Thomas, 20; MYLER, Mary E., 96; Samuel, 96; Urnal E., 95; MYNATT, Mary J., 311; MYRICK, Thomas, 153; NAPIER, Gerald W., 224; NASH, Alice M., 262; Allen G., 262; Charles A., 262; Charles T., 262; Cheston A., 235; Edna F., 262; Elza, 235; Eva, 235; Henry B., 262; James H., 262; Louisa, 307; Mabel C., 262; Mable, 235; Marvin, 235; Mary J., 235; Reford, 235; Veta C., 236; NAYLOR, Libbie, 56; NEAL, Paray, 119; NEALEY, Barbara, 193; NEBERGALL, Sarah A., 166; NEEDHAM, Frennie, 203; NEEL, O. W., 180; NEFF, Barbara, 168; Charles, 168; Donna, 168; Lavern, 168; NEILL, Joseph, 118;

NEILL, Nellie M., 106; NELSON, Angelina,196; Ross, 280; Samuel, 175; NESBIT, B. B., 137; NEVILL, Adaline, 137; Alexander H., 145; Alfred, 150; Alice, 146; Amelia A., 138; Anderson, 145; Anne, 128; Antoinette, 152; Araia, 145; Avnell, 141; Barbara A., 136; Barbara H., 136; Bathsheba, 129; Benjamin, 128, 129, 130, 137, 139, 143, 145, 178; Benjamin O., 138, 146; Caroline, 138, 143; Charles, 150, Clara A., 146; Clarence C., 143; Clyde, 145; Cora L., 143; Cornie, 145; Cynthia, 130, 152; Cynthia A., 130, 178; Daisy B., 146; David B., 146; David C., 143; Dora K., 146; Edmund, 129; Edward W., 136; Edwin J., 136; Edwin R., 136; Edwin W., 136; Effie, 16, 136, 141; Effie D., 142; Eleanor, 128; Eliza, 145;

NEVILL, Elizabeth, 128, 129, 130, 131, 136, 138, 140, 150, 152, 175; Elizabeth A., 146; Elizabeth V., 137; Elizabeth W., 136; Ella F., 145; Ella M., 141; Eliza J., 141; Emma, 152; Emma A., 145; Esperan, 153; Eugenia, 136; Eula M., 136; Florence, 128; Frances, 137; Fred, 143; G. F., 145; G. M., 145; George J., 153; George R., 140; Gibb, 143; Goodman, 129, 130, 149; Goodwin, 130; Granderson D., 136; Hardin, 138, 140, 143; Harrel R., 141; Henderson, 145; Indiana, 137; Irma, 136; Isaac, 149; Jackie, 143; James, 136, 153; James H., 143; James M., 145;

NEVILL, Jane, 150, 152; Jesse, 129, 130, 137, 139, 149; Jesse P., 136, 138; John, 128, 129, 153; John G., 150; John L., 140, 141, 146; John O., 145; John S., 136; Joseph, 128; Josiah H., 136; Julia F., 138; Katherine, 141; Ladonna L., 141; Laneter, 149; Lucy, 142, 146; Lucy J., 41, 140; Marsha L., 141; Marshall G., 141; Martha, 128, 139, 149, 150; Martha C., 137; Martha J., 138, 146; Martha K., 146; Martha L., 145; Mary, 128, 150, 152; Mary A., 140, 142; Mary E., 143, 146; Mary L., 145; Mary R., 152; Matthew, 149, 152, 153; Maud, 143; Minerva, 143; Mirt S., 141; Nancy, 143; Nancy A., 146; Nancy C., 140; Nancy E., 149; Nancy W., 138; Nimrod, 136; Norwood, 149; Ora Pinkney, 145; Oswin, 139; Patience, 128;

NEVILL, Pearl A., 136; Penelope, 128; Pleasant, 138, 145; Pleasant O. H., 145; Rebecca, 149; Richard S., 137; Roberta, 142; Robertson, 138, 139, 190, 191; Roger, 128; Rosella, 137; Ruby E., 141; Ruby M., 136; Ruffin, 153; Sallie B., 145; Samuel, 153; Samuel H., 140, 142; Samuel P., 130, 152; Sarah, 142; Sarah A., 143; Sarah L., 146; Sarah O., 146; Selah, 130, 149; Solomon, 130, 136, 138, 139; Solomon C., 136; Stroud, 143; Susan, 138, 145; Susanna O., 136; Thomas, 128, 129; Thomas E., 138; Thurza, 142; Turley, 149; Virgil G., 141; Weschina A., 152; Whitley W., 149; Wiley W., 130; William, 128, 129, 149, 150; William B., 140; William N., 152; William P., 145; William W., 143; Willie A., 145; Wilma, 143; Winifred, 149; NEVILLE, Bryant, 153; Delia, 153; Esperan, 153; Julia, 153; Martha, 153;

NEVILLE, Perian, 153; Samuel J., 153; William D., 153; NEW, Anna, 92; R. E., 102; NEWBERRY, Ida, 274; NEWCUM, Charles E., 231; Ethel J., 231; NEWLIN, Deborah, 120; John, 120; NEWMAN, Donald, 276; George E., 219; Robert W., 219; Simpson, 94; NEWPORT, Cavanaugh, 66; Richard, 66; NEWSOM, Cynthia A., 201; Frank, 201; NEWSOME, Hancel, 305; NEWTON, Edward, 177; Ella, 144; NICHOLLS, Agnes, 252; Alison C., 249; Alva E., 252; Amy L., 250; Andrew B., 249; Andrew B. C., 247, 248, 250, 251; Augustus H., 248; Avalee, 250; Barry C., 248; Barry G., 250; Benjamin, 94, 246, 247; Benjamin F., 247, 249, 250, 251, 252; Brooke M., 250; Cassandra, 247; Catherine, 247; Catherine M., 248; Claire E., 249; Doris, 250; Doris C., 250;

NICHOLLS, Dorothy, 252; Edward, 252; Eleanor, 246, 247; Eliza E., 252; Elizabeth, 247; Elizabeth L., 251; Eolia B., 252; Fannie S., 252; Florence E., 248; Frank, 249; George, 246, 247, 248, 249, 252; George J., 248, 249; George W., 247, 251, 252; Gregory D., 248; Hugh, 250; Irene R., 250; James A., 250; James K., 250; James Z., 248; Janet, 250; Jean C., 250; Jesse C., 248; Jesse D., 252; John, 252; John A., 252; John B., 249; John C., 250; John M., 247; Joseph, 247; Joseph K., 251; Julia L., 250; Kate, 252; Katherine L., 251; Katherine M., 247; Kristin, 250; Lena, 252; Lottie L., 247; Lucy V., 250; Margaret A., 252; Margery, 93, 246; Marjorie E., 249; Martha S., 250; Mary, 247; Mary D., 250; Mary E., 249;

NICHOLLS, Mary N., 250; Mary P., 252; Nancy, 246, 250; Nancy A., 250; Oscar, 252; Pamela A., 250; Rebecca E., 250; Richard M., 250; Robin K., 248; Samuel J., 247; Susan L., 250; Tallulah K., 252; Walter L., 252; William M., 247; William W., 249; NICHOLS, Darlene L., 93; David, 93; Harry, 197; Jacob, 210; Louise, 233; Martha B., 222; William, 93; NICHOLSON, Ida Jane, 194; James, 124, 125; Samuel, 306; NICKOLS, Barbara E., 230; Deborah L., 230; Jimmie L., 230; John, 230; Lila J., 230; William W., 230; NIMMO, James A., 217; NISLER, Marilynn, 194; William Cargile, 194; NOBLIN, Dora, 284; NOBLITT, Ray J., 19; NOCERA, Dixie L., 90; Frank 90; Frank L., 90; Thomas E., 90; Vicki M., 90; NOELL, Billie M., 83; Flossie E., 83; John, 83; Murriel V., 83; Willard L., 83; NORMAN, Frances G., 202; Jack, 202;

NORMAN, James G., 98; Seth, 202; Thomas J., 202; NORRIS, Boone, 55; Lee, 55; Mary, 27, 30; Morgan, 55; NORTH, Eleanor R., 169; Thelma, 177; NORTHCROFT, Frances, 245; NORTON, Fred L., 172; Margaret, 301; Sarah, 105; NORVELL, Albro, 221; NORWOOD, Elizabeth, 28; John T., 214; Mary, 131; William, 149; Winifred, 149; NOVAK, John, 82; John A., 82; NUNLEY, Bessie, 45; Mary A., 215; NUNNALLY, Mary P., 241; NUNNLEE, John W., 27; Joseph A., 27; William N., 27; NUTT, Billie L. (Yaws), 229; O'BANION, Barbara A., 226; Constance E., 226; Curtis P., 225;

O'BANION, David L., 226; David S., 226; Gary N., 226; Hulda M., 226; James L., 226; James R., 226; John M., 225; John W., 225; Julia E., 226; Marcus A., 226; Mary E., 226; Susan P., 226; William C., 226; O'DANIEL, Jesse, 150; O'NEAL, Eliza A., 271; O'NEILL, Florence M., 226; OAKWOOD, Henry, 51, 52; Mary, 51;Sarah, 52; Susanna B., 50; OCONNOR, J. H., 55; ODELL, Elizabeth, 277; ODGERS, Harold L., 251; OEST, John N., 152; John R., 152; Thomas N., 152; OGAN, Barbara, 310; Elizabeth, 310; Erwin, 309; George, 310; George E., 310; Hannah, 310; Hannah L., 310; Helen, 309; Henry L., 310; James, 310; Jane, 310; John, 309; M.H. Burket, 310; Margaret, 310; Martha, 310; Mary, 310; Mary A., 310; Mary F., 310; Nancy, 310;

OGAN, Narcissus, 310; Peter, 309, 310; Robert P., 310; Susan, 310; William, 310; Winnie J., 310; OGDEN, Effie C., 194; Robert V., 194; OGILVY, Margaret, 85; OGLE, Venita J., 230; OGLETREE, Rebecca T., 8; OKEEFE, Constance, 58; Frank J., 57; Irene, 58; OLIVE, Maxine, 134; OLLIFF, Gladys, 222; OLSEN, Alice, 74; Gertrude, 74; Ivan, 74; Peter J., 74; Raymond, 74; OLSON, Mark A., 93; Virgil, 93; ONEAL, Bernard, 34; ONLEY, Mary, 271; OPPE, Frances A., 147; ORGAN, Otis L., 275; ORMSON, Shirley, 93; ORR, Charles D., 294; Charlie R., 294; George W., 294; Joe S., 294; John D., 294; Nettie L., 294; Rachel B., 303; OSBORN, Aaron, 159; Benjamin, 34; Enoch, 158; Ephraim, 159; Hannah, 159; James, 159; John, 159;

OSBORN, Mary, 159; Nancy, 159; Noah, 159; Rachel, 159; Richard, 159; Robert, 159; Samuel, 159; Samuel M., 159; Sarah, 159; Solomon, 159; Stephen, 159; Susanna, 265; Tabitha, 159; William, 159; OSBORNE, Beulah, 270; David, 304; Frances, 296; James M., 270; James S., 254; OSWALD, Margie, 278; OTT, Fred, 89; Sarah, 86; OTTERBERG, Leonard G., 77; Mary E., 77; Neva L., 77; Ole, 77; Richard C., 77; Richard E., 77; OUTLAW, Myrtle, 224; OVERBY, Lois, 202; OWEN, Brady, 29; OWENS, Frank T., 232; John L., 232; John R., 232; John W., 232; Kent L., 232; Mary A., 232; Mary J., 232; Stanford L., 232; Sue, 232; Thomas D., 232; OWINGS, Minerva, 66; Samuel S., 66; OYLER, Cornelia, 296; Louise, 277; PACE, Estelline, 85; James W., 85; William, 128; PADDLEFORD, Nancy, 18; PAGE, Evie W., 117; PAINE, Mary,160;

PALMER, Daniel, 94; Fannie, 235; Thomas, 74; PANGBORN, Corinne, 79; PARCELL Judy K., 165; Mary J., 165; Patricia J., 165; Roy F., 165; Shirley J., 165; W.T., 165; PARHAM, Benjamin, 183; PARITY, Margaret, 50; PARK, Annie, 186; PARKE, Elizabeth, 129; PARKER, Ann, 24; Benjamin, 161; Caledonia, 161; Cephas, 101; Daniel, 29; Esther Mae, 187; Frances A., 200; George T., 101; Henry, 101; Ira, 160; John, 161; Lucetta, 101; Lucinda, 103; Lucy F., 220; Margaret R., 286; Mary, 24, 50; Miles, 161; Robert, 214; Robert T., 205; Sally, 219; Samuel, 129; Sandra, 144; Susannah, 209; William, 24, 101, 161; William T., 219; PARKS, George, 210; John, 129; Ruth, 66; Thomas, 242; PARNALL, Benjamin, 179; PARR, Richard, 174;

PARRISH, Edna L., 300; Elizabeth W., 99; Fleming, 99; Nellie, 100; Rhoda, 151; PARSONS, Isabel, 76; William, 43; PARTRIDGE, Jessie, 12; PASCHAL, Betty L., 135; Harold A., 186; Lenore, 186; Mary N., 185; Mitchel, 135; Pauline, 186;Sherill, 135; Thomas E., 186; Thomas M., 185; PASSMORE, Phoebe, 118; PATE, Elizabeth, 271; Mary, 271; PATTERSON, Chesley P., 131; Eva, 202; Kathline, 77; Mary, 121, 230; Max E., 77; Nathaniel, 9; Neena A., 77; Sarah, 131; Tina L., 77; PATTIE, William B., 146; PATTON, Abner F., 249; William, 113; PATY, Cinderella, 200; Eliza J., 200; John W., 200; PAXON, Ollie B., 229; PAYNE, George W., 99; Jack, 308; Julia I., 41; Julius, 121; Swannie, 121; PEAKE, Benjamin, 256; PEARSON, Bertha O., 194; Cleveland, 194; Emerson, 194; Emery P., 194; Frances E., 194;

PEARSON, Francis W., 194; Harvey, 76; Malissa, 194; Martha E., 194; Minerva F., 194; Oramae B., 194; Robert W., 194; Shelby M., 194; Thad O., 194; William H. M., 194; PEDEN, Benjamin, 95; Letitia Y., 95; PEDIGO, Audrey M., 97; Emma, 114; Oscar A., 97; PEEBLES, C. R., 46; Elizabeth A., 136; PEEL, D. E., 79; PEEVEY, Arthur, 108; Bonner, 108; J. M., 108; Lottie, 108; Nelle, 108; PEMBERTON, William B., 211; PENCE, Ruth, 199; PENDERGRASS, Donna J., 47; Ernest E., 47; Nancy M., 47; PENETON, Timothy, 61; PENNEL, Chester, 231; Donna K., 231;

PENNEL, Frank, 231; Roger L., 231; PENNINGTON, Abigail, 159, 163, 166; Ada, 164; Addie, 162; Albert S., 169; Alfred A., 163; Alice, 167; Alice L., 167; Allen 160; Allen J., 166; Alonzo, 166; Altamira, 161; Amanda M., 163; Ava J., 162; Avis L., 167; B. S., 162; Bertha P., 162; Billie, 167; Bryan, 167; Caleb M., 160; Caledonia, 162; Calvin D., 163; Carmen, 167; Carroll A., 164; Carroll W., 163; Catherine, 161; Charity, 161; Charles, 160, 166; Charles W., 169; Chester P., 164; Christopher, 163; Dan W., 162; Daniel,32, 33, 158, 162; Daniel B., 161, 163; Daniel R., 164; David, 167; Daymond, 164; Dixie, 167; Earl, 162; Earl M., 167; Edmund G., 161; Edward E., 169; Elizabeth, 160, 161, 163, 168; Elizabeth H., 163;

PENNINGTON, Elizabeth J., 166, 169; Elkanah D., 163; Ella M., 169; Elmer, 166; Elmer N., 167; Elmora F., 169; Elzie A., 163; Emily, 161; Esther, 163; Esther A., 164; Eva M., 167; Evadean H., 163; Fannie M., 161; Florence, 162; Florence T., 167; Florine F., 167, 168; Francis F., 167; Frank, 166; Fred, 167; Freiley, 163; Gladys, 167; Granderson, 160; Grannell M., 166; Hannah B., 166; Hardin, 162; Harry, 167; Henry A., 161; Hope, 167; Hugh A., 162; Ida, 161, 164; Ina, 167; Isaiah C., 163; Jack W., 162; James H., 161; James J., 166; James M., 166; James R., 162; Jane, 161; Jane C., 169; Janet, 167; Jemima, 166; John, 160, 161, 164; John A., 169; John C., 163; John E., 214; John L., 166; Joseph, 161, 163; Joshua, 158, 160, 161, 162; Joshua J., 166; Kathie, 168; Lambert, 166;

PENNINGTON, Lavesta, 163; Lavesta J., 164; Lawson J., 161; Leander W., 166; Leonard A., 167; Lola, 164; Lorenzo D., 163; Lucinda, 161; Lucy, 161; Malinda J., 161; Mamie J., 163; Marcene, 167; Margaret, 161; Martha, 160, 163; Marvin, 167; Mary, 161, 163, 167; Mary A. L., 162; Mary C., 169; Mary E., 162; Mary J., 160; Mary M., 166; Melvin, 166; Meredith, 168; Minnie, 164; Nancy, 161, 163, 164,166; Nancy J., 166; Nicholas, 162; Nicholas H., 166; Nora, 164; Pat, 167; Patty, 161; Paul, 167; Peg, 167; Prudence E., 163; Ray, 164; Red, 167; Rex, 167; Rhoda A., 161; Richard, 158, 160, 161, 166, 167, 168; Richard W., 169; Roy, 167; Ruth, 168; S. Boone, 162; Sam H., 162; Samuel F., 160, 163; Samuel H., 162; Sanford, 163;

PENNINGTON, Sarah, 161; Sarah A., 160; Sarilda A., 169; Stephen, 168; Stephen A., 166; Steven C., 163; Stewart, 159, 162, 163, 165; Stewart M., 166; Susan, 161; Thomas, 160, 161; Thomas J., 166; Timothy C., 161; Tolbert P., 164; Ulysses S., 166; Vera Lee, 163; Virgie, 164, 167; Wade L., 162; Walter, 162, 164; Warner, 166; William, 160, 163; William B., 166; William H., 214; William P., 160; William T., 166; PENROD, Betty, 146; Dale, 146; Lewis W., 146; Nancy, 146; PEOPLES, Allen H., 7; Ann, 7; Foster, 7; Hillery L., 7; Ruth, 7; PERKINS, Anna, 83; Jurdine C., 134; Lewis, 66; Patricia, 134; PERRIN, George N., 247; Jane E., 247; Katherine L., 247; Thomas S., 247; PERRINE, Elizabeth, 20; Garrett, 20; Julia,20;

PERRINE, Louisa, 20; PERRY, Abner, 119; Albert, 105; Artina, 105; Blanche E., 106; Charles, 105; Chester F., 106; Cora, 105; Delilie I., 175, 176; Dorothy 106; Edward, 106; Edward N., 175; Ethyl, 106; George, 105; Harry, 105; Homer, 106; Ida, 106; Jacob, 251; Jean, 106; John, 105, 106; John A., 175; Leland F., 106; Lilly, 106; Lola, 106; Lora I., 105; Lucille, 106; Mamie, 105; Manly M., 175; Marjory, 106; Mary E., 105; Murphy M., 175; Nancy, 252; Nancy C., 175; Nannie B., 295; Peter C., 175; Peter F., 175; Sallie C., 251; Sarah, 105; Sarah A., 175; Sudie B., 177; Walter, 106; Wayne, 106; William L., 106; PERSON, Thomas, 129; PERVINES, Nancy A., 18; PETERS, Jacob, 268; Jeannine A., 299; Lillian B., 222; Robert H., 299; Walter B., 299; Wayne B., 299; William, 301;

PETERSON, Calvin L., 97; Eulas, 106; Frank, 53; Jurgen, 53; Katherine, 53; Lance E., 97; Larisa M., 97; Lincoln C., 97; Lou, 53; Lynette J., 97; Margaret, 53; Ralph, 53; Raymond, 53; Robert, 53; Susan, 53; William, 285; PETTIT, Fanny, 276; PEUGH, Barbara A., 47; Edward A., 47; Jettie A., 47; Norman A., 47; Norman H., 47; PHELPS, John, 28; Maggie, 254; PHENIX, Abraham, 174; Barbara, 174; Cordelia, 174; John, 174; PHIFER, James, 219; Marilyn J., 219; William G., 219; PHILLIPS, Eliza, 222; Maxine, 78; Sarah, 206; Solomon N., 15; William P., 176;

340

PICKEL, William, 106; PICKETT, Oscar, 177; PICKETTS, Halene, 231; PIERCE, Charlotte A., 225; Cynthia K., 165; David G., 165; Glenda F., 165; Glenn, 165; Irene, 286; Jesse, 118; William, 26; PIGGOTT, Abigail, 75; William, 75; PIKE, Sarah, 75; PILE, William B., 166; PIRTLE, Elizabeth C., 223; William H., 223; William L., 224, 223; PITCOCK, Angie, 117; PITSINGER, Barnes, 201; Edwin E., 201; Everett E., 201; PITTS, Allie M., 252; Peyton, 252; Sarah, 51; PITZER, Tabitha J., 21; PLAW, Samuel, 124; PLEASANTS, Joseph, 24; PLEMONS, Donald C., 44; Dwight C., 44; Gerald D., 44; PLUMER, C. F., 58; PLUMMER, Jiggs, 141; POE, Dennis M., 148; POGUE, Inez, 272; POINDEXTER, Dollie, 164; POLAND, Jane A., 64; POLLARD, Charles T., 261; Jackie B., 261; John T., 261; Pearlie M., 261; Thomas, 261;

POOLE, Abraham, 246; Cassandra, 246; Frederick B., 147; John, 246; Margaret, 246; Milton J., 147; Myrtle M., 146; Ola E., 146; Robert J., 146; Walter A., 146; POPE, Mary, 26; Valentine, 267; PORTER, Carl S., 201; Harvey D., 201; POSEY, Andrew T., 256; Ann, 256; David T., 256; Elihu A., 256; Elizabeth F., 256; Frances C., 256; John T., 256; Louise, 256; Malinda, 256; William, 256; Zephaniah, 256; POSTON, Cora G., 298; Fleet, 297; Willie R., 298; POTEET, Winfred, 230; POTTS, Frank, 57; POWELL, Alexander, 204; Charlotte, 190; Erma, 116; H. T., 185; Harriet, 191; John, 188; Joshua, 26; Malinda, 6; POWERS, Amanda, 303; Fannie, 204; Herbert, 201; POYNTER, Woodrow, 272; PRATER, Cecil D., 217; Larry C., 217; Nick A., 217; PREECE, J. C., 306; Terry L., 306; PRENTISS, Charles, 63;

PRESCOTT, Owen L., 121; PRICE, Anna, 175; Frances K., 100; Johannah M., 101; PRICHETT, Jane T., 10; PRIDE, Eugene T., 215; PRINTY, Nancy, 11; PRIOR, Ellen, 279; PRITCHARD, Ann, 259; David, 53; Fledra, 53; Frank P., 53; Lyle, 53; Sarah E., 153; PROFFITT, Authur, 42; Corinne, 43; Findlay, 117; James A., 42; PROTHRO, Elizabeth, 120; Emily, 120; PROVINE, Carl G., 171; Ross, 171; William G., 171; PROVOST, Jack, 240; PRUDEN, Achsa, 57; PRUGH, Katherine, 170; Pridmore, 170; Ruth, 170; Thornton, 170; William, 170; PRUITT, M. B., 20; McCormick, 256; PUCKETT, Robert, 101; PUGH, Edward L., 77; Elizabeth, 63; PULLEY, Hallie, 43; Rowena, 171; PURCELL, Elizabeth B., 196; Myrtle E., 293; Philip, 25; PUTMAN, Dale, 89;

PUTMAN, Edith, 89; Robert, 89; QUESENBERRY, Maxine, 219; QUILLEN, Juanita, 293; Livingston, 293; Mary, 268; Milligan W., 293; Tate B., 293; Vesta E., 293; QUINN, Thressa, 79; RACICH, Dorothy R., 278; RADER, Don, 271; Frederick, 271; Landon, 271; Ruby, 271; RAGLIN, Daniel E., 20; RAGSDALE, Ernest, 43; RAIBONE, Richard, 28; RALSTIN, Amanda, 22; Elizabeth, 22; Ellen M., 22; Jane, 22; Marcus, 22; Matilda, 22; Moore, 21; William, 22; RALSTON, Moore, 9; RAMBO, Chad, 217; Denis, 217; Donna, 217; Justin, 217; RAMSEY, A. B., 195; Andrew, 197; Andrew J., 197; Belle, 196; Betty, 197; Callie, 195; Charles C., 195; Claude F., 291; Daphne, 291; David, 139, 195, 197; David A., 222; Dessie D., 222; Dora, 197; Dorothy H., 218; Drucilla, 195; Elizabeth, 195, 196, 219; Ella, 195; Euclid S., 218;

RAMSEY, Flora, 197; Floyd, 196; Foster, 196; Frances, 195; Frank, 196; Fulton, 195; George S., 196; George W., 195, 197; Gula, 195; Hence, 197; Horace, 219; Isabel, 196; James C., 195; James R., 196; Jane, 195; John, 195, 196; John L., 291; Joseph, 197; Joseph L., 302; Laura, 195; Lytle, 195; Martha A., 197; Mary, 195; Mary S., 197; Mollie, 196; Nancy, 195; Samuel, 197; Sarah E., 218; Walker, 291; William, 190, 195, 197; William R., 195, 196; William T., 196, 218; RAMSKILL, William F., 64; RANCIER, Lalla B., 232; RAND, Levisa, 189; William, 184; RANDOLPH, Athelia, 196; Sarah, 66; William, 24; RANKIN, Horace, 103; Mary A., 227; RANS, Blanche, 223; RASSMUSSEN, Dana, 193; Jerry, 193; Sherryl, 193;

RATCHFORD, Charles, 263; RATCLIFFE, Mildred, 135; RATHERT, Dianna Raye, 223; Edwin C., 223; Ronald A., 223; RATLIFF, Lynn, 98; Teen S., 218; RAVEN, Mata I., 93; RAWLINGS, Elizabeth, 3; Gregory, 3; John, 3; RAY, Annis, 18; Dixie, 148; Emily, 42; Emma, 18; Fannie, 150; George, 54; John, 18; Nancy, 40; Nancy L., 165; Sandi, 82; RAYBURN, Amanda, 198; REACH, Christine, 284; Louis, 284; REAGAN, Alvin J., 221; Robert C., 221; REASOR, Charles, 294; REBAR, Emma, 284;

RECTOR, Absalom, 66; REED, Alfred N., 254; Allie, 254; Benjamin, 138; Carrie, 79; Charles, 46; Charles W., 46; David, 254; Dicie, 254; Elmer N., 298; Fena E., 281; Isaac, 138; James, 254; Lizzie, 254; Minnie, 254; Myrtle, 254; N. A., 254; Nancy, 138; Norma T., 298; Patsy J., 46; Robert, 254; Samuel, 138; Twila, 46; REESE, Samuel, 62; William, 61; REGAN, James, 82; James R., 82; Penny A., 82; Rhonda S., 82; Sandra, 82; REGISTER, Rena M., 96; Troy, 96; REICHWALDT, Geraldine, 83; REID, Kenneth, 164; Malcolm, 164; Melba, 164; REINERT, Carrie, 264; Catherine, 264; Charles, 264; Connie, 264; Norbert, 264; REINHOLD, Elmer, 55; REMINGTON, Cynthia, 251; George, 304; Philip J.,251; REMLEY, Bertha, 261;

RENFRO, Bud, 272; Nancy Jane, 161; Schuyler M., 95; RENSHAW, Katherine C., 85; REYNIERS, Pamela G., 116; Victor, 116; REYNOLDS, Clifford, 217; Elisha, 190; Georgia, 214; Hamilton L., 140; Herman, 221; Jenkin, 190, 214, 227; Katherine, 53; Laura, 53; Louise, 53; Michael C., 53; Minerva, 214; Rebecca, 227; Tee, 303; Thomas M., 221; RHEA, Bonnie, 219; J. L., 282; RHODES, Byno R., 44; Karen L., 44; Michael R., 44; Myra G., 44; Noah E., 44; Pattye R., 44; William T., 44; RHOTEN, Ida, 117; RHOTON, Lucile, 46; RICE, Caroline, 64; Edward, 64; Henry, 64; Patrick, 64; Sarah E., 242; RICH, Albert, 110; George C., 110; Geraldine, 110; Hallie J., 110; RICHARDS, Stephen, 308; RICHARDSON, Dorothy, 56; Lovie, 98; Mary, 118;

RICHARDSON, Mary J., 112; Mathilda, 197; Richard, 63; Sallie L., 102; RICHMOND, Gladstone K., 285; Julian R., 285; Rebecca A., 285; W. G., 285; RICHTER, Charles E., 111; RICK, Rosella, 278; RICKETTS, Merchant, 255; Nicholas, 255; Virlinda, 255; William, 255; RIDENOUR, Ann, 117; RIDGE, Benjamin, 270; Elizabeth E., 270; John, 270; Laura A., 270; Martha, 270; William, 270; RIDLEY, Doris L., 234; George, 26; Margaret R., 232; RIGGS, Phoebe, 211; Vela M., 224; RIGNEY, Henry, 62; RILEY, Earl, 41; Herbert, 41; Phenton, 76; RINER, John, 304; RING, Louise, 233; Nathaniel, 70; RIPLEY, Lenora A., 84; William, 102; RIPPY, Elizabeth, 253; RISDON, Juanita, 250; RITCHIE, Gregory E., 255; H. M., 255; Rodney C., 255; RITTER, Kathleen, 79; Lawrence J., 79; RIVERS, Hope, 291;

ROACH, Frances M., 233; George, 189; James O., 233; ROADES, Billie R., 111; Carla A., 111; Homer C., 111; Margaret F., 111; ROARK, Charles A., 233; Charles E., 233; Richard L., 233; Susan M., 233; ROBBINS, Charles, 117; Earl, 117; George B., 151; Lynn A., 117; Pam, 117; ROBBS, Elizabeth, 67; ROBERSON, Allen, 175; Allison J., 150; Arlula E., 150; Bazel M., 150; Edward J., 150; Eliar F., 150; Jennie N., 150; Louisa M., 176; Mary J., 151; Ola M., 151; Pinkney, 176; Rosa B., 151; Stephen, 150; Stephen W., 150; Woodson L., 150; ROBERTS, Albert, 107; Cyrus, 228; Elizabeth, 157; James V., 170; Janet A., 170; Joseph, 108; Thomas, 108; William, 137; ROBERTSON, Addie, 179; Angie, 179; Athanasius, 174;

ROBERTSON, Berta, 179; Bertha M., 21; Clarence C., 21; Claudine, 180; Donald, 180; Dove C., 180; Eliza, 180; Elizabeth M., 178; Ella, 179; Ennis B., 180; Eula M., 180; Ezelle, 180; Fred, 180; George M., 180; Grace, 180; Hannah, 178, 179, 204; Harriet, 179; Hattie, 180; Hazel, 180; Henry, 180; Henry C., 180; Herbert, 180; Hugh, 180; James L., 180; James O., 180; James R., 21; Jane, 179; Jesse, 178; Margaret, 179; Marriott, 178; Mary, 174, 178; Mary L., 180; Mattie, 179; Nancy, 137, 178, 179; Nathaniel, 126, 174, 175, 178; Odia, 121; Percy, 180; Reba, 180; Robert B., 21; Samuel, 179; Samuel H., 179; Sarah, 178, 179; Thomas, 178; Thomas N., 179; Wayne E., 180; William, 130, 178, 179; William C., 21;

ROBERTSON, William H., 180; William J., 179, 180; William N., 180; ROBINETTE, Beulah V., 284; Ebbie, 282; G. B., 282; Georgia L., 284; James C., 282; Shelton, 284; Shirley J., 284; Theodore, 284; U. L., 282; W. L., 282; ROBINSON, Bess, 229; Jenny L., 55; John S., 159; Joseph M., 179; Magdalene, 5; Nancy, 153; ROBUCK, Murrell D., 45; ROBY, Robert P., 140; ROCKFORD, Joseph, 275; Walter J., 275; ROCKMAN, Adelia, 92; Bernard, 92; Fred, 92; John, 92; Luann, 92; Mae, 92; Martha, 92; Martin, 92; Mary, 92; Nancy, 92; Nicholas, 92; Niles, 92; Roslyn, 92; RODDY, Robert, 214; RODGERS, John B., 190; Katherine D., 299; ROEBUCK, George, 298;

ROEBUCK, Gladys E., 298; ROGERS, Cyrena, 213; Huldah, 201; Jacob, 213; Jesse K., 287; Margaret, 185; Mary J., 166; Monnie P., 287; Richard, 3; Thomas B., 176; William A., 287; ROLLER, Clara, 301; George P., 300; Gladys, 300; Lucile, 300; Scott H., 300; ROLLINS, Donald E., 82; Harriet, 297; Lloyd, 13; Pat, 82; ROOKER, Cora A., 222; ROOMSBURG, Robert, 165; Steven R., 165; ROOS, Gertrude M., 83; ROSE, George, 183; George C., 79; John, 124; Ken, 89; Tabitha, 124; ROSS, Alan North, 169; Albert S., 169; Anna K., 169; Charles, 55; Charles W., 169; Edith C., 169; Elizabeth I., 282; Ellis, 281; Especia L., 169; Eva, 55; Gertha G., 281; Harold K., 169; Jean, 193; Lawrence E., 282; Lucy, 55; Marion J., 282;

ROSS, Mark, 55; Mattie E., 282; Nannie B., 282; Robert C., 282; Vonnie, 148; William T., 169, 282; ROTHWEILER, George, 98; James, 98; Michael, 98; Nancy J., 98; ROWE, Elvie, 111; ROWLAND, Gail A., 134; James B., 134; Jenna L., 134; Sharron G., 134; ROWLETT, Kittie, 102; RUCKER, Betty A., 224; John B., 224; Margaret, 307; Sarah, 310; RUEHL, Carolyn, 221; RUMBLEY, Thomas, 215; RUNKEL, Charles, 77; Francis, 77; Fred, 77; Nina, 77; RUNYAN, Cora A., 272; RUSCHELL, Estelle, 264; RUSH, Alexander, 39; Beatrice, 114; Isaac, 164, 165; William H., 164; RUSHTON, Joseph, 119; Joseph C. D., 119; RUSSELL, Avalon, 100; Belle, 200; Benjamin H., 282; Benjamin L., 281; Carl R., 225; Cyrus, 43; E. Glenn, 225; Edna G., 43; Gypsy H., 43; Jeanne L., 225; Jimmy W., 100; Lillian J., 43; Lois O., 43; Marshall K., 43; Nannie B., 281; Robbie, 43; Teresa G., 100; Thomas, 38; Victoria, 121; William, 29; William J., 282; RUST, Littell, 228; RUTAN, Allen, 55; Carl, 55;

RUTAN, Fred, 55; Howard, 55; Jennie, 55; John, 55; Joseph, 55; Kenneth, 55; Mabel, 55; May, 55; RUTLEDGE, Elizabeth, 221; Frances, 203; Garland M., 203; Henry M., 139; RUTON, Mabel P., 249; SACHS, George, 233; Irene L., 233; SADLER, Betty A., 44; Ira B., 108; Lynda, 44; Margaret, 219; Margaret G., 44; Ralph S., 44; Smith R., 44; Whack, 55; William H., 44; William R., 44; SAFFEL, Allen B., 294; Eugene S. L., 294; Fletcher W., 294; Minerva, 294; SAFLEY, Robert, 227; SAIN, Ada C., 220; Alfred F., 220; Alice, 220; Anna L., 201; B. F., 220; Basil G., 220; Bessie, 221; Bettie B., 220; Carl, 221; Charles G., 200, 203; Charles J., 202; Daniel, 199, 213, 220; Daniel P., 221; Dorothy B., 221; Earl, 220;

SAIN, Edward, 220; Elizabeth F., 221; Elizabeth L., 202; Ellis B., 220; Ervin J., 201; Ervin T., 201; Finis E., 201; Frances, 202; Frances L., 217; Fred W., 216, 217; George C., 200; George K., 214; George L., 202; George M., 199, 220, 221; George T., 199, 200, 201, 202; Gloria, 202; Grace P., 203; Henry P., 221; Hyman, 200; James, 221; James B., 199; James C., 220; James E., 220; James L., 202; James M., 214; James P., 200; James W., 221; Jennie F., 200; John, 214; John R., 217; John W., 200; Joseph, 220; Kathy D., 217; Lillian, 200; Lillie, 220; Linda, 217; Little B. D., 213; Lorenzo B., 200; Louisa, 220; Lucy L., 201; Margaret A., 202; Martha, 220; Mary, 214; Mary B., 202; Mary C., 217;

SAIN, Mary E., 216, 220, 221; Mary G., 202; Mary L., 221; May R., 201; Mildred I., 217; Myrtle A., 201; Nancy, 220; Naomi R., 221; Norman, 217; Pearl, 200; Philip R., 202; Porter F., 201; Raymond L., 217; Robert F., 201; Robert J., 202; Robert L., 202; Sarah, 220; Sarah W., 213; Stephen T., 202; Stroud L., 201; Susan G., 202; Thomas E., 221; Wade, 202, 221; Wade J., 202; William, 220; William H., 197, 220; William L., 202, 214; William M., 199; William T., 200, 201, 202; Willie E., 201, 203; Willie N., 221; Wilmuth, 220; SALLADAY, John B., 56; SALWAY, John, 125; SAMPSON, Jacob S., 269; SAN MARTIN, Marie I., 111; SANBORN, Abner, 118; SANDER, Dianne, 92; Richard, 92; Sandra, 92; Terry, 92; Willis W., 92;

SANDERS, Anne, 255; Annie R., 96; Ardyce, 235; Clarence L., 96; Douglas L., 96; Evermond J., 96; Jeffery L., 96; Lee S., 96; Lewis N., 96; Lucy, 149; Michael J., 96; Nelson A., 96; Ray, 135; Rita R., 135; Samuel B., 96; Stephen J., 96; Terri C., 236; William, 38; SANDIFER, Ethel I., 52; Jean B., 52; M. F., 52; SANDLIN, A. K., 213; SANDUSKY, Margaret, 57; SANSOM, Alexis J., 264; Carroll T., 264; Frances B., 264; Janet K., 264; Leisla J., 264; Martha N., 264;

343

SANSOM, Richard R., 264; Richard T., 264; Robert N., 264; Russell O., 264; Thomas N., 264; William T., 264; SAPP, William, 191; SARTIN, Martha, 6; SARVER, Maxine, 81; SATTERWHITE, Alex, 235; Joe D., 236; Patricia A., 235; T. B., 235; SATTLEY, Dale, 193; Jackie M., 193; Lawrence P., 193; Talbert L., 193; SAUNDERS, John, 51; Mary, 285; SCALF, Patricia, 87; SCATES, Fountain, 30; SCHAEFFER, Frieda, 41; SCHARMEN, Gary, 89; Jackie S., 89; Larry, 89; Loralee, 89; Lynne, 89; Pam, 89; Sara, 89; SCHLEICHER, Barry M., 250; Frank C., 250; SCHLICHTMEIR, Margaret E., 238; Paul, 238; SCHOETHAL, Galeon, 168; Norman, 168; Shelly, 168; Stewart, 168; Terry, 168; SCHOOLCRAFT, James, 14; SCHRICKRAM, Ann P., 234;

SCHRICKRAM, Arthur L., 234; Charles A., 234; Horace J., 234; Karen L., 234; Louis A., 233; Martha X., 234; Rita M., 234; Scott L., 234; SCHULLEN, Nancy, 169; SCHULTE, David M., 81; John W., 81; Lester, 81; Mary K., 81; Ronald, 81; SCHULTZ, Carl, 289; Charles, 289; Ernest, 289; Lawrence, 289; Melva, 291; SCHWEITZER, Howard, 261; Louis, 261; Raymond, 261; SCOBY, Matthew, 185; SCOGGIN, Mildred, 177; SCOTT, Alexander D., 73; Alwilda, 73; Charles, 73; Clara G., 73; Elizabeth, 18, 159; Elmer H., 73; George, 18; Hattie, 232; James C., 43; John, 213; John H., 73; John W., 228; Leta, 18; Lewis H., 73; Mary E., 73, 74; Myrtle, 18; Nancy J., 228; Philip D., 43; Robert, 74; Rowena M., 261; Roy, 18;

SCOTT, Virgil B., 261; Wanda E., 261; William, 18, 73; SCOTTEN, Pearl, 234; SCOVILLE, Cecil, 105; Clarence, 105; Eugene, 105; George, 105; Harold, 105; Perry, 105; Stella, 105; SCREWS, Laura E., 192; SCROGGIN, Eliza, 272; SCROGGINS, Thomas, 8; SCRUGGS, Drury, 26; Jane, 26; SEABROOK, William, 37; SEARCY, Rebecca E., 216; Susan C., 216; Walter H., 216; Walter K., 216; SEAY, Thomas, 192; SEDESTRUM, Christin A., 170; SEE, Ianthana, 272; SEIDENSTRICKER, Eleanora, 16; SEITZ, Jack, 93; Sherry D., 93; Troy A., 93; SELL, Ben, 87; Catherine J., 87; Jessie, 87; John, 87; Mary J., 87; Rose M., 87; Rosetta, 87; Victoria E., 87; William, 87; SELLARS, Lizzie, 177; SELLERS, Victor B., 19; SENTALL, Samuel, 174;

SETZER, Barbara, 291; Charles C., 291; Emory D., 291; Marvin D., 291; Ralph R., 291; Violet, 291; William C., 291; SEVIER, George W., 40; SHACKLEFORD, Isola, 198; SHADD, Della, 277; SHAFER, Herbert, 262; SHAMBLIN, Jane S., 228; SHANNON, Charles, 168; Delila, 168; SHAPPARD, Grace, 19; SHARP, Claude, 137; SHARPE, Elizabeth, 65; Mary P., 246; SHAW, Alan M., 235; Alice F., 235; Don M., 235; George M., 235; John Q., 178; Martha E., 272; Mary, 159; Mary A., 178; Pearl L., 235; Sally, 185; Wiley, 214; SHEARMAN, John, 182; SHEEHAN, Kathryn, 102; Thomas, 102; Thomas A., 102; Walter B., 102; SHELBY, Altha L., 287; SHELDON, Allan V., 226; Avery, 291; Carol R., 226; SHELFER, Douglas M., 46; James D., 46; Loren, 46;

SHELL, Winifred, 270; SHELTON, Alec N., 285; Augusta M., 284; Avery, 283; Basil B., 283; Bernice R., 283; Bessie, 151; Bettie, 282; Bettie A., 281; Betty A., 284; Betty G., 284; Betty J., 216; Beulah E., 284; Bobby D., 285; Buena A., 283; Clauda I., 282; David, 281; David J., 283; Earl, 283; Eli C., 216; Erma R., 282; Eula, 282; Fitzhugh L., 283; Georgia L., 284; Glenna S., 285; Grover, 283; Gussie M., 283; Harry J., 284; Henry C., 282; Henry F., 282; Hubert A., 284; James L., 281, 283, 284; John W., 281, 282; Joseph, 283; Kate, 198; Lakie, 285; Laura G., 285; Lelia E., 284; Lillian G., 283; Lockie L., 282; Luther, 282; Malcolm L., 283; Margaret J., 216; Mary, 209; Mary B., 283; Mary S., 284;

SHELTON, Monnie E., 285; Nannie K., 284; Nell, 282, 283; Nellie L., 283; Ola M., 284; Ora I., 284; Patty R., 284; Pauline, 201; Peggy J., 284; Ralph, 282; Rebecca I., 283; Richard T., 284; Robert A. D., 282, 284; Ruby G., 284; Ruth A., 283; Sallie K., 282; Sam, 283; Stephen C., 284; Stephen M., 282, 284; Thomas, 282; Trula C., 284; Willard G., 285; Willard S., 285; William B., 281, 282; William C., 284; William R., 284; Willie, 283; Willie M., 141; Winifred, 283; SHEPHERD, Byrle B., 14; Daisy L., 109; Donald E., 14; Elizabeth S., 124; Harry A., 14; Henry T., 14; Lloyd, 14; Robert, 14, 124; Sally, 14; Stanley T., 14; SHEPPARD, Clara, 248; Monte, 234; SHIELDS, Dice A., 45; Harriet, 253;

SHIELDS, Josephine P., 277; SHILLING, Oliver, 87; SHIPLEY, Nathan, 32; Sarah, 99; SHIPMAN, George, 103; James, 103; John V., 103; Nicholas, 103;Robert, 103; Ruth E., 103; Sarah E., 103; SHIPP, John V., 178; SHIPPS, Ann, 272; John M., 271; SHIRES, Ruth, 70; SHIREY, Martha, 86; William, 86; SHIRLEY, Gordon, 74; SHOEMAKER, Dolly, 285; Jane, 301; SHOOP, W. B., 169; SHORT, Robert, 42; SHORY, Richard, 57; SHREVE, Daryl L., 84; Dennis L., 84; Omar L., 84; SHROPSHIRE, Jay, 235; SHROUT, Job, 103; SHULTZ, James, 79; SHUMATE, Carl, 56; Charlene, 56; Charles, 56; Hortense, 56; Virginia, 56; SHUTTERLY, Eugene, 137; SIDELL, James, 280; SILVEY, Alter E., 41, 43; Bedford J., 42; Benjamin B., 41; Bertha B., 45; Clel T., 41; Cynthia A., 45; David C., 45; Electa, 41; Ermine, 41; Fred P., 45;

SILVEY, Glade, 42; Grace, 44; Hiram H., 41; Hiram J., 41; Imogene, 41; Joy F., 45; Kirkpatrick, 41; Kittie E., 41, 43; Lockie, 41; Martin, 126; Mary E., 41, 42; Nannie L., 41; Paul, 41; Preston H., 42, 44; Ray H., 45; Robert H., 41; Robert J., 41; Ruth, 41; Trigg, 41; Walter C., 45; William L., 41; SILVIUS, Edna G., 91; SIMMONS, Allie A., 252; Mary L., 74; Wilburn C., 43; SIMMS, John, 27; Ross, 215; William P., 146; SINCLAIR, George R., 45; Lura D., 45; Margaret J., 45; Patricia A., 45; Richard G., 45; William S., 45; SINGLETON, Elizabeth, 52; Robert L., 139; SINGREY, Gertrude, 86; William O., 86; SIPES, Lucinda, 104; William, 104; SIVER, Pamela M., 84; SKAGGS, Dora N., 19; SKINNER, Arthur, 128;

SLACK, Ada C., 301; Barbara, 219; Clara R., 301; John C., 301; Sharon, 93; SLADE, Lois M., 193; Richard, 192; William R., 193; SLATER, Carl, 201; SLAUGHTER, Ann, 209; John, 209; SLAYTON, Clarissa, 7; George, 7; SLEMP, Venus, 293; SLOAN, Elvira, 160; Miranda, 160; SMALL, Goldie, 305; SMALLIN, Ozina, 307; SMARTT, Anita, 219; Ann W., 196, 218; Euclid R., 196; George, 196; I. B., 197; Joseph C., 195; Vesta A., 196; SMITH, Albert, 236; Alfred C., 236; America C., 199; Barbara A., 133; Beatrice O., 236; Benjamin, 179; Benjamin F., 237;Blanche, 179; Bruce F., 226; Cala B., 133; Caleb, 26; Charles A., 54; Chesley, 132; Craig, 179; Cynthia J., 98; Danny W., 237; Donna S., 237; Dorothy B., 135; Duncan, 164;

SMITH, Ed, 214; Elizabeth, 46; Elizabeth K., 132; Ella, 289; Ellen, 249; Ellie C., 63; Ephraim, 50; Ettie, 179; Evelyn, 179; Florence, 164; Frances, 209; Frances E., 133; Francise C., 236; Frank A., 133; Genevieve B., 227; Gladys, 179; Harry L., 54; Hayden T., 97, 98; Herschel, 132; Herschel K., 132; Hiram, 139; Hoagie, 179; Homer, 164; Ida E., 215; Inefa, 44; Jake M., 150; James E., 135; Jesse L., 236; Jo L., 236; Joe A., 132; Joseph D., 236; Josephine, 238; Joy K., 236; Juanita, 43; Judith I., 236; Julia, 179; June, 145; Laura A., 89; Lessie, 179; Lisa M., 89; Lloyd, 16; Lorena A., 236; Lucinda S., 132; Madelin, 104; Maidee A., 133; Margaret A., 149; Mark, 81; Marshall, 81; Mary E. P., 112;

SMITH, Mildred, 179; Minnie B., 229; Moses, 174; Natalie, 132; Nellie E., 217; Nora, 97; Philip, 36; Philip D., 98; Porter, 164; Preston, 179; Richard, 89, 174; Robert M., 133; Rosie, 306; Sallie E., 295; Sallie W., 133; Samuel H., 132; Samuel K., 132; Sarah, 28; Sarah S., 227; Seth M., 215; Stephanie, 81; Terry C., 236; Thomas, 128; Thomas A., 98; Uphremia, 96; Vina L., 237; Viola A., 236; Virgie L., 254; Walter L., 218; Walter W., 236; William E., 80; William J., 80; William N., 132; SMOCK, Debbie, 144; John, 144; SMOOT, J. T., 198; James, 198; Jennie, 198; John, 198; John C., 198; Mabel, 198; Maggie, 198; Mathilda, 198; Matthew, 198; Myra, 198; Sutton, 198; William, 198; Willie M., 198; SNAPP, Margaret, 296; SNAVELY, John A., 86; SNELL, Anna, 199; Charles, 200;

SNIDER, Amy J., 92; Beulah, 92; Carol, 92; Catherine R., 93; Clifford, 92; Donna, 93; Eleanora, 92; Elmer E., 92; Gearald, 92; Glen, 92; Ilene, 92; Kelly, 92; Kim E., 93; Michael, 92; Robert, 92; Roger, 92; Sharon, 92; Troy C., 93; Virgil, 93; SNIPES, Albert H., 151; Alfred G., 150; Angeline E., 150, 151; Ann, 188; Arthur P., 149; Bellefield T., 149; Brack, 149; Charles M., 150; Edna R., 149; Elbert, 149; Eva B., 149; Fanny, 149; Frances, 188; Frances J., 150; John, 150; John A. J., 149; Letitia A., 149; Lucile, 149; Manley E., 150; Marion, 150;

345

SNIPES, Martha F., 150; Mary H., 150; Mary W., 174; Matthew J., 150; Miranda, 150; Ophelia, 149; Presley J., 150; Sarah, 175; Sarah A., 150; Susan, 150; William C., 149; William G., 150; Winfield S., 149; Yonge, 149; SNODGRASS, William, 50; SNYDER, Bettie, 90; Glen, 90; Iva, 54; James R., 277; Louis, 171; Phyllis, 90; Sandra S., 277; SODERLUND, Donald, 89; SOMERS, Elsie, 134; SONJU, Jared O., 83; Oliver M., 83; Sandra D., 83; SORGE, Edward A., 89; Lynn E., 89; Mark E., 89; SOURBEER, John H., 296; SOUTHERN, Naomi, 106; SOWERBEER, Anthony, 51; SOWERBY, Thomas, 3; SPAIN, Eliza, 64; SPALDING, Bert, 138; Sarah, 100; SPANGLER, Mary, 68; SPARKS, America A., 108; Ruth, 107; Sarah A., 189; SPARROW, Buren S., 150; Leonidas, 150; Ralph L., 150; Roberta J., 150; William A., 150;

SPEARMAN, Braxton R., 203; Grace P., 203; Jo L., 203; Joe E., 203; Mary L., 203; Paty V., 203; Robert I., 203; Solomon J., 203; SPECK, Maxine, 44; SPEER, Lyle E., 278; SPEIGHTS, Elizabeth, 119; SPELLMAN, Nancy J., 273; SPENCE, Jack, 162; SPENCER, Barry P., 249; Gail A., 249; John M., 249; Lillian F., 249; M.A., 74; Mary J., 249; Philip R., 194; Shirley, 264; Susan E., 249; William, 124; William E., 194; William H., 249; SPICER, Eleanor, 216; SPINKS, Enoch, 258; Sarah, 258; SPOONMORE, Robert D., 107; Willa J., 107; William, 107; SPRINGER, Elizabeth B., 39; SPROLES, Ella, 293; SPROWLS, Willadean, 114; ST. GAUDENS, Lydia M., 186; ST. JOHN, Coy, 220; Susan, 225; STAFFORD, Ellen, 151; Ethel F., 80; STAHLMAN, Carolyn, 228; George W., 228; Margaret A., 228; Sylvia, 228;

STAIR, Alpha, 290; STALKER, Ara, 57; Fay, 57; Owen, 57; STALLARD, Dewey H., 297; Don E., 297; Frank W., 297; Jalah, 304; James C., 297; STALLINGS, Clyde, 96; STAMPS, Hosea, 190; STANALAND, Betty J., 240; Irving D., 240; Mary F., 240; Robert L., 240; STANFIELD, Addison, 131; STANFORD, Frances S., 150; Mary L., 150; STANGER, Emsley, 270; STARK, David J., 133; Donald K., 133; Malissa A., 272; STARNES, Carrie V., 293; Grover C., 283; Hobart W., 283; James M., 283; Mildred, 283; Olie, 283; STARR, James, 159; STATON, Allen T., 263; Barbara L., 263; Caroline J., 263; Carrie J., 264; Carroll A., 263; Catherine, 263; Dorothy, 263; Garnet G., 263; Gladys L., 263; Halbert W., 263; Henrietta, 270; Jacklyn, 263;

STATON, James, 262; James W., 262, 263; James W. J., 263; John, 263; John A., 263; John E., 263; Joseph F., 263; Joyce, 263; Lettie W., 264; Logan M., 263; Lowell, 264; Octa J., 263; Patricia A., 263; Robert E., 263; Ruth, 263, 264; Thayer, 263; William L., 263; Younger, 263; STEINGASSER, Joseph N., 148; STELL, Dennis, 120; STEPHENS, Beulah A., 236; Cordie M., 236; Daniel, 130; Hazel, 90; John W., 236; Louise, 225; Peggy P., 236; Wesley W., 236; William H., 236; STERLING, Sarah, 256; STEVENSON, James, 39; STEWART, Addie A., 289; Afton, 290; Bessie A., 293; Charles R., 290; Elizabeth, 158, 159; Eugene, 290; Evelyn V., 290; Ezekial, 289; Frank E., 290; Fred, 290; George W., 289; James H., 289;

STEWART, John, 158, 290; John E., 230; Josephine, 290; Margaret, 290; Margaret N., 290; Mary, 158, 159; Mary W., 290; Nannie L., 289; Omer, 290; Robert P., 289; Robert S., 230; Sarah, 158, 159; Sarah A., 230; Sarah E., 289; Scott N., 230; Sidney L., 290; STICKLE, C. W., 77; STILES, Mary E., 138; STINE, L. L., 77; STITH, Drury, 182, 205, 206; STOCK, Jessie A., 78; STOCKTON, Pearl G., 294; STOFFEL, Louise R., 296; STOKE, Adam, 267; STOKES, Martha, 203; STOLTZ, Bobbie, 47; Ray, 47; Rita, 47; Ronnie, 47; STONE, Elizabeth, 62; James, 304; John, 29; Joseph, 113; Martha A., 307; Nancy, 29; Thomas, 137; William, 29; STONESTREET, Abner, 138; Benjamin, 138; Benton C., 138, 139; Elizabeth, 138; Martha, 138;

STONESTREET, Matilda, 138; STOREY, Bruce, 108; STORM, Alfred, 104; Blanche M., 107; Fred O., 107; Judith A., 107; Landis R., 107; Mary F. O., 108; May, 280; Wyoma B., 107; STORY, Eva L., 223; STOUT, Jacob V., 221; Mary A., 74; Mary J.C., 221; STOVER, Jacob, 156; STRAIGHT, Charles, 87; Paul, 87; STRANGE, Benjamin, 136; STRATT, J. L., 142; STRATTON, Albina, 21; Amanda E., 21; Anastatia, 21; Clara, 21; Francis M., 21; Lot, 21; Louisa, 21; Lucinda, 21; Martin V., 21; Mary L., 21; Nancy J., 21; Napoleon B., 21; Rachel L., 21; Robert, 21; Roderick R., 21;

STRATTON, Susan, 21; Thomas B., 21; William, 21; William A., 21; STREET, William, 29; STRIBLING, Patricia A., 216; Rex E., 216; STRICKLAND, Dayton, 280; STRICKLER, Hattie, 222; STRNOT, Rudy, 79; STROM, D. F., 73; STRONG, Elsie, 292; Retta, 56; STROTHER, John, 206; STROUD, A. Madison, 192; Abraham, 189; Albert G., 191; Alfred, 185; Alice, 204; Allie N., 192; Amelia E., 192; Anderson, 184, 189; Andrew E., 205; Anna, 190, 197; Annie M., 192; Arthur B., 192; Bartlett S., 191, 192, 203, 204; Belle, 196; Benjamin F., 204; Betty, 206; Beulah Mae, 204; Bryant, 188; Calvin, 185; Claudia L., 193; Columbus, 189; Columbus G., 192; Cora, 192; David, 182; David H., 196; Delilah, 188; Dickson A., 204; Dixon, 185;

STROUD, Dorothea N., 193; Ed, 192; Edward C., 193; Effie, 192; Elam, 192; Eliza, 189; Elizabeth, 184, 185, 188, 189, 190, 191, 194; Elizabeth M., 204; Emmett S., 205; Espy M., 192; Eugene, 196; Fannie C., 193; Fielding, 188; Frances, 184, 191, 199; Frances C., 191; Frances M., 192; Frank, 196; Genarah, 192; George, 139, 189, 190, 191, 196; George A., 192; George H., 205; George N., 205; George R., 193; George S., 196; George W., 197, 203, 204; Grace E., 192; Grady, 205; Hannah, 204, 206; Hannah I., 205; Harrington, 192; Harry, 196; Harry B., 205; Hawkins, 188; Hence A., 204; Henderson, 192; Herschell M., 192; Hester J., 204; Hettie M., 191; Homer A., 193; Horace B., 204; Howard, 205; Ida C., 205;

STROUD, Inez, 192; James, 206; James M., 191, 192, 193, 196; Jane, 189; Jane A., 191; Jeanne J., 204; Jeff A., 193; John, 182, 183, 184, 187, 189, 205, 206; John A., 191, 193; John D., 191; John M., 204; John S., 188, 191; John T., 205; Jonnie M., 193; Joseph, 182; Joshua, 182, 205, 206; Josie, 192; Josie B., 205; Kate, 204; Lawson P., 193; Leonidas, 189, 192; Lillie B., 193; Linnie, 205; Lonn K., 204; Louisa, 189; Love, 204; Lucinda, 204; Lucy, 139, 191; Luther, 205; Maggie, 192; Marcus L., 191; Margaret, 184, 185, 188, 189, 191, 199, 206; Mark, 206; Marshall, 184, 185; Martha, 189; Martha E., 193, 194; Martha I., 193; Martha J., 191, 193, 205; Mary, 184, 185, 188, 189, 190, 197, 206; Mary A., 205;

STROUD, Mary B., 192; Mary F., 193; Matthew, 206; Mattie L., 205; Max H., 193; Medrith L., 192; Michael H., 196; Minerva, 191, 193; Minerva E., 192; Mystice, 192; Nancy, 188, 189, 190, 191, 197, 204; Nancy B., 192; Nancy E., 205; Ninah A., 192; Olive, 206; Oliver H., 191, 193; Oscar A., 205; Pamela S., 204; Patsy, 188; Perry L., 193; Peter, 183, 184; Philip, 204; Pleasant H., 204; Preston A., 191; Reziah, 191; Richard A., 193; Robert H., 193; Robert W., 196, 205; Robertson M., 204; Sally, 206; Sarah, 183, 184, 185, 188, 189, 190, 191, 204; Sarah E., 205; Sherod, 184; Sophia, 189; Susan, 183; Tabitha, 188, 206; Taylor M., 193; Thomas, 178, 182, 184, 185, 190, 191, 204; Thomas B., 204, 205;

STROUD, Thomas J., 191; Viola, 192; Wade H., 189, 213; Walter, 189, 227; William, 139, 182, 183, 184, 185, 188, 189, 190, 204, 205, 206, 212; William B., 192; William D., 205; William I., 205; William J., 192; William L., 193; Yearby, 184; STROWD, Caroline, 153; STUART, Edward, 118; Maria, 20, 21; STUBBLEFIELD, Agnes L., 231; Albert G., 229, 237, 238; Albert N., 230; Alethea, 224; Alfred C., 234; Allen C., 225; Allen L., 229, 230; Allene C., 230; Alva B., 235; Alzira E., 228, 232; Amanda C., 228; America, 212; Amy E., 229; Amy L., 216; Anderson, 238; Ann, 209, 211; Ann M., 219; Anna, 209, 212; Anne R., 223; Annie, 241; Annie L., 221, 224; Armstreet, 242; Arthur T., 228; Asa F., 214, 215; Barbara J., 215; Barry, 237; Berta L., 240; Betsy A., 239; Betsy J., 239; Beulah, 235, 236;

STUBBLEFIELD, Beverley, 209; Beverley B., 242; Bradley D., 224; Bradley O., 229; Brian S., 219; Buena V., 219; Carl T., 216; Carla S., 216; Carol J., 225; Carter, 241; Catherine, 211, 213; Charles B., 225; Charles E., 218; Charles R., 241; Clara B., 216; Clark C., 239; Claud B., 229, 231; Clay, 228, 229; D. W., 239; Dalores N., 215; Dandridge A., 241; Daniel W., 227; David A., 230; David A. W., 241; David R., 227; Demie T., 229; Denise, 237; Dennis D., 231; Dessie D., 223; Dewey P., 241; Dillard R., 215; Dixon, 239; Dolores E., 231; Don T., 235; Donna J., 220; Dora E., 240; Druella, 217; E. Page, 241; Earl B., 231;

STUBBLEFIELD, Ed A., 229; Edgar P., 215, 217; Edward, 209; Edward M., 218; Edwin H., 241; Edwin P., 224; Elisha D., 228; Elisha J., 214; Elizabeth, 209, 210, 211, 212, 213, 220, 223, 242; Elizabeth I., 218; Emma A., 222, 225; Emma O., 230; Emma S., 220; Ernest E., 215; Etalee, 229; Ethel, 229; Eunice, 239; Evelyn J., 238; Fannie, 239; Flora E., 215; Frances, 213, 242; Frances I., 215; Frank, 229; Frank W., 220, 229; Fred H., 216; Gale L., 231; Garfield, 229; Garrison, 242; Gary D., 231; George, 209, 210, 211, 212, 213, 227, 234, 242; George H., 222, 223; George J., 227, 228; George T., 214; George W., 211, 228; Georgia, 239; Gertrude, 229; Gilbert C., 230; Glenn E., 234; Glenna D., 224; Gregory, 237; Hannibal, 227; Hattie L., 223; Hazel M., 235; Hence W., 215; Henry, 209, 240;

STUBBLEFIELD, Henry P., 227; Herman H., 224; Herman P., 223, 224; Hermy B., 215; Hiram B., 227; Horace G., 240, 241; Howard G., 223; Howard H., 224; Howard L., 224; Hubert, 240; Hugh C., 210; Hugh H., 216; Hugh T., 215, 216; Hugh W., 215; Ida, 239; Inez C., 223; Irene, 239; Isaac N., 228; Jack G., 224; James, 209, 211; James A., 240; James C., 218, 228, 241; James E., 237; James F., 218; James G., 224, 225; James J., 225; James L., 231; James M., 214, 228, 239; James R., 222, 223, 227; James S., 218, 228; Jane C., 225; Jay E., 217; Jean A., 238; Jefferson P., 228; Jeffrey A., 230; Jeremiah, 242; Jerry E., 219; Jerry J., 237; Jessie, 234; Jessie M., 215; Jessie N., 240; Jethro E., 239; Joel, 210, 239;

STUBBLEFIELD, John, 209, 210; John D., 224; John H., 239; John L., 227, 228; John M., 227; John O., 234, 240; John W., 211; Johnnie L., 223; Jon D., 216; Jonathan S., 227; Joseph R., 211; Julius M., 238; Katherine, 220; Katie E., 216; Keith A., 235; Kelly, 241; Keziah, 211, 212; Kimmey, 240; King A., 235; Kitty, 227; Laura K., 219; Lavona, 228; Lee, 241; Lee A., 229; Leland A., 231; Leona L., 230, 231; Leonidas, 227; Leslie A., 216; Leslie J., 216; Lisa C., 215; Lisa R., 216, 225; Locksley S., 224; Lorita, 222; Lota A., 224; Lota E., 224; Lou, 214; 241; Louisa, 213; Louisa E., 241; Louise, 227; Lowell R., 231; Lucille M., 215; Lucretia, 227; Lucy, 241; Lula B., 240; Lusk, 214; Lycurgus J., 227;

STUBBLEFIELD, Lydia K., 216; Lyle L., 231; M. Elizabet, 239; M. J., 239; Mabel B., 218; Mahala J., 228; Malinda A., 211; Malissa V., 228; Marcena, 239; Margaret, 239; Margaret E., 214, 215, 218; Margaret L., 240; Margarette, 230; Marie, 240; Marilyn, 222; Marilyn K., 222; Marjorie A., 238; Mark A., 230; Mark R., 219; Mark T., 216; Martha, 210, 212, 213, 227, 241, 242; Martha A., 239; Martha C., 218, 228; Martha J., 221, 239, 240; Martin, 211; Mary, 209, 211, 212, 213, 228, 239; Mary A., 228; Mary C., 216, 225; Mary D., 217; Mary E., 220, 238; Mary F., 217; Mary K., 222; Mary L., 221; Mary M., 241; Mary P., 241; Mary S., 224; Matilda, 240; Maude E., 222; May, 214; Melinda A., 224; Michael L., 218;

STUBBLEFIELD, Minnie L., 240; Murna A., 224; N. O., 240; Nancy, 189, 211, 212, 213, 239, 241, 242; Nancy E., 216; Nancy W., 242; Napoleon, 227; Nathan, 242; Nellie R., 215; Nora, 234; Norris J., 235, 237; Ora L., 216; Orlianna, 212; Oscar F., 234; Park L., 230; Patricia F., 237; Paul, 219; Paul R., 219; Peter, 209; Peter B., 211; Peyton M., 241; Peyton T., 241; Polly A., 239; Raymond R., 223; Rebecca, 211; Rena, 231; Reuben L., 229; Richard, 210, 241, 242; Richard C., 242; Richard D., 237; Richard J., 241; Richard R., 231; Ricky, 237; Robert, 209, 210, 241, 242; Robert C., 235, 237, 242; Robert D., 224; Robert E., 219; Robert G., 229; Robert K., 224; Robert L., 26, 211, 212, 213, 221, 227, 228, 239;

STUBBLEFIELD, Robert R., 231; Robert S., 229; Robert W., 211; Roma, 227; Rosa E., 240; Roy, 240; Roy I., 241; Royce B., 229; Royce E., 220; Royce L., 223; Ruby, 222; Ruby I., 215, 216; Rufus W., 241; Russel B., 231; Ruth M., 238; Samuel, 239; Samuel M., 215, 219, 220; Sandra, 225; Sarah, 189, 211, 212, 213, 214, 227, 239, 241, 242; Sarah B., 214; Sarah E., 224; Sarah F., 240; Sarah J., 218; Sarah M., 241; Sarah S., 225; Scott E., 238; Simon, 209; Stacy L., 219; Stephen, 212, 238, 239, 240; Stephen A., 239; Stephen C., 224; Stephen R., 239; Steve B., 216; Susan, 212, 214; Susan L., 238; Susannah, 212, 242; Thaddeus, 227;

STUBBLEFIELD, Theodorick, 241, 242; Thomas, 209, 210, 211, 212, 213, 227, 239, 242; Thomas J., 219, 239; Thomas M., 219, 240; Tilman, 242; Tilman I., 242; Verdayne B., 231; Victoria, 229, 230; Victoria A., 241; W. Fulton, 214; Walter, 239; Wanda J., 219; Warren L., 222; Wesley, 211; William, 211, 212, 213, 214, 241; William A., 240; William D., 217; William H., 214, 222, 238, 239; William J., 227; William L., 217, 241, 242; William M., 217, 229; William P., 228, 234; William R., 214, 219, 240; William S., 224; William T., 221, 222; William W., 222; Willie, 241; Willie T., 240; Wilmuth, 212, 213; Wilson M., 239; Winifred, 213; Woodruff, 242; Wyatt, 210, 212, 239; Wyatt M., 239; STUBBS, Jesse, 65;

STURTEVANT, Daniel, 82; Darla, 82; Donald, 82; SUGGETT, Edgecomb, 126; Elizabeth, 126; SULLINS, Rebecca, 211; SULLIVAN, Lola, 107; SUMMERS, Annalee, 83; Elizabeth, 220; SUMNER, Mills, 93; SUNDMAN, Gordon M., 132; Susan, 132; SUSONG, Jacob, 51; SUTLIFF, William, 189; SUTTLE, Josias, 122; SUTTON, Ann, 53; Betty J., 296; Charles, 53; Edith A., 296; Elizabeth, 53; Fred W., 296; James, 53; John, 18, 53; Luther J., 296; Nathan E., 296; Rose, 225; William, 24, 53; SVEJDA, Angeline, 98; SWAIM, Lora M., 163; SWARTZ, Beulah, 281; SWATTS, John, 51; SWEARINGEN, Van, 9; SWEET, Frankie, 200; SWICK, Ed L., 200; SWITALA, James, 92; SWOFFORD, Emmett S., 254; Lois, 254; Stephanie L., 254; William E., 254;

SWOPE, Darrel W., 42; SYLVESTER, Claud, 106; Ralph, 106; TABLER, George, 1; TABODA, Eloisa, 237; TACKETT, Mary, 149; TALBOT, Eliza D., 11; TALBOTT, Anna M., 84; TALIAFERRO, Mildred, 20; TALLEY, Larry C., 219; Mary S., 219; Willard, 219; TANNER, Paul W., 104; TARR, Donna, 167; Frank, 167; Jerome, 167; TARVER, Beulah, 294; TATE, Campbell B., 293; Carmine S., 293; Charles D., 293; Charles E., 287; Emmanuel P., 293; Ethel M., 104; Frances C., 293; George G., 293; Guy E., 286; James S., 293; John R., 104, 293; Joseph C., 293; Joseph E., 293; Joseph R., 104; Joyce M., 293; Loretta, 105; Maggie E., 293; Melba E., 293; Minnie, 165; Nancy C., 293; Nancy V., 293; Nannie M., 293; Samuel W., 286; Sarah I., 293;

TATE, Susan J., 293; Virginia E., 294; William A., 293; William D., 293; TATUM, Dickie A., 148; Karen S., 148; Marlene, 148; Marlin, 148; Mary R., 148; TAYLOR, Anna E., 177; Blanch, 200; Carl C., 292; Catherine, 54; Charles W., 99; Claud L., 278; D. R., 80; Danelle R., 80; David, 99; Denny M., 99; Elizabeth, 8; Frances, 163; Glenn, 99; Helen, 214; Hiram H., 292; Jennie, 204; John, 130; John C., 301; Julia E., 222; Karen J., 278; Kent W., 292; Lily, 215; Linnie I., 292; Lockie L., 282; Marion F., 228; Mary, 12, 54, 196; Michael E., 278; Nelson G., 301; Patricia A., 278; Rhea, 292; Robert M., 99; Ruby V., 292; Sarah, 54; Stephen, 260; Susan Y., 131; Thomas, 228; William, 54; TEAGUE, Louise, 147; Marie, 300;

TEAGUE, Simon, 119; TEDFORD, James B., 144; TEEGARDEN, Alonzo, 261; Anderson, 261; Charles P., 261; Charles R., 261; Charles S., 261; Christine, 261; Edna P., 262; Fannie B., 261; George, 261; Jeremiah, 261; Julia, 261; Laura B., 261; Lucien A., 261; Lucien M., 261; Lucy P., 262; Maurice P., 261; Minnie B., 261; Penn B., 261; Virginia L., 261; William A., 261; William T., 261; TEMPLETON, Helen F., 84; William F., 301; TENNIS, Florence, 77; TERRAGAS, Guadalupe, 237; Miguel, 237; TERRELL, Katie, 177; TERRY, Julia, 109; TEUTCH, Celeste, 187; THACKER, Jesse E., 220; Nannie, 220; THACKSTON, James, 206; THARP, Thelma, 134; THAYER, Yale, 275; THERIEN, Greg, 116; Leonard, 116; Linda, 116; Mark, 117;

THERIEN, Sherry, 116; THIERSE, Ida M., 78; THIGPEN, Exa, 180; THOMAS, Albert S., 262; Alexander B., 262; Betty J., 277; Catherine, 261; Chalmos, 252; Charles M., 115; Donna M., 99; Elmer, 292; Frank, 274; Gene, 292; Georgie L., 262; Gilbert R., 98; Howard A., 261; Ileen B., 262; James F., 262; Jane, 4; Joseph, 115; Nadine, 292; Queen, 196; Samuel, 59, 157; Stanley H., 262; Vivian L., 262; William G., 98; William P., 98; THOMLINSON, Edward R., 291; Louis, 291; Merle D., 291; THOMPSON, Arthur J., 240; Barbara, 132; Charles L., 109; Christopher J., 82; Edward C., 286; Edward T., 286; Fauchie B., 240; Frances, 151; G.W., 138; Grace F., 286; Helen M., 240; Jeffrey, 109; John, 40, 82, 121; Kelly L., 82;

THOMPSON, Lucy S. G., 241; Margaret, 135; Martha, 206; Maynor, 109; Natalie, 132; Nora B., 286; Oleta, 148; Robert S., 151; Robert W., 132; Sadie, 121; Stephen, 61, 109; Terry M. A. J., 240; THRASHER, Helen, 279; THRELKELD, Harriet, 6; THRIFT, David, 188; Delilah, 188; Drury, 188; Elizabeth, 188; Isham, 188; Levisa, 188; Margaret, 188; Mary, 188; Nancy, 188; Perry, 188; Sarah, 188; Susanna, 188; William, 188; THURMAN, Clifton, 42; THWEAT, Jean, 203; TICE, Neil W., 238; Ralph J., 238; Robert W., 238; Roberta S., 238; TICER, Goldie, 141; TIDWELL, James M., 152; TIGRESS, Beruta, 279; TILFORD, Sarah, 195; TILGHMAN, James, 177; Kate, 177; TILLEY, Margaret A., 153; TILLMAN, James T., 307;

TILMAN, Willis, 138; TINDLE, Samuel, 65; TINKER, Glen L., 80; Janice E., 80; Kenneth, 80; TINSLEY, Flossie, 42; TITTSWORTH, David, 295; Elizabeth, 295; Ella K., 295; George A., 295; Georgia E., 295; John, 295; Lois F., 295; Lula, 295; Mary, 221; Mary K., 295; Mary V., 295; Sallie, 295; Walter D., 295; William D., 295; William K., 295; TOBIN, Daniel, 82; Susan A., 82; Tracy L., 82; TODD, Elizabeth, 242; Iva S., 80; Lillie, 231; William M., 151; TOLMAN, Eliza, 164; TOM, Ellison, 143; TOMBERLIN, Susannah, 166; TOMPKINS, Hannah A., 18; James, 18; TORBETT, Etta, 270; Eula, 270; John, 270; Kate, 270; Robert L., 270; TORGERSON, Alvin, 167; Arthur, 167; Harold, 167; Harvey, 167; Kenneth, 167; Milton, 167;

TORGERSON, Opal, 167; Roger, 167; TORRANCE, Glenn, 170; TOW, James, 175; TRABUE, Bruce A., 97; Bruce W., 97; Joe R., 97; Robert D., 97; TRAIL, Airy, 246; Ann, 245; Archibald, 245; Ashford, 255; Basil, 256; Cassandra, 245, 256; Charles, 245; David, 245, 255, 256; Dorcas, 256; Edward, 245; Edward N., 255; Eleanor, 245, 246, 255, 256; Elizabeth, 245, 256; Frances, 255, 256; Gulielma M., 255; Hamilton, 256; Henry, 245; James, 245, 247, 255; Jane, 245; Jean, 245, 252; John, 256; Kinsey, 246; Margaret, 256; Margery, 245; Mary, 256; Mary A., 255; Massa, 256; Nathan, 245, 255; Notley, 255; Osborn, 246; Rachel, 245, 255; Sarah, 245, 256; Solomon, 256; Susanna, 255, 256; Thomas, 245; Wesley, 246; William, 245;

TRAIL, William T., 246; TRAVIS, Annette, 136; Lula, 223; TRAYLOR, Priscilla E., 187; TREADWAY, Cynthia D., 171; Deborah M., 171; Monica E., 171; Swithen L. R., 171; TREGO, Margaret, 118; TRENT, Daniel, 302; Mack, 302; Margaret, 302; Robert, 302; Susan, 302; Sylvia, 302; Victoria, 302; TRIBBLE, Shadrack, 190; TRIGG, Ross, 43; John, 76; Martha, 76; TRILLIA, Lucia A., 64; TRIMBLE, Homer B., 16; Rachel, 273; TRISSLER, James, 107; John, 107; Marylu, 107; William, 107; TROTTER, Robert, 130; TROUP, Sharon, 226; TROUT, Catherine M., 43; TROXELL, Daniel, 51; Susan, 51; TROXLER, Dorothy, 216; TRUMAN, Connie S., 275; James H., 275; Mary R., 275; Ruth D., 275; TRUSLER, Mary, 121; TRYON, A. G., 41;

TUBBEVILLE, Jennie, 152; TUCKER, Forrest, 200; Gwendolyn, 225; Lucy, 200; Mildred E., 194; Wayne, 200; TUELL, Chester, 137; TURNER, Barbara J., 226; Dolores, 11; Douglas H., 89; Ethel J., 46; George, 304; Harry G., 89; Jesse, 226; John, 103; Jonah, 273; Lois, 231; Louise, 273; R. R., 20; Roger, 114; Scott S., 89; Silence, 86; TURPIN, Thomas, 24; TURRENTINE, Annie E., 194; TWENTE, Lucy, 98; TYRELL, Mary E., 105; UFHEIL, Delores, 170; UNDERWOOD, Gladys, 106; H. V., 105; Neva, 105; Robert, 106; Thomas J., 256; Wilmoth, 256; UNRUE, Lela, 263; UPPEY, Sarah, 156; URBAN, Kurt J., 84; Marilee, 84; VAIL, Amelia C., 169, 171; Ebenezer, 169; James M., 169; John S., 169; Mary E., 169; Mary H., 166; Perry, 169;

VAIL, Sarah A., 169, 170; Thomas P., 170; VALENTINE, Barry, 219; Elizabeth, 30; Nancy L., 219; Susan, 219; VAN CLEVE, Jane, 157; VAN COUPLAND, T., 144; VAN GILDER, Dixie J., 299; Shirley J., 299; W. W., 299; VAN HOOZER, Louis, 231; VAN HORN, J. J., 299; Lillie M., 300; VAN SANT, Clifford, 235; Ramona M., 235; VAN SLYKE, Clara E., 232; E. E., 232; VANCE, Clone, 43; VANZANT, Allison B., 19; Deborah S., 19; Robert E., 19; Valerie, 19; VARNER, Eliza J., 231; John S., 231; VAUGHN, Abraham, 37; Alexander, 7; Granderson, 136; Susannah, 7; Virginia A., 285; VEACH, Carmelita P., 84; VEATCH, Rosalind E., 196; VELTHOEN, Aart A., 80; VENABLE, Mary, 241; VENTERS, Margaret, 305; VESPER, Griffen, 92;

WEST, Charles, 260; Columbus, 253; Constant, 258, 259; David, 265; Eber, 253, 254; Elinor, 253; Eliza, 261; Elizabeth, 253, 259, 260; Elmira, 253; Emma, 262; Enoch, 258, 259; Ephraim, 260; Ferdinand, 253; Frances, 253; Francis, 262; Francis A., 262; George, 253; Georgia A., 254; Hannah, 260; Harvey, 253; Hester A., 253; Innetia, 261; Isaac, 259, 265; Jacob, 265; James, 253, 259, 265; James M., 253; Jane, 253; Javan, 253; Jennie, 253; Johannah, 260; John, 253, 258, 260, 265; Jonathan, 258, 260; Joseph, 245; Julia A., 254; Kendrick, 253; Levina, 253; Louisa A., 253; Lucy B., 262; Lydia, 265; Margaret, 260, 265; Martha, 260, 265; Mary, 12, 13, 253, 258, 259, 260, 262; Michael, 260, 262; Missouri, 254;

WEST, Monroe, 253; Myrick H., 253; Nancy, 260; Octavius, 253; Osborn, 256; Perry, 253; Priscilla, 258; Pulaski, 253; Rachel, 253; Rebecca, 260; Richard, 260; Robert, 34, 258, 259; Rosella, 254; Rowland, 140; Roxanna, 254; Samuel, 259, 262; Sarah, 258, 259, 260, 265; Sarah E., 262; Solomon, 253; Susan A., 253; Susanna, 258, 265; Thanotia, 253; Thomas, 259; Tripena, 253; Virginia E., 261; Virginia M., 262; Walter, 200; William, 252, 259, 265; Willis, 253; WESTHUE, William, 125; WHARTON, Ann, 197; WHEELER, Laura, 233; WHEELESS, Alba J., 110; Annie B., 110; Annie R., 109; Bertha B., 109; Carol Y., 111; Emma N., 111; George H., 111; Grace M., 111; Helen R., 109; James L., 109; James T., 109, 110; Janet L., 111; Jesse G., 110, 111; Jesse L., 111; Jessie D., 110; Joseph A., 110;

WHEELESS, Justin L., 109, 110; Katherine E., 111; Kim Ann, 110; Lucile A., 109; Lunsford J., 109; Mark P., 111; Mary L., 111; Mildred M., 109; Nora F., 111; Paul D., 111; Ruth A., 110, 111; Sam W., 111; Sharon A., 111; Silveetus J., 109; Silvester V., 109; Valta E., 110; William R., 111; Willie E., 111; Young B., 111; WHERRY, Robert, 162; WHIPPLE, Ann, 70; WHISNAND, Elihu, 270; Elizabeth, 270; Emanuel, 270; Franklin, 270; Jacob, 270; John C., 270; Laura C., 270; Margaret, 270; Rebecca, 270; Sarah J., 270; Susan, 270; Thomas, 270; William E., 270; WHITAKER, Ernest T., 235; Galor J., 235; Jimmie, 235; Karen L., 235; Mark, 258; Thomas, 258; WHITE, Agnes C., 29; Asbury, 100; Bercha O., 100; David, 110; Edna, 57; Elizabeth, 6; Elizabeth B., 6; Gordon, 110; Gretta, 17; Jack, 17; James, 7;

WHITE, Jean M., 148; Jesse, 7; John, 7, 256; Lou, 113; Lucy, 6, 7; Margaret C., 225; Mary J., 160; Melissa, 270; Micajah, 6; Patricia A., 110; Robert G., 146; Sophronia, 7; Thomas, 34; William, 12; Willis C., 225; WHITEHOUSE, Jean, 263; WHITEMAN, Frederick, 51; WHITESELL, Robert, 119; WHITFIELD, Robert C., 222; Robert L., 222; WHITLOCK, John, 190; WHITLOW, Oscar, 103; WHITMAN, Homer E., 299; Wilma J., 299; WICKER, Mace, 57; WICKLIN, Elias L., 63; WIDDING, Patricia M., 275; WIENER, Minnie, 224; WIGHAM, Mary A., 160; WILCOX, Betty J., 82; Judy J., 82; Ralph, 82; William R., 82; WILCOXEN, John, 157; WILDMAN, Nancy, 139; WILEY, George, 7; Ollie, 234; WILHELM, Charles R., 297; Dana, 297; Ed R., 297; Frances E., 295; Geneva, 297; Joseph H., 297; Lula, 286; Nannie, 295; Rebecca V., 300;

WILHELM, Richmond K., 297; William F., 297; William K., 297; WILKINS, Betty K., 227; WILKINSON, Batley B., 96; Dean R., 97; Franklin P., 96; George M., 96; James N., 95; Jehu T., 96; Julia G., 96; Lewis, 95; Lucy A., 96; Mary E., 95; Nancy J., 97; Rand A., 97; Samuel W., 96; William, 95; WILLIAMS, Benjamin, 112; Billy E., 42; Edwin M., 42; Elizabeth, 240; Elwood, 187; Florence E., 111; Floyd O., 285; George, 1; Ida, 141; Ina, 180; James, 129, 184; Jedidiah, 160; Joseph, 36; Kathryn M., 172; Leroy, 172; Louis, 179; Monnie L., 285; Myrtle A., 293; N. J., 186; Nathaniel, 175; Ola F., 284; Ralph, 209; Robert, 25; Wenona, 57; Winfield, 176; WILLIAMSON, Grace, 305; WILLIS, Alvin S., 222; Anderson F., 139;

WILLIS, David J., 215; Elynor L., 215; Farmer, 215; Linda K., 222; Philip L., 222; Rosemary, 222; Ruby P., 305; William B., 139; WILLSON, Rebecca, 242; WILSON, Ada, 97; Ada L., 144; Adam, 27; Alice M., 171; Charity, 102; Doris J., 171; Dosha, 201; Elizabeth, 305; Hugh, 147; James, 20; John, 38, 130; John R., 272; Lucy, 101; Martha, 188; Mary, 34; Mary A., 225; Melvin, 171; Noel J., 225; Romyn S., 226; Samuel, 39; Sarah E., 151; WIMPEY, Dorothy J., 101; WIMPY, Clorene, 145;

WINANS, Seymour, 53; WINBURN, Lafayette, 15; WINCHELL, Zelda L., 17; WIND-
ROW, John L., 135; Nancy B., 135; Paul M., 135; WINEGAR,Cora G.,297; Dovie J., 288;
Eldridge L., 288; Eldridge V., 288; Jeanette E., 287; Kenneth G., 288; Louvenia,
284; Mary, 288; Thomas, 297; WINFIELD, April D., 230; Bill, 230; Cheryl A., 230;
Sandra J., 230; WINKLER, Susan, 307; WINN, David L., 171; Lee T., 171; WINSLOW,
Franklin E., 85; WINTON, Ida, 274; Nancy, 203; Stephen, 203; WISE, Barbara A.,
237; Freda N., 237; Peggy L., 237; Roy D., 237; WITHERS, Albert G., 211; Elijah,
211; Elizabeth, 211; James, 211; John A., 211; Lewis W., 211; WITHROW, Mary, 140;
WOFFORD, Rhoda, 253; William, 38; WOLF, Beulah, 198; Davis L., 197; Della. 197;
Grace, 198; Kenneth W., 172; Lena, 198; Martha, 198; Newsome B., 197;

WOLFE, Abraham L., 280; Adaline, 285; Adam, 268, 272, 301, 302, 306; Addie,
270, 305; Albert E., 276, 304; Alice, 272; Allie, 309; Alois, 309; Alvin, 279;
Amanda, 302, 309; Amanda J., 303; Amelia V., 294; Angie, 272; Anita H., 276; Ann
C., 270; Anna, 271; Anna L., 280; Archibald, 301, 308; Arnold E., 279; Arthur,
272, 302; Arthur L., 280; Audrey I., 299; Barbara, 267, 307, 309; Barbara E.,
292, 293; Benjamin F., 272; Bert, 271; Bert J., 299; Bert P., 300; Berta, 298;
Berta E., 299; Bertha, 272; Bertha C., 280; Bertha M., 280; Bessie, 272, 293;
Beulah, 271; Carlton, 277; Carol A., 279; Caroline, 308; Carrie L., 294; Cath-
erine, 268, 271, 301, 302, 307; Charles, 267, 268, 274, 289, 306, 307, 308;

WOLFE, Charles A., 275, 276, 305; Charles D., 299, 305; Charles E., 276;
Charles H., 280, 286; Charles M., 276, 303; Cheryl S., 279; Claiborne, 302;
Clair M., 275; Clara, 272; Clarence W., 276; Clark S., 271; Cleo M., 294; Clyde,
289; Connie, 279; Cordelia E., 285, 291; Cornelia, 275; Cornelius W., 288; Cor-
rine M., 279; Courtney A., 300; Creed T., 270; Crystal E., 300; Curtis, 289;
Dale B., 300; Daniel, 302; Darrell W., 300; David, 278, 302; David L., 276; Dean
J., 279; Deborah A., 279; Della, 272; Della M., 305; Delores A., 276; Dewitt C.,
298, 299; Diana, 276; Diane, 279; Dionysius, 304; Dixie J., 300; Don F., 275;
Donald L., 279; Donald R., 278; Donna M., 279; Doris E., 276; Dorothy, 275;

WOLFE, Dorthula, 270; Edgar, 289; Edith, 277; Edley, 307; Edna, 275; Edna
M., 280; Edwin, 274, 278; Effie, 270; Effie, 272; Effie L., 299; El, 198; Elbert
S., 270; Eldon F., 276; Eliza, 309, 311; Eliza J., 273; Elizabeth, 269, 270, 280,
302, 307, 308, 309; Ella, 270, 272; Ellen, 274; Elmer B., 280; Elmo, 275; Elnora,
274; Elvira, 280, 295; Emaline, 285; Emaline E., 286; Emeline, 307, 309; Emily
F., 304; Emmanuel, 280, 285, 289, 292, 298; Ernest R., 299; Ethan, 272; Ethel G.,
275; Ethel M., 272; Ethel O., 275; Eugene F., 294; Eugene O., 278; Eugenia P.,
294; Eunice, 277; Eva M., 274; Evaline, 285, 300; Evert, 271; Ewell, 302; Fain,
300, Fannie L., 286; Fannie R., 294; Ferman, 272; Florence, 197; Frances,275,311;

WOLFE, Francis, 278; Frank, 289; Franklin M., 270; Fred I., 275; Frederick
R., 276; Gail D., 278; Gale, 293; Garnett, 298; Gary R., 276; Gayle P., 300;
Gene E., 278; Geneva A., 299; Genone, 278; George, 267, 268, 280, 285, 301, 302,
308, 309, 311; George C., 306, George D., 279; George G., 275; George M., 306;
George S., 307; George W., 269, 271, 274, 277, 279, 293, 300, 301, 303, 304, 305,
George W. S. 298, 300; Georgina, 280; Geraldine, 279; Gideon, 301; Gladys L.,
278, Glenn, 279; Grace E., 275; Greenberry G. M., 303; Hannah, 268, 302, 307,
309; Harley, 279; Harold, 279; Harold C., 278; Harold M., 276; Harold W., 276,
305; Hazel A., 299; Hazel G., 287; Hazel L., 288; Helen M., 300; Henry, 15, 51,
268, 269, 273, 274, 279, 302; Henry C., 271; Henry J., 272; Henry M., 274, 275;

WOLFE, Henry T., 277; Hiram, 285, 288, 298, 311; Howard L., 280; Hugh, 293;
Hulda, 274; Ida, 272; Ida L., 289; Ida P., 286; Illa I., 300; Ina G., 287; Irvin,
272; Isaac, 273, 280, 285, 298; Isaac C., 269, 271; Isaac J., 303; Isaac W., 303;
Isabel M., 292; J. Harrison, 301; Jackson B., 294; Jacob, 269, 303, 307; Jacob
H., 269, 272; Jacob J., 304; Jacob M., 304; Jacqueline M., 275; Jalah C., 304;
Jalah E., 304; James, 285, 289, 302, 311; James D., 274, 276; James H., 299;
James J., 279; James K., 293; James M., 296, 298, 304; James N. V., 303;

WOLFE, James P., 305; Jane, 302, 308; Jasper M., 304;Jeff, 307; Jefferson, 309; Jemima, 307; Jervis L., 300; Jesse, 302, 311; Jessie, 272; Jo Ann, 305; Joanne, 278; Jodilee, 301; John, 1, 267, 268, 269, 270, 271, 280, 285, 302, 309, 311; John B., 270, 272, 294, 306; John E., 299, 300; John H., 276; John J., 273, 274, 275, 298, 299; John L., 294; John M., 280, 293, 294; John P., 303; John S., 304; John W., 270, 305; Jonas, 268, 303; Jonas H., 303; Joseph E., 294; Joseph M., 270, 271; Josephine A., 294; Josephine E., 294, 300; Joshua, 309; Judith, 277; Julia, 274; Julia B., 274; Julia C., 303; Karen, 277; Karrie A., 279; Kate, 271; Katherine, 309; Kathryn, 276; Katie M., 298; Kelly H., 300; Kenneth R., 299;

WOLFE, Kermit S., 305; Kraig, 279; Laban T., 305; Laura, 279; Laurence H., 305; Leigh, 279; Lela, 275; Lena G., 298; Leon E., 305; Leonard 272, 277; Leroy, 302; Leslie L., 278; Lillian G., 299; Linnie K., 293; Lola, 271; Loretta, 271; Lorraine, 289; Lottie, 289; Lou A., 285, 290; Louella, 275, 277; Louisa C., 303; Loula C., 185; Lucian I., 298; Lucinda, 280, 297; Lucy, 304; Lula, 272; Lydia, 302; Lyla L., 276; Lyle L., 276; Lyman C., 275; Malinda, 303; Manuel, 301; Margaret, 268, 269, 302, 309; Margaret G., 305; Margaret I., 280, 292, 296; Margaret R., 303; Marion, 311; Mark H., 299; Marrilan, 276; Martha, 302, 307, 309; Martha B., 280; Martha J., 304; Martin V., 304; Mary, 267, 268, 269, 271, 302; 303; 304, 307, 308, 309, 311;.Mary A., 273, 277; Mary B., 305, 306;

WOLFE, Mary E., 272, 276, 286, 287, 303; Mary F., 280; Mary J., 285, 288, 295; Mary L., 292, 294, 298, 304; Maryle E., 275; May, 271; Melissa, 309; Melvina, 307; Merab E., 304; Merle A., 278; Michael G., 278; Mila, 301; Mildred G., 306; Mildred N., 299; Minerva N., 285, 289; Mollie C., 294; Myrtle A., 286; Myrtle G., 288; Nan E., 295; Nancy, 285, 301, 303, 304, 308, 309; Nancy A., 285, 303; Nell, 271; Nellie, 270; Nicholas, 309; Nora, 289; Oliver M., 303; Oliver P., 303; Ora, 279; Orin A., 286; Patricia, 276; Patricia L., 305; Pearlie M., 305; Peggy A., 251; Penelope J., 271; Perlina, 308; Perry, 309; Peter, 307, 308; Philip, 307; Phillip L., 278; Queenie E., 275; Ranae S., 278; Randall T., 276;

WOLFE, Ray E., 276, 278; Raymond, 289; Raymond D., 186; Raymond G., 289; Rebecca, 303; Rebecca B., 294; Reginald, 299; Rena L., 305; Reuben D., 304; Richard, 289, 302; Richard R., 279; Richard U., 276; Robert C., 289; Robert W., 276; Roderick D., 305; Roger D., 279; Roscoe C., 280; Rose, 274; Roy, 275; Ruby D., 304; Ruth A., 289; S. Merton, 270; Sallie I., 298; Sallie M., 294; Samuel G., 299; Sandra L., 305; Sarah, 309, 311; Sarah A., 269, 272; Sarah E., 299; Sarah I., 303; Serena, 302; Sherry L., 276; Silas D., 305; Simeon, 302; Sonora E., 304; Stephen D., 298; Susan, 15, 269, 273, 276, 302, 308, 309; Susan B., 276; Susanna, 307, 309; Teresa A., 275; Thomas B., 295, 303; Thomas C., 270; Thomas G., 301;

WOLFE, Thomas H. B., 270; Thomas M., 303; Timothy C., 276; Timothy J., 278; Tracy, 279; Turner, 272; Valentine, 309; Vena, 289; Vera, 276; Victor L., 278; Victoria, 274; Virginia, 272, 304; Virginia L., 299; Virginia V., 287, 384; Vivian O., 300; Walter, 274; Walter B., 270; Walter F., 299; Wanda A., 305; Warren, 271; Wayne, 279; Wayne R., 279; Wiley, 301, 308, 311; Wiley H., 294; Willard E., 299; William, 285, 302, 307, 311; William A., 269, 272, 303; William D., 305; William E., 270, 298, 299; William F., 54, 271; William G., 274, 305; William H., 303, 305; William M., 293; William W., 270; Winburn W., 280; Winfield S., 271; Winifred, 271; Woodson T., 311; Worley, 298; WOLLEN, Alberta F., 80;

WOLLEN, Alberta J., 81; Alice, 79; Alice L., 81; Andrew, 81; Anita A., 82; Arch M., 78; August H., 78, 79; Barbara J., 81; Beryl M., 79; Carol J., 80; Catherine F., 81; Cynthia S., 81; Debra S., 80; Denise L., 80; Edna E., 79; Effie D., 78, 82; Elizabeth R., 80; Ernest A., 78; Esther M., 80; Ethel G., 80; Florise V., 79, 83; Flossie E., 79; Floyd, 78; George L., 79; George W., 79, 80; Glen E., 80; Heloise O., 79; Ina M., 80; James W., 81; Jane A., 81; Juanita M., 81; Kenneth, 79; Kristy, 81; Leslie A., 79; Liliana R., 81; Linton L., 80; Lloyd P., 80; Lorigene M., 80; Mabel E., 79; March C., 78; Marvin E., 81; Mary G., 80; Mary J., 79;

WOLLEN, Mathias, 78; Nancy, 79; Nancy J., 80; Naomi O., 82; Olin G., 81; Orville R., 80, 81; Philip, 79; Ray J., 81; Rebecca S., 81; Rex L., 82; Roscoe D., 79; Roy, 79; Ruth E., 79; Sarah B., 81; Sharon, 79; Teresa K., 81; Terry S., 81; Valentine, 77, 79; Violette, 78; Walter, 78; William C., 78; WOLVERTON, Elizabeth, 185; WOMACK, Abraham, 24, 210; Ann, 210; Dorothy J., 218; Elizabeth, 210; Ellie, 196; George C., 218; George E., 218; Irene, 218; Jehu, 210; Jeremiah, 210; Josiah, 210; Levi, 210; Lucy, 210; Mary, 210; Morris W., 218; Pauline, 218; Sina, 210; William, 210; WOOD, Benton H., 97; Cornelia M., 274; Curtis, 94; George, 211, 212; Gwendolyn, 97; Henry M., 274; Inez, 151; John, 72; Jonathan, 97;

WOOD, Joshua, 258; Leah, 164; Margaret A., 97; Mary, 274; Mary J., 98; Nancy J., 97; Patricia H., 97; Sadie, 279; WOODARD, Albert E., 110; Cathy M., 110; Daniel, 110; Susan, 110; WOODCOCK, Alta, 44; Gipsy, 44; Wiley S., 43; WOODRUM, B.A., 268; WOODS, Albert, 18; David, 260; Dean, 114; Henrietta, 63; Margaret T., 42; Sarah, 262; WOODSIDE, Francis A., 73; Fred, 73; L. D., 73; Lela, 74; Lewis, 74; Lewis M., 73; Mattie, 74; Ralph, 74; Walter, 74; WOODSON, Ann, 27; John, 24, 27; WOODWARD, Anne B., 251; Eli, 103; Jane, 262; William, 183; WOODWORTH, Hiram C., 232; Sadie, 232; Virginia, 223; WOOLDRIDGE, Ann E., 227; WORD, Hattie, 96; William, 96; WORKMAN, Cornelia, 120; WORKS, Anthony, 81; Beth, 81; Joseph, 81;

WORSHAM, Sarah, 211; WORTHINGTON, Emma, 218; WRAY, Francis, 68; John, 68; WRIGHT, Belinda Nell, 215; Benjamin H., 215; Eleanor E., 205; Ernest B., 221; Gerald, 263; Granville, 240; H. E., 87; J. W., 15; Jessie L., 240; John, 25, 68; Joseph, 68; Josephine, 64; Karen Jo, 215; Martha, 204; Nathan D., 240; Robert L., 275; Rodney H., 215; Ronald, 275; Solomon, 68; Sue, 250; Thomas, 68; Virginia H., 221; WRIGHTSMAN, Ethel, 275; WUNDERLICH, Bernice, 276; Edwin, 276; Ross, 276; WYCHE, Ruth, 149; WYNE, Margaret, 58; WYNNE, Nancy, 211; YAGER, Clint W., 147; Clyde T., 147; Dorothy G., 147; Harry P., 147; James P., 147; Karen S., 147; Katherine V., 147; Margaret, 147; Mary A., 147; Mayme G., 147; Raymond L., 147;

YAGER, Roy W., 147; Royal M., 147; YAKEY, Henry, 160, 162; YANCEY, Eleanor, 209; YARBER, Dorene, 289; Emma, 289; Fay, 289; Iva, 289; Janet F., 289; John, 289 Levi, 289; Ralph, 289; YARBOROUGH, Archibald, 210; YATES, Mary M., 136; Roberta K., 84; Ruvilla, 272; YEARY, Betty, 144; Howard, 144; Howard E., 144; YENKO, Sally, 105; YORK, Braxton, 121; Lucinda, 121; YOST, David A., 85; George A., 85; John, 245; Joyce, 264; YOUNG, Audrey, 263; Austin, 231; Evelyn, 196; Letitia, 95; Margaret, 231; Rozella, 77; Susan F., 143; William, 38; YOUREE, William E., 197; ZETTLE, Charles, 170; Donna J., 170; Mary L., 170; Thomas E., 170; ZIKE, Lucinda, 103; Margaret, 103; Martha, 103; ZIMMERMAN, Ada V., 145; Alfred R., 144;

ZIMMERMAN, Benjamin H., 144; Billy F., 144; Clementine, 203; Connie, 144; Diane, 144; Eleanor M., 144; Ellis, 144; Gladys, 143; Hardin M., 143; Henry R., 145; James A., 143; James B., 144; James G., 144; James H., 143; James T., 144; James W., 143; Jeff W., 145; John, 144; Kerry, 144; Lydia B., 144; Mary A., 145; Mary S., 143, 145; Matt B., 144; Mattie, 143; O. B., 144; Oscar B., 144; Paul, 144; Ruby C., 144; Sally L., 144; Susan A., 144; Terry L., 144; Thomas W., 145; Walter E., 144; William, 143, 144; William A., 144; William R., 145; Winifred L., 144; ZIMS, Zolla, 171;

Made in the USA
San Bernardino, CA
10 May 2015